MIDDLESEX

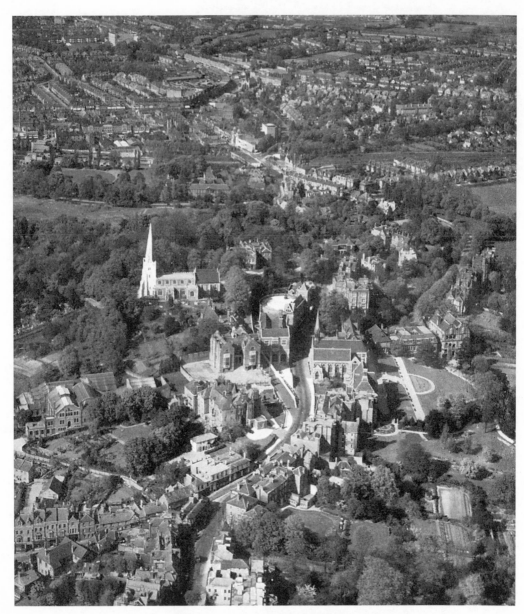

*Harrow from the air. In front, the Hill, Church, and School;
in the background, modern Harrow*

MIDDLESEX

MICHAEL ROBBINS

PHILLIMORE

First published in 1953 by Collins

This edition published 2003 by
PHILLIMORE & CO. LTD
Shopwyke Manor Barn, Chichester, West Sussex

ISBN 1 86077 269 2

Printed and bound in Great Britain by
THE CROMWELL PRESS
Trowbridge, Wiltshire

CONTENTS

CONTENTS

PART TWO

ILLUSTRATIONS

All the illustrations are from photographs taken at the time of the first edition in 1953, except where a date (sometimes approximate) is attached in this list. All are to be found between pages 216 and 217 except the frontispiece.

MAPS AND DIAGRAMS

LIST OF ABBREVIATIONS
USED IN NOTES

The following abbreviations and short titles are used throughout the notes:

Clapham, *Concise*
      J. H. Clapham, *Concise Economic History of England to 1750* (1949).
Clapham, *Modern Britain*
      J. H. Clapham, *Economic History of Modern Britain*, i (1926), ii (1932), iii (1938).
Cooke   G. A. Cooke, *Topographical and Statistical Description of the County of Middlesex* (ed. 2, *c.* 1825).
Darby   *Historical Geography of England before A.D. 1800*, ed. H. C. Darby (1936).
Dowdell   E. G. Dowdell, *A Hundred Years of Quarter Sessions* (1932).
Foley   H. J. Foley, *Our Lanes and Meadowpaths* (*c.* 1890).
H.C.M.   *Home Counties Magazine.*
Hassell   J. Hassell, *Picturesque Rides and Walks, with Excursions by Water, Thirty Miles round the British Metropolis* (1817).
Jackman   W. T. Jackman, *Development of Transportation in Modern England* (1916).
Lysons   D. Lysons, *The Environs of London* (1795; ed. 2, 1811) and *An Historical Account of those Parishes in the County of Middlesex which are not described in the Environs of London* (1800).
M.C.R.   *Middlesex County Records*, ed. J. C. Jeaffreson, i [1886], ii [1887], iii (1888), iv (1892); ed. W. J. Hardy, v (1905).
M.C.R. Reports
      W. J. Hardy and W. le Hardy, *Middlesex County Records Reports 1902-1928* (1928).
Mx. & H. N. & Q.
      Middlesex and Hertfordshire Notes and Queries.
Marshall   W. Marshall, *Minutes, Experiments, Observations, and General Remarks on Agriculture in the Southern Counties ... The Vale of London* (ed. 2, 1799).
Middleton J. Middleton, *View of the Agriculture of Middlesex* (ed. 1, 1798).
Thorne   J. Thorne, *Handbook to the Environs of London* (1876).
Trans. L.Mx.A.S.
      Transactions of the London and Middlesex Archaeological Society.
V.C.H.   *Victoria History of the County of Middlesex*, ed. W. Page (vol. ii only published, 1911).
Vulliamy   C. E. Vulliamy, *The Archaeology of Middlesex and London* (1930).
Willatts   E. C. Willatts, *Middlesex and the London Region* ('The Land of Britain,' Land Utilisation Survey, part 79, 1937).

In references to articles in periodicals, the first page only is cited. Periodicals are dated by the year in which the completed volume appeared.

MAP REFERENCES

In the gazetteer which forms Part II of this book the map references (B4, G9, etc.) can be found on the Ordnance Survey half-inch map.

N

A1	B1	C1	D1	E1	F1
A2	B2	C2	D2	E2	F2
A3	B3	C3	D3	E3	F3
A4	B4	C4	D4	E4	F4
A5	B5	C5	D5	E5	F5
A6	B6	C6	D6	E6	F6

W   E

S

PUBLISHER'S NOTE TO THIS EDITION

THE New Survey of England set out in the 1950s to describe the local history of England. Like so many series (before and since), this also foundered, but not before two outstanding county volumes—*Middlesex* (Michael Robbins) and *Devon* (W.G. Hoskins)—had been published. In its scope and objective the Survey represented something of a return to the methods of the earlier English local historians—Leland, Camden and Dugdale. Though Leland—The Father of them all—was the King's Antiquary interested chiefly in the past, the account given in his *Itinerary* of the revolution in progress around him is still of great value to us, more than four centuries later. Michael Robbins' view of Middlesex, commissioned by Professor Jack Simmons to be the most comprehensive history and description of an English county ever attempted in one volume, is of similar value to us, half a century after its first publication.

In this new edition of a work, still regarded by many as the single most important study of Middlesex's somewhat elusive history, the opportunity has been taken to update the tables of population and to mention significant additions to the bibliography. For this we are grateful to Miss Andrea Cameron, formerly responsible for the Local History Collections in the London Borough of Hounslow. James Robbins, the author's son, kindly agreed to write the Foreword.

We are delighted that this monumental work, the product of deep knowledge and great love of Middlesex, is once more in print, while regretting that the author's death in December 2002 deprived him of his share in this delight, fifty years after his book's first appearance.

FOREWORD TO THE 2003 EDITION

'An acre in Middlesex is worth a principality in Utopia'
Thomas Babington, 1st Baron Macaulay—writing in 1843

I am not sure Michael Robbins would have gone quite as far as Macaulay but, by the time my father died in December 2002, an acre in Middlesex was certainly worth far more, in real terms, than Macaulay could ever have dreamed.

Michael Robbins loved Middlesex. He shared a delight in it with John Betjeman, and even inspired the Poet Laureate to write three poems connected with the county—'Harrow-on-the-Hill', 'The Metropolitan Railway: Baker Street Station Buffet' and, of course, 'Middlesex':

> Gaily into Ruislip Gardens
> Runs the red electric train ...[1]

Public transport, one of Michael Robbins's consuming passions, held the key to Middlesex. It helped Londoners to colonise the county steadily through the nineteenth and twentieth centuries. And public transport made it possible for him to research this book. At weekends he would set aside his work for London Transport, and set off from home in Earl's Court, first on the Underground, and then on foot.

My father said he was not an obvious choice as author. He was not a professional, academic historian. When Jack Simmons (Professor of History at Leicester University and a friend since schooldays together at Westminster) told Michael in 1947 he was planning a series covering all the English counties, my father said, and called it a foolish thing to say, 'When it comes to Middlesex, you'll have to ask me.'

Jack picked up on it at once, and introduced my father to W.G. Hoskins, the author of *Devon* (the only other book completed in this series). According to my father, Professor Hoskins gave him a precious piece of advice: 'First of all do the bits that you feel least attracted to, then the rest will fall into place'. So he started with the Middlesex entries

---

[1] From *A Few Late Chrysanthemums* (1954).

in Domesday Book and the ancient archaeology; industrial archaeology was much more his thing.

Middlesex took four years to research and write, in the gaps between a full-time job and some time with my older sisters. I arrived a few months after the finished book. Michael was proud of his pace. Hoskins's *Devon* was not far behind, but it was Middlesex which was published first, in May 1953. The series, sadly, foundered almost immediately. My father blamed the academics who had been commissioned to tackle other counties. They, he said, got nowhere, and a big project simply fizzled out.

This book, however, consummated my father's relationship with the county, got him heavily involved with the London and Middlesex Archaeological Society, and led to his contribution of the Middlesex section to Betjeman's *English Parish Churches* of 1958. More than that, I think *Middlesex* persuaded him he could combine life as a professional transport administrator with a great deal of writing—as historian and industrial archaeologist.

Although my father travelled far from the county of his birth during a long, richly fulfilled life—he was born in Hendon in September 1915— he was very content to spend the last few years of that life in Teddington. He worked hard there to try to bury the local misconception that the village takes its name from 'Tide End Town'. He deals with the issue in this book, and he was content that *Middlesex* had stood the test of 50 years, as he put it, 'pretty well'.

JAMES ROBBINS
Twickenham
August 2003

ACKNOWLEDGMENTS

THE author's special thanks are due to the Rev. E. B. J. Armstrong, lately vicar of St Margaret with St Nicholas, King's Lynn, for the loan of a manuscript volume of the diary kept by his grandfather, the Rev. B. J. Armstrong, and for permission to quote extracts from it; to Miss Eila M. J. Campbell, of Birkbeck College, University of London, for access to her study of the Middlesex Domesday Book before publication; to Dr. W. G. Hoskins, reader in economic history in the University of Oxford, for help at several points; to Mr. F. A. A. Menzler, C.B.E., F.I.A., a colleague at London Transport, for reading the typescript with critical care; and to Dr. F. W. M. Draper and Mr. Richard Capel for reading the proofs and making valuable suggestions.

The following are also thanked for information on particular subjects: the Rev. Luther Bouch, minister of Old Meeting Congregational Church, Uxbridge; L. Crisp, editor, *The Middlesex Advertiser*, Uxbridge; W. N. C. Clinch, lately general manager, Northmet Power Co., Southgate; the Rev. B. B. Edmonds, Oxhey, president of the Organ Club; the Rev. Prebendary Stanley Eley; C. H. Rock, curator, Tottenham Museum; F. W. Scouse, editor, *The Middlesex County Times*, Ealing; the Rev. G. S. S. Scovell, assistant secretary, London Diocesan Fund; the Rev. H. Sellers, Congregational History Society; J. D. Swain, Eastcote; A. S. Tribe, lately secretary, Foreign Office Sports Association, Swakeleys; the Statistical Branch of the Ministry of Agriculture and Fisheries; and Col. W. le Hardy, M.C., F.S.A., County Archivist, and the staff of the Middlesex County Record Office.

Grateful acknowledgement is also made of willing and courteous service given by the staffs of libraries consulted during the preparation of this book, especially at the British Museum (Bloomsbury and Hendon), the Guildhall Library of the City of London, the Westminster and Kensington Public Libraries, Dr. Williams's Library, Gordon Square, and those belonging to the Bishopsgate Institute and the London and Middlesex Archaeological Society, the Victoria and Albert Museum, the Society of Friends, the Congregational History Society, the Royal Agricultural Society of England, and the Royal Statistical Society. The staffs of the public libraries within the county of Middlesex have invariably (with a single exception) shown a lively interest and desire to help in inquiries relating to local studies.

'Lord Finchley' from Hilaire Belloc's *More Peers* in *Cautionary Verses* is included by courtesy of the author and of Messrs. Gerald Duckworth & Co., Ltd.; the passage on the battle of Albuera from *Years of Victory* is quoted by permission of Mr. Arthur Bryant, and that on Victorian domestic building from Clapham: *An Economic History of Modern Britain, Vol. II*, by permission of Cambridge University Press.

The thanks of the editor and publishers, as well as of the author, are due to Mr. J. F. Trotter for the line maps and diagrams in the text of the book; to Miss Rosemary Gilliatt for many of the photographs, namely Nos. 19, 20, 22-24, 26, 27, 29-34, 36, 38-42, 44-49, 58, 61, 63, 69-71, 74, and for untiring patience in pleasing author, editor, and publisher; to Mr. J. Allan Cash for Nos. 21, 28, 37, 43, 53, 54, 60, 68; to Aerofilms, Ltd., for the Frontispiece and No. 73; to the Curator of the Ashmolean Museum at Oxford for No. 6; to the Trustees of the British Museum for Nos. 11, 14, and 16; to British Railways for Nos. 5 and 55; to The Central Press Photos, Ltd., for No. 67; to Messrs. Frederick B. Daniell & Son for No. 4; to Mr. Ian Dunlop for No. 13; to the Rt. Hon. the Earl of Durham for No. 7 and to Messrs. B. T. Batsford, Ltd., for the loan of the print; to Messrs. Arthur Guinness, Son & Co., Ltd., for No. 65; to Her Majesty's Stationery Office for Nos. 25 and 35 from *An Inventory of the Historical Monuments in Middlesex* (1937); to Hornsey Borough Council for No. 62; to London Transport for Nos. 57 and 64; to the Medici Society, Ltd., for No. 3; to the Metropolitan Museum of Art, New York, for No. 1; to Mr. S. W. Newbery for No. 59; to Mr. H. W. Newby for Nos. 52 and 56; to His Grace the Duke of Northumberland for No. 2; to the Royal Institute of British Architects for No. 9; to Mr. Michael Sadleir and Messrs. Constable & Co., Ltd., for No. 10; to the Curator of Sir John Soane's Museum for No. 8; to the Director of the Whitworth Art Gallery, Manchester, for No. 15; and to the Willesden Public Libraries for Nos. 50 and 51.

Acknowledgment is made of permission given by the Controller of Her Majesty's Stationery Office for the use of maps in official publications as a basis for maps and diagrams in the text. The diagram on page 5 is taken from *London and the Thames Valley*, by R. L. Sherlock (British Regional Geology, 1947), the map on page 18 and the plans on pages 270 and 354 from *An Inventory of the Historical Monuments in Middlesex* (1937), and the plan on page 262 from *Hampton Court Palace*, by G. H. Chettle (1947). The map on page 283 (Crown copyright reserved) is reproduced by permission of Winchester Publications, Ltd., from *Harrow School, Yesterday and Today*, by E. D. Laborde (1948).

AUTHOR'S INTRODUCTION

THE story of Middlesex has a good many individual features that deserve some word of explanation, for they have determined the particular way in which this book has been written.

The county of Middlesex has a history and traditions of its own, but it has throughout historic times been overwhelmingly influenced by its relations with London. No other English county has been dominated to the same extent by a single town—not even any of the other Home Counties, which are all larger in extent and have had, at least until the present age, a much stronger independent life of their own. This close relation with the capital has meant that Middlesex has always been very much involved in the development of the English state, and outstanding events in national history inevitably impinge a great deal upon its local history. Middlesex was the scene of the critical stage in Julius Caesar's principal invasion of Britain, of the important battle of Barnet in 1471, and of the encounter at Turnham Green in 1642 which decisively turned back Charles I from London. In the first two hundred years of its existence, from 1514 to 1714, Hampton Court played a greater part in English politics than any other house in the country except Whitehall. The Middlesex elections of 1769, and to a smaller degree those of 1804 and 1806, are important in the constitutional history of England.

These things happened in Middlesex because it lay at the doorstep of London. The ruling power in the capital has always understood the county's special place as part of the outer defences of London, as the history of the ownership of land in Middlesex demonstrates very clearly. Even before the Norman Conquest, the Church had become the principal landowner, and, after a sharp lesson from the turbulent Geoffrey de Mandeville, the Conqueror's successors were careful to prevent great secular lordships being formed so close to the seat of government. At the Dissolution of the Monasteries these ecclesiastical estates fell into the hands of Henry VIII. The Crown, though it continued to hold a more substantial block of Middlesex land than it had in the Middle Ages, did not retain all that Henry had acquired; here, as elsewhere, economic pressure forced it to part with much that it had gained. But still this did not give rise to a powerful local gentry. Estates were constantly changing hands in the succeeding centuries, with the one great exception of Syon. Even that was of little importance, for the earls and dukes of Northumberland played no great part in the local government and life of Middlesex; their vital interests lay in London and the North, and Syon was no more to them than one of their three principal residences.

The historic domination of Middlesex by London is also shown by the retarded development of its towns. None of the Middlesex towns was incorporated before the twentieth century. Some of them were important commercial centres for products on their way to London, but none—not even Uxbridge, which came nearest to it—ever became an important community in its own right, like Romford or Gravesend or Croydon. There was never even a county town. Brentford was the polling-place for parliamentary elections, but the administration of Middlesex has always been established in London.

In another respect also, which has come to be the most significant, Middlesex is overshadowed by London. For at least three hundred years past, if not for longer, it has provided residences for Londoners who preferred to live outside the city itself; and more recently it has supplied many of the services—water, transport, power—that the capital requires. During the past seventy five years—above all, since the 1914-18 War—it has become increasingly important for its industrial development. These three functions are today the foundation of its economic life.

Middlesex, then, cannot be understood apart from its special relation to London. The two are complementary. But Middlesex is *not* London; it has a peculiar and highly interesting story of its own. Anyone who visits the places in the county with his eyes open must see that. The face of the modern county is varied, not uniform; some places are thriving London dormitories, others, no further from town, have remained small and almost rural. The population today is far from evenly distributed, and the chronology of development in the nineteenth and twentieth centuries is not simply that of successive concentric belts of building as houses spread outwards from London. One of the things I have tried to do in this book is to indicate how the geology of the county, its water supply, and the development of its communications have formed the character and affected the appearance of modern Middlesex. The broad outlines of these three important influences are set out on pages 193-197. As part of the same inquiry, railway stations and tram lines occupy an unusually prominent position in the descriptions of particular places in Part II; without them it would be impossible to explain how each place has come to be what it is.

AUTHOR'S INTRODUCTION

I have tramped a good many miles through Middlesex suburbs while preparing this book. I began it with no formed opinions about the contemporary problems of the county; but the historian of a live community cannot avoid thinking of it as it is and as it might be. Some discussion of present-day Middlesex is printed here in Chapter XIV, 'The Suburban County,' at the conclusion of the historical survey; I hope that some readers who may find that Domesday Book does not interest them, and perhaps do not think the Gothic Revival fascinating, will nevertheless have a look at that chapter. Few authorities are referred to in it; indeed, there are very few that one can refer to. Too many writers (may one say, far too many historians, in particular?) have thought the suburb beneath their notice; and yet the thing has been with us long enough, and enough of us dwell in suburbs, to make study of the subject respectable. But the growth, and sometimes the decline, of the suburb; its special advantages, and its difficulties; what sort of life goes on there— these things are very inadequately noticed by writers, if at all. I have written something about these matters, viewed in their historical perspective.

It is a rash thing for an ordinary citizen to write anything about the peculiarly difficult problems of local government—difficult both because they are highly technical and because discussion of them seems to arouse very warm feelings. Still I have risked it. It seems to me specially important that these problems should be discussed now, because of the proposition—only temporarily shelved—that the county of Middlesex ought to be included within the territory of the London County Council. I have come to think, as I have written on pages 209 -214, that there are many other things to be thought of besides administrative efficiency in considering this problem, and I cannot feel sure the the accepted policy of amalgamating the ancient units into large modern aggregations is really the best for the people who live in them. A study of Middlesex history must, I think, lead one to question the wisdom of the developments of this kind that have happened in the last fifty years.

The reader is owed a few words on the methods I have adopted in presenting the complicated story of Middlesex, in which so very many events and persons and things appear. I have been obliged to be concise, especially in Part II. In that Part, I have given separate accounts (necessarily repeating some of the information in Part I) of each ancient parish, together with the new places that do not fit into the old parish framework, and of the most important houses. These were completed by the autumn of 1951, when the book was first put into type.

I have altered the punctuation and spelling of the older authors whose words I have quoted so that they do not distract by their quaintness. A few single phrases taken from previous writers are not attributed or put in quotation marks, to make reading easier. I have not been afraid of anachronisms–to write that Caesar crossed the Thames 'at Brentford' is as intelligible as 'at the place where Brentford was later built' and conveniently shorter. I have written the years throughout in the New Style (beginning the year on 1 January, not 25 March), but I have not altered days and months before 1752. In the two or three cases where there are alternative spellings of place-names, I have followed the current one-inch Ordnance Survey map. This is a survey of human history in Middlesex, and I have therefore not touched upon natural history except where it has had a direct bearing on economic life. (Fortunately, the reader who wants to know more about it can be recommended to Mr. R. S. R. Fitter's *London's Natural History* (Collins), published in 1949.) The territorial boundaries of this study are those of the existing administrative county of Middlesex, which are outlined on page 4. I have attempted to refer in the Notes to all my written sources which are outside what may be called the general topographical tradition: if a statement about, say, Enfield is in the Enfield histories, I do not give it a specific reference. The reader will, I hope, on balance approve.

The material on which this book is based is scattered all over the place, in a way that is (I suppose) unusual for an English county. There is no great county history; there are histories of separate places and buildings, some of them admirable; but there is no Middlesex bibliography, and even the British Museum lacks copies of many of the works published locally. I have tried to run these to earth (not always with success), and the bibliography on pages 371 to 392, which cannot be complete, is the result. It is offered here as a working foundation for historical study, not as a full bibliography of the county.

The writer of a new book about an English county would be ungrateful indeed if he did not express his obligations both to his predecessors in print and to his contemporaries working in the same field. My thanks to the former are expressed by my bibliography; my acknowledgments for help given personally are placed in a single list at pp.xv-xvi.

If, in spite of all this help, mistakes or questionable statements are found, the fault is entirely mine. Some of those to whom I have referred will disagree with my bald statements on disputed points. They are all that the length and scope of my text will permit; but I do not affect the omniscience that seems, now that I read them again, to lie heavy on these pages. No doubt the word 'probably' should occur much more often in them than it does; yet it becomes tedious by repetition, and there is, after all, a duty to make up one's mind, except in cases of very great doubt. I can only hope that, in silently correcting some errors current in

Middlesex historiography and omitting some subjects that all previous writers have thought worthy of mention, the following pages do not in turn introduce a greater number of mistakes; but I have no illusion that it is easy to avoid doing so in a book which necessarily states matters of fact in almost every line. Will readers who notice mistakes, or who can add to the bibliography or to the dates and attributions of buildings, please tell me? I shall be grateful.

MICHAEL ROBBINS

MIDDLESEX

The face or superficies of this country is most beautiful, the fields fresh and green, the valleys delightful to behold; the towns, villages and stately buildings interlaced with the pleasant woods are glorious to be seen.

JOHN NORDEN, *Speculum Britanniae* (1593)

All Middlesex is *ugly*.

WILLIAM COBBETT, *Rural Rides* (1822)

PART ONE

CHAPTER I

THE COUNTY OF MIDDLESEX

*'There is no place in the world which has the same
interest for an Englishman as the county of
Middlesex.'*
W. J. LOFTIE[1]

AS the traveller in a train to the north or the west of England passes
out of the town and into the suburbs of London, he can see from the
carriage window a panorama that owes little to any century before the
twentieth. For several miles the ground is covered with streets of small
red-brick houses, with their gardens, and the shops and cinemas and
schools that supply the daily needs of their inhabitants; there are modern
factories and office buildings; motor buses and electric trains ply among
them; tall trees and expanses of grass appear only on sports grounds or
public parks; there are canals and reservoirs, perhaps an airfield; here
and there is an old house, brown or grey, looking forlorn among so much
red; and a medieval church tower may be seen. This is the modern
aspect of the ancient county of Middlesex.

Middlesex, the smallest of all the historic English shires but one, is
yet in some respects the greatest. More people live under its county
administration than any other in England outside London; but its
inhabitants know less about it, and seem to care less for it, than any
others for theirs. It has a history of first-class interest, continuous since the
Roman invasions: so many events of importance to the whole nation
have taken place on its soil, and so many men of distinction have dwelt
within it, that few other counties could challenge a comparison; yet its
present appearance is almost entirely owing to the last sixty years. It is
commonly thought of, if it is thought of at all, as one huge and featureless
suburb; but beneath the apparent uniformity of the scene lie a rich
historical texture and significant diversities between the different parts.

Good reasons for these paradoxes can be found: they are its
geography and its great neighbour, London. The geographical setting has
impressed a particular stamp on local modes of life: the soils and waters
of Middlesex have supplied the firm framework within which the

[1] W. J. Loftie, *History of London* (1883), ii., p. 31.

modern pattern has been woven. The inescapable facts of geography determined early and enduring characteristics, and they have not been obliterated by the later and more obvious influence of London, exerted over an increasing radius from the south-eastern corner of the county. London's effects on the parts adjoining it on the north and west appear almost throughout recorded history, bearing more and more directly on the life of Middlesex until at the present day this influence appears to be supreme. But, if London overshadows, it does not yet entirely dominate Middlesex; it is the interaction of these two forces, the geographical setting and the influence of London, that supplies the key to the historical development of Middlesex and the features of its society and economy at the present time.

It is difficult for the passing traveller to know where the county begins and ends. Only where the river Thames flows on its sinuous course from Staines to Chiswick on the south, and the Lea runs in its well-defined valley on the east, is the boundary really evident; but most people cross the less obvious borders. In its earliest form, Middlesex probably extended over the whole tract between the Thames, the Lea, and the Colne that flows past Watford and Uxbridge, except only towards the south-east corner where the City of London exercised its own authority within its bounds.[1] When Hertford became a shire about the beginning of the 11th century, the northern border was most curiously drawn; the southern one from Stoke Newington to Hammersmith was made irregular, and irrational, when the greater part of the county of London was carved out from Middlesex in 1888. Some of the inhabitants do not know that they are living in Middlesex; the Middlesex Guildhall and the Middlesex Hospital are situated in London; and it surprises a good many people that the county itself has managed to survive. This volume deals with the area of modern Middlesex, not (except where it is unavoidable, as in some places it must be) with the ancient county. The limits of its territory include Uxbridge and Staines on the west, follow the line of the Thames from there to Chiswick on the south, take in Willesden, Highgate (but not Hampstead), and Tottenham on the London border, and run by an indented line including Enfield and Harrow (but excluding Barnet) on the north. These limits include fifty ancient parishes, the former market towns of Enfield, Harrow, Uxbridge, Staines, and Brentford, and the habitations of more than two million people.

Within this area there are marked geographical features. Middlesex lies in the trough of the London basin, which rests on the great concave fold of chalk extending from the Chilterns to the North Downs. The chalk itself is only on the surface in the county seen at Harefield and South Mimms, the extreme north-west and north points. Above the chalk

[1] H. J. Mackinder, *Britain and the British Seas* (ed. 2, 1930), p.199.

are deposits known as the Thanet beds (not seen on the surface), Reading beds (visible in the north-west), and the London clay. The landscape in the north of the county is modelled from the eroded clay, and its distribution has affected the areas of early settlement and forest clearing, the kinds of agriculture formerly practised, and the types of suburban development in the last hundred years. 'Clay of the most adhesive and ungrateful kind,' John Loudon the landscape-gardener called it about 1830[1]—a description that farmer, road-mender, and back-gardener have in turn endorsed.

Above the main bed of the clay further deposits, the Claygate and Bagshot beds, were laid down as the basin was rapidly filled up by

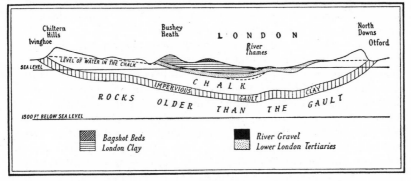

DIAGRAMMATIC GEOLOGICAL SECTION
ACROSS THE LONDON BASIN
(Vertical scale greatly exaggerated)

alluvium. The Bagshot beds, fine sand with some clay and flint pebbles, with their typical landscapes of heath and pinewood, form the caps of the shapely eminences of Highgate, Hampstead, and Harrow. The distribution of these sands has had an enduring economic influence: dry surface and ready water supply made them preferable to London clay as building land, and the sand was valuable material for sale.[2]

Scouring and erosion, together with the action of the Thames, combined to produce the features of modern Middlesex, until the Great Ice Age laid down new deposits in the form of glacial gravels. These consist of debris pushed beyond the main ice-sheet, which even at its greatest extent did not extend quite so far south. The chief feature from this age is the Boulder Clay, grey-blue, full of stones of all sorts and sizes, including large lumps of chalk pushed forward from Lincolnshire by the ice sheet. The glacier that left this clay as its residual deposit probably reached almost as far as the Hampstead-Highgate ridge; when it melted,

[1] J. C. Loudon, *Encyclopaedia of Agriculture* (ed. 2, 1831), p.1125. [2] R. L. Sherlock, *London and Thames Valley* (British Regional Geology, ed. 2, 1947); Vulliamy, chapter I.

the contents became deposited in the form of gravels over a large area about Finchley.

The gravel deposits laid down by the Thames extend in an almost unbroken sheet across the south of Middlesex, with occasional overlays of alluvium and extensive patches of brick-earth. This brick-earth, 'inundation mud' or ancient alluvium, is a mixture of sand and clay, containing small stones; a large deposit extends from Southall to Hounslow Heath, with other blocks between Hayes and Harlington and between Harmondsworth and Yiewsley and an extension up the Colne valley to Uxbridge. As the name implies, these deposits are used for the manufacture of bricks and tiles, and in some places they have been completely removed for the purpose. They have been highly important in the economic development of the area. Equally important, in a negative sense, is the entire absence of stone.

Middlesex thus presents two faces, flat alluvial plain and gently undulating clay lands rising in places to respectable eminences. In the south-west the surface is almost dead level between the Thames and the line of the Bath road; north of this there is a very gentle rise up to the Uxbridge road. Above this line, which roughly follows the division between alluvium and clay, irregular ridges run from Harefield through Harrow and Hendon to the heights of Hampstead and Highgate and on to Muswell Hill and Wood Green. The highest point is at Stanmore Common, on the Hertfordshire border, 505 feet above sea level; early 19th-century writers declared, with some improbability, that the German Ocean and the smoke of steamboats plying on the Thames could be seen from this point, and that ships on the river found it a useful navigation mark.[1] Not far south-west Harrow Hill, rising fairly steeply from the plain, commands good views north, west, and south, though its height is only 405 feet. The young Ruskin could see it from Herne Hill on fine summer evenings.[2] A man going due east from Harrow, as from many places on the eastern side of England, will not come to such high ground again until he meets the Ural mountains.

The northern part of the county was one vast forest well into historic times: Domesday Book of 1086 records large tracts devoted to swine, which fed on acorns. The oaks have mostly disappeared, though in 1895 they still sprang up every year and were cut down with the hay in the fields about Harrow.[3] The elm remains the characteristic Middlesex tree, both in the surviving woodlands along the northern border and in the hedgerows and copses of the south-west. The situation, and the inhabitants, of the elm trees in Hyde Park cost the builders of the original Crystal Palace of 1851 much anxious thought.[4]

The natural features, apart from some pretty hills, are thus not remarkable. The clay and gravel, however, have characteristics of their

---

[1] Hassell, p. 224; B. J. Armstrong, *Some Account of the Parish of Little Stanmore* (ed. 2, 1861), p. 16. [2] J. Ruskin, *Praeterita* (ed. 1949), p.26. [3] *Builder* 68 (1895), p.57. [4] C. Hobhouse, *1851 and the Crystal Palace* (1937), p. 6.

own which directed the types of agriculture that men adopted and the buildings they could erect, in the days before railways carried red bricks and Welsh slates impartially into every corner of the kingdom. While transport of heavy materials remained costly and difficult, houses had to be built from what could be had locally—walls of timber framing filled with rubble or brick, with red tiled roofs, and later of brown stock bricks. They gave the countryside a modest charm of homely peacefulness and repose; it was part of what Vanbrugh called 'the Tame Sneaking South of England.'[1]

A writer in 1890 called Middlesex 'unideal,' an imprecise adjective that well expressed its nature:[2] no picture-postcard beauty, no spots that tourists travelled far to visit, but a region of orchards and market-gardens, or meadows that were a pleasure to see in June when all the grasses were in flower, and here and there a village that looked as though it might be a hundred miles from London.[3] It was this Middlesex that cockneys, whether literary men or plain trippers, had in their mind's eye when they thought of the country. The Londoner thought of it as full of typical country scenes: a Duke of Norfolk wrote in 1536, in reference to an improbable allegation, 'Tottenham shall turn French,' as one might say, 'Then I'm a Dutchman'; Charles II, hearing 'the church visible' mentioned by his divines, remarked that they must mean Harrow church, whose slim spire is still a landmark far over the surrounding vale; and when statesmen and improving landlords wanted to bring home their arguments with forceful illustrations, they appealed to Middlesex examples. Sir John Sinclair, president of the Board of Agriculture, declared in 1803: 'Let us not be satisfied with the liberation of Egypt, or the subjugation of Malta, but let us subdue Finchley Common; let us conquer Hounslow Heath; let us compel Epping Forest to submit to the yoke of improvement'[5]—two out of three in Middlesex. It could be assumed, in speaking or writing for an audience in the metropolis, that these allusions would be telling; the subjects were thoroughly familiar. Middlesex was understood to be the county an educated person knew about, whatever other local affiliations he might have; it was, before the term was appropriated to other uses, London's country.

In modern times, Middlesex has come to stand for something else: no longer the rustic scene but the suburban residence. A journalist of the present day writes of the professional middle classes: 'Behind the neat privet hedges of Hendon and Edgware, Putney and Kew, Ealing and Pinner, Wood Green and Finchley there is real hardship—and sometimes tragedy.'[6] With perhaps excessive emphasis on privet (there is not much in Wood Green, for example), he includes six Middlesex places among the eight in his list of typical middle-class areas. It has become the suburban county *par excellence*. This has not happened all at once, and it

[1] L. Whistler, *Sir John Vanbrugh, Architect and Dramatist* (1938), p. 267, quoting letter of 1721. [2] Foley, p.viii. [3] Foley, p. 14; Hassell, p. 233 (of Willesden); A. Heales, *Trans. L.Mx. A. S.* OS 3 (1870), p.105 (of Stanwell); C. G. Harper, *Rural Nooks round London* (1907), p.98 (of Heston). [4] Quoted by D. Mathew, *Catholicism in England* (1936), p. 16. [5] Quoted by E. Halévy, *History of the British People in 1815* (Penguin ed., 1937), ii., p.45, from *Memoirs of Sir J. Sinclair* (1837), ii., p.111. [6] Quoted by R. Lewis and A. Maude, *English Middle Classes* (1949), p.203.

has happened in different ways in different parts of the county; it has been early in some and later in others as the state of communication with London has invited or retarded development; but it has nearly all taken place since 1890, and the pace was accelerated remarkably between 1920 and 1939.

In this process the individual character of old Middlesex seems almost to have disappeared. It was never very strongly distinctive, for there are no very sharp geographical differences from the neighbouring shires, and there was no vigorous and continuing local life and culture of a recognisable kind. Yet the visitor to the sites of the old villages may still find characteristic evidences of previous centuries remaining amidst the mediocre erections of the last 50 years. He will also find some signs that not quite all the works of the 20th century are so feeble or so ugly as the hasty traveller may think as he looks at the backs of suburban houses from his passing train, or as he is driven into London along an arterial road from the Middlesex airport that gives him his first view of Britain. Middlesex does not easily reveal itself to the tourist, and it hardly caters for him at all; but it is rewarding to one who has eyes for other things besides what is obviously picturesque. That is not to say that it is entirely unattractive; it contains one building, Hampton Court Palace, of the very first rank, and many other things of note. But in general its interest for the visitor lies in the more modest kind of sights—not the cathedral or the castle, but the church detail, and the dwelling-house, and the way life is lived in the 20th century.

Though traces of past character and individuality remain and can be discerned, London's most recent expansion has been so sudden that these traces have been almost submerged. During the last sixty years the number of people who live in Middlesex has vastly increased. By immense efforts the authorities have supplied the essential services for their daily wants and for the education of their children; but the new inhabitants hardly feel themselves citizens of the community they are dwelling in. Many, perhaps most, suppose and hope that they are living there only for a short time; they have to find some place to live from which they can get to London, or to some place of employment on its periphery, and they find one in Middlesex for lack of anywhere better. London's powerful economic attraction overshadows the life of the old county; today it is hard to find a theatre, a shop of the highest class, or a first-rate handicraftsman in Middlesex. For these things people go to central London. Their attention is concentrated on London, too; the public affairs of Middlesex, and of the smaller units within it, are not followed with any great interest except by the few people immediately concerned with them. The separate lives of the places within the suburban belt are all but submerged by uniformity and indifference.

Middlesex is in danger of undergoing the same horrid fate that overtook the pleasant parishes of south London a century ago—of becoming a husk round the kernel of London. The danger is serious, and imminent; but a few signs show that it may not yet be quite too late for men who value flourishing life in their local communities to save Middlesex. There may just be time.

CHAPTER II

EARLIEST HISTORY

'If one thing is more certain than another in the formation of Saxon England, it is the utter insignificance of Middlesex.'

SIR MORTIMER WHEELER[1]

SHAPED flints, found about a line running from West Drayton almost due east as far as Acton, are the earliest evidence of man in Middlesex. All these remains come from the alluvial soil of the Thames valley and not from the clays farther north, heavily wooded and uninviting for settlement. The western area has been much more intensively excavated than the rest, mainly for extraction of gravel; the excavations themselves, and the recording of finds, have been fortuitously distributed, and the very considerable palaeolithic remains found on the clay just over the London border at Stoke Newington make it unwise to suggest that the Middlesex clays were quite uninhabited by man in the Neanderthal age. In the west, however, it is clear that men successfully hunted the mammoth with worked flint 'hand axes,' for these have been found in actual contact with mammoth bones at several places, notably at Norwood Lane, Southall. No human remains have yet come to light.[2]

In the succeeding, or neolithic, age, distinguished by the general use of pottery and the practice of polishing stone implements, there was a more complex social system, with settlement, agriculture, and the partial domestication of animals. No structural remains of this age have been found in Middlesex, where there was no natural supply of large stones; only comparatively small objects have survived—worked stones, horn or bone tools, and pottery, mostly from the Thames. Fragments of pottery, coarse, dark, and decorated with repetitive impressions made by some simple implement like the finger-nail, have been found in the river, with flint 'picks' (bars from 4 to 14 inches long)and celts (chipped and polished axes).

The two next eras in south-eastern England are related to the beaker folk,' so named from their most characteristic pottery vessel. The beaker phase, reached by about 1800 B.C., was associated with immigration from

[1] R. E. M. Wheeler, *London and the Saxons* (1935), p.70. [2] Based on Vulliamy, chapters I to VI.

10

western Europe; similarly the approximate beginning of the Bronze Age, about 1000 B.C., was linked with the arrival of the Goidels. The beaker period is represented by pottery and flint knives, and the Bronze Age by a large number of bronze tools and weapons and some flint and bone implements of the same era, mostly from the Thames. Bronze-Age burials were normally cremations: four cemeteries, consisting of ashes in urns just below the surface of the ground, have been found in the west and north-west, and three tumuli, now destroyed. 'Hoards' marking the site of bronze-casting operations have been excavated at Hounslow and Southall.

The Early Iron Age, which followed, is divided into a period known by the name of Hallstatt, in Tyrol, and a later development called after La Tène, on lake Neuchâtel, which was the type of civilisation that the Romans found in Britain in the last century before Christ. Remains of the Hallstatt period (c. 600-450 B.C.) are rare in Middlesex, but there are many of the late La Tène period, as there are over most of south-east England. Almost all the objects have come from the Thames, and some have been found near Harefield. A curious discovery at Hounslow, in the same field as the Bronze-Age hoard already mentioned, was some bronze animal figures, each just over two inches long, together with a tiny wheel; they are probably trinkets or amulets. Fragments of pottery survive from this period, and some crude tin coins have been found on Eel Pie Island, Twickenham, and at Gunnersbury and Brentford. Gold coins of the same age have been found at Kew Bridge, Harlington, Enfield Chase, and New Southgate.

It has generally been thought that the alluvial soil was too waterlogged, and the clay uplands too hard to work, even with the comparatively heavy Belgic plough, for any important permanent settlement to have taken place away from the river. A discovery of singular interest, however, was made during the construction of Heathrow airport during the war of 1939-45, when remains were found of a small rectangular building, presumably a temple, with a surrounding colonnade. It was clear from associated pottery that this dated from the Early Iron Age, perhaps about 300 B.C. These important, indeed unique, remains had to be destroyed, but they have cast a new light on the prehistory of Middlesex. The plain in the west of the county, away from the Thames, may have supported a settled population much earlier than has previously been admitted.[1]

The earliest literary record of events in Middlesex is Julius Caesar's account of his crossing of the Thames during his second invasion of Britain in 54 B.C. The narratives of Latin writers incidentally give valuable, if sometimes tantalising, information about the history and characteristics of his opponents on the north bank of the river. The

[1] *War and Archaeology in Britain* (Ministry of Works, 1949), p.16.

Catuvellauni ruled the whole of the area that later became Middlesex, together with Hertfordshire and Essex and parts of adjacent counties, from a capital at Wheathampstead, near St Albans.[1] Their pre-eminence was due not only to military success, but also to the position of the territory they occupied, commanding the lowest Thames fords. This tribe had led a Belgic invasion about 100-50 B.C.; Cassivellaunus, its earliest known ruler, had recently overrun the territory of the Trinovantes in Essex, and added it to his dominions when faced with Caesar's invasion. There is no certain indication that Middlesex, apart from the valleys of the Thames and Lea, was inhabited by a settled population at this time. Caesar says that inhabitants and cattle were driven from the cultivated clearings during his march northwards from the Thames, but this is a slender basis for supposing an agricultural population of any consequence. It was clearly unattractive to settle on clay land, heavily wooded, until all the easier land had been occupied, and the district was probably an uncultivated common.[3]

A likely reconstruction of Caesar's expedition is that he left the Kentish coast for his attack on the Catuvellauni, whom he recognised as the dominant power in the south, about 2 August 54 B.C. He reached the Thames basin at Eltham and marched along the southern edge of the marshes which then lay over the site of south London as far as Brentford. A large force under Cassivellaunus defended the ford, which was also protected by stakes in the river. Caesar's army rushed the ford without waiting for low tide and turned the Britons out of their camp.[4] After pausing here to receive the submission of some British tribes, the army marched north past Stanmore, harried by British skirmishers in chariots. Cassivellaunus' capital fell about the end of August; the Romans immediately returned to the coast and embarked for Gaul at the equinox.

This summary account of Caesar's expedition across Middlesex disposes quickly of some thorny questions, which have been much argued. Like the number of cities competing for the honour of Homer's birth, seven different places have been suggested for the river crossing. The older antiquaries upheld a tradition that Cowey Stakes, Shepperton, was the site; Sir Montagu Sharpe argued strongly for Brentford; Napoleon III, in his life of Caesar, favoured Sunbury; Gordon Home's *Roman London* argued for Chelsea; Manning and Bray were for Petersham; and C. E. Montague in his novel *Rough Justice* suggested Isleworth. Brentford appears the most likely place, corresponding best with Caesar's distance of 80 miles from the coast.[5]

The third Roman invasion of Britain, which led to the annexation of the greater part of the island, took place in A.D. 43 under Aulus Plautius, joined later by the emperor Claudius. Dio Cassius, who wrote about a

---

[1] R. E. M. Wheeler, *Antiquity* 7 (1933), p.32. [2] The Catuvellauni may not have been of Belgic origin: G. Home, *Roman London* (ed. 2, 1948), p.27. [3] E. Guest, *Origines Celticae* (1883), ii., p.391, quoted by Vulliamy, p. 200. [4] M. Sharpe, *Middlesex in British, Roman, and Saxon Times* (ed. 2, 1932), p. 54, and map opposite p. 52. [5] For this paragraph and throughout the Roman period, see R. G. Collingwood in Collingwood and Myres, *Roman Britain and the English Settlements* (1936), whose view on the river crossings is adopted here; for references to the other places, Home (note 2), p.35.

century later, described the campaign at some length but without enough topographical detail to fix the army's route. Plautius' objective was Camulodunum (Lexden, near Colchester), now the capital of the Catuvellauni, under Caractacus, the son of Cunobelinus (Cymbeline). After a check at the Thames crossing, Plautius halted to await reinforcements coming with Claudius; when these arrived the whole army crossed the river and established a camp on the north bank. Claudius went on from the river-crossing to capture Camulodunum and then returned home, leaving Plautius to establish Roman rule in south-east England. A permanent camp was soon constructed on an elevation between the outfalls of the Fleet and the Lea into the Thames, where a small trading-post already existed; London was effectively founded.

The Roman occupation, though it lasted nearly 400 years, has left few archaeological remains in Middlesex compared with the numbers found in neighbouring counties. Three main roads, probably built soon after the conquest, passed across the district: one from London past Brentford to a place named Pontes in the 3rd century 'Antonine Itinerary'—probably Staines, though no remains indicating Roman settlement have been found there; a second, later known as Watling Street, from the Marble Arch along the present Edgware Road, on which there was a station called Sulloniacae; and a third through Tottenham on its way to Lincoln and York. Between these great roads the Ordnance Survey map of Roman Britain is forced to leave a complete blank: not a single villa or other find indicating permanent settlement has come to light. Waterlogged and wooded soils alike were still avoided; the 'forest-ward shift' to good soil wherever it might be found had not yet begun. Some trifling Romano-British objects have been turned up at Enfield and Turnham Green and dredged from the Thames, and some of the bricks in Kingsbury church may be of Roman origin; but only at Brockley Hill and at Brentford have any substantial remains been found.

A Roman-age settlement is being excavated at Brockley Hill, near Stanmore, on the northern border. Its position fits well enough with the Itinerary's indications of Sulloniacae, but identity is not yet proved. Belgic pottery on the site points to an existing pre-Roman settlement of some kind, and pottery was apparently being made there in the Flavio-Trajanic period (A.D. 70-117). Possibly there was a Roman posting-station there, but it is unlikely that the place was ever more important than that.[1] At Old England, beside the Thames at Brentford, remains of a pile-dwelling of the Romano-British age were excavated in 1928 by R. E. Mortimer Wheeler. This was a humble riverside dwelling, apparently occupied in the 2nd century A.D.; it was rectangular, unlike the round lake-dwellings of Glastonbury. Below it were relics indicating earlier occupation in the Hallstatt period.[2]

[1] See Bibliography, Brockley Hill, p.403. [2] R. E. M. Wheeler, 'Old England,' *Antiquity* 3 (1929), p. 20.

The tangible remains of Roman occupation are thus very few. Written history adds next to nothing. It can only be supposed, for there is no direct statement, that Middlesex lay within the *territorium* of Verulamium, near St Albans; this was a town of municipal rank exercising local government over the old lands of the Catuvellauni. London was certainly an important place, where a Christian bishopric was established about A.D. 250; but it was neither an old tribal capital nor so far as is known a Roman *colonia* or *municipium* and cannot have possessed the *territorium* peculiar to towns of municipal rank. Its importance came from commerce and industry, and it belonged in a special sense to itself.

The end of Roman rule was foreshadowed under Valentinian I (368), when marauding bands of barbarians penetrated into Kent and made raids close up to London, renamed Augusta about the middle of the 4th century. The life of the whole south-east of Britain must have been in great upheaval well before 400, and by 410 the Romans had withdrawn completely. It appears that they resumed administration of parts of the island from about 417 to 429 or earlier; in this twilight of the Roman rule, London was the seat of the civil government of the triangle bounded by a line from Weymouth to the Wash.

After that the faint light that occasionally casts a gleam on places in the Middlesex area during the first four centuries A.D. goes out completely. The Dark Ages followed: dark not only because we cannot detect what happened in those times, except with difficulty and almost certainly with error, but also because they gave little reason for encouragement to the men of southern England, except what was brought to them by the firm establishment of the Christian faith.[1]

During this barely penetrable darkness Middlesex was converted from a thick forest, crossed by a few tracks, to a countryside varied with dwellings, cultivation, and pasture. Nothing of this process is known in detail, but it lies behind and beneath the few events that chroniclers have recorded. By the end of the dark age Middlesex had received its pattern of village and market-town, field and common, which survived in essentials until 18th-century enclosures completed another revolution in historic modes of life and economy.

It is not clear whether the first wave of Anglo-Saxon invasion, about 450-460, reached the area north of the middle Thames; it is not even known, though there is plenty of conjecture, whether London retained any recognisable municipal entity throughout. But it is almost certain that there was Saxon settlement in the Middlesex area by 550-570. Place-names ending in *-ing*, a termination indicating 'the men of ...', suggest settlement during the early stages of sporadic immigration; these survive at Yeading and Ealing, and they are found in the earliest forms

---

[1] The main authority for the rest of this chapter is F. M. Stenton, *Anglo-Saxon England* (ed. 2, 1947), supplemented in the earlier portion by J. N. L. Myres in Collingwood and Myres (page 12, note 5).

of Hayes and Harrow—*Linga Haese* and *Gumeninga Hearh*. The word *hearh* in the last is particularly significant; it means 'the holy place,' the tribal sanctuary on the hill-top—the only indication of Saxon heathenism in the county. All these places are in the western part of the county, on or close to the valley soils. Near them is another remarkable group of names, Uxbridge, Waxlow, near Southall, and Uxendon at Preston, which apparently refer to the tribe of the Wixan; these equally come down from the earliest Saxon times when the tribe was still the significant unit. North and east of the Uxbridge road, on the clay land, settlement was later; names of a later stratum are found: -*wood*, -*ley*, -*field*, like Northwood, Finchley, Enfield, implying settlement and clearance in woodland. Thus the evidence of place-names reinforces the conclusion that is probable in any case: settlement began along the Thames and on the easily-worked alluvial lands in the west, slowly spreading northwards into the clay and forest belt.[1]

How were the inhabitants of Middlesex organised in the 6th century? Was Middlesex ever an independent political entity? This is the crux of all Middlesex history. There is no direct evidence that it was; indeed, the question would hardly arise but for the name. Middlesex belongs to a series of which the other members, Essex, Sussex, and Wessex, were all in historical times independent political units with well-established dynasties of their own, and it is natural to deduce that Middlesex was also an independent kingdom. One other puzzling feature in the names of the Thames valley could be explained if this was in fact so: the name of Surrey, *Suthrige*, the southern district, implies that there was a corresponding district to the north. If Middlesex was this corresponding district, the two together may have formed a Middle Saxon kingdom of sufficient weight to withstand for a few decades the pressure of more powerful neighbours from east and south—just long enough to affix these names to the areas.

There is, however, no direct evidence or any tradition to support this view. Early Saxon remains in Middlesex, a region that has been pretty thoroughly dug over within the last hundred years, practically amount to no more than a cemetery at Shepperton and a settlement at Hanwell. In Vulliamy's phrase, 'the scarcity of early Saxon relics in our district is best accounted for by the scarcity of early Saxons.'[2] If the place-names are really good evidence of early settlements, the villages can only have been very thinly populated. There is no known trace of any settlement suggesting a political capital of even such a minor kingdom as the hypothesis requires, unless there is one buried under modern Brentford. No tradition mentions a Middlesex royal family, and by the time written history begins again, soon after 550, the territory was already a dependency of Essex. Again, London stood at a point commanding the

---

[1] *Place-Names of Middlesex* (English Place-Name Society, vol. xviii, 1942), introduction; Darby, pp. 129, 166. [2] Vulliamy, p. 238.

communications of Middlesex and Surrey; whether the history of London was continuous or broken, Middlesex seems at this period to have been politically separate from it. Yet it is difficult to see how a viable state of Middlesex-cum-Surrey could have been formed without London.

No more, in short, can be said than this: the settlers in Middlesex, who may have had some kind of loose association with those in Surrey, were independent of outside control but never linked together in a close political grouping, until they fell before the first serious pressure from Essex. The problem of the names remains; perhaps Middlesex, first found in a copy of a charter of 704, was the description used to designate the tribal *regiones*, not combined in any higher grouping, that filled the unnamed area between Essex and Wessex.'

There is one piece of evidence dating from this period, as is usually supposed, whose significance is very difficult to assess. This is the Middlesex Grim's Dyke, a ditch and earthwork now traceable from the west side of Pinner in a north-easterly direction as far as Harrow Weald. It can hardly have been a military defence work, for it is sited quite uselessly for that purpose; it looks as though it must have delimited two spheres of influence—perhaps Teutonic invaders pressing down from the north and the Middlesex tribes clearing the forest from the south. If the northern people constructed the work, some more potent influence than a loose association of settlers must have been blocking their way south; if the Middlesex people did, it again argues a stronger organisation existing among them than appears from any other indication. If any conclusion is to be drawn from this rather mysterious feature, it may be that London, with a continuing sub-Roman tradition, retained more influence than has commonly been allowed and the Dyke marked its farthest north-westward extent. But it may yet turn out that it is a pre-Roman work.[2]

The notion of continuity in cultural and economic life in Middlesex from Romano-British to Saxon, and so to Norman, times has proved attractive for other reasons. Sir Montagu Sharpe devoted great energy to demonstrating that there was such a continuous tradition. The essence of his theory is this: 'The rights and services of the former Romano-British *tributarii* and *coloni*, fixed by the usage of centuries, had become crystallised into a well-known unwritten or customary law, and so firmly established that upon it was grafted much of the Saxon manorial system, while its fundamental feature, the village farm with appendant pasturage, has lasted down to the enclosure of parishes in modern times.'[3] This contention, which in the nature of the subject can never be completely established or refuted, is backed by different kinds of argument, and much ingenuity. Later writers have been inclined to view the economy of

---

[1] On 6th-century Middlesex, Myres (page 12, note 5), p.371, and review by R. E. M. Wheeler, *Journal of Roman Studies* 29 (1939), p.92; R. E. M. Wheeler, *London and the Saxons* (1935); Darby, p. 124, quoting Mackinder, (page 4, note 1), p. 182. [2] Wheeler, *Saxons* (see preceding note), p.59; Vulliamy, p. 270; see also Grim's Dyke in Part II, page 257, and Bibliography, page 380. [3] Sharpe (page 12, note 4), p.116.

the early Saxon settlement differently. J. N. L. Myres writes: 'Even if the possibility of some influence of the old agriculture on the new be allowed, yet the whole structure of rural society was shattered and reformed, and the towns and manors of the late Saxon England can claim no demonstrable connection with the Roman past.'[1] (This does not necessarily imply that the Romano-British population, as opposed to its institutions, was supplanted by the Saxons; more probably large elements survived and were assimilated.) Secondly, it is not agreed that the Saxons were incapable of providing an organisation of their own; indeed, the Anglo-Saxon forms of organisation have been traced back to Germany, and it is now held, with growing knowledge of Teutonic antiquities, that the essential fabric of social order, the fundamental technicalities of law, and the organisation by which they were administered, are all of obvious Germanic origin.[2] If these objections are well founded, as they seem to be, the old view appears to be correct: the Saxon conquest marked a sharp and real break in the rural economy of Middlesex.

Political history is a little clearer. By 600 London had become the chief town of the East Saxon kingdom; Surrey was already in 568 a territory disputed between Kent and Wessex. From then onwards Middlesex was a border province falling under the influence of the kingdoms of Essex, Mercia, and Wessex in turn. Because of its central position between these three, places in it were several times chosen for negotiations and councils, both royal and ecclesiastical. Throughout the Saxon period succeeding kings presented large Middlesex estates to the sees of London and Canterbury, and the Church became steadily more influential in the temporal as well as the spiritual life of the inhabitants. The diocese of London has throughout, with a very short break from 1540 to 1550, when there was a see of Westminster, included the whole of present Middlesex, apart from the archbishop of Canterbury's peculiar jurisdiction on his own manors of Harrow and Hayes and a tiny portion of Stanwell parish on the extreme west of the county in the diocese of Oxford. The see of London, which had originally existed under the Roman administration, was refounded in 604 with Mellitus as its bishop; its area—Essex, Middlesex, and the southern part of Hertfordshire—presumably corresponded with the East Saxon kingdom at that time. Secular boundaries were moved to and fro over Middlesex in succeeding centuries, but the diocese remained substantially unaltered until 1845.[3]

The assignment of the area into the six 'hundreds' of Middlesex, which retained some administrative significance until the 19th century and are still remembered in the names of some parliamentary and petty sessional divisions, probably took place in early Saxon times. The most important was Ossulston, in the south-east, comprising all the places in

---

[1] Myres (page 12, note 5), p.444.   [2] Stenton (page 14, note 1), p.311.   [3] For diocesan boundaries before 1845, see B. Williams, *Whig Supremacy* (1939), map 1, based on Church Commissioners' report, 1835.

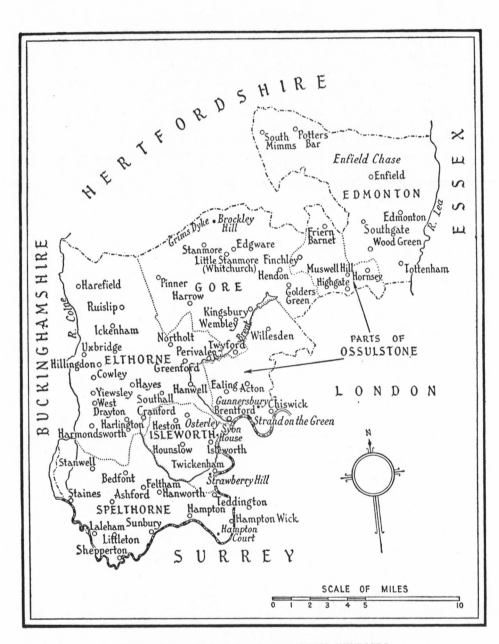

MIDDLESEX, SHOWING THE DIVISION INTO HUNDREDS

Isleworth hundred was called Hounslow at Domesday
(The places named are treated separately in Part II)

the county lying between the lower Lea and the Brent, except Hanwell; the name was derived from Oswulf's stone, the hundred meeting-place, probably near South Street, Park Lane. Hounslow hundred lay between Heston and Hampton, and Spelthorne (named from a thorn-tree at a place rather uncertainly identified near Ashford Common, and positively commemorated there by a public-house) between Hanworth and Staines; Elthorne, from another thorn-tree (perhaps in Southall near Hayes bridge, almost certainly not at Elthorne Park, Hanwell), extended from Brentford to the north-western corner at Harefield; Gore, whose meeting-place was at a *gara* or wedge-shaped piece of land in Kingsbury, comprised Harrow, Stanmore, Kingsbury, Edgware, and Hendon; Edmonton (perhaps meeting near Potters Bar) comprised Edmonton, Tottenham, and Enfield. These were the allocations to hundreds in the Domesday Survey; apart from a later transfer of Hampton and Teddington from Hounslow to Spelthorne, the boundaries remained unaltered for eight hundred years after, until the hundreds dropped out of use.

The successive allegiances of the Middlesex territory cannot be learnt from chronicles; they have to be pieced together from stray indications, mostly furnished by charters recording transfers of land. These are dated precisely, and the countersignatures of the overlords show the sphere of influence within which the area was lying at the time. The power of Essex suffered shocks during the 7th century, and Ine of Wessex, who reigned from 688 to 726, referred to Eorcenwald of London as 'my bishop'; but the earliest Middlesex charter—a deed signed in 695 by the same Eorcenwald relating to land at Isleworth (in the Saxon form of Gisleheeresuuyrth) and preserved, as most of them are, only in a later copy—is countersigned by the three joint kings of Essex. The next charter, dated 704, is specially significant: it is the earliest evidence for the name of Middlesex. It relates to land at *Tuicanhom in provincia quae nuncupatur Middelseaxan*, granted to Waldhere, bishop of London, by Suebraed, at that time sole king of Essex, with the additional signature of Coenred, king of Mercia—the earliest appearance of Mercia in connection with Middlesex. In the same year or the next Waldhere wrote to Berhtwald, archbishop of Canterbury, about a proposal to hold a council at Brentford concerning a dispute between the kings of Wessex and Essex. Middlesex must have been finally detached from Essex by the accession of Aethelbald of Mercia, for in 716 he granted land at Acton and Brentford without any other signature. His son Offa also granted Middlesex land as he pleased, at Harrow in 767 and at Hayes, Yeading, and Twickenham (these to the archbishop of Canterbury) in 790. Councils of the kingdom or synods of the church were held at Brentford in 780 and 781.

Under Offa's successors, Cenwulf and Beornwulf, the authority of

[1] Loftie (page 3, note 1), ii., p. 10; Sharpe (page 12, note 4), p. 192.

Mercia was recognised in Middlesex; but in 825 Egbert of Wessex defeated Beornwulf at Ellendun (Wroughton, near Swindon) and assumed the overlordship of all south-east England. In 830, however, Wiglaf recovered Mercia, and in 831 he made at Wychbold a grant of land at Botwell, Hayes, to the archbishop without any reference to Egbert. From that time London and Middlesex remained Mercian under Wiglaf and his successor until they were overrun by the Danes about the middle of the century. It is possible that from 879 to 886 Watling Street formed the boundary between Wessex and the Danish territories throughout its length; it is known, however, that by the treaty which Alfred, king of Wessex, signed with Guthrum, king of the Danes, in or soon after 886, it became the boundary of the Danish domains (or Danelaw) only so far south as a point about 50 miles north-west of London, from which the border ran to the river Lea and so down to its confluence with the Thames. In the following years Middlesex was crossed and recrossed by contending armies, the Saxons led by Alfred, his eldest son Edward, and Ethelred of Mercia, and there were engagements at a place called Thorney, an island in the Colne on the Middlesex-Buckinghamshire border, and in the Lea valley.

During the reigns of Edward the Elder, 899-924, and Athelstan, 924-c.939, Middlesex was left in comparative peace. It was probably overrun by the revolt of Aethelwold, Edward's cousin, supported by the Danes, in 902, but Edward's campaigns of 911 and the next few years drove the Wessex border farther north and east. There must have been much lawlessness within his territory, however, for a remarkable association for mutual protection, described as a 'peace gild,' was formed in Athelstan's reign. The leading members were the bishop and reeves of London; the ordinary members were the countrymen of a region which certainly included all Middlesex and may also have comprised Surrey and part of Hertfordshire. While providing for the spiritual benefit of its members, its chief object was the maintenance of law and order by means of a voluntary association for the pursuit of thieves and compensation for persons injured. Royal authority had become inadequate to guarantee the public peace.

About this time the northern boundary of Middlesex was fixed. The formation of shires is generally attributed to the reign of Ethelred II, 978-1018, and Hertfordshire is first mentioned in 1011; this was a 'shire,' a piece 'shorn,' and thus a deliberate creation for administrative purposes, not an existing region. The old northern boundary of the diocese of London and the extraordinary patchwork of hundreds in south Hertfordshire indicate that the country south-east of the Colne was detached from Middlesex at this time. The new boundary ran fairly straight along a low ridge from Harefield to Barnet, thence due north

---

¹ Clapham, *Concise*, introduction.

before turning east, so that it took the whole of Enfield Chase into Middlesex; but Totteridge, Chipping Barnet, and East Barnet (not Friern Barnet), which lay south of this line, were also included in Hertfordshire, being lands of the abbey of St Albans or of Hatfield, which belonged to Ely.[1] This strangely indented and inconvenient boundary has lasted down to the present day, except that Hadley was transferred to Hertfordshire in the 20th century.

Administration, however, could not be the unfortunate Ethelred's main care, From 980 onwards the Vikings renewed their incursions, and London was attacked several times, with stronger forces and greater determination. In 993 or 994 Olaf Tryggvason sailed with 93 ships up the Thames as far as Staines, and expeditions of 1009 and 1012 almost certainly included ravages in Middlesex. Under Sweyn in 1013 they made an unsuccessful attack on London from the west; but the city was finally brought to submission three years later, when almost all the rest of England had been overrun. Middlesex thus came under direct Danish administration, but, although a distinctive form of customary law deriving from Danish sources was recognised in the laws of William the Conqueror, it seems unlikely that there was intensive Danish settlement. The only place-name in the county formed from a Danish root is Gunnersbury, based on the feminine name Gunnhild; this single example contrasts strikingly with the number of Danish names on the Thames below London, like Sheerness, Northfleet, and Woolwich. Viking weapons and implements have been found in the Thames and Lea, but not elsewhere on Middlesex soil.

After 1016 Middlesex seems to have remained comparatively untroubled, until the events of 1066 opened a new chapter in its history.

[1] J. C. Russell, *British Medieval Population* (Albuquerque, 1948), p.20.

CHAPTER III

THE ECONOMIC BACKGROUND

*'Of all varieties of history the economic is the most
fundamental. Not the most important: foundations
exist to carry better things.'* SIR JOHN CLAPHAM[1]

DOWN to the 11th century, the economic, political, and ecclesiastical
histories of Middlesex (and of every other English county) cannot
be told separately. As successive disturbances made their impact upon
the area, economy, administration, and Church were affected directly
and equally; their affairs were so much intermingled, and they changed
so often in response to the same influences, that it would be tiresomely
repetitive to treat them apart.

From a time soon after A.D. 1000 things were different. The south-east
of England settled into a relatively stable political condition, broken only
for a moment by the great conquest of 1066 and by later commotions of
smaller significance. Organised life now had a fair prospect of security to
develop in its own way: agricultural organisation could be pushed
forward with a reasonable hope of return on outlay and experiment; the
Church no longer needed to fear pagan attacks or the quarrels of regional
rulers; and the king's administration could assume a more permanent
form. From this time forward developments in these three spheres can be
considered separately, though naturally they did not cease to influence
one another. Economy must be put first here, as it should be in any local
history; one does not have to be a Marxist to agree that the soil and its
products, trades and industries, and the means of communication existing
in each age of Middlesex development have been the things that
primarily determined its character. Politics and schisms may change the
nature of historical development; the local economy forms it.

The 11th century in England is illuminated, as none before and few
since, by the precious statistics of the Domesday Survey made in 1086.
They show a flourishing and developed agricultural society fully in
being; the Norman Conquest, however important in a political sense,
came in the middle of an economic age and did not by itself create a new

---

[1] Clapham, *Concise*, introduction.

set of economic conditions or coincide with any great economic change. In social affairs, of course, the changes it made were important, though not fundamental.

Domesday Book shows Middlesex with the general features it was to retain throughout the Middle Ages: the best manors belonging to the Church; scarcely any land held by the king; a good deal of infertile forest in the north and north-west; no towns. With less forest, and a few local market towns, this was still generally true in 1500. Domesday, however, also showed one feature that did not persist—a great noble as an important lay proprietor: Geoffrey de Mandeville, whose grandson lost all his inheritance through rebellion against Stephen in 1144; and after that great lords kept their estates at a distance from the seat of royal power. The Middlesex holdings of lay proprietors in the later Middle Ages were politically unimportant, and most of the lay owners were nonentities; the Church, assisted by the favour of pious monarchs, slowly gathered more and more land to itself.

Though the Roman roads were overcome by decay, travellers still had to pass through Middlesex to get from London to three-quarters of the places in the kingdom, and Middlesex men made good earnings from the carrying trade, by land and on the Thames and Lea. Already in the 13th century trees were being cut in Windsor Park for the bridge at Staines, and Middlesex fairs were attended by traders from far beyond the county. Brick-earth was used for bricks and tiles for London houses, where tile was nominally essential for all roofs after the great fire in John's reign; an account exists for tiles burned at Harlesden in 1500. There were no other industries worth the name; the working of woollen cloth, the great medieval industry, was not carried on in Middlesex.

This sketchy picture of medieval Middlesex needs to be filled in with much more detail still lying in manuscript records. The district was too obscure to merit much attention from the older writers, and modern scholars have largely ignored it; neither the poll tax returns of 1377, a first-rate economic document, nor the chantry certificates of 1545, stating the number of persons receiving Holy Communion in each parish, have ever been printed for this county.[1] The surveys and extents of Hendon have been published—a remarkable series perhaps unexcelled for completeness and the span of time (from 1321 onwards) that they cover; but the local affairs of other places whose records have survived have not yet been fully examined. Meanwhile, Middlesex generally appears on distribution-maps of population and wealth in medieval England with a disproportionately high attribution that is quite misleading. Even when 'London' is specifically left out of the county totals of population or taxation assessments, this only means that the City, properly so called, has been excluded; all London outside the City boundaries—

Westminster, the districts round the Tower, and Smithfield—is left in Middlesex, and the county average is thus inflated. All statistics about the county are subject to this qualification in some degree until 1889, when it became administratively separate from London; there is consequently less known about its present area in former centuries from the statistical sources familiar to students of English life than might be supposed.[1]

The Middle Ages, in the social and economic affairs of the county, came to an end very suddenly between 1530 and 1545. Henry VIII helped himself to most of west and south-west Middlesex, partly as a gigantic rounding-off to the manor of Hampton so as to form a royal chase extending over Surrey and Middlesex from Epsom to Staines, and partly because the monasteries had owned most of the land on that side of the county. What enclaves were left in other hands were soon drawn into the Crown's possession, either by forced sale, as the archbishop of Canterbury's manors of Harrow and Hayes, or by unwilling exchange, like Lord Windsor's manor of Stanwell, sadly given up for Bordesley abbey in Warwickshire. Almost every manor in the county passed to the Crown between 1537 and 1545; only a few escaped—the estates of the bishop of London and the dean and chapter of St Paul's, those of All Souls at Edgware, Harlesden, and Kingsbury, and of King's at Ruislip, and a group in the north-west at Harefield, Ickenham, and Hillingdon, and Tottenham in the north-east. Henry endowed the new bishopric of Westminster with some, kept many included in the honour of Hampton Court for himself, and sold others to the rising men of the time—Acton to Russell, West Drayton and Harmondsworth to Paget, Harrow and Hayes to North. Edward VI granted Brentford to Seymour, Duke of Somerset, and Hendon to Herbert, Earl of Pembroke; Elizabeth made over Heston to Sir Thomas Gresham; finally, James I disposed of a block in the south-west—Isleworth, Staines, Stanwell, and Sunbury. The Crown was forced to realise the huge capital that it had taken from the monasteries in order to pay for its wars; more readily, perhaps, because it was actually losing money, in that century of rising prices, on some of the properties where rents were fixed and low. A century after Henry VIII's acquisitions, it owned little more in Middlesex than it did before then, except around Hampton.[2] In some counties like Nottinghamshire the transfer of lands after the Dissolution entrenched the old land-owning families still more firmly; but in Middlesex there were none already established in the county who could profit in this way. Almost every one of the owners who came in was a new man, either attached to the service of the court, like Thomas Lake at Stanmore and Lionel Cranfield, created Earl of Middlesex in 1625, or grown wealthy in the City, like Thomas Gresham of Osterley and Edmund Wright of

---

[1] On the materials for the early economic history, see *V.C.H. ii.*, p. 102 (appendix I). [2] S. J. Madge, *Domesday of Crown Lands* (1938), pp. 42, 50; Clapham, *Concise*, p. 201.

Swakeleys—the new middle class busily making its way up to the ranks of the nobility.

From that time land changed hands so often that no dominating gentry had time to take root and form a county interest. Northumberland at Syon, Child and Villiers at Osterley, Byng at Wrotham, owned acres but hardly ruled them. This is the clue to much of the fragmentary, independent tendency of Middlesex affairs, political, economic, and social, which means that almost any generalisation about life in the county can be easily rebutted.

Elizabethan writers dwell on Middlesex as a wheat country—in his poem *Poly-Olbion* Michael Drayton wrote of 'Peryvale ... prank'd up with wreaths of wheat,' and Heston is traditionally supposed to have provided the special grain for Elizabeth's own table. But it was not only an arable country: there was a good deal of variety in rural occupations—cattle breeding and fattening, carrying to and from London, ferrying and fishing on the Thames. Market gardens for supplying London's food crept up the Thames valley into the area during the 17th century, and fruit and vegetable cultivation has remained a characteristic feature into the first decades of the 20th. They have not yet quite disappeared, though houses and airports have almost stamped them out.

In spite of all this activity, very much of the county still lay in unenclosed common and waste by the time enclosure by private acts of Parliament began soon after 1760. The greatest commons, Enfield, Finchley, and Hounslow, were successfully enclosed (subdued, contemporaries called it) during the Napoleonic wars; the process was practically complete by 1825. The early 19th-century farmer had a secure market in London; he was prosperous, and in consequence often unenterprising in his practices. In the south of the county, the rich alluvial soil was splendid arable ground, either for corn or for more specialised fruit or vegetable crops; in the north, on heavy clays, grass farms supplied hay for London horses. Hay was the characteristic north Middlesex crop from about 1750 to 1900; it needed little attention except at the mowing, which was mostly done by itinerant labour, and the resident population of places like Kingsbury and Edgware was small.

Elsewhere, especially along the great roads and the Thames valley, there had always been since late medieval days some settlement of Londoners, either great ones who had country houses or more modest ones who went to the city daily. From 1800 onwards this element in the county grew more quickly; after 1837, with the opening of railways, it invaded quiet country places like Southall and Harrow, hitherto rather self-contained; after 1885, as tramways spread first in the north and then in the west, it overran the nearer districts; then, as railways and tramways were electrified after 1900, it became a flood; and in the two decades from 1920 to 1940 it submerged almost everything left of the old Middlesex, its fields and its market gardens and its ways of life.

There were few industries down to the middle of the 19th century: brickmaking, brewing, milling (mostly at Uxbridge and Staines), powder mills on Hounslow Heath, and a few miscellaneous undertakings along the Thames and Lea. But since 1875, and especially since 1918, Middlesex has become one of the most important manufacturing districts of Britain, mainly for small and easily transportable products. With improved transport, firms no longer need to establish their works close to their principal raw materials, and there is enough labour to man factories near to the bulk of consumers; it is being close to the market that matters now. Thus manufacturers have preferred to set up new plant in the south-east of England, and in Middlesex in particular. This process was at its peak in the late 1920s and early 1930s. At the same time firms moved their factories from the congested areas of inner London to suburban districts generally in the same sector—Long Acre to Acton in the west, Whitechapel and Hoxton to the Lea valley in the north-east. There was not properly speaking a drift of industry from the north of England to the south-east; it was new industries that were established in the south-east and not in the old industrial districts.

Only since 1945 has government intervention effectively diverted this incursion of new industrial development to other industrial areas on grounds of general social policy; otherwise the lighter industries would probably have continued to congregate in Middlesex. One industry, however, cannot be planned away: extraction of the gravels from the Thames valley proceeds fast enough to make experts inquire what is to happen when within a measurable period the accessible supply has been exhausted.

Apart from the industries that properly belong to Middlesex there are those that provide services for London. Viewed in one way, the provision and servicing of dwellings for London workers might be called the staple industry of the county; but besides this it affords very many of the services that a great modern community requires. Some of those that it formerly supplied have disappeared, as needs and capacity have changed: field sports and many other kinds of country recreation have now to be sought by the citizen much farther away; there is no demand for hay, and there is no supply of firewood; the brickfields have been worked out. But still most of London's water is treated at the works beside the Thames, the Lea, and the New River; some of its gas is made at Brentford; the immense transport network is largely based on Middlesex ground for depots, repair shops, and railway yards; factories outside the London boundary supply many of the consumer goods, from tinned food to vacuum cleaners, that modern life demands; and many of

London's laundries are in the outer suburbs. London's two main civil airports lie on Middlesex land, at Heathrow and Northolt; so do cemeteries of metropolitan boroughs, mental hospitals of its county council, heaths and parks, and something of a 'green belt,' playing fields of schools and clubs; and beside the canal at Yeading is a gigantic rubbish dump built up from the city's refuse. If there were no such place as Middlesex, it would be necessary to create something very much like it merely to keep London going. The two areas, tolerably distinct in function and activity, complement each other.

The economic background of Middlesex has thus been formed by its geography—the two dominant soils, alluvium and clay, one well suited to intensive arable cultivation and the other to grass-farming, and the rivers Thames and Lea. The foreground has always in historic times been shadowed by the existence of London, as a market, as a centre of communications, and finally as an agglomeration of incessantly increasing population. Great towns inevitably cast their influence over the districts surrounding them; London's action on Middlesex is not peculiar. Effects of the same kind as Middlesex has felt may be traced in the history of the country round Paris. There also agricultural development was stimulated when fields were broken up into market gardens very early, well before the Revolution; commons almost vanished; and finally Paris overflowed with a flood of dwellings and industrial expansion. Like London, it drove the sources of its food supply further away from the hungry mouths of the capital and made the maintenance of its daily economy ever more delicate and precarious.[1]

The sequel may prove to be the same in both cases. Great cities need their home counties, both for sustenance and for recreation; but 20th-century cities swallow their surrounding country. It is certainly bad for their appearance, and it may well turn out to be disastrous for their economic digestion.

[1] J. H. Clapham, *Economic Development of France and Germany, 1815-1914* (ed. 4, 1936), pp. 9, 32.

CHAPTER IV

AGRICULTURE

'An acre in Middlesex is better than a principality
in Utopia'   MACAULAY[1]

THE Norman Conquest marks an epoch in English economic history:
not that its effect on daily life was revolutionary, but because its great
economic record has been preserved—the Domesday Survey, ordered by
William and completed in 1086. Whereas there is plenty of evidence
from documents before this date bearing on particular questions at
individual places, Domesday was the first general statistical inquiry into
England, answering the same questions on a comparable basis almost
throughout the whole kingdom; and it has survived.

The Middlesex Domesday, like Hertfordshire but unlike the East
Anglian counties, is a summary compiled from the original returns,
arranging the principal information not geographically but under the
landowners. Apart from a few small difficulties, understanding of the
document itself is relatively uncomplicated, by comparison with the
crucial topographical problems met in other counties. The places named
are all identifiable with their successors; the hundreds are exactly the
same as they always remained down to the 19th century, except that
Hampton and Teddington, then included in Hounslow, were later
transferred to Spelthorne. There is in each case a complete statement of
the annual value at three dates: in 1066; when the existing owner
received the land; and in 1086. There is, however, one considerable
lacuna: the land from Barnet to the London border, Finchley, Friern
Barnet, and Hornsey (together with Monken Hadley, then in Middlesex,
and possibly, though less probably, Edgware), is not mentioned in the
survey. Sir Montagu Sharpe suggested that these lands, part of the St
Albans abbey domains, had been seized for the Crown in 1066. If so,
they should appear in the survey with the king's other possessions; but
they do not. Hornsey and Finchley are later found in the ownership of
the bishop of London, and they were probably included in Domesday as
part of his lordships of Stepney and Fulham.[2]

[1] Macaulay, *Essay on Bacon.*
[2] Sharpe (page 12, note 4), p.211; S. J. Madge, *Early Records of Harringay alias Hornsey* (1938),
p.31; C. J. Féret, *Fulham Old and New* (1900) i., p.13.

The outstanding economic fact revealed by the survey is that the annual value of Middlesex was £909 in 1066 and had fallen to £748 in 1086, though this was past the lowest point. It used to be thought that 'Beorhamsted,' where William made peace with the Londoners, was Berkhamsted, in Hertfordshire, and routes for his devastating army were deduced from the greatest depreciations in value recorded in the parishes. But it is now held that Bearsted, in Kent, is the place referred to, and it is no longer useful to trace a line of 'scorched earth' through Hampton and Harrow and attribute it to the invasion.[1] Still, it is worth noticing that Edmonton hundred actually rose in value; the others, especially Elthorne in the west, declined heavily.

The measure of assessment was the 'hide'—a fiscal unit, not an area of land, though it probably represented in practice something like 120 acres. The county was assessed at 880 hides; a five-hide basis of assessment can be traced down to each parish. There were 664 'plough lands' in the county; but an important part of the evidence is still a mystery. If only we could possibly tell what the constantly repeated expression, *et quinque adhuc possent fieri*, 'and five (or whatever the number is) more could be made,' really means! Was this some 'target', of agricultural experts, or a statement how much land had gone out of cultivation? We do not know, and perhaps we never shall know. What is clear, however, is that the density of population and plough teams on the Middlesex gravel lands is above the general average for south-east England.

The return, after the principal matters of arable farming are dealt with, recites the other sources of rural wealth. Pigs were important in the economy, though the numbers given are round guesses: there was 'pannage,' or feeding in the woods, for 2,000 swine in Harrow manor and on Geoffrey de Mandeville's great estates at Enfield and Edmonton. There were 33½ water-mills in the county (the odd half lay across the Colne at Colham, shared with Buckinghamshire); 20½ fisheries, mostly for eels; and seven vineyards. The belt of woodland along the northern border of the county was completed by two large hunting parks—*parcus est ibi ferarum silvaticarum* at Ruislip, and another at Enfield.[2]

After the great survey, references to the agricultural life of Middlesex are fragmentary. Records of the manors of Hendon, Harrow, and Harmondsworth can be made to reveal much of their local affairs, but the general level of prosperity can be deduced only from comparison of the tax assessments with those for other counties. Conclusions must become more tentative as the buildings of London overspread the City boundaries, and thus the profits of trade as well as agriculture came to be reflected in the county valuations.

Middlesex recovered quickly from the Conquest and the anarchy

[1] E. Ekwall, *Concise Oxford Dictionary of English Place-Names* (ed. 3, 1947), art. Bearstead and Berkhamstead, and supplementary note, p.525. [2] There is no discussion of the Middlesex Domesday in *V.C.H.* (so far). Summaries of the figures appear in F. H. Baring, *Domesday Tables* (1909), p.79; M. Sharpe, *Middlesex in British, Roman, and Saxon Times* (ed. 2, 1932), p.219, and *Middlesex in the Eleventh Century* (1941). For the text see W. Bawdwen, *Dom Boc: a Translation of the Record called Domesday, so far as relates to the Counties of Middlesex, Hertford, Buckingham, and Gloucester* (Doncaster, 1812); facsimile (1861) and *Literal Extension of the Latin Text and an English Translation of Domesday Book in relation to the County of Middlesex* (1862); G. H. Harrison, *Facsimile of the Original Domesday Book with translation by General Plantagenet-Harrison* (1876).

under Stephen. The great pipe roll of Henry II, compiled in 1156, shows
the county assessed for Danegeld, as the royal tax was still called, at £85
os. 6d., with £10 lying in waste.[1] The proportion of waste to total—nearly
an eighth—is remarkably small for the time; only Sussex and Kent of all
the English counties show less. Soon after, certainly by 1183, the monk
William FitzStephen wrote[2]: '[To the north of London] are pasture lands
and a pleasant space of flat meadows, intersected by running waters,
which turn revolving mill-wheels with a merry din. Hard by there
stretches a great forest with wooded glades and lairs of wild beasts, deer
both red and fallow, wild boar and bulls. The cornfields are not of barren
gravel, but rich Asian plains such as make glad the crops and fill the
barns of their farmers with sheaves of Ceres' stalk.'

Throughout the 12th and 13th centuries the work of clearing the
forests and wastes, grubbing up the trees, turning the land over to
cultivation, and settling more villages continued. Early in the 13th
century Middlesex obtained complete exemption from forest laws; a
grant by Henry III in 1227 permitted cultivation and enclosure within
the warren of Staines, extending over the whole south-western district
up to Hounslow. This does not imply that all this area had previously
been waste or uncultivated; it was land outside the Common Law,
subject to a special law with the sole object of preserving the king's
hunting.[3]

It is difficult to judge how important sheep-farming was in medieval
Middlesex. It is mentioned in a charter of 1227, by which the house of
St John of Jerusalem at Hampton was permitted to have unlawed dogs to
guard the sheepfolds. (To 'law' a dog meant to mutilate its feet so as to
make it unable to hunt.) A return of 1338 from Hampton to the grand
master of the order in Malta showed 2,000 sheep. Middlesex wool is
included in a valuation of 1343 with the remark that, being 'marsh wool,'
its value was less than that from the Midlands. Though Middlesex wool
production was never of primary importance, it came second only to
Norfolk when the 'wool tax' of Edward III was levied in 1341. Then
Middlesex (excluding London) had to pay 236 sacks, or one to 760
acres; Norfolk was rated at 1 to 610 and all other counties less—
Hertfordshire 1 to 1,200 and Surrey 1 to 1,250 acres.[4] The 'nonae rolls,'
or records of ninths paid as tax to Edward III for his wars in France,
Scotland, and Gascony, show Middlesex outside London as an entirely
agricultural county. The most profitable parish was Staines, which paid
£50 and 1 mark; Harrow, Edmonton, and Enfield each paid over £40;
Great Stanmore, at the other end of the scale, paid 20 shillings. There
were complaints of poverty from Harmondsworth and Littleton,
attributed the sandy soil; at Littleton and Shepperton things were said to
be so bad that the peasants could not sow their lands; and at Sunbury it

---

[1] Quoted by Darby, p. 173. [2] H. E. Butler's translation: F. M. Stenton, *Norman London* (1934),
p. 26. [3] Darby, p. 176; *V.C.H.* ii., p.224. [4] *V.C.H.* ii., p. 61; Darby, p.242; E. Yates, *Hampton
Court* (1935), p.8.

was declared that most of the land was lying fallow and most of the sheep had been sold.[1]

A progressively greater area cultivated was one important feature of the agricultural economy; equally significant was the process by which personal services rendered on the manors were commuted for money payments. The Black Death of 1348-9 and the consequent shortage of agricultural labour only hastened a process already at work by the beginning of the 14th century, by which the farmers became free tenants and the owners of the manors hired labourers to do their work. One would perhaps expect that the neighbourhood of London, by providing tenants with a market and landlords with a supply of labour, would have accelerated commutation. In fact, however, commutation in Middlesex was on the whole later than in other counties, and there are few cases in the manor rolls of tenants deserting.[2] It may be that the large amount of land in Church ownership accounts in part for the lateness of the development; when temporal lords fell into financial embarrassments, they often raised ready cash by the sale of rents, but the wealthy Church owners had no need to. The clergy were on the whole conservative landlords.[3]

There was striking continuity—indeed, stagnation—in the manor of Harmondsworth, belonging to the abbey of the Holy Trinity at Rouen. In Richard II's reign the services rendered on the manor coincided absolutely with those existing in 1110, and again under Henry VI in 1433-4 exactly the same number of holdings was rendering the same services and receiving the same dues in return. Much is known of this manor because there were constant disputes between the abbot and his tenants; whether because the absentee landlord was oppressive, or had bad agents, or the tenants were unusually turbulent, the royal courts were repeatedly invoked to settle quarrels, in 1233, 1276-8, and 1289, and again in 1377-80. The abbot won each time.[4]

The field system of Middlesex, so far as it is possible to reconstruct it from the scanty indications we have, seems to have been a hybrid. The Middlesex tenant commonly held scattered strips of land of different sizes dispersed about several fields; resemblance to the Midland system, based firmly on three more or less equal pieces, has been found at only two places—at Little Greenford about 1300 and at Feltham in 1605. Nearly all the evidence, from 1203 at East Greenford to 1605 at Kempton, shows numerous unequal fields or furlongs, with holdings distributed irregularly among them. This suggests that Kentish and East Anglian influences had worked more effectively along the line of the Thames during the formative period than those from the Midlands, cut off by the belt of hills and forest to the north. Forest districts like Middlesex were in any case unfavourable to the true open-field system. The curious shapes and

[1] *H.C.M.* 6 (1904), p.47; 13 (191), p. 205. [2] *V.C.H.* ii., pp. 73, 80. [3] Clapham, *Concise*, p. 111. In the same book, p.52, however: 'It is possible, though on this point there is no scrap of evidence, that churchmen may have encouraged better use of the land and improved rotation of crops.' What is known of Middlesex points to the opposite conclusion, stated in the text. [4] *V.C.H.* ii., p. 66.

extreme fragmentation of the fields may well have arisen while the land was being gradually won from waste and forest and converted to field; as each piece was added to the farming land, it was presumably divided up immediately among the tenants in small and scattered plots. Nothing short of general enclosure could then alter the pattern.

Much unenclosed land, principally arable, remained in Middlesex until the great enclosures under parliamentary acts in the 18th and early 19th centuries. There had been some movement towards enclosure by private agreement in the 17th century; certainly Edgware, Harlesden, and Edmonton were in the main enclosed by 1600.[1] The county was not brought under the acts of 1536 and 1597 to prevent depopulation, which suggests that enclosure was proceeding slowly, or at any rate not so fast as to produce distress. Ruislip is mentioned as depopulated under Henry VIII and 'the praise of God decayed.' (The surviving records are, however, very incomplete.[2]) One important attempt at enclosure was made in 1545, when an act was passed for the partition of Hounslow Heath. The heath then in the king's possession, after the dissolution of Syon monastery and the acquisition of other properties, amounted to 4,293 acres of waste, extending into fourteen parishes and hamlets. The act recited that the 'barrenness and infertility thereof, by want of industry and diligence of men, ... breedeth as well scarcity and lack of all manner of grain, grass, wood, and other necessary things amongst the inhabitants of the said parishes; ... even so the conversion thereof into tillage and several pasture by men's labour and pains, besides that it shall be an exile of idleness in those parts, must of necessity cause and bring forth to all his said subjects plenty and abundance of all the things above remembered.' The sentiment, if not the language, is the same as that behind the 18th-century enclosures.

Elizabethan Middlesex still depended much on corn crops, though Leland on his journeys made about 1540 had noted a good deal of pasture, especially by the rivers. The excellence of the corn was celebrated by John Norden, the surveyor and author of *Speculum Britanniae* (1593), the first county topography, who probably lived at Hendon. This lively account of his home county, a beguiling example of his style, has often been quoted before, but it has such charm of language and of content that too much would be lost by paraphrase:

'Middlesex is a small shire, in length not twenty miles, in circuit (as it were by the ring) not above 70 miles, yet for the fertility thereof it may compare with any other shire; for the soil is excellent, fat and fertile and full of profit; it yieldeth corn and grain, not only in abundance, but most excellent good wheat, especially about Heston, which place may be called *granarium tritici regalis* for the singularity of the corn. The vein of this especial corn seemeth to extend from Heston to Harrow-on-the-Hill,

---

[1] W. E. Tate, 'Enclosure Acts and Awards, County of Middlesex,' *Trans. L. Mx. A. S.* NS 9 (1948), p.268; H. L. Gray, *English Field Systems* (Harvard, 1915), pp. 355, 381; Clapham, *Concise*, p.199. The view that Middlesex was not seriously, if at all, affected by 16th-century enclosure (Lord Ernle, *English Farming, Past and Present*, ed. 3, 1922, p. 66) is now hardly tenable. [2] *V.C.H.* ii., p. 89.

between which, as in the midway, is Perivale, more truly *Purevale* .... It may be noted also how nature has exalted Harrow-on-the-Hill, which seemeth to make ostentation of its situation in the *Purevale*, from whence towards the time of harvest a man may behold the fields round about so sweetly to address themselves to the sickle and scythe, with such comfortable abundance of all kind of grain, that the husbandman which waiteth for the fruits of his labours cannot but clap his hands for joy to see this vale so to laugh and sing. Yet doth not this so fruitful soil yield comfort to the wayfaring man in the winter time, by reason of the clayish nature of soil, which after it hath tasted the autumn showers waxeth both dirty and deep; but unto the country swain it is as a sweet and pleasant garden, in regard of his hope of future profit, for

> The deep and dirty loathsome soil
> Yields golden gain to painful toil.

The industrious and painful husbandman will refuse a palace to droil in these golden puddles.' (Thomas Fuller, living at Cranford, knew something else about Perivale wheat—'the purity thereof is much subject to be troubled with the mildew.'[1])

Not that Norden was entirely satisfied with the methods of these husbandmen; he added: 'It seemeth they only covet to maintain their ancient course of life and observe the husbandry of their fathers without adding anything to their greater profit.' And again: 'Things are more confounded by ignorance and evil husbandry in this shire than in any other shire that I know.' The complaint was echoed by every writer on Middlesex agriculture down to 1870.

Norden also noted the secondary products of the county's agriculture—cattle breeding and fattening, carrying to and from London, and ferrying and fishing on the Thames:

'Not meddling with the higher sort, I observe this in the meaner, and first of such as inhabit near the Thames: they live either by the barge, by the wherry or ferry, by the sculler or by fishing, all which live well and plentifully, and in decent and honest sort relieve their families. Such as live in the in-country, as in the body or heart of the shire, as also in the borders of the same, for the most part are men of husbandry, and they wholly dedicate themselves to the manuring of their land. And these commonly are so furnished with kine that the wife or twice or thrice a week conveyeth to London milk, butter, cheese, apples, pears, frumety, hens, chickens, eggs, bacon, and a thousand other country drugs which good housewives can frame and find to get a penny. And this yieldeth them a large comfort and relief .... Another sort of husbandmen or yeomen rather there are, and that not a few in this shire, who wade in the weeds of gentlemen .... These only oversee their husbandry and give

[1] T. Fuller, *History of the Worthies of England* (ed. P. H. Nuttall, 1840), ii., p.313.

direction unto their servants, seldom or not at all setting their hand unto
the plough, who having great feedings for cattle and good breed for
young often use Smithfield and other like places with fat cattle, where
also they store themselves with lean. And thus they often exchange, not
without great gain …. There are also that live by carriage for other men,
and to that end they keep carts and carriages, carry meal, milk, and many
other things to London, and so furnish themselves in their return with
sundry men's carriages of the country, whereby they live very gainfully.'[1]

Few points of farming practice specially characteristic of the county
have been recorded. One, however, has been preserved in Thomas
Tusser's *Five Hundred Good Points of Husbandry* (1557): the local rotation
was barley, wheat or rye, fallow, instead of the usual wheat or rye, barley,
fallow:

> But drink before bread corn with Middlesex men,
> Then lay on more compas, and fallow again.

There is little evidence about the progress of enclosure in the 17th
century, but what can be deduced from Ogilby's *Britannia* (1675)
suggests that only waste commons and common arable fields remained—
the common pastures had mostly been enclosed by agreement into dairy
farms and market gardens.[2] Gervase Markham, in *A Way to Get Wealth*
(1628), wrote that anyone taking the trouble to ride into the hard parts of
Middlesex would find that where sufficient industry was being used the
results everywhere justified the pains.[3] John Evelyn, visiting Mr. Secretary
Coventry's lodge in Enfield Chase in 1676, was surprised to find so
much land open and unused so near London, which suggests that most
of the rest of Middlesex was already enclosed: 'That which I most
wondered at was that in the compass of 25 miles, yet within 14 of
London, there is not a house, barn, church or building, besides three
lodges. To this lodge are three great ponds and some few inclosures, the
rest a solitary desert, yet stored with not less than 3,000 deer.'[4]

Almost a century later, the chase was viewed with disfavour by
Arthur Young, riding home to North Mimms at the end of his *Six Months
Tour through the North of England* (1770): 'Passing through London I
returned home by Highgate and Barnet, through a prodigious fine tract
of grass farms that let from £1 15s. to £4 an acre. Enfield Chase cannot
be viewed by any lover of his country, or of husbandry, without much
regret; so large a tract of waste land, so near the capital, within the reach
of London as a market and as a dunghill, is a real nuisance to the
public.'[5] In 1777 an act was passed for disafforesting the chase and
dividing it among the parishes and individuals having common rights,
but the first clearances were not all satisfactory. At South Mimms the
reclaimed land was successfully put under cultivation within 20 years,

[1] J. Norden, *Speculi Britanniae Pars*, ed. H. Ellis (Camden Society, 1840) p.xi. [2] Darby, p.469.
[3] Quoted by M. Campbell, *English Yeoman under Elizabeth and the Early Stuarts* (Yale, 1942),
p.173. [4] J. Evelyn, *Diary*, 2 June 1676. [5] A. Young, *Six Months Tour through the North of England*
(1770), iv., p.29.

but the Enfield and Edmonton portions were disappointing. Marshall wrote in 1788 of fortunes being lost in vain efforts to reclaim the chase, and Middleton noted in 1798: 'Three-fourths of Edmonton allotment is covered with bushes and has about one solitary, unthrifty, and unsightly tree to an acre. And as these are deficient in side-branches, they look like may-poles encumbered with ivy. The live stock, of course, is proportioned to the scantiness and poverty of the pasture.' From 1801 onwards, however, when the common land assigned to each of the parishes concerned was enclosed under a fresh act, it began to assume a prosperous appearance, as arable field or parkland.

Young's reference to London as a dunghill was not abusive but a terse way of pointing out the great advantage of being so close to a supply of good manure—not only animal droppings but, as a list of 1793 put it, 'woollen rags, sugar-bakers' scum, night soil, coal ashes, and soot.' The best land was constantly improved with London manure, which made a convenient back-load for the carts that took the produce to market. Even so, London manure was reckoned to cost 6s. a load at Hendon, 10s. at South Mimms. Two hundred years earlier Norden mentioned 'moor earth,' river sludge, as enriching the fields, and some chalk was later sent by barge down the Lea from places in Hertfordshire to Enfield for the same purpose.[1]

The earliest precise indication of land-use in Middlesex is John Rocque's map of 1754. This shows the parts immediately north of London, from Tottenham to a line running from Edgware to Acton, mostly enclosed and under grass, producing hay for the London horses, with a little arable, heath, and wood. London and Westminster, lying so close, had evidently hastened the development of Hendon and Hornsey as areas devoted to permanent grass, whereas farther west the land remained largely unenclosed, with grazing on unimproved commons and ploughland still lying in scattered strips on great open fields. The arable was subject to constant cropping in the 18th century; an example given is: wheat, followed by peas at the end of October, gathered green for market in May or June, or fed off early in July; then plough for turnips, off by next January; kidney beans sown in April and gathered in September.[2]

The classic descriptions of Middlesex agriculture were made by three reporters writing for the Board of Agriculture—Thomas Baird in 1793, Peter Foot in 1794, and John Middleton in 1798 (with a second edition in 1807). The three cover much the same ground, though Middleton allowed himself to diverge from the main theme more often and touched on a good many other aspects of economic life in the county. They described a state of agriculture both old and new, for the great enclosure movement was half-way through; they condemned the remaining

---

[1] *Annual Register*, 1794, p.304; Campbell (page 34, note 3), p.175, quoting J. Norden, *Surveyor's Dialogue* (1607), p.227; Cooke, p.37. [2] Willatts, p. 283; G. E. Fussell, 'Eighteenth-Century Crop Husbandry in Hertfordshire and Middlesex,' *Journal of the Ministry of Agriculture*, 43 (1936-7), p.944, quoting R. Bradley, *Complete Body of Husbandry* (1727), p.247.

commons and urged on improvements. They thought well of the soil but badly of the farmers and their methods, spoilt by the ease of selling their products to London and consequently not spurred on to improve their land like those in counties less fortunately situated—Norfolk, for example. William Marshall, writing in 1799, noted that land of equal quality in the Vale of Pickering, in Yorkshire, yielded a higher rent—the farming was better, and living (though not labour) cheaper. Middlesex farming was much inferior to Hertfordshire, which since about 1700 had the reputation of being the best corn country in England.[1]

Middleton estimated that one-eighth of the whole area of the county was under cultivation—23,000 acres (something less than in 1935), with 73,500 acres under grass. Only 3,000 acres of arable land were enclosed; the remainder lay in common fields. Wheat was grown on 7,000 acres; the land at Heston, Cranford, and Norwood gave splendid yields. Straw for the London stables was an important part of the crop. Barley was grown on 3,800 acres of the lighter soils, mostly for seed or for malting grain; oats and rye were unimportant; peas (mostly for hogs) occupied 3,000 acres and beans 2,800—these for horses or for export to the plantations of Africa and the West Indies as diet for negro slaves.[2] Clover for draught horses was grown on the enclosed arable land in regular succession with the corn crops. Of the grasslands, 70,000 acres lay on upland areas, 3,500 on low-lying tracts, often flooded. On these lands there was still Lammas tenure, in which common grazing rights were exercised each year from 12 August until 5 April, when the tenants began to sow their individual holdings, varying from about a rood to four or five acres each, divided by landmarks. The names of Lammas fields still survive at Tottenham, Ealing, and Staines. Milk and butter were not important in rural Middlesex; London was supplied from Islington and the other villages nearer at hand. There were not many sheep; they were originally of Wiltshire breed but degenerated—'poor half-starved, ragged-coated, and wretched looking sheep,' said Middleton, to be found on the commons; another writer called them 'greyhound-like.' Some house-lambs—that is, lambs kept indoors—were bred for meat, but there was no land used for the fattening of cattle for the butcher. (This was a change from Camden's time, 200 years before, when London butchers commonly hired grazing in the Home Counties.[3]) Horses were not bred in the county—the grass was too valuable as hay crop—but they were brought in from Leicestershire; and even in 1798 there were still 13 oxen used for draught. It was still the practice to pollard the hedge timber and allow the hedges to grow to a considerable size for the sake of getting a crop of brushwood every seven or eight years for firewood, and there were a good many copses—'nurseries for thieves.' Farms in

[1] Marshall, p. 17; Ernle (page 32, note 1), p.190. [2] *H.C.M.* 13 (1911), p. 167, quoting J. Middleton, *View of the Agriculture of Middlesex* (ed. 2, 1807), p.246. [3] Darby, p. 361.

general were small, being worked more as a kind of gardening than husbandry.

Such was the appearance of agriculture; a good many things needed correction. The rural artificers and labourers were stupid and refused to adopt new machinery (a complaint heard again for the next fifty years, until the railway took away most of the advantage of being close to the London market). The plough in general use was a 'very worthless one,' a swing plough of the most clumsy construction, though the Hertfordshire wheel plough was used in some districts in the north. Middleton noted: 'In May 1796, I saw in one day two teams, with six horses in each and three men to attend each team, namely one to hold the plough and two to drive the horses, ploughing with a wide furrow about three-quarters of an acre per day.' Few wagons were employed.[1]

The peculiar excellence of Middlesex farming was the hay crop. Middleton wrote: 'This branch of the rural art has by the farmers of Middlesex been brought to a degree of perfection altogether unequalled in any other part of the kingdom .... Even in the most unfortunate weather, the hay made according to the Middlesex manner is superior to that made by any other method in similar circumstances.' The mowers, each having five hay-makers, both men and women, with them, usually began at three, four or five o'clock in the morning and continued at work until seven or eight at night, with an hour or two to rest in the middle of the day. The whole business, taking four days, was made as systematic as possible, and it had its own technical terms; the process was from grass through single wind-rows, small cocks, straddles, double wind-rows, medium cocks, straddles again, and large cocks to the stacks themselves. There were no haystacks more neatly formed or better secured than those of Middlesex. Near Harrow, Hendon, and Finchley, where the best grass was grown on the heavy clay soil, there were many hay-barns with a capacity of 30 to 50, and even 100, loads. When the hay had been got in, the after-grass was let for grazing heavy cattle. William Marshall adds two notes: the stack was usually a 'long square,' which was convenient for square trusses, and the itinerant bands who did the mowing generally met near London and worked home by stages.[2]

The other staple of Middlesex agriculture was fruit gardening. Middleton observed: 'From Kensington, through Hammersmith, Chiswick, Brentford, Isleworth, and Twickenham, the land on both sides of the road for seven miles in length, or a distance of ten miles from market, may be denominated the great fruit-garden, north of the Thames, for the supply of London. In this manner much, some say most, of the ground in these parishes is cultivated.' An upper and an under crop were grown at the same time: the upper crop a complete orchard of fruit trees and the under crop of berries growing between and below the

---

[1] The preceding paragraphs are based on Middleton. [2] Middleton, p. 237; Marshall, pp. 39, 41.

trees. Twickenham and Isleworth were especially noted for their strawberries and for raspberries, sold to London distillers. There were perhaps 3,000 acres of fruit gardens, giving employment to five persons an acre, including children, in the winter and five more (mostly women from Wales and Shropshire) in the summer; they supplied three-quarters of the fruit sold at the London markets. The Welsh women carried the fruit some nine miles to Covent Garden, sometimes twice in a day, for sixpence a heavy basket.[1] Kitchen gardens for vegetables were at this time mostly closer to London, at Chelsea, Brompton, and Hammersmith. Evidence about potato-growing conflicts: Middleton says that few or none were grown for sale, but A. Wilkinson of White Webbs House, Enfield, stated in 1793 that many were produced in Middlesex and sold to dealers at two to four guineas a ton. The country people were allowed to enclose wide road verges to grow potatoes during the near famine of 1796.[2] Lavender was grown as a commercial crop in the early 19th century at Baker Street, Enfield, and near Hanworth.[3]

While part of the county was thus most intensively cultivated in separate plots, very much was still common land and waste. One of the cardinal doctrines of the Board of Agriculture, subscribed to without hesitation by Foot and Middleton, was that all this land ought to be enclosed. Sir John Sinclair, president of the Board, spoke in 1803 of the need to cultivate Finchley Common and Hounslow Heath in a manner prophetic of the 'Dig for Victory' campaign of 140 years later.[4] Middleton estimated that about a tenth of the surface of Middlesex, or 17,000 acres, was lying in uncultivated common which was 'capable of receiving improvement.' The soil and the grass on these commons were so bad, he suggested, that they were no more use to the community than if they were consigned to the bottom of the deep. Three-quarters of the commons in Middlesex, as in most other districts, were covered with heath and furze, from which a little of the worst sort of firing was obtained by the poor. What was more serious, they were 'the constant rendezvous of gipsies, strollers and other loose persons, living under tents which they carry with them from place to place, according to their convenience …. In short, the commons of this county are well known to be the constant resort of footpads and highwaymen, and they are literally and proverbially a public nuisance.' Furthermore, there were 20,000 acres of common arable fields on which each owner's property lay in small strips and patches; if these were united and enclosed, they could be turned over to permanent grass with great advantage.

Sir John Sinclair and his collaborators, however, need not have worried; enclosure by private act had been well under way since 1759. The acts together accounted for nearly a fifth of Middlesex acreage, almost all on the poorer soils. Enclosure went forward in Middlesex

---

[1] Middleton, p. 382; F. M. Eden, *The State of the Poor* (ed. A. G. L. Rogers, 1928), p. 239: Cooke, p. 51. [2] *Annual Register*, 1794, p. 304; evidence of Post Office witness to a Highways Committee, 1809, quoted by T. F. Ordish, 'History of Metropolitan Roads', *Report of the London Traffic Branch of the Board of Trade, 1910* (Cd. 5472, 1911), p. 170 (appendix H). [3] S. Tymms, *Compendium of the History of London and Middlesex* (c. 1841), p. 16* (Enfield); G. S. Maxwell, *Highwayman's Heath* (ed. 2, 1949), p. 142 (Hanworth). [4] Halévy (page 7, note 5), ii., p. 45.

without much open incident, though not entirely without opposition from the smaller men on the land. The *Annual Register* recorded under 6 March 1767: 'On Tuesday evening a great number of farmers were observed going along Pall Mall with cockades in their hats. On inquiring the reason, it appeared that they all lived in or near the parish of Stanwell in the county of Middlesex, and they were returning to their wives and families to carry them the agreeable news of a bill being rejected for enclosing the said common, which, if carried into execution, might have been the ruin of a great number of families.'[1] That particular act was postponed for another twenty-two years, but enclosure went on until, with the Northolt act of 1824, practically all the land worth cultivating was enclosed.

William Cobbett had something to say about the result in south-west Middlesex: 'A much more ugly country than that between Egham and Kensington would with great difficulty be found in England. Flat as a pancake, and, until you come to Hammersmith, the soil is a nasty stony dirt upon a bed of gravel. Hounslow Heath, which is only a little worse than the general run, is a sample of all that is bad in soil and villainous in look. Yet this is now enclosed, and what they call 'cultivated.' Here is a fresh robbery of villages, hamlets, and farm and labourers' buildings and abodes.'[2] By 1834 there were only 4,316 acres of common and 1,567 of common field out of a total area of 178,466 acres in Middlesex. Two further small pieces were enclosed under a new procedure, requiring specific consent of Parliament in cases within fifteen miles of London, under the General Enclosure Act of 1845; the act of 1854 prohibited enclosure within a ten-mile radius, and the Metropolitan Commons Act of 1866, arising from agitation against proposed enclosure of Wimbledon Common, provided for commons within the Metropolitan Police District to be preserved for the general benefit. In effect, it stopped enclosures in Middlesex. Several schemes were carried through under this act, but only one affected more than 100 acres.[3]

The cultivation of the enclosed portions did not satisfy the improvers of 1800. They thought the rural labourers were corrupted by being so near the metropolis, and the farmers themselves seemed the wrong type of men. There were four classes of farmers, according to these critics: only a few were professionals; the others were men who made farming their secondary occupation only, their first being in London, or who had made fortunes and retired, or who had changed to farming from a life spent in a different line. As for the farm hands: 'The labourers of this county are ruined in morals and constitution by public houses, whose number is greatly increased by reason of many brewers and distillers being in the commission of the peace .... Gentlemen's servants are mostly a bad set, and the great number of them kept in this county is the

---

[1] *Annual Register*, 1767, p. 68; for a full account of the Stanwell enclosure, J. L. and B. Hammond, *Village Labourer, 1760-1832* (1912), p. 378 (appendix A10), and for Laleham, p. 364 (appendix A7). [2] W. Cobbett, *Rural Rides* (Everyman ed.), i., p. 124. [3] Lord Eversley, *Commons, Forests and Footpaths* (ed. 2, 1910), p. 331; Clapham, *Modern Britain*, ii., p. 259; *V.C.H.* ii., p. 99.

means of the rural labourers acquiring a degree of idleness and insolence unknown in places more remote from the metropolis.'[1]

Whatever the reason, there was not much agricultural progress in Middlesex. In 1843 Henry Tremenheere found a four-ox team ploughing at Norwood, and the only machine of a comparatively modern construction he saw in the parish was a winnowing machine. 'There is a strong prejudice,' he wrote, 'in this district against the use of all modern inventions for facilitating or abridging labour, and the dislike to many admirable machines, now much used in husbandry, originates in a conscientious though mistaken solicitude for the welfare of the labouring classes.' At Ealing: 'Only one threshing machine exists in this parish, and that has been recently introduced. On its being mentioned by its owner at a farmers' ordinary at Uxbridge, and some of the straw and grain which it had worked being exhibited, he was generally blamed for using an invention so injurious to the labourer!' In Greenford he found four, sometimes six, horses yoked to one plough. At Perivale sheep were brought from 'distant counties' after the hay harvest and driven back to folds in the Midlands at the approach of winter.[2]

The Rev. James Clutterbuck, reporting his observations on the farming of Middlesex in 1869, found that labourers resented mowing machines for the hay crop, and there were very few of them; only tedding machines for spreading out the hay were in general use. Everything else was done by hand, parties of labourers coming in from Berkshire, Buckinghamshire, Oxfordshire, and other counties during the season; the influx of Irish labour, formerly a very large proportion of the haymakers, had almost died out. Hay farming was a 'precarious and anxious occupation' because of the weather. Not to the farmer alone: when the crop failed in 1830 there were deaths from starvation among the Irish labourers at Acton, Willesden, and Hampstead, and there was a riot among the Irish at Barnet.[4] Most of the land between Harrow and Uxbridge—great open arable fields until about 1800—was now turned over to grass, extending over many square miles where scarcely a single habitation was to be found; but south of the line of the Uxbridge road the whole area was 'of a marked and peculiar character,' with intensive cultivation of the alluvial and brick-earth plain, where farms were gradually giving way to market gardens. There was little interest in stock-raising, and no trace of the fattening of house-lambs, already declining in Middleton's day, nor was there much dairying.

The age of high farming in Middlesex lasted well after the 1870s, which marked the beginning of its decline in most of England. The principal crops, hay and market-garden produce, were specialised and not in competition with the new bulk imports flowing in from America and Australia, and they still commanded a ready market in London. The

[1] Middleton, pp. 383, 384.   [2] H. Tremenheere, 'Agricultural and Educational Statistics of several Parishes in the County of Middlesex', *Journal of the Statistical Society of London*, 6 (1843), p. 120, quoted by Clapham, *Modern Britain*, i., p. 461 (who mistakes Norwood for Northwood).
[3] J. C. Clutterbuck, 'The Farming of Middlesex', *Journal of the Royal Agricultural Society of England*, 2nd series, 5 (1869), p. 3.   [4] *H.C.M.* 13 (1911), p. 167.

London horse ate as much hay as Middlesex could produce until the internal combustion engine drastically reduced the demand from about 1905 onwards; at the same time the spread of houses over the north and north-west of the county, restrained until then by comparatively poor communications and the expense of building on the clay, effectively stopped the supply. In general, agriculture in the county held its own, unaffected by depression in corn products, until a common blight fell on all the farms in turn as the land on the brink of the advancing waves of houses waited to be cut up into building plots. There is no inducement to farm well on the very doorstep of a modern city; it is a luxury that men do not indulge in.

Middleton's estimate of the area under crops and grass in the middle of the 1790s was 96,500 acres, 23,000 of them arable, out of a total county area of about 180,000 acres. In 1866, when the modern agricultural returns began, there were nearly 110,000 acres under crops and grass; in 1879, 118,000, the highest figure; during the next forty years it fell at the rate of about 2,600 acres a year to 43,000 in 1934; and the 1948 return showed a total of 32,000 acres, of which 19,300 were under crops (5,100 of them orchards and vegetable gardens). Cattle decreased from 26,500 in 1876 to 17,000 in 1906 and 7,600 in 1948, roughly in proportion to the area of permanent grass; most are for dairying, not for beef. Sheep are now scarce, being maintained mostly on parks or public commons. There were something over 40,000 before 1871, but only 2,640 in 1948. There was no decline in the number of horses between 1876 (6,015) and 1906 (6,402), because the increase in carriage horses had balanced the fall in farm horses; in 1948 the county (with London) returned 967, of which 248 were employed in agriculture. Pigs, on the other hand, perhaps because they are more easily fed with the scraps of a city community, increased from 12,500 in 1876 to 16,300 in 1906 and 21,500 in 1948.[1]

Market gardening, already important in 1800, had become a flourishing industry by 1870. By 1885 a seventh of all the market gardening of England and Wales was situated in Middlesex, which actually had more acres devoted to it than any other county. Peter Kay started a glasshouse business at Finchley in 1874; by 1899 he had 19½ acres covered, growing grapes and tomatoes. Cultivation under glass in the Lea valley began about 1880. In 1935 Middlesex had 5,788 acres used for growing food for direct human consumption, and another 288 acres for hardy flowers. These were sold not merely in London but through Covent Garden market all over England. Nursery gardens occupied 994 acres, including 262 acres in the Lea valley and south-west Middlesex under glass, 106 acres with tomatoes.[2] West Middlesex, especially land reclaimed from Hounslow Heath near Harlington and Harmondsworth,

---

[1] Statistics conveniently collected in Willatts, pp. 163, 299. [2] W. E. Bear, 'Fruit Growing under Glass', *Journal of the Royal Agricultural Society of England*, 3rd series, 10 (1899), p. 267; Clapham, *Modern Britain*, iii., p. 92; Willatts, pp. 157, 200, 220.

was filled with orchards in the latter part of the 19th century. Richard Cox, a retired brewer, produced his famous orange pippin in his garden on the Middlesex side of Colnbrook in 1830; in 1908 and 1910 new varieties of apple were being named 'Feltham Beauty' and 'Hounslow Wonder.'[1] These orchards are now mostly commemorated by a few old fruit trees in suburban gardens and some names like Cherry Orchard Lane; they have given way to intensive cultivation of vegetables. At the same time the hedge timber has been felled—market gardeners dislike old elms, a waste of ground and harbourage for greedy birds—and thus the aspect of the level plain has been changed in the last forty years, even where it has not been invaded by houses or flattened into an airport. By 1924 Middlesex, with only 0.9 per cent of its area in woodland, mostly on the Hertfordshire border, had a lower proportion than any other English county.[2]

Agricultural labourers' wages in the 19th and early 20th centuries, for which regular statistics exist, were comparatively high in Middlesex, owing to the high prices round London, but they were not the highest in the country: these were found on the borders of the industrial districts in the north. The influence of London was already at work during the Napoleonic wars: from 1794 to 1824, when wages were falling in the south and south-east of England, they rose in Middlesex. In 1798 a labourer earned 10s. a week in winter, 12s. in summer. The system remembered by the name of Speenhamland, near Newbury, was not common in the county; few of the Middlesex wages in 1824 were supplemented from the rates. Cash wages, without allowance for cottage, overtime and harvest pay, and payments in kind, ran higher than the average in the south-east and east Midlands throughout the 19th century. H. Rider Haggard in his *Rural England* of 1902 remarked that near Potters Bar labour was dear; 18s. was paid for six days' work, or with Sunday £1, carters and shepherds earning more.[3]

Agriculture is not quite extinct in Middlesex: it was returned in 1948 as the occupation of 4,936 workers. There is an Agricultural Executive Committee to direct it, which has even tried to cultivate the wide verges of by-pass roads. But playing-fields, airports, and gravel pits, as well as suburban houses, are likely to attenuate what cultivation still remains. The soil of southern Middlesex is as valuable for intensive cultivation as any in England; an expert committee has recently called it 'one of the finest and most easily worked market-garden soils in this or any other country.'[4] Nevertheless, the 20th century, with its usual foolhardy rapacity, goes on destroying the value of this portion of its inheritance, as it does most of its other legacies.

---

[1] *Times*, 1 November 1934; A. Simmonds, 'Mr. Cox of 'Cox's Orange Pippin'', *Journal of the Royal Horticultural Society* 68 (1943), p. 347; H. V. Taylor, *Apples of England* (ed. 3, 1946), pp. 98, 112, 128. [2] Willatts, pp. 144, 198. [3] Clapham, *Modern Britain*, i., pp. 124 (quoting Select Committee on Labourers' Wages, 1824), 129; Middleton, p. 380; Ernle (page 32, note 1) [p. 468]; H. Rider Haggard, *Rural England* (1902), p. 551. [4] Ministry of Town and Country Planning, *Report of the Advisory Committee on Sand and Gravel* (1948), p. 17.

CHAPTER V

TRADE AND INDUSTRY

*'So the process of growth continues market and
population acting and reacting upon one another to
build up an ever greater collection of people and
industries. Nothing succeeds like success.'*

THE BARLOW REPORT, 1940[1]

THROUGHOUT most of the recorded history of Middlesex, its
trade has been principally carried on at fairs and markets. It has had
no 'staple,' or single dominant commodity: what it bought and sold was
until the 19th century the same as any other agricultural county, with
the pull of London making itself felt all the time on prices and the flow
of trade. The fairs and markets had two origins: the local mart for the
satisfaction of the needs of the district, and the commodity market
where London dealers met country suppliers. The commodity market
naturally grew more important and tended to submerge the local marts,
which languished and gradually died out. Thus most of Middlesex
commerce came to be conducted at a few centres on the main roads to
London: Staines, Hounslow, Brentford, Uxbridge, Enfield, and
Edmonton.

Staines was the first of these to receive a grant of a market from the
king; the abbot of Westminster was given permission in 1228 to hold a
weekly market and an annual four-day fair. The weekly market still
survives; the fair has disappeared, though in 1825 it was noted as
celebrated for onions. It never seems to have had more than local
importance.

Hounslow, the junction of the Staines road and the Great West road,
was a natural place to meet for business. The Trinitarian friary there was
granted a licence for an eight-day fair and weekly market in 1296; the
fair, begun on Trinity Monday, existed until the 19th century, but the
weekly market was discontinued some time earlier, except for cattle. A
short-lived fair was started on Hounslow Heath under licence from James
II, mainly for the benefit of his troops in camp there.

The most prosperous commercial centre in Middlesex was Brentford;

[1] Royal Commission on the Distribution of the Industrial Population, *Report* (Barlow Report,
Cmd. 6153, 1940), para. 352.

43

situated where the road from the west approached the Thames and being the first place of any consequence outside the metropolis on that side, it had evident advantages. London merchants made their bargains at Brentford and could leave the stock there, in fields if live, in warehouses if dead, to be forwarded by road or river as called for. Its charter was granted in 1307 for a weekly market and a six-day fair at the festival of St Lawrence. After the Restoration its prosperity increased, and a market-house was built. Cox noted in 1724: 'This town, being a great thoroughfare for the western counties and lying near London, is enriched with a very great trade, the market drawing a considerable concourse of citizens to flock to it on purpose to buy up such commodities as it affords.' The place was, in fact, the *entrepôt* for buying London's corn from the west; some was milled there, and some was sent to mills by the river Wandle on the Surrey side. In 1875 it was still a place of a good deal of trade; but its importance as a place of exchange had gone with the coming of the railways, and the market-house had been demolished in 1850.[1]

Uxbridge was the most important mart of the local kind. Its district included much of south-east Buckinghamshire as well as north-west Middlesex, for which its situation on the Oxford road at the Colne bridge was favourable. Mills driven by water power were established by the bridge, and after the Grand Junction Canal was opened to the town in 1798 it enjoyed admirable communication with Brentford and London. Market rights were granted to Henry de Lacy, Earl of Lincoln, in 1294, with an annual fair. The number of fairs increased—in 1784 there were four, the 'statute fair' being ingeniously doubled by holding it on the old style date of 29 September and on the new style date eleven days later. A pillared market-house was built in 1788 and still stands to cover a Saturday market. It was noticed as remarkable when it was built that it contained warehouses for storing grain from one week to the next. Corn was sold there in bulk as in the western counties, not by sample as at Croydon. Lysons in 1800 declared the weekly Thursday market one of the greatest corn markets in the kingdom; Loudon in 1831 called it the greatest corn market in the kingdom next to Mark Lane. In 1875 there was a corn market on Thursday and a general market on Saturday; four fairs were held annually, as well as one specially for wool.[2]

Nearer to London on the Uxbridge road an important cattle market was established at Southall under a grant of 1695 made to Francis Merrick. The market was 'a considerable mart for cattle' in 1800; 75 years later there was a weekly market, which still survives, but the two annual fairs had disappeared. Ealing Fair was not of a serious kind; William Cobbett wrote on 24 June 1822 of meeting 'in all the various modes of conveyance the cockneys going to *Ealing Fair*, which is one of

[1] T. Cox, *Magna Britannia et Hibernia Antiqua et Nova*, iii. (1724), p.21; F. J. Fisher, 'The London Food Market, 1540-1640', *Economic History Review* 5 (1935), ii., p. 46. [2] Middleton, p. 408; Marshall, p. 35; Loudon (page 5, note 1), p. 1125; Clutterbuck (page 40, note 3).

those things which nature herself would almost seem to have provided for drawing off the matter and giving relief to the overcharged *Wen.*' (He pursued his medical metaphor rather far.) It was held for three days on the Green.[1]

In the north-western angle were two local markets in medieval times, at Harrow and Pinner: at Harrow dating from 1262, but extinguished by Norden's time; at Pinner from 1336, 'long since disused' in 1800. With no main road communicating with London, these two places were left quite out of the movement of internal trade. Annual fairs went on until 1872 at Harrow, and one still survives at Pinner, celebrated on the Wednesday after Whit Sunday. At Edgware, on a main road, an important annual fair took place as late as 1825; a weekly market was still held fifty years later, with a special cattle-market once a month. Finchley Common was the scene about 1795 of a very large market where lean hogs from Shropshire were sold to hog-butchers, to be fattened by malt-distillers in London; it was extinct by 1869.[2] Hendon fair was suspected by the magistrates in 1697 of being merely an excuse for a concourse of disorderly persons to assemble, and the constables of Gore hundred were ordered to prevent its taking place. In 1786 there was a fair at Hendon including 'a burlesque imitation of the Olympic Games.'[3]

On the northern approaches the principal market was at Enfield, where a group of middlemen controlled much of the trade in Midland grain to London. They fought and lost a struggle with the London brewers, who promoted the Lea navigation in 1571 to cut them out, and the town petitioned Elizabeth as 'Her Majesty's decayed town of Enfield'. Its original grant of two three-day fairs was made in 1304; these went on until 1869, when they were declared illegal by the local bench with the consent of the Duchy of Lancaster, owner of the rights. A weekly market was also granted in 1304; it had to be revived under James I and again in 1778, petering out about 1800. A market is now held on Saturdays.[4]

Hiring fairs, where the country people came up and were hired for yearly engagements as domestic or farm servants, were still held at Enfield and Edmonton in September about 1825. Edmonton also had the ancient 'Beggars' Bush Fair,' granted under James I, which fell into abeyance about 1870 after being 'an inconsiderable holiday fair' for some years.

The free economic operation of Middlesex markets was affected by two special influences. The clerk of the market of the king's household exercised jurisdiction over markets held within twelve miles of the king's palace, a radius including nearly the whole of the county; he had authority to detect and punish trading offences, principally the use of false weights and measures, and collected fees for his work. There was a

---

[1] Cobbett (page 39, note 2), i., p. 90; A. T. Bolton, *Pitzhanger Manor, Ealing Green* [1918], p. 22. [2] Middleton, p. 375; Clutterbuck (page 40, note 3). [3] Dowdell, p. 30; E. T. Evans, *History ... of Hendon* (1890), p. 227. [4] *V.C.H.* ii., p. 86; E. Ford and G. H. Hodson, *History of Enfield* (1873), p. 101.

series of actions about his activity in the Uxbridge market from 1726 to 1730 in which the justices supported the complainants against the clerk. The other influence was the special legislation of Tudor and Stuart times regulating middlemen's practices in trade. An act of 1552 provided that traders in foodstuffs or drovers of cattle must be licensed; cattle might be resold only at a distance of forty miles or more, which prevented middlemen from buying stock in Middlesex for sale in London. Similarly there were licences for 'badgers' and 'kidders', dealers in grain and in other kinds of food. Buying for resale, or 'regrating', was forbidden; between 1660 and 1670 there was a system of information for forestalling, engrossing, and regrating, especially against butchers, in respect of intercepting cattle for London markets at Finchley, and in 1709-10, years of high prices, there were similar prosecutions on account of grain transactions at Brentford and Uxbridge.[1] The justices had very limited power to enforce the detailed and complicated regulations prescribed, and they naturally failed to make any real impression on the practices they set out to put down; as the 18th century progressed, *laissez-faire* supplanted the paternalistic notions of the previous age, and the laws became a dead letter, to be repealed in 1772.[2]

The London markets were, of course, always important to Middlesex farmers. Land-borne corn and malt from the county was being sold at Newgate in 1316.[3] The most important of the produce markets, however, were for hay, at the original Haymarket in St James's and at Whitechapel and Smithfield. There is a reference to engrossing of hay near London in 1630 'of purpose to keep the same from the market until the price thereof be extremely raised.' By the end of the 18th century it was customary to sell hay by the load or short ton of 18 cwt.—it was calculated that 2 cwt. on 20 was lost by evaporation from the field state.[4] The hay market near Charing Cross was already in use by the time of Suckling's *Ballad on a Wedding*, of 1641; it was removed in 1830 to the Cumberland Market, on the Regent's Canal. Standing ricks were sometimes sold direct to jobbers, it was reported in 1869, but a good many farmers carted their hay to London and brought back a load of manure on the return journey. In 1856 London consumed over 4,000 loads of hay and straw a week; the greater part of this must have come from Middlesex.[5]

The purely local market in Middlesex began to decline after about 1700 as the retail shop became the normal method of distribution; likewise the fair ceased to have any significant economic function and if it survived did so merely as an adjunct to holiday-making. Evelyn noticed this in 1683 on the other side of London: 'I went to Blackheath to see the new fair ... pretended for the sale of cattle, but I think in truth to enrich the new tavern at the bowling green ... There appeared nothing but an innumerable assembly of drinking people from London,

[1] Dowdell, p. 162; *M.C.R. Reports*, p. 7. [2] Halévy (page 7, note 5), ii., p. 48. [3] N. S. B. Gras, *English Corn Market* (Harvard, 1915), p. 66. [4] Gras (see preceding note), p. 126; Marshall, p. 44. [5] *H.M.C.* 13 (1911), p. 167; Clutterbuck (page 40, note 3); Cooke, p.37; P. Cunningham, *Handbook for London* (1849), i., p. 372.

pedlars, etc., and I suppose it too near London to be of any great use to the country.'[1] The remark might apply equally well to Middlesex. About 1825 the fairs at Beggars' Bush (Edmonton), Chiswick, Edgware, Edmonton, Staines, and Twickenham are shown as dealing in 'toys.'[2] The fair was declining into the thing of roundabouts and steam-organs that most people know today.

New kinds of commercial organisation, exchanges and banks, were developing. Banking in Middlesex, as indeed in Britain generally outside a very few of the largest cities, belongs to the comparatively recent stages of economic activity. Until the second half of the 18th century nearly all the country's banking was concentrated in London; Burke stated that in 1750 there were not twelve banks outside London, but by 1793 there were over 400.[3] One of these was in Middlesex, at Uxbridge, founded in 1791 by two millers, Norton and Mercer (the Old Bank House is still in the High Street) (Plate 40); it was taken over by two Quaker families, Hull and Smith, in 1820. The Uxbridge Old Bank issued notes circulating in parts of Buckinghamshire as well as in north-west Middlesex; its first branch was opened at Southall in 1879, followed in the next twenty years by five more between Pinner and Isleworth, as well as at Slough, Eton, and Windsor. About 1890, as Woodbridge, Lacy, Hartland, Hibbert and Co., it was removed to new premises in part of the old White Horse inn, and in 1900 it was absorbed by Barclay and Co. Thomas Ashby of Staines founded a bank in 1796 in association with his brewery; this bank also issued some notes. Ashby and Co. bought La Coste's Bank, Chertsey, in 1876, and later opened branches at Hampton Court, Hampton, Sunbury, and Feltham, with others in Surrey, Berkshire, and Buckinghamshire. Barclay and Co. absorbed it in 1904.[4]

The London and Middlesex Bank, founded in 1862 and taken over by the Westminster in 1863, had no branches in rural Middlesex.[5] The Union Bank of London, absorbed in 1918 by the National Provincial, opened branches at the end of the 19th century at Muswell Hill and East Finchley.[6] The famous private bank of Child and Co. had several personal connections with Middlesex: Sir Francis Child bought Osterley Park in 1711, and the family interest in the bank descended to the Earls of Jersey. The Mills family, of Glyn, Mills and Co., which absorbed Child's bank in 1924, lived at Hillingdon, from which C.H. Mills took his title in 1886.[7] The first genuine savings bank was established at Tottenham by Priscilla Wakefield in 1804, on the foundation of an earlier one (for children only) of 1798; but this belongs properly to social history and not to commerce.

In the 17th century, when private enterprise had to supplement the scanty means of exchange provided by coin of the realm, 'tokens' for small amounts were issued by traders and innkeepers at 28 places in

[1] J. Evelyn, *Diary*, 16 June 1683. [2] Cooke, p. 15. [3] Quoted by M. C. Buer, *Health, Wealth, and Population, 1760-1815* (1926), p. 49. [4] P. W. Matthews and A. W. Tuke, *History of Barclays Bank Ltd.* (1926), p. 290; W. F. Crick and J. E. Wadsworth, *Hundred Years of Joint Stock Banking* [Midland Bank] (1936), p. 313. [5] T. E. Gregory, *Westminster Bank through a Century* (1936), i., p. 233. [6] Information from National Provincial Bank, Ltd. [7] E.G.B., *History of the House of Glyn Mills & Co.* (c. 1933), pp. 39, 77.

rural Middlesex. Uxbridge, with 13 recorded varieties, issued most; 10
are known from Isleworth, 9 from Brentford, 8 from Chiswick; even the
villages of Cranford, Harmondsworth, Heston, and Pinner produced one
each.[1]

A wide range of specialised trades and occupations was followed in
rural Middlesex before London overran it. At Chiswick in 1839, with 91
nobility, gentry, and clergy at the apex of the social pyramid, there were
all the usual traders in foodstuffs, with builders, blacksmiths, and men
engaged in river trades, as well as coachbuilders, cricket-bat makers,
milliners and dressmakers, printers, toy dealers, and 21 taverns and
public houses—all for a population of about 5,700.[2] At Roxeth, in 1848,
still an outlying settlement distinct from Harrow, the list is headed by
nine gentry, followed by nine farmers; to provide for their wants were
four beer-shop keepers, four laundresses, a timber and coal merchant, a
carpenter, a butcher, a baker and grocer, a bricklayer, a farrier, a pig-
killer, a relieving officer, and a land measurer and collector of poor rates.
In other settlements within the parish were a hayseller, a straw-hat
maker, a bird-stuffer, a dairy woman, a chandler, a cheesemonger, a
hurdle maker, and a dealer in faggots.[3] This diverse structure of
production and sale has been superseded by the multiple shop and the
branded article.

*   *   *   *   *

The machinery of distribution existed, as it must in every inhabited
area that is past the primitive stage, throughout the development of
Middlesex; but until comparatively late the county's productions were
almost entirely agricultural, not manufactured. In the 20th century,
however, especially between 1925 and 1935, it has developed into an
important manufacturing district. The part of the county lying between
the Edgware road and the Great West road is now one of the most
important industrial areas in Britain, and there is also a considerable
settlement of industries in the Lea valley.

Until well into the 19th century manufacturing industries were
established where the facts of geography dictated, either where the raw
materials were to be found, or where an important element in the
manufacture (notably water, required in the processes of cloth-making or
for the supply of power) was at hand, or where easy communication,
normally by river or sea, could bring together the principal material and
the constituents and permit the transport of the finished product. In most
cases all three conditions existed together, as in medieval East Anglia
and Somerset, and in Staffordshire, Yorkshire, Lancashire, and South
Wales in the 18th century. But in Middlesex the only useful raw material

[1] W. Boyne, *Trade Tokens issued in the Seventeenth Century* (ed. 2, 1889), ii., p. 811; G. Redford
and T. H. Riches, *History ... of Uxbridge* (1818), p. 96. [2] W. Draper, *Chiswick* (1923), p. 166.
[3] *Handbook for the Use of Visitors to Harrow on the Hill*, ed. T. Smith (1850).

was brick-earth, and the rivers Thames and Lea provided the only adequate carriage for goods until the canal and railway age. Industries consequently remained few and scattered until conditions changed in the 20th century. Then greater technical control and improved transport, especially by road, overcame the geographical disadvantages, and the important merit of being close to the largest concentrated mass of population in Britain brought an influx of certain kinds of industries into the county. These have transformed its appearance and its economic life quite as much as the residential settlement of the spreading London suburbs.

The brick and tile industry occupies a special and primary place in the economic history of Middlesex because it was the only manufacture that sprang directly from the physical composition of the county. It also had a profound influence on the topography of large areas from about 1750 to 1900, as the level of the soil was constantly altered while the earth was being extracted. This was particularly marked around Heston during the 1860s, when the whole brick-earth belt, extending on each side of a line from Brentford to Yiewsley with a greatest width of about four miles between Yeading and Hounslow, was being exploited most actively.[1] Northolt bricks were then noted for superior quality and used for lining the London sewers.[2] There were also useful deposits in the Lea valley.

Roofing tiles were probably rare in Roman London, but after numerous fires in the medieval city, culminating in the disastrous one of 1212, the use of tiles for roofing was made compulsory.[3] No doubt most of these tiles were burnt within the present London county area; but already in the late 15th century John Maier and Agnes his wife were making tiles for William Code of Harlesden Green at a kiln, presumably close by, at the rate of 11d. a thousand.[4] The beautiful red bricks of Wolsey's Hampton Court were burned locally; 4s. 6d. a thousand was paid for those used in Henry VIII's great hall when it was building in 1530-2.[5] By the middle of the 18th century the county brickfields were beginning to supply the characteristic London stock brick of dark yellow-brown, with which tens of thousands of houses were built. Most of the brick in Buckingham Palace came from John Nash's kilns near Southall.[6] It has a good sound quality of its own, even if no particular beauty of texture; it was often faced with stucco or stone or another brick, and even today simple persons who think that all proper bricks look red cover it with colour-wash. Some of the finest examples of 16th- and 17th-century brickwork outside East Anglia are to be found within the county: Hampton Court itself, Swakeleys at Ickenham, Forty Hall at Enfield, and, best of all, Cromwell House, on Highgate Hill. Batty Langley in 1748 commended the dark purple glazed pantiles made 'first in Holland, now

[1] Clutterbuck (page 40, note 3). [2] Thorne, art. Northolt. [3] Home (page 12, note 2), p. 78; Clapham, *Concise*, p. 135. [4] *V.C.H.* ii., p. 129. [5] *Builder* 61 (1891), p. 294. [6] J. Summerson, *John Nash* (1935), p. 264.

by Mr. Barret of Brentford.' In 1777 the practice near Brentford was to mix the clay in the autumn, let it lie through the winter, and then fire the bricks not in kilns but in piles with coal or straw at the bottom and coal between each layer.[1]

John Middleton, the agricultural reporter of 1798, made some interesting observations on the commercial arrangements between landowner and brickmaker:

'About twenty years ago the sum usually paid by the brickmaker to the owner of the soil for an acre of brick-earth was £100. But the price of this, like other commodities, has been rapidly increasing, and indeed has gone as high as £350 per acre. The common way now is for the proprietor to receive from one shilling to half a crown per thousand, and after the brick-earth is completely manufactured and carried away the ground is returned in a level state. The common calculation is that there are one million of bricks per acre in every foot in depth including the ashes that are mixed with the earth, and, one field with another, that the brick-earth is four feet deep. The bricks called grey-stocks for the outside of houses sell at a guinea and a half per thousand, carriage included. Place bricks for inside work at twenty-four shillings. These fields lie close to the town, where manure is to be had in any quantity; and as the carriage costs but little, they are repeatedly dressed, by which means they soon recover their former fertility. There are many who object to such a manufacture being suffered in the neighbourhood of the metropolis, considering it offensive and unwholesome. On the other hand, it is contended that fire is a great purifier of the atmosphere; and that in close and hot weather a number of brick-kilns near London is of real use to the health of the inhabitants by promoting a change of air.'[2]

Until about 1835 the stock bricks were made from dustbin refuse and road sweepings mixed with clay and largely burnt by their own combustible contents; later they were made of London clay and chalk mixed with coal-dust. Modern machines, however, required new materials; formerly soft weathered clays, the brick-earth, alone were used, but most bricks are now made from hard clay or shale—the Fletton type from the Midlands which is now the standard brick for use in London and Middlesex—and brickmaking is almost extinct in the county.[3]

The extraction of gravel from surface pits is now, measured by bulk, second only to coal among the mineral products of England and Wales. Middlesex contributes for its size a large proportion of the total; the country's output was estimated at 23 million cubic yards in 1935, of which the western area of Middlesex, including small parts of Surrey and Buckinghamshire by the Thames, produced 3.6 million cubic yards. Until 1919 gravel was mainly used for road metal, but since then its use for concrete, together with immensely increased demand for road

[1] B. Langley, *London Prices of Bricklayers' Materials and Works* (1748), p. 20; *Diary of John Yeoman*, ed. M. Yearsley (1934), p. 47. [2] Middleton, p. 25. [3] Sherlock (page 5, note 2), p. 62.

surfacing, has increased consumption tenfold. Future demand is estimated at 30 million cubic yards a year, of which west Middlesex is expected to produce some 3½ million cubic yards. At this rate the known workable deposits (that is, those not sterilised by building, airports, or other immovables) should last until soon after 1980. The extraction of gravel, ugly and noisy while it is going on, leaves unsightly and useless pits which fill with water and are then politely called 'lagoons,' with a problem of 'after-treatment' to be faced. The most recent inquiry finds, however, that filling of pits is feasible; it has recently been extensively done at Edmonton and Feltham, and the ground rendered fit for use again. This consideration, together with a fresh calculation of the available gravel reserves round London, led a Ministry of Town and Country Planning committee in 1948 to reject Sir Patrick Abercrombie's proposal made in the Greater London Plan of 1944 to prohibit further extraction of gravel in the area.[1]

Next to the 'extractive' industries is the group concerned with the vegetable and animal products of the soil: agriculture, market-gardening, the nursery industry, forestry and timber, and animal products. Agriculture has been considered, as befits the primary occupation and interest of the county until recent times, in a separate chapter, together with market-gardening and the nursery industry; the story of the woodlands is brief. Though originally covered with forest, especially in the north, Middlesex was never notable for its timber products. Enfield Chase provided the best: in 1220 Henry III obtained oak shingles from it for the roof of his house at Westminster. In 1542, as appears from a 'Decree for the Commoners of Enfield Chase' by which the Crown attempted to regulate the use of the chase, firewood for sale was collected there; a heavy penalty, 3s. 4d., was set on any such 'as gather green boughs to sell to London out of any part of the chase.' Norden remarked at the end of the 16th century that depredations had so much reduced the wood available that the chase hardly provided enough firewood for the inhabitants. But there was also more substantial timber to be had. In 1650 the Council of State had to deal with the embezzling of timber trees in the chase, where 2,500 oaks, valued at £1 apiece, were reserved for Admiralty use. The rest of the trees were valued at £12,500 all told. In 1654 it was reported that the destruction of timber was going on at the rate of £2,000 a year, and by 1658 the valuation of the whole was only £6,979 12s.[2] In spite of these inroads, enough remained for one particular tree to form the keel of the *British Queen* of 1838, one of the earliest steamships on the Atlantic route.[3] The woods of Edgware were valuable enough in 1587 to give rise to a serious dispute between All Souls College, Oxford, the owners, and Lady Jane Stafford, who wanted to lease them. The college's timber in Edgware, Kingsbury, and

[1] Ministry of Town and Country Planning, *Report of the Advisory Committee on Sand and Gravel* (1948); P. Abercrombie, *Greater London Plan 1944* (1945), p. 59. [2] *V.C.H.* ii., pp. 49, 225, 228; Madge (page 24, note 2), p. 175 and map opposite p. 112; Darby, p. 395, quoting J. Evelyn, *Sylva.* [3] Thorne, art. Enfield Chase.

Willesden was valued in 1662 at £408 9s. 11d.[1] At the other end of the scale may be put the osiers cultivated on Thames islands and at sewage farms; early in the 19th century they were classified as of three kinds, used respectively for baskets, corn-sieves, and binding for packages. Osiers from Chiswick Eyot were sold for basket-making until about 1935.[2]

Turf was cut on Finchley Common for use on London fires when the sea-coal trade from the north was interrupted by the Scottish occupation of Northumberland and Durham in 1640; in 1798 peat was cut in the marshes near Uxbridge. In 1799 Marshall noted that faggots were of decreasing value in London, as the bakers were now using coal, but as late as 1875 wood was still gathered at Northwood as fuel for London.[3]

The catching of fish for food was prominent in the earlier centuries of Middlesex history. At Domesday fish-weirs were recorded at four places on the Thames and two on the Lea. Stanwell, Harmondsworth, and Harefield had valuable eel-ponds. About 1795 there were 100 families at Brentford living by fishing; fifty years later there were less than twenty. Even as late as 1864 it was worth adding fish-ladders to Molesey lock.[4]

A subsidiary occupation was bird-catching. J. E. Harting saw several siskins and redpolls taken by a birdcatcher near Hendon in the 1860s, and he knew a Middlesex gamekeeper who paid his rent by the capture and sale of nightingales; in one season he sold 180 in London for 18s. a dozen.[5] Three 17th-century pigeon-houses, or dovecotes, survive, at Boston House (Brentford), Breakspear (Harefield), and Swakeleys (Ickenham). In the early 19th century pigeons were kept in empty wine pipes set up on posts 15 or 20 feet high.[6]

Milling has been an important occupation in Middlesex at least since Domesday; then there were 33 water-driven mills on the Lea, Brent, and Colne (and one shared with Buckinghamshire at Colham); FitzStephen, who described 12th-century London, wrote of the mills 'whose clack is very pleasant to the ear' standing in the meadows on the north side. There was certainly a windmill at South Mimms in 1289—one of the earliest recorded in England—and many names in the county recall demolished windmills: Mill Hill in Hendon parish, Mill Hill Park at Acton, Windmill Hill at Enfield. Mills at Enfield and Heston survived until the 1890s, but not a single one is left. There were water-mills on the Crane at Isleworth for Syon abbey in the Middle Ages, and Norden noted at Osterley just after Sir Thomas Gresham's time 'great use for mills, as paper mills, oil mills, and corn mills, all which are now decayed (a corn mill excepted).' Modern commercial milling began in the 18th century at Uxbridge, from which 4,612½ tons of milled flour were put on the Grand Junction canal in 1799; meal was ground at Colham not far

[1] Oxford Historical Society, *Collectanea, First Series,* ed. C. R. L. Fletcher (1885), p. 179. [2] Middleton, p. 278; Cooke, p. 39; Willatts, p. 147. [3] *H.C.M.* 1 (1899), p. 234; Middleton, p. 313; Marshall, p.20; Thorne, art. Northwood. [4] T. Faulkner, *History and Antiquities of Brentford, Ealing, and Chiswick* (1845), p. 9; F. S. Thacker, *Thames Highway: Locks and Weirs* (1920), p. 447. [5] J. E. Harting, *Birds of Middlesex* (1866), p. 48. [6] Loudon (page 5, note 1), p. 1125.

away.[1] There was a quaint experiment in commercial milling at Teddington, where in 1832 a Royal Engineer officer began grinding in an old steam vessel, the *London*; unhappily it sank under the combined load of grain and machinery.[2] Flour is still milled at Uxbridge, but the place has lost its former eminence in this respect.

There were four malt-houses at Enfield in the 14th century, and it remained a profitable trade until, like everything else at Enfield, it was upset by the improvement of the Lea in the middle 16th century.[3] There were malt-houses in the 19th century on the Thames at Brentford, Chiswick, Isleworth, and Staines; but on the Lea side of the county malting had moved into Hertfordshire, mostly around Ware.

The early establishments of manufactures that were not associated with the products of the soil were, naturally enough, situated near the Thames and the Lea, in the only districts where transport was easy and assured. From about 1582 onwards there was a copper and brass mill at Isleworth, where John Brode and partners built a works for producing copper 'lattin' and 'battry.' These terms denoted copper alloy plates (often used for the metal of church 'brasses') and hammered brass or copper vessels for the kitchen or table. The metal was produced from copper and calamine ore brought from Worley Hill in the Somerset Mendips by Christopher Shutz, a German who had 'great cunning and experience' in its use. Norden noted that 'many artificial devices' were used in the manufacture. The enterprise did not prosper at first, for there was a long dispute about the management between John Brode and Sir Richard Martin, lord mayor of London in 1593, which came before the Privy Council in 1596.[4] But according to Lysons the works were still in existence two centuries later, at Baber Bridge on the edge of Hounslow Heath, rented from the Duke of Northumberland by the incorporated Society of the Mines Royal. Somewhere close to this place was a manufactory of swords in the 17th and 18th centuries.[5] A bell foundry is said to have been established by Thomas Swain at Longford about 1740.[6] Enfield was a minor centre of industry in the later Middle Ages: there were four tanneries there in the 14th century, and a fulling-mill, one of the only two in the London area, was at work soon after 1300.[7] Fuller in the 17th century said that it was the staple place for tanning, as London was for slaughter of beasts,[8] and there was still a tanyard there in 1800.

A paper-mill existed at Osterley during Sir Thomas Gresham's time (1562-79)—not, as sometimes stated, the first one in England. In the 17th century mills were worked at Hounslow and East Bedfont, which ground rags infected with the plague of 1636. There was a paper-mill operated by one Burneby at Stanwell in 1675.[9]

There was a fulling-mill at Harefield in 1518; another Harefield mill

---

[1] Lysons, art. Hillingdon. [2] Thacker (page 52, note 4), p.468. [3] *V.C.H.* ii, p.127; Norden (page 34, note 1), p.xi. [4] *V.C.H.* ii, p. 128; J. Norden, *Speculum Britanniae* (ed. 1723), p. 41 (much cut down from the version cited in preceding note); the standard work, H. Hamilton, *The English Brass and Copper Industries to 1800* (1926), p. 48, has only a brief reference. [5] G. E. Bate, *And So Make a City Here* (1948), p. 278; Maxwell (page 38, note 3), pp. 42, 85. [6] *V.C.H.* ii., p. 167 (evidence not cited). [7] Clapham, *concise*, p. 155. [8] Quoted by Cox (page 44, note 1), iii., p.31. [9] *V.C.H.* ii., p. 195; E. Lipson, *Economic History of England* (ed. 4, 1947), iii., p. 352.

made paper and then copper. The copper used for sheathing the bottoms of Nelson's ships was supposed to have come from this mill, which was still at work in 1850.[1]

At the end of the 18th century there were a few industrial establishments near the rivers manufacturing for general trade and not merely for the needs of the local population. At New Brentford were a starch manufactory and one for cotton wicks; at Isleworth a factory for calico grounds and a pottery; at Colnbrook a tannery and a glue-boiling plant; in the Lea valley an oil mill, the only manufacture at Tottenham, and the tanyard already mentioned at Enfield. It appears from research, including excavation on the sites, that the Isleworth potteries never manufactured porcelain ware, which they have sometimes been credited with, but were restricted to earthenware of various kinds, including one variety with a peculiar finish like bright red sealing-wax.[2] In 1774 there was a pottery at Brentford making only tun pots and 'sugar loafs.'[3] At Teddington about 1840 there was a wax-candle factory, 'the most complete in the kingdom.'[4] A crape factory existed at Ponders End in 1809 and another at Tottenham soon after. A Tottenham silk-mill had a very short life; the premises were taken over for the manufacture of rubber garments, then called 'caoutchouc,' but the stench of naphtha was too much for the district, and it was given up by 1843.[5]

A factory for oil of vitriol (sulphuric acid) was established at Twickenham in 1736 by Joshua Ward, a celebrated quack doctor of the time, and John White, who probably contributed the scientific knowledge required. Although manufacture at Twickenham was limited to 40-50 gallons at a time by the size of the glass globes employed as containers, it reduced the price of acid from 2s. 6d. an ounce to 2s. a pound. About 1840 there were vitriol mills at Heston and Norwood.[6]

The Grand Junction canal, opened in 1798, attracted a few factories to its banks, though it served rather to carry manure and other refuse away from London into Middlesex than to stimulate industrial settlement in the county. Railways attracted no fresh industries into districts hitherto cut off from transport; the expansion in the 20th century was principally caused by other influences. The census reporters of 1831 observed: 'In the appropriate application of the word manufacture, none of importance can be attributed to Middlesex ... other than that of silk'—and this was at Spitalfields, not in the present county area. In Augustus Petermann's map accompanying the 1851 report, which showed the local distribution of manufactures, the shower of straw hats, envelopes, and other symbols, including those denoting lace and silk, that is scattered freely over Hertfordshire and Buckinghamshire stops short at the Middlesex border; apart from a solitary rifle at Enfield there is nothing to denote production for more than local needs except a general hatching of the eastern and

[1] Hassell, p. 146; Tymms (page 38, note 3), p.16. [2] W. J. Pountney, 'Isleworth Potteries, 1750-1850', typescript in Victoria and Albert Museum library; H. Clay, 'Isleworth Pottery', *Burlington Magazine* 49 (1926), p. 83. [3] *John Yeoman* (page 50, note 1), p. 16. [4] Tymms (page 38, note 3), p. 16*. [5] Tymms, p. 16*; [J. Dean], *Tottenham and its Institutions in 1843* (1843). [6] Williams (page 17, note 3), p. 362; Tymms, p. 16*; MS. Diary of B. J. Armstrong (for Norwood).

southern portions of the county with the word 'Gardening' superimposed.[1]

The manufacture of synthetic dyes has no place in Middlesex today, and it was not carried on in Britain on any great scale until the 1914 war. Yet Middlesex, by the accident of being the birthplace of William Henry Perkin, the discoverer of aniline dyes produced from coal tar, was the birthplace of the whole industry. Perkin, who lived at Sudbury, discovered violet or 'Tyrian purple' in 1856 at the age of 18 while trying to produce synthetic quinine. He set up a factory in 1857 beside the canal at Greenford Green and developed its use with the help of Robert Pullar of the Perth dye firm. These dyes soon became popular, under the names of magenta and solferino given them by French chemists. Perkin continued to develop perfumes and fresh colours, including the first satisfactory Turkey red or alizarin in 1869; but in 1873 he abandoned manufacture and devoted the rest of his life to research at his house at Sudbury.[2]

In 1875 the distribution of industry had hardly developed since 1800; it was still tied to water communications. At Brentford were varnish and soap factories and sawmills; at Isleworth the brass mill still functioned, and there was a cement factory and boat-building yards; at Southall chemicals were manufactured, at Yiewsley oil and varnish, at Staines *papier-mâché* and linoleum; at Poyle near Stanwell was a paper-mill. A group of powder-mills had existed, probably since the 17th century, in the seclusion of Hounslow Heath, the scene from time to time of explosions that shook Horace Walpole, among others. In 1653 John and Henry Wroth had gunpowder made at Enfield Lock. The important small arms factory there, originally established in the Napoleonic wars, was re-equipped in 1855, and its products carried the name of Enfield all over the world, first coupled with Lee and later, combined with the pronounceable part of Brno in Czechoslovakia, in the 'Bren' gun. Joseph Whitworth had been invited in 1854 to construct rifle-making equipment for Enfield, but the arsenal at Harper's Ferry, West Virginia (soon afterwards made more widely known by the exploit of John Brown), was chosen as the model, and American machinery was installed in 1858.[3]

In the last quarter of the 19th century, however, influences began to operate which changed the face of Middlesex and, working with increased force after 1920, produced the mixed industrial and suburban county of today.[4] So far as industry was concerned, existing plants in inner London needed to be moved away to less cramped and insanitary sites; manufacturers looked for lower-rated areas in which to establish their works; and new industries, especially those depending mainly on assembly of partly-fabricated parts, were placed near to the most concentrated market. Sites in Middlesex meeting all these needs were to

[1] Clapham, *Modern Britain,* i., p. 67; ii., p. 26; Petermann's map at end of vol. ii. [2] Clapham, *Modern Britain,* ii., p. 106. [3] J. W. Fortescue, *History of the British Army,* xiii. (1930), p. 170; *V.C.H.* ii, p. 131; Clapham, *Modern Britain,* ii., p. 77; C. W. Whitaker, *History of Enfield* (1911), p. 169. [4] For these paragraphs, D. H. Smith, *Industries of Greater London* (1933); *Fourth Annual Report of the London Passenger Transport Board* (1937), p. 22.

be found in areas not yet built on because their situation was unsuitable for housing or there had been no easy communication with central London. Industries in east London, Hoxton, and Clerkenwell, especially clothing, metal-working, and cabinet-making, tended to move out to Tottenham and places farther up the Lea valley; in west Middlesex, especially along the Brent valley and the line of the canal, new industries grew up which needed clean air, like food processing, or had links with those formerly carried on in the West End of London, like coachbuilding and manufacture of musical instruments. New arterial roads built in the 1920s and 1930s opened up new districts for factory siting.

The Lea valley, a broad swampy bottom avoided by roads and residential settlement, remained comparatively untouched by modern development, apart from the small arms factory at Enfield Lock, until about 1880. There were good transport facilities by railway and canal; the London-Cambridge road ran through Tottenham and Edmonton, one to two miles west of the valley, giving off very few cross roads, and development was consequently mostly on the Middlesex bank of the river. By 1900 linoleum was being manufactured at Angel Road, Edmonton, jute at Enfield, and furniture at Tottenham; from that time onward clothing, light metal-working, and cabinet-making in the district increased, at a quicker pace after 1918. Clothing and electrical components are characteristic products of this area—small and easy to transport when finished, requiring skilled labour but no heavy raw materials. Little food is processed in this district.[1]

The rest of north Middlesex has not been much used by industry; there are no rivers, the railway communications in general are not so favourable as in the Lea valley, and the country was retained until comparatively late in large parks and private grounds. There has been a 'horticultural pottery,' making flower-pots of local clay, for over 150 years at White Hart Lane, Wood Green, and there are some recent factories at New Southgate.

The state of west and north-west Middlesex, however, is very different. At Acton, Brentford, and on the canal from Southall to West Drayton, there were sporadic establishments of industry in the 19th century, but in general the poverty of communications made the area unattractive for industry until between 1904 and 1914. In those years electric railways, the new Great Western line from Acton to Greenford and Ruislip, and the motor bus opened what had remained until then the most inaccessible and backward part of the county. Already between 1900 and 1908 factories from London, especially engineering and coachbuilding works, had moved to Acton Vale, and the site of the unsuccessful 'Park Royal' showground, north of Acton, had been earmarked for commercial and industrial development. Communications

[1] Willatts, p. 220.

with the Midlands and with the West End of London by road and rail were now good, and there was no other region of the same size still so little developed within seven miles of Charing Cross. After 1919 firms set up factories in the north-west at a remarkable rate. An almost continuous belt of factories lines the Edgware Road beyond Cricklewood; there is a cluster on the Wembley exhibition site, and another at North Wembley. The biggest concentration is at Park Royal, where disposal of government premises after 1920, with the building of the Western Avenue and the North Circular road, gave industry its chance. Farther out the arterial roads are lined with modern factories, some of them respectable and some of flashy appearance; they line the Western Avenue to Greenford and the Great West Road north of Brentford. One of these, the Firestone factory at Brentford, turned out its first tyre in 1929, eighteen weeks after work began on the building site.[1] There are also important groups of factories, mostly established between 1900 and 1919, farther west, at Southall, Hayes, and West Drayton, and some at Twickenham and Harrow. These are mainly producers of 'consumer goods,' in which organisation and labour are more important elements than raw materials. The factories are mostly run by electric power and are free from obnoxious by-products, which makes them less objectionable neighbours in residential areas. Many of them are engaged in food preparation of various kinds; many others are assembly industries making proprietary products. These are in general new industries not competing with those existing in the Midlands and the north of England; foodstuffs, electrical products, chemicals, motor vehicles, components and equipment, and musical instruments predominate.

The movement of industry to these areas was naturally influenced by where the workpeople lived. After the Great Eastern Railway branch from Hackney Downs through Tottenham and Edmonton to Enfield was opened in 1872, with workmen's trains at specially cheap fares, immense numbers of cheap, and often bad, houses were built close to the stations; when economic pressure and the need to expand their plants drove London factory owners to look for fresh sites, they naturally chose places close to where many of their workmen already lived. From 1900 onwards, when railways and tramways turned to electric traction and the motor bus began to make its characteristic contribution to suburban London, industries within the region had to worry less about their nearness to labour supply. Now, indeed, suburban transport services are taken so much for granted that workers at a Middlesex factory may come daily from ten or twelve miles away, much as office workers in central London do; more than a quarter of the workers at a New Southgate factory have been found to live over five miles away. Dispersal of industry has not necessarily implied shortening the daily journey to work.[2]

[1] *Builder* 137 (1929), p. 27. [2] K. K. Leipmann, *Journey to Work* (1944), pp. 144, 204; *London Travel Survey, 1949* (London Transport, 1950), p. 29.

Some useful indications of the movement of industries into these areas since 1900 were compiled in 1932; the general conclusions may be taken as valid for the whole period.[1] Inquiries from 627 manufacturing firms in the district (which for this purpose extended somewhat beyond the county border on the country side, without distorting the general accuracy for Middlesex) showed that 313 had migrated to the district between 1900 and 1932, and 314 had been originally established there. Of those that migrated, the great majority—243—had come from inner London; 43 had been set up by overseas firms; 27 had come from other parts of Britain, and of these only 14 from the Midlands and the north. Of the local firms which had always operated in the district, 82 were already there by 1922; the remaining 232 had been established since. These figures show that the 'drift of industry to the south,' as it is usually understood, is a fallacious notion; what was happening between the wars was not that factories were being transferred from the Midlands and north to the London region, but that the new light industries were established in the south and so altered the industrial pattern that the 19th century had left.

One Middlesex institution occupies a special place in the structure of modern British industry—the National Physical Laboratory and the other installations of the Department of Scientific and Industrial Research grouped round Bushy House, Teddington. The conception of scientific research undertaken under government sponsorship for eventual application to industrial processes was slow to take root in England—far slower than in Germany, where certain leaders of the Royal Society in the 1890s saw with envy the flourishing and useful *Physikalisch-technische Reichsanstalt* in Berlin fostering technical advances in industry. Lord Rayleigh, president of the Society, interested A. J. Balfour, his brother-in-law, in the creation of a similar institution in England, and the National Physical Laboratory was established in 1900. The original conception was limited to the establishment and maintenance of precise standards of measurement, but this inevitably developed into experiment and research in a wider field, supplying the link between the 'pure' scientific research of the universities and technical application by industrial research associations and individual firms. During the 1914-18 war, which reinforced official appreciation of the value of scientific research, the Department of Scientific and Industrial Research was set up as an independent department and assumed responsibility for the National Physical Laboratory.[2]

The Radio Research Station and Chemical Research Laboratory, under the D.S.I.R., are also at Teddington. Another branch of the department is the Road Research Station at Harmondsworth, opened in

[1] Smith (page 55, note 4), p. 171.   [2] R. Glazebrook, *Early Days at the National Physical Laboratory* (1933).

1930. The General Post Office transferred its research department to Dollis Hill in 1931.[1]

Middlesex has thus become an industrial area of the first importance. The county does not merely manufacture for consumption in London and round about; its production is of national significance. Many people, inside Middlesex and out, do not care for the fact, but it is too late to alter it.

[1] H. F. Heath and A. L. Hetherington, *Industrial Research and Development* (1946), pp. 248, 285, 292.

CHAPTER VI

COMMUNICATIONS AND WATER SUPPLY

*'There be three things which make a nation great
and prosperous—a fertile soil, busy workshops, and
easy conveyance for men and commodities from one
place to another.'*   FRANCIS BACON

THE river Thames, forming the whole of the county's southern
boundary, is the prime geographical fact about Middlesex; the
second is the river Lea on its eastern side. The parts of the county that
could be easily reached from these rivers are the only ones where
primitive man has left evidence of settlement; there are enough traces to
testify to a comparatively brisk traffic along the rivers from the neolithic
age onwards. The Thames stream was broader then than the river we
know now, flowing more rapidly at the centre, with more shallows and
small islands. In the Roman era, roads, fords, and bridges became more
important than the river itself, but with the arrival of the Saxons, and
later during the Viking invasions, the course of history in the area shows
that it had again become the great line of communication.

The first indication of the Thames as a highway organised for traffic
is found under the year 851, when Asser in his life of Alfred referred to
the City of London having certain rights over the river up to Staines—
rights still commemorated by London Stone on the left bank there.[1] Until
about 1350 the general jurisdiction of the Thames, as of the Severn,
Trent, and Great Ouse, remained a Crown prerogative, exercised through
special temporary commissions under letters patent; the City's specific
jurisdiction up to Staines was established by charter at the end of the 12th
century. By 1205 there was river traffic between London and Oxford; by
1274 there was some sort of dredging or other conservancy throughout.
Clause 23 of Magna Carta—*omnes kidelli deponantur*, let all kiddles, or fish-
weirs, be removed—presumes (what was far from being true) that the
common law for all navigable rivers is that they shall be open highways.
Domesday Book recorded fish-weirs at Staines, Shepperton, Hampton,
and Isleworth; Henry IV granted the right to a weir at Strand on the

---

[1] For references to the Thames, F. S. Thacker, *Thames Highway: General History* (1914) and
Thames Highway: History of the Locks and Weirs (1920); W. T. Jackman, *Development of
Transportation in Modern England* (1916); T. S. Willan, *River Navigation in England, 1600-1750*
(1936).

Green in 1411, only six years after the City had had all weirs below Staines destroyed; Edward IV made a similar grant in 1468, cancelled in the next year on complaint from the City. In 1580 the Privy Council demanded to know from the lord mayor, whose jurisdiction had been confirmed by an act of 1489, how many weirs there were anciently between Staines and London Bridge and how many had been put up in the last seven years, 'for that Her Majesty had been informed that by the many weirs the river in many places was being choked up and made unnavigable, and she was disposed to have present redress taken.' In 1590 the lord mayor was more sharply commanded to remove obstructions.

Some progress had been made by 1605, when an act recited that 'the river of Thames is from the city of London till within a few miles of the city of Oxford very navigable and passable with and for boats and barges of great content and carriage'; and in 1636, for further improvement of navigation, the Crown granted to certain individuals the right to dredge gravel from the river. It was in good enough condition to allow regular freight services to be operated; they were advertised in Taylor's *Carriers' Cosmography* (1637), a kind of early *Bradshaw*.

'To Bull Wharf (near Queenhithe) there doth come and go great boats twice or thrice every week betwixt London and Kingston; also thither doth often come a boat from Colnbrook. Great boats that do carry passengers and goods betwixt London and Maidenhead, Windsor, Staines, Chertsey, with other parts of Surrey, Berkshire, Middlesex, and Buckinghamshire, do come every Monday and Thursday to Queenhithe, and go away upon Tuesdays and Thursdays.'

Under an act of 1751 an immense body of Thames Commissioners was appointed, the City's rights being reserved below Staines. In 1777 the towpath, not yet fit for horses, was freed from toll in exchange for a navigation charge. Complaints about the state of the river, which must have been too shallow to navigate for some months in most years, were made with monotonous iteration during the later 18th century. It was said in 1793 that in summer time with favourable water it took two days to get from Isleworth to Maidenhead, 37½ miles, and there were several proposals for building artificial cuts. But these complaints do not show that water-borne traffic was seriously hampered, merely that a profitable trade might, in the opinion of the carriers, be made more so. Already in 1677 Andrew Yarranton, projector of not entirely visionary schemes for inland water communication, had written in his *England's Improvement by Sea and Land*: 'London is as the heart is in the body, and the great rivers are as its veins,' and proposed a canal linking Thames and Severn.

There was a good deal of river traffic. In 1715, 90 loads of flour left the Kennet mills in Berkshire for London by barge; in 1729-30, 2,375 tons of cheese left Abingdon and Newbury for London; and in the other direction 80,000 London chaldrons of coal went up the river, 3,000 of them as far as Abingdon. In Defoe's time barges drawing almost two feet of water were carrying 1,000 quarters of malt or meal from Abingdon to Queenhithe market.[1] These are casual figures from odd references; it is perhaps more significant that almost every picture of Thames-side houses of the 18th century shows a laden barge in the foreground. In 1747 the bargemasters protested against the new Walton bridge, whose openings would be too small for the safety of their craft. (Nearly all the early bridges were very difficult to navigate.) The act of 1751 laid down that boats were not to draw more than four feet of water, which is fair evidence for supposing that some of them previously did.

Throughout this period there was a running dispute between the owners of riverside mills and the bargemasters. It needed constant vigilance to maintain the rights of through navigation and haulage against the riverside owners' natural anxiety to make the river a continuous private water.[2] The ancient and clumsy method of 'flash' locks or weirs, at which enough water was let out of a single gate when required to float a barge up, began to be supplanted in 1623 when the first 'pound' lock on the Thames with two gates was built on the upper section of the river; but it persisted on the Middlesex and Surrey portion until 1810-15, when, with Sir John Rennie as its engineer, the City corporation built new locks (*Plate 3*). Bargemen did not all take kindly to the new devices; they did their best to smash Teddington lock soon after it was opened in 1811.

Until 1819, when a continuous towpath fit for horses was completed below Staines, barges were drawn by gangs of men called 'halers.' An observant visitor to Brentford in 1774 described them: 'I saw vast numbers of barges coming up the river; they had wind and tide but they had all men to draw them up. I saw 34 men to draw up one but there was several more tied to him.' Horses had, of course, been used on certain parts of the river from much earlier; one Richard Chippes, charged with negligently running down a rowing-boat at Kew in 1600, was the steersman of a three-horse barge.[3]

The decline of the Thames Navigation came quickly in the 1840s. In 1848 all the lock-keepers' wages had to be reduced because of railway competition, but on the tidal river there was still a very fair traffic—116 laden barges reached Brentford from London in one week of February 1849, and the Great Western Railway discharged traffic from the west at Bull's Bridge, Southall, for forwarding by water through Brentford to the London docks. From 1840 the City became engaged in a wearisome dispute with the Crown on the jurisdiction of Thames tidal waters. In

[1] D. Defoe, *Tour through England and Wales* (1724-6) (Everyman ed.), i., p. 345. [2] Jackman, p. 432, quoting *Public Advertiser*, 11 October 1786. [3] *John Yeoman* (page 50, note 1), p. 22; *M.C.R.* i., p. 261.

1856 the City withdrew its claim; next year the Crown conveyed its rights to the new Thames Conservancy Board, successor to the Thames Commissioners. In 1908 control of the river below Teddington passed to the Port of London Authority.

Freight on the Thames in recent years has been largely coal for the Metropolitan Water Board's pumping stations near Hampton and for the electric power station at Kingston. Some 20,000 tons a year were hauled past Teddington for places up to Staines in 1928-9; in addition, about 1,200 tons went beyond Staines.[1]

Passenger traffic has grown to be of greater consequence. Londoners early selected Hampton Court, Twickenham, Isleworth, and Chiswick as residences because of their easy access by water. Pepys visited Brentford by boat in 1665; in 1822 the table of authorised watermen's charges from London Bridge showed fares all the way up to Staines, which cost 18s. The first regular steamboat on this part of the river was the *Endeavour* of 1830, plying to Richmond; by 1842 there were four companies in the business. It was not without inconveniences: the owner of the *Diana* protested that the shallows caused his vessel to ground, thus 'detaining families of the first respectability until a late hour at night.' In 1843 there was actually a steamboat called the *Locomotive*; the City tried to restrict its speed to 2 m.p.h. In the forties steamers were still prevented from going through the locks above the tideway, beyond Richmond; but the river steamer on its way to Hampton Court or even Oxford, in two days from Kingston, is now a familiar summer sight.

The only other Middlesex river comparable with the Thames is the Lea—spelt Lee officially but never otherwise. With its comparatively broad and marshy valley running north and south, it early provided a natural communication and at times a natural frontier. It was probably the boundary of the territory of the Trinovantes to the east and the Catuvellauni to the west in the 1st century B.C., and throughout the Saxon age it defined the Middlesex territories from Essex proper. In later times the river has been canalised, and some of the ancient course is obliterated by reservoirs; but that course remains the boundary between the administrative counties of Middlesex and Essex.

Its history as a means of communication is long and interesting.[2] The first known English example of money borrowed by a statutory body for a public work is an act of 1430, setting up commissioners with power to borrow in order to remove obstructions from the Lea, as there were so many 'shelfs' in the river from Ware to London that boats could not pass along it. The commissioners were permitted to charge 4d. for each freighted boat for three years. A complaint of 1448 against the bishop of London, for allowing too much water to pass through the sluice at his water-mill at Hackney, recited: 'There is in Middlesex a water called le

[1] Smith (page 55, note 1), p. 28. [2] For references to the Lea, Jackman and Willan (page 60, note 1).

Ley, running from Tottenham to the Thames, by which ships and boats have been accustomed from time immemorial to go from the City of London to the said village of Tottenham and elsewhere with various goods.'[1] 'Time immemorial' is a doubtful indication, but it must at least imply water-borne trade to Tottenham in the 14th century.

A fresh attempt was made in 1571 with similar machinery to make the river navigable to Ware; this aroused much controversy and opposition from vested interests. The counties of Middlesex, Essex, and Hertfordshire were authorised to build a cut, or navigation, which was apparently completed by 1581. One of the earliest pound locks in England seems to have been in existence at Waltham on the Lea in 1574; the earliest known was on the Exeter canal in 1564. A chorus of complaint arose against these innovations; Enfield took a large part, protesting about the damage done to its carrying trade for grain, malt, and provisions, which now went throughout by water instead of being landed there. Burnings of the locks, violence to the lock-keepers, and damage to the banks ensued.[2] Improvements went on, against resistance, through the 17th century, and during the 18th the river head was carried up to Hertford. The opening of the railway up the Lea valley in 1840 naturally affected traffic on the river, but a substantial amount continued to pass, varying in the years 1878 to 1928 between a maximum of 784,000 tons in 1901 and a minimum of 532,000 in 1920: mostly coal and coke, then timber, oil, and flour for the factories in the lower part of the valley.[3]

The river Colne was probably navigated by small craft up to Uxbridge from fairly early times; Norden in 1593 mentions a statement that there was shipping on it as far as St Albans, only to dismiss it with the remark: *Minime credendum.*[4] The Brent was too small to signify.

Londoners, if not Middlesex men, were not content with the water communications provided by nature; they early sought to run canals across the county. The history of its artificial navigable waterways begins as usual with several unsuccessful projects. In 1641 Sir Edward Forde, soldier and inventor, published a proposal to bring a navigable cut from Rickmansworth on the Colne to St Giles in the Fields. This scheme had begun as a project for water supply, and navigation was an afterthought; it was republished in 1720.[5] A different proposal was promoted or supported by the owners and bargemasters of the Thames, who petitioned the common council of London in 1791 for a canal from Boulter's Lock, Maidenhead, to Isleworth.[6] It had been under consideration since about 1770, but, though supported with strong technical arguments, it succumbed to the opposition of landowners who asserted that a canal, which could not pay, would become 'green mantled pools of stinking water' which would 'contaminate the passing breeze with noxious exhalations.' In 1793, however, the Grand Junction Canal's

[1] *H.C.M.* 13 (1911), p. 231. [2] E. Lipson, *Economic History of England* (ed. 4, 1947), ii., p. 447; Fisher (page 44, note 1); *V.C.H. Hertfordshire* iv. (1914), p. 209; Gras (page 46, note 3), p. 127. [3] Smith (page 55, note 4), p. 43. [4] J. Norden, *Speculum Britanniae* (ed. 1723), p. 11. [5] Willan (page 60, note 1), p. 10. [6] For canals, Jackman, and J. Priestley, *Historical Account of the Navigable Rivers, Canals, and Railways of Great Britain* (1831).

first act was passed; it ran from Brentford past West Drayton and Uxbridge to join the Oxford Canal near Braunston, Northamptonshire, and was opened to Uxbridge in 1798 and throughout in 1805. This was an immediate success, unlike the Coventry and Oxford canals; it contributed much to the prosperity of Uxbridge, whose corn-mills flourished, and it gave a strong impetus to the development of brickfields about Isleworth and Heston. In 1829 its shares paid 13 per cent. But eight years later it delivered the Great Western Railway's first locomotive at West Drayton, and it settled down to a less dazzling prosperity. It was supplied with water from reservoirs established at Ruislip and Kingsbury (the Welsh Harp), but these lakes are now ornamental rather than useful.

A cut running to Paddington basin from the Grand Junction at Norwood was opened in 1801. The Regent's Canal of 1820 continued this link to the docks. The canals did not secure much of the coal traffic to London—in 1826 only 1,484 tons of the two million tons burned in the capital came into the Paddington basin; mostly it dealt with hay inwards and dung out, at any rate after the railways were opened.'[1]

For a few years in the early part of the 19th century passenger travel flourished on these canals. An engraving of 1801 shows the 'accommodation boat,' hauled by two horses and filled to overflowing with passengers, leaving rural Paddington on a bright morning. *The Ambulator (or a Pocket Companion for the Tour of London and its Environs)* wrote in its 1811 edition: 'At the [Paddington] Basin, a passage boat to Greenford Green and Uxbridge sets off daily during the summer months at eight o'clock in the morning: a breakfast is provided on board, and other refreshments may be obtained. The terms are reasonable, viz. five miles for a shilling, ten miles for eighteen-pence, and the extent of this *still* voyage to Uxbridge may be enjoyed for half a crown.' Evidently the canal boat could be no rival to the stage coach for the serious traveller, but pleasure trips continued on the canal to Greenford Green as late as 1853; the Packet Boat inn at Cowley still reminds the passer-by of this agreeable form of transport. It was so pleasant that Benjamin West, P.R.A. 1792-1820, painted a picture of it with himself and many of his friends on board.[2]

Rivers and canals, however, have to serve men in other ways than for communication. Large concentrated communities need, before anything else, a constant and assured supply of pure water. London, sited at the lowest bridgeable point on the river, owed its foundation to two reasons: it was the lowest point on the Thames with ground high enough to be free from marshes and with a supply of reasonably clean water. As the London population increased the wells were exhausted and the Thames became polluted; so the city's requirements had to be satisfied from places outside its limits. There was little to be got from the Surrey side, and the story of London's water supply since the late 16th century

[1] Clapham, *Modern Britain*, i., p. 233; ii., p. 201. [2] *V.C.H.* ii., p. 123; *Times*, 11 July 1849; J. T. Smith, *Nollekens and his Times* (ed. 1949), p. 188.

is mostly concerned with the Thames and Lea and engineering works for filtering their waters and conveying them to London. Most of these works were situated in Middlesex, and the waterworks and the artificial river are characteristic features of its scenery.

The earliest known evidences of water engineering in the county are, however, connected not with London but with the domestic supply of Hampton Court. One of the few relics of the preceptory of the Knights Hospitallers at Hampton Court is a piece of jointed water main dug up in 1926 under the foundations of the palace. When Wolsey built his house he took care to have good water brought in pipes from Coombe Hill in Surrey. In 1794 this water was said to be 'efficacious in the gravel, excellent for drinking and washing, but unfit for culinary use': it turned vegetables black.[1] This supply was reinforced by the Longford river (also called the Queen's or Cardinal's river), constructed in Charles I's reign from the Colne at Longford past Hanworth to Bushy Park and Hampton Court, where it still feeds the ornamental waters.

The county away from the rivers was indifferently supplied. Harrow, Hendon, Highgate, and Muswell Hill were early inhabited because of the springs in the Bagshot sands that capped the clay at those places, though their development was later restricted by the limited amounts so obtained;[2] but the clay meadows in between lacked water and remained sparsely settled until the 20th century, when 'company's water' could be brought from a distance in mains to provide the large—water engineers would say excessive—requirements of suburban houses. The area between Harrow and the Uxbridge road was especially waterless; the incumbents of Greenford and Northolt sought to remedy the scarcity by digging wells in 1791, and at Greenford it was still not easily available in 1875. Artesian wells were used to maintain supplies at Uxbridge and Tottenham in 1869.[3]

Almost all the water projects in Middlesex, however, have been carried out primarily for the benefit of London.[4] In 1544, a London conduit act gave the lord mayor authority to convey water from Muswell Hill and Hampstead Heath to the City. The first successful project was Hugh Myddelton's remarkable 'New River,' the admiration of its age and the envy of later capitalists. It was originally promoted in 1605 by the City; Myddelton offered in 1609 to execute the work and raised £19,000 to do so with assistance from the Crown and 28 'adventurers.' The river was inaugurated in 1613, running from Amwell springs in Hertfordshire by a somewhat circuitous route of 38 miles past Enfield and Wood Green to the New River Head at Islington. The most remarkable piece of work was the 'flume' or boarded trough, 660 feet long, at Bush Hill Park, which lasted until a clay sluice was built to replace it in 1788. The New River produced a dividend of £3 4s. 2d. per cent in 1633, £214 in 1720,

---

[1] Thacker, *Locks and Weirs* (page 60, note 1), p. 455. [2] H. Hunter, *History of the Environs of London* (1811), p. 85. [3] Clutterbuck (page 40, note 3); Lysons, art. Northall; Thorne, art. Greenford. [4] For the following paragraphs, H. W. Dickinson, 'Water Supply of Greater London', *Engineer* 186 (1948); *Water Supply of London* (Metropolitan Water Board, 1949); on the New River, Jackman, p. 179.

and £431 5s. 8d. in 1794—a good yield, even for a public utility in the 18th century, though much of it certainly came from rents on land owned by the company. Some of Myddelton's successors were men of note in their profession: Henry Mill, d. 1771, who shortened the course of the river, installed Sir Robert Walpole's water supply at Houghton, Norfolk, and invented an early form of typewriter; and three generations of the remarkable Mylne family—Robert Mylne, d. 1811, engineer and architect, designer of Blackfriars bridge, who made further cuts in the river, William Chadwell Mylne, d. 1863, and Robert William Mylne, d. 1890. Wells were sunk along the New River to supplement failing supplies from the Amwell and Chadwell springs, and some notable early steam engines by Smeaton (1766) and Watt (1786) were installed for pumping. Apart from its technical interest, the New River affords some pleasing variation to otherwise undistinguished tracts of north Middlesex like Finsbury Park, which needs it (*Plate 53*).

Such a successful undertaking could hardly remain without competitors. The Grand Junction Canal company took powers in 1798 to supply drinking water to Paddington from its reservoirs at Kingsbury and Ruislip, but canal water was found unfit for human consumption. The drinking-water part of the project was separated from the canal by the formation of the Grand Junction Waterworks company in 1811, with John Rennie as its engineer; it constructed an intake from the Thames at Chelsea. The principal works were established at Kew bridge in 1835, where the East and West Cornish engines by Boulton and Watt (1820) were re-erected and kept in regular use till 1944. They are still maintained in reserve.[1]

Meanwhile other London water companies were drawing their supplies from the Lea at Old Ford and the Thames within the London area. This was fairly satisfactory in 18th-century conditions, but it became intolerable as the tidal Thames became increasingly used as the receptacle for water-borne domestic sanitation. The great London cholera epidemics of 1832, 1848-9, 1854, and 1866 can be attributed directly to the sanitary improvement of the water closet: sewers discharged the effluent from the more prosperous districts only a few yards above the intakes of the water companies.[2] The Thames became so foul that the terrace of the Houses of Parliament was unbearable in summer and the windows of the chamber had to be closed against the stench. The Metropolis Water Act of 1852 laid down that all domestic water must be filtered and all intakes removed above the tidal limit at Teddington weir by 1856. The nearest available sites were on both banks above Hampton, and there the companies established their works in the prevailing Italianate style favoured by architects working with engineers. On the Middlesex side the Grand Junction, West Middlesex, and

---

[1] *Proceedings of the Institution of Mechanical Engineers* 156 (1947), p. 236. [2] G. Gibbon and R. W. Bell, *History of the London County Council, 1889-1939* (1939), p. 17.

Southwark and Vauxhall companies went to Hampton in 1852; the East London, a Lea valley undertaking, went to Sunbury after the last serious cholera epidemic in 1866. Charles Greaves of the East London, a notable water engineer, decided to use water drawn not only from the river but also from the excavations made for a reservoir in the gravel beds at Hanworth. This company was supplied in 1871 with three large pumping engines by Harvey & Co., of Hayle, Cornwall, adorned with the Horatian motto *Fies nobilum tu quoque fontium.*

After agitations during the 1890s, in which the new London County Council joined, the Metropolitan Water Board was established in 1902; it took over all the installations of the London companies and the Tottenham and Enfield undertakings in 1904. The Colne Valley Water Company continued to supply west and north-west Middlesex. The board completed some important works begun by the companies—the Banbury and Lockwood reservoirs in the Lea valley (1903) and the two Staines reservoirs (1904)—and it constructed the King George V reservoir (1913) in the Lea valley, the Queen Mary (1925) at Laleham, and the King George VI (1947) west of the Staines group. The huge Queen Mary reservoir covers 707 acres, almost as large as St James's Park, Hyde Park, and Kensington Gardens together; it has a central bank to break the waves that form in windy weather. These vast testimonies to Londoners' high consumption—over 51 gallons per head a day in 1947-8—obliterated good farming land, but they afford consolation to birdwatchers (*Plate* 72). The remark of a Royal Commission in 1874, that the Thames basin would remain an ample water supply for the wants of any possible increase in the population, still holds good; but for new developments the board has begun to look beyond the Middlesex border to the Enborne valley in Berkshire.

*   *   *   *   *

After communication by river—a long time after—came regular use of tracks and roads on land. As London lies towards the south-eastern extremity of England, and Middlesex is the strip of territory immediately north, north-west, and west of the city, all land communication with the greater part of the country, that part lying between lines running from London through Cambridge to the north-east and through Salisbury to the south-west, has to pass through Middlesex, but in no case is the distance within the county much more than ten miles. Some of the earliest turnpikes were set up in the county, and the most successful of the turnpike trusts controlled most of its main roads; in the present age the face of Middlesex has been transformed by new arterial roads. Many of the inhabitants have derived their livelihood from road communications, either from posting, or from tavern-keeping, or from more straight-forward plundering of travellers.

Trackways—the term 'roads,' which implies some degree of engineering, is unsuitable here—were the first means of land communication. It seems that Brentford was the lowest permanent ford over the Thames until Roman times, at the site known as 'Old England,' now covered by the railway goods yard and dock. It was approached from the south by a track, which existed until 1803, across Kew Gardens. On the Middlesex side there may have been three trackways leading away from the ford: one east through Strand on the Green, Fulham, Chelsea, and Tothill Fields to Old Ford on the Lea and so to Camulodunum, near Colchester; the second north through Ealing and past Horsendon Hill, Sudbury, and Brockley Hill to Wheathampstead and St Albans; the third north-west by Hanwell over the Brent to Hayes and Uxbridge.

These tracks have left only the faintest indications of their course, for they were not metalled and nature reasserted herself quickly when they were abandoned for a deviation that was less muddy or for the engineered roads of the Romans. They are mainly presumed from the indications of pre-Roman occupation at the Thames fords and at certain inland centres, which must have been linked by some such network; but H. S. Braun has adduced some slender pieces of actual evidence that, taken together, appear to point to two more tracks in the north-west of the county.[1]

Knowledge of the British ways is based on fragmentary indications and is speculative, but there is good archaeological evidence for the Roman roads, which were laid down within a few years of the conquest under Claudius and have remained the framework on which most later road development has been built up, though in places it has been curiously disregarded. The famous Watling Street, the axial road of England in Roman and later times, is known in Middlesex as the Edgware road. From the Marble Arch, where one route from Thorney Island, Westminster, over St James's Park was joined by another from London Bridge along Oxford Street, the Edgware road led almost without deviation to Brockley Hill, where there was a settlement of Roman date; then, after a remarkable kink, it resumed its general north-westerly direction and ran straight to St Albans and thence to Chester. The second road ran from Oxford Street by Notting Hill and Shepherd's Bush past Acton Green to Brentford, over Hounslow Heath to Staines, and on to Silchester, in Hampshire. The third, Ermine Street, ran north by Stoke Newington, Tottenham, and Enfield to Braughing in Hertfordshire and on to Lincoln, skirting the Fens.[2]

Leofstan, abbot of St Albans in the reign of Edward the Confessor, is credited with cutting through the thick woods that stretched from the edge of the Chilterns nearly up to London, building bridges, and

[1] H. Braun, 'Some Earthworks of North-West Middlesex', *Trans. L. Mx. A. S.* NS 7 (1937), p. 365; Sharpe (page 12, note 4), p. 3. [2] Vulliamy, p. 207.

levelling the roads. In Saxon times bands of travellers passed through the district with loud shouting and blowing of horns—a demonstration of strength, no doubt, but an odd way of preventing the attentions of the numerous robbers infesting the forest.[1] The principal road in medieval times was a new route from London to St Albans through Barnet. Because of the 'deepness and dirty passages in the winter season' of the original way by Colney Hatch Lane, a new road was formed over Highgate Hill and Finchley Common to Whetstone about 1386.[2] At the same period (1380) the right of exacting tolls from wayfarers, except ecclesiastics, was granted to John Crowcher of Knightsbridge to be applied to repairing the highway from London to Brentford.[3] Some of the wealthier inhabitants made bequests for improvement of specific roads: John Armstrong left money for the repair of Mapes Lane, Willesden, in 1352; in 1374 Thomas Frowyke of South Mimms left £10 to repair the old road between Barnet and 'the two Crouches'; Roger Evelyn, ancestor of John Evelyn the diarist, left 20 loads of gravel in 1508 for the highway near his house at Stanmore 'where that most need is'; and John Lyon, yeoman of Preston and founder of Harrow school, left valuable property in Marylebone for repair of the roads from London to Harrow and Edgware at his death in 1592.[4] Henry VII found the journey from Windsor through Staines, Richmond, and Southwark to Canterbury so bad that he left £2,000 to repair the road and the bridges along it; it was to be substantially ditched on both sides, well gravelled, raised to a good height, and made wide enough to admit two carts abreast.

Norden in 1593 complained of the Middlesex roads; Ogilby, writing his *Britannia* in 1675, approved them, if only by contrast with others; he noted that after the first 20 or 30 miles out of London the road was generally bad. Thoresby recorded in his diary on 18 May 1695: 'Rode to Edmonton (where we had our horses led about a mile over the deepest of the wash), to Highgate, and thence to London. I have the greatest cause of thankfulness for the goodness of my heavenly protector, that being exposed to greater dangers by my horses boggling at every coach and waggon we met, I received no damage, though the ways were very bad, the ruts deep, and the roads extremely full of water, which rendered my circumstances (meeting the loaded waggons in very inconvenient places) not only melancholy but often really very dangerous.'[5]

Before the end of the 17th century the first turnpike trusts had been set up—the administrative expedient which did most to reform the English roads, often under severe criticism, until the railways killed them in the 19th century and fresh authorities were vested with their duties. The old system of parish responsibility for road repair, linked with county upkeep of the most important bridges, was inadequate to deal with main highways, and in 1663 the first act was passed authorising a

---

[1] Loftie (page 3, note 1), ii., p.3. [2] *Mx. & H.N. & Q.* 4 (1898), p. 91. [3] Jackman, p. 11, quoting H. G. Davis, *Memorials of the Hamlet of Knightsbridge* (1859), p. 24. [4] S. Potter, *Story of Willesden* (1926), p. 118; F. C. Cass, *South Mimms* (1877), pp. 5, 77; P. Davenport, *Old Stanmore* (1933), pp. 32, 94; J. F. Williams, *Harrow* (1901), p. 17. [5] For this section, Jackman, pp. 30, 37, 61, 80, 99; J. Parkes, *Travel in England in the Seventeenth Century* (1925), p. 208.

new system, which soon developed into the turnpike trust—one of the
'statutory authorities for special purposes' characteristic of 18th- and early
19th-century attempts to deal with administrative problems beyond the
ability of the older bodies. All the principal Middlesex roads were
turnpiked in the first 20 years of the 18th century.[1]

Turnpiking undoubtedly improved the roads, in the earlier years at
least, but the inhabitants of Middlesex looked on it as a mixed blessing.
There are no records of 'turnpike riots' in the county, like those between
1735 and 1750 in the west of England, but about this time petitions
against extending the turnpike system were frequently presented to
Parliament. Near London the farmers did not want the turnpikes
extended back into the country, for that would impair their advantage in
communication with the capital—the same grievance that the Middlesex
farmers felt against the railways 100 years later. Another ground of
objection, from shopkeepers, was that with improved communications
the wealthy began to supply all their wants from London, even those
living as far as 60 or 80 miles away.[2]

The agricultural writers of the 1790s have left a picture of the roads,
as of so much else in Middlesex. Peter Foot stated that the roads, both
public and parochial, were in general good: William Marshall thought
them 'a pattern to the roadmakers of the kingdom' and noted that they
were watered with carts adapted to the purpose; John Middleton was
more critical. The roads were not so bad as in Sussex—a byword for
badness, on the evidence of Horace Walpole and many other travellers;
but there was much to complain of. After saying that the parish highways
were 'hard and clean in every sort of weather; so much so that gentlemen
may ride along them even directly after rain and scarcely receive a
splash,' Middleton continued:

'The turnpike roads, on the contrary, are generally very bad;
although at the toll-gates of this county there is collected a very large sum
of money, probably not less than £30,000 a year, which is uselessly
expended in sinking wells, erecting pumps, building carts, and hiring
horses and men to keep the dust down by watering, instead of more
wisely scraping it off.' [Mr. Middleton always pointed the way to
improvement, as well as condemning shortcomings in what he saw.] 'By
the folly of this practice, the roads are kept many inches deep in mud;
whereas if they were raked and swept clean winter and summer, there
would neither be dust in such quantity as to offend nor any of the present
obstructions. There is now double the draught necessary for conveying
every carriage on the roads, along which there is no riding even in boots
and horseman's coat during half the year. The mud indeed is so very
deep all the winter and so fluid after rain as to render it unsafe to meet
horses, owing to their feet throwing the mud not only over a horseman's

[1] Dowdell, p. 130; Darby, p. 428. [2] A. Smith, *Wealth of Nations* (World's Classics ed.), i., p.
167; Jackman, p. 235, quoting R. Phillips, *Personal Tour through the United Kingdom* (1828), p. 30.

clothes, but also into his eyes. (Note: This is no exaggeration: I have repeatedly experienced the truth of it. J.M.)'

In particular: 'The turnpike road from Hadley through South Mimms is insufferably bad and a disgrace to the trustees'; the Edgware road as bad; during the whole winter 1797-8 there was only one passable track on the Uxbridge road, less than six feet wide and eight inches deep in fluid mud, thronged with waggons, many drawn by ten horses, and farmers' carts, which made it very difficult, even dangerous, for horsemen and light carriages to pass; the only labourers to be seen on the road were those of a gentleman, employed in carting the footpath into his enclosures; the road from Hyde Park Corner through Brentford and Hounslow was equally deep in filth, in spite of the king travelling it several times every week; Highgate and Hampstead hills represented 'a tax of one horse in every team on the farmers of the Finchley and Hendon side of the county, and a new road ought to be built avoiding them.' He concluded with a prophetic footnote: 'On the waggon-ways belonging to the coal-works in the north of England' [the early railways], 'one small horse usually draws a waggon containing 2 tons 13 cwt. of coal, which is more than four of the same horses could do over the turnpike roads of this county.' All the goods went on carts; packhorses, a west-country visitor noted in 1774, were not to be seen on the Brentford road, nor 'a woman on horse back. Every one that keeps a horse keeps a cart.'[1]

For centuries the road through Brentford had been proverbial for dirt. James Thomson made his herd of prickly swine revel in the mire of 'Brentford town, a town of mud'; Gay wrote of 'Brentford, tedious town, for dirty streets and white legged chickens known'; in 1787 John Byng noted in the diary of his travels that the road from Wantage to Faringdon in Berkshire was 'as dirty as old Brentford at Xmas.'[2] Middleton, finding the town particularly offensive, suggested that it might be avoided by a new road being made on the north side; a report of 1837 proposed a new road from Gunnersbury to Syon House, to avoid the loss of five minutes that fast coaches incurred in negotiating Brentford High Street;[3] but it remained undone until the early motor age.

Stage coaches running from London for public conveyance, adhering to a published timetable, are first heard of in 1637 when two weekly coaches ran between London and St Albans. Twenty years later there were coaches three times a week to Chester, taking four days, and in 1669 there was a 'flying coach' to Oxford in one day '(if God permit)' in summertime for a fare of 12s. Regular services, however ill performed, testify to a higher standard of road maintenance than the reader might gather from casual and crotchety references in contemporary writers. The first daily coach to Bath began to run in 1716, the first mail coach

[1] Middleton, p. 393; *John Yeoman* (page 50, note 1), p. 45.   [2] *Torrington Diaries*, ed. C. B. Andrews, i. (1934), p. 252 (23 July 1787).   [3] Ordish (page 38, note 2).

in 1784—John Palmer's Mail Diligence, again to Bath; and the mail coach soon supplanted the mounted post-boy on the trunk roads.

At the height of the coaching age smart driving, good horses and equipment, and smooth road surfaces produced some fine runs. On Telford's new Holyhead road, a great improvement on the road from Barnet to South Mimms by Dancers Hill that he had called 'a succession of unnecessary bendings and inconveniently steep ascents and descents,'[1] the Holyhead mail used to run from the Swan with Two Necks in Lad Lane to South Mimms, 15 hilly and difficult miles, in 1 hr. 40 mins.; rival coaches on this road ran some stages at more than 14 miles an hour. In 1834 'The Age' ran from Oxford to London in 3 hrs. 40 mins., 14 miles an hour, and from Wycombe to London, 29 miles, in 1 hr. 40 mins. But coaches were not the only, or the most important, traffic: packhorses in the earlier years, great waggons from long distances, carts from the farms within the county, chaises and private carriages of all descriptions passed to and fro on the roads to London, mingled with single horsemen and herds of cattle and sheep being driven up in the summer to the London markets. The Middlesex towns and villages grew prosperous from this press of traffic. At Hounslow about 1800: 'The principal business of the inns consists in providing relays of post-horses and exchanges of horses for the numerous stage-coaches travelling the road. All here wears the face of impatience and expedition. The whole population seems on the wing for removal.' Even Barnet, on the north road, allowed that Hounslow was the first posting town in the kingdom.[2]

The traffic flowed into London from all parts of the northern, midland, and western counties, and the onlookers could often tell exactly where it came from: William Cobbett, writing at Kensington in June 1822—'one of the finest years that I ever knew'—looked out of his window and saw the Wiltshire waggon-horses going by with their harness covered with the chalk dust of that country; so the fine weather continued in the west.[3]

Just before the end of this age a few strange coaches were seen on Middlesex roads, reminding those who believed in such things of the prophecy of Mother Shipton (perhaps a spurious one): 'carriages without horses shall go.' Goldsworthy Gurney travelled from London to Bath and back in 1829 in his steam carriage, and he demonstrated it to the Duke of Wellington on Hounslow Heath; Colonel Maceroni's coach ran something like a regular daily service to Edgware, attaining 15 miles an hour.[4] But, though this development for a time alarmed coach proprietors more than the railways did, the day of the self-propelled road vehicle was not yet. The coaching age did not decline; it was snuffed out all at once. Gilbert Scott wrote of the north road as he saw it between 1835 and 1837, when the London & Birmingham Railway was being built: 'As far

[1] Ordish (page 38, note 2). [2] Brayley and Britton, *Beauties of England and Wales* (1816), x., ii., p. 441; Hassell, p. 201. [3] Cobbett (page 39, note 2), i., p. 90. [4] Jackman, pp. 328, 332, quoting F. Maceroni, *Memoirs of the Life and Adventures of Colonel Maceroni* (1838), ii., p. 474; R. W. Kidner, *Short History of Mechanical Traction and Travel* (1947), i., p. 17.

as Barnet on the north road seven mails ran together with their choicest trotting teams passing and repassing one another, the horns blowing merrily, every one in a good humour, and proud of what they were doing.'[1]

That is the last picture of crowded roads before their comparatively short eclipse, which looked so much like extinction to the Victorians. In 1829 there were 17 coaches daily each way between London and Birmingham, and in 1831 the Whetstone turnpike tolls were let for £7,530 a year; but in 1838 there was no bidding for them at the old rates.[2] In Middlesex the contrast with the preceding era can never have been so complete as in other counties; gentlemen still drove between their houses and town, hay and market-garden produce went to London by road, not rail, and at holiday times the citizenry made for its favourite resorts in every kind of wheeled vehicle.

Horse buses, too, plied from London along most of the main roads: there was a regular omnibus from Brentford in 1836, and in 1879 regular services ran to London from most places in the county.[3] There were also local omnibuses (*Plate 56*). There were sporadic revivals of coaching on the Uxbridge road and to Thames valley villages between 1860 and 1890 and Sir Alfred Somerset drove the 'Hirondelle' coach between Enfield and Hitchin for 16 years with four teams on the road.[4]

Bicycles began to use the road from 1870 onwards. Charles Spencer, who claimed to have introduced the bicycle into Britain in 1868, rode daily from Harrow-on-the-Hill to the City and back, exercising special care on the hill. From 1876 an 'annual monster meeting' of cyclists took place on a May Saturday at Hampton Green; disputes arose with the toll keeper at Hampton bridge because the 'instrumentalists,' each carrying his machine on his shoulder, demanded to cross as foot-passengers.

During the brief golden age of the old English road, from about 1800 to 1830, some notable improvements in road construction and administration were made in Middlesex. Much that has been carried out since 1900 might have taken place a century before if the rise of the railway had not been so sudden and its triumph so complete. A new road was cut from the foot of Highgate Hill under the Archway (first a tunnel, which collapsed, then a viaduct, replaced by an iron bridge in 1897) (*Plate 4*) to Finchley, and another from Barnet straight through the middle of South Mimms village and on to St Albans as part of Thomas Telford's improved Holyhead road. Another, the Finchley road, was constructed under an act of 1826 from the West End to join the Barnet road at Tally Ho! Corner, between Finchley and Whetstone. A new age of good and direct roads with good surfaces seemed to be opening. To promote better administration, fourteen of the metropolitan turnpike trusts in Middlesex were consolidated by an act of 1826 into a single

[1] G. G. Scott, *Personal and Professional Recollections* (1879), p. 84. [2] Jackman, p. 312; *Mx. & H. N. & Q.* 4 (1898), p. 91; *H.C.M.* 6 (1904), p. 215; Ordish (page 38, note 2). [3] *Dickens's Dictionary of London* (1879), p. 167. [4] Dickens (see preceding note), p. 72; *Mx. & H. N. & Q.* 4 (1898), p. 101; *Middlesex: Biographical and Pictorial* (1907) art. Somerset. [5] C. E. R. Sherrington, *Hundred Years of Inland Transport* (1934), p. 155, quoting C. Spencer, *The Bicycle; its Use and Action* (1870); H. Ripley, *History and Topography of Hampton-on-Thames* (1885), p. 138.

authority under 46 commissioners. This body, which became the wealthiest and most important road authority in the kingdom, with an annual revenue of £60-70,000, controlled 172 miles of street and road lying between Isleworth and Uxbridge on the west and the Lea on the east (including of course much now lying within the county of London) (*Plate 50*). J. L. Macadam, the famous road-surface engineer, became surveyor-general, but his son James Macadam, who succeeded him shortly after, was in fact the driving force; he in turn was succeeded on his death in 1852 by his son William Macadam. All the commissioners' debt was paid off by 1856, though it is recorded that not half the mileage of its roads was macadamised with broken granite by that date; in 1863 the tolls were abolished within the Metropolitan Board of Works area (later the county of London) and responsibility for the roads transferred to the parishes. The bishop of London gave up his Highgate toll in 1858, and the remaining roads under the commissioners were freed from toll in 1872.[1]

In 1815 Middlesex, with 31 per cent of its roads turnpiked, had a higher proportion than any other county. But turnpikes were not the whole story; most of the inhabitants, as opposed to travellers, had to use the parish roads, and in some parts of the county these were still very primitive. Edward Ford wrote in his *History of Enfield,* published in 1873: 'Within the last 50 years the late Lady Elizabeth Palk, who resided at the Rectory, was accustomed when she intended to call on Mrs. Elphinstone at East Lodge' [in Enfield Chase] 'to send out men two or three days in advance to fill the ruts with faggots to enable her carriage to pass.' It was characteristic of the by-roads in north-west Middlesex that they had no metal surface and remained green lanes until the 20th century. A writer remarked in 1908 that these lanes were scarcely ever passable for pedestrians before July, and the lane from Harrow to Wood End, Northolt, was alternatively called Love Lane and Mud Lane.[2] J. B. Firth noted in 1906 of the green lanes that survived to that date: 'Some of them almost impassable after heavy rains, and others so choked with brushwood that only a narrow footpath is left in autumn … Their chief drawback is that they are apt to be infested by tramps and gipsies, who choose them as secluded camping grounds.'[3] Most of those in Firth's list disappeared in the road improvements put in hand for the Wembley Exhibition of 1924, but one or two remain today near Ickenham, leading south from the village to nowhere in particular.

* * * * *

Crossing of rivers, whether by bridge, ford, or ferry, was always one of the worst difficulties facing the traveller by road. The valuable right to

[1] Ordish (page 38, note 2). [2] *H.C.M.* 10 (1908), p. 296; Foley, p. 89. [3] J. B. Firth, *Middlesex* (1906), p. 36.

operate ferries was jealously regarded in medieval times. Monopoly was granted by the Crown on conditions and when granted was enforced. All the Middlesex Thames ferries were probably included in a list of those forbidden in 1659 to work between sunset and sunrise; they were at Brentford, 'the Lymekile in Brentford,' Richmond, Twickenham, Hampton Court, Sunbury, and Shepperton. (There were already bridges at Kingston and Staines.) As late as 1908 the Earl of Dysart, owner of Twickenham ferry, attempted to assert his monopoly of all ferrying between Twickenham and Ham against an interloper operating from Marble Hill with the support of the London County Council, and only in the House of Lords was the case decided against him.[1]

Middlesex had an important interest in bridges, as the county was crossed by important roads and the Thames formed the whole of its southern border.[2] The bridging of the river was a special concern to successive kings who wished to assure passage to Windsor castle, and the upkeep of the only important bridge wholly within the county, over the Brent west of Brentford, was equally a link in this communication. Responsibility for maintenance of bridges, and consequently the right to exact toll, was cast upon several different authorities. In the Middle Ages the Crown granted rights of 'pontage,' collection of tolls towards expenditure on bridges, for limited periods only. A new principle was laid down by an act of 1530: the upkeep of bridges was a county responsibility unless it could be proved in any particular case to fall on some other person or body. The Privy Council kept an eye on bridge repairs, especially near London; in 1589 it called the attention of the Middlesex justices to the disrepair of Hackney bridge over the Lea. In 1670 the king was indicted for failing to maintain the bridge at Hampton (Kingston bridge at Hampton Wick), but the complaint was not pressed.

Down to 1786 the county justices maintained only three bridges—at Brentford and Hanwell over the Brent and at Chertsey over the Thames (the last jointly with Surrey); but in the next forty years they took over or built 27 more, partly owing to the new requirements of better roads and more traffic, partly to a shifting of old burdens.[3]

Thames bridges were naturally the most important.[4] There was one at Staines by 1228, for three oaks out of Windsor forest were granted in that year by the king for its repair and again in 1236 and 1237. A succession of unlucky erections between 1791 and 1830 preceded the present bridge, of three granite arches, designed by George Rennie and opened in 1832. A bridge existed between Kingston and Hampton Wick at least as early as John's reign. At the time of Wyatt's rebellion against Mary in 1554 it was the first Thames bridge above London, and Wyatt used it to cross the river. Leland in 1530 wrote of a timber bridge at Chertsey. Several bridges were opened in the middle of the 18th century:

---

[1] Thacker, *Locks and Weirs* (page 52, note 4), pp. 478, 495. [2] For the following paragraphs, S. and B. Webb, *King's Highway* (1913); Jackman; Dowdell, throughout. [3] *Report of the Committee of Magistrates appointed to make Enquiry respecting the Public Bridges in the County of Middlesex, 1825* (1826). [4] Thacker, *General History* and *Locks and Weirs* (page 60, note 1).

at Walton in 1750, Hampton Court in 1753, Kew in 1759. Richmond bridge, the most attractive on the Middlesex and Surrey stretch of the river, was built by James Payne in 1777; he also designed new bridges at Chertsey (1785) and Kew (1789). The Thames railway bridges add nothing to the attractions of the scene, but three road bridges, Chiswick (by Herbert Baker), Twickenham (at St.Margaret's, by Maxwell Ayrton), and Hampton Court (by Edwin Lutyens) (*Plate 67*), all opened on the same day in 1933, are worthy of their situations.

The most troublesome of all the Middlesex bridges, however, was not across the Thames but that carrying the western road over the little river at the west end of Brentford town—'Brent ryveret,' as Leland called it with some condescension.[1] In 1280 Edward I granted the right to levy toll for the passage of goods over it, with a special tax at the rate of 1d. each for Jews and Jewesses on horseback, ½d. each on foot; other travellers were exempt. Similar pontage grants for short periods were made in 1332 and 1375. A document of 1446 relating to a chantry chapel at the Isleworth end refers to a new stone bridge existing beside the old wooden one. There was a serious complaint about it to the county justices in 1618: 'Of late the Marquess of Buckingham, his coach and horses, were in great danger in passing over the bridge upon the river at New Brentford by reason of the lowness of the battlements of the said bridge.' In 1712 it was closed to horses and vehicles except when the river was too deep to ford, and in 1739 it was at length decided to build a new one. Charles Labelye, designer of Westminster bridge, completed the work by 1742. Like the city fathers of Hamelin, the county justices grudged payment; they allowed Labelye a fee of £100, a committee having recommended £120, and they paid him 20 guineas for out-of-pocket expenses which he had estimated at £30. This bridge was replaced in 1824.

*   *   *   *   *

Roads and road bridges altered very little during the 70 years from 1830 to 1900, when inventive skill and new capital were devoted almost entirely to the railway. There is no place in Middlesex today where the whistle of the railway locomotive or the milder clatter of the electric train is not heard, except perhaps in the middle of Hounslow Heath at the very centre of the airport at Heathrow, where other sounds occupy the ear. But the county was not quickly filled up with railways; down to 1900 there was a considerable tract of country between Ealing, Harrow, and Uxbridge that the rail had not yet invaded.[2]

The first railways in Middlesex were not local lines like those to Greenwich, Blackwall, and Croydon on the other side of London, but main trunk routes to the north and west of England. The first section of

---

[1] Dowdell; *M.C.R. Reports.* [2] On the railways in Middlesex, E. T. MacDermot, *History of the Great Western Railway* (1927-31); W. L. Steel, *History of the London & North Western Railway* (1914); C. H. Grinling, *History of the Great Northern Railway* (1898); C. E. Stretton, *History of the Southern Railway* (1936); M. Robbins, *North London Railway* (ed. 3, 1946); V. Sommerfield, *London Transport: a Review and Survey* (1935).

the London & Birmingham Railway, the forerunner of the famous London & North Western, was opened from Euston Square to Boxmoor (north of Watford) in 1837, passing not very close to Willesden, Sudbury, Harrow, and Pinner; a station was provided at Harrow from the outset and at the other three places in 1844. Short-distance travelling was not encouraged: in the summer of 1845 there were only three down and five up local trains each week-day, with three each way on Sundays, and only one train a day took third-class passengers. This company was preoccupied with main-line traffic, and no branches were thrown off in Middlesex until 1860. One monument of the early operation of the line is a striking piece of verse, to be seen on a tombstone not far from the south door of Harrow church; the whole epitaph reads:

'To the Memory of Thomas Port, son of John Port, of Burton-upon-Trent, in the County of Stafford, Hat Manufacturer, who near this town had both his legs severed from his body by the Railway Train. With the greatest fortitude he bore a second amputation by the surgeons and died from loss of blood, August 7th, 1838, aged 33 years.

> Bright rose the morn, and vigorous rose poor Port,
> Gay on the train he used his wonted sport;
> Ere noon arrived his mangled form they bore
> With pain distorted and o'erwhelmed with gore.
> When evening came to close the fatal day
> A mutilated corpse the sufferer lay.'

The railway age had set in with a vengeance.

The main Paddington line to the west was opened through Middlesex in 1838, with a station at West Drayton for Uxbridge; others followed within a year at Ealing, Hanwell, and Southall. This was the historic ground of the old Great Western broad gauge, measuring seven feet between the rails, which lasted until 1892; its traces are still to be detected in the greater spaciousness of the works on the fast lines. It has been stated that Uxbridge, Hounslow, and Brentford, all places depending greatly on road traffic, agitated successfully to prevent the Great Western passing through them; but the line taken by the railway is almost direct from Kensal Green to Maidenhead, and the stories may well be later inventions.[1]

The effects of the railway on a peaceful village have been described: 'A remarkable change for the worse took place about this time in the hitherto retired neighbourhood of Southall Green. The Railway spread dissatisfaction and immorality among the poor, the place being inundated with worthless and overpaid navigators' [the word, transferred from canal construction, then applied, as 'navvies,' to labourers on civil engineering works generally]—'the very appearance of the country was

[1] M. S. Briggs, *Middlesex Old and New* (1934), p. 205 (Uxbridge); Maxwell (page 38, note 3), p. 46 (Hounslow); R. Henrey, *King of Brentford* (1946), p. 13 (Brentford). The alleged opposition and deviations are not mentioned in MacDermot's history of the Great Western (preceding note).

altered—some families left, and the rusticity of the village gave place to a London-out-of-town character—moss grown cottages retired before new ones with bright red tiles—picturesque hedgerows were succeeded by prim iron railings, and the village inn, once a pretty cottage with a swinging sign, is transmogrified to the 'Railway Tavern' with an intimation gaudily set forth that 'London Porter' and other luxuries hitherto unknown to the aborigines were to be procured therein.'[1] All the places were not thus affected in the twinkling of an eye; this happened only quite close to the stations, and within the limitations imposed by an infrequent train service—in 1845 there were only eight down and ten up local trains on the Great Western line, and no local service on Sundays.

Farmers in the same parish had their grievances against the railway: in 1843 they were complaining of the fall in their livestock prices, which they were sure was due to the stock brought in by the railway; they complained too of the lower price of hay, attributed to the decline in the number of posthorses—again the fault of the railway. 'Some farmers,' it was reported, 'loudly express their apprehensions that it is not only ruining their business and depreciating the value of landed property, but that it will ultimately bring about a revolution in the state.'[2] It did, but perhaps not in the way they apprehended.

The third railway in Middlesex was also built broader than the standard gauge, in this case five feet—the Northern & Eastern, opened in 1840 through Tottenham and Ponders End on its way from Stratford towards Cambridge. It was absorbed in 1844 by the Eastern Counties (later the Great Eastern) and the standard gauge was adopted. In 1845 eight trains each way called at Tottenham on weekdays, three on Sundays. Four years later Enfield achieved railway communication by a branch from this line at Angel Road through Edmonton. The last of the early lines was the London and Windsor, part of the London & South-Western Railway, which was opened from Richmond straight across the southern part of Hounslow Heath to Staines in 1848.

Not much new railway was added in the fifties: the Great Northern line was opened from King's Cross in 1850, running through Wood Green and Potters Bar; and in the same year the Brentford and Hounslow loop of the South-Western was completed. In 1853 this line was linked with Willesden, and in 1858 a branch was built from Acton to 'Hammersmith and Chiswick,' enabling inhabitants of Turnham Green to travel to their City offices by way of Willesden, Bow, and Fenchurch Street. Uxbridge at length achieved railway communication by a branch from West Drayton in 1856.

The Hampstead Junction Railway, from Camden Town to Willesden Junction by Hampstead Heath, came in 1860; a South-Western loop from Twickenham by Teddington and Hampton Wick to Kingston in 1863;

[1] MS. Diary of B. J. Armstrong.   [2] Tremenheere (page 40, note 2).

and the Thames Valley Railway in 1864. The last was a grand name for a branch from Strawberry Hill through Fulwell, Hampton, and Sunbury to Shepperton; the state of these districts may be judged from the careful provision of boot-scrapers built into the station buildings at the booking-office doors. In 1867 the Edgware, Highgate & London Railway brought communication to a large area lying behind the Highgate and Hampstead heights that had been comparatively isolated until that time, and in 1868 the Midland completed its main line through Mill Hill and Hendon into the grand and very Gothic terminus at St Pancras.

Not a mile of new railway was built in the west and north-west of Middlesex during the seventies until the District line from Chiswick Park to Ealing Broadway in 1879. At this period the north was being rapidly filled in by branches of the Great Northern and Great Eastern. The Metropolitan emerged from its sulphurous tunnels into Middlesex air with an extension from Swiss Cottage to Willesden Green in 1879, carried on to Harrow-on-the-Hill in 1880; it did not then think it worth putting a station between Neasden and Harrow. In 1885 this line was pushed on to Pinner and in 1887 beyond the Hertfordshire border to Rickmansworth. The only other railways built in the eighties were a Great Western branch from West Drayton to Staines and a District line from Acton to Hounslow. In 1890 a local company opened the Harrow & Stanmore Railway, worked by the L.N.W.R.; the Stanmore terminus was a pleasing little station of ecclesiastical appearance designed not to spoil the amenities of that select village.

In 1900, therefore, when the age of the motor car and the electric suburban train had not yet begun, Middlesex was comparatively little exploited by the railway companies for local passenger traffic—far less so than Surrey and the nearer parts of Kent and Essex, where there was not the valuable main-line traffic and the heavy bulk of goods and coal enjoyed by the northern and western lines. Moreover, few Middlesex lines ran to London terminal stations in the City, where most people still went to work. The Royal Commission on London Traffic of 1905 found that the journeys made to the terminals in the western sector (Paddington, Marylebone, Baker Street, and Euston) amounted to 27 million a year—less than a tenth of the 310 million made into all the London terminals.[1]

A potent force had been at work on some of the lines, the workmen's train: providing transport from and to outer suburban districts at a return fare of 2d., it transplanted large sections of the populace and changed the character of whole districts. The Great Eastern, in particular, had to provide a workmen's service to compensate for dwellings acquired for its extension into Liverpool Street, under an act of 1864. The 1905 royal commission showed in a striking table what happened to Edmonton in consequence: the population, just moving up at about the natural

[1] Royal Commission on London Traffic, *Report* (1905), i., p. 64; Smith (page 55, note 4), p. 35; F. A. A. Menzler, 'London and its Passenger Transport System', *Journal of the Royal Statistical Society* 113 (1950), p. 299, especially table 14.

increase rate in 1861, was growing a little faster in 1871, when two workmen's trains had just been started; after that, increase in the number of these trains and in population went hand in hand (*Plate 55*). The Cheap Trains Act of 1883 obliged all lines to provide workmen's facilities, but a London County Council inquiry of 1892 found the London & North Western and Great Western unsatisfactory. 'Both these lines,' the report stated, 'touch Willesden Junction, and probably no part of the area of suburban London is so poorly provided with workmen's trains as the district around this junction. A police constable at Ealing says that he has to call workmen as early as 3.30 a.m. to enable them to walk to Shepherd's Bush—a distance of four miles—the nearest station at which they can get a workmen's train to take them to London. This also occurs at Acton and Hanwell; in the latter case the distance the men have to walk is stated to be about six miles.'[1]

With the new century new lines and local services were pushed into the unoccupied spaces on the Middlesex railway map: from Ealing to South Harrow in 1903, and next year from Harrow to Uxbridge; in 1905 a new line from Paddington through Greenford to High Wycombe; in 1906 a Great Central link from this line to Neasden; in 1910 a Great Northern extension beyond Enfield. The District and Metropolitan lines were electrified in 1905; some of the older lines followed suit; and tube railways burrowed beneath the London border out into Middlesex between 1907 and 1939. The details of these developments give the most valuable clues to the growth of particular places at particular dates, but the inquiry is too complex to be followed here.

The railways made it possible for men living almost anywhere in the county to travel daily to work in London. Most of these railways carried goods as well as passengers, but comparatively few large works and factories were established near them during the 19th century, when coal and heavy materials had to be conveyed to railway sidings; the great industrial development came in the age of electricity and motors. But many Middlesex acres were covered with yards and depots for the goods passing into London, or round it, by railway; the biggest lie close to the London border.

* * * * *

Meanwhile, the tramway had been playing a humble but far from insignificant part in the formation of present-day Middlesex.[2] Some local lines were opened between 1876 and 1887, worked by horses, with abortive attempts at mechanical traction; then there was an interval until electricity was applied to street railways; and a complete and ramified tramway system sprang into being in the decade 1901-10. With equal

[1] C. E. Lee, *Passenger Class Distinctions* (1946), p. 49; Royal Commission on London Traffic, *Report* (1905), i., pp. 14, 43. [2] C. E. Lee, 'Some Notes on the History of the London United Tramways', *Omnibus Magazine* 3 (1932), no. 32, supplement; 'Some Notes on the History of the Metropolitan Electric Tramways', *Omnibus Magazine* 3 (1932), no. 34.

speed, the decade 1931-40 saw the Middlesex trams completely replaced by electric trolleybuses.

The earliest line, called the Southall, Ealing, & Shepherd's Bush Tram-Railway Co., came into operation in 1876 between Shepherd's Bush and Priory Road, Acton, only, and this became the nucleus of the London United Tramways. The first regular electric working in the London area began on this system between Hammersmith and Kew Bridge in 1901 (*Plate* 57). It was extended by 1904 to Hounslow, Twickenham, Hampton Court, and Uxbridge. But this was nothing to the schemes the company applied for: lines to Staines, Cranford, and Sunbury were authorised, though an extension to Maidenhead was just too much for the Board of Trade to swallow. The tramway changed the face of Brentford—rather, of that side of the High Street that had to be pulled down to give it passage; and it clearly meant the end of the old, detached Middlesex air of places like Hayes and Hillingdon.

To the north lay the territory of the Metropolitan Electric Tramways; spheres of influence were delimited and agreed with the county council, which played an important part in the promotion of tramway schemes. The M.E.T. succeeded in 1902 to a group of lines 7½ miles long from Finsbury Park to Wood Green and from Stamford Hill through Tottenham to Edmonton, which had been opened in 1881-7. Steam haulage had been employed from 1885 to 1891, the only regular steam operation of tramways in the London area. By 1910 the M.E.T. was working an electric network extending from Edmonton in the north-east to the Harrow Road and Acton in the west.

Soon after the tramway system had been laid, its successor, the hybrid trolleybus, appeared on the scene. The first regular trolleybuses in Middlesex, and in the London area, were operated at Twickenham in 1931. By the end of 1939 the tram had entirely disappeared from the county. Its monument remains in the Metropolitan Electric style of architecture—a term which may be applied not unfairly to the parades of shops built between 1900 and 1914 at Cricklewood, Palmers Green, and most places in between, derived indeed from the style employed by advanced architects in Sloane Square and the surrounding districts about 1880 but transplanted to these Middlesex suburbs only by the civilising influence of the tram.

If the tramlines were the framework of the new suburban Middlesex in the 20th century, the motor-bus wove the pattern within the frame. Most of the old London horse-bus services stopped just inside the county boundary; in 1907 the longer routes ran to Willesden (the Spotted Dog), Harlesden, Finchley, Muswell Hill, and Crouch End, and motor-buses were plying to Willesden (the White Hart) and Cricklewood. In 1911 Ealing was the farthest point in the west served by a regular motor-bus.

During 1912 Twickenham and Southgate were reached, and routes were begun from Hounslow down the Bath and Staines roads.[1] From that time Middlesex has been criss-crossed with the red buses of the General company and of London Transport; the last village to be reached by General services was Stanwell in 1932, and now in 1952 there is still one settlement, Charlton by the Littleton reservoir, that feels cut off from the 20th century without a motor-bus.

*   *   *   *   *

The Middlesex main roads, barely adequate to deal with local traffic in the suburbs near the London border, were mostly too narrow and congested to cope with the through traffic that suddenly came back on to them about 1900. The Uxbridge road was the scene of many early motor trials, second favourite only to the Brighton road, and Thornycroft's factory at Chiswick turned out in 1896 some of the first steam waggons for heavy duty on the roads.[2] By 1939 a new network had been imposed on the county's road-map: the Great West road, by-passing Brentford and Hounslow (*Plate 68*); the Western Avenue, from Wormwood Scrubs, driven through the most rural part of the county past Greenford and Northolt; the Barnet and Watford by-passes of 1926-8, running through Hendon and past Mill Hill; the new Cambridge road of 1923-4; the North Circular road of 1923-34; and the Chertsey road from Chiswick to Hanworth, not yet finished.[3]

Main roads in Middlesex thus have three distinct origins: they may be descended from deliberately engineered ancient roads, like the Roman Watling Street and the 19th-century Finchley road, or promoted from a rambling succession of country lanes linking local hamlets, like the Harrow road, or a newly-built arterial road. The new roads are almost without exception melancholy instances of wasted opportunity: schools, dwelling-houses, shops, and cinemas have been built along them without regard for the through communication that they should afford. Most of the economic life-blood of Middlesex has to pass along these clogged arteries: awful examples how not to develop a road.

The most modern form of transport is not absent from Middlesex. The county has had a few passing associations with speculations on flying and with actual flight in previous centuries: John Wilkins, rector of Cranford 1661, wrote in 1640 a *Discourse concerning the Possibility of a Passage to the World in the Moon*, partly devoted to the principles of bird-flight; Dr. John Sheldon, one of the first Englishmen to make an ascent, accompanied J. P. Blanchard in his balloon from Chelsea to a point between Sunbury and Hanworth (an event noticed by Horace Walpole from Strawberry Hill) in 1784; the ascent of Biggin and Mrs. Sage from

[1] For the early motor-bus period, Reports of the London Traffic Branch of the Board of Trade, 1908-15. [2] R. W. Kidner, *Steam Lorry, 1896-1939* (1948), p. 2. [3] Smith (page 55, note 4), p. 28; R. Jeffreys, *King's Highway* (1949), pp. 52, 119, 229.

St George's Fields, Newington Butts, in 1785 terminated when Harrow schoolboys rescued the aeronauts from an angry farmer; Charles Green, one of the most notable balloon pilots, who made over 500 ascents between 1821 and 1852, had an adventure with a tree at Osterley Park in 1837; Henry Coxwell, who with James Glaisher made the celebrated balloon ascent to seven miles near Wolverhampton in 1862, was a Tottenham dentist; Horatio Phillips' 'experimental aerial machine,' a heavier-than-air engine that did manage to lift itself from the ground, was tested in 1893 at a Harrow factory. In the early 20th century Hendon and Stag Lane aerodromes were the favourite London starting-points for the early races, and the first British air mail was carried between Hendon and Windsor for a few weeks in 1911.[1] Several firms of aircraft builders have worked in the county since that time—Handley Page at Cricklewood, de Havilland at Stag Lane, and Fairey at Feltham; but there is too little room for them, and they have moved farther from London. Now Hanworth and Heston airfields can only accommodate smaller aircraft, while the airliners from overseas, circling round as they are stacked in the skies for landing at Heathrow and Northolt, fill the west Middlesex air with their continuous roar.

---

[1] J. E. Hodgson, *History of Aeronautics in Great Britain* (1924); R. D. Brett, *History of British Aviation 1908-1914* [1934]; P. G. Masefield, 'Some Economic Factors in Air Transport Operation', *Journal of the Institute of Transport* 24 (1951), p. 79.

CHAPTER VII

POPULATION

'Where is as essential as when to a man's being.'
THOMAS FULLER[1]

THE population of the area now within Middlesex was about 5,800 in 1086; 70,827 in 1801; 792,476 in 1901; and 2,268,776 in 1951. Figures act on some people like an emetic; the reader who cannot interest himself in figures, or in some of the more elementary technicalities of historical population study, had better leave it at that and pass on to the next chapter. The rest of this chapter is no more than an elaboration of these statements, with the appropriate qualifications and explanations.

Some of the figures that follow are mere guesses, others have been carefully enumerated; but, however arrived at, they represent the history of Middlesex in shorthand. Within the broad picture they present, an immense amount of significant detail may be found; it is not the general outline that counts so much as the particular information about numbers in individual parishes. In the tables appended after Part II (pages 365-70) the parishes are grouped by existing local government areas, and not alphabetically throughout, because in the latest period the census recorders have abandoned the smaller units—the civil parishes—within the boroughs and some urban districts; the most convenient way of setting them out is therefore a synoptic table, with the least possible explanation in footnotes.

Population estimates for 1086[2] may be deduced from Domesday Book. The returns included the number of men who were stated to be landholders or men working on the land; though there were variations between the practices adopted in the different parishes, the numbers are the result of actual enumeration and are likely to be fairly reliable in themselves. The number shown in the present Middlesex parishes is 1,552. Something has to be added for the villages not separately shown in the survey; perhaps there may have been 1,650 in all. There are a few evident anomalies: at Ashford, for example, no inhabitants at all are mentioned although land was being farmed. The clergy were not consistently dealt with: it is fairly certain that there was a priest in a good

---

[1] Fuller (page 33, note 1), i., p. 73. [2] The following paragraphs are much indebted to J. C. Russell, *British Medieval Population* (Albuquerque, New Mexico, 1948). On Domesday, see page 29, note 2.

many Middlesex places where none appears in Domesday; the return
shows them only where they owned land, but there were no questions to
be answered about them where they did not, and therefore no
information was given. So far, these discrepancies are of comparatively
small account; but a considerable element of estimation comes in with
the attempt to translate the exact figures of the landholders into total
population. Nobody can yet do better than multiply the number of men
by 3.5, which is a reasonable guess at the average size of a rural family.
Adopting this multiplier, it may be estimated that the Middlesex
population of 1086 was somewhere about 5,800.

A few scattered figures from the 13th and 14th centuries show the
Middlesex population, where it is known, as more than double the
Domesday figures: at West Drayton, where there were 17 tenants in
1086, the St Paul's Domesday return of 1222 shows 39; at Hendon the
46 of 1086 were nearly trebled (126) by 1321; at Harmondsworth 46 of
1086 had grown to 129 in 1338.[1]

The plagues of 1348 to 1374 reduced the population from these
levels to something like one and a half times the Domesday number. The
poll-tax return of 1377, enumerating all lay persons over 14 years old,
shows 11,243 persons in the ancient county. If this figure is increased by
one-half, to take account of children of 13 and under—again a reasonable
guess, but nothing more—the total for all Middlesex outside the City of
London becomes 16,865; and allowing for the clergy, who paid different
taxes, 17,000 may not be very wide of the mark. The returns have not
yet been published in detail, and no close estimate can be made for the
present county area; if the proportion of 3 : 2 to the Domesday figure is
valid, it must have been approaching 8,000.

The next series of figures comes from the chantry certificates of
1545, which rendered a return of the 'houseling' or communicating
persons within each parish (normally those of 14 years and over). These
figures are subject to the important qualification that, while they are fairly
good evidence for the smaller parishes, they are clearly rather indifferent
estimates, almost all in round numbers, in most of the larger ones. The
estimated population in the whole ancient county in 1545 is 36,763, the
stated figure being again increased by a half to allow for those under 14.
This can give no guide to the number in the present Middlesex area.

These results are admittedly produced by multiplication of basic
numbers by a more or less arbitrary figure, but they acquire a status of
almost demonstrable accuracy in comparison with the guesses that have
to be made about succeeding centuries. From 1545 until 1801 there is no
enumeration within the county on any common basis that can be
brought by a similar kind of adjustment to something representing the
total population of the county. Hearth-tax returns in the 17th century,

[1] *Domesday of St. Paul's of 1222*, ed. W. H. Hale (Camden Society, 1858); N. G. Brett-James,
'Some Extents and Surveys of Hendon', *Trans. L. Mx. A. S.* NS 7 (1937), p. 1; Public Record
Office, Special Collections 11,443, quoted by Russell (page 85, note 2), p. 88.

and all statistics based on the number of inhabited houses in given areas, do not produce results which can pretend to an accuracy comparable with those derived from the medieval returns.

The figures shown in the table for the 17th and 18th centuries (pages 365-367) are the baptisms recorded in parish registers over certain 10-year periods.[1] The figures are crude and unadjusted; in one case, Heston, it is known that the registers were badly kept because the vicar was long living abroad, at Leghorn; and others were no doubt erroneous for various reasons. It is less misleading to leave them in their existing state than to impart a spurious validity by tampering with them. (The only adjustment made is to average out arithmetically some shorter periods to decennia when for some reason the books are not complete over the decade; such cases are marked *a* in the table.) These figures need to be quite clearly understood for what they are worth: they take no account of population moving in and out (for Middlesex, mostly in), or of dissenters who did not bring their children for baptism (perhaps not in this case a very significant number). In relatively stable districts, it may be reasonable to multiply the 10-year total of births by 4 as a clue to the total population during that period;[2] but in the Middlesex parishes lying along the north roads and in the Thames valley immigration was going on so fast that this often gives too low a result. (As an indication of the fallibility of this rule of thumb, the enumerated total at the first census, of 1801, may be used for comparisons.) The only conclusions that should be drawn from these parish register figures are about the periods when increase, or decrease, took place in each parish; the degree of probable error, which misleads in comparing one place with another, is likely to be fairly constant at each place taken by itself, though it depended on the habits of different incumbents.

Few foreigners settled in rural Middlesex at any time in the way the Huguenots settled in the eastern counties. Three Flemings who took an oath of fealty to Henry VI in 1436 settled in north-west Middlesex, John Antony of Antwerp at Ruislip, Peter Antony and Leonard Vanderlyvyn at Uxbridge.[3] In 1635 the sessions records show two persons of Cowley called Joachin Chareavent and Massy Le Chesne (the clerk's orthography was not equal to this sort of test) coining King Charles ten-shilling pieces;[4] a gravestone of 1781 at Shepperton commemorates two negro servants, Benjamin and Cotto Blake; and there is one at Tottenham of 1827 to a little Greek boy, Constantine Sotiris, a Suliot refugee.[5] But such immigrants were unusual in Middlesex; natural increase and movement outward from London filled up its numbers.

After the beginning of proper census returns, in 1801, problems of computing the population of the districts concerned do not arise; the census showed, or attempted to show, the actual number of persons

[1] Extracted from Lysons. No doubt inaccuracies can be found here and there in Lysons' computations, but the general accuracy of the registers is not so dependable that small errors weaken their value much further. In most cases the trend of population is shown fairly enough.
[2] The multiplier 4 is used for this period by H. L. Smith, *History of East London* (1939), p. 299 (appendix D), for parishes on the other side of London; R. Pickard, *Population and Epidemics of Exeter in Pre-Census Times* (Exeter, 1947), includes estimates of the Non-conformist baptisms there in addition to the parish registers and gives a combined total of recorded births over each 10-year period; this figure is multiplied by 3.71 to produce the estimated total population.
[3] *Calendar of the Patent Rolls*, Henry VI, ii., 1429-36 (1907), pp. 556, 568.   [4] *M.C.R.* iii., p. 57.
[5] T. Compton, *Recollections of Tottenham Friends and the Forster Family* (1893), p. 52.

within each parish on the day selected. As experience was gained from each decennial count, the technique of census-taking was improved and accuracy became more refined; substantially no correction or adjustment is required except so far as the boundaries of the districts themselves were altered. Only in 1841 did a serious error come into the Middlesex returns, if they are read as indicating the resident populations; in that year the census was taken on 7 June—the others have been in March or April, except in 1811, 1821, and 1831, when they were late in May—and in consequence the numbers in the hay villages were inflated by the migrant labour that had moved in for the mowing.

The 19th-century census returns selected for the tables on pages 368-370 are 1801, the earliest; 1851, the middle point of the century; and 1881, when the population of places on the inner ring had begun its immense expansion, while some of the less accessible parts of the county were stationary or actually declining. The figures for these three censuses have been standardised on the areas of civil parishes fixed by the act of 1844. Although the boundaries of the Middlesex civil parishes were not very seriously altered in the period, and the figures are therefore reasonably certain, they have been adjusted to a small degree and are not identical with individual census figures.[1] In the 20th century, 1911 is selected as the first census after Middlesex passed the million mark, when the effect of electrified tramways and railways was just becoming felt; 1931, half-way through the expansion between the wars; and the 1951 census. The 1931 figures are adjusted to the 1937 areas, which are the same as those used for the latest figures; there are some insignificant differences from the 1911 areas. Where the area covered by the 19th-century series differs considerably from the later ones, it is set on a different line, with an explanation in a footnote.

The totals for Middlesex outside the county of London area, at these three censuses of the 19th century and all those in the 20th century, are:

Population Census Figures : County of Middlesex

	Old County	New County
1801	70,827	—
1851	139,972	—
1881	368,599	—
1901	812,690	792,476
1911	—	1,126,465
1921	—	1,253,002
1931	—	1,638,728
1951 *Provisional*	—	2,268,776

The totals in this table have been adjusted to take account of the complete parishes transferred to London in 1889, which are not included.

[1] They are taken here from *V.C.H.* ii., p. 110 (appendix iv., with notes on the areas involved).

The difference between 'old' and 'new' Middlesex at 1901 is due to some transfers of parts of old parishes, principally accounted for by South Hornsey, which went to Stoke Newington, in London, with about 15,500 inhabitants, and part of South Mimms, which went to Barnet, Hertfordshire, with about 4,800.

Finally, a comparison may be made between the growth of the Middlesex population and those of its neighbour Hertfordshire and of England and Wales as a whole; the Willesden and Harrow figures, representing the most striking 19th- and 20th-century rises, are also set out overleaf (page 90).

It would be interesting to know where these immense increases have come from. Over and above the 'natural' growth in population, people have moved into Middlesex both outward from London and inward from the provinces. Evidence could only be assembled by a detailed survey taken from a representative sample of Middlesex, with full inquiry made not into the immediately preceding address of each family but into their places of origin. This has not yet been done, and only a few indications from personal observation can be put forward. Londoners are born either north or south of the Thames, and they generally remain on the side where they began life. They tend to remove outwards along radial lines from the centre. Bloomsbury in one generation, Primrose Hill in the next, and Hendon in the third is a typical progression. Brixton generally moves to Banstead, not to Golders Green; Whitechapel moves to Hackney, Hampstead or Willesden, and Edgware; and then, if it can, to Gerrards Cross. Settlements of Irish, Welsh, Midland, and Yorkshire people tend to form in areas along the lines of railway leading to their native districts.

A few comparisons may make it easier to understand the scope and significance of the most recent figures in the tables. At the 1951 census, the population of Harrow, at 219,463, was greater than that of some English counties and several cities—than Plymouth, with 208,985; Norwich, with 121,226; Lincoln, with 69,412. Ten places in Middlesex had over 100,000, and another was within 2,000 of the mark. The administrative county, at 2,268,776, numbers more inhabitants than any except the county of London (the areas administered by the county councils of Lancashire and the West Riding of Yorkshire do not contain so many inhabitants, though they include greater populations within their geographical boundaries). There are over two and a quarter million inhabitants of Middlesex—not much less than the whole population of Wales with Monmouthshire; the actual figures are 2,268,776 against 2,576,000.

So much may be quickly learned from the numbers themselves. Their full significance is, in effect, the whole theme of this book, and each chapter is in some form a commentary upon them.

Population Census Figures : Middlesex and certain other Areas

	1801	1851	1881	1901	1911	1931	1951 (Provisional)
Middlesex (old)	70,827	139,972	368,599	812,690	–	–	–
Increase over previous figure, per cent	–	97.6	163.3	120.5	–	–	–
Middlesex (new)	–	–	–	792,476	1,126,465	1,638,728	2,268,776
Increase over previous figure, per cent	–	–	–	–	42.1	45.5	38.4
England and Wales	8,892,536	17,927,609	25,974,439	32,527,843	36,070,492	39,952,377	43,744,924
Increase over previous figure, per cent	–	101.6	44.9	25.2	10.9	10.8	9.5
Hertfordshire	97,393	167,298	203,069	258,423	311,284	401,206	609,735
Increase over previous figure, per cent	–	71.8	21.4	27.3(a)	20.5	28.9	52.0
Willesden	751	2,939	27,453	114,582	154,214	185,025	179,647
Increase or decrease, per cent	–	291.3	834.1	317.4	34.6	20.0	-2.9
Harrow	4,392	8,252	14,970	28,419	41,924	96,656	219,463
Increase over previous figure, per cent	–	87.9	81.4	89.8	75.3(b)	130.6	127.1

(a) 6,000 gained by transfers. (b) Increase on 23,900 (after transfer of Wembley).

CHAPTER VIII

POLITICAL AND MILITARY HISTORY

'Battles are the principal milestones in secular history. Modern opinion resents this uninspiring truth.' WINSTON S. CHURCHILL[1]

T HE history of Middlesex is overshadowed by London. Political and military events within its present county area were significant only because it was the approach to London, the last campaigning ground on which the authority established there could deal, by arms or diplomacy, with movements arising in the western or northern provinces. It formed a kind *of glacis*, in the military sense: a cleared space round the capital. The Crown learned a lesson from Geoffrey de Mandeville's rebellion in Stephen's reign and took care to prevent hostile combinations forming within striking distance by keeping the Middlesex lands in weak or friendly hands; the great nobles for their part chose to establish their castles and domains at a distance from the seat of royal power. Likewise in France throughout medieval times the nobility, far stronger rivals to their king than the English lords, kept their distance from Paris.

As part of the royal policy, the Church was granted very extensive estates in Middlesex, and the remaining manors came to be held by the Crown or its dependents. There was no county gentry with an independent and continuous influence. The result of these arrangements—for they clearly flowed from the Crown's deliberate policy—was that the county's political history is a series of events linked by the impact of national movements on the capital.[2]

There is nothing to record in Middlesex under the first two Williams except an incident in the quarrel between Rufus and Archbishop Anselm. Anselm, summoned in 1095 by the king to Windsor, stopped on his way at his manor of Hayes, where most of the bishops unsuccessfully urged him to come to terms. Anselm's determination and a threat of rebellion in the north forced William to send conciliatory messages to Hayes, and the quarrel was patched up for the time being.

In the civil war of Stephen's reign continuous military operations

---

[1] W. S. Churchill, *Marlborough: His Life and Times* (1947 ed.), ii., p.381. [2] For political history, *V.C.H.* ii., p. 15, with detailed references.

caused havoc in Middlesex; the Pipe Roll of Henry II shows one-eighth of it lying in waste. Geoffrey de Mandeville, grandson of the Geoffrey to whom William I had granted Enfield, Edmonton, and Northolt, swayed the issue by changing sides, first from Stephen to the empress Matilda in 1141, then back to Stephen, and finally to the empress again. On his death in 1144 from a wound received in a fight with Stephen's troops at Burwell, in the Fens, his estates passed to endow Walden abbey, Essex, which he had founded in 1136.

In 1215, during the comings and goings before the signing of Magna Carta, safe-conducts were granted to all who should come to treat with the king at Staines. The actual signature, though commemorated by sculpture on the Middlesex Guildhall, took place just over the boundary at Runnymede; the barons transferred a tournament from Stamford to Hounslow Heath for the better protection of London. When Henry III succeeded, Louis, dauphin of France, attempted to arbitrate between the barons and the king at Hounslow, and the conference known as the treaty of Lambeth was perhaps held at Staines. Henry's struggle with the barons culminated with Simon de Montfort's revolt in 1263; Richard, Earl of Cornwall and King of the Romans, the king's brother, arbitrated during negotiations at his manor of Isleworth, when de Montfort's demands were conceded. In the next year, when Richard joined the king in actively opposing de Montfort, the Londoners sallied out, burned down his manor house, and destroyed its 'water-mills and other commodities.' After Henry had gained the upper hand, a fine of 1,000 marks was levied on London to make good the damage.

Little is recorded of Middlesex in the 14th century. Humphrey de Bohun, Earl of Hereford, having served Edward III well in France, was given licence to fortify his manor house at Enfield in 1347. This was the only regular fortified place in the county, apart from an earlier castle belonging to de Mandeville near South Mimms. The land at Enfield passed to the Crown by the marriage of Mary, one of the de Bohun heiresses, to Henry of Lancaster, and the whole area of Enfield Chase was henceforth preserved as a royal hunting-ground.

A strong detachment from Middlesex joined the Peasants' Revolt of 1381. The revolt sprang from economic rather than political causes; its principal incidents happened north-east of the city, within the present county of London, at Clerkenwell, Highbury, and Mile End. Twenty-three Middlesex men from fifteen parishes were excluded from the general pardon, more than from any other district except London itself: two were outlawed, eleven acquitted, and the others perhaps never brought to trial. The list of exclusions is, however, hardly evidence for Sir Charles Oman's statement that 'inhabitants of almost every parish in Middlesex' were excluded; in the present county area it mentions only

Hendon, Hounslow, Heston, Ruislip, Greenford, Chiswick, and Twickenham. Local disturbances are known only at Harmondsworth (where there was a long-standing quarrel with the Church owners of the manor), Heston, and Pinner.[1]

Jack Cade's revolt against Henry VI did not affect the county, and in the early part of the Wars of the Roses the tide of battle did not come nearer than St Albans (1461). But in 1471, after Henry VI's short restoration, the decisive battle was fought just north of Barnet, mostly within Middlesex near Wrotham Park. Edward of York had marched from Nottingham to London, which had always supported the White Rose, with Warwick close behind him. Warwick camped on Gladesmore Heath, near Hadley, and Edward advanced from London to attack him in a misty sunrise on Easter morning. Warwick's right wing routed the Yorkist left, which fled back through Barnet and carried to London the news of a defeat. But the Yorkist right was winning, and in time the position of the two armies was almost reversed, with Edward facing south and Warwick north. As the victorious Lancastrian right returned from their pursuit to aid the centre, Warwick's men mistook them for Yorkists and attacked them. In the confusion Edward pressed his advantage and overwhelmed the Lancastrians; Warwick himself was slain.[2]

Under the Tudors Middlesex became a favourite place of residence for the royal family and the principal families at court. At the Dissolution of the Monasteries Henry VIII retained much of their Middlesex land for himself, especially in the south-west, and he added to it by forcing exchanges of manors. Many of the most important transactions of Henry VIII and Edward VI took place at Hampton Court and Syon House; Katharine Parr, Lady Jane Grey, and the young princess Elizabeth lived at Hanworth; Northumberland proclaimed Lady Jane queen at Syon House in 1553. Sir Thomas Wyatt, who raised the men of Kent against Mary in 1554, marched on London by Kingston bridge and Brentford. Elizabeth was often at Elsing Hall, Enfield, both as princess and queen, and at Hampton Court. Some particulars are known of the preparations made in Middlesex against the expected Spanish invasion of 1588. In April, 1,500 men were raised, in June another 1,000 and in July 123 horsemen; some of the Middlesex trained bands were specially detailed to guard the queen.

James I abandoned Enfield palace in favour of Theobalds, near Cheshunt in Hertfordshire, where he had stayed on his way to be crowned in London. White Webbs House in Enfield Chase was the scene of some of the preparation for the Gunpowder Plot conspiracy of 1605, to which Northumberland was presumed to be a party. He offered his Isleworth estates to the king in payment of the fine of £30,000, but these were not accepted, and he remained in prison until 1621.

[1] C. Oman, *Great Revolt of 1381* (1906), p. 91; *V.C.H.* ii., p. 83.   [2] F. C. Cass, 'The Battle of Barnet', *Trans. L. Mx. A. S.* OS 6 (1890), p. 1; J. C. Wall, 'The Battlefields of Middlesex', *Memorials of Old Middlesex*, ed. J. Tavenor-Perry (1909), p. 102; A. H. Burne, *Battlefields of England* (1950), p. 108.

Early in Charles I's reign Middlesex showed many symptoms of the discontent with his methods of raising money which was to take it into the Civil War on the Parliament side. There was contumacious opposition to the forced loan of 1626, and there was an outcry against the ship-money assessment of £5,500. William Noy, a commissioner of the 1626 loan, who lived at Brentford, was according to Strafford the man who discovered the precedent for ship-money among the records at the Tower. In 1639 collectors of ship-money were resisted in Gore hundred, and 40 distraints were taken at Harrow. Next year the levies were so much resented that the trained bands were ordered to be exercised on all holidays to prevent riots.

The critical year of the Civil War in the south-east was 1642, when the campaign reached Brentford and Turnham Green. Early in November, when the king advanced after Edgehill as far as Colnbrook, Parliament sent a petition to him 'for the removal of these bloody distempers.' Parliament had supposed that no new positions would be occupied while the negotiations continued; but by misunderstanding or sharp practice Charles ordered Prince Rupert's troops forward to Brentford. There they thrust back two Parliamentary regiments—Holles's and Brook's—in a sharp little action and proceeded to plunder the place (12 November 1642). The tale is recounted in a pamphlet entitled *A True and Perfect Relation of the barbarous and cruel Passages of the King's Army at Old Brentford, near London.* Many of the inhabitants had notoriously royalist sentiments; but at such times victorious armies are apt to overlook distinctions of that kind.

The story may be continued in S. R. Gardiner's words. 'If Charles expected to deal as easily with London as he had dealt with the isolated regiments at Brentford, he must have been grievously disappointed with the result. All through the evening of the 12th the City trained bands were streaming forth along the western road. On the morning of the 13th Charles's way was barred by an army of some 24,000 men, drawn up on the common at Turnham Green. The Parliamentary force was probably about twice as numerous as his own. Its composition was, no doubt, heterogeneous. Soldiers who had borne the brunt of war at Edgehill stood shoulder to shoulder with new levies which had never seen an enemy. Such an army might easily be defeated if it attempted complicated manoeuvres, especially against an enemy strong in cavalry, but as long as it stood on the defensive it was irresistible. Its spirit was undoubted. Even those whose voices had been raised for peace had no wish to see London given over to pillage. The fear which inspired the half-jesting sonnet in which Milton implored the royalist captain or colonel who might find his way into Aldersgate Street to spare the poet's home, as Alexander had spared the house once inhabited by Pindar, nerved the arms of hundreds of men who were perfectly incapable of writing sonnets.'[1]

Throughout 13 November the two armies faced each other without fighting, except for a cavalry skirmish at Acton, and in the evening Charles drew off his army towards Kingston. It is not clear why he did. Although the Parliamentary forces under Essex were large, they were mostly raw, and Charles's army was composed of the veterans of Edgehill; a vigorous attack round the north flank might have settled the issue. A force under Sir John Ramsay, holding the bridge at Kingston for the Parliament, may have seemed to be threatening; Essex in fact sent orders for it to fall back on London, but Charles may have thought it a menace to his flank, for he occupied Kingston before finally withdrawing to Reading and Oxford. Whatever the reason, the retreat marked a turning-point in the war; the king never again came so close to winning London. 'Turnham Green,' in Gardiner's phrase, 'was the Valmy of the English Civil War.'

These events confirmed Middlesex in its adherence to the Parliament, and there was a liberal contribution in aid of the plundered inhabitants of Brentford. There were camps and exercise grounds for Parliamentary troops in 1643 on Hounslow Heath and at Colnbrook and Uxbridge. In 1644, after the second battle of Newbury, all the county forces were concentrated at Staines to defend the London approaches. These things, however, meant billeting of troops, which Middlesex relished no more than any other county: the inhabitants petitioned in January 1644 against it, calling the soldiers 'so many Egyptian locusts who feed upon us at free costs.'

There was an abortive conference at Uxbridge in January and February 1645—a 'treaty' in the old sense of a negotiation. Each party had a 'best inn' reserved to its use, and meetings were held in Sir John Bennet's house, still to be seen as the Crown inn at the north-west end of the High Street (Plate 6). Throughout these proceedings there was no genuine desire for conciliation. Puritan divines ranted against the king in sermons in the town; Charles suggested to Sir Edward Nicholas, secretary of State, that if during his arguments with the Parliamentary commissioners 'in your private discourses ... you would put them in mind that they were arrant rebels and that their end must be damnation, ruin, and infamy, except they repented, ... it might do good.' If Nicholas did try this argument, it did not do good; the negotiation broke up with nothing achieved.[2]

In May 1646 Charles rode, accompanied only by a handful of attendants, through Hillingdon, where he spent a few hours at the Red Lion, past Harrow to Barnet, and thence to the Scots at Newark.[3] In August 1647 a Parliamentary army of 20,000 was drawn up in review

[1] S. R. Gardiner, *History of the Great Civil War, 1642-1649* (ed. 1893), i., p. 57. [2] G. Davies, *Early Stuarts, 1603-1660* (1937), p. 32, quoting *Diary and Correspondence of John Evelyn*, ed. W. Bray [1906], p. 796; Lord Clarendon, *History of the Rebellion and Civil Wars in England* (ed. 1843), p. 520. [3] F. Peck, *Desiderata Curiosa* (1779), ii., pp. 350, 360.

order on Hounslow Heath so that Fairfax could demonstrate its loyalty to the Independents in the presence of influential members of the Parliament. The demonstration convinced, and London surrendered to the army. Charles was thereupon moved to Hampton Court in dignified captivity. His children stayed at Northumberland's house at Syon. Negotiations went on, but the temperature was rising, and Charles decided to escape. In spite of suspicion aroused among the guards, he managed to get away on 11 November 1647 to Carisbrooke in the Isle of Wight, where he was no better situated than before. In the rising of 1648, the second Civil War, Lord Holland crossed from Surrey into Middlesex and marched north through the lanes about Harrow to St Albans and St Neots, where he was captured.

Under the Commonwealth Middlesex supplied country houses for the winning side: John Ireton at Highgate, Bradshaw at Hanworth, William Waller at Osterley, William Roberts at Neasden, Skippon and Rous at Acton, and Fauconberg, who married Cromwell's daughter, at Chiswick. Favourable references to Oliver Cromwell remained in the popular memory in different parts of Middlesex with a persistence that confirms that the county was generally affected to him. He lived at Hampton Court and was styled lord of the manor there; but the house on Highgate Hill that bears his name had no connexion with him, and there is no evidence to support his alleged association with houses at Brockley Hill, Neasden, or East Acton. The most curious tradition—that his body was secretly conveyed after the exhumation from Westminster abbey in 1660 and buried at West Drayton—is equally unsupported.[1]

The principal royalists were Sir Francis Rowse of Headstone, Sir Henry Wroth of Durants, Enfield, and Sir Henry Spiller of Laleham. Delinquents (from the Parliament's point of view) were heavily visited by the Committee for the Advance of Money in 1643: Sir Thomas Allen of Finchley was assessed at £1,000, and there is a fairly long list of fines between £200 and £2,000. Sir John Wolstenholme was said to have lost £100,000 in all by fines and the seizure of his estates, though he still had enough money left in 1670, after the end of it all, to get himself a very handsome monument in Stanmore church.

Whatever feelings Middlesex as a whole may have had about the Civil War, it welcomed the Restoration of 1660 as most of the country did. Sir Robert Vyner of Swakeleys went farther than most: in 1672 he set up on the site of the present Mansion House a statue of Sobieski trampling on a Turk, altered to do duty for Charles II trampling on a prostrate Cromwell.[2] Certainly Nell Gwyn is almost as popular a figure as Cromwell in the traditional local history.

In April 1686 James II established a camp on Hounslow Heath to overawe London by an exhibition of power, but London preferred to

[1] P. Norman, *Cromwell House, Highgate* (1926), correcting statements in F. Prickett, *History and Antiquities of Highgate* (1842) and J. H. Lloyd, *History ... of Highgate* (1888); J. B. Firth, *Middlesex* (1906), pp. 51, 237 (Acton, West Drayton); W. Keane, *Beauties of Middlesex* (1850), p. 81 (West Drayton); *Gentleman's Magazine*, 1822, part ii., p. 578 (Neasden); J. C. Collins, 'What Became of Cromwell?', *Gentleman's Magazine*, 1881, part i., p. 553; J. E. C. Welldon, 'The Fate of Oliver Cromwell's Remains', *Nineteenth Century* 57 (1905), p. 928.   [2] *Mx. & H. N. & Q.* 4 (1898), p. 2.

regard the camp as a pleasure ground. Macaulay has a celebrated passage about it:

'The king was resolved not to yield. He formed a camp on Hounslow Heath, and collected there, within a circumference of about two miles and a half, fourteen battalions of foot and thirty-two squadrons of horse, amounting to thirteen thousand fighting men. Twenty-six pieces of artillery and many wains laden with ammunition were dragged from the Tower through the City to Hounslow. The Londoners saw this great force assembled in their neighbourhood with a terror which familiarity soon diminished. A visit to Hounslow soon became their favourite amusement on holidays. The camp presented the appearance of a vast fair. Mingled with the musketeers and dragoons, a multitude of fine gentlemen and ladies from Soho Square, sharpers and painted women from Whitefriars, invalids in sedans, monks in hoods and gowns, lacquies in rich liveries, pedlars, orange-girls, mischievous apprentices, and gaping clowns, were constantly passing and repassing through the long lanes of tents. From some pavilions was heard the noises of drunken revelry, from others the curses of gamblers. In truth the place was merely a gay suburb of the capital.'[1]

London infected the troops, indeed, and they held to a strong Protestant bias. They acclaimed the acquittal of the Seven Bishops with a shout so loud that James, who heard it, knew he could not rely upon them any more than their commanders when it came to the test. The arrangements for the camp were very complete: a letter survives setting out proposals for a hospital made by Surgeon General Pearse. There should be enough single beds for 90 men, but 'they being pretty large, as men grow into a state of recovery they may lie 2 in a bed.'[2]

William III often passed to and from Hampton Court, his favourite residence. A plot was formed in 1696 by Sir George Barclay and others to murder him as he rode back to Kensington after a day's hunting in Richmond Park. The spot selected was the narrow lane (Sutton Lane) between Turnham Green and the ferry at Kew, a little below the present bridge; but two of the conspirators gave the plot away, and though Barclay escaped to France many of the band were captured.

Under the Georges the only active military operations in Middlesex occurred in 1745, when the Duke of Cumberland collected his army at Finchley common. Hogarth's picture 'The March of the Guards to Finchley,' showing them opposite the Adam and Eve public house in Tottenham Court Road, refers to this episode. (George II did not like the picture: he said, 'Take this trumpery out of my sight!') The common was again used in 1780 as a camp during the Gordon riots, and 102 soldiers who died of dysentery were buried at Finchley.[3]

Throughout the 18th and 19th centuries Middlesex provided country

[1] Lord Macaulay, *History of England* (ed. 1858), ii., p. 102.　[2] Historical Manuscripts Commission, *Dartmouth MSS.*, iii. (1896), p. 148.　[3] *H.C.M.* 1 (1899), p. 234.

retreats for politicians: Bolingbroke pulled strings behind the scenes from his house at Dawley, near Harlington; the elder Pitt lived for a time in Enfield Chase; Fox and Canning both died at Chiswick House; Lord Aberdeen lived at Stanmore; and Gladstone was often at Dollis Hill. Lady Jersey gave magnificent tory garden-parties at Osterley in the first half of the 19th century. Disraeli drew her, it is supposed, as Zenobia in *Endymion*; much of her 'exuberant eloquence about the salvation of the country' consisted of extracts from Lady Jersey's conversation. Long after her day the Osterley garden-parties were a feature of London's Saturday political holiday.[1] Politics of a different kind flourished at Twickenham, where the Duke of Orleans, later Louis Philippe, settled in exile. Orleans House was again occupied by the family after 1852, and other French royalties lived close by.

*　*　*　*　*

The parliamentary history of Middlesex begins in 1282, when the counties south of the Trent were summoned to send representatives to Northampton. The earliest known knights of the shire were William de Brok and William de Staunton, chosen in 1294; de Brok and Stephen de Gravesend went in the next year, and Richard de Wyndesor and Richard le Rous sat for the county in 1297. Throughout the 14th century the names of de Wyndesor, le Rous, de Enefield, de la Poile, de Badyk, Frowyk, de Swanland, Wroth, and Shordych appear recurrently.[2] These names, and those in the much less complete returns between 1400 and 1550, are mostly familiar to students of the county's manor records and church monuments, but hardly one of them belongs to a figure of note in national history. (It is just possible that Sir Thomas More was one of the county members between 1509 and 1523.) The name of Wroth appears most often in the 16th century; this family, originally of Wrotham in Kent, settled in London and acquired the manor of Durants at Enfield late in the 14th century. Sir Thomas Wroth, knight of the shire between 1544 and 1563, was a gentleman of the bedchamber to Edward VI; after Suffolk's rising in 1554 he fled to the Continent and lived at Frankfurt and Strasbourg until he returned on Elizabeth's accession in 1558. His son, Sir Robert Wroth, after sitting twice for boroughs, assumed his father's seat for the county and held it until his death in 1606. Sir Robert's grandson, Sir Henry Wroth, a royalist, was engaged to take part in a rising in 1659. With his death in 1671 the family came to an end.[3]

Royalism in the 17th century was also represented by three Middlesex peerages. Lionel Cranfield, created Earl of Middlesex in 1622, was the first of a new type of peer. He began life as a London

---

[1] *Manchester Guardian*, 20 October 1948.　[2] 'List of Middlesex Knights of the Shire from 1295 to 1832', *Trans. L. Mx. A. S.* NS 6 (1932), pp. 343, 534.　[3] See Enfield histories; J. E. Neale, *Elizabethan House of Commons* (1949), p. 311; *Letter-Book of John Viscount Mordaunt, 1658-1660*, ed. M. Coate (Camden Society, 3rd series, 69, 1945), p. 19.

apprentice and made a fortune in the City before going to court and winning favour by his management of the finances. His elevation made old-fashioned people angry: Sir Anthony Weldon complained that Cranfield was of so mean a condition 'that none but a poor-spirited nobility would have endured his perching on that high tree of honour, to the dishonour of the nobility, the disgrace of the gentry.'[1] This was in fact the first conferment of a peerage solely for success in the Commons, without either ancient family or great estates to sustain the dignity. Cranfield lost his offices on impeachment in 1624; on the death of the 3rd earl in 1674 the title became extinct. It was revived in 1675 in favour of his brother-in-law and became one of the honours of Sackville, Duke of Dorset, whence it comes that the portraits and papers of Cranfield are to be found at Knole.

The Bennet family, of Harlington and Uxbridge, secured two peerages in one generation: John Bennet, Lord Ossulston, who married Lionel Cranfield's daughter, and his brother, Henry, Lord Arlington, one of the *a*'s of the Cabal. Henry Bennet was born at Harlington in 1618 and was 'intended to be parson there,' according to Evelyn, who became well acquainted with him; but he entered Charles II's service during his exile in France and was a prominent politician after the Restoration. The Duke of Grafton, Charles's son, married Bennet's only daughter. If Clarendon's account of the preparation of his patent is right, the dropping of the 'H' was merely careless. None the less Arlington Street, Piccadilly, and the earldom, now merged with the Grafton honours, commemorate the clerk's mistake.[2]

Among the Commons, Sir Roger Cholmeley, founder of Highgate school, sat for the county in 1554; Francis Bacon in 1592; Sir William Waller, of Osterley, Parliamentary general, in 1660; and Sir Roger Newdigate in 1741, who 64 years later founded the Newdigate prize for English verse at Oxford.

The polling-place for the county elections was removed from Hampstead Heath to Brentford (*Plate 21*) at the end of the 17th century; the date is usually given as 1701, but there were certainly earlier elections at Brentford in 1659 and 1685 and at Uxbridge in 1614.[3] It is stated, on the evidence of a passage in Bubb Dodington's diary, that the assembly-place before the polling was on Stanwell Heath; but it is difficult to imagine the freeholder of St Giles in the Fields going first to Stanwell in order to return to Brentford. It was more likely Hanwell.[4]

During the century before the Reform Act of 1832 Middlesex in effect enjoyed a democratic franchise, and it exercised it by returning members of a distinctly radical tincture, and doing so amid scenes of rowdiness and violence that became a byword. The Middlesex freeholders, mostly Londoners living outside the City itself and

[1] Davies (page 95, note 2), p. 465, quoting *Secret History of the Court of James I*, ed. W. Scott (1811). [2] J. Evelyn, *Diary*, 10 September 1677; Lord Clarendon, *Continuation of the Life of Edward, Earl of Clarendon* (ed. 1843), p. 1133. [3] T. Faulkner, *History and Antiquities of Brentford, Ealing, and Chiswick* (1845), p. 37, quoting *The Post-Boy*, 9 January 1701; F. Turner, *History and Antiquities of Brentford* (1922), p. 76; W. D. Cooper, 'Uxbridge and its former Inhabitants', *Trans. L. Mx. A. S.* OS 2 (1864), p. 120. [4] Bate (page 53, note 5), p. 235, quoting *Diary of the late George Bubb Dodington, Baron Melcombe Regis*, ed. H. P. Wyndham (1784).

Westminster, expressed their lack of respect for Government by electing John Wilkes, the ugly, witty 'patriot by accident,' in 1768. He had already been prosecuted by Government and outlawed for a libel published in the *St James Chronicle* and for the obscene *Essay on Woman*. He was expelled by the Commons early in 1769; Middlesex returned him unopposed; this election was declared void; and Middlesex returned him unopposed again. Then Colonel Luttrell resigned his seat at Bossinney to stand against Wilkes, and the election that followed was exceptionally turbulent, even for the 18th century. The popular party, managed by Wilkes himself, Serjeant Glynn, and the Rev. John Horne, then curate of Brentford, rallied to the cry of 'Wilkes and Liberty' and the symbolic 'No. 45' (the issue of *The North Briton* which criticised the king's speech in 1763); the Duke of Northumberland, lord lieutenant of the county and no radical, was forced by a mob to drink Wilkes' health; pamphleteers, journalists, and caricaturists poured oil on the flames; Philip Francis launched the *Letters of Junius*, the most forceful political broadsides in the English language; and Samuel Johnson assiduously wrote for the Government. Wilkes polled 1,143 votes to Luttrell's 296, whereupon the Commons declared that Luttrell ought to have been returned, and the defeated candidate took the seat. But Wilkes was the winner in the end; he was elected sheriff of London and Middlesex in 1771 and became lord mayor of London in 1774. He had achieved respectability indeed. In the same year he was returned to Parliament for Middlesex unopposed, in spite of the king's personal anxiety that Sir Charles Raymond and Mr. Clitherow should stand against him, and he retained the seat without further commotion until 1790. The events at the Middlesex hustings led, through the Yorkshire Association of 1779-80, to a thoroughgoing radical programme. John Cartwright, one of the leaders, was buried at Finchley. The name of the Ballot Box inn beside the canal under Horsendon Hill perhaps testifies to the same spirit.[1]

The contests of 1802 and 1806 recalled the scenes of 1769. Francis Burdett, a champion of free speech and opposition to Government, opposed George Byng, of Wrotham Park, who sat for the county as a whig from 1790 to 1847, and William Mainwaring, the county magistrate who had most strenuously objected to Burdett's investigation of abuses in the management of prisons. Byng and Burdett were elected, but in 1804 Burdett's election was declared void on the ground that over 300 persons had been admitted to the polls as freeholders only by virtue of a part share in the 'Good Intent Mill' at Isleworth.[2] In a fresh contest Mainwaring's son defeated Burdett by five votes. In 1806 George Byng was returned with William Mellish of Enfield, 'a thick and thin man for the government and a jolly, comely, hereditary protestant.' They sat together until 1820. Joseph Hume, county member from 1830 to 1837,

---

[1] E. Porritt, *Unreformed House of Commons* (1909), p. 247; E. Halévy, *Growth of Philosophical Radicalism* (ed. 2, 1934), p. 122; *Cambridge Modern History* (1909), vi., p. 455; G. M. Trevelyan, *British History in the Nineteenth Century and After* (ed. 1937), p. 16.   [2] Bate (page 53, note 5), p. 125.

was the last representative of the strong radical element; he was 'Middlesex Joseph' in a *Times* leader of 1837.[1] By mid-century the county was tory; but there was a good deal of radical, and at times revolutionary, activity within its borders. J. G. Barmby, who claimed to have invented the word 'communism' during a discussion in Paris in 1840, lived for some time at Hanwell; he 'must be distinguished,' as G. M. Young wrote, from Mr. Baume, who planned a communist university at Colney Hatch. Mazzini was a frequent visitor at Muswell Hill; Alexander Herzen, leader of the Liberal Russian exiles of the 1850s and 1860s, lived at Teddington; Prince Kropotkin lived at Harrow. At a meeting of Russian exiles in 1903 at a corrugated-iron mission hall somewhere in the Hornsey Rise district Bolshevism was born, or at any rate cast off Menshevism for ever.[2]

The Reform Act of 1832 removed the metropolitan areas from the county constituency, which continued to return two members. In 1867 Chelsea was given two members, but all the rest of the county, urban, suburban, and rural, retained the county franchise—only freeholders had a vote. Anthony Trollope's *American Senator* of 1877 made great play with this in his lecture at the St James's Hall. 'When I came' [from London] 'to Brentford, everything was changed. I was not in a town at all, though I was surrounded on all sides by houses. Everything around me was grim and dirty enough, but I am supposed to have reached, politically, the rustic beauties of the country. Those around me, who had votes, voted for the county of Middlesex. On the other side of the invisible border, I had just passed the poor wretch with 3s. a day who lived in a grimy lodging or a half-built hut, but who at any rate possessed the political privilege. Now I had suddenly come out among the aristocrats, and quite another state of things prevailed.'[3] Ironical enough; and in 1884 the county outside the metropolitan boroughs was given the household vote and divided into seven single-member divisions. With the usual lag in time, this representation has been increased by stages to take account of the vast increase in population, and 28 Middlesex seats were contested in the 1950 and 1951 elections.

The later military history of Middlesex is that of the regular and auxiliary units recruited from the county. The Middlesex trained bands were merged into a reorganised militia in 1663; the quota was 1,160 in 1757, raised to 1,600 in 1761. They were disbanded at the end of the Seven Years' War in 1763 and embodied again from 1778 to 1783.

The Middlesex Regiment traces its origins to the 18th century; it was formed in 1881 by the union of the 57th (West Middlesex) and 77th (East Middlesex) regiments of foot, with two militia battalions.[4] The 57th was originally raised (as the 59th) in 1755, principally in Somerset and Gloucestershire; in 1782, when it was given the additional title 'West

[1] *The Times*, 21 June 1837, reproduced in G. M. Young, *Victorian England: Portrait of an Age* (1936), opp. p. 16. [2] Young (see preceding note), p. 19; *Mazzini's Letters to an English Family*, ed. E. F. Richards (1920); E. H. Carr, *Romantic Exiles* (1933); H. N. Brailsford, 'Trotsky the Brilliant Lieutenant', *Listener*, 29 August 1940, p. 302; P. Dukes, *Come Hammer, Come Sickle* (1947), pp. 41, 80. [3] A. Trollope, *The American Senator* (World's Classics ed.), p. 536. [4] C. L. Kingsford, *Story of the Duke of Cambridge's Own Middlesex Regiment* [1916]; E. Wyrall, *Die-Hards in the Great War* [c. 1926]; H. H. Woollright, *History of the 57th West Middlesex Regiment* (1893); *Historical Records of the 57th or West Middlesex Regiment of Foot 1775-1878*, ed. H. J. Warre (1878); H. H. Woollright, *Records of the 77th Foot*; E. J. King, *History of the Seventh Middlesex* (1927); E. T. Evans, *Records of the Third Middlesex Rifle Volunteers* (1885); C. Rudd, *Early History of the 17th (North) Middlesex Volunteer Rifles 1859-1889* (1895); C. Stonham and B. Freeman, *Historical Records of the Middlesex Yeomanry, 1797-1927* (1930); *V.C.H.* ii., p. 60.

Middlesex,' most of the men were Scots and Irish. It had a moderate reputation at this time—other regiments called them the 'Steelbacks' because they were flogged so often; but in the Peninsula they earned their honourable nickname, 'The Die-Hards,' at Albuera on 16 May 1811. Albuera was a dreadful battle. Arthur Bryant has described the advance of Hoghton's brigade—the 29th (Worcesters), 48th (Northamptons), and 57th. 'They passed straight through the Spaniards, killing several of Zayas's dauntless survivors with a volley, to disperse the Polish horsemen, and then, throwing their caps in the air and giving three cheers, breasted the hill which Girard was about to occupy. Immediately in front of them, looming like giants out of the rain, they saw the advancing French, formed in column of grand divisions with *tirailleurs* and artillery in the intervals and extending over almost the whole of the shallow valley. Though outnumbered by more than five to one and without a single gun in support, the three English battalions immediately opened fire ... Colonel Inglis of the Middlesex was mortally wounded by a charge of grape-shot. 'Fifty-seventh, die hard!' he kept crying to his men as his breath failed. All the while the dwindling line continued to close in on its centre and still, scarcely more perceptibly than a glacier, to advance on the dazed and astonished French until it was no more than twenty yards away, leaving its dead in rigid lines with every wound in front. Pride in their regiments and a dogged refusal to admit themselves beaten in the presence of old rivals and comrades and some invincible spark in an English heart kept these stubborn soldiers there.' Sir Charles Oman has called Albuera 'the most memorable of all Peninsular blazons on a regimental flag,' and the 57th fully earned it: 22 out of 25 officers and 425 men out of 570 were lost that day, and the regimental colour had 21 bullets through it. The most striking of Lady Butler's large battle-pieces, 'Steady the Drums and Fifes!' has made the scene familiar.[1]

The 77th, raised in 1787, served in India, notably at Seringapatam, and arrived in the Peninsula in 1811, winning the honour of Badajoz. It had received the title of 'East Middlesex' in 1807, under the half-formed territorial system of the time. There was little practical significance in the names; most of the recruits for the 77th in 1808 came from the North and South Mayo Militia, and from 1811 to 1833 only two per cent of all the recruits were Middlesex men. Nevertheless, in the way the British Army has, the traditions of the old line regiments have been fused with those of their successor battalions in the Middlesex Regiment.

The militia was called up for full-time service from 1793 onwards, being stationed within the United Kingdom to relieve line regiments; the East Middlesex Militia, for example, spent most of its service in the north of England. The numbers in the militia fell to 338 in 1802, but rose to 12,162 in 1812. Their quality varied; an inspecting officer reported of

[1] A. Bryant, *Years of Victory* (1944), p. 436; W. F. P. Napier, *History of the War in the Peninsula* (ed. Warne & Co., *c.* 1900), iii., p. 168.

one Middlesex militia regiment in 1807: 'The colonel is old and infirm and gives the words of command so indistinct, if it was a well-disciplined Regiment (which is not the case), it could not manoeuvre correctly.'

Part-time duties, mostly for preserving the peace within the county, were performed by 'Loyal Associations' of volunteer infantry and yeomanry. The Tottenham Loyal Association was formed in 1792; the Hadley and South Mimms Volunteers were among the forces reviewed in Hyde Park by George III in 1799; the Ealing and Brentford Armed Association and Volunteer Corps of 1797 was dissolved in 1806. Other districts, such as Finchley, did not proceed beyond the designing of uniforms. Volunteer cavalry corps were raised at Uxbridge and Twickenham. A report in *The Times* of 8 June 1801 indicates their purpose and activities: 'The active corps of Uxbridge Yeomanry, which has rendered such essential service to the public in repressing every appearance of riotous inclinations through all that neighbourhood during the course of that year, was among the foremost of the volunteer associations that assembled on the 4th to commemorate the joyous anniversary of his Majesty's birthday. The corps had a grand field-day, fired several volleys as *feu de joie*, and dined together at the White Horse, in Uxbridge, where many loyal toasts, sentiments, and songs expressive of affection to Church and State, closed with true convivial harmony the pleasing service of that day.'

These associations were disbanded at the Peace of Amiens in 1802, but in the next year the lord lieutenant was given power to raise local forces to meet the threatened invasion. Most of these, when again disbanded in 1813-14, maintained themselves in the form of shooting clubs.

In 1830 disturbances in the county, which no regular police force existed to check, led to local associations of infantry and cavalry being formed. In the west, where the Old Berkeley Hunt provided the nucleus of a mounted corps, the Uxbridge Yeomanry Cavalry was re-formed, with the appropriate motto *Pro Aris et Focis*—'for 'ares and foxes,' as the old soldier translated it for the recruit. It was reconstituted in 1870 as the Middlesex Yeomanry Cavalry, which served in South Africa from 1900 to 1902 and in the 1914-18 war in Gallipoli, Macedonia, and Palestine. In 1920 it was reorganised as a signal unit, still bearing the title and badge of the Middlesex Yeomanry, and it has since been reconstituted as an airborne signal unit.

The threat of war with France in 1859 caused several of the old volunteer units to be revived. In that year the 3rd Middlesex Rifle Volunteers were formed at Hampstead, the 12th at Barnet (not ashamed to be reckoned with Middlesex for this purpose), the 13th at Hornsey, and the 14th at Highgate, where its title is still to be seen graven on the

wall of the drill hall in Southwood Lane. The 33rd at Tottenham and the
41st at Enfield Lock were raised in the next year. In 1880 all these were
consolidated into the 3rd Middlesex Rifle Volunteers, and after various
reorganisations all the county volunteer battalions took their place within
the Middlesex Regiment as territorial battalions in 1907.

Until the Cardwell reforms of the seventies the two Middlesex line
regiments had little connexion with the county area. Both were in the
Crimea, and by 1880 the 57th had been overseas for 85 out of the 125
years of its existence. In 1873 the 57th and 77th were brigaded together,
with the Royal Elthorne Light Infantry and the Royal East Middlesex
Militia associated with them respectively; these in turn became the four
battalions of the Duke of Cambridge's Own (Middlesex Regiment) in
1881. The regiment was in South Africa at the relief of Ladysmith and
raised 46 battalions in the 1914-18 war, of which 26 served overseas. In
the 1939-45 war the regiment was re-formed into support battalions for
infantry divisions. Companies and platoons of mortars and machine-guns
were attached to infantry brigades, and so the Die-Hards came, like
gunners and sappers, to share in the battle honours of almost every
county regiment in the British army. The 1st battalion took part in the
defence of Hong Kong in December 1941, and its successor was with the
first British battalions in Korea in 1950. The depot is Inglis Barracks, Mill
Hill. The other regular regiment locally associated with the county is the
Royal Fusiliers (City of London Regiment), the Third of the Line, which
had its depot at Hounslow from 1875 to 1949.

The Grahame-White school of instruction at Hendon aerodrome was
impressed by the Admiralty on the outbreak of war in 1914 for the
training of naval pilots. A flight of aircraft was stationed there for the
defence of London, and the first recorded ascent of an aeroplane by
night took place there on 5 September 1914—on a false alarm. The
annual Royal Air Force display was held there until 1937.

In the 1939-45 war Bentley Priory, Stanmore, was the headquarters
of Fighter Command, Balloon Command, and the Royal Observer
Corps, and was thus the centre of the country's air defence system.
Uxbridge was the headquarters of No. 11 Group, Fighter Command,
which was responsible for the defence of London and south-east England.
Northolt was the station of the Polish fighter wing, now commemorated
by a memorial there, until April 1944 and was also an important air
transport terminal. Heathrow, close to a landing ground of the 1914-18
war, came into official use under the Ministry of Civil Aviation in 1946.
No. 604 (County of Middlesex) Squadron of the Auxiliary Air Force,
formed in 1930, was one of the most successful night-fighter squadrons.[1]

The headquarters for 'Operation Overlord,' the cross-channel assault
of 1944, was intended to be at Bushey Heath, just north of Stanmore, for

[1] Information from the Air Ministry.

convenience of communication with the Air Force headquarters; but by some mischance the United States army engineers placed it in Bushy Park, Teddington. General Bedell Smith, being told of the difference, cried: 'My God, I've married the wrong woman!'; but it was too late.[1]

Two well-known features of military life can claim a connection with Middlesex—barbed-wire entanglements and Ordnance Survey maps. Proposals for the former were submitted to the War Office in 1884 and afterwards demonstrated at Chatham by Lt. Col. E. M. Donnithorne, of Twickenham;[2] the latter are based on a line measured by General Roy on Hounslow Heath in 1784 and still marked, with proper piety, on the one-inch map.[3]

[1] F. Morgan, *Overture to Overlord* (1950), p. 259. [2] *Middlesex: Biographical and Pictorial* (1907), art. Donnithorne. [3] C. Close, *Early Years of the Ordnance Survey* (1926); C. Close, *Map of England* (1932), p. 28.

CHAPTER IX

ECCLESIASTICAL HISTORY

*'Nothing in England is quite so hard for the
Continental observer to understand as the Anglo-
Saxon attitude to religion and the Established
Church.'*   WILHELM DIBELIUS[1]

THE Church occupies a significant place in the history of most
English counties, both because it was interesting and influential in
itself and because there is generally ample documentary evidence about
it. In Middlesex, however, the case is different. It was an important area
for the Church because it supplied great revenues to clerical proprietors;
but no cathedral, no great monastic or collegiate foundation (with one
late exception) lay within its present borders.

The story of the see of London under the Saxons, connected closely
with political developments of those times, has already been sketched in
Chapter II. At the Conquest the Church already owned large portions of
Middlesex. In 1086 it had some two-fifths of the county—more even than
its third of Kent, and that proportion was high for the country as a
whole.[2] The Church went on adding to its Middlesex lands, until early in
the 16th century only 10 of the 52 principal manors were not in clerical
ownership.

Domesday Book records 17 priests resident with glebe land in the
present county area; there were, however, certainly more churches than
that. The names of a few eminent medieval churchmen who came from
Middlesex have been preserved: William of Northall, bishop of
Worcester, 1190; Adam de Brome, rector of Hanworth, who founded
Oriel College, Oxford, d.1333; John and Ralph Acton—the former
flourished about 1330 and was a canon of Lincoln; Richard Northall,
archbishop of Dublin, d.1397; and Robert Hounslow, d.1430, provincial
of the Trinitarian friars in England, Scotland, and Ireland. Muswell Hill
and Willesden were important centres of pilgrimage until the
Reformation; 'Wilsdon' was well enough known to be linked with
Walsingham, Norfolk, in the Homilies of the Anglican Church in 1562,

---

[1] W. Dibelius, *England* (ed. 1934), p. 339.   [2] Clapham, *Concise*, p. 52.

as an illustration against the Peril of Idolatry. Muswell, attached to Clerkenwell priory, was traditionally associated with a miraculous cure performed on a king of Scots, perhaps Malcolm IV, d.1165.[1]

No monastery, nunnery, or priory is indicated in the Middlesex Domesday. A few foundations were made later: the abbey of Bec in Normandy had a cell at Ruislip from about 1090; Bentley priory, at Stanmore, was founded by Ranulf de Glanvil in 1171 for Austin canons; the Trinitarian or Maturin priory of Hounslow was established in the 13th century; and there were smaller cells, *camerae*, of the order of St John of Jerusalem, at Moor Hall, Harefield (whose chapel still survives, mutilated), and at Hampton.[2] These were only of local importance; the one great monastic house was Henry V's foundation at Syon. This was a Brigittine convent, the only one in England.

This order, founded by St Brigit, a Swedish princess, in 1346, was perhaps introduced through the interest of Henry's sister Philippa, who married Eric XIII of Sweden. It consisted of sixty nuns and twenty-five brothers, living separately, with an abbess as principal of the whole house under a modified form of the Augustinian rule.[3] The first monastic profession took place in 1420, and Henry VI confirmed his father's grants in 1423, with a recital of all its endowments from St Michael's Mount, Lancaster, Minchinhampton, and many other places, mostly the lands of alien houses recently forfeited to the Crown. The monastery was originally in Twickenham parish; it was removed by 1431 (perhaps in 1426) farther north to Isleworth, 'more meet, healthful, and salubrious for them to inhabit,' where Syon Abbey was built on a site originally intended for a Celestine house.[4] Henry VI continued to present it with lands and revenues. In 1492 a survey of all the monastery's possessions showed a clear annual income of £1,616 18s. 5½d.; by 1539, when it was surrendered to Henry VIII's commissioners, the income was £1,731 8s. 4¾d. On the dissolution the abbess, Agnes Jordan, had a pension of £200 and the sisters various amounts from £13 6s. 8d. to £6.

Middlesex had its martyrs in the religious upheavals of the 16th century. Though the monks and nuns of Syon were mostly willing to accept Henry VIII's Act of Supremacy in 1534, John Hall, vicar of Isleworth, was executed at Tyburn in 1535, together with the prior of the London Charterhouse and Richard Reynolds, confessor of Syon monastery, for rejecting it. John de Feckenham, the last abbot of Westminster, who was rector first of Greenford and then of Finchley, refused to conform on Elizabeth's accession and was imprisoned until his death in 1585.

On the opposite wing, Foxe in his *Book of Martyrs* named eight inhabitants of Uxbridge who suffered for conscience' sake in 1521 and onwards.[5] Three protestants were burned at Uxbridge in 1555, but they

[1] J. G. Waller, 'On the Pilgrimage to Our Lady of Wilsdon', *Trans. L. Mx. A. S.* OS 4 (1875), p. 173; S. Potter, *Story of Willesden* (1926), p. 74; F. W. M. Draper, 'Muswell Farm; or Clerkenwell Detached', *Trans. L. Mx. A. S.* NS 6 (1932), p. 633. [2] M. Morgan, *English Lands of the Abbey of Bec* (1946); *H.C.M.* 14 (1912), p. 241 (Hounslow); T. Hugo, 'Moor Hall in Harefield', *Trans. L. Mx. A. S.* OS 3 (1870), p. 1. [3] *Catholic Encyclopaedia* (1907), art. Brigittines. [4] Bate (page 53, note 5), p. 74. [5] *The Acts and Monuments of John Foxe* (ed. Pratt, 1856), iv., p. 217.

apparently had no previous connexion with the district; they were condemned in Bishop Bonner's court in London, and their place of execution was presumably selected to warn the neighbourhood. In 1558 six men, arrested in Islington, were burnt at the Butts in Brentford.

After Elizabeth's accession, however, Roman Catholicism became until about 1840 as nearly extinct in rural Middlesex as anywhere in England. The returns of papist recusants made under Elizabeth and the Stuarts, taken with the evidence furnished by the sessions records, show that the old faith was given over by all but a very few isolated households. The diocesan return of 1577 showed 9 recusants, including at Ealing Henry Cole, doctor of law, 'little or nothing worth'; at Uxbridge the wife of Dr. John Story, active persecutor of protestants under Mary, recently executed at Tyburn; and at Harlington the wife of William Byrd, the composer. In the 1588 list there were 6, including Byrd himself; in 1592-3, 11. From 1581 onwards individual names appear in the sessions records for failing to go to church; in 1583 the Bellamy family is mentioned—Katherine Bellamy, widow, Jerome and Richard Bellamy, gentlemen.[1]

The Bellamys figure in a series of incidents of some importance in the history of the Elizabethan government's dealings with Roman Catholics. William Bellamy was the owner of Uxendon manor house, near Harrow. Edmund Campion, the Jesuit, visited the house in the 1570s, but it appears from entries in the Harrow parish register that the family conformed to the Establishment, at any rate nominally, until William died in 1581. In the following years Robert Parsons and William Weston, both Jesuit priests, were lodged in the house. In 1586 Anthony Babington arrived there in disguise after the discovery of his plot to assassinate Elizabeth; Camden in his *Annals* describes how the conspirators 'were openly proclaimed traitors all over England. They, lurking in woods and by-corners, after they had in vain sought to borrow money of the French ambassador and horses of Tichborne, cut off Babington's hair, besmeared and soiled the natural beauty of his face with green walnut shells, and being constrained by famine went to an house of the Bellamys near Harrow Hill, who were greatly addicted to the Romish religion. There were they hid in barns, fed and clothed in rustical attire, but the tenth day after they were found brought to London, and the city witnessed their public joy by ringing of bells, making of bonfires, and singing of psalms, insomuch that the citizens received very great commendations and thanks from the queen.'

Katherine Bellamy, William's widow, was imprisoned for her part in harbouring Babington and died soon afterwards in the Tower; her son Jerome was executed; his brother Robert, in prison at the time, escaped abroad and was later recaptured; another brother, Bartholomew, died in

[1] *M.C.R.; Catholic Record Society* 22 (1921), p. 47 (for 1577), p. 123 (for 1588); 18 (1916), p. 142 (for 1592-3).

prison. The fourth brother, Richard, was not involved and went to live at Uxendon later in 1586, with his uncle William Page, who was also a recusant. Richard's elder daughter, Anne, fell into the hands of the notorious Richard Topcliffe, bounder of Roman Catholics, whose name gave the law latinists a new verb, *topcliffizare*. The wretched Anne was prevailed on to reveal a visit of Robert Southwell, the Jesuit, to Uxendon; he was arrested there in 1592 and finally put to death in 1595. Richard Bellamy, his wife Katherine, a son, and two daughters were imprisoned, apparently after resisting blackmail by Topcliffe.[1]

The Bellamys were not characteristic of the Middlesex gentry. As in most of the south and east of England, anti-Spanish, and consequently anti-Catholic, feeling was strong, and though some of the courtiers who had country houses in the Thames valley professed the Roman faith it had no firm roots. Francis Cottington, envoy to Spain, who built Hanworth House in the 1630s, was one, and George Calvert, Lord Baltimore, original grantee of Maryland, who had a house at Isleworth, another.[2] In 1674 27 papist recusants were returned, all from the western parts except 5 at Enfield; in the whole of London and Middlesex no more than 52 paid the £20 fine in that year.[3] A private and portable chapel (later, if reports are true, converted into the church of Holy Trinity, Conduit Street) was established for James II in the lines of the camp on Hounslow Heath.[4] In 1695 papists were ordered to remove more than ten miles from the cities of London and Westminster.[5]

The 17th-century Anglican Church in Middlesex had more to contend with on the side of protestant nonconformity than in respect of Roman Catholics. James I held a conference at Hampton Court between the Established Church and the Presbyterians in 1604. After hearing the Presbyterians' arguments, the king told them that they were aiming at a Scottish presbytery, which 'agreeth as well with monarchy as God and the devil.' It was a decisive moment in the history of the Anglican Church. S. R. Gardiner summed up in an eloquent passage:

'In two minutes he had scaled his own fate and the fate of England for ever. ... 'If this be all they have to say,' he observed as he left the room, 'I shall make them conform themselves, or I will harry them out of the land, or else do worse.' Browbeaten by the bishops, and rebuked in no measured or decorous language by James, the defenders of an apparently hopeless cause went back to their labours, to struggle on as best they might .... Many a man who cared nothing for minute points of doctrine and ritual, and who was quite satisfied with the service as he had been accustomed to join in it at his parish church, would feel his heart swell with indignation when he heard that men whose fame for learning and piety was unsurpassed by that of any bishop on the bench had been treated with cool contempt by men who were prepared to use their wit

---

[1] W. D. Bushell, 'The Bellamies of Uxendon', *Trans. L. Mx. A. S.* NS 3 (1917), p. 71, quoting W. Camden, *Annals,* iii., p. 78; *V.C.H.* ii., p. 35 (attributing the incidents to Okington, Wembley, another house of the Bellamys); *Catholic Record Society* 5 (1908), pp. 132, 211, 334. [2] Mathew (page 7, note 4). [3] *Catholic Record Society* 6 (1909), p. 75. [4] J. Evelyn, *Diary,* 18 July 1691; P. Cunningham, *Handbook for London* (1849), i., p.231. [5] Dowdell, p. 39.

to defend every abuse and to hinder all reform.'[1]

James was in fact unable to make them conform, or to harry them out of the land, and the two religious parties were strong enough in the middle decades of the century to make sharp differences inevitable. Twenty-two of the Middlesex parish clergy are recorded as being sequestered or otherwise losing their benefices between 1642 and 1656; on the other side there were 32 ejections in 1660-2, when at least five of the sequestered ministers returned to their parishes.[2] The most notable among these latter was Dr. Bruno Ryves, who after being ejected from Stanwell in 1642 edited the *Mercurius Rusticus*, a royalist periodical; he regained his benefice in 1660 and was appointed to Acton in 1662. Lewis Hughes, rector of Shepperton, was committed to the Tower as a royalist in 1642 and was punished in 1647 for stirring up his late parishioners against the intruded parson; William Grant had an unseemly dispute with his parishioners, culminating in the publication of his pamphlet *The Vindication of the Vicar of Isleworth*; Robert Mossom, curate of Teddington, later bishop of Derry, was sequestered in 1650 for reading the Book of Common Prayer. Patrick Young of Hayes, ejected in 1645, was a scholar, the most celebrated Grecian of his age, and a translator of the Septuagint (the Old Testament in the Greek version).

The nonconforming clergy were more distinguished. These were men who lost their benefices, either in 1660 or 1661 on the simple ground that they were intruders and had no good title to their livings, or in 1662 for refusing to conform to the tests prescribed by the Act of Uniformity. There were 17 ejections in Middlesex under the first head and 14 under the second, with one other of uncertain date; almost all of those who lost their livings on legal grounds in 1660 would have been ejected on the religious test of 1662, for only two of all the 32 afterwards conformed to the Establishment. Thomas Malthus, for example, ejected from Harlington in 1660, went to Alfriston, Sussex, and was in turn ejected from there in 1662. Most of the Nonconformists, however, continued to live and teach in Middlesex. In 1665 they were forbidden to live within five miles of any corporate town or of a place where they had formerly held a benefice. In consequence a small colony of nonconforming ministers was formed at Brentford (as at Hackney and Stoke Newington), outside the limit but conveniently close to London and Westminster. They were in some danger of imprisonment until the survivors gained successively larger measures of toleration, being granted licences to preach in 1672 and to form their own churches in 1689.

The most celebrated Nonconformist divine of the Restoration period was Richard Baxter, author of *The Saints' Everlasting Rest*. He was invited to accept a bishopric in 1660, but refused and was ejected from the Church in 1662.[3] He settled at Acton and there wrote the greater part of

[1] S. R. Gardiner, *History of England from the Accession of James I to the Outbreak of the Civil War, 1603-1642* (ed. 1883), i., p. 156. [2] A. G. Matthews, *Calamy Revised* (1934), for the Nonconformists, and *Walker Revised* (1948), for the high churchmen; biographies of Anglican clergy, R. Newcourt, *Repertorium Ecclesiasticum Parochiale Londinense* (1708-10), and G. Hennessy, *Novum Repertorium Ecclesiasticum Parochiale Londinense* (1898). [3] F. Bate, *Declaration of Indulgence* (1908), pp. 9, 15.

his autobiography, the *Reliquiae Baxterianae*. He held a conventicle in his own house and then went with his flock to the parish church; for the former he was imprisoned, not too harshly, in the New Prison, Clerkenwell, in 1669. He received a licence to preach in 1672, but was again fined and sent to prison in 1685 by Judge Jeffreys for an alleged libel on the Church in his paraphrase of the New Testament. Acton had already been distinguished for puritanism, political as well as doctrinal: Philip Nye, who became rector in 1643, was a prominent figure in the ecclesiastical politics of the Commonwealth. He lost his preferments in 1660 and was specifically excluded from the Act of Oblivion. Thomas Gilbert of Ealing, saluted as the 'proto-martyr to the cause of nonconformity' or first to be ejected at the Restoration, emigrated to New England and became the pastor of Topsfield, Massachusetts. John Doddridge, against whom Lewis Hughes tried to stir up the parishioners of Shepperton in 1647, was ejected in 1660 and settled at Brentford; he was the grandfather of Philip Doddridge, the 18th-century Nonconformist divine and hymn-writer. Richard Swift, curate of Edgware till 1660, who set up a school at a house called Jeannetts, Mill Hill, was reported as 'led away with Fifth Monarchy notions' of the sectarian extremists.[1]

It is difficult, from these and many more biographical particulars, to judge how far Middlesex folk supported one side or the other in the controversies of the day. It seems that they accepted the independent ministers in most cases without demur. There was certainly a dispute at Twickenham when the congregation objected to Thomas Willis maliciously preaching against the king[2]—it is odd that Willis was one of the two ejected Middlesex clergy who afterwards conformed; the other was Timothy Hall of Hayes, nominated bishop of Oxford by James II and denied installation by the canons of Christ Church. Thomas Fuller, author of *The Worthies of England* and a well-known royalist, was presented to Cranford by Lord Berkeley in 1658 without open objection raised. But the other dispute on Church affairs that we know of in this period, at Northolt, was in the opposite sense: there the parishioners, or the Independent part of them, petitioned Cromwell to remove the vicar, Robert Malthus (great-grandfather of Thomas Malthus the political economist), 'a very fruitless and unprofitable minister ... that hath not only a low voice but a very great impediment in his utterance' and, more important, had uttered invective expressions against the army in Scotland and failed to observe appointed national thanksgivings.[3] Commotions during church services at Ashford, West Drayton, and Finchley found their way into the sessions records; but these were no more than brawls.

Not all the religious activity at this time was within, or on the borders of, the Established Church. The Society of Friends, or Quakers,

[1] N. G. Brett-James, 'Nonconformity in Mill Hill Village before 1807', *Transactions of the Congregational History Society* 16 (1949), p. 33. [2] *M.C.R.* iii., p. 308; A. G. Matthews, *Calamy Revised* (1934), art. T. Willis. [3] Lysons, art. Northall. I cannot agree with the church guide-book, which sees in this document evidence of 'virtually continuous high-church tradition' (p. 6); and it is unlikely that in 1642 Malthus would be presented to the living by Cromwell (p. 16).

founded a number of meetings and built several meeting houses between 1658 and 1700. There is a reference to a meeting in 1658 at Uxbridge, where Edward Burrough had first preached the Friends' doctrines a few years earlier. In the same year Philip Taverner, the puritan minister of Hillingdon, held a public disputation with Quakers at West Drayton.[1] In 1669 a 'monthly meeting' was established at Longford, having meeting houses there and at Colnbrook, Staines, and Uxbridge. There was apparently some persecution of Friends in the district, for in 1671-2 money was collected for their relief in London and Ireland, and even in Jamaica. George Fox was constantly in north Middlesex, especially at Winchmore Hill and Enfield, where meeting houses were built in 1688 and 1697 (*Plate 45*). There were 17th-century meetings also at South Mimms, Hendon, Mill Hill, Hounslow, and Brentford.[2]

When the Church commissioners appointed by the Commonwealth made their visitation of Middlesex they recommended, among other things, some adjustments of the ancient parish boundaries to conform to growth of settlement: Uxbridge and Pinner, for example, should become parishes, not chapelries.[3] Most of these proposals had to wait two centuries for fulfilment; meanwhile the dissenting sects took the opportunity to establish chapels in the outlying hamlets, many of them, like Longford, more populous than the parish centre but not provided for by the Establishment. Many Presbyterian, Independent, and Quaker congregations grew up in such places, as well as in the populous market towns. All in all, with allowance made for local variations, it seems that rural Middlesex was fruitful soil for puritan doctrines during the Commonwealth and for nonconformity in the next half-century. In the first list of licences drawn up under the Declaration of Indulgence of 1672, there were 17 resident ministers in the rural parts of Middlesex (15 of them Presbyterian) and twelve places besides licensed for holding of services.[4] In 1684 the justices were told that conventicles were usually held 'in places where no person dwelleth and the owners unknown.'[5] The Presbyterians had a chapel in Southwood Lane, Highgate, from about 1680; one in Baker Street, Enfield, from 1686 with registers from 1662; and one at Shackler's Yard, Edmonton, by 1686.[6] Dissenting preachers licensed by the Middlesex magistrates in 1689 included in addition ministers at Ealing, Chiswick, and Old Brentford.[7]

In the 18th century the old nonconformity gently declined, in Middlesex as everywhere else. Meeting-houses were still licensed by the justices; a list of 1745 has survived in the county records.[8] Some of the old Independent or Congregational chapels disappeared; the only substantial chapel put up between 1700 and 1750 was the Old Meeting

[1] Cox (page 44, note 1), iii., p. 26. [2] *Journal of Friends' Historical Society* 13 (1916), p. 67 (Uxbridge), 35 (1938), p. 23 (Winchmore Hill); W. Beck and T. F. Ball, *London Friends' Meetings* (1869). [3] *H.C.M.* 1 (1899) – 3 (1901). [4] Bate (page 110, note 3), appendix vii. (from *Calendar of Stat Papers, Domestic,* 1672-3). [5] Middlesex County Records, Sessions Book 422 (January 1684). [6] *Journal of the Presbyterian Historical Society of England* 9 (1949), p. 104; Middlesex County Records, Sessions Book 437 (April 1686); *Transactions of the Unitarian Historical Society* 2 (1922), p. 42; *Baptist Historical Society Transactions* 7 (1921), p. 181. [7] Middlesex County Records, Sessions Book 467 (July 1689), fol. 89; A. A. Walmsley, 'An Early Nonconformist Father of Freedom: John Jackson of Brentford', *Transactions of the Congregational History Society* 11 (1932), p. 96. [8] *M.C.R. Reports,* p. 125.

at Uxbridge, built in 1716 (*Plate 46*).[1] The Presbyterians dwindled away or became Unitarians.[2] The most notable Nonconformist divine was Richard Price, moralist, political economist, and statistician, who began his ministry at Edmonton; he wrote *Observations on Civil Liberty*, which contained dangerously liberal thoughts on the French Revolution and was censured by Burke in his *Reflections on the French Revolution*. The Friends, after a recession—the Longford monthly meeting reported in 1740: 'We don't pretend to prosperity'—rose in wealth and standing from about 1770 as the prosperous millers and bankers of Uxbridge and Staines and the intellectual Quaker colony at Tottenham advanced to influence in the world.

The Church of England did not supply any famous figures from Middlesex parishes during the 150 years after the Restoration. Names of note in their day were John Hall, rector of Finchley 1666-1707, author of *Jacob's Ladder, or the Devout Soul's Ascension into Heaven*, a popular devotional work which went through 19 editions by 1764,[3] and three men of science, John Theophilus Desaguliers, rector of Whitchurch, Stephen Hales, of Teddington, and John Lightfoot, botanist, minister of Uxbridge chapel. Joseph Trapp, rector of Harlington 1733-47, was an anti-enthusiast: he preached four discourses 'on the nature, folly, sin, and danger of being righteous over-much.' Two other Middlesex clerics of the 18th century were interesting if not notable: Samuel Glasse, rector of Hanwell 1780-5, later prebendary of St Paul's and master of a school at Greenford;[4] and his son George Henry Glasse, who succeeded him at Hanwell, rendered *Samson Agonistes* into Greek, 'spent a fortune; committed suicide,' as the *Concise Dictionary of National Biography* laconically puts it.

The Methodist movement in the Church had no special feature in the county. John Wesley's *Journal* records frequent visits to Brentford, where there was open opposition to his preaching in 1742, 1744, and 1746; when his doctrines were more freely accepted the society there melted away. It was restored about 1760—'the work of God is broke out afresh,' he exclaimed—but in 1786 it had diminished almost to nothing, only to rise again by 1790. Evidently Brentford Methodism was a wayward growth. Charles Manning, vicar of Hayes 1739-57, was a friend of Wesley's who preached in the church there several times between 1749 and 1753. In 1750: 'All behaved well but the singers; whom I therefore reproved before the congregation; and some of them were ashamed.' Some of the parishioners went off and took pews at Hillingdon to hear more acceptable doctrines; Wesley followed and preached to them there in May 1754; some of them consequently moved on to Uxbridge, but in 1758 he caught up with them: 'Now,' he wrote, '[the Gospel] is come to torment them at Uxbridge also.' He also preached at Staines and at Lauderdale House, Highgate.[5]

[1] W. H. Summers, *History of the Congregational Churches in the Berks, South Oxon, and South Bucks Association* (1905), p. 66; *Middlesex Advertiser*, 12 June 1936. [2] W Wilson, *History and antiquities of the Dissenting Churches and Meeting Houses in London, Westminster and Southwark* (1808-14); Dr Williams's Library MSS. 35-5, 'State of the Dissenting Interest of England and Wales, 1715 and 1773'; also MSS. 35-4 and 35-6. [3] *H.C.M.* 3 (1901), p. 248. [4] *Shardeloes Papers*, ed. G. Eland (1947), p. 115. [5] *Journal of the Rev. John Wesley* (Everyman ed.) especially i., pp. 366, 482, 549, ii., pp. 183, 493, iv., pp. 362, 459, 495 (Brentford); ii., pp. 92, 136, 246, 275 (Hayes); ii., pp. 280, 402 (Hillingdon and Uxbridge); iii., p. 455 (Staines); iv., pp. 246, 334, 418, 455 (Highgate).

The church at Hayes needed reform. The rector entered some particulars in the register of a disturbance which lasted from 1748 to 1754. The singers ordered a carpenter to pull down part of the belfry without leave from the minister and churchwardens; when the clerk gave out the 100th Psalm, the singers sang the 15th instead. As the quarrel went on, the churchwardens ordered the belfry door to be broken open for the benefit of a visiting party of ringers; the service was disturbed by some of the inhabitants ringing the bells and going into the gallery to spit below; most scandalous of all, a fellow came into church with a pot of beer and a pipe and remained smoking in his own pew until the end of the sermon.[1] But Hayes was not typical.

In the more tolerant 18th century some notable Roman Catholics lived in Middlesex. In 1745 the justices thought it worth seeking out 'papists or reported papists' and compelling them to take the oath of allegiance. But these people were exceptional and isolated; there was no body of Catholic squires and yeomanry as in Lancashire. James Radcliffe, Lord Derwentwater, brought up in the exiled court at St Germain and executed after the '15, had a house at Acton; Alexander Pope lived at Twickenham and was buried in the parish church; Mrs. David Garrick went regularly from Hampton to services at Isleworth; foreign artists working in Middlesex, Verrio, Laguerre, Zoffany, were at any rate nominally Catholics.[2] In the household of the Talbots, Earls of Shrewsbury, at Isleworth, the old religious observances persisted, with a chapel and resident chaplain. The foundation of the chapel is traditionally given as 1675; the earls professed the faith from 1718 onwards, and there are registers from 1746, covering an area extending from Brentford to Sunbury, with some places on the Surrey side. The register mentions 'Weafers at Teddington Factory' in 1757, and from 1811 soldiers from Hounslow barracks; but entries are few.[3] The settlement at Hammersmith probably served places closer to London.

The Jews do not figure largely in the history of old Middlesex, or indeed of any rural part of England. There is a curious, it may be thought incredible, story recounted by Lockyer in Joseph Spence's *Anecdotes*:

'The Jews offered my lord Godolphin to pay £500,000 (and they would have made it a million), if the government would allow them to purchase the town of Brentford, with leave of settling there entirely, with full privileges of trade, etc. The agent from the Jews said that the affair was already concerted with the chiefs of their brethren abroad, that it would bring the richest of their merchants hither, and of course an addition of above 20 millions of money to circulate in the nation.' But Godolphin was too wary to provoke both the clergy and the City, and the proposal was dropped. There seem to have been few Jewish inhabitants: Moses Hart won a lottery in 1720 and bought a house at

[1] W. E. Tate, *Parish Chest* (1946), p. 168.   [2] Mathew (page 7, note 4).   [3] 'Parish Registers of Isleworth, Middlesex, 1746-1835', *Catholic Record Society* 13 (1913), p. 299.

Isleworth; Aaron Capadoce of Stanmore, who died in 1782 at the reputed age of 105 and was sent to Holland to be buried, is remembered in the topographies; and there are traces of jewish settlement at Brentford and Harrow between 1782 and 1839.[1]

After about 1775 the older nonconformist sects revived. The Presbyterians (such as had survived the drift to Unitarianism), Congregationalists, and Baptists began founding chapels. In the Congregational connection, Staines, Poyle, and Uxbridge belonged to the 'Berks, South Oxon and South Bucks Association.' A string of chapels nearer London was 'supplied' from 1798 to 1844 by preachers from the London Itinerant Society. This preaching gave rise to rioting at Ealing in 1801 and 1805, and there was a great commotion at Harrow in 1812 when supporters and friends returning to Greenford for the canal boat to London after the opening of a Baptist chapel were set upon with stones by the schoolboys. There had been a Baptist church at Brentford in 1692, and others at Barnet and South Mimms at the same period, which did not survive. New Baptist chapels were founded from 1800 onwards. They were not all successful; after three separate attempts in Hendon, the cause collapsed for the time in 'this dark village,' as it was despairingly called.[2]

An influx of Roman Catholic priests and institutions from France and the Low Countries began during the revolutionary period, but these for some reason settled principally south of the Thames; Tottenham, exceptionally, has the church of St Francis de Sales of 1793. Only four more Roman Catholic foundations had appeared by 1860, and most of the 69 parochial churches now in the county date from the 20th century. They first grew up in the west, perhaps largely to minister to immigrant Irish labour. There are now many collegiate and religious institutions, including both Strawberry Hill and Pope's Villa at Twickenham. Perhaps the most important, and certainly the most conspicuous, is St.Joseph's College for missionaries at Mill Hill, founded by Cardinal Vaughan in 1869.[3]

The state of affairs in the Church of England early in the 19th century was much as it was everywhere else. Writing in 1850, B. J. Armstrong, rector of Whitchurch, declared that an old bellringer told him that on Sunday afternoons some 15 years before he had locked up the church for want of a congregation. Most of his parishioners, he observed, were decidedly puritan, but nevertheless Tractarian principles were beginning to be approved, and in six adjoining parishes the round of fast and festival was observed.[4] At Willesden in 1820 the vestry recorded a resolution that throws light on the condition both of the Church and of dissent at that time: 'That it appears that the parishioners of Willesden have long had cause to regret that Divine Service is only

---

[1] C. Roth, *Rise of Provincial Jewry* (1950), pp. 16, 17; Lysons, art. Stanmore Magna. [2] 'Echoes of Past Pastors in Highgate', *Transactions of the Congregational History Society* 7 (1918), pp. 310, 350; Summers (page 112, note 9); W. W. Druett, *Harrow through the Ages* (ed. 2, 1936), p. 216; W. T. Whitley, *Baptists of London 1612-1928* [1928]. Mathew (page 7, note 4); *Catholic Directory* (annual). [4] MS. Diary of B. J. Armstrong.

performed once on Sunday, and that by reason thereof not only many of the inhabitants and their families who would be happy to attend in the afternoon, but numbers of their servants and of the poor, are deprived of the benefit of the performance of Sunday duty; and that there has lately been erected in the parish a dissenting meeting house tending to cause religious divisions among them and which they fear is chiefly to be attributed to the want of Divine Service at the parish church.' The 'divisions' had their origin in one Mr. Nodes, who used to visit his mother's cottage every Sunday and read to her from the *Village Sermons*, gradually a congregation assembled week by week to hear him.[1]

Parish boundaries remained generally unchanged since the Middle Ages (Brentford, divided from Hanwell in 1723, and Pinner, from Harrow in 1766, were exceptional) until an act of 1843 permitted new parishes to be formed for ecclesiastical purposes without special legislation. From that date, however, the parishes could keep pace with the new settlements of population: Hampton Wick, Harrow Weald, Southgate, and Uxbridge became independent within a few years, and parish life revived. The diocese of London remained unaltered since Saxon times (apart from a brief period, from 1540 to 1550, when the bishopric of Westminster was established) until in 1845 its boundary was retracted to the Middlesex border.[2] The most notable Middlesex divines of the 19th century (not counting Christopher Wordsworth and Charles Vaughan, headmasters of Harrow) were J. M. Neale, who was educated at Shepperton 1823-9 and wrote a high-church romance, *Shepperton Manor* (1844); Theodore Williams, vicar of Hendon for 63 years, from 1812 to 1875; his successor, F. H. A. Scrivener, one of the New Testament revisers; Edward Monro, at Harrow Weald 1842-60, a prolific religious writer; Derwent Coleridge, second son of S. T. Coleridge, rector of Hanwell 1864-80. Among the Nonconformists, Hugh Price Hughes, Methodist minister at Tottenham 1875-8, and Sir John McClure, headmaster of Mill Hill school 1891-1922, became figures of national repute.

Since about 1900 there has been a considerable settlement of Jews on the London fringe, especially in the parts contiguous to their favourite area of Hampstead. More than half of the 450,000 Jews in the whole country live in greater London, and most of these outside the East End and Hackney are in Middlesex districts. Golders Green, Willesden, and Edgware are particularly well supplied with synagogues—there are 50 in the county.[3]

Most of the 19th-century Anglican churches were built by subscription within the new parishes, which were nearly all wealthy enough to be able to pay for buildings without outside help, by the ordinary means of raising money known to church treasurers. The new church at Stanmore

[1] Potter (page 107, note 1), p. 162. [2] For diocesan boundaries before 1845, Williams (page 17, note 3), map i, based on Church Commissioners' Report, 1835; J. Caley and J. Hunter, *Valor Ecclesiasticus* (1810-31), map; M. F. Bond, G. Crosse, and S. L. Ollard, *Dictionary of English Church History* (ed. 3, 1948), art. London. [3] *Jewish Year Book*, 5710-1 (1950).

(1849), costing £6,000, was half paid for by a church rate; but this method was abolished in 1868. There was of course a London diocesan church-building fund, and Bishops Blomfield and Tait were active church-builders; but their efforts were mostly devoted to the town districts.[1] The Ecclesiastical Commission made grants for stipends and vicarages; occasionally a single donor presented a building, like Christ Church, Ealing, 1852, built by Miss Rose Lewis in memory of her father W. T. Lewis ('Gentleman' Lewis, the actor), and St Peter, Staines, 1894, by Sir Edward Clarke. At East Acton the Goldsmiths' Company built the church of St Dunstan, 1879, and endowed the benefice. In Tottenham outside generosity provided St Mary, Lansdowne Road, the Marlborough College mission church of 1885. In the late eighties money was given at Hornsey and Teddington on condition that something superior to the ordinary run of suburban churches should be put up.[2] Only at Teddington and St Anselm, Hatch End, was there opposition of any account on the ground of alleged irregular ritual practices; the rood-screen at Hatch End gave rise to a famous case decided in the ecclesiastical courts in 1904.

The economics of church-building have been changed during the last 50 years. Whereas formerly local energy, solidly based on generous gifts of land or money from the wealthier inhabitants, was able to keep pace with the needs of the expanding suburb, the immense expansion of the housing estates has forced the churches to adopt new methods. In many of the new suburbs there was not as before a mixture of classes, so that large individual donations could not be made; the higher cost of living farther from the centre, and the burden of mortgage and hire-purchase payments, made it impossible for the new congregations to contribute nearly so much to the total church expenses as had been usual half a century before. As well as this, there was noticeably less desire to build churches. In housing-estate Middlesex it is generally true to say that before 1914 the demand for a church came from the people, whereas today the church has often to create the demand by pioneer evangelistic work.[3]

In general, therefore, the planting of churches has come more closely under central supervision, and the diocese or other central authority has been more firmly organised to guide and supplement local efforts. In some places funds for hall, church, and vicarage—usually in that order— have been secured by union of benefices within London, principally in the City: the foundation of the churches of St Peter le Poer, Muswell Hill, and St.Benet Fink, Tottenham. (1910 and 1911), for example, were assisted by this device. Similarly the Glasshouse Yard Baptist chapel of 1680 has been transplanted to Winchmore Hill. In a few cases landowners or estate developers have themselves provided sites for churches, but the diocese or the central fund of the denomination

[1] B. F. L. Clarke, *Church Builders of the Nineteenth Century* (1938), p. 217; W. W. Druett, *Stanmores and Harrow Weald through the Ages* (1938), p. 152. [2] *Builder* 55 (1888), p. 233. [3] For these paragraphs, S. Eley, 'The Great Adventure: Planning a New Church', in *Post-War Church Building*, ed. E. Short (1947).

concerned has had to make provision for most sites. Between 1918 and 1939 the diocese of London, whose building operations were almost entirely in Middlesex, spent £80,000 on sites.

In this state of things, the achievement of all the ecclesiastical bodies in providing halls, churches, and clergy has been remarkable. Very few Anglican parishes in the years before the 1939-45 war could expect to raise more than a fifth to a quarter of the building costs involved, though in denominations with little or no central endowment the local congregation might have to do very much more than that. Most of the churches in the new districts are thus newly built. There are now 227 Anglican parishes within the county; 74 of their churches were built between 1851 and 1900 (not counting complete reconstructions of existing buildings, like Heston and Ealing) and 82 between 1901 and 1950 (not counting reconstructions and new buildings erected beside existing ones, like St Andrew, Kingsbury, and Greenford). Twenty-seven new parish churches were consecrated between 1931 and 1942 (*Plate 61*). In addition to these parochial churches, there are 51 chapels of ease, mission rooms, and halls devoted partly to secular uses; some of the chapels of ease, like St Catherine, Feltham, and St John, Friern Barnet, are, as far as the buildings go, larger and more convenient than the mother churches.[1] The Free Churches have been almost equally active in building. In proportion to their numbers, the Roman Catholics have perhaps done most of all, by establishing 48 new (not reconstructed or resited) churches in the first half of the 20th century.[2]

The old rural parishes have been subdivided, and there has been immense expansion of work by all the churches. Nevertheless, Greenford had become by 1939 the most populous parish in the whole country, and the provision of churches is still far from adequate. The Church of England aims in suburban districts at working towards a network of parishes each having the making of a self-supporting unit, almost, if not quite, able to pay its way, covering an area inhabited by about 7,000 to 8,000 people; and this may take a long time. Meanwhile, the lambs are certainly there to be fed.

---

[1] Calculated from *London Diocese Book* (1950). [2] Calculated from *Catholic Directory* (1950).

CHAPTER X

SOCIAL HISTORY

'Derbyshire for lead,
Devonshire for tin,
Wiltshire for hunting,
Middlesex for sin.'

OLD RHYME[1]

VIGOROUS local societies with a continuing tradition of their own
have flourished in England when three distinct conditions have
been present simultaneously. First, the district must be reasonably secure
and prosperous; social and intellectual life does not flourish when times
are hard. Second, the local centre must be at least some 20 or 30 miles
distant from a rival in point of size. Third, the wealthier inhabitants must
lend their patronage to organised social activity; this has always required
subsidy, at any rate down to our own day, when the welfare state at once
dries up the springs of private generosity and assumes many of its
obligations.

Middlesex has never yet had an independent and continuing social
life of its own. The county has been prosperous and secure enough, but
the other two conditions were never fulfilled. The attractions of London
have been too influential for much local feeling to endure in the county.
Outside London, too, there has never been a county town in the proper
sense; Brentford never filled the bill. Most important, perhaps, there
were few county gentry firmly rooted through generations in the soil of
the rural parts. Thomas Fuller noted about 1660 that the Wroths of
Enfield were the only family in Middlesex out of all those mentioned by
Norden (in 1593) that had not become extinct by his time; and of all
Norden's list only Wroth and Shordych were among the 33 families of
gentry returned by commissioners of 1433.[2] E. P. Shirley, compiling his
list of *Noble and Gentle Men of England* (1859) whose families had held
land since before the battle of Bosworth in 1485, found no such family
in Middlesex. The Newdigates of Harefield indeed went back to the 14th
century (even further back in the female line to Roger de Bacheworth,

---

[1] Quoted by Druett (page 115, note 2), p. 237. [2] Fuller (page 33, note 1), ii., p. 328.

who was settled there in 1285), but their Middlesex tenure had been interrupted. Clitherow at Boston House, Wood at Littleton, and Taylor at Staines had held their lands for over 200 years when W. J. Loftie wrote his *History of London* (and Middlesex) in 1883, but these cases were exceptional enough to be worth recording.[1]

The lengthy inscriptions on the older monuments in the parish churches tell the story. Most of the Middlesex proprietors were men who achieved means, if not fortune, at court or in the City of London and held estates in the county for a generation or two before the family failed or moved on to broader acres farther from the capital. Local life was much less under the leadership of landed proprietors than in almost any other county, and it was fragmentary in consequence.

With great prosperity there was little corporate unity.[2] Lower down in the social scale, among the yeomen and farmers, some families in the north-west, like Page at Harrow and Nicoll at Hendon, persist through centuries, and names like Atlee, Greenhill, and Robins are constantly found in parish records or on tombstones; but in the Thames valley it was otherwise. In 1867 the extraordinary migration and change in family names about Shepperton within the previous 200 years was remarked.[3]

Until the Reformation there had been one stabilising influence—the Church. In 1086 four great church proprietors already owned almost two-fifths of Middlesex land, most of it in the productive west and south, and the only great lay proprietor, Geoffrey de Mandeville, had more important interests in Essex and Hertfordshire. No great feudal castles were built after the Conquest; there was a small motte-and-bailey near South Mimms, which may have been a minor fortified place of the Mandevilles, and Humphrey de Bohun had licence in 1347 to fortify his house at Enfield. In the main, however, the history of the 12th to the 15th centuries is that of lay estates passing to church ownership. The Crown held little except Enfield. It is difficult to discover how the life of the people was affected by this almost universal absenteeism of the landlords. Whether clerical management meant agricultural and economic stagnation or more rapid improvement (there is not much evidence either way),[4] the absence of great noblemen's estates must have been an advantage in the age when castles still invited attack and ravage which necessarily involved the surrounding country.

Enclosure was the outward sign of revolutionary changes in the 16th century. Henry VIII's attempt to establish a hunting reserve enclosed by a wall round a great tract about Hampton would have destroyed the life of the villages within the area. The villagers knew it, and demonstrated; but fortunately Henry died before things had gone very far. Minor riots were caused by enclosure of common land at Enfield later in the century.[5]

[1] Loftie (page 3, note 1), ii., pp. 4, 16. [2] *V.C.H.* ii., 28; G. N. Clark, *Later Stuarts* (1934), p.16.
[3] Anon., *History of our Village: or a few Notes about Shepperton, Ancient and Modern* (1867), p. 27.
[4] See Chapter IV, page 31; Clapham, *Concise*, p. 52. [5] *V.C.H.* ii., p. 91.

After the Restoration of 1660, estates changed hands more often and were generally subdivided into smaller lots each time. All these changes were within the accepted social framework and on an intelligible scale; even the ostentations of the Duke of Chandos' Canons were not inordinate. This society lasted in Middlesex until about 1870; in 1873, when the 'New Domesday Book' was compiled, there were still 11 individual owners of 1,000 acres or more, but the advance of the housing estates had begun.

Owners of property exercised their authority through the administrative functions of the justices of the peace, a system successful enough in general but inadequate to deal with the large and disorderly population of the town districts. Men of a lower degree than the gentry had to be put on the commission of the peace, and the 'trading justices' of the Middlesex bench got a peculiar and undesirable reputation. Burke described some of them in 1780: 'The scum of the earth— carpenters, bricklayers, and shoemakers; some of whom were men of such infamous character that they were unworthy of any employ whatever, and others so ignorant that they could scarcely write their own names.'[1] The county records reveal that there was indeed inefficiency and some arbitrary action, and occasional corruption; but in general, apart from the period 1781-1822, the Middlesex justices strove hard to discharge their varied and onerous duties, devising expedients that in several cases were the forerunners of regular institutions that were generally adopted.[2]

It has been claimed, indeed, that the first stages in the transition from the Tudor system of local government, based upon the county and the parish, to modern forms of administration were nearly always found in Middlesex. Various expedients were adopted to cope with the congestion of business cast by a paternal Parliament on the county bench. The first was a separation of the rural from the town business by the holding of small sessions for outlying areas. There was a regular meeting at Brentford, mostly for highway matters, from 1651 onwards; as early as 1675, half a century before Parliament enacted the requirement, there were special sessions in each hundred for licensing public houses; and by 1727 there was a district meeting of magistrates held at Edgware for the hundred of Gore. Committee meetings between sessions, beginning with an audit committee, became usual about 1750, foreshadowing the characteristic procedure of modern local authorities.

The mass and specialisation of the local government work in the urban and suburban areas made it impossible to maintain the old system of unpaid service. As late as 1785 Lord Mansfield held it illegal to pay a person to act as assistant overseer of highways, and Parliament did not authorise it until 1819. Nevertheless, a staff of paid officials was slowly

---

[1] *Parliamentary History*, 8 May 1780, xxi., p. 592, quoted by S. and B. Webb, *Statutory Authorities for Special Purposes* (1922), p. 387; K. B. Smellie, *History of Local Government* (1946), p. 18. [2] On these paragraphs, Dowdell, throughout; S. and B. Webb, *Parish and County* (1906), especially chapter vi.

developed throughout the 18th century, through an intermediate stage in which contractors were employed. Finally, new *ad hoc* bodies, like turnpike commissioners and improvement commissioners, were formed under statutory authority to discharge certain new functions which could not have been imposed on the existing county machinery without breaking it down completely. At the same time the regulation of trade was tacitly, sometimes openly, laid aside by the justices as the doctrine of *laissez-faire* became generally accepted.

The great names of the Middlesex bench belong to the 18th century: Henry Fielding, his brother Sir John Fielding, and Sir John Hawkins. Henry Fielding, the novelist, became a magistrate in 1748 and took his duties seriously.[1] In his *Enquiry into the Causes of the late Increase of Robbers* (1750) he attributed much social evil to excessive gin-drinking, and in 1753 he propounded an elaborate scheme for the building of a county poorhouse to accommodate 5,000 at Acton Vale. He suggested making two great divisions of the poor, a County House for the industrious, which should also contain wards for the sick and aged, and a House of Correction for vagrants, which 'beside work-rooms and lodgings should be equipped with dungeons and fasting rooms' with prison-like discipline. After his death in 1754 his work was carried on by his half brother, Sir John Fielding, blind from birth, who in 1753 enrolled the first 'Bow Street runners,' predecessors of the modern police force.[2] Sir John Hawkins, who lived at Twickenham, better known as a member of Johnson's circle and author of a *General History of Music*, was a Middlesex magistrate who paid particular attention to road business and published *Observations on the State of the Highways* in 1763.[3]

The first effective measure to get rid of the 'trading justices' was the Middlesex and Surrey Justices Act of 1782, which established a stipendiary magistracy and regulated its relations with the police. It was important in itself and a step towards Peel's Metropolis Police Act of 1829. The area covered by the Metropolitan Police was meant from the first to extend some 15 miles from Charing Cross, and by 1839 the whole of Middlesex was policed by the new force. Bow Street horsed patrols had been at work since 1805.[4]

The yeomen and labourers formed the mass of the rural inhabitants. No account of ordinary village life survives; no 18th-century Middlesex parson left a diary (there is none published, at all events). There are indeed full records of the county sessions from 1549 onwards, almost complete, and a selection has been printed; but these deal with the exceptional events, the crimes and recusancies and shortcomings, and not with the commonplaces of life. It seems from the records that Middlesex men outside London were normally law-abiding, with a strain of independent thought and action. Collection of ship-money was

[1] G. M. Trevelyan, *British History in the Nineteenth Century and After* (ed. 1937), p. 23; Dowdell, p. 156. [2] D. Marshall, *English Poor in the Eighteenth Century* (1926), p. 49; Williams (page 17, note 3), p. 132; R. Leslie-Melville, *Life and Work of Sir John Fielding* [1934]. [3] Jackman, p. 218. [4] W. L. M. Lee, *History of Police in England* (1901), pp. 170, 195, 268; J. F. Moylan, *Scotland Yard and the Metropolitan Police* (1929), p. 132.

resisted in 1639 in the hundred of Gore; the county was strongly, though not unanimously, on the Parliament side in the Civil War; and it was radical enough in 1769 to elect Wilkes as its representative three times against the declared wishes of Government. The gentry could not lead their tenants to the polls as they wished, and there were no rotten boroughs.

Middlesex produced its fair share of eccentrics and characters. Peter Fabell, the 'merry devil of Edmonton,' was supposed to have made a compact with the devil, in the manner of Faust, and, unlike Faust, to have bettered him. Roger Crab, the hermit of Ickenham, is a better authenticated figure; he was a Parliament soldier who became a vegetarian, subsisting on dock leaves at a cost of a farthing a day, and earned some local reputation as an astrologer and wizard.[1] Daniel Dancer was an 18th-century inhabitant of Harrow Weald who earned a place in the *Dictionary of National Biography* with the simple description 'miser.' He let his land lie fallow to save the expense of cultivation, and for clothing he used 'hay bands, which were swathed round his feet for boots and round his body for a coat.' He went to law against a tradesman whom he suspected of cheating him of threepence.

In every county there is some district reputed to be especially backward. In Middlesex this was Hayes, considered in the 18th and 19th centuries to be a neighbourhood of peculiar uncouthness and barbarism. Of Yeading nearby a writer of 1861 declared: 'Sure I am that at Yeading dirt, ignorance, and darkness reign supreme'; and Botwell was but little more civilised. Cock-throwing was practised in Hayes churchyard on Shrove Tuesday down to the 1750s; in the 19th century a vicar, imprisoned in the King's Bench for debt, used to go every week and preach with the sheriff's officer behind him in the pulpit; mummers and handbell ringers still made their rounds at Christmas in 1875.[2]

In many parts there were unfortunate women reputed to be witches. The sessions records contain accounts of 22 indictments for witchcraft under Elizabeth and James I. The law, it seems, was administered with some degree of mercy; only five of the accused were put to death.[3] Elizabeth Sawyer of Edmonton and Elizabeth Rutter of Finchley achieved local notoriety, and Gillian or Jill of Brentford was a figure of some note in literature. In *The Merry Wives of Windsor* Falstaff disguised himself as the old fortune-telling Fat Woman of Brentford, evidently a well-known figure to Elizabethan audiences.

Ghosts no less than witches played a part in Middlesex folk-lore. There were of course several at Hampton Court—one of Katharine Howard and another of Edward VI's nurse. They were numerous at Hayes, and at Cranford House there was one in the kitchen, 'dressed as a maidservant, with a sort of poke-bonnet on, and a dark shawl drawn or

---

[1] *Mx. & H. N. & Q.* 1 (1895), p. 160. [2] Thorne, art. Hayes, quoting E. Hunt, *Hayes Past and Present* (1861). [3] *M.C.R.*, ii., pp. 1-1iii.

pinned lightly across her breast.'[1] The suburbs were not always as prosaic as they seem to the passing visitor today.

The names of Finchley and Hounslow had a sinister ring in the ears of 17th- and 18th-century travellers; they were the haunts of the highway robbers who infested the commons and alehouses on the approaches to the metropolis. Even in 1876 Anthony Trollope would write in his autobiography that Edward Chapman looked at him 'as he might have done at a highway robber who had stopped him on Hounslow Heath.'[2] Nowhere in the kingdom, except on Blackheath in Kent, could such a constant stream of travellers with valuables be found within a small compass as on the Middlesex approaches. Hounslow Heath was the worst area; the Green Man inn at Hatton, lying in the angle between the Bath and Staines roads, was particularly well situated as a base for their operations.[3] The palmy days for highwaymen were from the Restoration to the death of Queen Anne, when violent men, disbanded soldiers and officers, 'took to the road.' The forces of law and order were not quite incapable of dealing with them, but most had a long run before they were caught. In 1698, the year after the peace of Ryswick and the ensuing disbandment of the army, three highwaymen near Hounslow robbed between 30 and 40 people one after the other, including two peers; James Maclean, a Scottish minister's son, who held up Horace Walpole in Hyde Park, committed his last robbery, from the Earl of Eglinton on Hounslow Heath, in 1750; John Rann—'Sixteen-string Jack'—was hanged in 1774 for robbing Dr. William Bell in Gunnersbury Lane of his watch and eighteen pence[4]; Kitty Clive, the actress, lost a little silver and her senses when threatened with a horse-pistol near Teddington church in 1776. In the later stages, the mounted highwayman gave place to the mere footpad; in 1802 three men assaulted Mr. Steele, who kept the Lavender Warehouse in Catherine Street, Strand, and battered him to death on the Hanworth road.[5]

The Oxford road was dangerous, too. In 1669 Sir Robert Vyner of Swakeleys and Bridget Hyde, his sixteen-year-old stepdaughter and heiress, were attacked by 11 robbers near Hillingdon. Two people were murdered at the bridge between Hillingdon and Uxbridge in 1702, and a monument in Gloucester cathedral commemorates Eli Dupree, 'abus'd unto death' at Hayes in 1741.[6] On the Great North road at South Mimms the parish register records the burial of an unknown man, 'a highwayman,' in 1689; in the next year £15,000, collected as taxes in the Midlands, was stolen from a coach there; and in 1692 Marlborough was robbed of 500 guineas on the road.[7] Jack Sheppard was captured at Finchley in 1724, wearing a butcher's blue frock, with a watch concealed under each armpit. In the next year two highwaymen, Everett and Williams, fell out about an agreement for sharing their profits acquired

[1] G. C. G. F. Berkeley, *My Life and Recollections* (1866), p. 209. [2] A. Trollope, *Autobiography* (World's Classics ed.), p. 107. [3] Harper (page 7, note 3), p. 107. [4] J. T. Smith, *Nollekens and his Times* (ed. 1949), pp. 12, 86. [5] Maxwell (page 38, note 3). [6] Parkes (page 70, note 5), p. 176; *M.C.R.*, iv., p. 88; Harper (page 7, note 3), pp. 108, 113. [7] F. Brittain, *South Mymms* (1931), p. 45.

on Finchley common and took the case to court. The common's reputation was so bad as late as 1790 that Sir Gilbert Elliot, later Earl of Minto, would not travel over it at night.[1] It was not only the wealthy who had something to fear: in 1719 a sawyer returning home to London with his week's wages earned on the building of Canons, Little Stanmore, was robbed and beaten to death near Highgate.[2]

The most remarkable exploit of the Middlesex robbers was in March 1674, when a band called 'Jackson's gang' robbed the Windsor coach in daylight on Hounslow Heath; two days later they held up two more coaches near Bedfont, and rode to Harrow, where 40 or 50 men were drawn up to defend the place against them. They were finally rounded up, after a good deal of shooting, near the hamlet of North End, Hampstead, and Jackson was hanged at Wildwoods.[3] Harrison Ainsworth credited Dick Turpin with exploits in Tottenham and Edmonton, and he connected Jack Sheppard with Willesden; but these are romances.

Still, romances apart, there was reason for the good folk of Middlesex to apprehend robbery on the roads, and they did not neglect their own defences. At Brentford there was some kind of fortification against attack; at Gunnersbury a small blockhouse was manned by soldiers to secure the king's passage to Kew or to Windsor; at Pinner Hill House in 1830 the family blunderbuss was fired once a fortnight to show the house was armed; and about the same time parties used to form to be escorted by the watchman from Battle Bridge (King's Cross) along the Seven Sisters Road to Tottenham.[4] Chiswick residents formed an 'Association for Prosecuting Thieves and Felons, etc.' in the 1790s; it was reconstituted in 1808 as 'The Chiswick Association for the Protection of Persons and Property against Depredations and for prosecuting Thieves, Felons, etc.,' with the Duke of Devonshire at the head. There was a similar association at Twickenham in 1784, and one at Hanwell fifty years later, where there were frequent fights between the population and Irish labourers working on the canal and railway.[5] No wonder that the whole of Middlesex clamoured to be brought within the area of Peel's police; for proper policing was the only way to put down the pest, combined with reduction of the commons and wastes and closing of the public-houses that harboured thieves.[6] No amount of exemplary punishment had been effective: gibbets with bodies hanging in chains stood at intervals along the roads on Hounslow Heath and Finchley common. 'All the gibbets in the Edgware Road,' said the *Annual Register* for 1763, 'on which many malefactors were being hung in chains, were cut down by persons unknown.' The more delicate taste of a new age—some say, of George III—had the Hounslow gibbets removed soon after 1800.[7]

Gipsies as well as highwaymen were to be met on the commons. In 1594 five yeomen were seen at Hounslow in the 'consort or society of

[1] *H.C.M.* 1 (1899), p. 234. [2] C. H. C. and M. I. Baker, *Life and Circumstances of James Brydges, First Duke of Chandos* (1949), p. 147. [3] Parkes (page 70, note 5), p. 183. [4] R. Henrey, *King of Brentford* (1946), p. 88; *H.C.M.* 13 (1911), p. 109; W. W. Druett, *Pinner through the Ages* (1937), p. 210; F. Fisk, *History of Tottenham*, second series (1923), p. 107. [5] W. Draper, *Chiswick* (1923), p. 155; Webb (page 121, note 1), p. 440; M. Sharpe, *Account of Bygone Hanwell* (1924), p. 96. [6] Trevelyan (page 122, note 1), p. 200, based on G. Borrow, *Romany Rye* (Everyman ed.), p. 145. [7] Jackman, p. 143, quoting P. Kalm, *Journey through England* (1752), p. 81; T. Pennant, *Journey from Chester to London* (1782), p. 288; *H.C.M.* 1 (1899), p. 311; 2 (1900), p. 6; T. C. Croker, *Walk from London to Fulham* (ed. 1860), p. 124; *H.C.M.* 14 (1912), p. 241.

vagabonds commonly called Egipcians,' and the three of them in custody were sentenced to be hanged. John Stanley, 'king of the gipsies,' was buried at Bedfont about 1765.[1] A hut at Enfield Wash belonging to a gipsy called Mother Wells was the place where Elizabeth Canning asserted she was imprisoned for a month after being kidnapped in London on New Year's Day, 1753. The prosecution of the gipsies, and then of Elizabeth Canning for perjury, split the town into rival factions of 'Canningites' and 'Egyptians' and caused as much commotion as the case of the Tichborne claimant over a century later.

Three celebrated forgers were connected with Middlesex. The Rev. William Dodd, after a career as a fashionable parson, forged a bond for £4,200 in the name of Lord Chesterfield, his former pupil, and, in spite of an agitation for pardon in which Dr. Johnson joined, was executed in 1777; he had been arrested at Whitton and was buried at Cowley, where his brother was vicar. William Wynne Ryland, engraver to George III, who first used the stipple manner of engraving in England, forged a bill of exchange and was hanged at Tyburn in 1783—not quite, as sometimes stated, the last man to be executed there; he was buried at Feltham. Henry Fauntleroy, partner in a bank, who lived at Hampton, was convicted in 1824 of forging a power of attorney for Government stock and executed.[2] Thomas Griffiths Wainewright poisoned his uncle and his mother-in-law at Linden House, Turnham Green, in 1828 and 1830.

Each century leaves fuller records of its crimes than of its virtues. The county's petty defaults can be read in the published sessions records,[3] and most of them seem small beer: 'keeping of a lewd strumpet of incontinent life' by a tailor of Isleworth in 1586; the theft of a 'blue cow' worth 40 shillings at Sunbury in 1596; refusing to aid the constables 'in apprehending a number of rogues in a barn' at Hillingdon in 1609; cheating at cards, in a game called 'Thy card and my card,' at a Hounslow inn in 1619. There was a quaint case in 1668 about a squatter, Amos Cox, a carpenter, who set up a cottage in the night time on the waste in Finchley without the 4 acres of ground laid on to it that an old Elizabethan statute still required. What sort of a cottage, as Sir John Clapham inquired, would go up in the night on the waste in Finchley?[4] Social unrest of any consequence does not appear before the disorders attending the enclosures of 1760-1800. Stanwell villagers marched to London in 1767 to protest against an enclosure bill, but there were few riots, or none at all, in the county. The Uxbridge Yeomanry Cavalry, formed in 1797 for service in an internal insurrection as much as a foreign invasion, was said to have 'repressed every appearance of riotous inclinations' in the neighbourhood in the succeeding years: it is not clear whether any such inclination in fact existed.[5] Charles Lamb, writing in 1830, mentioned rick-burning at Enfield 'with strange chemical

[1] M.C.R., i., p. 221; Gentleman's Magazine 1825, part ii., p. 201. [2] Trial of Henry Fauntleroy, ed. H. Bleackley (1924), with notes on Dodd and Ryland; on Dodd, Times Literary Supplement 7 December 1922, p. 780. [3] Bibliography, section A, page 371. [4] Dowdell, p. 82; Clapham, Concise, p. 303. [5] Times 8 June 1801; Stonham and Freeman (page 101, note 4), p. 7.

preparations, unknown to our forefathers.'[1] As late as 1883 there was a
serious riot at Hounslow, where an attack was made on Dr. Whitmarsh
of Albemarle House on account of suspicions aroused by his partner's
suicide. At the time of the 'Battle of Sidney Street' in 1911, when a
foreign gang had to be shot out of a house in Stepney, there was a similar
battle at Tottenham.[2] But all in all, apart from highway robberies, it was
a peaceful county.

Not every one, however, found the state of affairs in the old rural
society good; when it was mentioned in print, it was usually adverted to
with the sourness appropriated by social commentators in every age.
John Middleton wrote in 1798:

'The moral principle of the rural servants and labourers of this
county is at so low an ebb that it is supposed not one in a hundred, or
perhaps in five hundred, are honest and faithful to their masters. Their
minds have been contaminated, and every honest idea banished, in
consequence of being continually assailed by women calling for rags,
broken glass, and kitchen-stuff; pretended gipsies, itinerant Jews, ballad-
singers and show-men, strolling from house to house, pilfering every little
article they happen to meet with, and tempting and encouraging servants
and labourers to do the same, by offering to purchase every portable
article. To these may be added millers, ostlers, and corn-chandlers,
dealers in eggs, butter and poultry, plumbers, blacksmiths and publicans,
chandlers' shops, old iron shops, old clothes shops, and rag shops, low
brokers of furniture, and pawnbrokers.'[3] J. C. Loudon, who lived at
Pinner, was less Pauline, more pithy in his summary of Middleton's
findings when he wrote of Middlesex 30 years later: 'Labourers ruined in
morals and constitution by the public houses. Gentlemen's servants a bad
and contaminating set.'[4] Sir Stamford Raffles, founder of Singapore,
wrote from Highwood Hill when applying for a commission of the peace
in 1825: 'We are more than four miles removed from our parish church
and the exercise of anything like police, and the consequences are as
might be expected: the poorer classes, left to themselves without control
in this world, and neither check by moral nor any other authority, are in
a sad degraded and irregular state. We are just on the borders of another
county, not famous for the moral character of its inhabitants .... We are
now concerting a plan for the erection of a Chapel of Ease; and the next
object is an efficient magistracy.'[5]

The most pressing social problem throughout these centuries was
pauperism, which led to vagrancy and thus to crime. As well as having
the almost unmanageable mass of the London poor within its county
area, rural Middlesex had the nuisance of returning paupers from
London to their home parishes. The thing became a regular business. In
1692 Andrew Ward, former constable of Finchley, pressed for payment

[1] *Letters of Charles Lamb*, ed. A. C. Ainger (1891), ii., p. 264.   [2] Maxwell (page 38, note 3), p.
85; Moylan (page 122, note 4), p. 52. [3] Middleton, p. 459. [4] Loudon (page 5, note 1), p. 1125.
[5] Letter of 31 December 1825, *Memoir of the Life and Public Services of Sir Thomas Stamford Raffles*
(1830), p. 591.

of £13 14s. 7d. expended on conveying vagabonds and cripples through the parish back towards their homes. Later the business was put out to contract: Mr. Davies, 'vagrant contractor' for Middlesex, gave evidence to a committee on mendicity in 1815 that he had undertaken, for £300 a year, to convey in and out of Middlesex all vagrants sent to him by the magistrates with passes to their home parishes. He had a large house capable of holding 50 to 60 at a time; as the vagrants were released from Bridewell they were brought straight to him by the constables. They were then despatched by the cartload to outposts like Staines and Colnbrook, where they were collected by the contractor for the next county. He reckoned that he dealt with 12,000 or 13,000 in a year—often, of course, the same person several times.[1]

Constant application of punishments under the stringent Tudor laws proved useless in repressing vagrancy, and in 1600 a joint meeting of the City of London and Middlesex and Surrey justices concluded that the best way to deal with the vagrants was to build houses of correction. A Middlesex house was completed in 1615; a 'workhouse' to accommodate 600 was built and opened in Clerkenwell in 1666, but it proved so expensive to run that it was closed nine years later.

Throughout the 17th century successive attacks of the plague added to the cares of the parishes.[2] The three worst years were 1603, 1625, and 1665; the villages lying on the main roads were worst affected, to judge from comparisons of burials recorded in the parish registers. In 1625 the Court removed from Whitehall to Hampton for security and then, as the infection advanced, farther on to Windsor. Hendon and Tottenham incurred the displeasure of the Privy Council for receiving refugees from London; the villagers were ordered to remove them and to receive no more.[3] In June 1636 the Privy Council ordered persons from London to be removed from places within ten miles of the court at Hampton Court, for fear of infection, and in August paper-mills in the district were ordered to stop work, as the rags used in manufacture might be infected.[4] In 1640 John Green was ordered to be put in the stocks at Brentford for refusing to kill his dog after it had gone among persons infected with the plague.[5] The great attack of 1665 was severely felt in some places; at South Mimms seven parishioners died and over 100 unnamed, probably Londoners smitten while fleeing away.[6] According to Defoe the inhabitants of Whetstone 'offered to fire' at two men attempting to travel along the Great North Road and turned them back.[7] On the other side of the county the barbarous men of Hayes clubbed Londoners to death for fear of infection.[8] At Old Brentford a new cemetery had to be made that year in 'Dead Man's Field.'

Much later, cholera epidemics were carried into Middlesex; it was reported at Mill Hill village and school about 1825 and at Southall in

[1] On these paragraphs, Marshall, pp. 165, 243, 281; Dowdell, p. 59; M.C.R., v., p. 69; M.C.R. Reports, p. 10; V.C.H. ii., p.92. [2] V.C.H. ii., p.95. [3] Parkes (page 70, note 5), p. 154. [4] Middlesex County Records, Acc. 249/819-821. [5] Middlesex County Records, Sessions Book 12/30. [6] Brittain (page 124, note 7), p. 42. [7] H.C.M. 6 (1904), p. 214. [8] Harper (page 7, note 3), p. 42.

1832, and it was specially serious at the Thames valley places from Brentford up to Staines in 1849.[1]

During the 18th century fresh provision for the poor was made, so much that Middleton in 1798 could not repress his indignation at the 'numerous efficient and comfortable funds raised for the support of the idle poor in this county, which operate against the general industry of the labouring poor.' The thriftless pauper, he wrote, was better housed and fed in the workhouse than the industrious labourer and his family; charity added to the evil by raising voluntary contributions during every temporary inconvenience. There were 61 workhouses in the county, outside the City and Westminster, in 1777.[2] At Sunbury the paupers had beer every day, and at Isleworth the accommodation and victuals were so good that it was hard to get the people out in the spring who had come in for the winter.

At Enfield about 1810 outdoor poor relief amounted to £60 a week. Peter Hardy, who produced four editions of a pamphlet *Hints for the Benefit of the Inhabitants of Enfield*, wrote that the parish had deprived itself of the means of supporting its poor liberally by spending charity money on roads and bridges and in aid of the general rate. 'No parish in England has had so fine an estate,' he wrote, with some bitterness, 'and no set of people could have made a more miserable use of it.'[3]

Sir Frederick Morton Eden, the historian of the Poor Law, who lived at Ealing, described the internal economy of two Middlesex workhouses, Ealing and Hampton, in 1796. The Hampton description may be quoted:

'The poor are partly relieved at home and partly maintained in a Poorhouse on Hampton Common, in an airy situation on gravelly soil. ... It is under the direction of a man and his wife, who, in addition to a small salary, receive 2s. 8d. a week for every pauper they feed. The food seems wholesome and good, and it is certainly much better than a labouring man could afford his family. Meat is served every day, with vegetables from the garden. The female paupers are not content with the ample allowance of food, and would be riotous without tea every morning. This is not allowed by the master, but they contrive to get tea, and sugar, cups, and teapots. The house seems clean and neat, and can hold 40 inmates. There are six bedrooms, each having three feather beds; seldom more than two sleep in a bed. The children are taught to read and say their prayers, but no kind of work seems going forward .... The Poor are clothed once a year, and wear a red badge on their shoulders, marked PH (parish of Hampton).'[4]

Nearly fifty years later improved arrangements obtained at Ealing, where allotments provided by the bishop of London in 1832 were reported to have acted admirably, especially for the aged 'in deferring

[1] N. G. Brett-James, *Mill Hill* (1938), p. 27; MS Diary of B. J. Armstrong; *Twelfth Annual Report of the Registrar-General, 1849* (1853), appendix, p. 70. [2] Clapham, *Modern Britain*, i., p. 355. [3] *V.C.H.* ii., p. 100, quoting *State of Population and Poor and Poor Rates in Middlesex* (1805); P. Hardy, *Hints for the Benefit of the Inhabitants of Enfield* (ed. 4, 1813), p. 46. [4] Eden (page 38, note 1), p. 239.

the period of refuge to the union workhouse.' There was a waiting list of fifty for the allotments.[1]

*   *   *   *   *

Very many schools, of various fortune and distinction, have existed in Middlesex. There were schools intended and reserved for the children of the inhabitants; others which began as local schools and achieved wider usefulness and fame; and others which were established to board Londoners' children. This last type was the characteristic contribution of Middlesex (and Surrey) to English education—the comparatively small boarding school of the 18th and 19th centuries, usually kept by a clergyman or a dissenting society, just far enough away from London for parents to be relieved of the care of their children, but not so remote that the journey became costly and difficult. When Rowland Hill was prospecting for a suitable place to establish a school of this kind, he 'examined every great road from London,' as he said, and picked on a place at Tottenham. Boarding schools were, of course, not peculiar to the Home Counties—Dotheboys Hall was in Yorkshire—but they flourished particularly in north Middlesex, at Tottenham and Enfield, and in the west at Brentford, Ealing, and Chiswick. It was probably at Chiswick that the German pastor C. P. Moritz, visiting England in 1782, saw a 'beautiful white house' and was astonished to learn that it was a boarding school.[2]

No Middlesex school can be traced back to an origin before the 16th century. A. F. Leach, in his *English Schools at the Reformation*, was unable to include a single one in the present county area in his long and detailed list of those which certainly existed before the time of Edward VI. Except for an indirect reference to schooling at Harrow in the 14th century, no record of a medieval school has yet been found.

Harrow school (*Plate 12*) must stand at the forefront of any reference to education in Middlesex.[3] Its continuous history goes back to a charter obtained in 1572 by John Lyon, yeoman, of Preston nearby. There had certainly been a school at Harrow before that time: John Intowne was brought before the manor court in 1384 for sending his son away to school, and in 1557 'Gerarde Richard, son of William Gerard, Gent., of Harrow Middlesex School,' was admitted scholar of Caius College, Cambridge. Lyon's charter recited that he intended *de novo erigere, creare, et in perpetuum stabilire* a certain grammar school within the township of Harrow-on-the-Hill. Whatever the exact import of the words *de novo erigere* may be—whether that a new school should be established or an existing one thoroughly renovated—Lyon's charter was certainly the significant event that Harrovian tradition (which prefers the old-style date

[1] Clapham, *Modern Britain*, i., p. 470; Tremenheere (page 40, note 2).   [2] C. P. Moritz, *Travels in England in 1782* (ed. 1886), p. 84.   [3] See Harrow bibliography, page 383, especially E. D. Laborde, *Harrow School Yesterday and To-day* (1948); for the endowments, J. F. Williams, *Harrow* (1901), appendix B.

of 1571) declares it to be. On the death of Lyon's widow in 1608, the appointed governors entered into their property and began to put up the building now known as the Old School. It remained the only building until the 19th century.

By a fortunate provision Lyon had laid down in one of his rules: 'The schoolmaster may receive over and above the youth of the inhabitants within the parish, so many foreigners as the whole numbers may be well taught and applied.' This rule, though the parishioners attempted to resist its application as late as 1810, prevented Harrow from remaining a local school—a Welsh boy speaking no English came in 1668—and enabled it to attain nation-wide fame and influence. Its rise began in the 18th century, largely owing to the skilful management of the Duke of Chandos; under this influence it took on a whig complexion in contrast to tory Eton, and to the outside world the two names have been bracketed ever since.

In 1721 there were 144 boys at Harrow—40 free scholars and 104 foreigners; but there was a fall soon after. Thomas Thackeray, headmaster 1746-60, restored the school's fortunes; after him, under Robert Sumner 1760-71), another Etonian, appointed at the age of thirty, the numbers rose to 250: at that time Eton had 480 and Westminster about 220-250, both exceptionally high for the period. It was assumed by the scholars that Sumner would be succeeded by Samuel Parr, the second master, and they so informed the governors; when Benjamin Heath—yet again an Etonian—was appointed, there was a riot. After unseemly commotions, Parr seceded with about 40 boys to open a rival school at Stanmore, which expired in 1777.[1] After Heath came Joseph Drury, 1785-1805, under whom were four future prime ministers— Goderich, Peel, Aberdeen, and Palmerston. Under his successor, George Butler, 1805-29, there was a good deal of strife—first on his appointment, when many of the boys, including Byron, wanted Drury's younger brother; there was a rebellion against infringement of monitors' privileges in 1808; and a Chancery suit was brought by the inhabitants of Harrow in 1809-10. During this period the school suffered some decline, which had become serious by the end of Christopher Wordsworth's headmastership (1836-44). Charles Vaughan, 1844-59, a pupil of Thomas Arnold at Rugby, who succeeded Wordsworth, was the real founder of modern Harrow, with Montagu Butler, 1860-85, son of George Butler and the first Harrovian headmaster. In the 20th century Harrow, with over 600 boys, has shown no signs of losing the place it attained in the 18th and 19th. Its eminence is mostly owing, no doubt, to the personalities of its strong headmasters during the last 200 years, but some of it is also due to its situation, ten miles north-west of London, which almost predestined it, as soon as it was firmly established, to be

[1] Historical Manuscripts Commission, *Dartmouth MSS.*, iii. (1896), p. 194; *Du Cane MSS.* (1905), p. 228.

Eton's rival. It has proved strong enough to flourish through the rivalry.

Highgate school was founded in 1565 under the will of Sir Roger Cholmeley, lord chief justice 1552-3, 'for the education, institution, and instruction of boys and youths in grammar at all times for ever to endure.'[1] Sir William Cordell, master of the rolls 1557-81, who carried through the building of the school after Cholmeley's death, was in effect joint founder. New buildings were erected in 1819, and a complete remodelling took place in 1866. It was no more than a modest local grammar school until the 19th century—there were only 19 boys in 1838. Dr. J. B. Dyne, headmaster 1838-74, an administrator as well as a scholar, virtually refounded the school.

Mill Hill school was founded in 1807 for Nonconformists, to whom the established public schools and the universities were barred, but from the outset it was not closed to sons of episcopalian parents.[2] The most famous of the earlier headmasters was Thomas Priestley, 1834-52, but after him the school declined, and in 1868 it was decided to close it. After reconstruction, however, it recovered and flourished, especially under J. D. McClure, 1891-1922.

The first mention of a 'school-house' at Enfield is in 1557, but the will of William Garratt, 1586, was the real foundation of the grammar school. It declined from about 1750 onwards, much as the schools at St Albans and Berkhamsted in Hertfordshire did at the same period. In 1817 there were 104 scholars, boarders having been given up; by 1873 there were no funds available for essential repairs.[3] The school recovered, and it was taken over by the Middlesex County Council in 1909. Robert Uvedale, horticulturist, headmaster 1664-c.1700, and at the same time proprietor of a private school at the Old Palace, was the most notable of the masters.

Hampton school dates, as the inscription on the building just east of the churchyard declares, from 1556, when Robert Hamonde left an endowment worth about £3 a year.[4] It was more liberally provided in 1697 with the proceeds of a fourth part of Nando's coffee-house in Fleet Street. After various rearrangements in the 19th century, a new school was built in 1880. It was similarly taken over by the county council in 1909.

Westminster school has a slight, but once important, connexion with Middlesex.[5] A house at the west end of Chiswick Mall was leased in 1571 to the dean and chapter of Westminster for use, after rebuilding, as a schoolhouse. In the 17th century the scholars were removed there from Westminster during the summertime; in 1603 and 1657 they used it as a refuge from the plague. Later, until about 1760, it was used as a summer residence for the headmaster. When the house was finally sold in 1866, some of the proceeds were applied to building new studies at

[1] C. A. Evors, *Story of Highgate School* (1938). [2] See Mill Hill bibliography, p. 386. [3] S. Smith, *Short History of the Enfield Grammar School* (1931); N. Carlisle, *Concise Description of the Endowed Grammar Schools in England and Wales* (1818), ii., p. 116. [4] *H.C.M.* 3 (1901), p. 90; B. Garside, *History of Hampton School from 1556 to 1700* (1931); Carlisle (see preceding note), ii., p. 118. [5] J. Sargeaunt, *Annals of Westminster School* (1898), p. 35.

Westminster (in Grant's, No. 2 Little Dean's Yard), which are known as 'Chiswicks.'

The villages on the high roads out of London contained many private academies of note and some of distinction between 1700 and 1850. The most famous was the Great School at Ealing, in the Old Rectory House near the church, which was at its best after 1791, when it was taken over by the Rev. D. Nicholas. The numbers soon rose to 300 and in 1820 there were 365 pupils. The father of T. H. Huxley, the scientist, was mathematics master.[1] Ealing was full of schools: Dr. Dodd, later executed for forgery, kept one at the Manor House, and Bulwer Lytton was at Ealing House school in 1817. Shelley, his biographer Medwin, and John Rennie, engineer, were all at Syon House Academy, Brentford End, between 1802 and 1805. This school was kept by Dr. Greenlaw, a Scottish divine of uncertain temper. Medwin wrote that 'Syon House was indeed a perfect hell' to Shelley. 'The least circumstance that thwarted him produced the most violent paroxysms of rage,' wrote Rennie; 'and when irritated by other boys, which they, knowing his infirmity, frequently did by way of teasing him, he would take up anything ... to throw at his tormentors. His imagination was always roving upon something romantic and extraordinary—such as spirits, fairies, fighting, volcanoes, etc.—and he not unfrequently astonished his schoolfellows by blowing up the boundary palings with gunpowder, also the lid of his desk in the middle of school-time, to the great astonishment of Dr. Greenlaw himself and the whole school. In fact, at times he was considered to be on the borders of insanity.'[2]

The young Anthony Ashley Cooper, later Lord Shaftesbury, was just as unhappy at the Manor House, Chiswick, from 1808 onwards. He wrote: At seven went to school—a very large one at Chiswick. Nothing could have surpassed it for filth, bullying, neglect, and hard treatment of every sort; nor had it in any respect one compensating advantage, except, perhaps, it may have given me an early horror of oppression and cruelty. It was very similar to Dotheboys Hall.'[3] That may be; but it is only fair to remember that he was just as miserable at home.

On the northern side of the county were several denominational academies. There was a short-lived Congregational academy at Pinner from about 1696 to 1704 under T. Goodwin the younger; there was a Baptist academy from about 1730 to 1756 at Enfield, under William Tonge, and another, under John Ryland, removed from Northampton to Enfield in 1785 (though this appears to have been an ordinary school and not an academy providing a Nonconformist substitute for a university education). In 1818 there was a 'considerable and respectable seminary for young gentlemen' attached to the Presbyterian church at Uxbridge, where there had been an earlier school kept by Hezekiah Woodward

[1] L. Huxley, *Life and Letters of Thomas Henry Huxley* (1900), p. 1; MS. Diary of B. J. Armstrong; E. Jackson, *Annals of Ealing* (1898), pp. 168, 210. [2] *Autobiography of Sir John Rennie* (1875), p. 2. [3] J. L. and B. Hammond, *Lord Shaftesbury* (Penguin ed., 1939), p. 12.

after the ejections of 1662.[1] In the middle 19th century there was a celebrated Jewish school kept by H. N. Solomon at Edmonton. A succession of Quaker schools flourished at Tottenham from 1707 to 1879. In 1827 the brothers Hill—including Rowland Hill, originator of the penny post—opened at Bruce Castle a branch of their school at Hazelwood, near Birmingham, which had already become well known. It was conducted on 'new principles of generous emulation,' the boys being grouped in circles of ten each, with one as guardian.[2] This school, continued in the family for 50 years, was closed in 1891. About 1810 the Rev. Stephen Freeman kept a school in Baker Street, Enfield, where Frederick Marryat, the novelist, was a pupil; he ran away as often as he could. Keats was until 1810 at the Enfield school founded by Ryland and then kept by John Clarke, father of Charles Cowden Clarke; Edward Holmes, author of the first English life of Mozart, was there at the same time.[3]

The ordinary primary schools of Middlesex developed as in the rest of England: modest origins in the 17th century, with small endowments; sporadic private activity flowing from evangelical and humanitarian motives, followed by reconstitution under the National and British & Foreign Societies, founded in 1811 and 1814; serious inadequacy in the middle 19th century, before the 1870 Education Act; immense expansion under local school boards and the county council since that date. A schoolhouse dating from the first period is happily still to be seen in use at Stanwell (*Plate 58*), founded and endowed by Lord Knyvett in 1624, as the inscription over the door testifies. There were 13 such endowed 'non-classical' schools in Middlesex outside the City of London and Westminster by 1698; a further 21 were established by 1720. An account of 1724 gives the total number of school children within the present county as 517. These schools taught the three Rs, some handicrafts, perhaps Latin; and they were often connected with a clothing charity.[4]

Enthusiasm for schooling abated during the middle years of the 18th century, but about 1780 interest, especially in Sunday schools, was renewed. This was principally owing to the evangelical revival in the Church of England. The pious and formidable Mrs. Trimmer, of Brentford, was a pioneer in the good work. The Sunday schools in Ealing, founded in 1786, were attended, according to Lysons, 'with the most beneficial effects to the morals and manners of the poor in consequence of their excellent regulations and the zealous and persevering attention of Mrs. Trimmer.' Schools of industry for weekday employment of Sunday-school children followed quickly and produced direct benefits: 'In 1787 a school of industry for 40 girls was grafted on the Sunday schools, which among other advantages has furnished to society many well-principled domestic servants. The chief employment

[1] *Transactions of the Congregational History Society* 6 (1915), p. 137; 11 (1932), p. 28; H. McLachlan, *English Education under the Test Acts* (1931), p. 12; S. J. Price, 'Dissenting Academies, 1662-1820', *Baptist Quarterly* NS 6 (1933), p. 125. [2] W. Keane, *Beauties of Middlesex* (1850), p. 84; *Sketch of the System, Moral and Intellectual, in Practice at Bruce Castle School, Tottenham, near London* (1837). [3] R. D. Altick, *Cowden Clarkes* (1948), pp. 11, 13; C. C. Clarke, 'The School-House of Keats at Enfield', *St. James's Holiday Annual for 1875*. [4] For these paragraphs, M. G. Jones, *Charity School Movement* (1938), pp. 22, 83, 150, 337, and appendices.

of the girls in the school is plain needlework; they are allowed half their earnings.' It was not, however, a success.

Mrs. Trimmer has a special place in the history of educational reform. She addressed some significant remarks to young ladies of the upper classes in *The Œconomy of Charity* (1801), urging them to teach in schools; ignorance need not deter them, she said, and the disgusting circumstances of a crowd of ragged children should not. She departed from the orthodox practice of teaching little children only from the Bible, Prayer Book, and Catechism by writing books suitable for their understanding; her *Story of the Robins* (1786) remained in the S.P.C.K. list for 70 years, and a quarter of a million copies were sold. Possibly Rousseau's ideas on education had influenced her—though she would certainly have repudiated any such suggestion.[1]

Progress was not fast. Marshall wrote in 1799 that the children of farm labourers near London were among the most illiterate in the island; few, unless of late years at Sunday schools, were taught even to read.[2] In 1843 Henry Tremenheere published a statistical account of the schools round about Ealing.[2] He found them on the whole in a low state. In his official prose: 'It is considered right to abstain from entering into any details respecting the efficiency of the schools; but it was obvious that with very limited exceptions they were not such as were calculated to satisfy those who would wish to see the education of the labouring classes effectively conducted.' Out of the 21 dame-schools in the area, 11 were kept by poor widows who derived their sole subsistence from them; two teachers solicited charity at his visits. There was a national school in each parish: at Ealing ('where Wilhelm's system of singing had recently been introduced') it was endowed; at Hanwell it was supplied by subscriptions; at Old Brentford, Mrs. Trimmer's girls' school, there was a charge of 1d. a week. At Acton the only reading was the Bible; needlework and knitting, in which the boys joined, filled the greater part of every afternoon. There was also an institution of another kind, Lady Noel Byron's school at Ealing, 'combining industrial training with elementary instruction.'

Under the 1870 Education Act, local school boards were elected to provide elementary education in areas where voluntary provision was not adequate. In Middlesex this meant in effect the inner part of the county bordering on London, where the high blocks of board-school buildings may be seen in Acton, Willesden, and Tottenham. The Middlesex County Council became responsible for elementary education in 14 out of the 26 local government 'county districts' under the 1902 act, and it is the authority for higher education throughout the whole county. The county council boldly dealt with an average increase of 4,500 children a year in its elementary schools in the decade 1928 to

---

[1] Halévy (page 7, note 5), ii., p. 155; *Edinburgh Review* 9 (1806), p. 177.   [2] Marshall, p. 25.
[3] Tremenheere (page 40, note 2).

1938 by much new building, most of it in an admirable style (*Plate 59*). Less grand, but not less notable, is the school for canal children on a barge at West Drayton.

* * * * *

Charity schools were only one among many benefactions enjoyed by the villages of old Middlesex.[1] Until the reforming brooms of the 19th century swept them into tidy heaps, parish charities supplied children with schooling, youths with apprenticeships, the poor with bread and coals, and the old with almshouses, as well as providing for more strictly ecclesiastical needs. Not every parish was equally well served: Uxbridge and Enfield were well endowed, and the feoffees of the Finchley charities were the most important people in the parish; but at Feltham, when Lysons was collecting material for his *Middlesex Parishes* about 1795-7, there were no charities, and at Shepperton there was nothing but the rental of an acre and a half for church purposes; both places later acquired some endowments. Not all the old charities have been rationalised away under 'schemes'; the inhabitants of the ancient parish of Hornsey still have a local fuel charity, and bread is distributed from a handsome 17th-century wooden cupboard in Ruislip church.

Most of the medieval endowments disappeared, to the benefit of the Crown, during the 16th century, but Hobbayne's benefaction at Hanwell, applied in 1781 to a school, was continuous from 1484 and the Finchley charity from 1486.[2] The 16th-century benefactions were mainly for bread, clothing, and fuel; in the 17th century donors preferred to build almshouses, like those at Tottenham by Balthasar Sanchez, a naturalised Spanish confectioner, and Harefield, by Lady Derby. After 1700 most new benefactions were devoted to schools, but Horace Walpole's gift at Twickenham was expended on coals.

All this is familiar in most English counties. Middlesex perhaps gained something more than its fair share by legacies under the wills of wealthy Londoners who had retired to live not far from the capital. Against this, land was constantly changing hands, and property being subdivided; this made it difficult to keep charity land identified, and much was quietly appropriated. Lord Coleraine compiled a history of Tottenham about 1705 expressly to leave a record and prevent further losses of benefactions.

There were a few curious features among Middlesex endowments. At Chiswick, Brentford, Ealing, and Hanworth, the church rate, from which some charities were supplied, was supplemented by the profits on public sports and diversions, especially at Whitsuntide; drinking in the church house was a favourite source of income. 'Throwing at cocks,' a popular

---

[1] For the charities, see Lysons and most of the topographers. [2] 1485, given by Lysons and by W. B. Passmore, *Bygone Finchley*, No 1 (1904), p. 4, is the old-style date.

sport at Pinner in the 17th century, earned money for charities; some of
the market profits at Uxbridge were similarly applied. At Brentford, with
singular good management, money left for a coal charity was used to
build a gallery in the church; the parson let the pews and, after deducting
the interest on the original sum to be applied to coals, appropriated the
remainder for himself. Mrs. Barbara Burnell overstepped the usual
parochial limits at Stanmore in her provision of clothing—'safeguards and
waistcoats'—for six poor women; they were to be chosen in alternate
years from Stanmore parish and from Bushey, Harrow Weald, and
Edgware. At Twickenham there were strange survivals of ancient
customs: two 'great cakes' were divided in the church on Easter Day
among the young people until Parliament commanded in 1645 that this
superstitious relic should be converted into an ordinary bread charity.[1]
Even then some gaiety attended the distribution: well into the 18th
century the bread was thrown from the top of the tower to be scrambled
for in the churchyard. Some of the distributions required attendance at
Divine Service, at any rate on the qualifying day: Paul Jervis left 20
shillings for an annual sermon in South Mimms church on Christmas Eve
and 40 shillings to be distributed among the poor attending it; Edward
Dickinson left money in 1781 for distribution to three poor couples,
being deemed labouring, honest, industrious, and sober persons, married
in Acton church during the preceding year; and John Crosse provided in
1772 for a copy of *The Whole Duty of Man* to be presented to every couple
married in Hendon church.

There were few medical charities among all these benefactions.
There was a lazar-house, or lepers' hospital, at the foot of Highgate Hill
from medieval times, but Middlesex has no long history of medical
foundations, and few of its past worthies have been doctors. If Middlesex
folk needed hospital treatment they were sent to London. The Hornsey
overseers' accounts for 1774 record 6s. paid for the admission of one
Horten or Haughton to St Thomas's hospital and another 13s. 10d. for
conveying him there.[2] A dispensary was opened at Brentford in 1818.
The first hospitals in the modern sense were at Tottenham, where a lying-
in charity was established as early as 1791 and a free dispensary was
opened in 1864. Dr. Michael Laseron, a German homoeopathic
physician, founded a deaconesses' institution and training hospital on
Tottenham Green in 1868, on the model of the German one at
Kaiserswerth (where Florence Nightingale was trained); this has
developed into the Prince of Wales's hospital on the same site. Five
general hospitals, established in the later 19th century by boards of
guardians, passed to the county council in 1930, and these, with two
large tuberculosis sanatoria at Harefield and Clare Hall, South Mimms,
were taken over by the regional hospital board in 1948.

[1] Davies (page 95, note 2), p. 394. [2] F. W. M. Draper, 'Two Studies in the Hornsey Church
Books', *Trans. L. Mx. A. S.* NS 10 (1951), p. 41.

There was more provision for mental illness, both publicly and privately. Humane methods of care for the insane, first effectively introduced by William Tuke, a Quaker philanthropist, at the Retreat, York, in 1793, were developed by his grandson, Samuel Tuke, who established an asylum at the Manor Farm House, Chiswick, in 1824; it was transferred under Dr. Seymour Tuke to Chiswick House in 1895. The first place where Tuke's principles, involving abandonment of instruments of severe restraint, were applied on a large scale was Hanwell asylum (it lay in fact in Norwood parish, but the name is firmly affixed to it). This institution, built by the county, was opened in 1831, and Dr. John Conolly introduced the new treatment there in 1839. The asylum printing press was working for outside contract in 1849.[1] Colney Hatch asylum, built in 1851, was an immense block for 2,000 patients. A private asylum was established by Sir William Ellis at Southall Park;[2] there were two at Hayes, and one at Wyke House, Osterley, in the later 19th century. These districts were favoured for asylums as they were for schools, being far enough away from town for the inmates to be secluded but not too far for an occasional visit.

* * * * *

Besides the necessary associations of the inhabitants in the parish or the manor for the transaction of their affairs, voluntary associations were formed to meet fresh needs that the parish and manor machinery did not satisfy. This naturally happened first where settlement was thickest and people wanted the amenities of town life. A book society, or circulating library, was begun at Highgate before 1789; there was a circulating library at Brentford, which Shelley used while he was at school in 1802-5, and one that Charles Lamb complained of at Enfield in 1830. Two book societies were established at Uxbridge in 1811 and 1815—the second one possessing 'besides a very respectable collection of volumes, amounting to near four hundred, ... an electrical machine and several other philosophical instruments.' A literary and scientific institution, which still flourishes, was founded at Highgate in 1839; there were others at Twickenham and Staines. An assembly room at Edmonton is referred to in 1776, but this must have been of a very modest character. Mechanics' institutions were established for the lower orders at Tottenham and Edmonton and at Brentford about 1835; a book of verse by members of the Brentford institution was published in 1843. But in the greater part of Middlesex—as at Acton, for example, and Chiswick—there was no library accessible to the public without charge until the last decade of the century. The first one at Harrow-on-the-Hill was opened in 1950.

Voluntary effort was early engaged in stimulating thrift among the

[1] Gibbon and Bell (page 67, note 2), pp. 12, 344; Draper (page 125, note 5), p. 187. The 1849 edition of B. J. Armstrong, *Account of the Parish of Little Stanmore*, was printed at the Hanwell asylum press.   [2] E. Mogg, *Handbook for Railway Travellers* (ed. 2, 1840), p. 231.

lower and middle classes. The Tottenham Quakers were responsible for the important innovation of a savings bank. Priscilla Wakefield began a bank for the poor at Tottenham in 1804, now generally accepted as the first true savings bank of the modern type; it had been preceded in 1798 by a children's bank.[1] The savings bank movement soon spread: one was set up at Uxbridge in 1816 and another at Brentford in 1818. Tottenham also had 'the Accumulating Fund Society,' a building society for the middle class operating in 1843.[2]

Armed associations for the preservation of order and social peace were formed as part of the auxiliary forces of the Crown; they had the blessing, if not always the very active encouragement, of the War Office. Fire brigades depended on local exertions. Uxbridge paid £48 for an engine in 1770, and another £14 for building an engine-house; the Sun Fire Office gave £20 towards these expenses. In 1772 Edmonton was presented with an engine, and Abraham Draper was appointed organ-blower at the church and at the same time 'unanimously elected to the office of engineer, or engine keeper, to the engine.' Five fire engines were on the scene at a rick fire at Tottenham in 1839.[3] Regularly organised volunteer fire brigades were formed in most of the urban areas from 1870 onwards; class distinctions were still observed in them, as in the Staines brigade, which consisted in 1880 of captain, first officer, second officer and engineer, nine gentlemen, and four working men.[4] As late as 1866 Acton, a place of nearly 5,000 inhabitants, had no fire engine of any kind; but from the 1880s local boards began to organise brigades seriously.

Newspapers, which might have reported all these local affairs and focused local interest, were singularly lacking in Middlesex until after the repeal of the stamp duties on the press in 1855. The standard *Census of British Newspapers and Periodicals* down to 1800 can show no Middlesex local newspaper. The oldest of the county papers is the *Middlesex Advertiser*, of Uxbridge, founded at Amersham, Buckinghamshire, in 1840 by William Broadwater, a dispensing chemist, as *Broadwater's Journal*. It soon gained a circulation over an area (the claim was 'from Hammer-smith to Oxford and Staines to Watford') more easily served from Uxbridge, and the paper was removed there, as the *Middlesex Advertiser*, in 1860. The *Middlesex Couny Times*, of 1863, includes the *Ealing Post* of 1842 as one of its constituents; otherwise the older Middlesex newspapers date from the late fifties, at Harrow, Hounslow, and Enfield.[5]

* * * * *

Sport has occupied no less a place in Middlesex social life than in any other English county. Indeed, Middlesex signifies to many thousands

---

[1] Clapham, *Modern Britain*, i., p. 298; H. O. Horne, *History of Savings Banks* (1947), p. 25. [2] Dean (page 54, note 5). [3] *Bruce Castle Magazine* (1839), p. 116. [4] *Dickens's Dictionary of the Thames* (1880), p. 198. [5] *Tercentenary Handlist of English and Welsh Magazines, Newspapers, and Reviews* (*Times*, 1920); R. S. Crane and F. B. Kaye, *Census of British Newspapers and Periodicals* (1925); *Johnson's England*, ed. A. S. Turberville (1933), ii., p. 351; *Middlesex Advertiser*, 5 November 1948; *Willing's Press Guide* (annual).

of people nothing more than the cricket team that plays at Lord's, and many thousands more who care nothing for Pope or Horace Walpole know the name of Twickenham well: it is the place where Rugby internationals are played. The 'Middlesex station' is the one selected by a confident captain who wins the toss in the university boat race; Wembley represents the summit of an Association footballer's ambition, for the cup final is played there; so is the Rugby League final; the Olympic Games of 1948 were principally held at Wembley, and the marathon race was run round Stanmore and Edgware. Almost all kinds of modern sport, except those which require large open spaces of land or water, have their headquarters or their principal contests in the county.

The great original sport, however, has been thrust out. The history of hunting in Middlesex has ended, giving way before the imperious demands of cultivation and housing, but in former ages it was of high importance. Royal hunting-grounds within convenient distance of the capital were retained by preserving large tracts round Hampton Court and Enfield Chase in their wild state, and the humbler citizenry found sport in the Middlesex woods.[1]

Deer and hares were hunted from Hampton by succeeding sovereigns; William III called it 'villainous country' for stag-hunting, but Anne and the first two Georges found it agreeable enough—George II indeed would not give it up in the summer. The other royal chase, Enfield, much larger, was not so much favoured, though Elizabeth hunted there from Enfield and James I from Theobalds Park.[2]

The earlier county records show singularly few prosecutions for breaking into game preserves. There was some poaching, of course: in 1569 Matthew Vincent of Ickenham, not having land worth 40s. a year, broke into the Earl of Derby's park at Hillingdon after rabbits; in 1574 three yeomen of Enfield broke into the chase; in 1649 there were two convictions for killing deer in Enfield chase 'with guns charged with gunpowder and bullets'; in 1658, when Cromwell was lord of the manor, three men of Teddington were charged with 'taking and destroying seventy hares with cords and other instruments nigh unto the hare warren of the Lord Protector within the honour of Hampton Court.' After this the records of such prosecutions are very scanty; probably it was beyond the power of the magistrates to restrain the dwellers round about the remaining parks, and they did not try. Still, the game laws remained in force into the 19th century; in 1869 there were 131 prosecutions in Middlesex, all but four for trespassing in pursuit of game in the daytime.

George Grantley Berkeley, who tried to maintain the sport at Cranford from 1824 to 1836, wrote that, for its size, no place had such a stock of pheasants and hares.[3] There was pheasant shooting at Osterley

---

[1] For these paragraphs, *V.C.H.* ii., p. 253.   [2] *V.C.H.* ii., p. 225.   [3] G. C. G. F. Berkeley, *Reminiscences of a Huntsman* (ed. 1897), p. 11.

in the 1830s, and at Southall 'considering the vicinity to London ... very fair sport.'[1] As late as the 1901 census 60 persons in Middlesex were returned as gamekeepers.

Berkeley formed a pack of staghounds at Cranford, for which the hounds were sent up from Berkeley Castle, in Gloucestershire, for the season. He wrote an amusing account of Middlesex hunting in his *Reminiscences of a Huntsman* (1854), which reveals plainly enough why he could never get on with his neighbours for long. His runs were mostly over the Harrow country, which was heavily farmed and populated by fellows holding strong views against hunting. 'The farmers of the Harrow Vale were certainly the most untoward set of men to deal with I ever saw,' he wrote. They served him with notice not to trespass and then made their own estimates of the amount of damage done; the hunt raised a public fund for damage, which only put up the price; then individual riders were cut off, impounded, and forced to buy their way out. Quaint incidents were bound to happen in country already so thickly populated; a stag enlarged at Kingsbury ran into London by Regent's Park and had to be taken on the steps of No. 1 Montague Street, Russell Square, whose owner threatened to send for the beadle if the animal was not removed; another was taken inside the house of a gentleman who burst out to Berkeley: 'Your stag, sir, not content with walking through every office, has been here, sir, here in my drawing-room, sir, whence he proceeded upstairs to the nursery, and damme, sir, he's now in Mrs. ——'s boudoir.' But the farmers would not be pacified, even by a dinner given to them and coursing for all who kept or could borrow greyhounds, with presents of game and occasionally venison. Finally a lawsuit brought for trespass and assault (summed up, Berkeley avers, with 'great partiality for the complainant's case' by Lord Tenterden) forced him to remove from the district.

In spite of his quarrels, Berkeley thought the country a good one: 'The land in winter is so wet and badly drained that, in the state it was when I hunted over it, it would not carry sheep. The grass and the absence of sheep made it the finest possible ground for holding a scent; at the same time I have no hesitation in saying that it was the deepest country I ever crossed with hounds.' The hunt ran a stag once from Harlington Corner nearly to Guildford; another time down the river to Brentford. Lord Alvanley, asked what sport there was on this occasion, replied: 'Devilish good run; but the asparagus beds were awfully heavy, and the grass all through was up to one's hocks; the only thing wanting was a landing-net, for the deer got into the Thames and Berkeley had not the means to get him ashore. They say that garden-stuff is ris since they saw us among 'em.'

A pack was started at Enfield by Sir Alfred Somerset in 1885, with

[1] MS. Diary of B. J. Armstrong.

Queen Elizabeth's uniform for the hunt servants, scarlet coat and orange cap, but was removed in 1899 over the Hertfordshire border.[1] The Royal Buckhounds hunted from Windsor into the west of the county; there were regular meets at Hounslow and Sunbury from 1698 to 1739, with runs up to 40 miles. This pack, too, was pelted with pitchforks if it got into the Harrow country.[2] B. J. Armstrong wrote of Middlesex meets in 1838: 'Nothing could be more brilliant than the meets of the Royal Pack at this time; they were attended by most of the sporting nobility then in London, and the show of horses and of elegantly dressed ladies on horseback and in carriages at the place of appointment was well worth riding a few miles to see, independently of the first-rate sport which invariably followed.' He was out with the same pack in January 1839 when a stag running from Southall towards Hounslow got on to the Great Western Railway and a train was derailed by running over a horse.[3] In 1868 the Prince of Wales took part when a stag ran from Denham Court past Pinner over Harrow Hill to Wormwood Scrubs; it was eventually taken at Paddington goods station, and the hunt then rode through Hyde Park and down Constitution Hill to accompany the Prince to Marlborough House.[4]

The only pack of foxhounds was the Old Berkeley (the 'old' was added in 1820), which hunted all the country from Scratch Wood (described rather puzzlingly by Nimrod as 'part of Wormwood Scrubs') to Cirencester, or alternatively from Kensington Gardens to Berkeley Castle and Bristol. (In another version, 'from Barnet to Bath, with leave to draw the Zoological Gardens.'[5]) The hunt wore tawny coats, in commemoration of the pack of an earlier Lord Berkeley, who hunted the country round Charing Cross in this colour. It constantly met opposition, even at the height of the hunting age: John Middleton the agriculturist was severe on it in 1798, when he referred to 'the greatest of all vermin, to a cultivated country, *hunters*. (Note) Those lovers of a savage life are as unfit for a cultivated country, as are the stinking objects (foxes) of their pursuit.'[6] In 1808 there was a well-attended protest meeting at Stanmore, representing landowners and farmers of Harrow, Pinner, Watford, and Stanmore, with the Earl of Essex in the chair and three other peers subscribing to a motion protesting against hunting. 'However harmless an amusement hunting might be in certain parts of the kingdom,' it declared, 'yet near the metropolis land was of so great a value, with scarcely an acre left unenclosed, the practice of hunting was attended with injuries too serious to be tolerated.' The hunt issued a counter-proclamation. The dispute was taken to law, and the hunt lost a claim for damages.[7]

The field at this time consisted of 100 to 150 horsemen, and the crowd attending the meets became embarrassing as time went on. Finally

[1] *V.C.H. Hertfordshire* i. (1902), p. 359.   [2] J. P. Hore, *History of the Royal Buckhounds* (1895).
[3] MS. Diary of B. J. Armstrong; *Times*, 14 January 1839.   [4] *V.C.H.* ii., p. 262, quoting Lord Ribblesdale, *Queen's Hounds and Stag-hunting Recollections* (1897), p. 147.   [5] *V.C.H. Hertfordshire* i. (1902), p. 356.   [6] Middleton, p. 135.   [7] *Mx. & H. N. & Q.* 3 (1897), pp. 74, 160.

the Old Berkeley was obliged not to advertise meets, 'in order to avoid the pressure of a swarm of nondescripts who, starting from every suburb in London, were glad to make a meet of foxhounds their excuse for a holiday on hackney or wagonette, overwhelming the whole procedure by their presence and irritating farmers and landowners, to the great injury of the hunt.' In 1878 there was still near Harrow 'a small stretch of as good grass as could be ridden over anywhere in England.'[1] Finally, however, the hunt was divided in 1883 into the Old Berkeley East, since 1885 at Chorleywood, Hertfordshire, and the Old Berkeley West, at Hazlemere, Buckinghamshire; they were reunited in 1952. The country of the Enfield Chase foxhounds also lies outside Middlesex. There has been foxhunting of a different kind since the packs withdrew from the suburban districts; wild foxes, which have interfered with domestic rabbits and fowls, have been reported recently as shot on Hampstead Heath and at Muswell Hill and Mill Hill.[2]

The parks at Hampton and Osterley provided coursing, and it was carried on by clubs in the Home Park till the end of the 19th century. There was a pack of harriers at Cranford about 1800, another at Hornsey and Southgate about 1817, Mr. Westbrook's at Heston soon after, at Bedfont in 1840 and at Hampton about ten years later.[3] John Norden reported 'a fair warren of conies' at South Mimms in 1593, and there was a great rabbit-warren on Uxbridge common until the enclosure in 1816.

The earliest mention of horse-racing in the county is at Enfield Chase in James I's reign, when a golden bell was the prize, and there were meetings on Hounslow Heath in the 18th century. The most important contribution to the sport, however, was the Royal Stud in the Home Park, Hampton Court. Prince George of Denmark, Queen Anne's husband, took a great interest in breeding, and the stud was much developed in her reign. Under George IV, William IV, and Victoria some of the best horses in the country were bred there. The earliest race-meeting under modern conditions was held at Enfield in 1788, but the company was neither numerous nor fashionable, and the races expired, like other Enfield festivals, soon after 1822. During the 19th century there were also races at Hounslow Heath, at Harefield, later at West Drayton (in 1875 'among the most frequented of the lower-class suburban gatherings'), at Hendon, near the Welsh Harp, at Headstone Lane, Pinner, and a revival at Enfield on Windmill Hill. The present racecourses are at Alexandra Park, established in 1888, and Kempton Park, in 1889. Polo was initiated in England about 1870 by a match at Hounslow between the 10th Hussars, who brought the game from India, and the 9th Lancers, and there was later a club at Wembley Park.

The most respectable of the ancient pastimes for the lower orders

[1] *Middlesex: Biographical and Pictorial* (1907), art. Old Berkeley Hunt; *V.C.H.* ii., p.260, quoting 'Brooksby' [E. P. Elmhirst], *Hunting Countries of England* (1878). [2] *Times*, 22 June 1939, 26 January 1948; R. S. R. Fitter, *London's Natural History* (1945), p. 194. [3] *H.C.M.* 1 (1899), p. 259; MS. Diary of B. J. Armstrong (Osterley and Bedfont); Hassell, pp. 30, 212 (Hornsey and Southgate); Berkeley (page 140, note 3), p. 18 (Heston).

was archery, which was officially encouraged in every village, even to the banning of its principal competitor, football. Under an act of 1541 a penalty of 40s. a day was imposed on the playing of unlawful games, including bowls, quoits, and tennis. This was intended to protect archery, and the statute was enforced; in 1557 a Twickenham bricklayer was prosecuted for being a 'maintainer' of bowls.[1] Archery had its dangers; accidental deaths during practice were recorded at South Mimms and Hendon in 1560 and at Hampton in 1568. At Harrow school there was a regular competition for a silver arrow until 1771, when Dr. Heath stopped it.

Pigeon-shooting became fashionable about 1790. The Old Hats inn at Ealing was a favourite place; another was Willesden; and Hornsey Wood House was the scene of notable matches about the middle of the 19th century until it was closed in 1866 to make way for Finsbury Park. High towers for shooting remained in use near Kingsbury until about 1930, and at Down Barns, Northolt, twenty years later. There were complaints of pigeon-shooting to the public danger on Eel Pie Island in 1881.[2]

By the beginning of the 19th century Hampton was renowned as an angling station. T. C. Hofland described the Thames fishing in his *British Angler's Manual* of 1839: 'Salmon have been driven from the river by the gasworks and steam navigation, not one having been caught to my knowledge during the last twelve or fourteen years ... the last salmon I saw taken, in a net, was opposite Twickenham meadow in the year 1818.' As late as 1839 the lord mayor held a court of conservancy on his barge at Teddington lock for illegal fishing cases.[3] The Thames Angling Preservation Society, founded at Hampton in 1838, has made the twenty miles above Teddington one of the finest stretches for coarse fishing in the country, by preservation and restocking.

Though the Thames is the premier river of Middlesex, it must always take second place to the Lea in the affections of anglers, for on its banks Piscator gently explained the mysteries of his art. The scenes of Izaak Walton's *Compleat Angler* have given way to a dreary landscape; it is even doubtful where his riverside inns stood. Still, the Lea has remained a well-patronised stream, and trout have been introduced into it. There is fishing in the Colne at West Drayton, but the Brent, apart from the Welsh Harp reservoir, must have been too much polluted to be worth fishing during the last hundred years.

A rustic game was being played at Twickenham in 1747 when Horace Walpole went to live at Strawberry Hill: 'Lord John Sackville *predecessed* me here, and instituted certain games called *cricketalia*, which have been celebrated this very evening in honour of him in a neighbouring meadow.' There had been cricket on Laleham Burway early in the 18th century, and village matches were being played in 1774

[1] *M.C.R. Reports*, p. 18. [2] Thacker, *Locks and Weirs* (page 52, note 4), p. 478. [3] MS. Diary of B. J. Armstrong.

when John Yeoman walked to Ealing to see 'a Grand Cricket Match, Eleven of a side Southall and Norwood People against Ealing; it is the same as the children play in our Country [Somerset] only they play to the Truth of the play,' whatever that may have meant.[1] The earliest school match recorded between Eton and Westminster was played on Hounslow Heath in 1796; Westminster won by 66 runs. Cricket was played at Harrow in 1772, and there was a match against Eton in 1800. Byron made 7 and 2 for Harrow in another match in 1805, and since 1822 the fixture has been an annual institution, played at Lord's from 1854 onwards. The greatest Harrovian cricketers were I. D. Walker, A. G. Maclaren, and F. S. Jackson.

Middlesex county cricket began in 1863, largely owing to the exertions of the Walker family of Southgate, commemorated by a tablet on their house, Arnos Grove. There were seven cricketing brothers, who formed a considerable proportion of the Sixteen of Southgate who played a United All-England team each year from 1858 to 1863. The county club, established in 1864, first played at the old cattle market at Islington; like Gloucestershire, the original team were almost all amateurs. Middlesex cricket has its great names: the Hearnes, B. J. T. Bosanquet, Alfred Lyttelton, P. F. Warner, E. Hendren, D. Compton, and W. J. Edrich; but its home ground has always been within the London county area. Middlesex has won the county championship five times and in 1949 tied for it with Yorkshire.[2]

The earliest mention of football in Middlesex is in the records of the justices of the peace; it was clearly a licentious occupation which aroused the worst passions. At Ruislip in 1576 five men of the village and seven from Uxbridge 'with unknown malefactors to the number of a hundred assembled themselves unlawfully and played a certain unlawful game, called football, by reason of which unlawful game there arose amongst them a great affray, likely to result in homicides and serious accidents.' At South Mimms in 1583 there was a homicide during a football match, but it appears that this arose out of an existing enmity. In 1618 a draper of Edgware was summoned for abusing the constable of Little Stanmore and 'telling him that he would not come to the musters, and dissuading others, asking them if they would go see a football play.'[3]

The principal Middlesex club is Tottenham Hotspur, which has played at White Hart Lane since 1899 and won the cup in 1901. Football Association cup finals have been held at Wembley since 1923, when 120,000 people attempted to witness the game. The majority of clubs in the original Rugby Union of 1871 came from Middlesex; its international ground was opened at Twickenham in 1908. Harrow school retains its own variety of football, evolved to suit the adhesive clay of its fields; the Rugby game has also been played at Harrow since 1928.[4]

[1] H. S. Altham and E. W. Swanton, *History of Cricket* (ed. 4, 1948), p. 31; *John Yeoman* (page 50, note 1), p. 46. [2] W. A. Bettesworth, *Walkers of Southgate* (1900), pp. 34, 168; Altham and Swanton (preceding note); *Middlesex County Cricket Club* (i., 1864-99, W. J. Ford; ii., 1900-20, F. S. A. Cooper; iii., 1921-47, N. Haig). [3] *M.C.R.* i., p. 97 (Ruislip), p. 138 (South Mimms); *M.C.R. Reports*, p. 32 (Edgware). [4] For these paragraphs, *V.C.H.* ii., p. 253.

The oldest surviving tennis court in England, built in 1529-30, is at Hampton Court. Henry VIII played there often; so did Charles II, William III, who renovated it, the Prince Consort, and Edward VII. As well as this court, called the 'close tennis play'—it was enclosed, with a glazed window protected with wire—there was an 'open tennis play.' The closed court is still in good repair and in regular use. The game of squash rackets originated at Harrow school about 1850.[1]

Rowing on the Thames as a sport for amateurs began early in the 19th century. Then endurance rather than high speed seems to have been the test: the Amicus cutter club's crew rowed from Westminster to Gravesend, Gravesend to Twickenham, and Twickenham to Westminster in 1821. Westminster school rowing began with six-oared boats, of which the earliest recorded is in 1813. Racing against Eton was stopped by the authorities of both schools in 1820, and long expeditions up the river took its place: to Hampton and back in 1820 in the *Defiance*, to Sunbury on 26 May 1821 ('it snowed during a great part of this expedition, and the crew were obliged to eat their provisions in an inn at Hampton'), and in the eight-oared *Challenge* to Eton and back, about 84 miles in 21 hours (14 hours' rowing), in 1825.[2] The university boat race was first rowed over the Putney-Mortlake course in 1845 when it was transferred from Henley.

This summary account has not touched on all the distinct forms of Middlesex sport and athletics even by name; lawn tennis, golf, swimming, boxing, and almost every other kind of organised sport and pastime have their place in the county. Sport links the Middlesex past with the present day, but its characteristic form changed about 1870 from something essentially individualist to a more highly organised social activity, for the benefit of spectators as well as contestants. The social structure was beginning to change very rapidly, in Middlesex even faster than elsewhere in England outside the industrial districts; this was the real watershed between the present era and the one before, which the label 'Victorian age' does its best to obscure. Since about 1700 there has been a fairly vigorous independent local life in Middlesex, though it was always subject to the pull of London. It was based on difference of class and occupation within the community of local interest, both in the comparatively prosperous villages that depended on agriculture and in the superior residential suburbs along the Thames and north of London. After 1870, as agriculture was resignedly awaiting extinction, the new suburbs as they arose belatedly tried to work out new ways of living together suited to communities leading split lives. This must be the theme of another chapter.

[1] [P. A. Negretti and M. G. L. Bruce], *Royal Tennis Court, Hampton Court Palace* [1950]; Laborde (page 130, note 3), p. 201. [2] Anon., *Rowing at Westminster from 1813 to 1883* (1890), p. 2.

CHAPTER XI

LITERATURE AND THE ARTS

'Cities and towns, the various haunts of men,
Require the pencil; they defy the pen.'
GEORGE CRABBE, *The Borough*

T HE list of writers and artists who have lived and worked in the villages and suburbs of Middlesex is long, and it contains many distinguished names, such as no city or county in England, except London itself, can rival; but very little of their work has its roots firmly planted in Middlesex soil. The surface and culture of the little county were hardly distinguishable from those of the surrounding area; so no provincial school arose with a distinctive Middlesex character. The main stream of metropolitan literature flowed too strong and deep and embanked to leave many local backwaters. There was no Middlesex peasant poet like John Clare in Northamptonshire or William Barnes in Dorset; there is no modern school of regional novelists; and few painters have drawn inspiration from its unpretentious landscapes or, presumably, would have found a very ready market for disposing of its scenes if they had painted them.

The Muses, then, have never fixed their bower in Middlesex; but they have sometimes taken lodgings in the best-favoured parts of the county for week-end visits from town. Throughout the finest age of English literature Middlesex villages and the Thames riverside supplied poets and novelists with patterns for their descriptions of rural life; indeed, some of these writers knew hardly any other countryside. Between 1700 and 1850 almost the whole English cultivated world was at Twickenham at some time, to call on Pope or Walpole or Turner or Dickens; and for a shorter period, while Charles and Mary Lamb were living at Enfield and Edmonton, the modest charms of the northern parts won some recognition. Since 1850, however, and especially in the last fifty years, the writer and the artist have been hard to find in Middlesex;

they have migrated from the outer suburbs, either inwards to Hampstead or Chelsea, or else to some thatched cottage farther afield.

Many places in the county, therefore, have been associated with literature and the arts in past ages. There are almost countless allusions in literature to Middlesex places, and some to Middlesex characters; but many of the associations have been almost accidental, and the following account can hardly avoid being scrappy, because it has no lasting and vigorous native tradition to record. Yet, with all this conceded, it emerges that Middlesex has imparted a characteristic cast to some periods in the grand succession of English art and literature.

Apart from an anonymous satirical ballad, 'The Tournament of Tottenham,' of about 1450, preserved in Bishop Percy's *Reliques of Ancient English Poetry*, literature specifically associated with Middlesex began at Hampton Court. John Skelton sourly adverted in his thumping satires against Wolsey to the magnificence of the palace buildings and appointments and the extravagant state that was maintained there; George Cavendish, the cardinal's gentleman usher, admirer, and biographer in prose and verse, treated the same subjects with respectful admiration. Thereafter down to the present century visitors, novelists, travellers, and diarists have viewed and appraised Hampton Court, and sometimes set their hands to describing it: John Evelyn, Samuel Pepys, and Celia Fiennes in their 17th-century diaries; Alexander Pope in *The Rape of the Lock*; John Wesley in his journal; and later writers from Nathaniel Hawthorne and William Morris to Jerome K. Jerome and John Galsworthy.

Writing about Hampton Court is thus in a class of its own, because it has been done by visitors. The descriptions have been travel sketches, or set pieces. Most of the earliest literary allusions to other parts of the county have had even slighter connexion with its own life. Brentford was slightly known by the dramatists of the Elizabethan age. Shakespeare did not place any of his scenes in Middlesex, but he got Falstaff out of Mistress Ford's house in *The Merry Wives* of *Windsor* by disguising him as Mother Prat, the fat woman of Brentford. The Three Pigeons inn, the principal hostelry of the place, appeared in Ben Jonson's *Alchemist* of 1610 and in George Peele's *Merrie Conceited Jestes* of 1627, and the town was unamiably mentioned by a good many later writers; Johnson placed it in unflattering comparison with Glasgow.

Higher up the Thames there was a flowering of writers among the aristocratic circle that settled within the influence of Hampton Court. At Whitton, in Twickenham parish, Sir John Suckling was born, remembered for the lyrics in his plays and for inventing the game of cribbage; Margaret Howard, whose marriage to Roger Boyle in 1641 was the occasion of Suckling's best-known poem, the *Ballad on a Wedding*, was born at Isleworth; William, Thomas, and Henry Killigrew, three dramatist brothers, were baptised at Hanworth. John Donne was often at the Countess of Bedford's house at Twickenham between 1605 and 1610 and wrote a poem called *Twicknam Garden*, but it contains no local reference. John Milton wrote his masque *Arcades* about 1633 for performance at Harefield Place by 'some noble persons of her family' before the Countess of Derby, whose gorgeous monument remains the most striking thing in the church; he was then living at Horton, Buckinghamshire, a few miles over the Colne. The battle of Brentford in 1642 gave him occasion to write the mock-heroic sonnet 'Captain, or Colonel, or Knight at Arms,' to affix to his door in Aldersgate Street and deprecate the sacking of the house by the royalist soldiery. As things turned out, it was not required. Thomas Traherne, metaphysical poet, curate of Teddington 1672-4, was slightly remembered as the author of works entitled *Christian Ethics* and *Roman Forgeries* until the manuscript of his *Poems* and *Centuries of Meditations* was discovered on a street bookstall in 1896. He is best known now for the anthologists' favourite, 'How like an Angel came I down.'[1] Two early miniaturists had Middlesex connexions. Elizabeth granted Poyle, in the manor of Stanwell, to Nicholas Hilliard for 21 years in 1587, and Peter Oliver lived at Isleworth for some time before his death in 1648.

The great age of the Thames valley as a home and school for poets began in 1719, when Pope, who had lived for three years at Mawson's Buildings, Chiswick, took a lease of a villa and five acres of ground at Twickenham which, enlarged and embellished, remained his home until he died in 1744. His letters and poems throughout the period are full of references to his gardening and grotto-making activity:

'I am as busy now in three inches of gardening as any man can be in three-score acres. I fancy myself like the fellow that spent his life in cutting the twelve apostles in a cherry stone. I have a Theatre, an Arcade, a Bowling-green, a Grove, and what not? in a bit of ground that would have been but a plate of sallet to Nebuchadnezzar the first day he was turned to graze.'[2] Twickenham is more often in his prose than his poetry; Hampton Court is the scene of *The Rape of the Lock*, and it has always been supposed, despite Pope's denial, that Canons, the Duke of Chandos' house near Edgware, was the original of Timon's villa in Epistle IV of the *Moral Essays.*[3]

His gloomy prophecy about the fate of Canons, where the house began to be sold up within three years of his death, was a more successful shot than Swift's similar forecast about Marble Hill, a little way down the river from Pope's villa. It was being built in 1727 for Mrs. Howard, later Countess of Suffolk, George II's mistress, when Swift wrote his satirical 'Pastoral Dialogue between Richmond Lodge and Marble Hill.' He

---

[1] *Poetical Works of Thomas Traherne*, ed. G. I. Wade (ed. 3, 1932), introduction. [2] Pope to Lord Strafford, 5 October 1725. [3] G. Sherburn, '"Timon's Villa" and Cannons', *Huntington Library Bulletin*, no. 8 (1935), p. 131, considers that Pope did not mean the epistle to apply to Canons. Most of his contemporaries thought that he did.

predicted that the outlay on the house would be excessive and it would
have to be sold to 'some South-Sea broker from the City'; but the
countess lived there till her death in 1767.

Twickenham was thus already visited by poets and wits when Horace
Walpole arrived in May 1747 and took the lease of a little house—'this
little rural bijou,' he called it, anticipating the auctioneers—from Mrs.
Chenevix, the toy-woman *à la mode.*[1] His description of Strawberry Hill,
often reprinted, is incomparable:

'Twickenham, June 8 1747.

'You perceive by my date that I am got into a new camp, and have
left my tub at Windsor. It is a little plaything-house that I got out of Mrs.
Chenevix's shop, and is the prettiest bauble you ever saw. It is set in
enamelled meadows, with filigree hedges:

> A small Euphrates through the piece is rolled,
> And little finches wave their wings in gold.

Two delightful roads, that you would call dusty, supply me continually
with coaches and chaises: barges solemn as Barons of the Exchequer
move under my window; Richmond Hill and Ham Walks bound my
prospect; but, thank God! the Thames is between me and the duchess of
Queensberry. Dowagers as plenty as flounders inhabit all around, and
Pope's ghost is just now skimming under my window by a most poetical
moonlight. I have about land enough to keep such a farm as Noah's,
when he set up in the ark with a pair of each kind; but my cottage is
rather cleaner than I believe his was after they had been cooped up
together forty days. The Chenevixes had tricked it out for themselves: up
two pair of stairs is what they call Mr. Chenevix's library, furnished with
three maps, one shelf, a bust of Sir Isaac Newton, and a lame telescope
without any glasses.'

To the cultivated *literati* of the 18th century everything in Middlesex
seemed to be in miniature, a few degrees less than life-size. Authors who
wanted to lead the country life without incurring the danger of being
forgotten in town found it convenient. Bolingbroke, living from 1726 to
1735 at Dawley on his *ferme ornée,* affected to employ his talents among
the minor country joys; Voltaire and Pope described him trying hard to
do so. Oliver Goldsmith retired to lodgings at Edgware in 1768 and at
Kingsbury in the last years of his life from 1771 to 1774; while there he
wrote *She Stoops to Conquer* and his *Animated Nature,* a natural history.[2]
Jean-Jacques Rousseau, withdrawing temporarily from France after the
publication of *Emile,* lodged with a grocer at Chiswick for a few weeks in
1766. Henry Fielding lived at Fordhook House, on Ealing Common:

'The month of May [1754], which was now begun, it seemed
reasonable to expect would begin the spring, and drive off that winter

---

[1] R. W. Ketton-Cremer, *Horace Walpole* (ed. 2, 1946), chapter viii.   [2] *Mx. & H. N. & Q.* 1
(1895), pp. 31, 82.

which yet maintained its footing on the stage. I resolved therefore to visit a little house of mine in the county of Middlesex, in the best air, I believe, in the whole kingdom, and far superior to that of Kensington Gravel-pits [Notting Hill Gate]; for the gravel is here much wider and deeper, and placed higher and more open towards the south, whilst it is guarded from the north by a ridge of hills, and from the smells and smoke of London by its distance: which last is not the fate of Kensington when the wind blows from any corner of the east.'

He left Fordhook on 16 June 1754—'on this day the most melancholy sun I had ever beheld arose,' he wrote—on the voyage to Lisbon from which he never returned.

Middlesex incurred a peculiarly large dispensation of bad, or at any rate minor, poets in the 18th century. Joseph Trapp, rector of Harlington from 1733 to 1747, was the earliest and perhaps the worst. Swift's passing reference to him is: 'Your parson Slap, Scrap, Flap (what d'ye call him?), Trap.' He became professor of poetry at Oxford in 1707, and his lectures, *Praelectiones Poeticae*, 'gained him the character of an elegant scholar and a good critic'; but, said Lysons pithily, 'his translations of Virgil [into English] and Milton [into Latin] were fatal to his reputation as a poet.' Dr. Johnson, however, allowed that his translation of the *Aeneid* might continue its existence so long as it was the clandestine refuge of schoolboys. Paul Whitehead, satirist, secretary and steward of the Medmenham monks, died at Twickenham; Henry Pye, 'postmaster and poet-laureate … a country gentleman of Berkshire,' as the *Dictionary of National Biography* epitomises him, died and was buried at Pinner; Mark Akenside celebrated the rustic pleasures of Golders Green in an 'Ode on Recovering from a Fit of Sickness, in the Country'; and Hounslow Heath was tediously described by the Rev. Wetenhall Wilkes in a long poem of 1747. This author, whose previous publication was *An Essay on the Pleasures and Advantages of Female Literature*, was saved only by the firmness of 18th-century poetic conventions from producing the worst of all topographical poems; it is compounded of halting invocation of the Muse to strike the warbling lyre, adulation of his noble patron, the Duke of Argyll, and a good deal of borrowing from Thomson's *Seasons*. One couplet perhaps deserves something one stage this side of oblivion:

> Convey me, goddess, to the western end
> Of *Hounslow Town*—to see a worthy friend.

The connexion between Middlesex and the 17th- and 18th-century stage was more distinguished. David Garrick, the greatest of its actors, bought a house and land at Hampton, had the house refronted, built a temple to Shakespeare in the grounds, and entertained the quality; he was lord of the manor at Hendon and built a temple to Shakespeare there also. Middlesex villages, especially on Thames-side, were favourite retreats for successful actors: Peg Woffington, who 'shone in the higher walks of comedy,' at Teddington; Kitty Clive, who was particularly noted 'in chambermaids, romps, superannuated beauties, viragoes, and all whimsical and affected characters,' and Mrs. Pritchard, 'the greatest Lady Macbeth of her day,' at Twickenham; Elizabeth Barry, whose career lasted from 1673 to 1710, at Acton; Charles Holland, Shakespearean actor and friend of Garrick, who wrote his epitaph, at Chiswick; Luke Sparks and Henry Giffard at Brentford; Barton Booth, joint manager of Drury Lane, and John Rich, the first and most famous English Harlequin, at Cowley; Charles Hart, 'the Roscius of his age' (the middle 17th century), at Stanmore; Mary Porter, unrivalled on the London stage from 1730 to her retirement in 1743, at Hendon; Thomas Rosoman, proprietor of Sadler's Wells theatre, and John Beard, manager of Covent Garden after Rich, at Hampton.

The earliest figure among musicians and composers that can be distinguished as a resident in Middlesex is William Byrd, who lived at Harlington from 1577 to 1592 in comparative obscurity as a Roman Catholic recusant, while remaining a gentleman of the Queen's Chapel Royal. During this period he was at the height of his composing powers. His house was probably near the pond in the middle of the village.[1] William Heather, who established the Oxford chair of music, was born at Harmondsworth about 1584. John Hingeston, a pupil of Orlando Gibbons, was appointed the Lord Protector's organist during the Commonwealth and had two organs at Hampton Court.[2]

Middlesex historiographers have done their best to make up for its lack of musical antiquities by enthusiasm for George Frederick Handel. In the fully developed form of the traditional account, he was installed as professional musician, composer, and organist to the Duke of Chandos in 1718, succeeding Johann Pepusch as *Kapellmeister* of the magnificent palace at Canons. While in residence there, he composed *Esther* (on the organ at St Lawrence church, Little Stanmore or Whitchurch), *Acis and Galatea*, the 'Chandos anthems,' and the *Suite de Pièces pour Clavecin*; the melody for one of these pieces, the 'Harmonious Blacksmith,' came to him while sheltering from a storm in the Edgware smith's forge. What was more, the smith, William Powell, was also the parish clerk of Little Stanmore. The whole of the harmonious blacksmith story, which was never heard of before 1820, was always regarded with some suspicion by good writers, and it collapsed completely under the searching criticism of R. A. Streatfeild and Newman Flower. As for William Powell, he was not even apprenticed to a smith until 1725, which is too late for any version of the tradition. The statement made on a brass plate affixed to the Whitchurch organ that Handel 'composed the oratorio of Esther' on it is

---

[1] E. H. Fellowes, *William Byrd* (1936), pp. 11, 39.   [2] Davies (page 95, note 2), p. 386.

improbable in itself; he had no need to be playing an instrument during composition. He may well have played this organ on occasion; there was another in the private chapel of the house which he would more probably use, though it is not certain exactly when this was built. But, beyond this, no documentary evidence has yet been produced that he resided at Canons at all. The details of Handel's life are remarkably obscure, for all that he lived among the most influential and fashionable of his day; recent research seems to show that Pepusch never left the duke's service at the time when Handel is supposed to have supplanted him. In addition, Handel was so much out of England in the years 1718- 21—the only period when he can have been under Chandos' patronage— that it is most unlikely that he was ever resident *Kapellmeister* at Canons. If he did live with the duke's household, it was probably at his London houses. It remains that *Esther*, for which he received £1,000 from the duke, was certainly performed at Whitchurch in 1720 and *Acis and Galatea* probably in 1721; he must have been present at least for those performances.[1]

It was, however, firmly believed before the end of the 18th century that the great composer had especially close associations with Whitchurch, for 'on the 25th of September 1790, a grand miscellaneous concert of sacred music, selected out of the works of Handel, was performed at Whitchurch in honour of that master; when, among other pieces, some parts of anthems composed by him at Canons were sung by Signora Storace, Mrs. Crouch, etc. The profits were intended for the benefit of the Sunday schools in some adjoining parishes, but it did not turn out productive.'[2] This may be taken as an adequate commentary on the state of musical culture in rural Middlesex at the time.

Painting was more highly appreciated. Some of the most celebrated artists of that age lived in the Thames-side villages. William Hogarth had a house at Chiswick from 1749 till his death in 1764. It had previously belonged to his father-in-law, Sir James Thornhill, painter of many ceilings at Hampton Court and elsewhere in the county, who was paid (according to Walpole) at the rate of 40 shillings a square yard.[3] Hogarth was buried in the churchyard, with an epitaph by Garrick. His particular moralising talent did not find much to adopt from the Middlesex scenes of his later years; but P. J. de Loutherbourg, buried at Chiswick in 1812, painted its river landscapes, and John Zoffany, who lived at Strand on the Green till his death in 1810, took local fishermen as models for his 'Last Supper,' still in Old Brentford parish church (the Peter is said to be a self-portrait), and he used riverside scenes as backgrounds for his portraits. Higher up the river, Peter Scheemakers the sculptor was living at Isleworth in 1771.[4] Godfrey Kneller, prolific and successful portrait painter under William III and Anne, and founder of an academy for

[1] R. A. Streatfeild, *Handel* (1909), p. 79; N. Flower, *George Frideric Handel* (ed. 2, 1947), p. 135, summarising earlier discussions; W. C. Smith, *Concerning Handel* (1948), pp. 42, 197; C. H. C. and M. I. Baker, *Life and Circumstances of James Brydges, First Duke of Chandos* (1949), p. 125. [2] Lysons, art. Stanmore Parva. [3] Williams (page 17, note 3), p. 376, quoting H. Walpole, *Anecdotes of Painting in England*, iv., p. 21. [4] *Johnson's England*, ed. A. S. Turberville (1933), ii., p.75. The death-rate 1770 given in *D.N.B.* is apparently wrong; K. A. Esdaile, *English Church Monuments 1510-1840* (1946), p. 64, says that he left England in 1771 and died in Flanders in 1781.

training young artists, built himself a house at Whitton (now called Kneller Hall), hiring Laguerre to decorate the staircase. He lived there in state as a county magistrate and had unseemly quarrels with Pope. At Twickenham lived Samuel Scott, marine painter, d. 1772, and Thomas Hudson, portrait painter, d. 1779. The sculptress Mrs. Damer, whose best-known work is the carving on the Thames bridge at Henley, lived at Strawberry Hill from Walpole's death in 1797 until 1811, when she bought York House, Twickenham.

It remained, however, for a later and a greater artist to seize the beauties of the Middlesex Thames. J. M. W. Turner, who had been to school at Brentford while living there with his uncle, a butcher, designed himself a house at Twickenham, first called Solus Lodge, then Sandycombe Lodge, and had it built in 1813. He lived there till 1825, the years in which his genius was developing most rapidly. 'He kept a boat, and spent day after day on the river, sketching and studying the water—surface, colour, and reflections—the ever-shifting cloud-forms, and the morning and evening mists. Here and in this way it was that he learnt, as no painter had learnt before, the mysteries of cloud and vapour. The grand landscape in the National Gallery, 'Crossing the Brook,' was one of the early fruits of his Twickenham studies, as the 'View from Richmond Hill' was one of the latest.'[1] In his younger days he often walked with Thomas Girtin to Bushy Park and back to make drawings 'for good Dr. Monro at half a crown apiece and a supper.'

The air, the scene, and the society at Twickenham made it a lively and attractive place. Horace Walpole could write without evident absurdity:

> Where Silver Thames round Twit'nam. meads
> His winding current sweetly leads;
> Twit'nam, the Muses' fav'rite seat,
> Twit'nam, the Graces' loved retreat; ...

and certainly, as well as the great names, a good number of the minor characters of literary history assembled there at one time or another: Lady Mary Wortley Montagu, letter-writer and introducer of smallpox vaccination, who incurred Pope's enmity and in return called him 'the wicked wasp of Twickenham'; Horace Walpole's Miss Berrys; Sir John Hawkins, author of a *General History of Music* (1776), editor of *The Compleat Angler*, and executor of Dr. Johnson; his daughter Laetitia Hawkins, novelist; Richard Owen Cambridge, author of *The Scribleriad*, wit, and man of many acquaintances—'a synonymous term for his friends,' said Lord Chesterfield. Walpole summed it up in 1755:

'Nothing is equal to the fashion of this village: Mr. Muntz says we have more coaches here than there are in half France. Mrs. Pritchard has

[1] Thorne, art. Twickenham.

bought Ragman's Castle, for which my lord Lichfield could not agree. We shall be as celebrated as Baiae or Tivoli; and if we have not such sonorous names as they boast, we have very famous people: Clive and Pritchard, actresses; Scott and Hudson, painters; my lady Suffolk, famous in her time; Mr. H[ickey], the impudent lawyer that Tom Harvey wrote against; Whitehead the poet; and Cambridge the everything.' But withal: 'There is not so untittletattling a village as Twickenham; and if Mr. Cambridge did not gallop the roads for intelligence, I believe the grass would grow in our ears.'[1] If *la douceur de vivre* was to be found anywhere in England, surely it must have been here.

All this activity was personal and individual. It is hard to find any trace of organised literary or cultural activity before 1800. There was the unsuccessful Handel concert at Whitchurch in 1790; a book society was formed at Highgate some time before 1789; but otherwise there were no concerts, hardly a playhouse, no societies of dilettanti in the county— naturally enough, with London so close. There were modest theatres in the 18th century at Edmonton, Highgate, and Chiswick; but there were no newspapers, and hardly a printer's name (except T. Lake of Uxbridge, working in 1774) is known until Charles Whittingham established the Chiswick Press in 1810. Horace Walpole had his private press at Strawberry Hill, the *Officina Arbuteana*, which produced collector's pieces.[2]

Away from the Thames, there was little either of literature or art in these years. An incumbent of Edgware, the Rev. Francis Coventry, was an author and versifier, whose satirical and faintly salacious little tale *Pompey the Little, or the Adventures of a Lapdog*, published in 1751, achieved some vogue. Two remarkable clerics were provided for Hendon by David Garrick: James Townley, vicar 1772-6, author of the successful farce *High Life below Stairs* of 1759, and Henry Bate (later Sir Henry Bate Dudley), his curate, known as 'the fighting parson,' who edited the *Morning Post* from about 1774 to 1780. Otherwise the Middlesex clays yielded nothing to English letters.

By 1800, however, a fair number of the productions called 'useful writings' had been written in these districts. There had been 17th-century scientists: Thomas Harriot, an accomplished mathematician and astronomer, pensioned by the Earl of Northumberland, lived at Syon House from 1607 to 1621; Brook Taylor, mathematician and secretary of the Royal Society, 1731, was born at Edmonton; John Theophilus Desaguliers, vicar of Whitchurch, 1714, was a physicist, astronomer, and experimenter with the steam engine; Stephen Demainbray, d. 1782, who lived at Northolt, discovered the influence of electricity in stimulating the growth of plants; and Stephen Hales, curate of Teddington from 1709 to 1761, physiologist and inventor, was the author of *Vegetable Staticks* and

---

[1] Walpole to R. Bentley, 5 July 1755. [2] *V.C.H.* ii., p. 199; *Journal of the Printing-Office at Strawberry Hill*, ed. P. Toynbee (1931).

works on distilling water, the preservation of food, and ventilation. George Keate, of Isleworth, was a 'miscellaneous writer,' an author who wrote only for pleasure, a painter and friend of Voltaire, whose best-known works were *Sketches from Nature, taken and coloured in a Journey to Margate* (1779) and *An Account of the Pelew Islands* (1788). Biography is represented by Thomas Fuller, author of *The Worthies of England*, rector of Cranford 1658-61; translation by William Page, of Harrow, whose version of Thomas à Kempis' *Imitatio Christi* came out in 1639; oriental studies by Sir William Jones, translator from Sanskrit, who lived at Harrow; natural science by Sir Joseph Banks of Spring Grove, president of the Royal Society 1778-1820; ornithology by William Hayes, who wrote on the birds of Osterley Park (1794); history by Robert Orme, historiographer to the East India Company and author of *The History of the Military Transactions of the British Nation in Indostan from 1745* (published 1763-1778), who lived at Ealing 1792-1801; Macaulay pronounced his work 'one of the most authentic and finely written histories in our language,' and it was Colonel Newcome's favourite book. One of the earliest social investigators, Sir Frederick Morton Eden, author of *The State of the Poor* (1797), also lived at Ealing. Horne Tooke, who as the Rev. John Horne was curate of Brentford during the Wilkes elections, after leaving the church acquired some reputation as the author of Ἔπεα Πτερόεντα, *or The Diversions of Purley* (1786), a philosophical and etymological work.

Some of the most eminent of the unassuming company of topographers have been Middlesex men: John Norden, whose *Speculum Britanniae* described Middlesex in detail in 1593, probably had a house at Hendon; Richard Gough, author of *Sepulchral Monuments in Great Britain* (1786) and translator and editor of Camden's *Britannia* (1789), lived from 1752 to 1809 at Gough Park, Baker Street, Enfield, where, as he wrote, he could 'with pleasure, from his earliest life, review many pleasing hours of retirement and antiquarian research spent in this parish, so happily situated as a centre of many curious monuments in the adjacent counties.'[1] John Nichols, whose history of Leicestershire was published between 1795 and 1815, often accompanied Gough on his tours, and his family, editors and later proprietors of the *Gentleman's Magazine*, settled at Hanger Hill, Ealing, after the marriage of John Bowyer Nichols with Gough's daughter. Isaac D'Israeli, compiler of *Curiosities of Literature* (1791) and father of the Earl of Beaconsfield, was living at Enfield as a boy when he ran away from home and was found in Hackney churchyard.

Early in the 19th century the northern parts of Middlesex enjoyed a brief popularity among writers. The Muses deserted Twickenham and the Thames and camped for a short time beside the New River and the

[1] W. Camden, *Britannia*, ed. R. Gough (ed. 2, 1806), ii., p. 107; on Gough, J. G. Nichols in *Trans. L. Mx. A. S.* OS 1 (1860), p. 319; on Norden, E. Lynam, 'English Maps and Map-Makers of the Sixteenth Century', *Geographical Journal* 116 (1950), p. 7.

Lea. Charles Lamb was the head and centre of this little regional school. He went in 1825 from Islington to lodge at 'a Mrs. Leishman's, Chase, Enfield,' and in 1826 he took what he called 'an odd-looking, gambogish-coloured house' at Chase Side: he also called it 'the prettiest, compactest house I ever saw.' Soon, however, he and his sister moved to lodgings 'twenty-five inches further from the town,' where they stayed until they went to Edmonton in 1833. In these modest cottages the Lambs were often visited by their circle—Wordsworth, Hazlitt, Hood, Leigh Hunt, George Dyer, Sheridan Knowles, George Darley; and they came to know the surrounding paths and lanes. At one time he would cry down the country life: 'O let no native Londoner imagine that health, and rest, and innocent occupation, interchange of converse sweet, and recreative study, can make the country anything better than altogether odious and detestable.' At other times he could find something good to say of this countryside, when he was not writing the praises of Mackery End and Blakesware in Hertfordshire: 'The way from Southgate to Colney Hatch, thro' the unfrequentedest blackberry paths that ever concealed their coy bunches from a truant citizen, we have accidentally fallen upon.' In 1833 the Lambs moved to Bay Cottage, in Church Street, Edmonton, where Charles died at the end of 1834. He is buried in the churchyard under a sentimental epitaph by H. F. Cary. A memorial inside the church, put up in 1892, is one of the feeblest works of the revived Gothic taste, with Lamb on the left and Cowper (who, so far as is known, was never at Edmonton in his life) on the right. Cowper's connexion with the place is that he wrote *The Diverting History of John Gilpin*, describing how the citizen intended, but failed, to stop his horse at the Bell at Edmonton.

Some of Lamb's contemporaries allowed themselves to be more enthusiastic about north Middlesex than he was. Keats had lived at Edmonton during his apprenticeship to Mr. Hammond, a surgeon, from 1810 to 1816, and he wrote some of his *Juvenile Poems*, published in 1817, in the district. One passage of 'I stood tiptoe upon a little hill' is attributed to a footbridge on the path from Edmonton by Bury Street to Enfield. Leigh Hunt, the only man of note who has ever expressed pride in his Middlesex birth, wrote in his *Autobiography*:

'It is a pleasure to me to know that I was even born in so sweet a village as Southgate. I first saw the light there on the 17th of October, 1784. It found me cradled, not only in the lap of the nature which I love, but in the midst of the truly English scenery which I love beyond all other. Middlesex in general, like my noble friend's [Lord Leigh's] county of Warwickshire, is a scene of trees and meadows, of 'greenery' and nestling cottages; and Southgate is a prime specimen of Middlesex. It is a place lying out of the way of innovation, therefore it has the pure sweet air of antiquity about it.' Henry Crabb Robinson, living at Southgate in 1812, described it: 'No distant prospect from the Green, but there are fine trees admirably grouped, and neat, happy homes scattered in picturesque corners and lanes.'[1] At Rose Cottage, Vicarsmoor Lane, Winchmore Hill, a little way from Southgate, Thomas Hood settled in 1829; and nearer London, at a house later called Lalla Rookh Cottage, Muswell Hill, Tom Moore lived for six months in 1817. Samuel Rogers, the banker-poet, was buried at Hornsey. All these were men of the capital, who may have remarked the picturesque rusticities of their retreat to adorn a tale or supply a paragraph in a letter to a friend, intended for later publication; but Middlesex was no rival to the Lakes as a school for writers.

Although the special character of Twickenham as a literary centre faded away with the 18th century, its natural advantages for the hard-working writer were yet great enough to commend it to Dickens and Tennyson. Dickens spent the summer of 1838 at 4 Ailsa Park Villas, St Margaret's, and wrote parts of *Nicholas Nickleby* there; the description of the journey of Bill Sikes and Oliver Twist along the Thames valley, through Isleworth, Hampton, and Shepperton, to the burglary at Chertsey must have been drawn from earlier rambles, for *Oliver Twist* was being published in parts during that year. He had Jerrold, Maclise, Talfourd, and Thackeray as visitors at Twickenham, and it may be that Thackeray was influenced to turn to writing novels during a stay there. Forster records that the figure of Mrs. Gamp first came to Dickens when he was lodging in a sequestered farmhouse at Finchley, identified as Cobley's Farm, near Fallow Corner on the Great North road. He buried himself there for a whole summer month to get away from interruptions and wrote part of *Martin Chuzzlewit* (1843). He was a constant visitor at Collins's Farm (now Wyldes), at the top of Hampstead Heath behind the Bull and Bush inn.[2] Tennyson took Chapel House, Montpelier Row, Twickenham, in 1851-2. F.T. Palgrave, vice-principal of the Kneller Hall training college from 1850 to 1855, became intimate with him at this period. This friendship led him to bring out his *Golden Treasury of Songs and Lyrics* in 1861.

But writers had begun to settle in other parts of the county, not only at Twickenham and Enfield. Anthony Trollope lived at Harrow for 17 miserable years, first from 1817-27 in a handsome house, Julians, on the south side of Harrow Hill, built by his optimistic and unpractical father; then at a farmhouse close to it, Julians Hill; and finally from 1830 to 1834 'at a wretched tumbledown farmhouse,' as he called it in his *Autobiography*, at Harrow Weald, from which he had to trudge three miles each way twice daily along the miserable dirty lanes to attend Harrow school as a despised day-boy. 'Perhaps the eighteen months which I

[1] Robinson to Mrs. Clarkson, 13 August 1812. [2] J. Forster, *Life of Charles Dickens* (Charles Dickens ed.), i., p. 73; U. Pope-Hennessy, *Charles Dickens* (1945), p. 188; *Bygone Finchley* (exhibition catalogue, 1947), p. 10; H. Pearson, *Dickens* (1949), p. 29.

passed in this condition ... was the worst period in my life,' he wrote. Nevertheless, his description of this countryside in the dramatic *Orley Farm is* not without charm for those who know Harrow today. He indeed placed it 'some five and twenty miles from London,' which Harrow is not, but there is no doubt of the attribution; the 'irregular and straggling but at the same time roomy and picturesque' house was drawn by Millais for the frontispiece of the first edition (*Plate 10*). It was, Trollope wrote, 'somewhat more than a mile distant from the town of Hamworth ... These fields lie on the steep slope of Hamworth Hill, and through them runs the public path from the hamlet of Roxeth up to Hamworth church; for as all the world knows, Hamworth church stands high and is a landmark for miles and miles around.'[1] His mother, Frances Trollope, used material from the local high and low Church controversy for her most effective tale, *The Vicar of Wrexhill* (1837). Anthony set a few scenes of his novels in Middlesex: Surbiton Cottage at Hampton appears in *The Three Clerks*, with a boating accident at Hampton bridge; Alexandrina Cottage at Hendon was visited by Ralph Newton in *Ralph the Heir*, a Willesden cottage and a Twickenham scene appear in *He Knew He was Right*, and some of the action of *Miss Mackenzie* takes place at Twickenham.

While the Trollopes were facing reduction in their fortunes, and finally the bailiffs, at Harrow, a different kind of family life was being led in a 'large, solid-looking old red-brick house' at Laleham, on the Thames just below Staines. Dr. Thomas Arnold settled there in 1819 and took private pupils until he was appointed headmaster of Rugby in 1828. He came to appreciate the flat meadow scenery. 'I have always a resource at hand,' he wrote, 'in the bank of the river up to Staines; which though it be perfectly flat, has yet a great charm from its entire loneliness, there being not a house anywhere near it; and the river here has none of that stir of boats and barges upon it, which makes it in many places as public as the highroad.' Here his son Matthew Arnold was born in 1822 and lived with a tutor from 1830 to 1836. He too had an eye for the west Middlesex scene; he described after a visit in 1848 'the journey to Staines, and the great road thro' the flat, drained Middlesex plain, with its single standing pollarded elms.' Matthew Arnold himself and three of his sons who died in childhood are buried in Laleham churchyard. He lived for five years, from 1868 to 1873, at Byron House, Harrow: 'I cannot tell you how the old countrified look of the house pleases me,' he wrote to his mother.[2]

The attractions of Harrow had been discovered and celebrated by Byron during his schooldays before either Trollope or Matthew Arnold was born. He went to Harrow in 1801 and left in 1805; he left it with regret, if his 'Lines written beneath an Elm in the Churchyard at

[1] A. Trollope, *Autobiography* (World's Classics ed.), pp. 3, 15; *Orley Farm* (J. Lane ed., 1906), pp. 2, 11. L. P. and R. P. Stebbins, *The Trollopes* (1946), pp. 30, 54, date Harrow Weald before Julians Hill; M Sadleir, *Trollope: a Commentary* (ed. 1945), p. 65, adopts the order followed here, which appears to agree better with the *Autobiography*. [2] *Letters of Matthew Arnold, 1848-1888*, ed. G. W. E. Russell (1895), i., pp. 2, 386; E. K. Chambers, *Matthew Arnold* (1947), pp. 2, 19.

Harrow' are to be taken as evidence, and he wrote of Harrow again and again. He wanted his daughter Allegra to be buried there; after controversy about the propriety of admitting the body of an illegitimate child into the church, it was finally agreed that she should be buried under the porch.

Edward Bulwer-Lytton was another Harrovian strongly attached to Middlesex scenes. From his early schooldays at Ealing he retained an affection for the valley of the Brent—an affection that, if it has existed, has not been echoed by any other author of repute. He recorded in his autobiographical notes: 'The country around the village in which my good preceptor resided was rural enough for a place so near the metropolis. A walk of somewhat less than a mile, through lanes that were themselves retired and lonely, led to green sequestered meadows, through which the humble Brent crept along its snake-like way.' It appears that he had some early and unhappy love-affair in these surroundings, which is reflected in the story of Kenelm and Lily in *Kenelm Chillingly*, written almost 50 years later, and the scenery of Ealing and Perivale is drawn upon as a setting for parts of *My Novel*. Lytton lived at Pinner Wood House in 1831-3 and wrote the greater part of *Eugene Aram* there.

Thomas Love Peacock was a week-end resident of Middlesex for many years, at Lower Halliford on the riverside between Shepperton and Sunbury. He passed much of his early life at Chertsey and wrote a poem 'The Genius of the Thames,' of no great merit, published in 1810. In 1823 he bought a cottage for his mother at Halliford and later moved his family to one adjoining. In 1851 George Meredith, who had married his elder daughter in 1849, went to live with him. They did not get on well together, and Peacock placed the Merediths in a cottage on the other side of the village green; but the ménage was not a success, and the marriage broke up in 1858. Meredith's side of the story was told in *Modern Love*. Peacock retired in 1856. His end was hastened by a fire (of which he had a morbid terror)—he stayed in his library shouting: 'By the immortal gods, I will not move!'; and did not, for he had to be carried to his room and remained bedridden till his death in 1866.[1] His writing contains scarcely any allusion to Middlesex, though there is a delightful aquatic excursion higher up the Thames in *Crotchet Castle*. He did leave, however, a touching epitaph in Shepperton churchyard on his daughter Margaret, who died in 1826, aged three, beginning:

> Long night succeeds thy little day ...

John Mason Neale, high-churchman, translator, and hymn-writer, who contributed one-eighth of *Hymns Ancient and Modern*, was privately educated by the rector of Shepperton from 1823 to 1829, and wrote an

---

[1] *Novels of Thomas Love Peacock*, ed. D. Garnett (1948), introduction.

historical romance, *Shepperton Rectory* (1844), with a good deal of High-Church moralising on affairs in the reign of James I.[1] Lower down the river, at Gomer House, Teddington, lived R. D. Blackmore, author of *Lorna Doone*, more interested in market-gardening than in historical fiction, from 1858 until his death in 1900. One of his stories, *Kit and Kitty*, is set in west Middlesex. Chiswick appeared in Thackeray's famous scene in *Vanity Fair* when Becky Sharp, leaving the Miss Pinkertons' school for the last time, flung the dictionary they had given her out of the window of her coach. Two houses contend for the honour of being the original of this school: Walpole House, on Chiswick Mall, facing the river, where Thackeray himself was at school, and Boston House, just north-west of the church, which has a plaque commemorating the fictitious event affixed to it; the second is less probable, though the gates shown in Thackeray's drawing of the scene are certainly those in front of Boston House.

During the 19th century some minor writers, and a host of minor artists, lived in Middlesex villages. For a few years at the close of the 18th century the north-western villages close to London had attracted painters of country scenes: Julius Caesar Ibbetson lived at Kilburn about 1780; George Morland was for a short time at Kensal Green in 1785-6 and later at the Bull inn, North Hill, Highgate; John Linnell was at Collins's Farm, in Hendon parish, from 1823 to 1827. But few writers or artists lived far from the Thames valley, apart from some near Enfield. Hampton Court attracted many artists of various kinds beside the straightforward topographical school—Thomas Rowlandson (*Plate 17*), Charles Wild, Joseph Nash, for example, but they did not live in Middlesex. T.C. Hofland, landscape artist and author of *The British Angler's Manual*, lived at Twickenham from 1817 to 1823; William Marlow, Samuel Scott's pupil, died there in 1813; James Hewlett, flower painter, died at Isleworth in 1836; Samuel Owen, marine painter, died at Sunbury in 1857; and J. Macallan Swan, animal painter, was born at Old Brentford in 1847. In the northern district John Nixon painted Edmonton statute fair in 1788[2] (*Plate 18*); John Clayton, still-life painter, died at Enfield in 1800; F. C. Lewis the elder, whose etchings of the *Scenery of the Rivers of England and Wales* were published in 1845-7, painted several scenes round Enfield, where he died in 1856.[3] Douglas Morison, water-colourist and lithographer, was born at Tottenham in 1814, and Myles Birket Foster, illustrator and landscape painter in the Victorian taste, was at the Quaker school there about 1830. J. M. Whistler was buried in 1903 near Hogarth's tomb at Chiswick, and Hamo Thornycroft cast some of his sculpture in a Chiswick Mall garden. There is a curious connexion with Vincent van Gogh, who taught Bible history in Mr. Jones's boys' school at Isleworth for a few months in 1876. In those days

[1] J. Julian, *Dictionary of Hymnology* (ed. 1907), p. 785. [2] H. M. Cundall, 'Edmonton Statute Fair', *Connoisseur* 76 (1926), p. 97. [3] Victoria and Albert Museum, *Catalogue of Water Colour Paintings* (ed. 2, 1927); H. M. Cundall, *History of British Water-Colour Painting* (1908).

he had an eye for the picturesque: 'It was beautiful in the park,' he wrote, 'with dark avenues of elm trees and the wet road through it, and a grey rainy sky over it all; in the distance there was a thunderstorm.' He was intending then to become an evangelist; he preached at Richmond and taught in a Turnham Green Sunday school.[1]

Frederick Delius was at the International College at Spring Grove, which was for some reason popular with Bradford parents, from 1876 to 1879. He had a passion for cricket at the time, but during convalescence after being hit on the head with a stump he had time to develop his musical gifts, and he composed his first song at the school.[2] Maurice Hewlett also went to the International College; R.L. Stevenson was at school in Witham Road, Spring Grove, in 1863. William le Queux was editor of the Hounslow *Middlesex Chronicle* in 1883, and W. E. Henley lived in the late 1880s at Chiswick and in the 1890s Muswell Hill.

These are chance associations; there is little truly local literature to record since 1850, compared with the galaxy before that. The Thames valley has continued to inspire most of the best work. C. E. Montague, who was born at Ealing and lived at Twickenham, laid the early scenes of *Rough Justice* at 'Gistleham,' where stakes used in the defence of the ford against Caesar are found at low tide—a thin disguise for Isleworth. Some of his short stories in the volume *Action* (1928) catch the atmosphere of the river and its ferries on this reach. Sir Alan Herbert, who fails by a few yards to qualify as a Middlesex resident, has happily preserved in one of his most *Misleading Cases* a record of the affair when Mr. Albert Haddock, navigating a small boat of shallow draught along Chiswick Mall in time of flood, had a difference of opinion with a Mr. Rumpelheimer, driving a motor car, whether in the circumstances the rule of the road or the Regulations for Prevention of Collision at Sea were applicable to the situation.

All in all, the last hundred years have been singularly barren. Middlesex no longer offered the contrast with town life that it formerly did. There were, it is true, *The Hill*, H. A. Vachell's novel of Harrow school life with characters not very difficult to identify, and G. K. Chesterton's allusions to Bedford Park (appearing as Saffron Park) in *The Man who was Thursday*; but no Arnold Bennett has built a saga out of the abundant material of Wood Green or Willesden. Modern writers sheer away from modern life of this kind. Unhappily, too, John Betjeman's suburban Muse, who does not disdain such scenes, has not yet alighted in Middlesex.

One thing, however, Middlesex has contributed: when the Debrett of the fictional House of Lords comes to be compiled, it will be found that this important institution is much indebted to the county. Anthony Trollope had Viscount Middlesex (a courtesy title, for its holder sat in the

---

[1] *Dear Theo: Autobiography of Vincent van Gogh from his Letters*, ed. I. Stone (1937), p. 7. [2] P. Heseltine, *Frederick Delius* (1923), p. 7; C. Delius, *Frederick Delius* (1935), p. 51; M. Hewlett, 'The Gods in the Schoolhouse', *English Review* 13 (1913), p. 43.

Commons), a fervent and uninteresting exponent of Church reform, in *Can You Forgive Her?* and an Earl of Brentford in *Phineas Finn*. Lord Harrowhill appears in Thackeray's *Pendennis*, and Lord Ickenham was P. G. Wodehouse's *Uncle Fred in the Springtime* (though Ickenham is un-accountably transplanted to Hampshire); Hilaire Belloc's tale of Lord Finchley should be very cautionary:

> Lord Finchley tried to mend the Electric Light
> Himself. It struck him dead: And serve him right!
> It is the business of the wealthy man
> To give employment to the artisan.

Lord Edgware Dies is one of Agatha Christie's stories.

Even the detective novel, which has become the recognised mental sedative for all ranks of society and has supplanted the Latin epigram as the pastime of dons, is not at home in Middlesex. It moves within predestinate grooves, in a convention requiring a limited—but not too limited—number of suspects: the boarding school, or college, the sleeping-car, and above all the country-house party, meet this requirement very happily; the semi-detached house in the suburban street does not. Among the thousands of detective stories, Anthony Berkeley's *Murder in the Basement* (1932), partly set in a new little house in a north-western suburb, is quite unusual. There seems to be no place in industrious suburbs for the artist or the writer. He finds them useful targets for satire, but he would rather not know much about them.

CHAPTER XII

BUILDING MATERIALS, BUILDINGS, AND ARCHITECTS

'Middlesex ... abounds with plain and excellent examples of the different styles, well adapted for the study of beginners.'   J. H. SPERLING[1]

T HE tale of Middlesex building materials is soon told. There is no building stone in the county, but there have been abundant supplies of brick-earth and in the earlier period some timber. In the last sixty years pits in the west and the Lea valley have yielded huge quantities of gravel for concrete. Until the age of canal and railway transport, therefore, when brick-and-slate construction became standard from Dover to Carlisle, Middlesex buildings presented the same general Thames-valley characteristics as Berkshire and Essex: good stone, which had to be carried by water, was used only within a convenient distance of the rivers, except for the most important buildings and details like church windows and doorways; otherwise construction was of the most homely kind, in rubble, timber, and brick, with a little flint.

Nearly all the surviving medieval building is contained in the churches. The ancient portions are mainly composed of rubble, with pebbles, untrimmed flints, and pudding-stone (composite rock formed of pebbles in a flinty matrix), with quoins and dressings of clunch (soft white limestone) from Hertfordshire and Surrey. The best stone, used only for doors and windows, came from quarries in Rutland or (for some of the riverside churches) from Caen in Normandy. Worked flints are not common in the county; they were used at Hayes, Hillingdon, and Ruislip, plain without patterning, and in chequer-work in Stanwell tower and at Shepperton. Purbeck marble from Dorset is found inside the chancels of West Drayton and Stanwell and in some 13th-century fonts.

Some Roman tiles were built into the miscellaneous fabric of Kingsbury church, but the manufacture of bricks, introduced first into the eastern parts of England from the Low Countries, did not take hold in

[1] J. H. Sperling, *Church Walks in Middlesex* (ed. 2, 1853), p. viii.

164

Middlesex until about 1500. From that date, however, with the abundant brick-earth deposits and the absence of stone, the manufacture flourished. Next after Essex and Lincolnshire, Middlesex was an obvious field for the use as well as the manufacture of brick; the castle was giving way to the country house. John Leland noted in Henry VIII's reign that brick and tile were replacing timber and thatch in the London basin.[1] Brick of the 16th century is found at Hampton Court—in warmth of tone and controlled fancy of ornament never since excelled—at Tottenham and Ickenham churches, and set in between the timber frames of a good many ancient cottages; the best early 17th-century work is at Swakeleys, Ickenham, and the old church at Stanmore (*Plate 34*). These were red bricks, relieved with a few burnt blue or black and laid in patterns. Later, in Wren's additions to Hampton Court, a warm orange-red colour was favoured. The 18th century came to prefer stock bricks of yellow-brown; Isaac Ware wrote in 1756 that 'they sort better with stone,'[2] though he had used red brick at Wrotham Park, South Mimms (1754) (*Plate 42*). 18th-century brown stock brick is to be seen at Strand on the Green and in innumerable riverside mansions and rural farmhouses in the county. But it had not yet driven out the older materials; although building in brick was comparatively cheap and easy, at the end of the century Marshall could write, with an exclamation mark, that farm buildings were still chiefly of wood.[3]

The Middlesex brown stocks give modest houses a sort of homely charm of texture when, as is usual in 18th-century buildings, there is a slight irregularity in bonding and the bricks are flecked here and there with pink and black (*Plate 22*). The effect is more agreeable than the duller yellow-brown brick from Sittingbourne, Kent, that came into London up the Thames. As the 19th century advanced, architects began to look for regular bonding and uniform colour; G. G. Scott indeed specified these requirements in his contracts.[4] The result may be seen at St Andrew, West Hillingdon, where Scott in 1865 managed to make the local Cowley brick look harsh. Most of the Middlesex churches between 1800 and 1850 were built not in brown stocks but a hard, soapy-looking yellow brick from Suffolk.

From 1850 onwards every kind of material was poured on to the unprotesting soil: harsh red bricks, sometimes glazed; in the north, yellow-green brick from Three Counties, near Hitchin; slates, pantiles, green tiles; stucco, artificial stone, and concrete. In the present age Middlesex, its own supplies exhausted by meeting 19th-century London's demands for its mild brown bricks, has itself been covered with hard pink brick of the Fletton type from the Midlands. Many of the best facing bricks for 20th-century buildings have come from Berkshire (Binfield and Bracknell), for Hendon town hall of 1904 they were

---

[1] Darby, p. 343. [2] *Johnson's England* (page 153, note 4), ii., p. 95. [3] Marshall, p. 18.
[4] *Builder* 102 (1912), p. 135.

imported from Ashby de la Zouch. Unhappily brick is the least admirable of Leicestershire's products.

An account of the buildings themselves must begin with the churches. The old Middlesex churches form a group which is highly interesting in detail without exhibiting many beauties of the kind that appeal to amateurs of the exceedingly ancient, the grand and stately, or the gothic picturesque.[1] They seem modest edifices in comparison with the characteristic village churches of Somerset or Northamptonshire, but they are specially valuable in preserving some link—in many places the only visible link—with the rural Middlesex of the past. Harrow is foremost in architectural interest, beauty of situation, and important associations (*Frontispiece*); Harefield encloses a collection of sepulchral monuments of the first class, ranking with Lydiard Tregoze in Wiltshire and Stanford on Avon in Northamptonshire; Little Stanmore is unique of its kind (most 18th-century churches are unique in some respect, but this one still merits special note) (*Plate 23*); and the group of tiny buildings at Perivale, Greenford, Northolt, Ickenham, and Cowley has a special character of great charm. Nevertheless, the broadminded ecclesiologist, if he exists, will probably agree that the most interesting and significant contribution the county has made to church-building is to be found in the 20th century, when traditional forms and materials have been used with great freedom or completely abandoned in favour of new ones.

The earliest remaining fragments of building are in the walls of Kingsbury church. 'Long-and-short' work in the quoins at the corners of walls has been thought a certain indication of pre-Conquest work, and Cowley and Bedfont, as well as Kingsbury, have been claimed as Saxon, on this ground alone. These two, however, are assigned by the Historical Monuments Commission to the 12th century; Kingsbury may be earlier.

There is a fair amount of 12th-century Norman work: the elaborate carving of the south door at Harlington is well preserved, with four rows of ornament, not too crude; there is a similar door, but not so good, nearby at Harmondsworth; and the south entrance and chancel arch at Bedfont are remarkable. The west door at Harrow, the north arcade at Laleham, and the plain built-up south door at Kingsbury are recognisable Norman features.

The 13th-century Early English style is best seen in Littleton chancel and at the remarkable but sadly decayed building of the Knights Hospitallers at Moor Hall, Harefield. It can be detected also in the nave arcades at Stanwell, the south arcade at Willesden, and most of the nave and transepts of Harrow, and in the chancels of several others. The main body of the ancient churches is mostly early 14th-century Decorated; Northolt nave is the best example on a small scale (*Plate 19*), and the south arcade at Harefield, the chancel at Harlington (both about 1360), South

[1] For the old churches, Sperling (page 164, note 1); J. C. Cox, 'The Ancient Churches of Middlesex', *Memorials of Old Middlesex*, ed. J. Tavenor-Perry (1909), p. 14; E. T. Long, 'Medieval Ecclesiology of Middlesex', *Builder* 148 (1935), p. 176; Royal Commission on Historical Monuments, *Middlesex* (1937); E. Freshfield, jr., *Communion Plate of the Parish Churches in the County of Middlesex* (1897); 'The Bells of Middlesex', *Trans. L. Mx. A. S.* NS 10 (1951), pp. 118, 310; 11 (1952), p. 27.

Mimms chancel (about 20 years later), Hayes nave, and Stanwell chancel are all good. The only complete Perpendicular fabric is West Drayton (too heavily restored); north chapels were added at Laleham about 1500 and South Mimms, with north aisle, c.1526, and clerestories at several churches; the one at Littleton (in brick, about 1500) is interesting. The principal additions during the 15th and early 16th centuries, however, were stone west towers, which form a recognisable group, mostly with square-headed windows, bold buttresses, and newel turrets: such are Chiswick (about 1425), Heston (the finest, about 1450), New Brentford, Harlington, Harmondsworth (in brick, c. 1500) (*Plate 33*), and over half a dozen more. Another group, less effective because unbuttressed, is formed by Hendon, Finchley, Tottenham (*Plate 1*), Enfield, and Shepperton. Small wooden cupolas were added to many of these towers in the 17th and 18th centuries; they set off the outline well and have fortunately survived at Hillingdon, West Drayton, Uxbridge, and some other places.

The medieval church furniture and fittings that the hands of time and the restorer have spared are not numerous, but some are worthy of mention. The fonts are particularly good: Norman at Finchley, Harrow, Hendon, and Willesden; transitional Norman at Harlington, Hayes, and Ruislip; Early English at Cowley (mutilated), Harmondsworth, Littleton, and South Mimms. There are nine 14th- and 15th-century examples; West Drayton is particularly fine, with open panel work and subject carvings. Heston and Littleton have good medieval carved font-covers.

There are original sedilia at Enfield, Harmondsworth, Hayes, and Stanwell; a well-preserved external stoup at Heston; and an Easter sepulchre at Harlington. There is little ancient seating, but some has survived at Harmondsworth, Littleton, and Ruislip. There are no pre-Reformation stone effigies, though there is an ancient carved coffin-lid at Shepperton. Enfield has a medieval brass of the first rank, probably made about 1470, of Joyce, Lady Tiptoft (d. 1446), in an heraldic mantle, with a coronet and jewel necklace, under a canopy, which has been compared with the brass of Eleanor, Duchess of Gloucester, in Westminster Abbey (1399); though the Enfield example is certainly not quite so good, it is still very fine and well preserved. There are a good many other brasses, mostly small, of the later Middle Ages; the earliest, to Robert Lenee or Levee at Hayes, dates from about 1370; those at Harrow and Hillingdon (Lord Strange and wife, 1509) are good of their kind.[1]

Little old glass has survived; the best is at South Mimms (early 16th century), and there are two seraphim at Hanworth and some odd pieces of the 16th century removed from their original sites to Tottenham and Greenford. Wall paintings at Bedfont (about 1300) and at Hayes and Ruislip (15th century) are notable. The most interesting church plate is at West Drayton (1507-8)—one of the three or four parish churches in the

[1] M. Stephenson, 'Notes on the Monumental Brasses of Middlesex' *Transactions of St. Paul's Ecclesiological Society* 4 (1898), p. 221; H. K. Cameron, 'The Brasses of Middlesex', *Trans. L. Mx. A. S.* NS 10 (1951), p. 267; 11 (1952), p. 48.

country to retain both chalice and paten from pre-Reformation times. The only certainly medieval altar is a Purbeck marble slab with consecration crosses at Laleham. There are ten medieval bells, the earliest (14th century) at Kingsbury and Greenford, and two of the late 14th century at St Paul, Finchley (brought from a city church) and Cranford. There are good parcloses (wooden screens) to the north chapel at South Mimms and a chancel screen, much restored, at Littleton.

Two undoubtedly medieval farm buildings survive, the magnificent tithe barn, just west of the church at Harmondsworth, 191 feet long by 36 feet wide, with twelve bays, and parts of the archbishop of Canterbury's farmhouse at Headstone manor, Harrow (*Plate 31*). Apart from these, there are a number of small buildings dated, generally from internal features, to the 15th century; a group at Uxbridge, including the house now numbered 112 High Street and the King's Arms and Queen's Head inns; the Harrow inn at Charlton, near Littleton; parts of Perivale rectory and Littleton old manor house; Sparrow farm, South Mimms; part of the King's Arms inn at Harefield; and perhaps the Frays, West Drayton. These smaller buildings are almost all timber-framed, but they have been extensively altered and in most of them brick has been substituted for the original plaster or weather-boarding.

Apart from Harmondsworth barn, these buildings are only noteworthy for their age and the chance that they have survived so long among great changes. The continuous story of domestic architecture in Middlesex begins with Hampton Court, the earliest and most splendid example of the important houses. Its influence has indeed been so profound that it is part of the national rather than the local heritage. Nevertheless, it was built where and how it was because of specific influences derived from its situation. It was the first great private house on the lower Thames above the immediate environs of London, chosen because it was at once easily accessible by water and far enough away to be outside the press of metropolitan business and the city's smoke and fogs; and the peculiar beauty of its material was owing to the Middlesex earth that went into its bricks. Londoners may see for themselves what the Great Hall would look like with different execution by comparing it with the hall of Lincoln's Inn; Philip Hardwick copied the proportion and the detail faithfully enough, but the texture and the bonding of Victorian bricks fail to reproduce the warmth and sympathy of the original. Generations of visitors have remarked on the English character of Hampton Court: oddly, in one sense, because many of the contributors were foreign, from Maiano under Henry VIII to Tijou, Verrio, and Daniel Marot under William III; but naturally, perhaps, when viewed from a later age, because the styles imported by these artists were very quickly incorporated into the main body of English design.

When the palace was being built it seemed the vast extravagance of a *nouveau riche*, indecently grand for a subject to own. The magnificent interior apartments are still striking today, when the bright colours have faded and many of the elaborate furnishings, as well as all the troop of liveried attendants, have disappeared. Yet Wolsey and his designers left a building that expresses the grave, mellow charm of English architecture in harmony with the soil it rests on: peaceful, warm, and comfortable. Even the moat outside its front cannot turn it into a castle or disguise what it really is: in form the last great secular building of the Middle Age, in fact the first of the great palatial English country houses (*Plate 17*).

Only fragments remain of other large houses of the 16th century: the stables of the royal palace at Hanworth and Sir Thomas Gresham's house at Osterley; parts of Bruce Castle, Tottenham; and the gatehouse of Lord Paget's house at West Drayton. All these were brick-built, but two of the smaller manor houses, Francis Awsiter's at Southall, of 1587, and Wyllyotts at Potters Bar, of about the same period, were still timber-framed (*Plate 32*). So were the smaller houses and cottages in the county; very many lasted until the early part of the 20th century, but then the old places were nearly all demolished. They had been neglected in their later years, when few landlords cared to renovate old property lying in the path of advancing suburban development, and many were in poor condition, though by no means irreparable. Survivors are to be found here and there on the fringes of the county (*Plate 29*). The names of Old Cottage at Cowley and Old Cote at Heston proclaim an antiquity of about 400 years, not much regarded in the Midland stone belt, but sufficiently remarkable in Middlesex. The best groups of these minor buildings are at Mill Hill (*Plate 20*), Ruislip (*Plate 30*) and Eastcote, Pinner, and Uxbridge. Individual 16th-century buildings of some note are the Manor farm at Ruislip, Fieldend Lodge at Eastcote, Manor farm at Ickenham, the Old Treaty-House (early 16th-century brick) at Uxbridge, 'King John's Palace,' as it is called, at Colnbrook, with some simple pargeting decoration on the plaster, and two in the north-eastern corner—Salisbury House on Bury Street, Edmonton, and the King James and the Tinker inn in Enfield Chase. The brick north aisle, larger than the nave, at Ickenham church dates from the Elizabethan period.

In the early 17th century Middlesex villages were increasingly favoured by wealthy Londoners for their country houses, and some notable examples were built, all in brick: Swakeleys at Ickenham (*Plate 41*), a winged house with gables of a flowing Dutch type, like Broome Court, Kent, and some other houses of the period between 1620 and 1640;[1] Forty Hall, Enfield (no longer attributed to Inigo Jones); Boston House, Brentford (*Plate 37*); and Cromwell House, Highgate, a street house with fine external details in rubbed brick. All these have good

---

[1] C. Hussey, 'Stratfield Saye', *Country Life* 104 (1948), p. 1050.

interior plaster-work on ceilings. The finest example extant of gauged and moulded brick-work of the Wren period was a window pediment from a house at Enfield, removed to the Victoria and Albert Museum; it is attributed to E. Helder, described as a bricklayer, who died in 1672.[1] York House, Twickenham, is a good and stately example of the latter part of the century (*Plate 44*); but all are eclipsed by Wren's addition to Hampton Court palace, one of his foremost works (*Plate 24*). 'The architect ought above all things,' said Wren, 'to be well skilled in perspective';[2] and here on the garden front is his precept carried out to perfection. The skill of Jean Tijou is displayed in the ironwork screens by the river (*Plates 25 and 26*), and the gardens, laid out in the taste of Le Nôtre's disciples and now filled with a wealth of flowers that they could not command, compose a grand harmonious setting to the buildings (*Plate 73*).

The only 17th-century church was a brick building (now a ruin) at Stanmore, consecrated by Laud in 1632, with handsome buttressed tower, round-headed windows, and nave and chancel on a simple rectangular plan (*Plate 34*). There is a west tower dated 1631 at Staines, and the north vestry at Ickenham was a mortuary chapel built about 1640-50. There is, however, a wealth of 17th-century work in the fittings of churches and their monuments, like the fonts of Greenford and Stanmore, the font-cover at Perivale, pulpits at Harrow and Ruislip, bread-cupboards at Ruislip and Enfield, and communion tables at Tottenham and Willesden.

A fine series of Renaissance and 17th-century monuments provides the old Middlesex churches with their principal claim to attention. There are good 17th-century monuments in almost every old church; the best of the earlier part of the century are at Hillingdon, Uxbridge, Ruislip, Cranford, and Enfield. Harefield church possesses a splendid series of memorials to the Newdigates and Ashbys and the notable tomb of Alice, Countess of Derby, 1636 (*Plates 35 and 36*); the 18th-century monuments, though not so conspicuous, are admirable examples of their age. There is a handsome monument of 1703 at Hendon, and the memorial by Grinling Gibbons to James Brydges, Duke of Chandos, and two of his wives at Little Stanmore, 1718, is something more than imposing. The Thames valley churches contain the best 18th-century work in the county, at Chiswick, Isleworth, and Hampton, and there are representative pieces by Thomas Banks, John Bacon, and John Flaxman among the hundreds of monuments of the last two hundred years in Middlesex churches, many of them worth more consideration than they generally get.[3]

Most of these memorials have been treated well by succeeding ages, and many are repaired and painted as occasion requires; in a few cases rather more than occasion requires. Only rarely have tablets and monuments been treated with contempt; it has been more common to

[1] N. Lloyd, *History of English Brickwork* (1925), p. 185; C. W. Whitaker, *History of Enfield* (1911), p. 176. [2] Quoted by Whistler (page 7, note 1), page 62. [3] K. A. Esdaile, *English Monumental Sculpture since the Renaissance* (1927); *Monuments in English Churches* (1937); *English Church Monuments 1510-1840* (1946).

relieve the walls of a new church by transferring the memorials from the old. At Great Stanmore, however, most of them were indecently huddled into the tower of the 19th-century church, some skied far out of eye-shot, and at Finchley some are hidden in the gallery. Outdoor memorials are generally modest affairs; too much Carrara marble and Aberdeen granite has made most churchyards unpleasing to modern taste. Still, there is good work in a local tradition that expired about 1800; headstones with restrained carving and sound lettering are to be seen at Shepperton, Sunbury, Pinner, and Tottenham, for example. The oldest headstone is to John Francklin, 1597, at Little Stanmore. Until about 1820 the wooden headboard was the most common memorial in Middlesex churchyards, and there are later examples.

Several Middlesex churches date from the early 18th century. These were old churches rebuilt for various reasons; except New Brentford, no new parishes were formed at this period, even where there was a considerable influx of population. At Isleworth the old church fell down and Wren submitted a design, but the new edifice was built in 1706 on somewhat more economical lines; at Twickenham the church fell in 1713, and a new one was built in brick by John James, architect of St George's, Hanover Square, with Doric pilasters and pediments on the north and south sides as well as in the more common position at the east and west ends (*Plate 15*); at Little Stanmore the Duke of Chandos resolved to have a church suitable to his new house at Canons and had one built in 1714-15, perhaps by John Price (*Plate 23*); fire destroyed Cranford nave in 1710 and a modest little thing was put up in its place. At all of these a 15th-century tower remains at the west end, having survived both accidental disasters and the hand of the rebuilder. Twickenham retains some of the 18th-century fittings, with galleries along both sides; Cranford is in good order but hardly an 18th-century interior; Little Stanmore, after neglect, is again in good repair; but Isleworth is a shell, accidentally burned out in 1943. Another collapse in the early 18th century, in which Middlesex spent as little as it could to prevent decay in its churches, gave Ealing a classical church in 1733, and sheer itch for smartness made the parishioners of Sunbury pull down their church in 1751 and have a new one built by Mr. Wright, clerk of the works at Hampton Court, with a distinctive tower and a cupola on top. These two, however, did not escape the correcting zeal of the 19th century.

Organs began to appear in the wealthier Middlesex churches about this time. They were not common until the 19th century; barrel-organs did service in a good many, with a limited repertory of tunes. Perivale church had no musical instrument until a twenty-tune barrel-organ was bought about 1861; West Twyford was then managing its chants with the help of an Eolina, or mouth-organ.[1] There are, however, a few 18th-

[1] J. A. Brown, *Chronicles of Greenford Parva* [1890], p. 123.

century organs and organ-cases, some in unexpected places. Enfield and St.George, Southall, have almost identical cases by Richard Bridge, about 1753; Hampton Court chapel has an instrument originally built about 1710, probably by Schreider (not, as usually claimed, by 'Father' Smith); and All Hallows, Twickenham, has the original organ and case from All Hallows, Lombard Street, by Renatus Harris, 1695, carefully restored and enlarged for its new situation. Few of the newer organs are noteworthy; perhaps the best is in Harrow school chapel, with case by Sir Charles Nicholson.[1]

In the 18th century, as the wealthier citizens of London increasingly sought houses just out of town, Middlesex began to be cut up for residential properties of a substantial, though not often very imposing, kind. An age began of good, solid mansions of brown brick, square, comfortable, without much ornament; they may still be seen in many parts of the county, especially along the river. Many of them are now in reduced circumstances, though it is still possible to detect the air of amiable, unexciting spaciousness that they once possessed.

Among these minnows there were some veritable Tritons, in size or distinction. Middlesex is fortunate in possessing three of the most famous examples of 18th-century building: Chiswick House, Syon House, and Osterley Park, the first an acknowledged masterpiece of the architect and dilettante Earl of Burlington (*Plate 14*), the second and third splendid reconstructions by Robert Adam. Sacheverell Sitwell has written: 'Syon, the plain exterior of which is so dull and unprepossessing and the interior so little known, and seldom seen, is among the greatest works of art in England.'[2] Now that it has been opened to the general public, few who have visited the house and compared it with others better known will disagree with this judgment (*Plate 2*). Another, though its life was short, merits mention with these three: Canons, the magnificent palace of the wealthy Duke of Chandos (*Plate 13*). Of a different kind, not a mansion but an overgrown villa, was Strawberry Hill, Horace Walpole's *jeu d'esprit*, which will enjoy fame as the forerunner of the Gothic revival in England so long as the history of architecture is studied (*Plate 16*). There were many other large country houses, which made Defoe exclaim in 1724: 'There's an incredible number of fine houses built in all these towns, within these few years, and England never had such a glorious show in the world to make before; in a word, I find two thousand houses which in other places would pass for palaces, and most, if not all, the possessors whereof keep coaches, in the little towns or villages of Middlesex, west of London only.' To the early part of the century belong the Duke of Schomberg's house at Hillingdon (1717); Arnos Grove at Southgate; Orleans House, with a beautiful octagon room by James Gibbs, and Marble Hill at Twickenham; Kneller Hall at Whitton, in

---

[1] Information from the Rev. B. B. Edmonds. [2] S. Sitwell, *British Architects and Craftsmen* (1945), p. 148.

which Vanbrugh may have had a hand. Later came Wrotham Park, built by Isaac Ware in 1754 for the unfortunate Admiral Byng (*Plate 42*); Trent Park in Enfield Chase; Sir William Chambers' villa in the Italian style at Whitton; Garrick House at Hampton; and scores of minor country seats. Smaller 18th-century houses are mostly to be found by the riverside, at Chiswick Mall (*Plate 43*), Strand on the Green, Isleworth, and above all at Twickenham, where Sion Row and Montpelier Row show how terraces ought to be built. Humbler dwellings have survived at Cowley, Chiswick away from the river, Enfield, Uxbridge; but the 20th century has been heavy on them. The finest surviving examples of medium-sized houses face the Butts at Brentford, behind the dreary High Street (*Plate 21*); there are some handsome houses on Hampton Green and in the village of Hampton; and Shepperton rectory has a beautiful front of about 1700 masking an older interior (*Plate 38*). Here and there in the north, as along Tottenham High Road, good old houses look out sadly; at Highgate they have been more fortunate (*Plate 22*); but most of them have been overwhelmed.

Church building in the classical idiom ended with a new church at Feltham in 1802 a decent brick room with plaster ceiling and patterned frieze, and round-headed windows that the churchwardens of 1856 respected enough to make their new aisles in the 'Norman' style. Both building and addition were about twenty years behind the times, for Feltham, then as now, was no leader of fashions (*Plate 49*).

The first forty years of the 19th century, the unregenerate youth of the Gothic revival, produced some charming works. Unfortunately nearly all of them were built in white or light yellow brick from East Anglia, difficult enough to admire at the best of times and unanimously reprobated by later ecclesiologists. Gothic forms, mostly of Perpendicular derivation, were treated with great freedom to decorate what remained in effect 18th-century preaching-houses. Hampton has a well-preserved example; the new parish of Hampton Wick was furnished with a similar but smaller church, without a tower; and others were put up at Enfield, Whetstone, Mill Hill (Wilberforce's church), Hounslow, and other growing places at a similar distance from town. They were pronounced 'very unecclesiastical' by the ecclesiologists—their chancels, if they had any, were rudimentary; they belong to the age of evangelical piety, and their light, unassuming interiors were constructed with all economy, sometimes quite baldly, with a severe eye on the cost expressed in £ per sitting. Their large clear or *grisaille* windows cast no air of Gothic gloom; these buildings were intended rather to give the preacher a good hall than to house a sanctuary. In some way, whether from their pitch-pine seating or their improved patent heating stoves, there still arises in them the characteristic odour of sanctity of the 19th-century Low Church.

But in the Middlesex of the eighteen-thirties George Gilbert Scott, an observant, ambitious young architect, was already making week-end walking tours and carefully noting the features of the surviving medieval parish churches. The first fruit of his studies was a batch of six churches; two of them are at Hanwell and Turnham Green. They were decidedly of the 'hard school,' as though designed to look well in a steel engraving. Scott wrote of them: 'The designs for these churches were by no means similar, but they all agreed in two points—the use of a transept of the minor kind, which happened to be suggested to me by those at Pinner and Harrow, and the absence of any proper chancel, my grave idea being that this feature was obsolete. They all agreed too in the meagreness of their construction, in the contemptible character of their fittings, in most of them being begalleried to the very eyes, and in the use of plaster for the internal mouldings, even to the pillars ... As I had not then awakened to the viciousness of shams, I was unconscious of the abyss into which I had fallen. These days of abject degradation only lasted for about two years or more, but, alas! what a mass of horrors was perpetrated during that short interval! Often, and that within a few months of this period, have I been wicked enough to wish my works burnt down again.'[1]

Scott and his contemporaries were protesting against the way churches were being built in their day, and even more at the way the old ones had been debased. In 1844 a correspondent of *The Builder* was protesting at the general bad treatment and neglect of west Middlesex churches, disfigured with whitewash, painted deal, and other evidence of the churchwarden era. In 1846 Heston church was said to be 'much injured by Messrs. Economy and Compo.'[2] Fortunately we have an accurate, if often too brief, account of every old church in the county as it appeared in 1849, written by one of the reforming party: the Rev. J. H. Sperling's *Church Walks in Middlesex*, often tart, always observant, a mirror of the notions of the new ecclesiologists (like the Cambridge Camden Society, he always spelt pews 'pues'). 'The general condition of the churches has within the last ten years greatly improved,' he wrote. 'Still there are many in a disgraceful state of neglect and dilapidation ... The large increase of population along the banks of the Thames has not enhanced the interest of its ecclesiology, all the churches in consequence having suffered more or less grievously from revived pagan additions during the last century.' At Harlington, 'the altar is vested in a decent covering'; at other places presumably this was not so. At Cowley, 'the interior is in a grievous state from pues and galleries ... the pues are of all sizes, shapes and colours'; at Edmonton, 'the pues and galleries are very offensive.'

The Rev. G. S. Master left an account of the state of Twickenham

[1] Scott (page 74, note 1), p. 86. [2] *Builder* 2 (1844), p. 119; 4 (1846), p. 210.

church when he became vicar in 1859: 'The entire area of the church was in the possession of a small number of families, and the poor were practically excluded altogether; a few uncomfortable brackets, placed sideways in the central passage, being the only accommodation provided for them. The fronts of the galleries were of unnecessary height, and the divisions of their seats were so contrived as to make them resemble stalls in a stable. The organ occupied the western gallery, above which, close to the ceiling, was another contrivance of the same kind, unsafe, unwholesome, and unsightly, devoted to the use of the children of the parochial schools. The vestry occupying the lower storey of the tower had been arranged at the expense of the blocking up of the tower arch, the destruction of the western door, and the substitution for it of a hideous window. The whole aspect of the church, from its circular east window, leaded apparently in imitation of a spider's web, to its glazed and wainscotted approaches at the west, was melancholy in the extreme, and truly lamentable from its exclusiveness and its inadequacy to the wants of the parishioners.' Mr. Master set to work, and within a year the pews had given way to open benches, the west galleries had gone, and the whole church had been 'opened out.'[1]

Between them these two writers expressed the whole indictment: the churches were unecclesiastical; they exhibited relics of pagan styles—that is, there were classical features in them; they were neglected; they were exclusive; they were inadequate. The restorers and rebuilders went to work putting things to rights with all but universal approval: *The Illustrated London News* did, it is true, lament 'those noble old Queen-Anne-like pews at Twickenham'[2]; but Sperling was confident that if the Duke of Chandos were still living he would probably have been the first to reform so grievous an abuse as the corrupt arrangement at Little Stanmore of having the organ at the east end of the chancel. With this temper among the incumbents and architects, and adequate contributions from an affluent laity, there was inordinate destruction of church interiors, and sometimes of their very fabrics. The wonder is not that so much that was good and serviceable perished, but that so many Middlesex churches and fittings that did not comply with the new demands managed to survive.

The ancient churches suffered equally with those of the preceding age, although these things were done in the name of the Gothic revival. Hillingdon, Harrow, and West Drayton, which Sperling's account shows to have been of great interest, were drastically rebuilt in the interest of the fidgety neatness that was required. Heston was 'most disastrously and inexcusably destroyed in a fortnight in 1865, except the tower and lych-gate—not without protest, which was joined by G. E. Street, whose wayward talent had something to answer for in the same direction.[3]

[1] R. S. Cobbett, *Memorials of Twickenham* (1872), p. 31. [2] *Illustrated London News*, 22 October 1859, quoted by Cobbett (see preceding note), p. 30. [3] A. Heales 'Heston Church', *Trans. L. Mx. A. S.* OS 2 (1864), p. 204; *Builder* 23 (1865), p. 67; *Memorials of Old Middlesex* (see page 166, note 1), pp. 48, 94; Cobbett (see note 1), p. 33.

It was easy enough to run up new naves and chancels east of the strong west towers of the medieval churches, using most of the old stones, rechiselled into the hard cold forms of Victorian masonry; but the 18th-century pagan edifices with their round-headed windows presented a peculiar difficulty to all but the most determined restorers. One such was found, S. S. Teulon, with the hardihood to turn the 'brick barns' of Ealing and Sunbury into what were confidently but rather wildly termed Byzantine basilicas. Ealing as a result possesses the ugliest tower in the county, of a shape that words are inadequate to describe. Sunbury church is a riot of apsidal excrescences on the original building, the whole decorated in high polychrome; it should be preserved intact, a monument to the taste of the eighteen-sixties, as curious and characteristic of its time as the Prudential building in Holborn and Peter Jones's store in Sloane Square of later periods. Sunbury had its admirers, who must have been sorry that the 18th-century tower was not altered to suit; some of the parishioners of Twickenham regretted that they could not profit 'by the excellent example [Sunbury] now affords of the truest and most successful manner of renovating churches built after their unwieldy and uneeclesiastical pattern.' One contemporary critic did complain that this treatment was unsuitable; the insertion of a few Byzantine window decorations, he wrote, made it 'like an elephant with a few feathers from the tail of a peacock.'[1] At Isleworth a bold experiment was tried: the addition of a Gothic chancel arch and chancel to a Tuscan nave 'with the happiest effect.' It depends what is meant by happy.

Nearly all the new churches built in the revived Gothic between 1840 and 1880 were mediocre. Scott, recognised in his day as the most eminent of his profession, stands first in output, but his Middlesex churches are not his best; none of them approaches the mastery he showed in St Mary Abbots, Kensington. Hanwell, a work of 1841 standing on an eminence beside the Great Western main line, is the most familiar, though not, as sometimes stated, his first church; Christ Church, Turnham Green, is another of the same vintage; Christ Church, Ealing (later altered by G. F. Bodley), and Southgate (*Plate 60*) are correct, etiolate Decorated; St Andrew, West Hillingdon, is an ugly thing. Works of some merit by his contemporaries are to be found: by William Butterfield, with characteristic use of contrasting coloured brick, at Ashford, Harrow Weald, St Mary, Edmonton, and St Mary Magdalene, Enfield (the last a late work, unusually plain); by Dawkes at Kingsbury (transplanted from Wells Street, Marylebone); by G. E. Street at SS. Peter and Paul, Teddington; but of the vast output of Benjamin Ferrey, after Scott perhaps the most prolific of the middle Gothic revivers, the only work in Middlesex was a couple of cemetery chapels at Hillingdon.[2] In

[1] *Builder* 17 (1859), p. 414. [2] *Builder* 25 (1867), p. 275; 39 (1880), p. 283; Clarke (page 117, note 1).

general the churches down to 1880 do more to interest than to attract the beholder; they are hard in material and execution, the ornament is lifeless when it is not downright ugly, and they seem in spite of elaboration of detail not to warm but to chill. With advancing age they do not mellow, and the hand of time does not heal.

The population of Middlesex doubled between 1800 and 1850, and a corresponding number of dwellings was built. Most were undistinguished. One or two were good: John Nash's Grovelands House, Southgate, was a superior example of 1797 (*Plate 9*); John Soane's reconstruction of George Dance the younger's building at Pitzhanger, Ealing, in 1802 was a striking and highly individual work, foreshadowing many things in his later house at 13 Lincoln's Inn Fields (*Plate 8*). But when Gunnersbury House was rebuilt about the same time it was done 'somewhat after the previous design' (by Webb, in 1663), and houses built in 1825 were recognisable derivatives in the vernacular from those put up fifty years before. Even in 1852 Lewis Vulliamy's house for Lord Kilmorey at St Margaret's, with its Doric portico, was in an outmoded style. Like other counties where brick and not stone was the staple building material, Middlesex stuck to the classical tradition in its larger houses long after Gothic, in one form or another, had come back into general favour in other parts of England. The soil was not favourable to fantastication of any kind, certainly not in architectural experiment; it was left to flightier neighbourhoods to lead the fashion. There were a few—but not many—eccentricities: Twyford Abbey of 1806 was a 'Cockney Gothic' affair by W. Atkinson, who was later to design Waiter Scott's Abbotsford, and a Gothic mansion of 1843 at Stanmore was saluted as 'the most beautiful building in that style of the last 50 years.'[1] The builders generally contented themselves with taking details out of the artistic architects' books and sticking them on as ornament to plain building. There were two monstrosities of the sixties at Pinner, charitably attributed to the owner's eccentricity. A few strange houses with loopy barge-boards appeared in the Thames valley, and an outbreak of Gothic villas occurred between Isleworth and Twickenham; but on the whole what was left of the classical tradition held on.

The Gothic revival never flourished in Middlesex outside the churches. Among the whole 343 'Selected Examples' appended to C. L. Eastlake's *History of the Gothic Revival in England*, which takes the story down to 1870, there is only a single one in this area—the International College at Spring Grove (1866-9) by Norton and Masey.[2] There were some more here and there, of course: ugly almshouses in Tottenham; Harrow school buildings; the Commercial Travellers' Schools at Hatch End ('Gothic and Elizabethan' by Lane and Ordish, 1854); and the Town

[1] Keane (see page 134, note 2), p. 193. [2] C. L. Eastlake, *History of the Gothic Revival in England* (1872), p. 414.

Hall at Ealing (1889), lacking the courage of its Gothic convictions. All these were institutional, but other institutions avoided the Gothic— Colney Hatch lunatic asylum (which caused the neighbourhood to rename itself New Southgate), by Dawkes (1851), described its huge bulk as Italian (or alternatively as 'the plain style');[1] the reformatory at Feltham and the Welsh charity schools at Ashford, both of 1857, were nondescript; and the Alexandra Palace at Wood Green (1875) was unclassifiable. A. Blomfield's St Katharine's training college for schoolmistresses at Tottenham of 1881 was already in a sort of developed 'Queen Anne' style, as it was beginning to be called. A few strange and horrible things happened on the river banks; a tea merchant's villa replaced Pope's at Twickenham; but the 19th century in Middlesex was not a time of architectural vulgarity. Dullness there was; but it was left to the 20th century to supply vulgarity.

The elevated style of the better kind of domestic building, which could be found in the prosperous suburbs, like Ealing, has been well described by Sir John Clapham:

'In London [more spacious ways of living] could only be got with any ease in the true suburbs ... The suburb was much the same all over the country. It had real gardens, if ever so little, and shrubs and hedges of holly or privet. When, as a suburb, it was old, there would be imbedded in it houses restrained, balanced, usually rectangular in mass and fenestration, of red brick and stuccoed, inconspicuously roofed, dating from before the railways and the publication of *The Stones of Venice* (1851-3). But whether old or new, the suburb was dominated by what average builder-architect opinion had made out of the Gothic Revival and John Ruskin. Slated roof and gable were assertive. There might be patterns on the slates. There was likely to be a wooden or iron finial on the gable end, and perhaps machine-made open work on its crest. Latterly, the half-timbered gable had become prominent. Turrets were possible; curved bays or some deliberate avoidance of the rectangular almost certain. True Gothic windows were awkward and scarce, but some of the windows could be given round heads, others small panes. Worked stone, for beauty and diversity, would be mixed with the normal brick in various ways, if only in the single bow window of the smallest semi-detached villa residence, or in the diminishing perspective of bow windows along the stretches of continuous house between the true suburb and the town. Attention had been called to the Venetian decoration of wall veils with inset marble slabs; so there could be patterns of red brick on white, and of blue or red. Porches gave great scope for Gothic detail, because they need not be comfortable. It was on a porch, but of a public-house in Ealing, that Ruskin had seen in 1873 brickwork which would have been in no discord with the tomb of Can

---

[1] *Builder* 5 (1847), p. 585; 9 (1851), p. 415.

Grande, had it been set beside it at Verona. Discord with the best Italian Gothic had not, however, been universally avoided.'[1]

Ruskin was driving from Ealing through Brentford on Waterloo Day of 1873 when he saw the red light of sunset after thunderous rain fade through the gaps between the rows of new houses which were springing up everywhere as unexpectedly as the houses in a pantomime. At Kew Bridge: 'I could not but be solemnly impressed by the appearance of a circular temple built since I last crossed the bridge, some thirty or forty times the size of that (so called) of Vesta, by the Tyber, which it otherwise in many particulars resembled, no less than that of the Sibyl at Tivoli. Its dark walls and singularly tall and narrow columns rose sublimely against the twilight at the extremity of the longer reach of the stream, and presented at once a monument to the art and the religion of the children of Thames; being no less beauteous a work of peace than the new gasometer of (I presume) the Brentford Gas Company, Limited.'[2]

It needed the imagination, and the irony, of a Ruskin to compare industrial installations of 19th-century Middlesex with temples of ancient Rome. It is a pity we have no comparison from his pen of the campanili of the waterworks with their remote progenitors at Venice and Siena. The latter-day Italianate towers and pump-houses at Brentford and Hampton, built between 1850 and 1860, displayed something of the strength and the ambition of the engineers in a more appropriate fashion than the Gothic gingerbread of the Tower Bridge. The new railways, however, had done little to embellish the county, apart from Brunel's magnificent Wharncliffe viaduct over the Brent at Hanwell (*Plate 5*); William Tite's little stations on the South-Western loop through Chiswick (*Plate 54*) and Brentford (1849-50) were tasteful and better than any other line could show.

In the churches a new respect for materials and a greater freedom in the application of the fundamental Gothic forms became apparent after about 1880. Still no great work of the revival was built in the county; the nearest was J. L. Pearson's St Augustine, Kilburn, a few yards over the London border. St John, Friern Barnet, in Pearson's favourite Early English style, with apsidal end and stone vaulted roof, comes near to being a fine church. The only one on the grand scale is the massive fragment of All Saints, Teddington, designed by W. Niven in 1886, so grand that it is still incomplete and may well remain so. The most successful church fully characteristic of this period is perhaps G. H. F. Prynne's red-brick St Peter, Staines, of 1894. James Brooks' stone St Mary, Hornsey, his only essay in the Perpendicular, and Temple Moore's St John, West Hendon, both uncompleted, were free from the prevailing orthodoxies, uncommon churches for their date; Brooks' St Andrew, Willesden Green (1886), shows his simple Early English style in brick,

[1] Clapham, *Modern Britain*, ii., p. 497.   [2] J. Ruskin, *The Stones of Venice*, preface to second edition, 1874 (ed. E. T. Cook and A. Wedderburn, 1903) ix., p. 11.

with a *flèche*. J. D. Sedding's St Peter, Ealing (1889), is a large and handsome affair in an experimental Perpendicular with a good deal of elaboration in window tracery and buttresses. J. O. Scott's St John, Palmer's Green (1905), in brick, may be cited as a moderate example of the feeble end of the revival.[1]

Very little remains of the chapels built by the other communions in Middlesex before the 19th century. Most of them were extremely modest, and they were demolished or abandoned as larger congregations and some degree of affluence arrived. The Congregational Old Meeting House at Uxbridge, set back a little shyly along a passage from the High Street, is a brick building of 1716, much rebuilt in 1883 (*Plate 46*); the Friends' Meeting House at Winchmore Hill, of 1688, rebuilt in 1790, is a plain building standing in a Quaker graveyard (*Plate 45*). Their 19th-century successors were not a distinguished lot; they were best when they carried on the classical tradition with a portico, as at Staines (Congregational, Laleham Road, pleasing Ionic of 1836) (*Plate 47*), Baker Street, Enfield (Emmanuel Old Baptist, 1862), and Harlington (Baptist, 1879, a very queer derivative of the classical). In other parts, where wealthy congregations built, they favoured the Gothic style and produced some of those edifices celebrated by contemporary guide-book compilers as 'conspicuous objects,' as at Chase Side, Enfield (1875), Turnham Green (1883), and Northwood (Wesleyan, 1924, a late example).

Much of the most important Roman Catholic building in the county throughout this period was in the hands of F. W. Tasker or the firm of Goldie. The Gothic tradition was expanded with some freedom by A. Young in St Edward the Confessor, Golders Green (1915), in silver-grey brick with a bold central tower.

At the end of the 1870s, when the first reviving effect of Gothic in church architecture had spent itself, domestic housing was at its dullest and most unsightly. Row upon row of dull brick boxes, chopped off with a blank wall where another street crossed at the distance prescribed by the by-laws, marched over the fields of Tottenham, Hornsey, and Edmonton. Some of this building, called forth by the new railways and tramways, was not merely dull but thoroughly bad. Two estates, at Queen's Park, Willesden, and Noel Park, Wood Green, laid out for the Artizans' and General Dwellings Company under architectural supervision—a luxury that the builders of the common working-class housing did not indulge in—show a level of domestic building for inner suburbs somewhat superior to the ordinary in the second half of the 19th century. These are long terraces of houses, with some architectural feature, generally a turret, at the corners, regular, decent, and dull. They complied with the building by-laws, and they demonstrate how much the

---

[1] The dates given for these buildings are the years in which an illustrated account appeared in *The Builder*; in some cases a date a year or two earlier or later appears on the building itself.

'garden suburb' movement was wanted to open out and refresh the whole conception of domestic housing.[1]

So far as the buildings themselves were concerned, the way out had already been pointed by Philip Webb's Red House, put up at Bexley, Kent, in 1859, which returned to traditional English materials and forms of gable and roof instead of reviving yet another foreign historical style. It found few imitators, however, and the next significant experiment in domestic building did not come until 1875, when the earliest garden suburb, called Bedford Park, between Chiswick and Acton, was begun. It consisted of a number of streets, carrying early 18th-century associations in their names, lined with moderately large houses based on study of the native English house of the 17th century; the whole was grouped round a church by Norman Shaw which was certainly not Gothic as it was then understood, nor what it was called, 'Queen Anne,' in style. Bedford Park is recognisably a product of its period—nobody could think that Queen Anne's Gardens are early 18th-century; but it pointed the road that architects were to tread, and houses almost exactly like the best of Bedford Park were still being put up, with the addition of a garage, in Bournemouth and Leicester and plenty of other places fifty years later.

Houses with 'traditional' features and plan crept slowly into some of the more select parts of Middlesex. A cautious beginning was made in 1881 on the Mount Park estate at Harrow, and from that time there was a more determined return to the picturesque in the north-west, at Harrow, Pinner, Northwood, and Stanmore, for those who could pay for it. R. A. Briggs was one of the ablest exponents of this type of design, and Arnold Mitchell was building houses at Harrow from 1893 onwards that pointed forward, with their half-timbering on the gables and bits of coloured glass in the porches, to the builders' patterns of the 1920s. More truly, perhaps, the builders' houses pointed back to Mitchell's.

The next significant housing development was the Hampstead Garden Suburb of 1905, lying within Hendon and Finchley. This was far from complete by 1914, and it was not continued quite in the way it began; but its early part shows Edwardian domestic building at its best (*Plate 66*). It was an experiment in town planning and building control in accordance with an overriding conception of the whole estate; its centre-piece was provided by a square of houses, enclosing two churches and an 'institute,' or communal centre, all based on designs by Edwin Lutyens. The suburb is built throughout of brick, some of it plastered over, with hipped roofs of early 18th-century type or steep tiled roofs with dormer windows. Besides Raymond Unwin and Barry Parker, who shared the general architectural control, M. H. Baillie Scott, E. Guy Dawber, Geoffrey Lucas, and T. M. Wilson designed individual houses or groups

[1] *Builder* 33 (1875), p. 933; 44 (1883), p. 880.

of dwellings in the formative period. The houses are good neighbours; the lines of the roofs combine well when seen from a distance; the backs look as good as the fronts; and the roads, though the plan is rather wilful in parts, are laid out to conform with the contours of the ground, not to ignore them. Important and novel virtues, these, in 1905; and not enough regarded since. The place is dated, of the age immediately before the private motor car; but the practice, if not the art, of designing suburbs has not advanced much since then.[1]

Many good houses of the Edwardian age are to be found in Middlesex, if the term 'Edwardian' may be extended to cover the quarter-century from 1890 to 1914 when the same architects were busy designing admirable houses and feeble public buildings. (The Middlesex County Council's own Guildhall in Parliament Square must be excepted from this last criticism; in a difficult situation, facing Westminster Abbey and the Houses of Parliament, it is yet a highly successful building.) The Hampstead Garden Suburb was a pattern book for cottages in the traditional manner—its principal planner, Raymond Unwin, called it the picturesque style; but its immediate influence was less strong in that department than in the larger detached house. Many good works of this kind were put up, especially at Southgate, Hendon, and in the north-west. Few of them, unfortunately, proclaim when they were built, as they should: a house, like a book, that claims to be anything at all should bear its date. The earliest considerable groups of smaller houses to adopt the new technique of terrace building, with varied layout and good treatment of corners and cul-de-sac roads, were built on the London County Council's White Hart Lane estate at Tottenham, the Government housing scheme at Stag Lane, Kingsbury (1917), and T. Alwyn Lloyd's estates for the Great Western Railway at West Acton and Hayes (1920). The London County Council's Watling estate, between Hendon and Edgware, is the principal large municipal development of the era between the wars. The outline plan provided for all existing large trees to be preserved where possible and for open spaces to be retained. The terrace house predominates, treated in different ways, with a good deal of variety in external finish, and the architectural effect is good. The general planning was less satisfactory; no space was provided for community services, shops, churches, and halls, and they had to be placed at the edges or fitted in later. None the less, a community spirit has grown up; the gardens are well looked after; and its neighbours no longer speak of 'Little Moscow.'[2]

Unhappily the characteristic building of Middlesex between the 20th-century wars was quite different from this kind of controlled, and often artful, development. It was the age of the arterial road, ribbon building, and the £595 or £695 house: semi-detached, three-bedroomed, with a

---

[1] *The Hampstead Garden Suburb: its Achievements and Significance* (1937). [2] A. G. Clarke, *The Story of Gold-beaters and Watling* (1931); R. Durant, *Watling: a Social Survey* (1939).

garage at the side. The thing was not peculiar to Middlesex; it was a national, not a regional, style, dumped down impartially at Newcastle, Bangor, or Plymouth. Still, the first 'little palaces' were at Colindale,[1] and Middlesex had more of them than most districts—one can travel from one end of the county to the other and see hardly anything else. The Middlesex examples set the standard from which regional variations in other parts of the country have sometimes slightly departed (*Plate 69*).

These houses stand in pairs with a strip of garden in front and a path running (not always straight) up to the front door from a wooden gate, usually bearing a name. There is a side door, too, more often used, and usually a garage. The building itself is brick, of two stories, with bow windows on ground and upper floors on one side, surmounted by a gable. The roof, of fairly steep pitch, is tiled, not slated. The gable is finished with plaster or rough-cast, with three or five vertical planks painted black affixed to the front. (These planks may seem a quaint conventional survival of half-timbering, like the grooves reproducing the grain of timber on the stone triglyphs of Doric temples, or the wood cut in canopy form on railway platform coverings to remind the traveller that he is lucky not to be standing under a canvas roofing; but they have in fact a purpose, to inform the observer that the house was not built by a local council.) There may be a porch with a decorative pattern of brick or tile; the casement windows probably have metal frames and leaded panes, and one window at least, perhaps the one in the door, varies the monotony by displaying some coloured glass in a design of uncertain inspiration. The front elevation asserts its individuality by picturesque variations in details, though the house is in fact exactly the same in height and plan as all its neighbours. The traveller by train, or the observer from the house in the road behind, sees that the backs are all the same, flat surfaces with windows cut into them as the interior needs dictate, relieved by a recurring pattern of external drain-pipes.

'Parades' of retail shops provide for the daily needs of the inhabitants. Though some of these in conspicuous positions on main roads affect a Tudor style, the architects have usually been content to design a plain front, perhaps diversified with a band of concrete or ornament of some other kind along the upper stories, which provide flats for some of the shop people to live in (*Plates 70 and 71*). Distinction of one shop from another is provided by ingenious application of the shop fitter's art: different colours on the fascias, variations in the entrances and the disposition of the windows, lettering of the trade-mark kind to call attention to the branch establishments of multiple providers, and ingeniously compelling signs hung at right angles to the shop, bearing such names as 'Suzanne' in oversize handwriting for a dress-shop, or 'Maison Frederick: Coiffeur de Dames' for the local barber. Here and

[1] Houses so described were being advertised soon after the tube railway was extended through Colindale in 1924.

there is a cinema, whose style defies classification as its embellishments, however familiar to the present age, beggar description. The front is probably finished in cream terra-cotta; the inside is opulent. The style is certainly striking, perhaps novel—sometimes Egyptian, or even (as at Southall) Chinese.

The banks, on the other hand, are concerned to show the good breeding of their managements. The Middlesex branches demonstrate how the head offices have always struggled to keep not too far behind the van of architectural fashion in street architecture. The London & Provincial (Barclay's) at Enfield (1897) is an essay in the Dutch gabled style; Lloyd's at Wealdstone (1909) is good of its period; the Westminster at West Ealing (1912) a pleasant 'Queen Anne' pastiche; the Westminster at Harrow (1917) a tortured composition in specially-made 2-inch red bricks. The National Provincial branches in the north-western suburbs (1926-8) are superior examples of their neo-Georgian style.

A different kind of building houses the communal services. In this field the county council has led the way with its schools and hospitals, flat-surfaced with large windows, relying on mass and composition, not elaboration of detail, to make their effect. The schools, by the council's architects, are a notable group, mostly in the north-west, as at Headstone Lane, Ruislip, South Harrow, Southall (*Plate 59*), and Alperton. Individual authorities have been more timid with their town halls and libraries: at Hendon, for example, and Tottenham the municipal buildings are dignified and lumpish. Wembley, Friern Barnet (*Plate 63*), and Hornsey (*Plate 62*) are exceptional in having built town halls that are not imitation 18th-century buildings but look their age (Hornsey, by R. H. Uren, 1935, is an altogether remarkable design), and Finchley has a good modern branch library on the Great North Road. The immense block of government offices at Bromyard Avenue, Acton Vale (1922), has a gaunt and slightly Teutonic aspect about it; but, if sinister, it compels respect by its clean lines. The British Empire Exhibition, held at Wembley Park in 1924 and 1925 in somewhat durable buildings wondering dubiously how to clothe their steel skeletons, is commemorated by the most satisfactory of them, the stadium, by J. W. Simpson and Maxwell Ayrton.

There are a few good factories in the melancholy area of North Acton and Park Royal, the three great blocks of Guinness's, by Sir Giles Gilbert Scott, claiming most attention by their good proportions and pleasing brickwork as well as their mere extent (*Plate 65*). The Great West Road demonstrates with many examples what to avoid in modern factory building; it is a pity there are not more showing how it should be done. Most of them try to look modern, by being rectangular compositions with flat concrete fronts, and most of them succeed in looking vulgar.

Apart from a house at Harrow Weald (Sunmore, Uxbridge Road) that fits easily into the surroundings though constructed entirely in the modern idiom, *Modernismus* has not had much chance in Middlesex; it seems to need the breezier air of the North Downs or the Chilterns, for it does not flourish in the *bourgeois* atmosphere of the north London suburban ring. There is one striking attempt at modern living, Highpoint flats at the top of North Hill, Highgate, built in 1935-8 and much admired at the time. Buildings like this have nothing to do with Middlesex, except that they happen to have occurred on its soil; neither their shapes nor their materials (nor, very often, their inhabitants) fit in. As Middlesex winters, fraught with damp and fog, go by, any one can see for himself that flat white surfaces get blotched and streaked while brick improves with age and weathering.

In other buildings, however, tradition and modern design have been mated with happy effect; the London Passenger Transport Board's series of stations on the Piccadilly line north to Cockfosters and north-west to Uxbridge shows that. The one at Arnos Grove, by Charles Holden, 1932, is a minor classic: standing by itself on a main road, geometrical in form with good use of reinforced concrete, glass, and brick, it looks like a station (*Plate 64*). Cockfosters (interior), Southgate, Ealing Common, and Sudbury Hill are almost as good. These stations, and adjacent buildings meant for baser uses like the car sheds at Northfields on the Hounslow line, show that new techniques injected into traditional building can produce a satisfying modern vernacular.[1]

In all, some housing estates and a few railway stations are the only secular building in this area put up since Soane went to live at Ealing in 1800 that can candidly be recommended as really worth looking at, though there are certainly many others of merit, and many again of curiosity.[2] The most recent churches, however, call for more attention; whether departing entirely from traditional planning and idioms, or retaining the Gothic spirit expressed in new forms and materials, they assert their religious purpose in a new fashion. They are light inside instead of dark, relying for emotive effect on line and mass and a few richly coloured fittings at the focus of attention, instead of their predecessors' diffused mysterious gloom, tinted, if the sun is shining, with strong reds and blues. The first fresh approach in the 20th century was Edwin Lutyens' pair of churches, St Jude-on-the-Hill and the Free Church, in the Hampstead Garden Suburb. Under great steeply-pitched tiled roofs covering both nave and aisles are bodies with interior round arches, barrel vaults, and saucer domes. This style has had few imitators; it was the novelty that was significant. At the same period, the Roman Catholic churches did not depart far from the orthodox Gothic-revival pattern, unless to adopt some Italianate elements. The Nonconformists,

[1] *Builder* 143 (1932), p. 599. [2] For the 1930s, H. Casson, *New Sights of London* (1938).

feeling perhaps that they had conformed too hastily in the 19th century to the long, narrow, and somewhat dark building that was essentially priestly and unprotestant, cast about for some style to express their own intentions more clearly. Their early 20th-century churches were often rectangular buildings with windows of a Perpendicular persuasion; there is a notable collection at Muswell Hill. The church at Mill Hill (1920), with deep roof and dormer windows, still Gothic, marks a departure from ecclesiological influence; the Unitarian church of All Souls, Golders Green (1927), is basilican in design; the Methodist church at Friern Barnet (1931), with a shallow dome, is a development from it. In the 1930s a group of churches at Perivale Park, Eversfield Gardens (Mill Hill), Wembley Park, Pinner, and Neasden provided interesting and sometimes sound solutions to the peculiar problems of Nonconformist church worship.[1]

The Church of England's experiments in building led it in different directions: the barn style, with heavy timber construction exposed in the interiors, handsome in its way, and with some affinity to Middlesex tradition, as at St Andrew, Sudbury (1924), and the new parish church at Greenford (1939); the modified traditional, as at Giles Gilbert Scott's St Alban, Golders Green (1932), cruciform, lit from windows in the tower over the crossing; the unorthodox plan, like the John Keble church, Mill Hill (1936), and the Ascension, Hanger Hill, Ealing (1939); and a really successful and satisfying group of the 1930s retaining the traditional arrangement of nave and chancel, while employing the new freedom of concrete construction: St Thomas, Boston Road, Hanwell, St.Alban, North Harrow (perhaps the best example) (*Plate 61*); St Paul, Ruislip Manor; St Paul, South Harrow; and St Michael, Tokyngton, Wembley.[2] These are proclaimed to be churches by towers freely treating the conventional pattern and, in most of them, by the pointed arch of the concrete-finished arcades; they have simple, almost austere, interiors, light and spare, and all the details are significant and harmonious, except the electric lighting at some places and the banners of the church guilds almost everywhere. The interior furnishings are important: too many churches have fittings of standard neo-Victorian types supplied by church furnishers; old churches where modern furniture has been installed seem to have had bad luck with the selection, and there is too much expensive *bondieuserie* about. In all the newest churches, however, the fittings have been designed with the building; while they certainly owe something to contemporary stage design, most of them show freshness and vitality in the architects' treatment of themes—pews, font, screen, reredos—that had become worn out in the traditional variations.

The architect has so far had little chance to show his hand in Middlesex since 1945: perhaps as well, to judge from the works without

[1] M. S. Briggs, *Puritan Architecture* (1946). [2] *Fifty Modern Churches*, ed. R. J. McNally (Incorporated Church Building Society, 1947); G. W. O. Addleshaw and F. Etchells, *Architectural Setting of Anglican Worship* (1948), p. 234.

form or character being produced elsewhere. Only on the London County Council's estate near Headstone is enough new work to be seen assembled together to allow a judgment to be formed. Here the community planning is more thoughtful and should be more successful than it was at Watling twenty years before, but the mere architecture will probably seem to the observer a generation hence to be outstandingly plain. Baldness is all. Watling was deliberately picturesque at many points, both in the shape and the disposition of the houses, and it was certainly not the last word in suburban design; but the groups of buildings at Headstone are a good deal less of a pleasure to look at. Something has been learned from experience, and something forgotten.

CHAPTER XIII

LONDON AND MIDDLESEX

'[Middlesex] is in effect but the suburbs at large of London, replenished with the retiring houses of the gentry and citizens thereof.' THOMAS FULLER[1]

LONDON overshadows Middlesex. Within the natural framework formed by the soil and the river waterways, London has been shown in the preceding chapters exercising its unmistakable influence on Middlesex, first on the settlement of the county and then on its social, economic, ecclesiastical, and political life. As the great trading centre of the land, London attracted the man-made communications from north and west, road and canal and railway; as the usual seat of the royal court, it drew into the home counties men who looked to the king for advancement; as the greatest agglomeration of consumers in the country, its needs governed the agricultural practices of the surrounding area, and later its industrial developments; and finally its demand for housing turned the county into one great suburb. This last has made London and Middlesex at first glance indistinguishable. But only to a very casual glance: the two areas are distinguishable, and distinct, and their relations with each other form a separate chapter in their history. It is a chapter that contains some obscure passages, and a significant epilogue is perhaps very soon to be added to it.

Almost at the outset of the story comes the obscurest passage of all: what were the relations of London (if there was a London) and Middlesex (if there was such an entity) in the darkest age, between A.D. 450 and 600? The state of the argument has already been briefly recorded in Chapter II; the question remains open, and inviting, to specialist debate. A second important controversy concerns the 11th and 12th centuries: was Middlesex then in some sense an appendage, or *territorium*, of London? The key point in this is the position of the sheriff: did the sheriff of London exercise jurisdiction over Middlesex as well, implying a subject status, or did the double shrievalty of London and Middlesex mean rather a partnership? The answer will suggest how the

[1] Fuller (page 33, note 1), ii., p. 313.

city and county were first linked, some time before A.D. 1000, though it will not necessarily cast light so far back as the dark age.

The older view was stated by W. J. Loftie in 1886: 'Middlesex affords the sole example in England of a district held as a Greek city held its περίοικοι, a German city its *Unterthanen*, or an Italian city its 'campagna';' in other words, it was subject territory. Supporters of this view rely on a charter of Henry I confirming the right of the citizens of London to 'have their chases to hunt, as well and fully as their ancestors have had, that is—to say, in Chiltre, in Middlesex, and in Surrey'—the rights mentioned by FitzStephen in a passage cited earlier.[1]

J.H. Round, however, controverted this view in his *Geoffrey de Mandeville* (1892).[2] He argued that the offices of port-reeve of London and shire-reeve (or sheriff) of Middlesex were united in the same person as equal dignities, the city of London and the county of Middlesex remaining distinct though not separated entities throughout. The joint office passed, with all his estates, from Esegar (or Ansgar), the 'staller' or master of the horse under Edward the Confessor and Harold, to Geoffrey de Mandeville I as part of the Conquest settlement; a charter of 1141 conferred the shrievalty on Geoffrey de Mandeville II on the same terms as were granted to his grandfather. After various alterations of the terms during the remainder of the 12th century, the right of appointing the sheriff was finally made over in 1199 to the citizens of London, and they continued to make the appointment until the county got a sheriff for itself as part of the revolution in county government made by the act of 1888.[3]

Throughout this time there was no alteration in the formal relations between the county and the city, which never formed part of the administrative county. Westminster lay within Middlesex; so did the Tower Hamlets and all the other suburbs outside the City area. These districts achieved various degrees of limited and delegated independence in some departments of administration as they developed into parts of a densely-populated city;[4] but that story belongs to the history of London and not to the area that forms present-day Middlesex. While London was profoundly affecting Middlesex life by its economic force, the administrative pattern remained substantially unchanged until the agitations and reforms of the 19th century. These economic effects have already been outlined; it remains to indicate how Londoners increasingly settled in the county for residences and visited certain places in it for recreation, and then to survey the most recent era when London burst and submerged the green of Middlesex under an advancing flood of brick.

Already in the 13th century citizens and merchants of London who could afford to maintain a house in the country as well as in town owned property in Middlesex villages. Humfrey Bocointe, son of a justiciar of

[1] W. J. Loftie, *London* (1886), p. 123. W. de G. Birch, *Historical Charters and Constitutional Documents of the City of London* (1884), p. 4, quoted in *V.C.H.* ii., p. 254, dates this charter between 1100 and 1129. [2] J. H. Round, *Geoffrey de Mandeville* (1892), p. 347. [3] *V.C.H.* ii., p. 18; W. Page, *London: its Origin and Early Development* (1923), p. 186. [4] Dowdell, p. 1.

London, held land at Edgware in 1170, and Andrew Buckerel, mayor from 1231 to 1235, whose family name is commemorated by Bucklersbury, had a country house at Edmonton. The FitzAlulfs held property at Acton early in the 13th century; the Blunds, London merchants, owned land at Edmonton, where the Paynes, aldermen of Castle Baynard, also settled.[1] Above all, the London clergy had important temporal interests in Middlesex; the St Paul's estates in Willesden, Clerkenwell lands in Harefield and Cranford, St Giles's land in Feltham, meant that ties of ownership and interest linked the city and the county.

The Church manors just outside the gates of London may have had the effect of constricting the City throughout the Middle Ages within narrow limits; the Church rarely let go a property it had once acquired.[2] (Later, it is true, the City itself resisted expansion of its boundaries.). Certainly the Dissolution of the Monasteries in the 1530s and the sale of their lands transferred much Middlesex property to London merchants, as well as to more immediate supporters of the king. There are four 16th-century brasses and one of the 17th century extant in Middlesex churches to officers of the royal household.[3]

When Hampton Court became a royal palace it was kept in close touch with London; the river banks and the roads joining the two became lined with houses, and men began making the daily journey to and from town. In 1636 the Privy Council, having forbidden communication between London and Hampton (where the court then was) on account of the plague, reported that 'divers Londoners obtained houses near Hampton Court and Oatlands, and these inhabit, going daily to and from London, which cannot be without great peril to their Majesties'; they were ordered to give up this practice and to stop their servants going up to London.[4]

'Daily-breading' from the Thames valley has thus an ancestry of three centuries. This was among the well-to-do; it was some time before London tradesmen lived outside the City and Westminster and the immediate neighbourhood. In 1709 Edmond Skinner claimed exemption from parochial office in Enfield, where he lived, on the ground that he travelled daily to the City, where he was a haberdasher of petty wares; fifteen years later a stage-coach proprietor of South Mimms was excused from serving as high constable of Edmonton hundred because he resided chiefly at his place of business in Goswell Street and could not execute the office without prejudice to his own affairs.[5]

Descriptions of Middlesex as a kind of pleasure-garden for wealthy Londoners begin with John Norden's in 1593:

'This is plentifully stored, as it seemeth beautified, with many fair and comely buildings, especially of the merchants of London, who have planted their houses of recreation not in the meanest places, which also

---

[1] Page (page 189, note 3), pp. 241, 255, 263; W. J. Loftie, *London* (1886), p. 79. [2] W. J. Loftie, *London* (1886), p. 121, and *History of London* (1883), ii., p. 4; N. G. Brett-James, *Growth of Stuart London* (1935), p. 223. [3] Stephenson (page 167, note 1). [4] E. Law, *Short History of Hampton Court* (ed. 1906), p. 214. [5] *M.C.R. Reports*, pp. 4, 84.

they have cunningly contrived, curiously beautified with divers devices, neatly decked with rare inventions, environed with orchards of sundry delicate fruits, gardens with delectable walks, arbours, alleys, and great variety of pleasing dainties: all which seem to be beautiful ornaments unto this country.'[1] Thomas Cox wrote in 1724: 'We may call it almost all London, being inhabited chiefly by the citizens, who fill the towns in it with their country houses, to which they often resort that they may breathe a little sweet air, free from the fogs and smoke of the City.'[2]

These charming descriptions hardly represent all the truth of the matter. Such scenes were to be found on some of the roads leading out of London, notably at Chiswick and Isleworth, and at Highgate, Tottenham, and Edmonton; but there were large areas, the commons of Hounslow and Finchley, the clay lands of the north-west, the wilds of Enfield Chase, and the backwaters like Perivale and Northolt, that were not yet beautified by 1750. Some were still strangely rustic in 1900; if a writer of 1898 may be believed, 'yokels in smocks with strangely and elaborately embroidered fronts that are really more primitive than anything we see in Cheshire or Staffordshire' were still to be met near Edgware.[3]

While it yet remained rural, the county provided pleasure grounds for the ordinary Londoner to relax in. The family rendezvous that John Gilpin, the citizen of credit and renown, so signally failed to keep was at the Bell at Edmonton. The George and Vulture at Tottenham was a well-known tea-garden in the 17th and 18th centuries, succeeded in the 19th by the Ferry Boat inn at Hale (*Plate 39*). Hornsey Wood House was a modest rural inn which became a noted tea house in the 18th century, a famous duelling ground, and later a place for anglers and pigeon-shooters, with an eel-pie house on the New River;[4] Johnson in the *Idler* of 1758 made it one of the places to which Zachary Treacle was dragged by his wife on Sundays.[5] The north-west, with few natural or artificial attractions, was not visited until the middle 19th century, when the earlier resorts had been built over; then the White Swan at Golders Green had a popular tea-garden, and the Green Man at Wembley Hill was favoured for trade dinners. Kingsbury reservoir, or the Welsh Harp, was visited for angling and the hay fields between there and Harrow for pigeon-shooting.[6]

On the west side the Thames afforded recreation to Londoners from very early times. The London Apprentice inn on the river at Isleworth was kept open all night at some periods for their benefit.[7] A little way upstream was Kendal House, advertised in 1750 as being open for public breakfasts.[8] Eighty or ninety years later the island opposite Twickenham was at the height of its popularity, of a somewhat lower order; it is described in *Nicholas Nickleby*: 'It had come to pass that

[1] J. Norden, *Speculum Britanniae* (ed. 1723), p. 12. [2] Cox (page 44, note 1), iii., p. 1. [3] A. Rimmer, *Rambles round Eton and Harrow* (ed. 2, 1898), p. 244. [4] Hassell, p. 30. [5] *Idler*, no 15, 22 July 1758, quoted in *Johnson's England* (page 153, note 4), i., p. 192. [6] Thorne, art. Golders Green, Kingsbury, and Wembley. [7] *H.C.M.* 7 (1905), p. 245. [8] *Daily Advertiser*, 4 April 1750, quoted by Lysons, art. Isleworth.

afternoon, that Miss Morleena Kenwigs had received an invitation to repair next day, per steamer from Westminster Bridge, unto the Eel-pie Island at Twickenham: there to make merry upon a cold collation, bottled beer, shrub [a drink prepared from orange or lemon juice, sugar, and rum] and shrimps, and to dance in the open air to the music of a locomotive band.'

For the 18th-century excursionist with a taste for the curious there had been Horace Walpole's collection of bric-à-brac at Strawberry Hill, which parties might see, upon application made in due form, between the hours of 12 and 3 in summer only; only one party, of not more than four persons, was allowed each day, and those who had tickets were desired not to bring children.[1] From the middle of the 18th century Hampton Court, falling out of use as a royal residence, became a favourite show-place, where the deputy-housekeeper conducted visitors round the state rooms for a fee, the greater part of which she retained. Queen Victoria gave orders very soon after her accession that the state rooms should be opened free to the public; 350,000 people visited them in 1851, and about a quarter of a million was the average annual number in the late 19th century. In 1932 it was estimated that 600,000 people visited the palace and gardens each year.

Of all the excursions from London into unknown Middlesex, perhaps the one that appealed as most novel and charming was the ride by canal barge from Paddington to Greenford and Uxbridge. J. T. Smith, in *Nollekens and his Times*, described the emotions that the trip called forth, not without a glancing allusion to the parsimony of his friends:

'When it was customary for so much company to visit Uxbridge by the barges drawn by horses gaily decked out with ribands, Mr. and Mrs. Nollekens, with all the gaiety of youthful extravagance, embarked on board, and actually dined out on that gala day at their own expense.' In letters after this trip 'Mrs. Nollekens most poetically expatiated upon the clearness of the water, the nut-brown tints of the wavy corn, and the ruddy and healthful tints of the cottagers' children who waited anxiously to see the vessel approach their native shores.'[2]

The rusticity of Middlesex impressed observers at this time. William Marshall wrote in 1799: 'The farmers of the vale of London, even within a few miles of the town, are (the higher class excepted) as homely in their dress and manners as those of the more recluse parts of the kingdom, and are far less enlightened and intelligent than those of many parts of it.' But a change was already coming over the parts easily accessible from London. Middleton noted in 1798: 'the entrance to Enfield from the windmill is charming; it abounds with smart boxes of from £30 to £60 a year.'[3] Horace Smith, writing of Brighton in 1813, began: 'The Cit forgoes his box at Turnham Green.' Londoners of more modest fortunes

---

[1] *Gentleman's Magazine*, 1803, part i., p. 203. [2] Smith (page 65, note 2), p. 188. [3] Marshall, p. 25; Middleton, p. 124.

were beginning to dwell in the nearer parts of the county. Smollett's prophecy, made in *Humphry Clinker* (1771), that London was growing so rapidly that soon the whole of Middlesex would be covered with brick, was showing signs of beginning to come true, though for the moment the smart boxes hid their brick behind a stucco facing.

Roads were good enough by the early 19th century for prosperous people of the middle classes working in London to live part of the week in London and part in villages on the west side. About 1823 Thomas Love Peacock, of the East India House, moved to live at Halliford at the week-ends; and in 1830 Benjamin Armstrong, a prosperous oil merchant of Hatton Garden, took 'a very pretty and rather commodious cottage-residence' at Southall Green, to live there for six months of the year and in town for the rest: two kinds of occupancy which are now mostly found farther away from town.[1] William Cobbett may have the last word on this subject; in a *Rural Ride* of 1822 he makes the damning judgment: 'All Middlesex is *ugly*,' and justifies it with a summary account of the road through Twickenham, Hampton, Sunbury, and Shepperton: The buildings consist generally of tax-eaters' showy, tea-garden-like boxes, and of shabby dwellings of labouring people who, in this part of the country, look to be about half Saint Giles's: dirty, and have every appearance of drinking gin.'[2]

At this time a great revolution was at hand: mechanical transport was on the point of bringing on the change in the face of Middlesex that turned it from an agricultural appendage to London into the suburb, all but continuous, that it had become by 1939. The distinction between present-day London and Middlesex has grown out of this: London is the area that was within daily reach of town for all classes in the age of horse-drawn transport; Middlesex is the next outer ring from north to south-west that had to wait for mechanical transport—railway, tramcar, and road motor—before it could effectively become a London dormitory. The formal boundary between them was arrived at on quite a different basis; but, though crude and not allowing for exceptions both ways at the fringe, the statement is true enough. These different origins have stamped the two areas with different characteristics.

Mechanical transport, then, has cast Middlesex in the pattern it now presents. The companies owning the three great main lines of railway running from Euston, Paddington, and St Pancras did comparatively little to stimulate building along their lines for the first fifty or sixty years of the railway era, for two main reasons: they concentrated on the more profitable long-distance passenger and goods traffic, and did not choose to fill their lines with suburban trains; and their terminal stations were unattractively far from the City and Westminster, where most London workers needed to go. The southern and eastern lines, on the other hand,

[1] *Novels of Thomas Love Peacock*, ed. D. Garnett (1948), introduction; MS. Diary of B. J. Armstrong. [2] Cobbett (page 39, note 2), i., p. 92.

with less valuable main-line traffic and their terminals in or close to the City, began very early to provide good services to the suburbs. Thus the nearer districts of Surrey, Kent, and Essex filled up with streets of houses long before places in Middlesex at the same distance from town. In the northern sector, however, the Great Eastern Railway, which like the southern lines could command no important long-distance traffic, turned Tottenham and Edmonton into artisan quarters in a very few years after 1870; and the Great Northern, although it had a large main-line traffic, tried to superimpose an intensive suburban service upon it—nearly throttling itself in the process—and caused Hornsey, Wood Green and Finchley to grow almost as fast. In this sector, too, street tramways were built in the 1880s; after electrification in the 1900s, they spread throughout the county, with a frequent service and workmen's fares. Houses and shops soon sprang up beside the roads the trams traversed.

In the south-west, at Hounslow, Twickenham, and other places on the London & South-Western Railway, development began in the fifties and sixties with some superior housing schemes, such as the Spring Grove estate at Isleworth, like the outer Surrey suburbs. Settlement along the Metropolitan line in the north-west did not begin seriously until electrification in 1905. Electric tube railways entered the county at Golders Green in 1907; their full effect was exerted in the 1920s and 1930s when, allied with motor buses, they made every part of the county easily accessible, and very few places in it more than an hour's travelling from Charing Cross. By 1940 many people did not think that excessively long for daily travel; in 1949 one in five of those who regularly used public transport in the London area took over an hour on the journey to work.[1]

Three principal kinds of suburban settlement may be distinguished. The first was beside the main roads leading away from London—Turnham Green, Ealing, Tottenham, for example. These were mostly mere lines of houses and gardens strung out along the main roads, ribbon development without depth, and the spaces between the radiating roads were left untouched. Second came settlements detached from the main mass, centred on some existing small town or village that had acquired a railway station. Railway companies gave free season tickets for house-holders at Enfield in 1849, when the original Eastern Counties branch from Angel Road was opened, and at Harrow in 1858, when the London & North Western offered a first-class season free for 11 years to every occupier of a new house over £50 annual value.[2] Harrow developed a good deal of settlement, though places much closer to London, like Wembley and parts of Willesden, were still farmland. Third within the Middlesex area—first, of course, in London—came settlement on the fringes of the existing continuous town, as the built-up city advanced upon and engulfed areas

[1] See page 57, note 2. [2] Anon., *Story of Enfield* (1930), p. 45; *Builder* 16 (1858), p. 296.

that had been left untouched by earlier settlement because they were inaccessible, low-lying, or otherwise undesirable.[1]

The suburbs thus began life at different times in the century from 1840 to 1940, and they arose in distinct forms. Useful clues to the characters of a suburb are to be found in the answers to the questions: 'When was it built?' and 'What sort of people was it built for?' with perhaps some allowance made for the answer to a third: 'Does that sort of people live there now?' The railway and tramway maps of the county suggest answers to the first and second of these questions, if it is remembered that the date when a railway was opened may be less significant for suburban development round its stations than the year when the line was electrified or an intensive service begun. Still, to provide a station at all usually meant that some development began at once; in 1875 James Thorne noted (a few hundred yards over the Middlesex border, but generally applicable): About the Barnet station has sprung up within the last few years one of those new half-finished railway villages which we have come to look on as almost a necessary to every station within a moderate distance of London.' All the same, a railway station and a tolerable service of trains did not always mean that building began; not a single house was built within a quarter of a mile of Palmers Green station between 1876, when it was opened, and 1888 because the local owners refused to sell their land.[2]

Even with such reservations made, however, it would still be too simple to explain away the process of settlement in the last 120 years altogether by reckoning the comparative accessibility of the different districts. Settlement in Middlesex followed, and was encouraged by, the provision of good communications; transport undertakings were usually at least prepared for, and sometimes well ahead of, development. But development does not everywhere wait for good transport. Ilford and south-west Essex generally have shown otherwise in the 20th century. Still, in Middlesex ease of access promoted the first two types of suburban development—the ribbon and the overgrown village; but other influences were also at work in shaping the final pattern. Several islands or wedges of country remained unused until, when all the surrounding areas had been developed, they were at last built over. Such late-used patches of land lay on valley ground between comparatively elevated stretches, as between Muswell Hill and Friern Barnet, and in the Brent valley. In most English towns the high ground is the wealthier quarter and the valley is the slum. People who went from London during the 19th century to live in Middlesex were mostly, except in the north-east, of the middle or wealthier sort, and, outside the Thames valley, they lived on the hills, at Ealing, Harrow, Hendon, Finchley, and Southgate. The valleys filled up with sewage-farms and isolation hospitals, or stayed

[1] Smith (see page 55, note 4), p. 9. [2] Thorne, art. Barnet; H. W. Newby, *'Old' Southgate* (1949), p. 59.

as they were, so that at the beginning of the 1920s they were still comparatively unoccupied, waiting for one of the new roads, factories, and housing for factory workers.[1]

The natural geography of the region has also affected suburban settlement in another way. The most significant division in the county for the farmer was the boundary between the clay and the alluvium that runs east and west just above the Uxbridge road. Modern Middlesex has assumed the form it now presents largely because modern technique and transport have enabled men to ignore the natural features of the soil; but nature will not be overriden completely, even in a London suburb, and the geographical division has had an evident, though indirect, effect on settlement. In 1869 an agricultural writer thought both types of ground repelled rather than encouraged the 'colonisation' of either part of the county, and made it unattractive as a residence for the rich; Londoners looked for gravel or chalk for building country residences, he observed, and Middlesex could only offer cold clays with poor water supply or flat loam and gravel.[2] Londoners have not been permanently repelled by these disadvantages, but the settlements have conformed with the soil. North of the line, on the heavy clays, water is scarce and drainage is difficult; house-building has therefore required considerable capital, and comparatively large estates were undertaken at one time by speculative builders, often companies, who had to carry out road works and arrange for main water and drainage to be provided. Each unit consequently being comparatively large, there was more uniformity in the appearance of the buildings, and usually more tidiness in planning; in general, also, the houses cost more than those south of the line. There water was easy to get, by sinking wells, and the brick-earth and gravel soil easy to drain; the 9,000 inhabitants of Ashford had no main drainage until 1934. In this sector, therefore, there was a good deal of sporadic small-scale building, often no more than one house at a time.[3] Much of the difference between the modern urban districts of Ruislip-Northwood, north of the line, and Hayes and Harlington, its neighbour on the south, is to be referred to the soils they stand on.

The other natural feature that has powerfully affected the settlement of Middlesex since 1800 is the prevailing wind. This is the south-west wind, and, as in most of the cities of Western Europe, it makes the East End the poorest part of the town. Londoners who can afford it have always had their private houses west of the smoky quarters of the City and the docks. Industries therefore went eastward, fashion and fashionable trades west; so that, apart from Brentford, whose exceptional position where the canal joined the Thames promoted some of the dirtier kinds of manufacture, Middlesex districts escaped those developments of the heavier industries and the housing for them that sprawl beside the

---

[1] Smith (see page 55, note 4), p. 167. [2] Clutterbuck (see page 40, note 3). [3] Willatts, pp. 193, 206.

Thames in south Essex and north Kent. The port and docks were partly responsible for this, of course; but so was the south-west wind.

Three things, therefore, combined to hold back the march of London building north-west and west in the 19th century, compared with the strides it was making in other directions: less developed communications; unattractive soil; and lack of industrial development. But this retarded state could not last for ever. London's population was growing, by immigration and natural increase, and crowded districts had to be thinned out. London had to expand over the adjacent countryside in every direction, to build its new houses and to plant its new industries, and services had to be provided for the whole gigantic mass. The change in Middlesex began in earnest about 1905, when tramway and railway electrification and tube railways began to improve the communications, and the internal-combustion engine at once removed the demand for the hay crop and made many industries independent of waterways and railways.

It will naturally be asked, either on a contemplation of the pleasant well-ordered rural Middlesex of the middle 19th century, or after a visit to the apparently endless suburbs of today: 'Did this have to happen?' and 'Did it have to happen like this?' Certainly something of this kind did have to happen, unless the British economy had taken a very different course, and a much less prosperous one, in the modern age. It will not do merely to lament the fields and rare cottages and tall elms of old Middlesex. A nation that does not adopt technical invention, and does not raise its standard of life and level of population, stands still; and in the modern world to stand still is to go backwards. Given the course of economic development since 1850, London was bound to grow, and Middlesex to bear crops of houses instead of hay. But the growth certainly did not have to happen as it did. Middlesex is ill-planned in its local streets and through communications, chaotic in outward appearance, and much of it downright ugly. More than that, some of the best soil in all England, which twenty and thirty years ago was yielding the finest crops for the market, has been sterilised.

Some people blame the notion that semi-detached or two-storey houses are the only possible habitations for Londoners: why not, they ask, put them into flats? The whole history of London suburban development is against them: Londoners will travel far from their work to have a garden at home. A royal commission was told by Lord Shaftesbury in 1884 that there had always been 'the greatest desire in London and other large towns that every man should have his own house ... It would be a great blessing. But in such a vast city as this it is next to impossible.'[1] The next fifty years did their best to achieve the next to impossible. In places like Paris and Vienna, where the line of

[1] Quoted by Clapham, *Modern Britain*, ii., p. 489.

fortifications existing until modern times has fixed the city limits and
forced buildings upwards instead of allowing them to spread outwards, or
in Venice and New York where the site is naturally limited, the citizens
may think it natural, or at least not intolerable, to live in blocks of
tenements; but the Londoner does not easily tolerate it. His idea is: 'One
house, one family'; it might be truer to say it is his ideal. It follows that
London building is greedy of land; this has its advantages in a war of
aerial bombardment, but it is all too wasteful.[1]

The damage is done, modern Middlesex is there, built up, and the
few portions that have so far escaped are being earmarked for this or that
particular purpose. Would the result have been better if it had been
conducted with the full benefit of town-planning? The town-planners' art
and science are still largely experimental, and they are not yet free from
the reproach that their principles are apt to be changed rather often, as
one particular preoccupation succeeds another, so that planning policies
are adjusted as fast as political ones. The present mode is to favour
independent satellite towns, having separate zones within them for
housing, shopping, and industry. This seems unduly wasteful of land and
of transport, and a fresh theory may perhaps arise to supplant it. Under
the full rigours of planning, too, it is fair to suppose that fewer houses
would have been built, or shops and services provided for them; and
only a very inhuman planner would welcome that result. It is open to
question, also, whether the whole would have functioned any better as a
community if it had been a planners' creation; tidiness, in most
departments of English life, is generally felt to be artificial.

Yet Middlesex today is a mess to look at, and in addition much of it
is a very awkward and impractical place to live in. Shops, communications, open spaces, and houses are intermingled without order or natural
grace or much practical advantage. If it had been planned in larger units
than the normal housing estate or builder's piece, the places would have
been more attractive to look at. Probably also they would have been
more conveniently arranged for their internal economy, and many
people would have been saved long journeys to work-places and shops
and schools and parks. Town-planning would have produced better
places, though it is equally certain that there would have been fewer.

*　*　*　*　*

Thus far the latest age has been considered only in respect of the
physical impact of London on Middlesex. Much has been altered also in
their formal administrative relations, and there has been and still is much
agitation for further change. The problem of administering the London
agglomeration was already before a royal commission in 1837, which felt
it to be a problem of a quite special and peculiar kind: 'The word

[1] For an appreciation of the single-family dwelling in London's development, S. E.
Rasmussen, *London: the Unique City* (ed. 1948).

suburb,' it observed, 'can no longer be applied with its usual signification to the vast extent of uninterrupted town which forms the Metropolis of the British Empire.'[1] Thus began a long discussion and agitation for reform of London's local government. In 1854 another royal commission reported that 'the two first conditions of municipal government, minute local knowledge and community of interest, would be wanting if the whole of London were, by an extension of the present boundaries of the City, placed under a single municipal corporation.'[2] Extension of the City's boundaries into Middlesex was not wanted either by the City or by the districts outside the City.

A new authority, the Metropolitan Board of Works, was constituted under the Metropolis Management Act of 1855 to discharge many local functions—principally control of streets and sewers—within the area covered by the Registrar-General's bills of mortality. The historians of the London County Council attribute this limitation of area to Sir Benjamin Hall, chief commissioner of works; he apparently, they write, 'decided on his own that the new Metropolitan Board of Works area should be the Registrar-General's district … [This] had its origin in the bills of mortality kept since the 16th century for parishes in the City and the neighbouring populous areas, largely so that the Court and others might be warned of plague and seek safer retreat … London, for the 1855 Act, comprised the 36 registration districts used for the census of 1851, and so substantially it remains.'[3]

The 1855 act hardly stemmed the debate on the government of London; it seemed to be necessarily implied that the completely urban districts must be severed from Middlesex, and smaller areas from Surrey and Kent. After several fruitless proposals the County of London was finally established by an amendment (an afterthought) to the Local Government Act of 1888.[4] In January 1889 the new county took over the Metropolitan Board of Works area, and apart from a transfer from Middlesex to London near Finsbury Park in 1899 the boundary of 1855 remains today as the dividing line between the two authorities. It is anomalous at many points. It was out of date at the start—parts, at least, of Willesden, Hornsey, and Tottenham would have fallen within the urban area if it had been determined afresh in 1888; and it is a very unpractical boundary, passing down the middle of busy streets in Kilburn, Highgate, and Seven Sisters Road, and at other places following the course of obliterated and long-forgotten streams.

Middlesex was not completely swept out from London. The seat of county administration remained at the Guildhall in Parliament Square, on the site in the city of Westminster where the Middlesex justices used to meet; the High Courts of Justice still acknowledge the old Middlesex area for many purposes (there never have been separate assizes for the

[1] Quoted by Smellie (page 121, note 1), p. 173.   [2] Quoted by H. Finer, *English Local Government* (ed. 3, 1946), p. 480; Smellie (see preceding note), p. 174.   [3] Gibbon and Bell (page 67, note 2), p. 22; Finer (preceding note), p. 506; Smellie (page 121, note 1), p. 175.   [4] Gibbon and Bell (page 67, note 2) (1939), p. 65.

county); and the acts requiring land to be registered at the Middlesex Deeds Registry continued for some time to apply throughout the ancient county. On the other hand, some London areas created during the 19th century for particular purposes had already spilled over beyond the new county borders: the commissioners for the metropolitan turnpike roads of 1826 took in north Middlesex and west as far as Hounslow; the Metropolitan Police Area of 1840 covered the whole county;[1] and the London postal districts of 1857 included Tottenham, Hornsey, Willesden, and Acton. The Metropolitan Water Board area of 1902 included most of the county, and the London Passenger Transport Area of 1933 the whole of it; the nature of their services could not conform with county boundaries. The City had adopted the western border of Middlesex as the limit of its outer jurisdiction from time immemorial; this was perhaps a relic of the ancient hunting rights. Staines was the up-river limit of the corporation's control of the Thames; the edge of the area within which it exacted duties on coal and wine, not finally extinguished till 1890, coincided in the west and north-west with the Middlesex county boundary. Small cast-iron obelisks beside the Great Western line at West Drayton, the London & North Western north of Hatch End, and at some other places still denote the points at which coal became liable to a duty of 1s. 1d. a ton payable to the City.[2]

The boundary of 1888 has so far remained untouched except in details, but not for want of proposals to alter it. The Royal Commission on London Government of 1923 considered, and its majority report rejected, a proposal made by the London County Council that its area should be extended to cover at any rate the Metropolitan Police district, thus including the whole of Middlesex. The Middlesex County Council, with the support of Hertfordshire, proposed that a regional joint committee of authorities should be established for town planning, garden city and housing schemes, and traffic problems, and a regional planning committee was set up which lasted, with modifications, until the 1939-45 war.[3] The Local Government Boundary Commission of 1945 had no power to deal with the boundaries of the County of London or—a significant indication—with the granting of county borough status to any Middlesex authority. The White Paper on the commission stated that the subject of Greater London was considered too big to be dealt with by the commission's procedure, and reforms would need to be carried out by enactment; further, it would be a mistake to change boundaries at a time when large schemes of planning and development were in preparation.[4]

So, in complete uncertainty, the matter stands now. Middlesex is on notice that great reforms in its status may be made, and it is freely prophesied that the county will disappear in the process.

---

[1] Lee and Moylan (page 122, note 4). [2] *Railway Magazine* 87 (1941), p. 448. [3] Finer (page 199, note 2), p. 506; Smellie (page 121, note 1), p. 186. [4] *Local Government in England and Wales during the Period of Reconstruction* (Cmd. 6579, 1945).

CHAPTER XIV

THE SUBURBAN COUNTY

*'Therefore Willesden, like London, the British Empire,
Parliament, and our other national institutions, has
grown up* naturally *and not* according to any
definite plan.'   SIMEON POTTER[1]

'Mind your own Middlesex.'
TITLE OF COUNTY COUNCIL PAMPHLET, 1949

'IN future times, when this little island shall have fallen into its natural
insignificancy, by being no longer possessed of a fictitious power
founded upon commerce, distant colonies, and other artificial sources of
wealth, how puzzled will the curious antiquary be when seeking amidst
the ruins of London vestiges of its past grandeur.' Lady Holland was
writing in 1800.[2] She sought to explain the meanness of the scene, the
absence of great public works, by referring them to the spirit of
independence and selfishness engendered by a commercial civilisation.
But the reason was not as simple as she thought: she was not English, and
she only partly understood what she saw; she certainly did not care for
it. Her 'curious antiquary' (not the first literary figure of his kind, but
surely the parent of Macaulay's traveller from New Zealand, who should
'take his stand on a broken arch of London Bridge to sketch the ruins of
St Paul's') will find ruins far wider spread than his author could have
imagined possible. This future archaeologist, if he knows no more of
what it signifies than we do when we peer at the remains of the Minoan
ages in Crete, may well turn to contemporary literature, if any has by
chance survived, for explanation and enlightenment; but he will find
precious little to help him there.

When the modern writer catches sight of a suburb, he either looks
quickly away for fear of what he may see or, if he does stop to look,
hates the sight of it. Thus G. D. H. Cole, quoted apparently with
approval by the author of *The Greater London Plan*: 'There are an

[1] Potter (page 70, note 4), p. 136. [2] *Journal of Lady Holland*, ii., p. 54, quoted by Halévy (page
7, note 5), iii., p. 117.

astonishing number of suburbs round London that are very like this suburb of mine ... and I doubt if, in the whole history of mankind, there has ever been a type of place so lacking in the spirit of community or in democracy or in any sort of unity save that of mere physical juxtaposition.'[1] 'In the whole history of mankind,' mark you! Again, the bishop of Croydon, opening a mission campaign in 1949: 'The mission is a crusade against the ignorance of Suburbia.' And a critic, wishing to indicate that an author wrote some work that was inferior: 'If the [excluded] essays are bad they ought still to have been included, for a collected edition should have everything, the suburbs as well as the West End of a writer's mind.'[2]

Few modern authors can mention a suburb without a snarl, as if suburban meant much the same as sub-human. It is apparently common ground that in suburbs each man is just like his neighbour; all life is standardised, but there is no sense of community; every one is lower-middle class, and nobody of any individuality could think of living there; every building is new and a misery to look at. Probably the last is the real reason why the suburb stands in the mind of the intellectual for all that is detestable. Architecture is so permanent, and so inescapable a memorial of its age, that its physical evidence dominates the judgment of all but the very shrewdest historians. It is common to think that the 18th century must have been a more agreeable era to live in than the 19th because its surviving buildings are more attractive, and it has been a vulgar error for some 30 years past to suppose that because the Victorians put up ugly buildings they must have been insensitive and unintelligent. In this form that error is now perhaps being dispelled; but it is being reproduced in another way by most writers who notice suburban life at all. Suburban houses are on the whole ugly; and the architectural fallacy misleads the commentator.[3]

Many things indeed are wrong with the suburban existence, but generally not the things the critics write about. They imply that this kind of life in itself has some baneful influence on responsibility and communal sense. Suburbs—so the complaint runs—enforce rigid stand-ards of behaviour and belief, and repress talent and genius. Anyway, it is argued, no great man grew up in a suburb. Yet Turner was brought up at Brentford, Huxley at Ealing, Ruskin at Herne Hill on the Surrey side; if he may be named in such company, H. G. Wells was born at Bromley. Modern suburbs have not yet produced men of their calibre; but there the charge lies against the age, not the suburb—Ruskins and Huxleys do not occur in every century. Still, ordinary men, something less than famous but gifted with character and decision, are the necessary ground from which genius springs, and they are not lacking in suburban places. Men from these new places did fully their share of distinguished actions

[1] P. Abercrombie, *Greater London Plan, 1944* (1945), p. 21. [2] *News Chronicle*, 12 May 1949; *Times Literary Supplement*, 17 June 1949, on Lytton Strachey. [3] J. M. Richards, *Castles on the Ground* (1946), must be excepted – a perceptive essay, mainly concerned with the more romantic and middle-aged suburbs.

in the battles of Britain and the Atlantic and Africa. The published lists of honours and awards in the war of 1939-45 testified to that.

People who bring this criticism against the new suburbs are expecting too much of them too soon. It is true that they have still to develop a way of life that can be thought full and flourishing and assured, but no kind of society has ever done so within 20, or even 50, years of its birth, unless, as in New England, there was some strong pressure from outside, forcing all the inhabitants to undertake communal duties for the sake of mere self-preservation. It may be judged, when the history of the 20th century comes to be written with detachment, that civil defence against air attack and the Home Guard of the 1939-45 war did something of the same kind for London suburbs.

If much of the current criticism is misplaced or muddled, what remains? What is the fire underneath all this smoke? It is evidently impossible to give a proper answer here. The life of modern Middlesex is far too complex to be described in the last chapter of an historical survey; this can do no more than indicate some of its features and the problems they pose. A much fuller and more subtle analysis would be required for real understanding—an analysis undertaken by people with knowledge of the background as well as the foreground of the scene, if its conclusions were to be valuable. A more modest task is attempted here: first, a statement of the 'challenge' (to adopt a convenient scheme), the special difficulties besetting social life in modern Middlesex; then an indication of the different responses made to this challenge; a discussion of local administration, in some ways the most important social problem of all; and finally a speculation whether a vigorous society can emerge from the shapeless aggregations of the present day, and how this might come about.

*   *   *   *   *

The *Shorter Oxford English Dictionary* defines suburbs as 'those residential parts belonging to a town or city which lie immediately outside and adjacent to its walls or boundaries.' Some more precise wording can perhaps be found to define the Middlesex suburbs of London. They share both physical and economic characteristics. The double connexion might be expressed thus: the suburbs are the districts adjacent to London and linked with it by continuous or nearly continuous building, a considerable proportion of whose earning inhabitants perform their daily work outside the district in which they reside. This is cumbersome, but it does indicate the two features of suburban life that stamp it as completely different from the traditional English pattern and set the social problems that have not been adequately dealt with. Men dwelling in suburbs have no compelling personal interest in the prosperity of the local community they live among, and they are cut off from direct connexion with the soil, taking, no part in the business of agriculture or the relaxation of field sport. This is the opposite of the old village life (though the modern village is not what it was); it is different from town life, either of the kind of Thomas Hardy's Casterbridge, where the interests of the market town and the surrounding countryside were inextricably interwoven, or of industrial towns where the prosperity of all is affected by the fortunes of one industry or even of a single factory. Suburban man, on the other hand, is severed from country life, and he can if he chooses remain indifferent to his neighbour's affairs. These two characteristics, both fundamental to a suburb as it is defined above, might by themselves be enough to breed selfishness and lack of communal responsibility; but they are most powerfully reinforced by a third, which is partly incidental—migration. One suburb will be much the same as another to people who merely look for a place to live at within a certain radius of their place of business in town, and there is bound to be less regular settlement in such places than in towns and villages. Over and above this there has been a quite exceptional movement of population and fluidity of ownership in modern Middlesex; the population, nearly 800,000 in 1901, has increased by some 1½ million people, or nearly trebled, since then. Over three-quarters of the adult population of Willesden at the end of 1946 had settled in the district since 1919.[1] This influx cannot go on in such an exaggerated form. During the 20 years from 1919 to 1939 not only were new houses built in the county at a rate that can never be repeated for so long a period, but there was also a transfer of industry into the area at a pace that is equally unlikely to be paralleled. In the future there is likely to be greater stability of occupation, more time to grow roots.

Special difficulties besetting social life in Middlesex arise from these conditions. First, many of the inhabitants, drawn from different places of origin, do not expect or intend to remain where they now live and are always temporary settlers, resident aliens. Second, the natural growth of social life has been frustrated because thousands of houses have been run up so fast that the newcomers could not be absorbed into existing institutions, and new facilities for communal life were not provided as part of the expansion. Third, the breadwinners scatter daily to their work at distant places; many of them are employed within London, and many again of the workers in Middlesex factories live outside the immediate neighbourhood. Fourth, the merging of places which were once separate into one endless 'built-up area' causes fellow-feeling to be lost as boundaries are blurred; most men need some visible limit for their

---

[1] *Willesden and the New Towns* (1947), p. 1.

loyalties. Finally, there are special difficulties caused by the prevailing organisation of local government.

*   *   *   *   *

People in Middlesex who care for a proper balance of social life have not neglected the challenge that these special difficulties present. The kind of full local life of former centuries, in which private interest and public duty operated together, is evidently impossible in these hastily-assembled conglomerations, in which the administration of public affairs is conducted somewhat remotely, and private interests, on a narrow view, do not promote communal activity. There is no parish meeting for the transaction of any kind of secular business—that is a privilege reserved, for some reason, to rural districts; there is nothing like the village inn, that prime 'community centre,' in the new suburbs, but only hotels that are generally too big for that purpose; and Women's Institutes survive only in a few overgrown villages. Instead, very many voluntary associations for the spending of leisure in common activities have sprung up, some sound and successful, others short-lived. Some are linked with churches of the different denominations, others with ratepayers' or residents' associations formed in the first place to watch the expenditure of local authorities. The mere multiplication of societies may not of itself be a sign of strength; but their scope is wide enough to include as well as leisure occupations all that field of voluntary social work—visiting, care of the old, providing proper facilities for the leisure of the young—that needs to flourish, alongside state organisation and private interest, if the social compromise of this century is to be made to work.

This much encouragement may be drawn from the intense activity of such societies: it means that people are taking root and beginning to feel themselves dwellers in the homes where they live, not squatters. But there is also one significant threat to their success. Community of employment is different from community of residence; wealthy or benevolent employers often provide attractive facilities for recreation of their staffs, and thus the community of employment is knit closer. This may help to secure the loyalty of employees; but it is almost impossible for a man to feel himself a member of the community where he lives if he both works and plays outside it. This makes a home become merely a place for sleeping in.

The firm has this advantage, indeed, over the locality: it usually has a personality, which most places in Middlesex apparently have not. Few of the inhabitants are aware that there is an individuality to be found in their own suburb, that it can become (if it is not now) a place to be proud of instead of being a place to be escaped from as soon as the chance is offered.

It may be thought impossible to develop individual characters in these places; it is supposed that they never have had any to start with. There is a notion that all the Middlesex suburbs are exactly the same; if you are set down in one you may go a long way before you have any idea where you are. This is to confuse the externals with the character, like saying that all the cotton towns in Lancashire are alike. There is a Queen Anne's Gardens in Bedford Park and a Queen Anne's Gardens in Bush Hill Park, but the resemblance ends with the name; there are in Middlesex fourteen roads called Meadway, but they are not identical and interchangeable. Each suburb, and each district of each suburb, has its own personality, each on a different step in the social scale and each with different kinds of interests. These distinctions are often subtle, and they do not readily reveal themselves to the outsider. Money incomes do not now often settle the matter as they once did. It is much more important whether the children go to the state schools as a matter of course or the parents give up other things to have them educated at their own expense; this creates a social distinction, with many implications, that money income has less and less to do with. Another kind of division is found in some districts where whole roads are occupied only by people who have moved in from Wales or Ireland or particular parts of the English Midlands or north; and a more elusive one appears where people who live in a suburban road feel its standing lowered when one of them comes back from work wearing a uniform. English society, in spite of the egalitarians, is infinitely but clearly graduated all the way up.

There have been, and there are still, serious attempts to obscure the outward distinctions that do exist; one is the obliteration of the old distinctive names. When Roxeth is called South Harrow, a good deal is lost. The practice of calling individual outlying settlements not by their proper names but by that of the parish centre prefixed by a compass point or the word 'New' began perhaps when Brompton insensibly put on South Kensington some time in the eighteen-sixties; it at once gratified social snobbery, by substituting the superior and better-known parish name for the local hamlet, was welcome to railway companies which could thus appear to serve a place that they did not approach very closely, and was liked by local authorities for its tidiness. It is a bad sign that many Middlesex district names have disappeared: Uxendon, Tollington, Waxlow, Halliwick should stand for separate places but are sunk to being street-names (one is a telephone exchange). Individuality of name is precious; it indicates the individual character of places, making them unique and not replicas. Suburbs can hardly afford to drop the distinctions they have got.

On a smaller scale, suburbans almost instinctively try to distinguish their own houses by difference of decoration, of garden layout, above all of name. Having escaped from identical town dwellings, they give their Middlesex houses names that are distinctive, and often just romantic. A characteristic sample of the period between 1890 and 1914 is provided by two roads of large superior middle-class houses lying by Hatch End station, The Avenue and Royston Park Road. In the former, 49 houses bear names: 18 of these may be classed as romantic (4 of them with special overtones of their own, Ivanhoe, Kenilworth, Tresco, and Newlyn), 17 as having a rural association (either vague, like Claremont and Fairholme, or more definite, like Cherry Tree or The Limes), 7 as asserting a certain dignity (Carlton House, Willoughby Lodge); and 7 are unclassifiable. In the second road, the exotic element is stronger: of 36 named houses, 14 bear romantic place-names (Iona, Talysarn, Malabar), 14 are rural (Woodthorpe, Roselands), 3 have genuine local associations (Oxhey Cottage, Old Redding Cottage, and Pinriver), and 5 are unclassifiable. After 1920, the proportions are much the same, though a certain jaunty illiteracy creeps in with Kozikot and Dunromin, a little lower down the social scale.

If the results are sometimes laughable, this almost universal search for a distinctive label, sternly repressed on council estates, does point to a natural anxiety to appear different, to establish a private plot with a name of its own instead of a mere number in a street. (Scarcely a single 'street' has been laid down in Middlesex for 30 years—a mute protest against the London that the migrants have left behind them; the map is filled with 'ways' and 'roads' and 'closes.') When he moves from the city to the suburb, a man thinks he is becoming an individual on his own account, and thinking so is more than half-way to doing so. Outsiders may think that a heavy burden of conformity and convention weighs down the man in the suburb; but it is much less a feature of life there than in a country village where the procession of the seasons and the business of agriculture tie man down far more inexorably. 'The romantic suburb,' wrote Lewis Mumford, 'was a collective attempt to live a private life';[1] and Middlesex, though it sounds odd to say so, contains plenty of romantic suburbs. Whatever kind of suburb they live in, most suburbans enjoy a freer, not a narrower, life than where they dwelt before, and they have a plot of garden.

The garden and the sports ground are the links with the soil. These are less satisfying than the field and the hunt (or the poaching), no doubt; but they are the best that our restricted island can afford to the greater part of its swollen population. Sport has inevitably become organised so that it can be played on small spaces, and, because almost every one

[1] L. Mumford, *Culture of Cities* (1938), p. 215.

wants a plot of ground for his own, the flower garden and the allotment naturally follow.

This is the justification for the suburb: the island is small; the population is great; each man to be a full man needs a dwelling of his own and some soil that is his to work on. The suburb is the most economical way of supplying these needs. In our circumstances it may be still too extravagant of our most precious possession, the land; but there will have to be a mighty change of mind before the argument is declared invalid and the generality of Englishmen consent with good will to live in blocks of flats. It is well to add this: the argument may justify the idea of the suburb; it certainly does not excuse the forms it has too commonly assumed.

* * * * *

These are the responses made by suburban man to the special difficulties of his environment: to live a distinctive and personal life, and to indicate this so far as he can in protesting against imposed conformity by stressing his individual difference in externals; and to join his neighbours in recreation, even though he cannot join them at work. Not every suburban man does these things, not perhaps very many; but when the challenge presented by external uniformity combined with absence of neighbourly interest is taken up, these are the ways of responding to it. These are the responses of individuals; are the communities collectively, as they are organised in units of local government, best fitted for the promotion of the diversity within the conditions imposed by the suburban pattern of development that will establish sound and vigorous local life? The question here is not the broad national problem of centralisation, whether local government is local enough, but simply whether the present scheme of local authorities in Middlesex is the best that can be devised in the very peculiar conditions of the county. None the less, some general remarks made in the Local Government Boundary Commission's report for 1947 are pertinent to the Middlesex area: 'The general aim, in our view, should be to make the local administration of a local government service as local, that is, the area of administration as restricted, as is compatible with securing an effective service. This fundamental consideration should be specially borne in mind at a time like the present when the practical advantages of large-scale organisation need no emphasis. It is of the first importance if local interest is to be preserved and encouraged and full use made of local knowledge. As the unit becomes larger, the element of public control by elected representatives tends to diminish and to be replaced by officialdom.'[1]

[1] *Report of the Local Government Boundary Commission for 1947*, ¶ 19.

The Middlesex County Council administers an area of nearly 150,000 acres, in which more than 2¼ million people live. None of the towns was large enough to achieve county borough status under the original act of 1888, and none has been elevated to that status since; the 15 municipal boroughs range from Wood Green with 52,000 inhabitants to Ealing with 187,000, eight of them having over 100,000; the 11 urban districts range from Potters Bar with 17,000 inhabitants to Harrow with 219,000. There have been no rural districts in the county since 1930. Piecemeal formation and alteration of local districts has produced a ring of boroughs along the London border and part of the Thames valley, with a line of urban districts beyond it. Edmonton is a borough while Enfield, with a larger population and rateable value, remains an urban district; Harrow, the largest, wealthiest, and most populous district in the county, has not yet achieved the status of a borough. There have been no alterations to status or boundaries since 1937.

Specialist writers have recognised that peculiar problems arise in the local administration of a completely urban county. Sidney and Beatrice Webb in *A Constitution for a Socialist Commonwealth of Great Britain*, proposed to divide Middlesex entirely among 4, 6, or 10 coterminous county boroughs, thus eliminating the county council altogether.[1] It has been more often urged in recent years that it would be sensible, and only keeping the Local Government Act of 1888 up to date, to extend the county of London so as to include all the continuously built-up area, and thus to swallow up all Middlesex. The reformers evidently feel that some alteration needs to be made, and their general conclusion is that the London area ought to be enlarged and its local affairs placed in the hands of one authority. The question usually asked is: 'What is the best arrangement for securing good administration of the local government services?'; not often enough: 'What does most to foster vigorous local life?' Of course, all local government reformers should strive for administrative efficiency, but this should not necessarily take first place in considerations of the subject. Enlargements of areas and consequent rise in status have often been urged in the past on the ground that administrative economies will follow (they have not always followed), and transfers of territory from one authority to another have been justified by appeals to administrative convenience. But this is making much of the means and forgetting the end; you cannot expect a community of any size to hold together if it has no common past and no pressing reason, other than the will of administrators, for seeking a common future. The test for local government should be: does it promote, or does it stand aside from, the full development of local life in all its forms?

How does the present scheme of local government in Middlesex respond to this test? No doubt a good many different answers could be

[1] S. and B. Webb, *Constitution for a Socialist Commonwealth of Great Britain* (1920), p. 232.

given; it might be said, 26 different answers, one for each district. Here only one indication is mentioned which appears strong enough to imply that the scheme fails to do what is properly required of it. If the local councils were fully and adequately functioning as the focal points for local opinion and action in administrative affairs, they would be the places where local views and grievances would naturally find expression, and perhaps satisfaction. But over the whole county there is a remarkable growth of unofficial bodies formed to press local authorities, among others, for the redress of grievances and the provision of facilities and amenities: ratepayers' or residents' associations, community clubs, and the like, so far as they deal (as they very largely attempt to do) with matters of local administration. Voluntary association for some purposes may be taken as a sign of strength, but here it is a disquieting symptom: the ordinary inhabitant thinks the local authority so remote that he joins a 'pressure group' to urge his wishes upon it. This implies that the union of several ancient parishes into one borough or urban district, the usual Middlesex arrangement, has failed to produce the authority that the residents feel confidence in to look after their local interests. The inhabitants of Great Stanmore, for example, are not entrusted with the running of their own affairs, or even with an organ of such limited powers as the parish council that exists in rural districts. Even if they cannot manage their affairs with reasonable convenience and economy, they can hardly be expected to rejoice at being incorporated in Harrow, a place of entirely different character and traditions. Local government would be stronger if some of the larger groupings, which have no common past or interests, were broken up into manageable districts, say of about 60,000 inhabitants, with authorities which could stand much closer to their residents.[1] They would have a fair chance of establishing a loyalty which the larger units do not command and of becoming the true centres of local life. If suburban life is to be rescued from the danger of impersonality that besets it, Middlesex would do better to take as its example for reform the urban district of Friern Barnet, with a population of 29,000 settled within the boundaries of a single ancient parish, rather than Ealing, with 187,000 in six ancient parishes, each having a tradition and interests of its own.

This conclusion will seem either retrograde or far-fetched to a good many people; but it has the merit of respecting genuine distinctions, not overriding them, and distinctions are what suburban life needs. If the general principle is accepted, proposals would need to be worked out in detail with an eye on the economies that really are secured by larger groupings, and joint arrangements between authorities should be made for those purposes. What is wanted is a working compromise between democracy and efficiency. The essential feature—real democratic control

[1] The number 60,000 has the support of P. Abercrombie (page 202, note 1), p. 113.

of local affairs, close enough to the individual for him to feel that his voice has a share in decisions—is one that could powerfully revive the life of Middlesex communities. Today they too rarely deserve the name.

In any such proposals the question of boundaries would arise, too technical and controversial for more than a mention here. The ancient limits of rural parishes form no useful boundaries for modern suburban districts. Many of them have been sensibly revised, but only in minor respects, and serious anomalies still disfigure the map: a Congregational church at Cockfosters, for example, lies partly in Middlesex and partly in Hertfordshire.[1] It is easy to lay down the principle that boundaries should be drawn along lines that are crossed by the smallest amount of necessary daily traffic; they should be fixed by the watersheds of retail trade and of travel to local occupations. This generally rules out main roads as boundaries—they link, not sever, the districts on each side. Large rivers with few bridges generally make good boundaries; small brooks, such as divided many Middlesex parishes, very rarely do so. Railway lines generally form the best border-lines by the test suggested here. But it must be agreed that drawing of local boundaries proves endlessly difficult in practice.

Over and above these questions of local areas, however, is the more significant question: 'Should the administrative county of Middlesex, anomalous fragment of the ancient county that it is, be allowed to survive?' This is clearly a matter of great doubt; the Local Government Boundary Commission of 1945 was not empowered to take Middlesex districts into consideration, as it was declared that the whole question of local government in the Greater London region was under review separately.[2] For some purposes, especially those embraced by the inclusive term 'planning,' most of the experts feel that the whole region should be administered as one. If county-council functions are transferred to such a regional authority, Middlesex inevitably disappears.

Middlesex has a history of a distinctive kind. It is affected by London, but it is not London. It can be developed, with wise concentration on its best features, into a union of distinct communities having many interests in common; and it is quite big enough to require a separate county administration. It might, indeed, more plausibly be urged that it is already ripe not for aggregation to another county but for division. This suggestion, however, need hardly be pressed; the county administration proved itself fully able to meet the unprecedented demands on its education service, for example, during the period of fastest expansion in the nineteen-thirties, and there is perhaps no good reason to break it up now.

There is no need, though, to regard the present boundaries of the county as the best that can be devised. Much sensible improvement could

[1] *Evening Standard,* 19 August 1947. [2] *Local Government* (page 200, note 4).

be made, especially on the London side where it is plainly out of date: all
the district south of the railway from Kilburn to Willesden Junction, for
example, where nothing but the sign at the end of the street indicates
whether it is in Willesden or Paddington, might well go to London, and
the Middlesex portion of Colnbrook village could better be in Buckinghamshire. It would be useful to adjust the curious salient of Hertfordshire
near Barnet. But it is possible to be too sweeping and regardless of proper
sentiment even in such cases. County boundaries within the Greater
London region have not quite lost all significance. A police inspector,
giving evidence at Beaconsfield in 1948 about a disturbance at Denham,
said: 'People come into the village from Middlesex and create a nuisance
after the dances.' That is how Denham feels about West Drayton.[1]

    If Middlesex is to be joined to London, it should only be done on
clear proof that the union would benefit both London and Middlesex
without valuable features of their local administration being lost in the
process. It would be a difficult thing to prove. It may be doubted whether
London would in fact gain by an enlargement of the responsibilities of its
county council; it is certain that it would be a wanton and retrograde
action to abolish Middlesex now, just when a community of purpose is
being discovered and a settled and vigorous local life has a chance of
emerging.

                    *   *   *   *   *

    'A settled and vigorous local life has a chance of emerging.' Is this a
reasonable expectation or a slender hope? In tracing the development of
Middlesex, previous chapters have shown that, while men's lives from
the earliest times have been constantly influenced by London, they have
still developed strong local attachments and carried on a vigorous
corporate life, producing characters of worth and distinction not only in
the rural villages of old Middlesex but also in places that were
recognisably suburban in character. There was never a truly independent
provincial life and sentiment, as there was in Norfolk or Devonshire or
Cheshire; London was too strong for that; but there was local loyalty in
the past to places not essentially different from their present-day
successors except that they were growing more slowly and therefore their
institutions could keep pace with their growth. Only when immigration
has swamped the existing villages has assimilation proved impossible; at
a reasonable rate of increase the thing has been achieved. New
Middlesex can become a home for real communities, provided that its
population is reasonably stable and certain right decisions are made
quickly. The county must continue as an entity, and the separate units
within it should be smaller. In addition, the residents should be enabled

[1] *Evening Standard*, 31 August 1948.

and encouraged to form voluntary associations for all kinds of activities; the Questors at Ealing, one of Britain's liveliest 'little theatres,' have shown how successfully this can be done on Middlesex soil.[1]

These matters, it may be objected, are all administrative and social; must not the physical replanning of the county have first consideration, to free it from the grosser mistakes made during the great expansion and to restore some of the balance between open and built-up land? It is true that the suburbs need all the grace and amenity that can be bestowed on them by official efforts. Nevertheless, it is too simple to suppose that good living flourishes automatically where the town planning has been good and the best architects have been employed. Ugliness in the surroundings is indeed a great bar to the good life; but men can love ugly places, as they often love plain people. The feeling of affection for a native or adopted place, the local patriotism that makes men unhappy when they are living anywhere else, is not necessarily fostered when tidy improvements are made according to the most approved outside advice. It is genuine character, not tidiness, that counts in attaching men to places; local patriotism is nowhere fiercer than in the unlovely Five Towns of the north Staffordshire Potteries. Let Middlesex be planned as well as can be, so long as the personality of its constituent elements is made more distinct, not more uniform. Let it be planned for variety rather than neatness, so that all that is characteristic in the different places may be enhanced.

The past and the present combine to produce the character of a place, as of a person; and, while the character of places, like persons, is originally determined by physical influences, it is far more effectively moulded by the procession of events impinging on it. History tells you more about places than geography does (in the south of England, at any rate). 'People will not look forward to posterity,' said Burke, 'who never look back to their ancestors': a judgment that needs quite as much heed in the 20th century as in the 18th. When men in considering their local affairs are aware that the present is no more than one point of time in a process that began in the far past and has very long to run yet, that they are the heirs to a tradition, then local character may be fully realised and tradition be fortified by a decent respect for former times. This will extend not only to institutions but to the whole environment—buildings, trees, and open spaces. So long as respect does not decline into conscious antiquarianism, or try to fix the organisation and appearance of a district in a pattern that is obsolete, it serves to knit together the successors to the tradition and enables them to enlarge it.

Some Middlesex communities recognise the value of tradition: the Pinner Association, for example, sets out to use its influence to make Pinner a more pleasant and convenient place to live in and by

[1] *Listener*, 15 December 1949.

conserving the evidences of its past to establish its distinctive character more firmly in the present. More of the same kind has been done at Ruislip, with promising material and considerable success, and at other places also. It may be more difficult in some parts of the county, especially where there is no village centre as a nucleus; but it is worth doing, and it can be done.

Something, then, is being done to stop the erosion of character and personality from the old Middlesex villages. But there is nothing to show that there is a general, informed interest in the county. It is on the whole poorly served by its local topographers and historians, though there are honourable exceptions; but what sort of a town is Uxbridge, with a long history that nobody has written since 1818, or Staines, that nobody has written at all? There is no county magazine; and yet this book, if it shows nothing else, should have indicated that there are still plenty of things in Middlesex worth writing about. Nobody marks the houses of famous men, or their sites; there are perhaps half a dozen tablets in the county, and those not to the best known or the most important of its former inhabitants. There is not even a Middlesex Association to stimulate conservation of what is good and improvement of what is bad. In a healthy society these things would not be left wholly to official bodies; the inhabitants would take care to mind their own Middlesex. They have a chance now, in this breathing-space that the 1939-45 war and the comparatively few physical changes since its end have afforded. One thing, of course, they must have if the chance is to be taken: they must be given some assurance that Middlesex will continue to exist as a unit in something like its present form.

Middlesex is worth conserving and improving, for the sake both of its ancient fame and of its modern importance. It will never be a county that attracts many people by its beauties, though these are not so negligible as most suppose; but, though it may not be much to look at, it is modern England.

ILLUSTRATIONS

1. Tottenham Church from the north about 1830.
From a painting by Constable in the Metropolitan Museum of Art, New York.

2. Syon House in 1752. From a painting by Canaletto in the possession of the Duke of Northumberland at Alnwick Castle

3. Hampton Lock in 1871. From a painting by Sisley

4. Highgate Hill and the Archway from the south about 1815.
Aquatint from a drawing by A. C. Pugin

5. The Wharncliffe Viaduct, Great Western Railway, in 1846.
From a lithograph by J. C. Bourne

6. *The Treaty House, Uxbridge, about 1810. From a water-colour drawing by Samuel Prout in the Sutherland Collection at the Ashmolean Museum, Oxford*

7. *Mr. and Mrs. Garrick and Mr. Bowden taking tea in the garden of the Garricks' villa at Hampton. From a painting (about 1770) by Zoffany in the possession of the Earl of Durham at Lambton Castle*

*8. Sir John Soane's house at Ealing (now the Ealing Public Library) in
1845. From a water-colour sketch, probably by C. J. Richardson, in Sir
John Soane's Museum*

*9. The north front of Southgate Grove, 1797, by John Nash; now
Grovelands Convalescent Home. From an engraving in 'The New Vitruvius
Britannicus,' 1802, by G. Richardson*

*10. 'Orley Farm.' From an engraving after a drawing by Millais,
published in the first edition of Anthony Trollope's novel in 1862.
This was the Trollopes' house at Harrow*

11. Mr. Forrest's Cottage, Syon Gardens, Brentford, in 1828. From a drawing by John Buckler in the British Museum: Add. MS. 36371, f. 16

12. Harrow School about 1840. From a lithography by Thomas Wood.

13. *The east front of Canons, near Stanmore. A conjectural restoration by Ian Dunlop*

14. *Chiswick House in 1822. From a drawing by John Buckler in the British Museum: Add. Ms. 36369, f. 160. The Palladian villa in the centre, the wings of 1788 to left and right*

15. *Twickenham on Thames in 1760. From a water-colour drawing by Samuel Scott in the Whitworth Art Gallery, Manchester. The Church and waterfront from Eel Pie Island; Scott's house facing the Church*

16. *Strawberry Hill in 1826 (south-east view). From a drawing by John Buckler in the British Museum: Add. MS. 36371, f.10*

17. *Hampton Court Palace in 1820. From a water-colour drawing by Rowlandson in the Victoria and Albert Museum. Right, the Great Gate House (before excavation of the moat); left, the Cavalry Barracks*

18. *Edmonton Statute Fair in 1788. From a water-colour drawing by John Nixon in the Victoria and Albert Museum*

19. Northolt Church: a rustic building in a new suburb

20. *Weatherboarded cottages at Mill Hill*

21. The Butts, Brentford, scene of the Middlesex elections

22. *Southwood Lane, Highgate: different textures in London stock brick*

23. *The Church of Little Stanmore, or Whitchurch*

24. *Sir Christopher Wren's Hampton Court, from the south-east*

25. A panel of Jean Tijou's ironwork screen at Hampton Court

26. Ireland: a detail from Tijou's screen
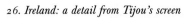

27. *The Gateway, Dyrham Park, South Mimms*

28. *Syon Park Gate*

29. The Harrow Inn, Charlton, near Sunbury. Perhaps the oldest inhabited house in Middlesex

30. Cottages overlooking the churchyard, Ruislip

31. Headstone Manor House and barn, near Harrow

32. Wyllyotts Manor House, Potters Bar

33. Harmondsworth Church Tower

34. The ruins of Stanmore Church

35. *The monument to Alice, Countess of Derby (d. 1637), in Harefield Church*

36. Detail of the Derby monument, Harefield

37. Boston House, Brentford

38. The Rectory, Shepperton

39. The Ferry Boat Inn, Tottenham

40. The Old Bank House, Uxbridge

41. Swakeleys, Ickenham

42. Wrotham Park, South Mimms: the central feature

43. Chiswick Mall from across the river

44. York House, Twickenham

45. The Friends' Meeting House, Winchmore Hill

46. Old Meeting Congregational Church, Uxbridge

47. Congregational Church, Staines

48. The Goldsmiths' Almshouses, Acton

49. Feltham Church

50. Kilburn Toll Gate, on the Edgware Road, in the 1860s

51. Bramley's Farm, Willesden, about 1865

52. The Woodman Inn, Southgate, about 1895

53. The New River in the 1950s near Bush Hill Park

54. Chiswick Station

55. An Enfield line workmen's train at Liverpool Street, 1884

56. The bus to Palmers Green station at Southgate about 1898

57. London United Tramcar, 1901

58. *Lord Knyvett's School, Stanwell*

59. *Lady Margaret School, Southall*

60. *Christ Church, Southgate*

61. *St Alban, North Harrow*

62. *Hornsey Town Hall*

63. *Friern Barnet Town Hall*

64. Arnos Grove Station

65. Guinness's Brewery, Park Royal

66. The Free Church from Erskine Hill, Hampstead Garden Suburb

67. Hampton Court Bridge from the air

68. The Great West Road at Osterley Station

69. Suburban building of the 1930s at Hillingdon

70. Eastcote High Street

71. Eastcote High Street

72. *Water-Board Middlesex: Sunbury to Staines, with the Queen Mary Reservoir (centre) and the Staines group (above)*

73. *Hampton Court from the air; centre, the Palace; right, the Fountain Garden; above, Bushy Park and the Chestnut Avenue.*

74. *Hampton Church from the Surrey side: right, David Garrick's temple to Shakespeare*

PART TWO

ACTON (c4) is a borough (1921) lying just W. of the London border; it extends from Willesden Junction in the N. almost to Chiswick High Road in the S., divided from Hammersmith (in London) on the E. and from Ealing on the W. by wandering lines representing the course of the old Stamford Brook and Bollo Brook respectively. There are no distinctive natural features. It is an historic place, with little to show for it now. The old village stood about the main Uxbridge road. Modern Acton has in the main grown up since 1860. London County Council housing estates in the NE. corner and Bedford Park in the S. provide agreeable variations on undistinguished streets, but the industrial district of North Acton presents a horrid example of the 20th century doing its worst.

Acton means 'farm by the oak-trees.' Thomas Fuller in the 17th century counted 17 Actons in England, 'the place nigh London the paramount Acton among them.'[1] This Acton was not mentioned in Domesday, being part of the bishop of London's manor of Fulham, but it is found from 1181 onwards.[2] The principal manor remained the property of the see of London; there was another manor, perhaps attached to Berrymead Priory, which was surrendered by St Paul's to the Crown in 1544, immediately granted to Lord Russell, and later held by Herbert, Earl of Worcester.

Acton was unimportant in medieval times; John and Ralph Acton, divines, fl. 1290 and 1320, may perhaps have been natives. From about 1600, however, its position on the main Oxford road made it a convenient country retreat for noblemen and lawyers who wanted to be within reach of town. After the battle of Brentford in 1642 the royalist forces advanced as far as Turnham Green, with cavalry skirmishes N. towards Acton village. During the Commonwealth several leaders of the Parliamentary side lived there. In the 18th century, when inland watering-places were popular, its wells acquired some repute; but the place was not important enough to justify the Great Western's building a station when its line was carried through the parish in 1838. The first Acton station (on the North & South-Western junction line) was opened in 1853; Acton (Great Western) followed in 1868, and seven others on different lines later. Horse trams began to ply from Shepherds Bush in 1876; the line was electrified by the London United Tramways and extended to Ealing and Southall in 1901. The Metropolitan Electric tramway along Horn Lane from Harlesden began work in 1909. Industries from the West End of London, particularly coach-building, printing, and music-engraving, moved out to Acton from 1875 onwards and displaced the pleasant lanes, market gardens, and orchards with a few wheat fields that Thorne described in that year. Since the 1914-18 war, when vacant land in the N. was used for government factories, engineering works and many

---

[1] Fuller (page 33, note 1), ii., p.324. [2] This is the date given by English Place-Name Society, *Place-Names of Middlesex* (1942) (from *Domesday of St. Paul's*). Sharpe (page 12, note 4), p. 170 (relying on the Saxon charter in W. de G. Birch, *Cartularium Saxonicum* (1893), p. 134), identifies an Acton mention in 716 with this place.

light industries have been established. The Western Avenue was driven across the N. part in 1921-6.

The centre of Acton wears the form but not the look of an ancient village. The church (St Mary), standing prominently on the N. side of the High Street, contains most of the remaining evidences of Acton's past. It was entirely rebuilt in red brick with stone dressings, not in the worst style, with a well-proportioned tower (H. Francis, 1865; tower 1876). It replaced a church recased in brick about 1760 with a brick tower of about 1550 and chancel of 1837.[1] Some monuments and furniture from the old church were transferred to the new, including the set of plate dating from 1639.

Tablets to the wives of Francis Rous and Philip Skippon recall the ecclesiastical affairs of Acton in the 17th century, which were much disturbed. Daniel Featly was rector in 1642 when the Parliamentary troops occupied Acton, plundered his rectory, damaged the church fittings, and tore down the altar rails—'(as Ducks do with a Frog) tear them limbless,' wrote the royalist newssheet.[2] He was removed in 1643 and succeeded by Philip Nye, a fiery independent with a memorable beard. Nye was ejected in 1660 in favour of Bruno Ryves, formerly of Stanwell, a fanatical royalist and author of *Mercurius Rusticus*. During the Commonwealth Philip Skippon, major-general, lived at Acton; his rank has been crossed out (it is supposed by Ryves) in the parish register and the word 'Traytor' inserted above; titles were similarly erased from the tablet to Philippa Rous, wife of Francis Rous, provost of Eton 1643. After the Restoration, Richard Baxter, leader of the nonconformist divines, settled at Acton in 1663, where he preached in his own house and then led his flock to the parish church. He wrote most of his autobiography, *Reliquiae Baxterianae*, there and moved to London on the Declaration of Indulgence in 1672.[3]

Other residents of consequence at Acton in the 17th and 18th centuries were Sir John Vaughan, Chief Justice of the Common Pleas, d. 1674; Sir Matthew Hale, Lord Chief Justice, d. 1676; George Savile, Marquess of Halifax (the Trimmer), d.1695; and Elizabeth Barry, actress, d.1713. John Erskine, Earl of Mar, who raised the standard of the 1715 rebellion, was married at Acton in 1714.

The High Street now contains no buildings of any interest. The Roman Catholic church of Our Lady of Lourdes is by E. Goldie (1899). Behind the heavy municipal buildings (baths 1904 and 1926; town hall 1938; library, M. B. Adams, 1900) is the Priory constitutional club, in Salisbury Street, incorporating whatever remains of Berrymead Priory, a religious house of which very little is certainly known. Bulwer Lytton lived about 1836 in the present building, and from 1849 it was occupied by Lola Montez, dancer and adventuress, who had precipitated the Bavarian rising of 1848. On the N. side of Acton Park is a handsome row of brown-brick almshouses built by the Goldsmiths' Company in 1811, with a pleasing stucco portico (*Plate 48*). To the E., across Acton Lane, is the site of East Acton manor house, a handsome brick mansion remodelled in 1712, demolished in 1911; the area is now occupied by sports grounds. Beyond, at Bromyard Avenue, is a great rectangular block of government offices (Ministry of Pensions; J. G. West, 1922), imposing in a grim fashion, and farther E., in Old Oak Road, is St Saviour's church for the deaf and dumb (E.

---

[1] J. H. Sperling, *Church Walks in Middlesex* (ed. 2, 1853), p. 85, wrote: 'The brick tower dates about 1660; the rest of the church a century later'; but this does not seem right. A brass tablet in the present building states that a new church was erected between 1550 and 1583. [2] [B. Ryves], *Mercurius Rusticus: or, the Countries Complaint* (ed. 1685), p. 192. [3] *Autobiography of Richard Baxter*, ed. J. M. Lloyd-Thomas (Everyman ed.), p. 204.

Maufe, 1930). S. of the main road is Acton Vale, with factories.

Little but the windings of East Acton Lane remains to indicate the separate settlement of East Acton; the red-brick church of St Dunstan was built in 1878 by the Goldsmiths' Company. N. of Western Avenue is a portion of the London County Council's Old Oak housing estate that has overflowed from Hammersmith. Part of Old Oak Common was occupied after 1870 by a *Biergarten* for the German colony of London. Just N. of the Great Western main line, the names of Wales (i.e. Wells) Farm Road and Acton Wells junction signal-box commemorate the watering-place that brought Acton into repute about 1750. There was an assembly-room and something of a fashionable season. John O'Keeffe, actor and dramatist, d. 1833, lived at Acton Wells. An old house of this period remains N. of the arterial road at the end of Wales Farm Road. Apart from this, trading estates, sports grounds, factories, and trolleybus wires continue Acton as far as the melancholy purlieus of Willesden Junction.

W. of Horn Lane things are better. The district near West Acton station has been agreeably laid out in garden-suburb form (T. A. Lloyd for the Great Western Railway, 1923). There is nothing of note in the crowded streets of central Acton about Horn Lane, except where the name Derwentwater Road continues the association of the unhappy James, Earl of Derwentwater, executed 1716 for his part in the '15 rebellion. There is one good old house, the Elms House, N. of the Uxbridge road at the Ealing end. S. of the High Street, extending as far as Chiswick Park station, is South Acton, an unattractive district filled with buildings of the 1860s and 1870s; All Saints,

Bollo Bridge Road, was built in 1872 (J. Kelly); its spire is now decapitated. Acton Green, at the extreme S. bordering on Chiswick, is the remnant of a fair-sized common where part of the engagement of Turnham Green, 1642, was fought; it is now much cut about by railways, and its only adornment is a sad-looking little church (St Alban; E. Monson, 1887). St Peter, Southfield Road, is in the Romanesque style (W. A. Pite, 1914).

The SE. corner is occupied by Bedford Park, so named from land formerly owned by the Russell family, which runs over into CHISWICK. It is not a park, but the first London suburb laid out in the picturesque style, with trees, gardens, and irregular housing lines as part of the plan. It was founded in 1875 by Jonathan Carr, d. 1915. Its architectural style bears the characteristic stamp of R. Norman Shaw; M. B. Adams, editor of *The Building News*, d. 1933, and E. J. May completed it. For some reason it chose to become known as the 'Queen Anne' style; but the historical inspiration dates from almost a century earlier, from the flowing Dutch gables and ornamental brickwork of 1600-50. There is picturesque variety and deliberate informality, with some flat gables and dormer windows. The principal public buildings lie just N. of Turnham Green station—the Tabard inn, of an old English type that brewers' architects copied and caricatured 25 to 50 years later, and the church (St Michael; Norman Shaw, 1875), in which a 'Queen Anne' body puts up with Gothic windows; the exterior is interesting, the inside dark and disappointing. There have been some well-known residents: William Terriss (W. C. J. Lewin), actor, murdered 1897; Myles Birket Foster, painter, d. 1899;

and A. W. Pinero, dramatist, d. 1934. The suburb came as a breath of air in the middle seventies, when places like Tottenham and Harlesden were being run up; indeed, Ernest Renan, the French critic, called it a *véritable utopie.*[1] It has worn well through 75 years; even if it may look a little close-packed and heavy to 20th-century notions, it marked a significant new movement in good suburban building, and it has merits of its own.

ALEXANDRA PALACE (E3). *See* WOOD GREEN.

ALPERTON (C4). *See* WEMBLEY.

ASHFORD (B6) is a district in the SW. Middlesex level (not to be confused with its better-known namesake in Kent), lying between the main London-Staines road and the road from Kingston over Sunbury Common to Staines. Until after the 1914-18 war its occupations were purely agricultural. There has been much recent building development, and its aspect is now suburban.

The name means 'ford over Eccle's brook'; the names Ash and Exe given to the river are recent back-formations from the name of the village.

The manor appears to have been an appendage of Staines from a very early date. At the Dissolution of the Monasteries it was vested in the Crown and annexed to the honour of Hampton Court. Hounslow Heath extended into the parish until the common land was enclosed in 1809; Lysons recorded in 1800 that the regiments of cavalry were frequently reviewed by the king on Ashford common.

The original chapel (St Michael), demolished in 1796, had a S. door said to be of Saxon (i.e. Norman)

architecture. It was succeeded by a plain brick edifice with a steeple and small spire. In 1858 this was in turn replaced by the present stone church by W. Butterfield, which contains a brass of 1525 from the original building and a brass coffin-plate to Lord Kinnoull, 1758.

Close to the station is the Welsh charity school (H. Clutton, 1857), called by Thorne 'a noticeable and picturesque building of a modified Elizabethan character.' Farther W. is the large West London District School of 1872.

BARNET, FRIERN (E2), the smallest urban district in Middlesex, lies between Finchley on the W. and an intrusive tongue of Hertfordshire that includes New and East Barnet on the N. and E. At the NW. corner it takes in the E. side of the Great North road at Whetstone; the old North road, from Crouch End over Muswell Hill, ran through Friern Barnet, but this route sank to a country lane after the 14th-century road was built through Highgate and Finchley. There is a good deal of open ground in the S., particularly about Colney Hatch; otherwise, except where there are signs of decay along Oakleigh Road in the NE. and at Whetstone, the district is pervaded by an agreeable suburbanity.

The name first appears in 1274 (*freren*, brothers—the Order of St John, which held the manor; *barnet*, a place cleared by burning). After the Dissolution of the Monasteries Henry VIII granted it to St.Paul's. Halliwick or Hollick manor house stood near the Orange Tree inn. Colney Hatch is possibly derived from a dam or sluice in a nearby Cole brook and not, as usually explained, from a gate of Enfield Chase.[2]

---

[1] Quoted by M. Gilbert, *Chiswick: Old and New* (1932), p. 20.   [2] F. W. M. D[raper], 'Notes on Two Place-Names', *Trans. L. Mx. A. S.* NS 10 (1951), p. 171.

Friern Barnet has no history. The Great Northern Railway opened a station at New Southgate in 1851. A tramway was laid along the High Road at Whetstone in 1905 and to Finchley by Woodhouse Road in 1909.

The Middlesex county lunatic asylum at Colney Hatch is a gigantic Victorian pile with Italian tendencies (S.W. Dawkes, 1851); it excited a melancholy awe at its vastness, with accommodation for over 300 staff and 2,000 patients kept (as Thorne marvelled in 1875) 'without shackle or even strait-waistcoat,' as well as admiration for its internal arrangements, like the patent steam-escape from the general kitchen to the soup and vegetable kitchens. The building rises to a certain impressiveness on its principal front, facing N. and 1,881 ft. long, with a central domed feature. It is now called Friern Hospital.

A little way W. is the church of St John (1892), a bold and characteristic work by J. L. Pearson, with stone-vaulted roof, side chapels, apsidal E. end, and ambulatory behind the altar. The windows of the N. aisle depict Anglican worthies, including John Keble. The wooden pulpit is in a restrained Jacobean style. Farther W. are the municipal buildings (Brown and Henson, 1941), on a quarter-circle plan in orange-red brick and green-slated roof with a small belfry. The curve of the front and its good proportions make this, with Hornsey town hall, the most satisfying of the modern civic buildings in the county (*Plate 63*).

About ½ m. N. along Friern Barnet Lane is the pleasant old churchyard, containing what remained of the parish church after rebuilding in 1853, probably on the old foundations and perhaps with the use of some old material. The S. doorway, a much-restored 12th-

century work with chevron ornament, is the only ancient portion remaining. Further NW., near Whetstone, are the brick almshouses built by Laurence Campe in 1612 (restored), a picturesque row of six tenements of two storeys with attic and dormer windows.

At the N. of the district is All Saints, Oakleigh Park, in unremarkable Victorian Early English (J. Clarke, 1882); near Oakleigh Road, in Manor Drive, is a Methodist church (Farrow, Turner and Cooper, 1931) with a dome. Friern Park is a 19th-century house on the site of the old preceptory, later occupied by Sir John Popham, Lord Chief Justice under Elizabeth, and the Bacon family, descendants of Lord Keeper Bacon.

BEDFONT (B5) (properly East Bedfont; West Bedfont is a hamlet in Stanwell parish) is a village on the Staines road 3m. W. of Hounslow. The parish, now included in Feltham urban district, is shaped like an irregular figure 8, with Bedfont village in the lower loop and the settlement of Hatton in the upper loop, which runs up to the Bath Road at Cranford Bridge. The river Crane forms the NE. boundary as far as the bridge on Hounslow Heath.

'Bedefunte' appears in Domesday Book; in succeeding centuries the name assumed many different forms—even 'Belfound' in 1806. It is interpreted either as 'Beda's spring' or as 'spring in the hollow' (though there is now no perceptible hollow in the dead-flat plain).

The manor was held by Azor before the Conquest; at Domesday it was held by Richard under Walter FitzOther. In the early 14th century it was given by John de Neville to the priory of Hounslow; after the Dissolution it belonged to the Crown until 1599 and then passed in succession to the families of Stanhope, Berkeley, and Percy, Duke of Northumberland. Two other manors in the parish, Pates and Hatton, were given to the priory of Hounslow in the 14th century.

Much of the parish was enclosed from the heath in 1813, and farming and market-gardening became the staple occupation. A writer in the *Gentleman's Magazine* of 1825 described Bedfont as 'a small pretty village' and attributed its trebled population since 1800 to the successful enclosure. Powder-mills were established on the river Crane in the 17th century (see HOUNSLOW HEATH), and various light industries have settled in the parish since 1919. There is a good deal of irregular and unsatisfactory housing development. The Middlesex Industrial Reformed School, built in 1859 and now called Feltham Borstal, lies within Bedfont parish at its SW. extremity.

The principal antiquity is the church (St Mary), standing on a green just N. of the main road. The chancel and nave date from the mid-12th century. The low tower, surmounted by a spire of peculiar design, standing to the S. of the nave, was built in 1865 to replace a wooden W. belfry. The interior shows work of all centuries from the 12th to the 16th; the earliest portions are the S. door and the chancel arch, which have round heads with strongly incised chevron ornament. The transeptal excrescence on the N. side (locally known as the 'annexe') was built of brick in 1829 and looks like it. Some remarkable wall paintings in red line on a dark-red background were uncovered at the 1865 restoration in recesses N. of the chancel arch; they date from the 13th century and show a throned figure of Christ with hands raised and exhibiting the five wounds, angels holding a cross and a lance, and the resurrection of the

dead.[1] On the N. wall of the chancel are brasses of 1629 and 1631.

A curiosity of the churchyard is at the gate

Where yew-trees into peacocks shorn
In vegetable torture mourn,

examples of topiary art dating from 1704, which used to display the initials (IH, IG, and RT) of the vicar and churchwardens of that date; Thomas Hood could not resist writing a poem on the legend that these trees represent two proud sisters who refused the hand of a neighbouring squire. A character of the 18th century, John Stanley, 'king of the gipsies,' was buried here about 1765.

Just N. of the church are the handsome 15th- and 16th-century manor farm and barn of Pates. There are other old houses on the green, and Bennet's Farm, SW. of the church, is a good 18th-century building. Fawns Manor is 16th-century, with a 17th-century wing. The Green Man inn at Hatton is an old house, much rebuilt.

Bedfont had a short-lived fame as the headquarters of the Bensington Driving Club, an association of wealthy men who drove their own teams on the road, which removed to the Black Dog inn from Benson, Oxfordshire. 'Nimrod' wrote in 1832 that the inn was 'then kept by a person named Harvey, famous for his beef-steaks, as also for the fish sauce which still bears his name.'[2]

BEDFORD PARK (D4). See ACTON.

BOSTON HOUSE (C4). See BRENTFORD.

BOTWELL (B4). See HAYES.

BOWES PARK (E2). See SOUTHGATE.

BRENTFORD (C5), which may be reckoned the county town of Middle-

[1] E. W. Tristram, *English Medieval Wall-Painting: the Thirteenth Century* (1950), p. 504.
[2] 'Nimrod' [C. J. Apperley], *Life of a Sportsman* (1832; ed. 1948), p. 305.

sex, lies on the Thames between Isleworth and Chiswick, where the Brent and the Grand Union canal flow into the river. This was the site in early historic times of the lowest regular ford over the Thames, and the town is certainly of very ancient origin. It has a generally unprepossessing appearance, owing to the industries established along the riverside.

Most authorities hold that Julius Caesar's crossing of the Thames in 54 B.C. took place at Brentford; traces of British trackways detected in NW. Middlesex point towards it,[1] and there was certainly habitation on the site called Old England, by the railway docks, in pre-Roman times.[2] With less likelihood, the river crossing by Aulus Plautius in Claudius's campaign of A.D. 43 has also been attributed to Brentford.[3] It is first mentioned by name, 'Bregunt ford,' in 705, when it probably lay on the border between Essex and Wessex. The name referred to a ford over the Brent, not the Thames; forms like 'Brainford' and 'Branford' were common from the 13th to 17th centuries.

Offa, king of Mercia, held synods at Brentford in 780 and 781, and in 1016 Edmund of Wessex and Canute the Danish king fought several actions in and about it. It did not appear in Domesday Book; Old Brentford, touching Chiswick and Acton on the E., was part of Ealing, in the bishop of London's manor of Fulham; New Brentford, the W. end of the town, was included in Hanwell until 1723. There was no visible demarcation between the two portions of the town. Patrick Ruthven, Earl of Forth, was created Earl of Brentford in 1644; W. Joynson-Hicks, M.P. for Brentford 1911-18, was created Viscount Brentford in 1929.

Brentford's position where the western road touched the Thames, at the point where craft going upstream have to turn from a westerly course for a wide southward loop, made it a likely spot for market, warehouse, and transhipment trade, and the corn produced to the N. and W. on the fertile brick-earths, as well as cattle and sheep from more distant points, naturally flowed towards it. A Thursday market, with an annual 6-day fair, was granted in 1307. In the later 17th century a timber market-house was put up, which lasted until about 1850, when market trade had sharply declined.

Next to the market, inns provided much of Brentford's living: there was a meeting of the order of the Garter at the Lion in 1445, and the Three Pigeons, an ancient house existing until 1848, was mentioned by several writers about 1600. The town was important enough for six protestants to be burnt there in 1558. There was some obscure story about a witch of Brentford—Falstaff in *The Merry Wives of Windsor* gets out of Mistress Ford's house disguised as Mother Prat, the fat woman (alternatively, the witch) of Brentford; there exists also a strange composition called *Jill of Brentford's Testament*. There is, too, some queer folk-lore about Two Kings at Brentford, which makes literary appearances down to a ballad by Thackeray; it now appears to be proverbial in the form 'There cannot be two Kings of Brentford.'[4]

The last and best-known battle of Brentford took place in 1642, when after Edgehill the royalist troops were feeling their way towards London. They forced a small detachment out of the town in a sharp engagement on 12 November and the next day decided to withdraw without pressing farther east in face of determined opposition assembling at Turnham Green. The

[1] H. Braun, 'Some Earthworks of North-West Middlesex,' *Trans. L. Mx. A. S.* NS7 (1936), p. 365. [2] R. E. M. Wheeler, 'Old England', *Antiquity* 3 (1929), p. 20. [3] Sharpe (page 12, note 4) was the protagonist for Brentford's share in both these events. A column erected close to the river in 1909 with inscriptions stating these views as facts is now lost to sight. [4] The most recent occurrence of this proverb that I have noticed is in an article by Lord Brand in *Lloyd's Bank Review*, April 1949.

populace of Old Brentford petitioned the Commons with a statement of their sufferings, and a collection was taken throughout Middlesex for their relief.

The place achieved notoriety in the 18th century for its dirty roads and rowdy elections. The dirt became proverbial—'as dirty as "Old Brentford at Xmas,"' Byng of the *Torrington Diaries* called a Berkshire road in 1787,[1] and Gough's edition of Camden's *Britannia* (1789) flatly calls it 'dirty, long, and ill-built.' In spite of these defects, a strange tale is found in Spence's *Anecdotes*, under the year 1730, of an offer by the heads of the Jewish community in England to buy the place for £500,000, rising to a million.

The polling-place for Middlesex elections was the Butts, a large square behind the market-house, formerly used for archery practice. It is not clear when polling first took place there, but certainly from the beginning of the 18th century the Middlesex elections were held there and nowhere else.[2] At election times, and especially during the famous contests of 1768 and 1769 when John Wilkes was repeatedly elected and in 1802 when Sir Francis Burdett was returned, the town was in uproar for weeks together.

By 1800 industry was beginning to settle on the town: Lysons mentions turpentine works, a steam corn and starch mill, and a manufactory of cotton wicks. The Grand Junction canal of 1798 brought more: Faulkner in 1845 mentions timber yards and steam saw-mills, soap works (of 1799), distillery and breweries, gas (1821), water works, and there was a considerable pottery at work in 1774.[3] Many of these may still be traced by the names of small streets and alleys in the town. Brentford's first railway station, lying at the back of the town, was on the

London & South Western's Hounslow loop line of 1849; more important for its economy was the Great Western branch of 1859 from Southall, with a station beyond the bridge at the W. end (actually in Isleworth parish) and docks that in time spread over most of Old England and a considerable area at the mouth of the Brent, where a large tranship traffic developed. In the late 19th century it had factories for soap, colours, mineral oil, varnish, and size, with gas works, potteries, sawmills, malthouses, a tannery and a brewery. It must have been a smelly place.

In 1901 the London United electric tramway was pushed through the High Street, at the cost of pulling down a good many buildings, and in 1925 the Great West road was driven over the fields and market-gardens N. of the town, which had not grown very far back from the river.

Brentford's title to be called the county town of Middlesex depended only on the holding of the elections; it was not an ancient borough, and it is only half a modern one (jointly, with Chiswick, 1932); it had no town hall; there were no assizes. Modern Middlesex does not allow primacy to Brentford in any respect. The main part is now a pretty plain industrial town, with some interesting and one or two attractive survivals from the 17th and 18th centuries. To the N. are newer and somewhat better streets.

The entry to Brentford from London, at the Kew Bridge end of the High Street, is a defile between cliff-like walls; on the left are gas works, on the right, with a campanile of 1867, water works, established by the Grand Junction company in 1835, where two Cornish steam pumping engines of 1820 by Boulton and Watt were installed and worked until 1944 (one still exists

---

[1] The turnpike road from Wantage to Faringdon: see page 72, note 2. [2] See Part I, page 99, and note 3. [3] *John Yeoman* (page 50, note 1), pp. 16, 47.

there).[1] In the shade of a gasholder is the church of St George, Old Brentford, the 19th-century successor to a chapel of Ealing parish built by J. J. Kirby in 1762. A modest and pleasing brick building, it was regarded with unaffected horror by the time it was 100 years old, and was demolished in 1886. The present church (A. Blomfield, 1887) has no particular merit; there is a panel of the royal arms of 1767; and a Last Supper by John Zoffany, with Strand on the Green fishermen as the Disciples, is in the side chapel. A schoolhouse of 1786 just survives at the W. end of the church; here Mrs. Sarah Trimmer, educational and pious writer, d. 1810, laboured in her Sunday school.

The S. side of the road, down to the river, is filled with industrial buildings, happily obscured from the Kew Gardens side by two aits until lately cultivated for osiers; there were some good houses in this area until about 1930.[2] Farther W., close to the road called 'Half Acre,' is the church of St Paul (1867), Victorian Decorated with a spire. The High Street, now broader and lined with shops (one or two with good old fronts, most in shabby condition), continues into New Brentford, which mostly looks older than Old. S. of the road is the church of St Lawrence, a yellow-brick structure of a feeble kind tacked on to a 15th-century tower in 1764. The interior is high, wide, and unhandsome; wooden Ionic columns support galleries. Some pieces were worked in from the old church—a good octagonal font of about 1500, a 14th-century carved stone with the Berkeley arms in the W. wall of the nave, and monuments to the families of Hawley and Clitherow (of Boston House). A tablet to John Clitherow, 1852, is notably good for its period,

and there is a charming Flaxman monument to W. H. Ewin, 1804. There are bits of a brass to Henry Redman, chief master mason of the king's works, 1528, and his wife; he is credited with designing Wolsey's Hampton Court, Lupton's Tower at Eton, and parts of St Margaret, Westminster, mostly in conjunction with William Vertue.[3] A tablet commemorates Thomas Hardwick, d. 1829, designer of Marylebone church and father of Philip Hardwick; he advised J. M. W. Turner to abandon architecture. William Noy, d. 1634, the lawyer who found a precedent for Charles I's ship-money and prepared the writ, lived at Brentford and was buried in the church (the brass inscription was defaced soon after his death). The most notable curate of New Brentford was John Horne (later Horne Tooke), 1760-73, radical politician, supporter of Wilkes at the Middlesex elections of 1768 and 1769, and philologist.

Beyond the church, over the Brent bridge, which had a long history of neglect and repair[4] from medieval times, are a few good old houses (in Isleworth parish), including Syon Park House, where Shelley, his biographer T. Medwin, and John Rennie, civil engineer, were at school in 1802-5; the house still stands as a transport office N. of the road. All traces of the medieval chantry chapel at the bridge end have disappeared.

N. of the church is a magistrates' court on the site of the old market-house; beyond is the open square called the Butts, lined on most of three sides by as fine a collection of late 17th-century houses as Middlesex can show, apart from Hampton. Beaufort House and Chatham House, at the top of the square, are splendid examples of serene domestic building of about 1700, and

---

[1] *Institution of Mechanical Engineers Journal and Proceedings*, 156 (1947), p. 236; H. W. Dickinson, 'Water Supply of Greater London', *Engineer*, 186 (1948), p. 406. [2] R. Henrey, *King of Brentford* (1946), contains a semi-fictional account of some of these. [3] J. Harvey, *Introduction to Tudor Architecture* (1949), p. 29. [4] See Part I, page 77, and note 1.

an unexpected refreshment to the eye in their dingy surroundings (*Plate 21*). Several others are good, especially Linden House and Cobden House on the E. side, and 1 Upper Butts; but there are horrific pieces of the 1870s to remind the visitor that he is still in Brentford.

To the E., on Windmill Road, are a few good 19th-century houses. NW. is the church of St Faith, Windmill Road, by G. F. Bodley and G. W. Hare (1907). Boston House, W. of Boston Manor Road, is a good 17th-century brick mansion; its ceilings and staircases were particularly noteworthy, but the whole fabric suffered damage during the 1939-45 war. The main block was built in 1623, after the property had passed to Mary, wife of Sir William Reade, in 1621. In 1670 it passed to the Clitherow family, and the N. wing and outbuildings on the E. side were added in 1671. The exterior, of dark-red brick with stone window-framing, porch, and entablature running all round above the first-floor windows, shows classical treatment of some features in an otherwise old-fashioned house with gabled roof (*Plate 37*). Inside, the ceilings and wooden panelling were good. The square building to the NE. was probably a pigeon house.

BROCKLEY HILL (c2) is an elevation between Edgware and Elstree, rising to 445 ft., where the road from London to St Albans (Watling Street) bends slightly E. of N. for a short distance before resuming its more or less straight NW. course. The Antonine Itinerary, or road-book of the Roman empire, placed a station called Sulloniacae on this stretch of the road. The actual position of Sulloniacae is generally supposed to have been on the E. side of the modern road (which is slightly to the W. of its ancient course[1]) at the top of the hill; there was probably a settlement on both sides of the street.

Excavations on this site are in progress.[2] They have already shown that there was a Roman-age settlement of some kind there, but it is not yet possible to form any judgment exactly what it was (it seems unlikely to have been more than a posting station) or when it flourished; it appears reasonably certain that pottery was being made there in the Flavio-Trajanic period, A.D. 70-117, and there are traces suggesting occupation from Belgic times to the 4th century.

The Royal National Orthopaedic Hospital buildings, in Brockley Hill House and grounds W. of the road, make excavation on that side difficult. There are several artificial mounds and hollows round the hill-top. There may still be a good deal more to be known about Brockley Hill.

BRONDESBURY (D4). *See* WILLESDEN.

BURNT OAK (D3). *See* HENDON.

BUSH HILL PARK (F1). *See* EDMONTON and WINCHMORE HILL.

BUSHY PARK (C6). *See* HAMPTON COURT and TEDDINGTON.

CANONS PARK (C2). *See* STANMORE, LITTLE.

CHARLTON (B6). *See* SUNBURY.

CHILD'S HILL (D3). *See* GOLDERS GREEN.

CHISWICK (D5) is the nearest Middlesex Thames-side parish to London, lying in a loop of the river between Kew Bridge and Hammersmith

[1] Mrs. H. E. O'Neil, 'Watling Street, Middlesex', *Trans. L. Mx. A. S.* NS 10 (1951), p. 137.
[2] See Bibliography, Brockley Hill, page 403.

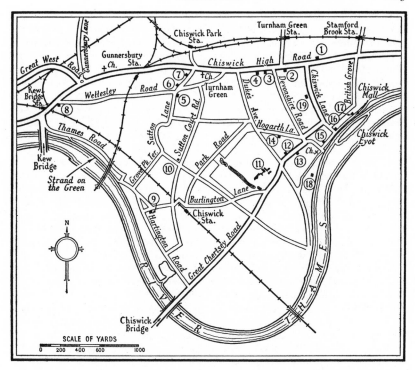

CHISWICK,
SHOWING THE SITES OF THE OLD HOUSES

*1. Bohemia House.   2. Annandale House.   3. Linden House.
4. Bolton House.   5. Heathfield House.   6. Arlington House.
7. The Chestnuts.   8. Stile Hall.   9. Grove House.   10. Sutton
Court.   11. Chiswick House.   12. the Cedars.   13. Fairfax House.
14. Hogarth House.   15. Beford House.   16. College House.
17. Walpole House.   18. Corney House.   19. Manor Farm House.*

(STRAND ON THE GREEN, separately noticed, is a little settlement on the river bank just below Kew Bridge); the line of the old Stamford brook, not now to be seen, divides it on the E. from Hammersmith. It has been joined with Brentford as a borough since 1932.

There are three distinct parts of Chiswick: the old riverside village; development along the Great West road across the N. of the district, mostly of the early and middle 19th century; and more recent building in the river loop on the grounds of the large estates that formerly divided it. Apart from the historic interest and quiet, but not uninterrupted, beauties of its riverside and one surviving great house,

Chiswick is a characteristic 19th-century London suburb, with the benefit of a good deal more open space than most.

The name of Chiswick, like Keswick, Cumberland, means simply 'cheese farm'; its first appearance is 'Ceswican' in a charter of about 1000. It was not in Domesday Book, being then part of the Bishop of London's manor of Fulham.

Manorial records relating to Chiswick from the 12th century onwards are in St Paul's cathedral archives.[1] The principal manor, called Sutton or the Dean's manor, was sequestered to the lord mayor of London and others during the Civil War. The lease was later held by Thomas Belasyse, Earl Fauconberg; Boyle, Earl of Burlington; and Cavendish, Duke of Devonshire. A second property, attached to one of the canons' stalls in the cathedral and called the prebendal manor, was leased in 1570 to the dean and chapter of Westminster and the house used as a country retreat for Westminster schoolboys, especially in times of plague.[2]

From the end of the 17th century a number of considerable houses were built for noble and wealthy persons from London. Chiswick's first historian, John Bowack, could write in 1705: 'It has for many years past boasted of more illustrious and noble persons than any of [its] neighbours.' He proceeded: 'Fishermen and watermen ... make up a considerable part of the town.'[3]

The most significant development in the parish was not, however, along the river, but to the N., by the road from Hammersmith to Brentford where Bowack noted 'several good brick houses' and as many inhabitants as in the old village. The middle-class villas were submerged during the next hundred years, as horse-buses, then the railways and a horse-tramway (1882, electrified 1901) combined to make the N. part of Chiswick an unattractive extension of Hammersmith. Turnham Green itself survived, but there was no sign of consideration for amenity in the rest, except at Bedford Park in the extreme N. where a garden suburb was laid out (see ACTON). To the S., building about the London & South Western Chiswick station (1849) (*Plate 54*) was generally hemmed in by large private estates until about 1900 and this district, with a good many private playing-fields and open spaces, escaped the flow of traffic until a road to a new Thames bridge was driven through in 1933. There was some unlovely industrial building by the river, notably Thornycroft's engineering works, and osiers were cultivated on Chiswick Eyot until the 1930s.

The old village centre, by the river in the E. part of the parish, contains many attractive and interesting buildings clustered round the church (St Nicholas), which is not itself notable. The W. tower is dated to the time of William Bordall, vicar 1416-35;[4] it is of the usual 15th-century Middlesex type, with square-headed windows and a bold stairway turret. No other portion of the old church, which was a jumble of bits dating from about 1550, 1710, and 1772, survived rebuilding in 1882, when the red bricks of the old fabric were ground up and mixed in the mortar for its successor. The new church, by J. L. Pearson, has nothing in particular to commend it. There are two brasses on the wall of the organ-chamber, and a good alabaster wall-monument in the S. chapel to Sir Thomas Chaloner, 1615, author of a treatise on the virtues of nitre and promoter of alum mining near Guisborough, Yorkshire.

[1] See *Domesday of St. Paul's of 1222*, ed. W. H. Hale (Camden Society, 1858). [2] 1572 has been given as the date, but this refers to a sub-lease of part of the property: W. Draper, *Chiswick* (1923), p. 51. [3] Bowack's account is reprinted in full by W. P. W. Phillimore and W. H. Whitear, *Historical Collections relating to Chiswick* (1897), p. 1. [4] His death is wrongly dated 1425 on an alabaster slab put up by Francis, Earl of Bedford, in 1631.

Also buried in the church or church-yard are: William Hogarth, d. 1764, with Garrick's lines beginning 'Fare-well, great Painter of Mankind'; Ugo Foscolo, poet of the Italian *Risorgimento*, 1827 (monument by Marochetti; body removed to Florence, 1871); Thomas Bentley, partner of Josiah Wedgwood, 1780 (relief by T. Scheemakers); Charles Whittingham, printer, 1840; Colin Campbell, architect, 1729; William Kent, architect and landscape-gardener, 1748; and Richard Wright, bricklayer, 1734—these three at the cost of the architect Earl of Burlington; Adam Cardonnel, Marlborough's secretary, 1719; Charles Holland, actor, 1769 (epitaph by Garrick, bust by William Tyler); P. J. de Loutherbourg, painter, 1812; J. M. Whistler, painter, 1903. There is also a monument to Sir John Chardin, oriental traveller, 1712, buried in Westminster Abbey. Mary, third daughter of Oliver Cromwell, d. 1709, and Frances, his youngest daughter, are buried at Chiswick, with no monument. Beside the churchyard a pretty little schoolhouse of 1707, much altered and in poor condition, was demolished in 1950.

From the corner of the lane at the E. end of the church, with Vine House (18th century) and the vicarage (1657/8), Chiswick Mall runs NE. along the river opposite Chiswick Eyot towards Hammersmith. Beside it is a handsome collection of fine houses of the late 17th and 18th centuries, not unbroken but well deserving attention. They are the Chiswick that Pope and Hogarth and Thackeray knew, far from characteristic of the place today (*Plate 43*).

The first notable building is Woodroffe House, about 1700, in red brick, spoilt by unsuitable later windows; there follow Bedford House and Eynham House (originally one), early 18th-century, extended 1749; Said House, reconstructed *c.*1935; Thames View House and Lingard House, early 18th-century; Red Lion House, about 1700, spoilt by a poor balcony and cement-rendering. Farther along is Walpole House, the finest on the Mall, with internal portions of the late 16th century and exterior mostly of the late 17th century, some as late as 1730. There is good wrought ironwork in front. Barbara Villiers, Duchess of Cleveland, d. 1709, is said to have lived in it during her old age, and Daniel O'Connell lodged there as a student about 1796. It was later occupied by H. Beerbohm Tree, actor-manager, d. 1917. Next is Strawberry House, about 1700 with a plain front of about 1730; beyond are Morton House, about 1730; Norfolk House and Island House, about 1840; Swan House and Cedar House, late 17th-century, refaced in the 18th century. In spite of some nasty intru-sions, notably Croswight and Orford House, an incongruous pair (J. Belcher, 1887), Chiswick Mall is on the whole well preserved, where preservation has not meant petrifaction.

On the corner of Chiswick Lane and the Mall was the old prebendal manor-house of St Paul's, where in the 17th century Westminster scholars took the country air. In 1816 Charles Whitting-ham moved his Chiswick Press into the house, and from then till 1852 he and his nephew Charles Whittingham brought out from it the most attractive and workmanlike English printing of the 19th century. The old house was pulled down in 1875; the Hollies, Suffolk House, Staithe House, and Thames Bank occupy the site.

There was not much development back from the river until the 19th century, apart from some buildings—

Mawson Row, named after Matthias Mawson, bishop of Ely 1754-70—in Chiswick Lane, a little way NE. of the church, and some in what is now called Hogarth Lane, farther W. Pope lived with his parents at the corner house of Mawson Row (now the Fox and Hounds) from 1716 to 1719, when he moved to Twickenham. Immediately N. and NW. of the church are some good buildings: Latimer House, with a fine wrought-iron gateway, and Holly House; some houses opposite, including one in weather-boarding and another now the office of a yeast factory; tenements in Lamb Yard; the George and Devonshire Arms inn, on Burlington Lane; and Chiswick Square, with choice houses of about 1680 on the E. and W. sides and the handsome front of Boston House (about 1650-1740) on the S. Boston House claims by an inscription to be the scene of Becky Sharp's hurling the dictionary from the carriage window as she left the Miss Pinkertons' school at the beginning of *Vanity Fair*; but Walpole House is the more probable claimant for this distinction. There are features of both houses in Thackeray's description, but he clearly places his school 'on Chiswick Mall.'[1]

On the W. side of Burlington Lane lies Chiswick House, one of the most admired pieces of Palladian architecture in England. Though additions have injured the effect of the Earl of Burlington's villa, and its condition had become distressing by the end of the 1939-45 war, it is still a very notable example of 18th-century building. It was designed in a singular mode—the circle-within-a-square plan copied from Andrea Palladio's Villa Capra at Vicenza; since the destruction of Nuthall Temple, Nottingham, by the housebreaker in 1929 and of Foot's

Cray Place, Kent, by fire in 1949, Chiswick and Mereworth, Kent (Colin Campbell, 1727), remain the only considerable examples of their type in England. Mereworth is large, but Chiswick is somewhat smaller than the Villa Capra; it is a miniature, 'too small to live in and too big to hang to one's watch,' as Lord Hervey said when it was built (*Plate 14*).

The site was previously occupied by a Dutch-gabled house built in the early 17th century for Sir Edward Wardour, occupied about 1624 by Robert Carr, Earl of Somerset, and his countess (together suspected of having procured the poisoning of Sir Thomas Overbury in the Tower); it was bought in 1685 by the 1st Earl of Burlington. The portion now called the Grosvenor wing (the stables) was added NE. of this house about 1700. Richard Boyle, 3rd Earl of Burlington, architect and patron, set about building a little *casina* or garden temple to his own designs at Chiswick in 1717, and in 1725, on his return with William Kent from a second tour to Italy, he began the villa; the exterior was finished in 1727 and the interior, largely to Kent's designs, was completed some years later.[2] It was meant to be a *villa*—not a residence but a setting for pictures and statues. The present house, therefore, with the wings added by James Wyatt in 1788 to turn a temple of the arts into a dwelling-house, is far from what Burlington conceived; nevertheless, its skilful arrangement of steps, portico, and dome remains admirable. The Palladian style had an able advocate in England.

Adjoining the villa on the N. is a stately gateway ascribed to Inigo Jones, 1621, formerly at Beaufort House, Chelsea, and given to Burlington by Sir Hans Sloane in 1738. The grounds were laid out and improved by Kent in his

[1] M. Gilbert, *Chiswick: Old and New* (1932), p. 66. [2] M. Jourdain, *Work of William Kent* (1948), p. 66.

informal manner, with water, a bridge, statues (some of the animals by Scheemakers), and classical buildings; they were somewhat impaired by planting of exotic trees in the 19th century but remain attractive. The whole estate, inherited by the Duke of Devonshire in 1753, was much visited by rank and fashion in the succeeding 100 years. Charles James Fox died in the house in 1806 and George Canning in 1827. Walter Scott described a garden-party there in 1828[1] at which 'the scene was dignified by the presence of an immense elephant who under charge of a groom wandered up and down, giving an air of Asiatic pageantry to the entertainment,' and one of the earliest giraffes seen in England was similarly shown there about 1860. Edward VII when Prince of Wales took the house for some years; later it was used as a private lunatic asylum. It is now a municipal park, and the house, needing much repair, became the property of the Ministry of Works in 1949.

During the time of the 6th Duke of Devonshire (succeeded 1811, died 1858) the land N. of the house was occupied by the grounds of the Royal Horticultural Society, to which the duke had a private gate. He noticed there an intelligent young gardener employed in training creepers at 12s. a week, called Joseph Paxton, and took him into his service—which led to the Chatsworth conservatories and the Crystal Palace. The grounds were established in 1821 under T.A. Knight, and by 1826 there were 1,201 varieties of apple alone in the list;[2] they were removed to Wisley, Surrey, in 1904, and the site is covered by the streets between Barrowgate Road Gardens and Hadley Gardens.

NE. of Chiswick House is Hogarth House, a pleasant 18th-century brick building with a wooden bow on the S. front, war-damaged but restored. Hogarth lived in it each summer from 1749 until his death in 1764; H. F. Cary, translator of Dante, occupied it between 1814 and 1826.[3] Between Chiswick House and the river are some industrial buildings, including Thornycroft's. Sir John Thornycroft's father, Thomas Thornycroft, sculptor, d. 1885, had his studio on Chiswick Mall, and there the *Nautilus* steam-launch was built in 1860. It was the first steam-launch able to keep up with the University boat-race (which it did in 1862), and from 1866, when the Chiswick shipyard was established, steam torpedo-boats and road vehicles were built there until the firm moved to Woolston, Southampton, in 1906.

To the S. are the Duke's Meadows in the loop of the Thames, with Chiswick bridge (Herbert Baker, 1933) at the SW. corner. NW. is the district of Grove Park, with some agreeable suburban houses of 1870 and later; the name is taken from Grove House (demolished 1928), an older building reconstructed with a pedimented portico in 1711.

Turnham Green is the N. part of the old parish of Chiswick, and its modern centre; it was the scene of a check to Charles I's forces in 1642 after the battle of Brentford, when the London trained bands, hurriedly drawn up and resolutely commanded by Essex, put up a stout enough defence to convince the king that he could not take the city. He withdrew, never again to come so close to London in command of troops. In 1698 William III was nearly assassinated between the river and the Green on his way back to town from hunting in Richmond Park; but the plot, in which Sir George Barclay and some 40 others were concerned, was given away.

---

[1] Walter Scott, *Journal 1827-28* (ed. J. G. Tait, 1941), p. 246 (17 May 1828).   [2] H. V. Taylor, *Apples of England* (ed. 3, 1946), p. 26.   [3] Sir James Thornhill, painter and father-in-law of Hogarth, is wrongly said to have lived in the house before him: W. P. W. Phillimore and W. H. Whitear, *Historical Collections relating to Chiswick* (1897), p. 244, quoting A. Dobson, *William Hogarth* (1880), p. 180.

The green itself is now a modest triangle of ground, with Christ Church (G. G. Scott, 1843) in the middle. On the N. side is Chiswick High Road, a broad thoroughfare much encroached upon since 1800, as surviving passages and property-lines on the S. side show. Two ancient roads led E. from Brentford, one along the parish boundary where the District railway now runs S. of Acton Green, by Bath Road to Shepherd's Bush; the other by Wellesley Road, Heathfield Terrace (along the S. of the Green), and the passages S. of the High Road to Hammersmith. The present course of the High Road combines parts of both.[1] It is an unpleasing thoroughfare, with only one or two good houses remaining along it; Afton House, on the S. side, now a club, is a decent late 18th-century building. W. E. Henley, author, lived at No. 64, 1887-8.

Inn signs commemorate the names of old taverns. Some old houses demolished within the last 150 years were notable. Corney House, S. of the church, demolished 1832, belonged to Russell, Earl of Bedford, in the late 16th and 17th centuries. The Manor Farm House, W. of Chiswick Lane half-way between the river and the High Road, was built about 1691 for Sir Stephen Fox, d. 1716, founder of the houses of Ilchester and Holland, who had previously lived in a smaller house on a site within the later grounds of Chiswick House. This stately, though not ostentatious, brick house was later used as a school and a private asylum; it was pulled down in 1896. At Turnham Green was Heathfield House, occupied by George Eliott, Lord Heathfield, defender of Gibraltar against the Spaniards, 1779-83; the house was demolished in 1837 and the site occupied by Christ Church

vicarage; its iron gates, after being re-erected before Chiswick House and then at Devonshire House, Piccadilly, now stand at the top of the Queen Victoria avenue in the Green Park. Linden House, in the High Road at Linden Gardens, demolished 1878, was the home from 1828 to 1830 of Thomas Griffiths Wainewright, forger and poisoner. Sutton Court, at the corner of Sutton Court Road and Fauconberg Road, W. of Chiswick House, stood on the site of the old manor house; it was occupied during the Commonwealth by Chaloner Chute, speaker 1659, who died there. Thomas, Lord Fauconberg, who married Mary, third daughter of Oliver Cromwell, in 1657, took it in 1676. It was later owned by Lord Burlington and the Dukes of Devonshire; a rebuilt house of 1790 was demolished in 1896.

Chiswick ought to have done better than it did when these good old mansions were being replaced with new streets between 1870 and 1914, but the results are disappointing. The place should be much more attractive than it is.

COCKFOSTERS (E2). *See* ENFIELD CHASE.

COLHAM (A4). *See* HILLINGDON and UXBRIDGE.

COLINDALE (D3). *See* HENDON.

COLNBROOK (A5). *See* STANWELL.

COLNEY HATCH (E2). *See* BARNET, FRIERN, and SOUTHGATE.

COWEY STAKES (B6). *See* SHEPPERTON.

COWLEY (A4) is a small parish in Ux-

---

[1] J. Tavenor-Perry, 'Strand on the Green', *H.C.M.* 13 (1911), p. 109.

bridge urban district between Uxbridge and West Drayton; until the 19th century it was almost completely surrounded by Hillingdon. There is an outlying settlement to the S. at Cowley Peachey, and the church lies to the E. of the village. There is no direct road communication leading E. towards London. The name has nothing to do with cows; the earliest form—'Cofenlea' in 959—shows it to be derived from a man Cofa, like Coventry. Bartholomew Pecche, granted land in Cowley and Ickenham in 1252, or one of his family gave his name to Cowley Peachey. The manor was part of the ancient possessions of Westminster Abbey.

Cowley was a remote agricultural village until the Grand Junction canal (1798) and the Great Western branch railway to Uxbridge (1858) were built through the parish. The name of the Paddington Packet Boat inn at Cowley Peachey commemorates the passenger service by canal barge. Towards the end of the 19th century considerable market-gardens and glasshouses were laid out. There are a few good if modest old houses shaken by constant heavy traffic on the main road, with modern development of a poorish kind between. The best buildings lie W. of the road near the Crown inn.

To the E., beyond the station, is the church (St Lawrence), the smallest parish church in Middlesex, 45 ft. by 18 ft; it is quite surprisingly primitive, more fitted for the remote parts of Essex than for this sophisticated county. The main portion was built in the 12th century; the chancel was rebuilt and widened in the 13th century. The bell-turret was reconstructed in 1780. There was a destructive restoration in 1897, but the interior with its quaint late medieval roof, supported by three king-post trusses, has many features of interest. There is a double-decker gallery at the W. end, with decorative panelling of about 1600 worked into it, and there are remains of a 15th-century wooden screen and a brass of 1505. The interior is very dark, in spite of a dormer window on the S. side of the nave; the small windows, every one of a different shape, are filled with coloured glass. There are some charity cottages of 1760 opposite the church.

Some persons of note resided at Cowley: Barton Booth, 18th-century tragic actor, the original Cato in Addison's drama, d. 1733, and his second wife, Hester Santelow, esteemed for her performance as the Fair Quaker of Deal, d. 1773. An inscription painted on the W. end of the church commemorates Dr. W. Dodd, executed at Tyburn for forgery in 1777 and buried in the churchyard (his brother being then rector).

CRANFORD (B5) is a village N. of the Bath road between Heston and Harlington, partly in Heston and Isleworth borough and partly in Hayes and Harlington urban district. The old village, with some once good houses, lies E. of Cranford Park; modern building extends down to and along the Bath road, with startling architectural treatment of the principal road junction. The park and the banks of the river have been preserved, but this has not prevented Cranford acquiring the characteristic W. Middlesex air of untidiness, and in places the hand of decay lies heavy upon it.

Cranford, so spelt in Domesday Book, means 'ford frequented by cranes or herons.' The river, originally called the Fishbourne, got the name of Crane by back-formation.

At Domesday Cranford manor was

held by William, son of Ansculf; it was later divided into Cranford St John and Cranford le Mote, the former belonging to the Templars and then to the order of St John, and the latter to the abbey of Thame, Oxfordshire. Both were vested in the Crown at the Dissolution and were granted to Lord Windsor in 1543, passing then to Sir Roger Aston; in 1618 Lady Elizabeth Berkeley purchased the 'sweet and well-seated manor' for £7,000.[1] Cranford House consisted of additions made to Sir Roger Aston's house by James, 3rd Earl of Berkeley, in the early 18th century; it was pulled down in 1945, except a portion of the stable block, which remains. The house had a well-attested ghost, 'dressed as a maid-servant with a sort of poke bonnet on and a dark shawl drawn or pinned lightly across her breast'; and there was another of a man.[2] Grantley Berkeley, the quarrelsome sportsman of the early 19th century, was the best known of its later occupants. His book *Reminiscences of a Huntsman* (1854) contains some curious passages on Cranford and the surrounding districts.

The little church (St Dunstan) stands in the park W. of the village, close to the site of the manor house. It is pleasantly situated but of no great architectural interest. It has a 15th-century chancel and W. tower, joined by a nave without aisles built in the classical style in 1716, after the original building had been damaged by fire; at the same time a top storey was added to the tower. The interior, generally too garishly coloured, has a 17th-century marble floor in the chancel. The monuments are noteworthy as the best collection in the county after Harefield. The earliest is to Sir Roger Aston and Mary, his first wife, executed in 1612 by William Cure at a cost of £180; it

is a handsome alabaster and black marble object on the N. side of the chancel. Against the S. wall is the marble effigy of Lady Elizabeth Berkeley, 1635, which has been attributed to Bernini but was almost certainly carved by Nicholas Stone.[3] There are also wall tablets to George, 8th Lord Berkeley ('the traveller'), 1658, and George, 1st Earl of Berkeley, 1698. On the E. chancel wall is an alabaster tablet to Thomas Fuller, rector 1658-61, author of *The Worthies of England.*

There were two other notable residents at Cranford in the 17th century: John Wilkins, rector 1661-2, and Sir Charles Scarburgh, physician, d. 1693 (tablet on N. chancel wall). Wilkins, bishop of Chester 1668, wrote a *Discourse on the Beauty of Providence* and *Discourses concerning the World in the Moon and a New Planet*; he was an original member of the Royal Society. Sir Charles Scarburgh wrote *A Treatise on Trigonometry*, a compendium of Lily's grammar, and an elegy on Abraham Cowley.

Apart from the church and manor house, there was very little at Cranford before the 20th century. There are some pretty houses in the High Street (so called); the circular building by the road in the grounds of Springfield (demolished) was an observatory where Warren de la Rue made important experiments in photography and photo-astronomy between 1857 and 1874. There is a tradition, which may be a good one, that Mendelssohn visited the church and played on the organ there. Not this place, but Knutsford in Cheshire, was the scene of Mrs. Gaskell's Cranford.

CRICKLEWOOD (D3). *See* GOLDERS GREEN and WILLESDEN.

---

[1] J. Smyth, *Lives of the Berkeleys,* quoted by *The London and Middlesex Notebook,* ed. W. P. W. Phillimore (1892), p. 11. [2] On the ghosts, Berkeley (page 124, note 1), p. 209. [3] K. A. Esdaile, *English Monumental Sculpture since the Renaissance* (1926), p. 167 (Appendix), pronounces it 'certainly the younger Nicholas Stone's.' A recent leaflet on the history of the church adheres to the attribution of the figure to Bernini.

CROUCH END (E3). *See* HORNSEY.

DAWLEY (B4). *See* HARLINGTON.

DOLLIS HILL (D3). *See* WILLESDEN.

DRAYTON (C4). *See* EALING.

DRAYTON, WEST (A4), lies on the W. border of the county S. of Uxbridge and Cowley and N. of Harmondsworth; it is separated on the W. from Iver in Buckinghamshire by the Colne river. The place is mentioned as 'Draegtun' in 989; 'draeg' may indicate a place where a boat might be dragged overland to avoid a river bend. 'West' is added to distinguish it from Drayton in Ealing.

At Domesday the manor belonged to St Paul's, which held it until 1547, when Henry VIII obtained it and granted it to Sir William Paget, created Lord Paget of Beaudesert in 1549. Drayton felt the impact of the Paget ownership: most of the village was pulled down for the new manor house of 1550 and the churchyard was enclosed in the grounds; Lysons in 1800 noted that only the vicar and inhabitants had right of free access. Thomas Paget, owner under Elizabeth, was a Roman Catholic recusant, and Sir Christopher Hatton, lord chancellor 1587-91, and George Carey, Lord Hunsdon, obtained the estate. It was later regained by the Pagets, earls of Uxbridge, but the house was pulled down in 1750 and the manor sold to Fysh Coppinger in 1786.

Standing on the fertile level land of W. Middlesex, Drayton was noted for its agricultural produce, especially fruit, until houses came to be of more account than crops. Industrial establishments had been built by the Colne and the Grand Junction Canal (1798); the Great Western Railway opened a station (for Uxbridge) in 1838. There were races at West Drayton in the late 19th century, 'among the most frequented of the lower-class suburban gatherings.' Now West Drayton is a suburban district showing some traces of the rural appearance which it retained until 40 years ago; it has been united with Harmondsworth in the urban district of Yiewsley and West Drayton.

The church (St Martin), S. of the station, has a sturdy 15th-century tower, capped by cupola (added about 1700), of a type common in W. Middlesex. It appears to have been rebuilt in the 15th century, though there are remains of 13th-century lancet windows in the chancel. It was severely restored in the 1850s. The present church has the dignity of a lesser 15th-century building. The chancel floor is higher than the nave, raised, it is said, because the Pagets were buried upright in their coffins in the vault beneath. The font has an octagonal bowl with side panels sculptured in high relief; they show the Crucifixion with the Virgin and St John; a large leaf and a figure of a man with hood and dagger (this may possibly represent a sculptor at work on foliage); the descent from the Cross; a vintner carrying a wineskin; and half angels with shields and scrolls, with other human and animal figures under the edge of the bowl and at the base. The church plate dates from 1507—the only inscribed pre-Reformation chalice and paten left in Middlesex; one of only four pairs in English parish churches. There are several brasses of interest, including a fragment to Richard Roos, mercer of London, 1406, and monuments to the family of de Burgh (the surname assumed by Coppinger in 1790); George Carey, Lord Hunsdon, 1603; James Eckersall, clerk of the kitchen to Queen Anne, George I, and George II, 1753; and Rupert Billingsley, captain of the *Royal George*, d. 1720, with a representation of some other vessel.

The gatehouse outside the church is all that remains of the old manor house; it is a red-brick building of the early 16th century, originally higher, much built about in modern times, though the oak doors are old. The vicarage, to the E., is a 17th- and 18th-century building; and to the W. and SW. are several pleasant old houses and cottages. The Frays, on the mill stream, contains 15th-century portions, refaced in brick. The N. part of West Drayton is noticed under YIEWSLEY.

One of the Middlesex Cromwell legends was attached to an old house known as Burroughs—that his body was buried there after being dug up and cast out from Westminster Abbey at the Restoration.[1] Burroughs stood between Swan Road and Colham Mill Road.

EALING (c4) is a considerable district lying about the Uxbridge road immediately W. of Acton. It became a borough in 1901—the first of the modern Middlesex boroughs—and since 1928 has stretched out to embrace the ancient parishes of HANWELL (without New Brentford), PERIVALE, GREENFORD, and NORTHOLT, with part of WEST TWYFORD. GUNNERSBURY is separately noticed; only Ealing proper (less Old Brentford in the S., separated from it in the 19th century) is dealt with here—an area nearly square, divided by the Brent river from Wembley, Perivale, and Greenford in the N., and by lines corresponding with no existing feature from Acton in the E. and Hanwell on the W.

Ealing stands on a slight elevation on the Middlesex plain, which rises between the Uxbridge road and the Brent to about 200 ft. at Hanger Hill in the NE. corner. The old village stood not on the main road but S. of it about the lane from Brentford. Most of modern Ealing takes its character from the solid, respectable residences of the 19th century that began to arise after the Great Western Railway opened its station in 1838; there are fringes of 20th-century development to N. and S. The town is solid, composed of buildings mostly respectable and sometimes superior, with the ugliest large church in Middlesex and a fair number of historic houses preserved. The municipal guide-book writer, with an unusual flash of phrase, calls it 'the Queen of the western suburbs'; it is, in fact, the Queen Victoria.

Ealing is named from the Gillings, or people of Gilla, who appear in records of the late 7th century; the G, or Y, survived until the early 17th century, in forms like 'Gilling' (1243) and 'Yelling' (1307).

Like Acton, Ealing formed part of the bishop of London's great manor of Fulham at Domesday, and it was not separately mentioned; the manor remained the property of the see. Subordinate manors were GUNNERS-BURY, owned in the late 14th century by Alice Perrers, mistress of Edward III, and in the 15th by Sir Thomas Frowyck, Lord Chief Justice; Coldhawe in the S.; Pitshanger, or Hanger Hill; and Drayton in the W.

Ealing first became something more than an agricultural village in the 18th century, when it began, because of its 'nearness to the town or court, [to] abound with retirements of the nobility and gentry.'[2] It became the centre of middle-west Middlesex, with well-

---

[1] See Part I, page 96, and note 1. [2] W. Camden, *Britannia*, ed. R. Gough (ed. 2, 1806), p. 91.

known schools, a royal residence, a poor-house, a fair on the Green much frequented by Cockneys, and pony races on Ealing Dean.[1] The first station out of Paddington on the original Great Western Railway of 1838 was on Haven Green (now Ealing Broadway station), and the centre of gravity began to shift away from the old village about the church. More railways and stations followed after the 1870s. A London United tramway along the Uxbridge road began work in 1901. The North Circular road was carried by existing roads from Gunnersbury over Ealing Common to Hanger Hill in the late 1920s and the Western Avenue across the NE. corner at the same time. With this proliferation of transport facilities, the Ealing population rose very quickly after 1861.

The centre of modern Ealing is the Uxbridge road along the Broadway, a street with no architectural merits. On the N. side are Christ Church (G. G. Scott, 1852; alterations by G. F. Bodley; blitz-damaged), grey Victorian Decorated with a well-proportioned spire, and the town hall (C. Jones, 1889; additions to E., G. H. F. Prynne and A. W. Johnston, 1931), in not a very courageous Neo-Gothic style; some of the interior is better than the outside promises. S. of the Broadway, on the W. side of Ealing Green, is the most interesting and attractive of the historic houses, now the public library (sometimes called Pitzhanger Manor).[2] A house was built here about 1770 for Thomas Gurnell by George Dance the younger (who married Gurnell's daughter in 1772). It was bought in 1800 by John Soane, Dance's successor as professor of architecture at the Royal Academy, who found the interiors of the S. wing such admirable examples of the taste introduced by the Adam

brothers that he retained that wing while completely reconstructing the rest. The main front, with 4 free-standing Ionic columns supporting female figures, is a reminiscence of Robert Adam's front to Kedleston, Derbyshire, on suburban instead of palatial scale. The interior, now very bare (in contrast to the over-furnishing indicated in water colours of the original[3]), is full of curves and ellipses, especially in ceilings and alcoves. Dance's S. wing, with the 'eating-room' on the ground floor (spoilt by modern lighting), has good plaster ornament. Soane's building, without being a masterpiece, is full of interest as the precursor of his house at 13 Lincoln's Inn Fields, where his singular talents are shown at their most mature. He left Ealing in 1811; the existing N. wing was built by a later owner on the site of some artificial ruins that Soane particularly liked (*Plate 8*).

The house was later occupied by a daughter of Spencer Perceval, prime minister, d. 1812, and with the neighbouring property (occupied by Spencer Walpole, d. 1898, 3 times home secretary 1852-67) became a public park in 1898. Additions, to house parts of the public library, have been made in brick that has not toned to the colour of the original, and perhaps never will.

Farther S., past some good old houses, is the parish church (St Mary), E. of the Brentford road. The old church fell down in 1729; it had been giving premonitory signs of dissolution for 50 years, and a wooden tabernacle had been set up beside it in 1726. It took 11 years and an act of Parliament before a new church was ready. William Cole, the Cambridge antiquary, visited it in 1773 and wrote of the interior: 'The altar is remarkably plain, only wainscoted, and Moses and Aaron

[1] Cobbett (page 39, note 2), i., p. 90; C. Jones, *Ealing* ... (1902), opp. p. 81 (posters of 1813 and 1819). [2] The manor or manor farm of Pitshanger lay on the N. slope of Ealing towards the Brent, where Pitshanger Park now is. It is difficult to connect this property with the manor house on the Green; the confusion (if it is one) may have arisen in the 18th century when Thomas Gurnell owned both the manor house and Pitshanger farm (C. Jones, *Ealing* ... (1902), p. 63), though neither Brayley and Britton, *Beauties of England and Wales* (1816), vol. x., part iv., art. Ealing, nor T. Faulkner, *History and Antiquities of Brentford, Ealing, and Chiswick* (1845), refers to the house as Pitzhanger Manor. [3] Soane Museum, 13 Lincoln's Inn Fields; reproduced in A. T. Bolton, *Pitzhanger Manor, Ealing Green* [1918], pp. 10, 12.

painted on the sides, with the Decalogue. A very handsome pulpit or desk stands just before it, and fronts the west door, but in my opinion a very indecent situation.'[1]

Such plainness and indecency could not survive the Victorian enlightenment in Ealing. The whole edifice was firmly reconstructed by S. S. Teulon in 1866 (tower, 1874) in a manner that the archbishop of Canterbury (Tait) described as transformation 'from a Georgian monstrosity into a Constantinopolitan basilica.' An apsidal chancel was thrown on to the E. end; buttresses were built between the windows; a semicircular baptistery was added on the S. side; a tower whose elaborate ugliness defies description took the place of the plain one at the W. end; and the whole was finished with horseshoe-shaped arches and bands of various coloured bricks: in brief, the Byzantine style that Mr. Teulon conceived, here as at Sunbury and at Holy Trinity, Leicester, to be the happy solution to the problem set by a classical church with round-headed windows. Monuments from the church of 1740 and its predecessor are stuffed into the W. end and may be discerned with difficulty. On the N. wall of the nave is a brass to Richard Amondesham (or Awnsham), merchant of the staple of Calais, and his wife, about 1490; at the W. end of the chancel is a striking alabaster tablet to Richard Taverner, vicar, 1638, displaying skull, cross-bones, and hour-glass. Sir Frederick Morton Eden, author of *The State of the Poor* (1797) and pioneer of modern sociological investigation, and Robert Orme, author of *A History of the Military Transactions of the British Nation in Indostan from the Year 1745*, d. 1801, are commemorated by tablets. There is also a tablet to John Horne Tooke, sometime curate of Brentford, radical

politician and author of the etymological *Diversions of Purley*, d. 1812. Tooke and John Oldmixon, historian, d. 1742, occasionally remembered as the butt of Pope's gibes, are buried in the churchyard.

Near the church Westfield House, a good building used as a Conservative club, and a row of cottages S. of the churchyard remain to hint what 18th-century Ealing looked like. There were three well-known private schools close to the church: Great Ealing School, at the old rectory, where, under Dr. D. Nicholas, Louis Philippe, later king of the French, and T. H. Huxley's father were assistant masters (Huxley was born in 1825 in a house close by), and the pupils included Cardinal Newman, his brother F. W. Newman, W. M. Thackeray, F. Marryat, R. Westmacott, sculptor, W. S. Gilbert, Hicks Pasha, Sir Henry Rawlinson, Lord Lawrence, and Sir Henry Lawrence; Ealing House, where Bulwer Lytton was at school in 1817 (scenes from Ealing and the Brent meadows appear in *My Novel*); and the Manor House (of Coldhawe manor, near Little Ealing) or Goodenough House, kept by Dr. W. Dodd, executed for forgery 1777. C. Sturgess, vicar 1775-97, set up one of the earliest Sunday schools after Robert Raikes' original one at Gloucester (1780); Mrs. Trimmer of Brentford was his 'zealous and active coadjutor.'

Little Ealing, now known as Northfields, is the SW. corner of the district. Rochester House, now a convent, is a house of about 1710-20, with a later block; it is named from Zachary Pearce, bishop of Rochester, d. 1774; General Dumouriez, victor of Valmy and Jemappes, lived there in exile for some years before 1822. Charles Blondin, rope-walker, d. 1897, lived at Niagara House, named from

---

[1] British Museum, Additional MSS. 5845; *Mx. & H. N. & Q.* 3 (1897), p. 183; E. Jackson, *Annals of Ealing* (1898), p. 67.

the scene of his most famous exploit (1859). Lammas Park was formed from land held on the old Middlesex Lammas tenure, which became common after 12 August each year.

Ealing Common, a broad green about the Uxbridge road on the Acton side, is mostly lined with large ugly houses of 1870 to 1900. St Matthew's church, at the SW. corner, is a large red-brick affair (A. Jowers, 1884). On the London side of the common, N. of the road, stood Fordhook House, where Henry Fielding, magistrate and novelist, lived for a short time in the year of his death (at Lisbon, 1754). Lady Byron afterwards lived there, and Byron's daughter Ada was married in the house, 1835. Elm Grove, formerly Hickes-upon-the-Heath, was a mansion on the common occupied by Sir William Trumbull, secretary of state and friend of Pope, d. 1716, and by Spencer Perceval, prime minister, assassinated in the lobby of the House of Commons 1812; part of the site is now covered by All Saints church (Perceval memorial, 1905). There are also numerous nonconformist churches about the Broadway and Ealing Common; M. Horder's Little Church attached to the Congregational chapel has merit.

S. of Ealing Common is Gunnersbury (see separate article); N. is the more modern district of Hanger Hill. The church of the Ascension (J. Seely and P. Paget, 1939) is notable. It is plain and light within, where the reinforced concrete limbs are displayed rather nakedly in the roof, and grey brick with plain windows outside; the central tower lights the chancel. The oak woodwork of screen and reredos is good. Modern houses fill up the area E. of Hanger Hill up to Park Royal station.

Ealing N. of the Broadway and Haven Green is the true upper-middle-class suburb of 1860 to 1900: rows of detached residences of red, and some brown, brick, with various fussy adornments, many of them bobbing a curtsey to the Gothic in the shape of the porch. The church of St Peter, Mount Park Road (J. D. Sedding, 1893, completed by H. Wilson), white brick and Box stone, is very original Perpendicular, with buttresses dividing the large clear W. window. Two rows of external turrets line the roof above the nave arcades; inside a triforium, without clerestory, runs above flat arches: a striking attempt to escape from the neo-Decorated tyranny. At the top of the hill is a reservoir, with an extensive view N. to Horsendon Hill, Harrow spire, and the heights about Stanmore. On the N. slope down to the Brent at Perivale is Brentham (a fabricated name), a garden suburb of 1910-14, with the large unfinished church of St Barnabas, Pitshanger Lane.

Farther W., towards Castlebar Hill, the houses are mostly smaller and date from the 1890s and later, with some earlier and larger ones at the top of the hill. St Stephen's church is a conspicuous object, stone-built Decorated with tall spire (H. Ashdown, 1876; spire, A. Blomfield, 1891), at the top of Castle Hill. On Castlebar Hill was Castle Hill Lodge, occupied by Mrs. Fitzherbert and the Duke of Kent, Queen Victoria's father (who unsuccessfully promoted a bill to allow him to dispose of it by lottery, 1819). Castlebar Lodge was occupied by G. Osbaldeston, foxhunter; Castlebeare House by Archibald Constable, Walter Scott's publisher, in 1821; the Grange by General Eliott, Lord Heathfield, defender of Gibraltar 1779-83. The large Princess Helena college was built in 1882 (S. Bannister), when it was removed from Regent's Park.

Ealing Broadway is continued to West Ealing (otherwise known as Ealing Dean or Drayton Green) by houses once good which have come down in the world. The Old Hats inn was in coaching days the first stage from London on the Oxford road. The only thing at West Ealing worth looking at is St John's church (E. Horne, 1876), a queer building with lancet windows and a Frenchified W. tower with conical cap and corner turrets, not unimpressive inside.

EASTCOTE (B3). *See* RUISLIP.

EAST TWYFORD (D4). *See* WILLESDEN.

EDGWARE (C3) is an ancient parish (now in Hendon borough) roughly triangular in shape, lying on the E. side of Watling Street (known as the Edgware road thus far from London) on the Hertfordshire border; BROCKLEY HILL is noticed separately. The N. boundary runs from the village of Elstree along the wooded Ridgeway, and the Dean's brook divides it on the E. from Mill Hill and Hendon. The old village lies at the S. extremity of the triangle; the buildings W. of the main road are in Little Stanmore (Whitchurch). The Watford by-pass road cuts across the middle of the district; to the N., some 1½ m. from the old village, is the hamlet of Edgwarebury, where one of the few Middlesex farms still remains.

'Æcges wer' (Ecgi's weir or fishing pool) is mentioned in a charter of about 978; it is not in Domesday Book. In the 16th-18th centuries it was commonly 'Edgeworth.' Domesday Book probably included the place under Little Stanmore, or perhaps under Kingsbury; it was first described as a separate

manor, belonging to the Countess of Salisbury, in 1216. 1n 1443 it was sold to Thomas Chichele and others as trustees for All Souls College, Oxford, which still owns property in the district. It was heavily wooded, and most of its value lay in timber; there was a sharp struggle between All Souls and Lady Jane Stafford in 1587, when the college maintained its refusal to lease its woods in Edgware to her, in which most of the prominent personages at court took one side or the other.[1] There were inns on the Watling Street, and at one period there was a weekly market on Thursdays, discontinued by 1800. In 1867 the Great Northern Railway's branch from Finsbury Park through Finchley was opened, and a monthly cattle market was licensed. Electric trams began to run from Cricklewood in 1904; but in spite of these advantages Edgware did not take on the air of a suburb. Only when the tube railway was extended from Golders Green in 1924 did Edgware begin to change with a vengeance. It is now completely covered with houses at the S., but there is open country N. of the Watford by-pass road.

Like most other things about Edgware, the church (St Margaret) is not of much interest. It has a sturdy buttressed W. tower, probably of the 15th century; the rest of the church was rebuilt in 1764 and 1845; aisles were added in 1928. There is a chrisom brass of 1600 in the chancel and a monument to Randolph Nicoll, 1658. In the parish was also a chapel of St John of Jerusalem, intended for the refreshment of pilgrims to St Albans, which has in some accounts been confused with the parish church.

The frontage of Edgware on Watling Street is uninteresting, except for the single-storey tenements of Atkinson's

[1] *Collectanea* (page 52, note 1), p. 179.

almshouses, c.1680, about ½ m. NW. of the church. Station Road, continued NE. as Hale Lane, displays the effect of development in the 1920s; there are fearsome specimens of 'brewer's Tudor' and the suburban commercial styles. Commonplace semi-detached houses run up to the Watford by-pass road and spill over it to the N. at some places. Edgwarebury Lane, formerly called 'Roman Road' by the locals,[1] meanders up to Bury Farm, a timber-framed weatherboard house of the 17th century, and on to Elstree. In the NW. corner of the parish Edgware shares Brockley Hill with Little Stanmore.

The only persons of note to live in Edgware were two of its clergy, Francis Coventry, d. 1759, author of a popular little tale, *Pompey the Little*, and Thomas Martyn, professor of botany at Cambridge 1762-1825. The family of Richard and Maria Edgeworth believed that their ancestors migrated from Edgware to Ireland in the 16th century and named their new home Edgeworthstown from the usual spelling at that date.[2]

EDMONTON (F2) lies on the E. border of Middlesex, between Enfield and Tottenham, divided from Essex by the course of the Lea. The ancient parish extended W. to the Hertfordshire border at East Barnet and took in some of the SW. parts of Enfield Chase, but Southgate, Bowes Park, Palmer's Green, and Winchmore Hill were formed into a separate parish of SOUTHGATE in 1881. The whole district, roughly square in shape, is dead flat, except for slight ridges in the NW. and SW. corners; the Pymmes brook flows across it from W. to E., not everywhere on the surface, and the New River cuts the NE. corner. The principal highway is the road from London to Waltham Cross; through Upper Edmonton (to the S.) and Lower Edmonton, the original village centre, it is called Fore Street. Silver Street and Angel Road, running E. and W., have become parts of the North Circular road; the Cambridge road of 1923-4 runs up the W. side of the district. There are a few remains of ancient buildings, and one or two good modern ones, but most of the E. portion is covered by dreary streets. It has some celebrity in literature owing to two personages whose recorded actions are largely fabulous—the Merry Devil of Edmonton and John Gilpin.

The parish, which gave its name to the NE. hundred of Middlesex, including also Enfield and Tottenham, appeared as Delmetone or Adelmetone (Eadhelm's farm) in Domesday Book. The manor was given by William the Conqueror to Geoffrey de Mandeville. It was held from 1190 to 1370 by Say of Berling and was later purchased by Henry VIII. Under Charles I it was settled on Queen Henrietta Maria. There were smaller manors of Willoughby and Deephams, and others, including Bowes, owned by St Paul's.

In the Middle Ages Edmonton was of much less consequence than Tottenham or Enfield, but in the 17th and 18th centuries it eclipsed Enfield, largely because of its fairs. The two Beggars' Bush fairs, re-granted by James I, were held on the Southgate side; they fell into abeyance in the middle 19th century. Edmonton fair, held from 1680 onwards at various public houses, was in origin a well-known hiring-fair for servants. By 1820, when it was estimated that some 30,000 persons attended, it was declared that, the original object of the fair being obsolete, it was no more than a noisy nuisance and a source of great moral injury;[3] it

---

[1] *H.C.M.* 10 (1908), p. 296. [2] The tradition further asserts that a daughter married into the family of Lake, of Canons; but the earliest Edgeworth of eminence (Roger Edgeworth, canon of Salisbury, Wells, and Bristol, d. *c.* 1560) was born in Denbighshire, and the Edgeworths were probably not originally a Middlesex family: *Black Book of Edgeworthstown*, ed. H. J. and H. E. Butler (1927), p. 7. [3] W. Robinson, *History and Antiquities of Edmonton* (1819), p. 9; Brayley and Britton, *Beauties of England and Wales* (1816), vol. x., part iv., p. 717.

ceased about 1870. There is a spirited picture of the 1788 fair by John Nixon in the Victoria and Albert museum[1] (*Plate 18*). Fairfield Road, just N. of the crossing of Fore Street and Angel Road, commemorates the ground where it was held from 1730 onwards.

Until about 1840 there was little manufacture—only a glass factory of 1776 and a hard soap works of 1789. The district shared the character that Tottenham then had, a pleasant residential village for wealthier citizens of London; it supported a public assembly room, which was flourishing in 1776.[2] It was also considered a salubrious place for schools. The Cambridge railway, with a station on Angel Road, was opened in 1840; the Enfield branch was driven through the Green at Lower Edmonton in 1849. In 1872 the Great Eastern line through Tottenham was opened, with workmen's trains and cheap fares that caused most of the parts within walking distance of the stations to be quickly covered with shoddy dwellings. Trams arrived at Edmonton in 1881 and were electrified in 1905. Since this period factories have been established in the Lea valley, many removed from E. and NE. London. In 1875 there were extensive market-gardens, especially for potatoes, and until after the 1914-18 war there was agricultural ground on the W. side, except at Bush Hill Park, in the extreme NW., where a detached suburb had grown up round the station. The building of the Cambridge road and new housing estates almost filled up the available land by 1939; E. of the railway towards the Lea the ground is mostly too marshy to be much use. The last brickworks in Edmonton gave up in 1936.

The village centre was the Green, where 17th-century two-storey houses can be seen above and behind new shop-fronts. The Golden Lion inn presents a decent bow-windowed front. Leading W. is Church Street, with the school house of 1784 on the S. side—'a Structure of Hope founded in Faith on the Basis of Charity'—and Lamb's Cottage (Bay Cottage, where he moved from Enfield with his sister in 1833 and lived till his death after a fall in the next year) on the N. Keats lived in Church Street, in the house of his grandmother, Mrs. Jennings; the site is now covered by Keats Parade, a terrace of shops. He was apprenticed from 1811 to 1815 to Mr. Hammond, a local surgeon, and most of his *Juvenile Poems*, published 1817, were written at Edmonton.

The old parish church (All Saints) is distinguished by a good buttressed W. tower of the 15th century with a bold corner turret. The main body of the church was built at the same date; remains of a 12th-century arch and doorway are set in the W. wall of the S. aisle. The church, apart from the tower, was encased in brick in 1772; in 1889 the S. aisle was built and the whole church restored, leaving it with a plain appearance. There are 16th- and 17th-century brasses. There are numerous monuments, including some in the dark chancel to the Huxley family of Wyre Hall, and one on the S. aisle wall of about 1530, with the indents of missing brasses in a wall recess under a carved canopy. Inside the N. door is a deplorable pair of Gothic-revival tablets to Lamb and Cowper (1892). The churchyard contains the graves of Charles and Mary Lamb. Vicarage Cottage, to the SE., is a building of about 1700.

Fore Street is a horrid jumble, featuring the Town Hall in municipal Perpendicular (1884, enlarged 1903)—

---

[1] Reproduced in *Connoisseur* 76 (1926), p. 97. [2] Harrison, *History of London* (1776), quoted by F. Fisk, *History of the Parish of Edmonton* (1914), p. 76.

'much more than a building; it is an institution,' according to the official guide; the church of St Mary (W. Butterfield, 1883, unfinished); some decent houses fast going to decay, notably at Angel Place; and the Bell public house, uninteresting successor (1878) to the one where Mrs. John Gilpin waited for her husband in Cowper's tale.[1] (Cowper was never at Edmonton in his life, so far as is known; he appears to have heard the tale from Lady Austen and written it in a summerhouse at Olney.[2]) Close to the Bell is St James's church (E. Ellis, 1850) and farther S., on the Tottenham boundary, Snell's Park Congregational church (F. Pouget, 1850) in a fiddling Gothic style, almost opposite the old Fore Street chapel building of 1788. Near Angel Road station is St John, Dysons Road (C. H. B. Quennell, 1924). W. of Fore Street is Pymmes Park; the mansion, which was 'a proper little house' of Lord Burghley, according to Norden (1593), was rebuilt twice in the 18th century and burned down in 1940. Weir Hall Gardens, farther W., indicates the approximate site of the Huxleys' house, demolished in 1818.

North of the Green, the Roman Catholic church in Hertford Road (1903) and the Anglican churches of St Michael (W. D. Caroë, 1901) and St Peter (1902)—both built in part with funds derived from the sale of St Michael Bassishaw in the City—are the only buildings of merit. To the W. there is creditable housing-estate development of the 1920s, and the good modern Latymer school (1924, successor of the parish charity school of 1624) and the County School (W. T. Curtis, 1931) on the Cambridge Road. W. of the arterial road are the suburb of Bush Hill Park, built when the 'Queen-Annery' of Bedford Park, Chiswick, was still the fashion; the slopes of Bush Hill itself, with the New River and good timber setting off comfortable houses in an unEdmontonian way; and Salisbury House (the name perhaps more correctly Sayesbury), a picturesque, irregular-gabled building of about 1600, with projecting upper storeys, standing in a small park S. of Bury Street.

Among past worthies of Edmonton[3] were John Tillotson, Archbishop of Canterbury 1691-4; Brook Taylor, d. 1731, secretary of the Royal Society and mathematical writer; and James Vere, d. 1779, 'a worthy charitable man,' who wrote *A Physical and Moral Inquiry into the Causes of that Internal Restlessness in the Mind of Man which has been the Complaint of all Ages*. Richard Price, d. 1791, nonconformist divine and author of *Observations on Civil Liberty*, which called forth Burke's *Reflections on the French Revolution*, began his ministry at the old Independent chapel. J. T. Smith, author of *Nollekens and His Times* (1828) and A *Book for a Rainy Day*, lived for some years at a cottage in the parish. John Bradshaw, president of the commissioners for the trial of Charles I, was never (as stated in most of the authorities) resident at Bury Hall.[4] The story of Peter Fabell, the 'Merry Devil of Edmonton,' who was supposed in the Elizabethan play to have cheated the Devil himself, was early regarded as mythical; the sedate Weever allowed himself a pun on the name in his *Ancient Funerall Monuments* (1632)—copied, indeed, from Norden (1593)—and Thomas Fuller could not resist reproducing it in his *Worthies*. 'If a grave bishop,' he wrote, 'in his sermon, speaking of Brute's coming into this land, said it was but a bruit, I hope I may say without offence that this Fabell was but a fable.' Elizabeth Sawyer, an old woman condemned to

---

[1] There has been confusion between the Bell (or Old Bell) and the Angel (or Blue Bell), exhaustively set right by Fisk (see preceding note), p. 106, and about its position in relation to the Wash of Edmonton, apparently crossed by Gilpin on the London side of the Bell. [2] The authenticity of the John Gilpin story has been extensively canvassed in *Notes and Queries*: reference in *Dictionary of National Biography*, art. William Cowper. [3] Thorne appears to be wrong in calling Nahum Tate, hymn-writer and poet-laureate, a holder of the living. [4] Fisk (see page 244, note 2), p. 147.

death for witchcraft in 1621, supplied a more authentic inspiration for Dekker, Ford, and Rowley's piece *The Witch of Edmonton.*

ENFIELD (F2), the second largest local government district in Middlesex, covers 12,400 acres at the NE. extremity of the county. The eastern third of the district is the flat ground of the Lea valley, the remainder the undulating land of ENFIELD CHASE. The character of the place corresponds to these differences of soil: in the W. mainly residential, with considerable open areas remaining; in the E. industrial, with some gravel-working and market-gardening; the shopping centre, successor to the old market town, lying towards the S. where the two kinds of country meet. The Lea divides Enfield from Essex on the E.; the New River flows from N. to S. just above the 100-ft. contour, imparting some pleasing touches to the scene. The main Hertford road and Cambridge railway pass through the settlements named from S. to N. Ponders End, Enfield Highway, Enfield Wash, and Freezy Water, towards the E.; the new Cambridge road lies parallel and slightly to the W.; Enfield Town itself, on the more ancient course of the main road,[1] is reached from London by the Green Lanes through Wood Green and Winchmore Hill. The Royal Ordnance Factory, at Enfield Lock in the extreme NE., is the home of the rifles that have carried Enfield's name into many remote places, and so many and various are the products of the 150 local factories that their annual exhibition can be entitled 'Enfield Can Make It.'

It must be confessed that at Enfield the past is a good deal more attractive than the present. The 19th century ruined the look of the E. portion:

Charles Lamb 'had thought in a green old age (O green thought) to have retired to Ponder's End—emblematic name how beautiful', but no one who could avoid it would retire there now; and the 20th century is busy doing the same for the rest. Nevertheless, enough fragments remain to bring its long and not uninteresting history to mind.

'Enefelde' is the name in Domesday Book; it perhaps means 'Eana's open space'—a clearing made in the N. Middlesex forest. The manor was given by William the Conqueror to Geoffrey de Mandeville; it was later held by Bohun, Earl of Hereford, and passed in 1399 to the duchy of Lancaster by the inheritance of Mary de Bohun, who had married the Duke of Lancaster (Henry IV) in 1382. The manor court leet and court baron were held until 1925. Like Edmonton and Tottenham, it was never in church ownership, an uncommon thing in Middlesex.

The site of the original manor-house, which Humphrey de Bohun obtained licence to fortify in 1347, is not certainly known; Camlet Moat, an earthwork on the N. side of the chase, and (more probably) Oldbury, some ½ m. E. of the church, have been suggested. Edward VI in his childhood and Elizabeth, before and after her accession, lived at Elsynge Hall, believed to have been close to Forty Hall, N. of the town. It is unlikely that the building in the market-place known as Enfield Palace, demolished in part in 1792 and completely in 1928, was ever lived in by any of the royal family. The manor of Worcesters, in the N. part, was made over by Thomas, Earl of Rutland, to Henry VIII in 1540, and there were other manors—Durants and Gartons, near Ponders End, belonging to the Wroth family (the house was burned down about 1800 through too many

---

[1] The Roman road from London to Lincoln probably ran through Stoke Newington and Tottenham to Lower Edmonton, thence to Enfield Town and past Forty Hill towards Theobalds Park; the Hertford road on the low ground through Enfield Highway and Waltham Cross appears to be medieval: T. Codrington, *Roman Roads in Britain* (1903); W. J. Roe, *Ancient Tottenham* [1949], p. 67.

logs being heaped on the fire at a tenants' meeting); Suffolks, in the same district; Honeylands and Pentriches, in the extreme N., by Capel House; and perhaps one called Goldbeaters.

Enfield early became the centre of trade for N. Middlesex; a market was granted in 1304 with two annual fairs, and by the 16th century there was also a Sunday morning meat market in the churchyard, which gave such offence in 1586 that Leonard Thickpenny, set on, it was believed, by the vicar, 'in a very outrageous manner very evil beseeming a man of the church, in a madding mode most ruffianlike' seized the meat and threw it to the ground.[1] The place, though not actually on the Lea, was well enough situated in relation to the head of the navigable river to make it an *entrepôt* for midland grain, especially barley for malting, on its way to London. It also had a fulling-mill (rare in this part of the country) and several tanyards in late medieval times. When the navigable stream was extended to Ware and Hertford, Enfield lost much of the carrying and warehousing trade, and in 1586 it was petitioning Elizabeth as 'your Majesty's decayed town of Endfield.' There was a disastrous fire in 1657, and Richard Gough, an inhabitant, wrote in his 1789 edition of Camden's *Britannia* that it was 'the skeleton of a market town.' In 1795 the only manufactures were a tannery and a mill for marbled paper. Dissent was strong in Enfield during the 17th and 18th centuries, with regular meeting-houses in Baker Street and Parsonage Lane and at Ponders End.[2]

Prosperity returned as regular coaches from London made it a rural but not remote retreat for citizens like Charles Lamb; by 1798 'the entrance to Enfield from the windmill is charming; it abounds with smart boxes of from £30 to £60 a year.' The fair, which declined at the end of the 18th century owing to strong competition from Edmonton, was revived in 1826 but was finally held to be illegal and closed down in 1869. Races were held from 1788 to 1821 at Green Street, Ponders End, and again from 1864 to 1880 on the Chase side. The government ordnance factory, established beside the Lea navigation in 1804, was much extended in 1854; the main Great Eastern railway up the valley was opened in 1840, with a branch to Enfield Town in 1849. The coach it displaced was later to be found by the traveller plying between Alexandria and Suez.[3] Industry crept up, and market gardens down, the valley from about 1880 onwards, encouraged by tramway and railway extensions. Residential building of a middle-class character extended to the W. and artisan quarters N. of the town.

The centre of Enfield Town, with its 'market house' supported by eight teak pillars (1904) in a square flanked on the N. by the church, retains some air of its origin when market stalls are set up on Saturdays. On the E. is a bank in the Dutch style of 1897 and the old vestry house, facing a weather-boarded house; the rest of the main street is commonplace.

The church (St Andrew) is of no particular architectural merit, principally dating from the 14th century with a clerestory of about 1530. The tower, its principal external feature, is a thin and feeble object. The whole S. side was rebuilt about 1820, when the porch, with a muniment room above it, was pulled down. The interior contains some noteworthy memorials, of which the altar-tomb and brass of Joyce, Lady Tiptoft, d.1446, on the N.

---

[1] *V.C.H.* ii., p. 86. [2] There are some curious particulars of a dispute in the congregation of Zion Chapel, Parsonage Lane, in 1791, which led to the foundation of a new chapel 14yds. away: *H.C.M.* 12 (1910), p. 213. [3] S. Beaven, *Sands and Canvas*, quoted by M. Phillips, *Enfield: Past and Present* (1917), p.19.

side of the chancel, is outstanding. This is a tomb of painted stone, with a canopy of *c*.1530; the brass shows Lady Tiptoft richly clothed, with an heraldic mantle. The whole tomb is decorated with shields of arms indicating the noble lady's connexions. This brass has been compared[1] with the somewhat similar one to Eleanor de Bohun, Duchess of Gloucester, d.1399, in Westminster Abbey; though the earlier one is certainly superior, the Enfield example is in the same class of excellence and good preservation.

Other notable monuments in the church are: Sir Nicholas Raynton, lord mayor of London, d. 1646, and his wife, of Forty Hall—a three-decker, Sir Nicholas reclining aloft in armour with mayoral cloak and chain, Lady Raynton below him, and kneeling figures at the foot; and Martha Palmer, 1617, an oval tablet by Nicholas Stone. Tablets commemorate Dr. Abernethy, surgeon, d. 1831, and Joseph Whitaker, of the Almanack, d. 1895. In the N. chapel is some glass of 1530 with the initials T. R. (Thomas Roos or Manners, Earl of Rutland, of Worcesters manor), and a pleasing 17th-century bread-shelf; some remains of brasses are in the N. and S. chapels. Over the W. gallery is a fine organ-case of 1752 by Richard Bridge. The New River Company is represented on a series of tombstones in the churchyard.

There has been a grammar school at Enfield certainly since 1557, in the building opposite the W. end of the church; the original two-storey school house, of brick with modern stone dressings, has survived in the middle of accretions built during the last 200 years. Dr. Robert Uvedale, d. 1722, who also ran a private boarding school in the so-called palace while headmaster of the grammar school, was a celebrated naturalist in his day and raised a famous cedar of Lebanon in the palace garden.

'Queen Elizabeth's Palace,' which stood on the S. side of the market square with its principal front to the W., was a brick building with elaborate and handsome internal decorations; the most important of them happily survived the demolition of the house in 1928. Built or substantially rebuilt about 1552 (the 'E. R.' of the fireplace probably refers to Edward, not Elizabeth), the 'palace' was used as a school from 1660 onwards; the greater part was pulled down in 1792 and what was left served until 1896 as a school, then as the town post office, and finally as a club. The best of the oak panelling, a carved stone chimney-piece, bearing the royal arms and symbols and the motto *Sola salus servire Deo; sunt caetera fraudes*, and a fine ceiling were re-erected in a house on the E. side of Gentleman's Row, immediately N. of the council offices, a little way NW. of the town centre.

This part of Enfield, with the stream of the New River's original course running between green banks and some houses of the 18th and early 19th centuries more or less faithfully preserved, has an air of the place Charles and Mary Lamb knew when they moved from Islington in 1827. They lived first at Mrs. Leishman's on Chase Side, then at another house—'an odd-looking, gambogish coloured house,' now Clarendon Cottage, with a tablet affixed—until 1829, and then at the Westwoods', next door and 25 in. farther from town, until they moved to Edmonton in 1833. For a hundred yards or so, the walk is picturesque, if the eyes are shut from time to time: Brecon House, Sedgcope, Fortescue Lodge, the council offices, and a weather-board cottage are good examples of Middlesex

---

[1] C. Boutell, *Trans. L. Mx. A. S.* OS 1 (1860), p. 67.

building. The Methodist church at the corner (1889) is dreadfully Gothic; so is the Congregational church farther along Chase Side (J. Tarring, 1874).

Silver Street and Baker Street, running N. from the town centre to Forty Hill, can still show a few of 'those good old red-brick houses ... standing for the most part in well-timbered grounds' that contributed so much to the character of the place when Thorne wrote in 1875; but most of them look rather sad now. The vicarage, largely modern, has two 16th-century wings; there is a group of three good houses on the W. side of Silver Street; a little way beyond, on the corner of Parsonage Lane, the lower school of the grammar school is accommodated in Enfield Court, built about 1690, where Sir Alfred Somerset, the last private occupier, who kept and drove a coach between Enfield and neighbouring towns, had a pack of hounds until 1899 and built a circular riding-house and a gazebo in the grounds.

Farther on, at Forty Hill, are handsome ironwork gates, which used to lead to Gough Park, the house of Richard Gough, antiquary, d. 1809, and some agreeable buildings in unkempt surroundings: the Hermitage (dated 1704), the Old Bakery (weatherboarded), Forty Hill House, Elsynge House (18th-century), and Worcester Lodge (17th-century, spoilt). On the W. side of the road is Forty Hall, standing in a finely-wooded park, a brick building of three storeys on an almost square plan, built between 1629 and 1632; like most houses of that period, it has been attributed without any very good reason to Inigo Jones.[1] It has belonged in turn to the Raynton, Wostenholme, Meyer, and Bowles families. It is a handsome example of 17th-century domestic work, and the interior plaster and panelling are fine. The courtyard and stables lying to the NW. are contemporary and contain an imposing moulded brick gateway; there is also a 17th-century Dower House to the S.

Beyond Forty Hill are Jesus church, in white brick (1835), a tiny infant school of 1848 by Maiden Bridge, Myddleton House (1818) with a fine garden, the hamlet of Bull's Cross with the old Pied Bull inn, and Capel House in a wooded park at the extreme N. of the district on the Hertfordshire border.

The parts E. of this line contain little to attract or interest. Enfield Wash is notable solely as the place where Elizabeth Canning, a servant girl, was, as she alleged, abducted and locked in a house belonging to Mother Wells, a gipsy, in 1753. (Her story was not believed, and she was found guilty of perjury and transported for 7 years amidst immense public excitement; Lysons cites the titles of 36 pamphlets on the case.) The electric power station at Brimsdown is best seen from a distance, with the Essex hills behind; at Ponders End are a good old house or two, some remnants of the Durants estate in a public park, and a weatherboarded mill of Hertfordshire pattern on the Lea. The church of St James, Enfield Highway (1831; chancel, 1864), is not a bad example of its periods; St George, Freezy Water (J. E. K. and J. P. Cutts, 1900), is commonplace. The ordnance factory lies beyond.

There is not much of Enfield S. of the town, where the Edmonton boundary approaches close. The Town Park occupies part of the grounds of Chase Side House, and farther W. a golf course is laid out in the estate of Enfield Old Park, given by Charles II to George Monk, Duke of Albemarle, in 1660. An extraordinary collection

[1] It is not listed in J. A. Gotch, *Inigo Jones* (1928).

of antiquarian relics was assembled there in the late 19th century by Edward Ford, historian of Enfield, including some good panelling and the old pulpit from the church and a Grecian temple brought from Canons, Little Stanmore. The districts W. of Chase Side are noticed under ENFIELD CHASE.

Enfield Town station stands on the site of a fine 17th-century brick house (demolished 1872), where John Keats, Charles Cowden Clarke, and Edward Holmes, author of the first adequate life of Mozart, went to school.[1] Before Cowden Clarke's father established the school, it was the birthplace of Isaac D'Israeli, 1766, author of *Curiosities of Literature* and father of the Earl of Beaconsfield. The window pediment of the front, a fine example of gauged, carved, and moulded brickwork of the Wren period, was fortunately removed to the Victoria and Albert Museum. The house is said to have been built in 1672 by E. Helder, a 'bricklayer' under Wren.

A number of other notables, not mentioned in this description, have been associated with Enfield. Sir Walter Raleigh is traditionally supposed to have lived at a small house where Gordon Road meets Chase Side; he certainly was in attendance on Elizabeth at Enfield, but there is no evidence for this attribution.[2] Major Cartwright, radical politician of the later 18th century, died at Enfield in 1824; he was buried at Finchley. Frederick Marryat, author of *Peter Simple*, and Charles Babbage, mathematician and inventor of the calculating machine, were at Mr. Freeman's school at Holmwood, Baker Street, near Gough Park, and Walter Pater lived in the town from 1842 to 1857.

ENFIELD CHASE (E1) was the general name given to the portion of the old forest of Middlesex stretching from the NE. corner of the county neat Waltham Cross SW. over large parts of the ancient parishes of Enfield, Edmonton, South Mimms, and Monken Hadley; it refers now to the much smaller area lying W. of Enfield Town and Forty Hill as far as Cockfosters. This is heavy clay land much less intensively built over than the surrounding districts, with a good deal of open country and some extensive views for a place only 10 m. from London.

In Domesday Book there is a note under Enfield, *Parcus est ibi*; this was the Chase, generally called *parcus extrinsecus*, the outer park. The property passed by marriage to Henry IV and thereafter was a favourite hunting-ground of the court, especially of Elizabeth and of James I. To acquire a convenient hunting-lodge, James induced Robert Cecil to give up Theobalds, just N. of the county border, in exchange for Hatfield.

The Chase, being Crown land, was seized by the Parliament on the death of Charles I, and a survey was made in 1650 with a view to profitable exploitation of the timber for the state revenues: the oaks were valued at £2,500 (excluding 2,500 trees earmarked for the navy), the other wood at £12,500, and the deer at £150.[3] It was intended to enclose and sell the Chase for the benefit of Colonel Fleetwood and his regiment; but the project aroused the Enfield inhabitants, who claimed rights of common, and there were disturbances which had to be dealt with by sending down soldiers, who became embroiled with the locals.[4] By 1658 felling and enclosure had reduced the value of the timber to £6,959 12s. At the Restoration of 1660 the Chase was

---

[1] Altick (page 134, note 3), p. 11. [2] E. Ford, *History of Enfield* (1873), p. 185, did his best to make Enfield the setting for the Raleigh story, cloak and all. [3] Madge (page 24, note 2), p. 175; part of the map made at the 1658 survey is reproduced by Madge, opp. p. 112. [4] At least four pamphlets were brought out in London on the affray, including *Bloudy Newes from Enfield; being a true . . . Relation of the bloody Fight . . . between eightscore Country-men and a Party of Foot-Souldiers* [1659].

regained by the Crown, restocked with deer, and planted with young trees.

John Evelyn recorded a visit in 1676: 'I went with my Lord Chamberlain to see a garden at Enfield town' [presumably Dr. Uvedale's]; 'thence to Mr. Secretary Coventry's lodge in the Chase. It is a very pretty place, the house commodious, the gardens handsome, and our entertainment very free, there being none but my lord and myself. That which I most wondered at was that in the compass of 25 miles, yet within 14 of London, there is not an house, barn, church, or building, besides three lodges. To this lodge are three great ponds and some few enclosures, the rest a solitary desert, yet stored with not less than 3,000 deer. These are pretty retreats for gentlemen, especially for those who are studious and lovers of privacy.'[1]

In 1700 the Chase was estimated to contain some 631,000 trees. It could hardly escape the zeal of the agricultural improvers; Arthur Young wrote in 1770: '*Enfield-chase* cannot be viewed by any lover of his country, or of husbandry, without much regret; so large a tract of waste, so near the capital, within the reach of *London,* as a market and as a dunghill, is a real nuisance to the public.'[2] He suggested that the king might profitably reclaim it out of his private revenue. In 1777, however, an act was passed for disafforesting and dividing the Chase and allotting it to the parishes and individuals claiming common rights. The were transported to Lord Bute's park at Luton Hoo. For some 20 years the results were disappointing: while the South Mimms enclosure was all under cultivation by 1800, there was hardly a beginning made on the Enfield portion.[3] The roads remained in a bad state much later; well into the 19th century faggots

had to be thrown into the ruts to make it possible for a carriage to get to East Lodge.[4] The whole district was rustic enough to force M. T. Bass, Liberal M.P. for Derby 1848-83, to abandon South Lodge because his family could get no sleep for the noise of the nightingales.[5]

The original boundaries of the Chase are still indicated by the names of Southgate and Northaw (in Hertfordshire, not far from Potters Bar: the north haw or bolt, i.e. wood). East Lodge, sometimes used by Charles I as a hunting lodge, was occupied in the late 18th century by Alexander Wedderburn, Lord Loughborough (Lord Chancellor 1793-1801); West Lodge, near Cockfosters, was where Evelyn visited Mr. Secretary Coventry; and South Lodge was the house of the elder William Pitt, Earl of Chatham, from which after spending a good deal of money on the grounds he removed to Hayes, Kent. Trent Park is named after Trent, South Tyrol, where Richard Jebb cured the Duke of Gloucester, George III's brother, of an illness; the estate was granted by the king in recognition. The Bevan family, of Barclay's Bank, lived there in the 19th century. The park and house are handsome; it was the residence of Sir Philip Sassoon until the Middlesex County Council took it over as a teachers' training college. The house, hitherto undistinguished, was reconstructed and refaced with brick from William Kent's Devonshire House in 1926.[6] In the grounds is an old earthwork called Camlet Moat; Scott, describing it in the scene of the murder of Lord Dalgarno in *The Fortunes of Nigel,* refers to the tradition that it was the site of the ancient manor-house of Enfield. Beech Hill Park, on the road to Potters Bar, was another good estate, cut into of recent years for houses

---

[1] J. Evelyn, *Diary* 2 June 1676: he was probably overstating the case a little; the keepers and foresters must have needed houses of some kind. This is the authority for Macaulay's famous passage on Enfield Chase (*History of England,* ch. iii. (ed. 1858) i., p. 323), which shows some characteristic heightening: Evelyn's 'not less than 3000 deer' become 'deer, as free as in an American forest, wandered there by thousands'. [2] Young (page 34, note 5), iv., p. 29. [3] Lysons, art. South Mimms; Middleton, p. 116. Maps of the enclosure, Madge (see page 24, note 2), opp. p. 240; Middleton, opp. p. 532. [4] Ford (page 250, note 2), p. 100. [5] Phillips (page 247, note 3), p. 30. [6] A. N. Gamble, *History of the Bevan Family* [1924]; *Country Life* 63 (1931), p. 40.

advancing E. from Hadley Wood station and N. from Cockfosters.

Cockfosters, strictly in Southgate borough, was a tiny village in a secluded part until the Underground railway was extended to it in 1933. The church is a curious little building in the revived Early English style of 1837.

On the Chase Side of Enfield itself are the more select houses and churches added to the town during the 19th century. The Bycullah estate is a prime example of upper middle-class suburban housing of late Victorian days, large detached houses irregularly grouped, in soapy yellow brick with a good deal of ironwork. The quaintly-named Bycullah Athenaeum club of 1870 has disappeared. St Mary Magdalene, Windmill Hill, is a stone building with a graceless spire by W. Butterfield (1883); St Michael, Chase Side (W. Slater and R. H. Carpenter, 1873), is unfinished; St Luke, Browning Road (James Brooks, 1898), is a characteristic essay in his 'Early English' style, in red brick with a curious little slated turret (a saddle-back NW. tower was designed but not built); St John Baptist, Clay Hill, is almost appealing in its steel-engraving ugliness (J. P. St Aubyn, 1857). This district is known as Gordon Hill, Brigadier Hill, and Clay Hill; there is a pleasant weather-boarded house (of a class above the cottage in which this construction is usually seen) at the corner of Brigadier Hill and Lancaster Road. To the north lies White Webbs, now a park and golf course; the mansion, built in 1791, is the successor to an earlier one, granted to Robert Huicke, d. c.1581, physician to Henry VIII, Edward VI, and Elizabeth. It was reputed to be a resort of papist conspirators at the time of the Guy Fawkes plot and was thoroughly searched without convincing proof being found. On the N. side of the road at Clay Hill is the Rose and Crown inn, principally of the 18th century; farther N., in Whitewebbs Lane, is the King James and the Tinker inn, incorporating some 17th-century portions, which Enfield historians associate with a ballad that more probably refers to an episode on the Scottish Border.

FELTHAM (B1) is a large village in the SW. Middlesex plain; the urban district includes HANWORTH, BEDFONT and HATTON. The river Crane forms part of the E. boundary.

Feltham (*feld*, open space) first appears in a charter of 969 (suspected of being a 13th-century forgery); it was granted to the abbey of Westminster. The manor was held by Robert, Earl of Mortain, at Domesday; it later passed to the hospital of St Giles-without-the-Bars, which relinquished it to the Crown in 1537. In 1631 it was acquired by the Cottington family and passed with Hanworth from them to Beauclerk, Duke of St Albans.

After the 1914-18 war the village was much changed by the building of a large marshalling-yard E. of the station for the goods traffic of the London and South Western Railway. Lines of suburban dwellings, with some factories, sprang up on the sites of the market-gardens and orchards, and the place is now a dormitory for London with a pleasant centre grouped about a village green.

The old parish church (St Dunstan) in Lower Feltham was a small pudding-stone building with a wooden tower and spire; it was pulled down in 1802, to be replaced by a new brick edifice, a simple rectangular building. This was enlarged in 1856, when two aisles were added in churchwarden's Norman. The interior is now strangely pleasing, especially at the W. end with its gallery and painted lettering; evidently there was not enough money to permit excessive elaboration, and the plainness of the two styles has good effect (*Plate 49*). A new church (St Catherine) was built near the railway station in 1880, with a handsome spire added in 1898. William Wynne Ryland, engraver to George III, executed in 1793 for forging East India Company bonds, is buried in the old churchyard.

The reformatory school (beside the railway and actually in Bedfont parish) is a plain building in brick (Banks and Barry, 1857). Longford school in Bedfont Lane is a good-looking piece of Middlesex County Council building (1936).

FINCHLEY (E3) is a borough (1933), shaped like a leg of mutton, stretching from the London border at the Spaniards inn, Hampstead Heath, in the S. to Hertfordshire, near High Barnet, in the N.; the SW. portion is included in the HAMPSTEAD GARDEN SUBURB. It is bounded by Hornsey and Friern Barnet on the E. and is separated from Hendon on the W. by the Dollis and Mutton brooks in a noticeable declivity. The ground is all high, for Middlesex, mostly above 200 ft. The Great North road enters from Hornsey near the foot of North Hill, Highgate, in the SE. and runs out through Whetstone (which stands partly in Friern Barnet) to High Barnet at the extreme N. The Finchley road from the west end of London was constructed in 1827 to a junction with the old road at Tally Ho! corner; it passes close to the church and old village in the W. extremity. The Barnet by-pass and North Circular roads cross the S. part. Almost the whole area, apart from

municipal open spaces, is built over with houses, except where a model dairy farm at Church End and large cemeteries on the East End Road give some relief.

Finchley, like Hornsey, was not mentioned in Domesday and similarly belonged to the bishops of London 'from time immemorial,' perhaps as part of their manor of Fulham. The name appears first in St Paul's records of 1208.

Most of the parish was uncultivated until the 18th century; the ancient forest is commemorated by Woodside in the NW. and by fragments of Coldfall Wood, on the E. towards Muswell Hill. Parts of Finchley common near the main road were used for military camps in 1660 when General Monk collected his forces before the Restoration, in 1745 when the army depicted in Hogarth's 'March of the Guards to Finchley' assembled for the Culloden campaign, and in 1780 when the Gordon riots caused alarm in the capital; 102 burials from the camp were noted in the parish register for that year. The common was notorious throughout this period as a haunt of highwaymen and a place for exhibiting their bodies on gibbets, and it was frequently coupled with Hounslow Heath when agricultural improvers denounced the wasteful folly of leaving land in common. The award for its enclosure was made in 1816. A weekly swine market, of some importance in the late 18th century, had died out by 1870.[1]

At the beginning of the 19th century the parish was an inconsiderable place of 1,500 inhabitants, mostly settled near the church and in the hamlets of East End (now East Finchley) and Whetstone. Great Northern Railway branches were opened in 1867 and

---

[1] Clutterbuck (see page 40, note 3).

1872. Tramways were laid in 1905 and 1909.

Most of Finchley's historical interest is now concentrated in the church (St Mary) in Hendon Lane, about ¼m. SW. of Finchley Central station, on the slope down to the Dollis brook. Some fragments of a 12th-century church are inserted in the W. wall of the N. aisle, but the main portion dates from a 15th-century rebuilding. In 1872 a S. aisle was added and other improvements took place; after controversy over further additions, finally resolved by the diocesan consistory court,[1] an outer S. aisle and vestries were added in 1932. The E. end was damaged in the 1939-45 war. The church, with its low W. tower, is not remarkable outside; the interior is of straightforward 15th-century type, clerestoried with square-headed windows. The W. gallery (1804) has not yet been restored away; it partly conceals two good monuments, to Alexander Kinge, 1619, and Sir Thomas and Mary Allen, by Edward Allen, 1681. There are several brasses. There is an early 13th-century font with octagonal bowl of Purbeck marble. Persons of note in their day buried in the church or churchyard were William Seward, d.1799, author of *Anecdotes of Distinguished Persons* (1798), and Major Cartwright, radical reformer of the 1770s and 1780s (d. at Enfield, 1824). John Feckenham, rector in 1554, was abbot of Westminster at the time of Elizabeth's coronation; refusing to conform to the new form of church government, he was imprisoned till his death in 1585. John Hall, rector in 1666, wrote *Jacob's Ladder, or the Devout Soul's Ascension into Heaven,* which ran through 19 editions in the century after its publication in 1672. Thomas Stackhouse, curate in 1731, was a prolific author of short histories and abridg-ments, notably a *History of the Bible* (1737).

There are one or two old houses near the church; Park House, a few yards S., is a good example of the early 19th century. Opposite the church is Christ College, founded 1857, a Gothic-revival building by A. Salvin in red and blue brick, culminating in a conspicuous round tower with conical cap.

On East End Road, about ½ m. E., is the manor house (18th-century); farther on, S. of the road, is Park Farm House with a good 18th-century barn. Beyond is East End, with a curious little village settlement of no great picturesqueness lying just W. of the main North road. The borough stretches S. from here over a more open tract rising to the Hampstead-Highgate ridge; Bishop's Avenue, lined with large and opulent houses of 1910-35, commemorates the bishops of London who owned a lodge on the site of the Highgate golf course just to the E. (see HIGHGATE). The Spaniards inn, at the S. extremity, is a 17th-century house much altered; in the tea garden there Mrs. Bardell was taking the country air when she was removed to the Fleet prison for the debt arising from her costs in the celebrated action of Bardell v. Pickwick.

North Finchley is a more closely-built area without much individual character. A few yards S. of Tally Ho! corner is Christ Church (J. Norton, 1870), an over-Decorated building; there are other churches of the succeeding decades, none good. Woodside Park, W. of the North road, is a late Victorian suburb of large spiky houses and heavy foliage; beyond the railway is a small Edwardian garden suburb. The church of Whetstone, to the N. (St John, *c.* 1830), is a characteristic white-brick

---

[1] The judgments, containing interesting observations on the principles to be applied in deciding how far ancient churches should be modified in expanding them for the requirements of increased congregations, are reported in *Trans. L. Mx. A. S.* NS 6 (1932), pp. 208, 662.

product of the early, unacademic Gothic revival.

FORTY HILL (F1). *See* ENFIELD.

FRIERN BARNET (E2). *See* BARNET, FRIERN.

FULWELL (C5). *See* TEDDINGTON.

GOLDERS GREEN (D3) is the SE. corner of Hendon bordering on Hampstead. It is here taken to cover all Hendon S. and E. of the Brent, including Temple Fortune, Child's Hill, and part of Cricklewood; the HAMPSTEAD GARDEN SUBURB, which lies partly in Finchley, is treated separately. These parts of the ancient parish were in the manors of Hodford and Clitterhouse.

The name Golders Green is presumably derived from the 14th-century family of Godere or Godyer. The green lay on both sides of the road towards Hendon, now Golders Green Road; there were few houses when Thorne described it in 1875 as 'a little outlying cluster of cottages, with an inn, the White Swan, whose garden is in great favour with London holiday-makers.' The Finchley road from Regent's Park (1827) cut across the green at its SE. end; a few large houses had been built by 1907, when the tube railway station was opened by the cross-roads. Electric trams were laid along Finchley Road in 1909-10; by 1914 the district was given over for building houses of a superior type. After the 1914-18 war, and especially after 1933, there was a considerable influx of foreign-speaking (mostly German) imigrants in fairly comfortable circumstances, and 'the British consul at Golders Green' became a subject for music-hall jokes.

The centre of Golders Green is formed by parades of shops near the tube station in the suburban style of 1910. St Alban (Giles G. Scott, 1932), SE. of the station, is a good modern church within the traditional Gothic framework. There are transepts but no aisles; the interior is lighted from a low centre tower, surmounted by a short octagonal spire. Farther SE., running over into Hampstead at the hamlet of North End, is Golder's Hill, now a public park, with a mansion in the Flemish style of 1880 on the site of an earlier one where the 18th-century poet Akenside celebrated the salubrity of the air. On Finchley Road, to the N., is the bold tower of St Edward the Confessor (A. Young, 1915), in silver-grey brick. E. of it, up Hoop Lane, are the towers and cloisters of the Golders Green crematorium (Ernest George and A. B. Yeates, 1911-31), in what is described as the Lombardic style; W. is the Unitarian church of All Souls (G. R. Farrow and J. R. Turner, 1927).

Temple Fortune, farther N., is probably named from the Knights Templars who owned land in Hendon and Finchley in the 13th century; the 'Fortune' part is obscure. Child's Hill, S. of Golders Green on the London border, is an old settlement which expanded quickly about 1850; the surname Child is found in 1321. All Saints, Cricklewood Lane, is by T. Bury (1856).

Cricklewood lies on both sides of the Edgware Road and is consequently divided between Hendon and Willesden; the name probably refers to a wood that was 'crickled,' either bent in outline or unusually impervious. There is a church, St Peter (T. H. Watson, 1902), but nothing else to look at. The place bears the impress of the

Midland Railway's goods yards and engine sheds. Clitterhouse Road, NE. of the railway, commemorates the name of the old manor, property of St Bartholomew's hospital.

GREAT STANMORE (c2). *See* STANMORE.

GREENFORD (c4)—sometimes Great Greenford, in distinction from Little Greenford or Perivale—lies between the meadows of the Brent valley above Hanwell and the S. slopes of Harrow Hill at Sudbury, and it takes in the knoll of Horsendon Hill (278 ft.) at its E. extremity, towards Wembley. The Paddington branch of the Grand Junction canal was built round the N. side of the parish past the hamlet of Greenford Green in 1801, but there were no roads better than country lanes until the Western Avenue plunged through the middle from E. to W. in the late 1920s. It has been included since 1930 in the borough of Ealing.

The name is first found in a charter of 845—*in illam famosam villam quae nominatur Grenanforda*. (Nobody has explained why it should have been *famosa* at that, or any other, time.) The manor was given by Ethelred to Westminster Abbey; it was appropriated to the diocese of Westminster in 1540 and to that of London in 1550.

Greenford is a characteristic place of the Middlesex clay belt. Norden in 1593 found it 'a very fertile place of corn'; it was later given over to pasture, and lack of water delayed development for suburban uses. At Greenford Green, on the canal to the N., W. H. Perkin of Sudbury established his chemical factory for the production of aniline dyes after his discovery of Tyrian purple, or mauve, in 1856, fuchsia, or magenta, in 1859 (which powerfully affected fashions in the 1860s), and turkey red in 1869.

No railway invaded, or came near, Greenford until 1904, when the Great Western line was opened. Greenford is now almost covered with building of no very high order. Factories are prominent on the Western Avenue.

The old church (Holy Cross) is almost the only ancient building left in the parish; 19th-century restoration did not seriously impair its characteristic family look of the NW. Middlesex group, and the 20th century has spared it by building a new church for the general requirements of its vastly increased congregation. It was probably built, or rebuilt, about 1500; it is flint-finished outside, with a timber structure at the W. end supporting a tower and small tiled spire. The S. porch is timber-framed, 16th-century, and the W. gallery with wooden panelling is 17th-century. The stained glass in the chancel, of the 16th century, said to have come from King's College, Cambridge (which purchased the rectory in 1731), shows armorial devices and an early type of windmill. The stone font with rounded bowl was given by Frances Coston in 1638; the carved and painted oak cover is probably contemporary. There are several brasses. The wall monuments are good: John Castell, rector, 1687, and wife, 1695; Michael Gardiner, rector, 1630, and wife, 1624; Bridget Coston, 1637 (signed on the cherub's wing by Hum. Moyer); and two 18th-century tablets on the E. wall. There are 5 handsome 17th-century marble floor-slabs in the chancel; outside in the churchyard are well-cut headstones. A 17th-century rector, Edward Terry, d. 1660, in 1616-17 accompanied Sir Thomas Roe in his embassy from

James I to the Great Mogul and wrote an account of the journey.

The new church, at right angles W. of the old, is somewhat in the barn style, open and airy (A. E. Richardson, 1939), with the timbers of the structure showing in an almost Scandinavian style. This and All Hallows, North Greenford (C. A. Farey, 1942), are the only 20th-century buildings that call for note; the rest is commonplace.

GREENHILL (c3). *See* HARROW.

GRIM'S DYKE (B3-C2), a deep ditch and bank, is a considerable earthwork now traceable for some 4 m. from the parish of Ruislip through Pinner to Harrow Weald. It is not known when or why it was built; it is generally attributed to the 5th and 6th centuries A.D., but a prehistoric origin cannot be ruled out.

The name, first found in the 13th century in the form of 'Grime's Ditch,' is the same as that affixed to similar works in Hertfordshire, Buckinghamshire, and Wiltshire; Grim is probably another name for Woden, or the Devil, who was often held responsible for ancient earthworks. Its topographical features only are indicated here; for a note on its historical significance, see Part 1, page 16.[1]

The limit of ditch that can be traced at its southern end is near Cuckoo Hill, Pinner Green. The line of the bank can just be discerned, first running N. and then turning E. round Pinner Green; on the E. side of the brook near Pinner Hill Road it remains well preserved for some 350 yards. The next portion is obliterated, but from Woodridings School on the road from Pinner to Hatch End it continues NE. as far as the main London and Birmingham railway. Building has destroyed traces E. of this for some distance along Royston

Park Road. From Oxhey Lane it runs parallel to Wealdwood Road across the Grim's Dyke golf course; this is the most perfect surviving section. The last portion of the dyke lies within the grounds of Grim's Dyke House, where part of it has been dammed to form an artificial lake.

In 1936, H. Braun adduced medieval field-names in Little Stanmore and the ancient name for Barnet Gate, near Elstree (Grendel's or Grim's Gate), as confirmation that the dyke extended E. beyond Harrow Weald. In his view, it was constructed for driving beasts during hunting; the parks at Enfield, Pinner, and Ruislip were later brought into the scheme as reserved 'chases' into which game could be driven along the line of the dyke.

Much more inquiry is needed before the place of Grim's Dyke in the history of Middlesex can be clearly understood. It is difficult to accept that so large a work could have been undertaken merely for the purpose of delimiting part of a tribal boundary or in connexion with hunting, at the time when it is generally believed to have been built. It remains a rather mysterious feature of the NW. Middlesex landscape.

GUNNERSBURY (c4) is a district in the NE. corner of Old Brentford taking its name from Gunnersbury Park, an estate now jointly owned by the boroughs of Acton, Brentford and Chiswick, and Ealing. It provides the only certain example of a Danish element in a Middlesex place-name— 'Gunnhild's manor'; the attribution to Gunhilda, niece of Canute, has no evidence to support it.

The estate, held under the bishop of London's manor of Ealing, was one of those enjoyed by Alice Perrers, mistress

[1] See also Bibliography, page 380.

of Edward III, in the late 14th century; in the 15th it belonged to Sir Thomas Frowyck, d. 1485; in the late 17th to Sir John Maynard, serjeant at law, prosecutor of Strafford and Laud, M.P. for various Devon boroughs between 1640 and 1690; and from 1761 to 1786 to Princess Amelia, daughter of George II. After passing through the hands of various owners, who divided the estate and pulled it about a good deal, it was bought by Nathan Meyer Rothschild and occupied by Baron Lionel de Rothschild, the first Jewish M.P. (1858) and the original of Sidonia in Disraeli's *Coningsby*.

The old manor house was presumably demolished in 1663, when a handsome porticoed building was put up by James Webb in a style influenced by his master Inigo Jones. William Kent laid out the grounds about 1740, and in Princess Amelia's time a temple, a 'bath,' and other embellishments were added in the grounds. After 1801, when the estate was divided, Webb's house was pulled down, and two different houses built—one by R. Smirke in 1834[1]—so that the park, re-united by the Rothschilds, presents the singular feature of two mansions side by side on the same terrace. A local museum is now housed in one of them.

HALLIFORD, LOWER (B6). *See* SHEPPERTON.

HALLIFORD, UPPER (B6). *See* SUNBURY.

The HAMPSTEAD GARDEN SUBURB (E3) is an estate of 317 acres, lying in Hendon and Finchley boroughs (and not in Hampstead at all) between Golders Green and East Finchley, grouped round the Hampstead Heath extension. It is one of the most attractive parts of modern Middlesex.

The suburb owes its origin to Henrietta Barnett, d. 1936, wife of Canon S. A. Barnett, warden of Toynbee Hall 1884-1906.[2] Novel social and architectural features marked the plan as a significant step in the art of laying out new suburbs. The estate was to consist mainly of cottages with gardens for people working in London; it was to be laid out as a whole on an orderly plan; social classes were to be mingled; and the natural beauties of the site were to be preserved.[3] Thus the self-contained character of earlier essays in town planning—Bournville, Port Sunlight, and Letchworth—was not to be aimed at; it was to be a dependent residential suburb, with provision for religious and cultural activities, but no public-houses and only a few shops on the fringe. Development has consequently been somewhat lopsided, and it has in the result not produced quite the kind of mixed but integrated community that the founder hoped for.

The suburb has proved more influential on architectural development than on community planning. Mrs. Barnett's plans were outlined in 1905; a company was formed in 1906 and the land bought from Eton College, owners of the Wyldes estate; and the Hampstead Garden Suburb Act of 1906 conferred powers (later made generally available by the Housing and Town Planning Act, 1909) to limit the number of houses to eight an acre and to relax certain municipal by-laws concerning road access and paving in the interests of the new, more informal type of development. Until the war of 1914 the original plan was followed fairly closely. This was prepared by Raymond Unwin and Barry Parker, who favoured construction in the traditional styles,

[1] R. Blomfield, *A Short History of Renaissance Architecture in England 1500-1800* (1900), p. 89.
[2] [H. Barnett], *Canon Barnett (1844-1913): His Life and Work* (1918), ii., p. 312. [3] H. Barnett, *Contemporary Review*, February 1905, and *Canon Barnett* (preceding note), vol. ii.; for the architectural and town-planning principles, R. Unwin, *Town Planning in Practice* (1909; ed. 2, 1911).

with brick walls (sometimes roughcast) and high tiled roofs, sash windows in the larger houses, and casements and dormer windows for the cottages. The roof-line was almost always carried in a long sweep without picturesque variations in the form of gables or humps. Edwin Lutyens designed the central feature—the 'Institute,' St Jude's church (named from Canon Barnett's church in Whitechapel), and the Free church, in modified Renaissance styles; these were disposed about a square at the highest point of the suburb, framed with substantial houses in the early 18th-century manner, also by Lutyens (*Plate 66*). W. and N. of these, smaller houses were built, many in 'closes' or blocks of two-storey dwellings; architects contributing at this period included M. H. Baillie Scott (Waterlow Court flats, 1909), W. Curtis Green, W. H. Ward (Woodside, Erskine Hill), E. Guy Dawber (Temple Fortune Lane), H. A. Welch, G. Lucas, T. M. Wilson, M. Bunney, and G. Cowles-Voysey.

After the 1914-18 war more of the larger houses were built, until the construction of the Barnet by-pass road—here called Lyttleton Way—improving communication across the N. part of estate gave a fresh opportunity for inclusion of flats and shops. Designs in this period were less uniform but still harmonious; fashion crept in with some modernist houses near East Finchley in the middle thirties. J. B. F. Cowper (Hampstead Way flats), C. G. Butler (shops and flats at Northway), Welch, Cachemaille-Day and Lander (Kingsley Close and Carlyle Close),and C. G. Herbert (24-30 Vivian Way) were some of the architects designing for the suburb between the wars. The earliest work is the best; after about 1925 it appears to be coarser, though there are good exceptions.

The whole estate looks well designed; most of the roads follow the contours of the ground; buildings turn corners as though they were meant to, instead of presenting one blank wall to the side road; and they seem to grow naturally from the gardens they stand in. Lutyens' terraces of houses and flats in North Square, South Square, and Erskine Hill are very good, in silver-grey brick with red-brick dressings; St Jude's church, a conspicuous object, is handsome in itself with its large steep tiled roof, but the tower and spire are ugly and the internal decoration detracts from the firm lines of the barrel-vault; the Institute, Lutyens' first public building, is fussy in its details; and the Free church, with a dumpy dome, though truly Protestant in character, is something too bald. The shops at Temple Fortune and the club house in Willifield Way betray some study of German models with their square, capped towers; apart from these, the inspiration is wholly English, well adapted to Middlesex, the most homely of all English counties. The estate has been well described as 'the most satisfactory and characteristic contribution of the Edwardian age to town planning and social architecture.'[1] It is a pleasure to walk through with the eyes open (which distinguishes it from most suburbs); there is nothing to shock, either with ugliness or audacity. It pleases, and it does not astonish.

HAMPTON (c6) lies on the Thames where it makes a curve SE. and then N. at the S. extremity of Middlesex. The parish anciently extended from HAMPTON WICK, a hamlet at the W. end of Kingston bridge, as far as Kempton Park, on the borders of Sunbury, and included all Hampton Court Park and most of Bushy Park; Hampton Wick

[1] C. Hussey, *Country Life*, 17 October 1936.

became a separate parish in 1831. Both parishes have been included in the borough of Twickenham since 1937.

Besides the old village of Hampton, lying on the river where the road from Brentford through Twickenham meets the Kingston-Staines road, there are the 19th-century residential districts of Hampton Hill (a hill not distinguishable by the eye) to the N. and Marling Park in the direction of Hanworth to the NW. The Queen's or Cardinal's river flows between these districts on its course from Longford to supply the ornamental waters of Hampton Court. More useful waters are stored in the Metropolitan Water Board's reservoirs by the river W. of Hampton village; this was the nearest place to London where the companies could find land to comply with the Metropolis Water Act of 1852, forbidding them to take water from the river below Teddington lock after 1856. The Thames Valley Railway (the Shepperton branch of the L.S.W.R.) was opened in 1864; an unattractive settlement grew up round Hampton station. Electric trams began to run from Twickenham in 1903.

Hampton (farm in the bend of the river) first appears in Domesday Book, when it was held by Walter de St Valéry. In the early 13th century it passed into the hands of the order of St John of Jerusalem; Cardinal Wolsey took a 99-year lease from the order in 1514 and surrendered it to Henry VIII in 1526; from that date its manorial history is merged with that of the royal palace.

The parish church (St Mary) stands at the centre of the old village and is well seen from the river: a not unpleasing edifice in the Gothic of 1830. The church that preceded it was according to Lysons 'a brick structure with a plain square tower'; the tower had been built in or about 1679. Thorne in 1875 thought this one 'a neat, commonplace, white brick Perpendicular building,' which will serve as a description. There is a W. tower, with sawn-off pinnacles. The interior retains its original galleries and roof, but an unsuitable screen in the fashion of modern church furniture has been inserted in front of the embryonic chancel. There are monuments to eminent persons, including a number of residents at Hampton Court Palace; the Paget family is well represented. Most of the old monuments are skied, and the handsome tomb of Mrs. Sibell Penn, nurse to Edward VI, d. 1562, is awkwardly placed in the entrance lobby. There are two 17th-century brasses. Modern brass inscriptions are affixed to some columns of the nave, and there is a painted royal arms of 1831. Among the tablets is one to Huntingdon Shaw, the smith employed at Hampton Court, called in his epitaph 'an artist in his way' (a description which, it has been suggested, was added to the epitaph about 1830),[1] and there are monuments to Mrs. Susanna Thomas, probably designed by Thomas Archer, 1731;[2] Thomas Ripley, architect of the Admiralty, 1758; Thomas Rosoman, proprietor of Sadler's Wells theatre, 1782; and John Beard, singer, 1782. Unhappily the inscription to Edward Progers of the royal household, who died aged 96 in 1714 'of the anguish of cutting teeth,' has disappeared. The grammar school, established in 1612 on the foundation of an earlier school of 1557, had a new room built for it in the churchyard in 1833; this is now the parish hall. The school moved to Upper Sunbury Road in 1880.

Hampton was a residence for a good many people of note from the century onwards. The most celebrated was

<hr/>

[1] R. G. Rice, 'Notes on Huntington Shaw', *Archaeological Journal* 52 (2nd series, vol. 2, 1895), p. 158. [2] H. M. Colvin, 'The Bastards of Blandford', *Archaeological Journal* 104 (1948), p. 179. The monument has also been attributed to Sir Henry Cheere (Lysons, art. Hampton; *D.N.B.*, art. Cheere); it is signed 'W. Powell Fecit'.

David Garrick; he lived in Hampton House (E. of the church, facing the river, now Garrick Villa) from 1754 until his death in 1779. He enlarged the house and gave it an entirely new front, designed by Robert Adam. The rebuilding took place in stages, in 1755, 1772, and 1779; the portico (of wood) is of Adam's later period. Rooms on the W. side were added in 1865.[1] The grounds, separated from the house by the main road, extended to the river, with a wide lawn on which a 'Grecian temple' was built to receive Roubiliac's statue of Shakespeare, for which Garrick sat as model. There was good company at Hampton House: Horace Walpole met there 'the Duke of Grafton, Lord and Lady Rochford, Lady Holderness, the crooked Mostyn, and Dabreu the Spanish Minister; two regents, of which one is lord chamberlain, the other groom of the stole; and the wife of a secretary of state. This is being *sur un assez bon ton* for a player.'[2] When Queen Charlotte called to visit Mrs. Garrick, however, without previous warning, she found her peeling onions for pickling, and calling for a knife peeled onions too.[3] Johnson visited the house and, when Garrick asked him how he liked it, observed: 'Ah, David, it is the leaving of such places that makes a death-bed terrible.' After Garrick's death, his widow lived in the house until 1822, when the contents were sold by auction and dispersed; the statue of Shakespeare went to the entrance hall of the British Museum. Today the public may picnic on the lawn in front of the temple (*Plate 7*).

A little way beyond, on the riverside, is St Albans, a 17th-century house alleged to have been built for Nell Gwyn, much altered in the 18th century and later. On the E. side of Church Street are good large houses, Orme House in particular, of the early 18th century, and there are old cottages in Thames Street. The whole place has managed to escape much improvement. Jessamine House, at the W. end, has been identified with the 'Surbiton Cottage' of Trollope's *Three Clerks*.[4]

To the N. are residential growths of the 19th and early 20th centuries; the church of St James, Park Road (1863-79; spire, 1890), is not bad. The Lady Eleanor Holles school, removed from Cripplegate, is at Hampton Hill. NW. towards Hanworth, waterworks and greenhouses lie on the level plain, and there is a striking display of public-utility architecture of the 1850s put up by the water companies beside the roads to Sunbury.

HAMPTON COURT (c6), the name given collectively to the palace lying 1 m. E. of Hampton village, its subsidiary buildings, and the park in which they stand, is an historic site without equal in Middlesex and deservedly ranking among the most celebrated places in England. The buildings are themselves beautiful in design and in texture, and the pleasing colours of their brick and stone are well set off by the gardens surrounding them. They exhibit the perfection of English building in the early 16th and late 17th centuries, and their details and decoration are as good as anything that has survived from those periods. Historic events and royal personages were associated with Hampton Court for more than 200 years, and it has been admirably preserved in recent times as one of the principal objects of pleasure excursions in the Home Counties.

The Development of the Buildings

The manor of Hampton passed from the family of de Saint Valéry to Henry

[1] *Country Life* 40 (1916), p. 756; *Builder* 98 (1910), p. 686. [2] H. Walpole to R. Bentley, 15 August 1755. [3] Smith (page 65, note 2), p. 80. [4] W. Jerrold, *Highways and Byways in Middlesex* (1909), p. 144; Jerrold lived in the house.

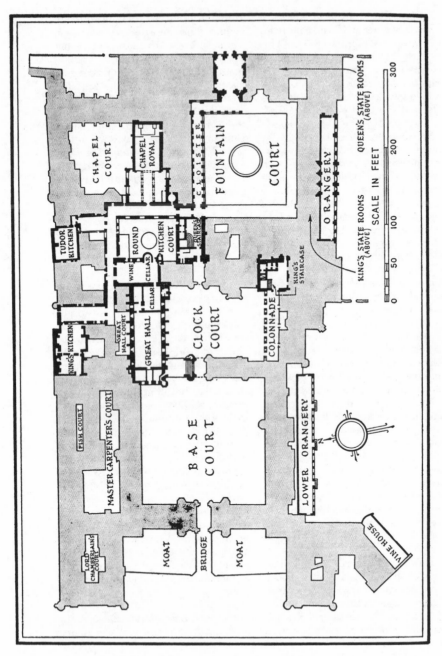

HAMPTON COURT PALACE: GROUND FLOOR PLAN

of St Albans early in the 13th century and was transferred by him to the order of St John of Jerusalem about 1217. (There appears to have been a preceptory of sisters of the order at Hampton before the end of the 12th century.) The manor was leased in 1514 to Thomas Wolsey, archbishop of York, for 99 years at £50 a year. Wolsey evidently chose it because it was far enough from London to be a peaceful place of residence, while the Thames made it possible to communicate with the capital comparatively quickly, and he began to build a house equal in magnificence to the position of cardinal and lord chancellor to which he had risen from humble beginnings by the force of his own abilities. It was in its way the product of a *nouveau riche*. The house is the earliest surviving example in England of purely domestic architecture on such a large scale, with only unimportant traces of military influence in the design; none the less the original building was surrounded by a moat, said to be the last one dug in England. This moat, and the small size and irregular disposition of the windows, mark Wolsey's Hampton Court as the last great medieval house rather than the first modern one.

The original design appears to have embraced only the quadrangle now represented by Clock Court, with the chapel and cloister E. of the court and the kitchen to the NE.[1] The house was built of red brick, mostly burned locally, with dressings of stone; the warm colour of this brick, varying from rose to crimson, is one of the most attractive features of the whole building, contrasting favourably with the less mellow colour of the 17th-century work and of the modern restorations. The name of the architect is not certainly known, though 'Mr. Henry

Williams, priest, surveyor of works' is mentioned in the building accounts. These have survived, not quite complete enough to enable the total cost to be stated. Henry Redman, king's mason from 1519, has been credited with the design of Wolsey's building, and John Molton and James Needham with the Great Hall and Henry VIII's additions.[2]

As Wolsey progressed in favour and wealth, his notions became enlarged, and the present Base Court, the Great West Gatehouse, and the subsidiary buildings round the Master Carpenter's Court were put in hand. They were well on the way to completion by 1523. One of the innovations in the cardinal's house was the inclusion of galleries running the whole length of each wing, in which he used to pace up and down—a new feature, included in several later 16th-century houses. In Wolsey's day, it has been conjectured, the palace was very much the same size as the present one, which covers eight acres and contains a thousand rooms.[3] The erection and lavish furnishing of this magnificent building made him as many enemies as any act of his whole career, and the most important of those who envied him was the king. Henry entered into effective possession when Wolsey fell in 1529, and he acquired the freehold from the order of St John in 1531.[4] Between 1529 and 1540 he had extensive alterations and additions made: the Great Hall and Chapel were rebuilt; the W. side of Clock Court was remodelled and the E. side altered; the Watching Chamber block was rebuilt and enlarged; a new quadrangle containing the royal lodgings was added to the E. of the original buildings (where Fountain Court now stands); and the Great Kitchens were enlarged. A stone approach bridge over the moat was also

[1] Royal Commission on Historical Monuments, *Middlesex* (1937), p. 30. [2] Harvey (page 227, note 3), pp. 29, 41. [3] E. Law, *Short History of Hampton Court* (1906), p. 22. [4] There is no direct evidence in support of the tradition that Wolsey made a present of it to Henry in 1525.

added. Many details of the expenditure incurred on these works are known from the surviving accounts: in 1530-2 the bricks cost 4s. 6d. a thousand; the bricklayers were paid 6d. a day and the freemasons 3s. a week;[1] tallow candles were bought so that work on the Great Hall could go on by night as well as day; overtime rates were paid; and the bills during 1531-3 came to £400 a week. Bricks came from Taplow in Buckinghamshire as well as from local kilns; stone was brought from Reigate in Surrey, the Cotswolds, and Caen in Normandy; and timber, mostly oak, came from Surrey, near Dorking and Banstead, arid from St John's Wood.

After Henry's remodelling the main structure was little altered for 150 years; but almost immediately after the accession of William and Mary in 1688 work was begun on rebuilding to Christopher Wren's designs. William had already created, in Macaulay's words, 'on a sandy heath in Guelders a paradise which attracted multitudes of the curious from Holland and Westphalia ... The king, in his splendid banishment, pined for this favourite seat, and found some consolation in creating another Loo on the banks of the Thames.'[2] It is believed that a project for an entirely new palace at the W. end of the village of Hampton was considered first, but was abandoned because of the long time required to complete it.[3]

Meanwhile, in April 1689, the old palace was adapted, and plain sashes were put in place of the old mullioned windows. Materials were collected during June, and new work began in July.[4] It was intended to reconstruct the whole palace except the Great Hall, and work began with the demolition of the State Rooms and private apartments of the sovereign to make way for the buildings that now surround Fountain Court. The new portion of the palace, of brick with Portland stone dressings, was carried out in Wren's most mature style, uniting grandeur with domestic repose. A fine, thin mulberry-coloured brick was used; enough Portland stone could not be secured because the French war was interfering with navigation in the Channel, and the S. front had to be dressed with Cotswold stone.[5] This was all replaced with Portland 200 years later. Wren was not unhampered in his activities. William Talman, designer of Chatsworth, comptroller of works, was certainly independent of him and perhaps in some respects his superior; he certainly thwarted Wren at some points. Grinling Gibbons and C. G. Cibber were employed for the carving.

After Mary's death in 1694, plans for complete rebuilding[6] were abandoned, but some work continued, and, in addition to the block of Fountain Court, the colonnade on the south side of Clock Court and minor alterations elsewhere were carried out before William died in 1702. A total of £132,000 was spent on the buildings in the years 1689-96. Some further building, mostly supervised by Vanbrugh, was done under Anne, and the decoration of most of the State Apartments was completed in her reign. The E. range of Clock Court was rebuilt, by William Kent, in 1732 under George II; but on his death in 1760 the palace was given up as a royal residence, and it became the practice to allot separate suites of rooms within the building for the use of residents nominated by the Crown; various minor alterations were made in consequence. In 1771-3 the Great West Gatehouse was rebuilt and reduced in height by two storeys. Much restoration took place in the 19th century. In 1909 the moat on the W.

[1] E. Law, *History of Hampton Court Palace* (ed 2, 1903), i., pp. 344-5. [2] Lord Macaulay, *History of England* (World's Classics ed.), iii., p. 47. [3] Law (page 263, note 3), p. 292. [4] Wren Society publications, vol. iv. (1927); J. Evelyn, *Diary* 16 July 1689. [5] *Builder* 90 (1906), p. 264. [6] Plan for the intended N. court: J. Belcher and M. E. Macartney, *Later Renaissance Architecture in England* (1901), p. 35; E. Law, *Chesnut Avenue in Bushey Park, Hampton Court* (1919), p. 28.

front was cleared, and the handsome stone bridge, buried for many years, was uncovered.

Historical Associations

The first personage of historical note associated with Hampton Court was Thomas Wolsey, who was constantly there from 1514, when he took the lease, until July 1529, when he saw the place for the last time. Henry VIII, who first visited it in 1514 in company with Katharine of Aragon, was often there, and many episodes of his matrimonial career are associated with the palace. In Edward VI's reign, the Duke of Somerset, Lord Protector, attempted in 1549 to put the palace in a state of defence against his enemies. Edward himself recorded that 500 suits of armour were brought out from the armoury for the servants in attendance. Proclamation was made in the villages round about, and some of the populace gathered on the green in front of the palace, impelled perhaps more by curiosity than sympathy; Edward appeared and addressed them: 'I pray you, be good to us and our uncle.'[1] Nevertheless, Somerset did not defend his position by force of arms; he fell and was executed without any military action being taken. After him both Mary and Elizabeth lived in the palace from time to time.

James I was often at Hampton Court, particularly for the hunting, which suited his not very adventurous taste. A more, serious matter was the Hampton Court Conference of 1604 between the established Church of England and the Presbyterians, with the king in the chair. An important result of this meeting was the decision to undertake a new translation of the Bible, which emerged as the Authorised Version of 1611; but no solution of the differences between the parties was achieved. Charles I retired from London to the palace in 1625, when a proclamation was published prohibiting all communication between the palace and London, Southwark, and Lambeth on account of the plague.

Charles continued to visit Hampton Court from time to time, and the Grand Remonstrance voted by the House of Commons was presented to him there in 1641. In 1645, after Naseby, Parliament took possession of the palace. Charles was again installed at Hampton Court in August 1647 in dignified captivity, which lasted until he escaped after withdrawing his parole in November. It is supposed that he passed through a room called 'Paradise' (later demolished) by a private passage to the riverside, where he was met with horses. He then travelled to the Isle of Wight, where he surrendered himself and was lodged as a prisoner of state in Carisbrooke castle.

In accordance with Parliament's policy of selling the property of 'the late Charles Stuart,' a full inventory of the contents of the palace was made late in 1649, and the sale, which began that winter, lasted on and off for nearly three years. Already, however, many of the tapestries were reserved for the use of the Protector; after various changes of mind it was decided that Hampton Court should be retained as his residence, and in 1657 Cromwell's name is found in the court rolls as lord of the manor.

A bill was presented to Parliament in 1660 to settle the palace and parks on George Monk, Duke of Albemarle, but he declined it. Charles II lived there a good deal in the earlier part of his reign and had alterations made in the gardens. William III, who could not tolerate the air of London, spent most

---

[1] *Literary Remains of King Edward the Sixth*, ed. J. G. Nichols (Roxburghe Club, 1857), i., p. cxxx; ii., p. 234.

of his time in England between Hampton Court and Kensington; his queen, Mary, superintended the construction and furnishing of the new buildings, the gardens, and (anticipating Marie Antoinette) a dairy. After her death in 1694 the works were stopped completely for several years, until the destruction of Whitehall palace by fire made William turn his attention to Hampton once again, and the completion of the King's Rooms was pressed on. In one of the parks William fell a victim to 'the little gentleman in black velvet' whose molehill caused his horse Sorrel to stumble and throw him, and so led to his death.

Anne preferred to live at Windsor and Kensington, but her visits to Hampton are chronicled for ever in the well-known lines in *The Rape of the Lock*:

> Close by those meads for ever crowned
>   with flowers,
> Where Thames with pride surveys his
>   rising towers,
> There stands a structure of majestic frame
> Which from the neighbouring Hampton
>   takes its name.
> Here Britain's statesmen oft the fall
>   foredoom
> Of foreign tyrants, and of nymphs at
>   home;
> Here thou, great Anna ! whom three
>   realms obey,
> Dost sometimes counsel take, and
>   sometimes tea.

George I preferred Hampton Court to London because he did not see so many Englishmen there, and George II used it a little. George III and his successors never lived in the palace, and during his reign the greater part was converted into suites of rooms occupied by the grace and favour of the sovereign; Dr. Johnson's application for lodgings in 1776 was rejected.[1] The remainder of the building was thrown open to the general public on Queen Victoria's accession in 1837.

Description of the Palace

The approach from London to Hampton Court was intended to be by water, and the principal front was therefore on the S. side, facing the river. The visitor today, however, enters by road from the W. through the Trophy Gates built in George II's reign, with his heraldic devices. On the left are Cavalry Barracks, built in the second half of the 17th century, now converted into flats (*Plate 17*). The way into the palace lies over the bridge across the moat built under Henry VIII and showing mason's marks on almost every stone. The carved beasts at the side are modern work of about 1910, good copies of the originals. The wings at the ends of the main W. front were added by Henry; they project into the moat, which was not dug round them, and the bricks at the junction are not bonded together. The Great Gatehouse in the centre of the W. front formed the most impressive feature of Wolsey's work, but its proportions were sadly affected when it was reduced by two storeys in 1771; Lupton's Tower at Eton perhaps gives a fair idea of the original. On the Gatehouse are terracotta plaques with busts of the emperors Tiberius and Nero, probably brought from Windsor in 1845. They were supplied to the king for Whitehall palace by Giovanni da Maiano at the same time as a set of 8 (farther inside) for which Wolsey paid £2 6s. apiece in 1521. (There are some similar but less elaborate medallions at Hanworth, 3m. away.) Beyond the gatehouse is the Base or West Court, built almost completely by Wolsey, two storeys high with battlemented parapets. The brickwork

---

[1] *Letters of Samuel Johnson*, ed. G. Birkbeck Hill (1892), i., p. 389.

here, red with irregular patterning in black, is especially noteworthy, and the various shapes and grouping of the windows and chimneys are striking. The whole court, in spite of its great width, which is perhaps disproportionate to the modest height of the flanking buildings, is a charming example of early 16th-century building.

On the E. side of the Base Court, leading to Clock Court, is Anne Boleyn's Gateway; the vaulted stone roof, of 1882, is an exact copy of the original, with the initials of Henry and Anne entwined in lovers' knots. On the E. face of the gatehouse is a handsome terracotta panel with the arms, hat, and staff of Cardinal Wolsey, supported by two cherubs and flanked by Corinthian columns, with his motto *Dominus michi adjutor* below. Cuts in the stone show where at one period Henry VIII had these arms removed and his own substituted. Above is the famous astronomical clock built in 1540, having three moving copper dials, recording the phases of the moon, the days of the month, and the signs of the zodiac; the sun is made, in accordance with the science of the time, to revolve round the earth. This clock, the work of a Frenchman, Nicolas Oursian, was taken down and thrown away during the 19th century, but was recovered and set to work again. One of the bells (for the hour) dates from 1471.

Clock Court, E. of this gateway, exhibits work of the four periods most characteristic of the building as a whole. The W. side is part of Wolsey's building and still carries his arms; the N. is filled by the Great Hall, built for Henry VIII; the colonnade on the S. dates from William III's reign; and the E. side was restored under George II in 1732, when William Kent remodelled the gateway and most of the windows, though the walls are still of the early Tudor brickwork. The fine Ionic colonnade was built by Wren between 1689 and 1700 to form a suitable approach to his Great Staircase by masking the irregular mass of buildings on the S. side of the court; it is a model of proportion.

The last of the courts, farther E., is Fountain Court, which dates entirely from the late 17th and early 18th centuries. It has a cloister running all round, with the tall windows of the State Apartments above it. The urns surmounting the whole are worth notice: no two are exactly the same, and the carving is fine on all of them. Wren's mastery of design is evident in the skilful fashion by which the difference in the centre lines of this court and the gardens beyond is disguised. He was not his own master altogether, for he protested against the instructions given him by which he was forced to provide an unsuitable shallow roof to the cloister so as to give greater height to the rooms above.

This beautiful court, with its contrast of red brick and white Portland stone, prepares the visitor for the striking and lovely view of the exterior of the block that is seen from the park: the façade presenting an appearance of stateliness and grandeur without losing the character of domestic repose that runs through all the buildings of Hampton Court (*Plate 24*). On the S. front of the palace is the Orangery, a gallery on the ground floor of William's main block; farther E., against the S. side of Base Court, is the Lower Orangery, a single-storey building of Anne's time, where the Mantegna cartoons of the Triumph of Caesar are now housed. On the opposite side of the garden is Wren's Banqueting House. At the N. end of the main E. front is a 16th-

century building containing Henry
VIII's tennis court. To the W. is a 16th-
century tower, built for spectators at
tournaments in the tiltyard.

The interior is reached by the King's
Great Staircase, leading from the SE.
corner of Clock Court. The State
Rooms are on the first floor, consisting
of two distinct suites, each having its
own guard room, presence chamber,
audience chamber, drawing-room, state
bedroom, and closet or dressing-room;
they are known as the King's Side,
facing S. over the Privy Garden, and
the Queen's Side, facing the Great
Fountain Garden on the E. The view
from the windows of the Queen's
Drawing Room is the most splendid at
Hampton Court; three radiating
avenues and a grand semicircle of trees
and water are presented to the eye.
Parallel with these suites, facing
Fountain Court, are communicating
galleries and private apartments. All of
them contain paintings, of various
merit; the state portraits and battle
pieces are on the whole the best.
Throughout the state apartments the
influence of Daniel Marot, a Huguenot
who had already worked for William
in the building of Het Loo, can be
traced in the detailed designs, especially
in the shelved mantelpieces for display
of china.

The Chapel Royal, entered from the
cloister on Round Kitchen Court,
originally built by Wolsey, was lavishly
embellished by Henry VIII in 1535-6,
when the magnificent fan-vaulted
wooden ceiling was constructed. This
is most striking, with carved and gilded
pendents and a blue vault painted with
stars. The chapel was much knocked
about and 'purified' in 1645, and, apart
from the roof, the existing fittings were
designed by Wren for Queen Anne;
the oak reredos with Corinthian

columns, carved by Gibbons, appears
sober in comparison with the ceiling.

The Great Hall, built by Henry VIII
to replace the more modest hall of
Wolsey's house, was begun in 1531 and
finished in 1536. It is a magnificent
piece of craftsmanship, perhaps the last
great work in England carried out
under the medieval gild system; the
same men designed and carved the
elaborate pendents of the roof. Fancy
and skill far outran structural needs,
but the effect of splendour and technical
mastery is superb. The external shape
of the roof—very steep pitch above the
walls, with the upper part truncated,
mansard-like—is uncommon.[1] The dais
at the E. end, lighted by a bay window
with an excellent vault above the bay,
was occupied by the high table for the
king and his invited guests; the rest of
the company sat in the body of the hall.
At the far end, behind screens which
support the Minstrels' Gallery, is a wide
stone stairway leading up from Anne
Boleyn's Gateway, which was the
principal entrance to the hall. Almost
exactly similar arrangements can be
seen in the hall of Christ Church,
Oxford, which was being built at the
same time. Below the hall are the king's
beer cellar and the king's new wine
cellar, of a size adequate for the
population of the palace in Tudor times
(probably about 500). At the ground
level are the serving-rooms and
passages necessary to accommodate the
troops of servants employed between
the kitchen and the hall. The Great
Kitchen itself lies at the N. end of the
passage.

A doorway beside the kitchen opens
into Tennis Court Lane, from which
the N. side of the palace is admirably
seen. The great chimney stacks of the
kitchen, with moulded brick shafts, are
picturesque and striking. Hardly one

---

[1] Sir Frank Baines, *Builder* 125 (1923), p. 760; 133 (1927), p. 968.

of these chimneys is original, but they are faithful copies of the 16th-century designs. The N. side, containing the domestic offices, has been much rebuilt and is not of such high interest as the state rooms; none the less, the small courts—the Lord Chamberlain's Court, the Master Carpenter's Court, and the others—contain many features that please.

The Pictures

The pictures are a selection from the different royal collections, mostly portraits. They were collected by men of widely different tastes, opportunities, and knowledge; some of the finest were bought by Charles I, who, in Sir John Clapham's phrase, 'like so many of our least fortunate kings—Henry III, Richard II, Henry VI—was a patron of art.' He attempted to form a collection which could worthily be called royal and in 1628 acquired the gallery of the dukes of Mantua, including Mantegna's nine great cartoons 'The Triumph of Caesar,' painted between 1486 and 1494; now hung in the Lower Orangery, they are Hampton Court's outstanding artistic possession. Cromwell himself prevented them from being sold in 1649, but they had so far decayed by William III's time that Laguerre was called in to restore them. His work was rather coarsely done, but recent cleaning and restoration have revealed that, while much of every canvas was irreparably disfigured by him, more of Mantegna's own work had survived than was hitherto suspected. Nos. IV, V, and VI, the finest of the set, contain much by Mantegna's own hand.

The Hampton Court sale under the Commonwealth disposed of 382 pictures for nearly £5,000, but some were returned afterwards. The most celebrated pictures of the Restoration period are Lely's 'Beauties'; Kneller's portraits of Queen Mary's ladies were painted in emulation of them. The paintings by Verrio, Laguerre, and Thornhill on the staircases and ceilings may best be regarded as architectural embellishments.

The Gardens

The accounts show that money was spent on gardens when Wolsey's house was being built, and the little enclosure on the S. side of the palace, known as the Pond Garden, probably represents the style of that age. The Tudor garden is a recent reconstruction from a late 17th-century picture. Great alterations took place under Charles II. Evelyn in 1662 described the park E. of the palace as 'formerly a naked piece of ground, now planted with sweet rows of lime trees, and the canal for water now near perfected.' This part of the garden was certainly influenced by the practice of the celebrated French gardener Le Nôtre, though he himself probably never visited England.[1] The Long Water, which now lies entirely in the park outside the gardens proper, was constructed at this time right up to the E. end of the palace; it was fed from the Longford river. Daniel Marot, however, under William and Mary planned the Great Fountain Garden in a semi-circular piece of ground enclosed by lime trees; the existing avenues, fanning out in the *patte d'oie* fashion, were cut back and the Long Water was filled in where it conflicted with this plan, which is generally the arrangement today. The Labyrinth, or Maze, originally of hornbeam hedges, later patched with holly and privet, was planted at the same period.

The magnificent Broad Walk through the Great Fountain Garden runs down

---

[1] E. Cecil, *History of Gardening in England* (1910).

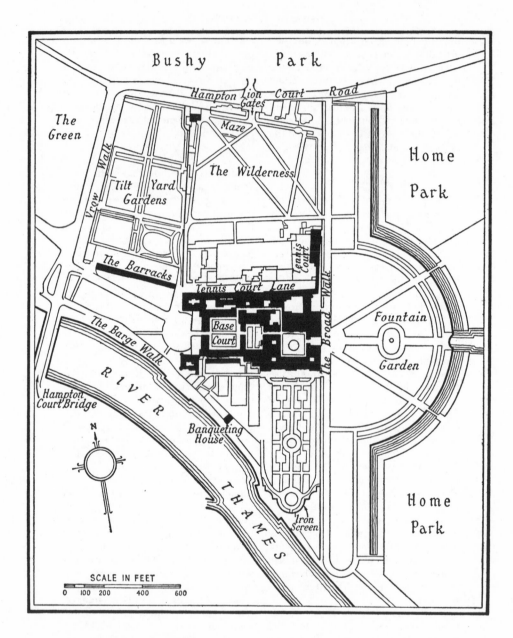

HAMPTON COURT: PARKS AND GARDENS

to the river. The Privy Garden, of a formal pattern, is terminated at the S. end by a beautiful wrought-iron screen, designed by Jean Tijou and executed by Huntingdon Shaw. There has been controversy about the respective parts played by the two men, but it seems to be established that Tijou was the designer and Shaw the artificer; at all events, the accounts show that money was paid only to Tijou (who sometimes appears as 'John Tissue'). In Anne's reign he was still praying for payment of £1,889 1s. 6¼d., and he died in poverty. Mr. J. Starkie Gardner's judgment may be quoted: 'No such sumptuous garden screen has since been attempted, and had Tijou's original embossed work been preserved it would have been among the finest extant works in wrought iron. The novelty and charm of Tijou's work were due to his masterly ability in designing and embossing masks, garlands, diapers, acanthus, etc., of sheet iron, and using them in discriminating profusion, combined, in the French manner, with smith's work (*Plates 25 and 26*). In these respects no work in our country approaches Tijou's before or since.'[1]

Queen Anne's gardeners reacted somewhat from the elaboration of the preceding age towards the 'plain but noble manner' that was coming into fashion. The Lion Gates, designed by Wren as part of a stately N. entrance to the palace, were begun under Anne and completed for George I; the initial 'A' appears on the stone work and 'G' in the iron. William Kent, the accomplished architect and gardener of George II's reign, left some traces of his work at Hampton Court, and so did Lancelot ('Capability') Brown, appointed royal gardener in 1750. He caused the Great Vine, one of the best-known features of the gardens, to be planted in 1769.

The Parks and Outlying Houses

Hampton Court was created an 'honour,' or group of manors, by act of Parliament in 1539. The lands thus annexed to the manor extended over a large tract of Middlesex and Surrey, and a new forest, to be called Hampton Court Chase and surrounded by a wooden fence, was delimited. This was naturally highly unpopular with the inhabitants of the region, and there were so many complaints that after Henry VIII's death the deer were removed to Windsor, the fence was taken away, and the land was restored to the old tenants. In 1639 Charles I revived the intention of creating a forest by enclosing about ten square miles of country as a hunting-ground, but the protests of the people, whose common rights were threatened, and the advice of Laud dissuaded him. Nevertheless, the inhabitants were disgruntled by the construction of the Longford river to supply the gardens, and in 1648 parts of the works were destroyed.[2] The park attached to Hampton Court by Wolsey consisted of about 2,000 acres within a red-brick buttressed wall, of which part still survives along the Kingston road. Henry VIII had a large rabbit or hare warren in the park, and he also reared pheasants and partridges there. The domain was divided, as it still is, into two by the Kingston road, the N. portion being called Bushy Park and the S. the Home Park (*Plate 73*).

The stud house in the Home Park was the official residence of the Master of the Horse. The royal stud occupied the paddocks and stables on both sides of the Kingston road until it was sold in 1837. Bushy Park was laid out in its present form, with a central road

---

[1] J. S. Gardner, *Ironwork, part III* (Victoria and Albert Museum guide, 1922), p. 81; Rice (page 260, note 1); Law (see page 263, note 3), pp. 317, 355. [2] B. Garside, *Incidents in the History of Hampton on Thames . . .* (1937), pp. 11, 21.

running N. and S. through the park, by Henry Wise under William III; the conception of the design was Wren's own.[1] Near the Hampton Court gate the road forms a circle round the 'Diana Fountain'; the statue is possibly a representation of Venus or Arethusa. The grand avenue of horse-chestnuts, flanked by four rows of limes, was intended to lead to a new entrance, never completed, on the N. side of the palace. The avenue, just over 1 m. long, remains one of the finest vistas in the surroundings of Hampton, though impaired at the Teddington end by squalid army buildings under the trees, put up during the 1939-45 war. The house now known as Bushy House, on the W. side of the avenue near Teddington Gate, originally Upper Lodge, was built by Lord Halifax, ranger of the park under George II. William IV lived at Bushy House until his accession to the throne. It is now the director's house of the National Physical Laboratory (see TEDDINGTON).

The Green and the Bridge

Some buildings of charm and character facing the Green are apt to be overshadowed by the altogether exceptional quality of the palace. Wilderness House, facing N. near the entrance to Bushy Park, is a pleasant building of about 1700; there is a row on the N. side of the Green—Craven House, late 18th-century, is notable; and on the S. side are some handsome houses of about 1700. Faraday House was occupied by Michael Faraday 1858-67, and Old Court House by Christopher Wren 1706-23. The Mitre is a good-looking hotel by the bridge. There has been a bridge since 1753. The first was of 7 wooden arches; the second, also of wood, had 11 arches, 1778; the third was a five-span iron

girder bridge by E. T. Murray, 1866; and the present one, by Sir Edwin Lutyens, was opened in 1933 (*Plate 67*). Beyond the bridge, in Molesey, is Hampton Court station (1849), which made the palace and gardens easily accessible to the excursionist, for whom in the 19th century it was one of the comparatively few show places near London open on Sundays.

HAMPTON WICK (c6) lies on the Thames opposite Kingston in the extreme SE. of the great loop of the river. The parish, which extends N. to Teddington and W. to the buildings of Hampton Court Palace, is mostly covered by Hampton Court and Bushy parks; only a small area at the bridgehead is built over. The road from Kingston to Staines runs from Hampton Wick to Hampton between the walls of the two parks, with a few pleasant old houses situated on it; several roads to Teddington branch NW. just by the bridge.

Hampton Wick first appears in the 13th century; 'wic' means a dairy farm. A bridge was already there in John's reign; it was dangerous in 1318, and a grant was made for its repair in 1449. When Wyatt crossed it during his revolt against Mary in 1554 it was the first one above London. The present bridge was opened in 1828. The London and South Western Railway's Teddington loop line, with a station, was opened in 1863; electric trams began to run over the bridge and to Twickenham and Hampton Court in 1903.

The church (St John the Baptist) was built of white Suffolk brick and Bath stone in 1830 by E. Lapidge, architect of the bridge; it has been reasonably described by Thorne as 'Decorated, of bald character.' The interior fittings and most of the glass represent the taste of

[1] E. Law, *Chesnut Avenue in Bushey Park, Hampton Court* (1919), p. 8.

that age. The domestic architecture of Hampton Wick is not remarkable; there is a group of good houses in the lower Teddington road opposite the Swan inn, and a pair of attractive 'Gothic' cottages stands in Park Road.

Steele dedicated the fourth volume of *The Tatler* 'from the hovel at Hampton Wick, April 7th, 1711'; it is not certain where this was. Another inhabitant attained local fame: Timothy Bennet, a shoemaker, who asserted the public right of way over Bushy Park in 1752, at the age of 75, 'being unwilling to leave the world worse than he found it.'

HANWELL (c4) lies on the Uxbridge road W. of Ealing, included in that borough since 1928. It is bounded on N. and W. by the river Brent, whose banks have retained some of their homely charms. The ancient parish extended in a narrow strip down the E. bank to the Thames, but the S. portion was cut off to form the parish of New Brentford (formerly a chapelry) in 1723. This north-and south alignment was perhaps a survival from British times when a trackway led from the Thames ford at Brentford towards Uxbridge. Hanwell was the only parish in Elthorne hundred E. of the Brent; the modern names Elthorne Park and Elthorne Heights are no warrant for supposing that the hundred meeting-place was within this parish. The place was until about 1850 a small village clustered about the bridge carrying the Uxbridge road over the Brent, noted for watercress grown in the meadows. After that its situation on the Great Western main line caused it to grow rapidly and ungraciously.

The name of Hanwell, mentioned in three 10th- and 11th-century charters, is explained as meaning 'cock-fre-

quented spring.' The Spring is still the name of a property just E. of the church. The manor was given to Westminster Abbey by Edgar and confirmed by Edward the Confessor; it passed, like Greenford, to the bishop of Westminster in 1540 and to the bishop of London in 1550.

The old bridge over the Brent (traces of which can be detected on the S. side of the present road bridge), first mentioned in 1280,[1] was the important feature of the place in medieval times. The Great Western Railway contributed its best architectural feature, the Wharncliffe viaduct, in the strong style of the early railway engineers (*Plate 5*), and a station in 1838. Electric trams began to run on the Uxbridge road in 1901 and along Boston Lane from Brentford in 1906. Practically the whole area away from the river, apart from two large cemeteries, is now covered with houses.

Overlooking the viaduct, on a knoll by the Brent NW. of the centre of Hanwell, is the church (St Mary; G. G. Scott and W. B. Moffatt, 1841), faced in black flint on the S. side, with a thin broach spire; the chancel (W. Pywell) was added in 1898. It was one of the buildings that Scott very soon regretted.[2] Its predecessor, rebuilt 1780, was described as neat, with light-coloured walls and an elegant little cupola; the school, of 1799, had pointed windows to give it 'an antique Gothic air';[3] it is still to be seen SW. of the church. Samuel Glasse, rector 1780-5, resigned to keep a private school at Greenford and was succeeded by his son G. H. Glasse, who translated *Samson Agonistes* into Greek verse, ran through a fortune, and committed suicide in 1809. Derwent Coleridge, author, second son of S. T. Coleridge, was rector 1864-80. Jonas Hanway, traveller,

---

[1] 1280 is given as the date of Edward I's letters-patent for building the bridge by M. Sharpe, 'The Mending of the Brynt Bridge', *Trans. L. Mx. A. S.* NS 5 (1928), p. 449. [2] Scott (page 74, note 1), p. 86. [3] *Gentleman's Magazine*, 1800, part i., p. 305.

philanthropist, introducer of the umbrella into England, and pamphleteer against midnight routs, late hours, crowded assemblies, and tea-drinking, was buried in the churchyard, 1786.

To the E., in Church Road, are curious small houses of about 1800 and farther on some larger 19th-century houses. The rest of Hanwell N. of the Uxbridge road dates mostly from 1880 to 1914, with St Mellitus' church, red brick and stone with a bell-cote (1910) S. of the Uxbridge road, on Boston Road leading towards Brentford, are St Mark's church (W. White, 1879). Farther on is St Thomas (E. Maufe, 1934), with a bare concrete-finished interior; all the details are good and significant. The reredos and organ came from St Thomas, Portman Square.

Across the Brent, in Southall, is the block of buildings known as Hanwell asylum (now St Bernard's Hospital of the London County Council), originally opened in 1831. Here from 1839 onwards, under Dr. John Conolly, humane treatment of mental disorder was introduced, without any of the instruments of severe restraint usually employed up to that time, apart from experiments at York and Lincoln. Hanwell's example effectively began a revolution throughout the country in the treatment of mental illness.[1]

HANWORTH (A1) is a village in the flat plain of SW. Middlesex lying on the S. edge of Hounslow Heath, now included in the urban district of Feltham. The river Crane divides it from Hounslow and Twickenham, and the Queen's or Cardinal's river flows through the parish. The principal features are the London air park, which occupies Hanworth Park, and the remains of a Tudor royal palace not far away.

The name first appears, in Domesday Book, as Haneworde; *hana* is the old English word for a cock, but it was in this case more probably a man's name. The manor was held in 1086 under Roger de Montgomery. In 1304 two-thirds of the manor was held under the honour of Wallingford, the remainder under the abbey of Westminster. The manor was in the hands of the Crown by 1519 and became a royal residence; Camden described it as 'a small royal seat, which Henry VIII took great delight in and made the scene of his pleasures.' Towards the end of his reign it was settled on Katharine Parr, who survived him; she later lived there with her second husband, Sir Thomas Seymour, Lord Admiral, and with the Princess Elizabeth, whose education was in her charge. Seymour was later accused by his enemies of undue familiarity with the princess, aged 15 at the time, and trifling details of his conduct at Hanworth were adduced in support. Elizabeth, when queen, revisited the park and hunted there in 1600. It was leased to William Killigrew in 1594 and was acquired about 1627 by Sir Francis Cottington (Lord Cottington of Hanworth, 1631). Parliament gave the estate to John Bradshaw, the principal regicide; after the Restoration it was acquired by the Beauclerk family (Baron Vere of Hanworth, 1750, later Duke of St Albans). The house, which contained little of interest except a ceiling painted by Kneller, was burnt down in 1797.

The parish church (St George) stands W. of Hanworth Park on the road to Lower Feltham. The medieval church was entirely rebuilt in 1812 by James Wyatt, and further reconstruction, including extension of the chancel, took place in 1865 under S. S. Teulon. The glass in the N. chapel is partly of the

[1] Gibbon and Bell (see page 67, note 2), p. 344.

15th and 16th centuries, taken over from the old church and made up with modern glass.

S. of the church a block called Tudor Court (now flats) represents the original entrance court of Hanworth House, with some terracotta roundels of Roman emperors by Maiano like those at Hampton Court but less elaborately bordered. The buildings have been much altered.

The only notable inhabitants of Hanworth were three Killigrew brothers— Sir William Killigrew, born 1606, and Thomas and Henry Killigrew, both dramatists, born 1611 and 1613. Sir John Berkeley, Lord Berkeley of Stratton, royalist general, was born there in 1607, and Sir William Berkeley, governor and historian of Virginia, in 1608. E. M. Pollock, Master of the Rolls 1923-35, became Baron Hanworth in 1926 and Viscount Hanworth in 1936.

HAREFIELD (A3) lies at the NW. tip of Middlesex, N. of Uxbridge and W. of Ruislip and Northwood, in undulating and wooded country; chalk comes to the surface in Middlesex only here and at South Mimms. The N. extremity of the parish reaches almost to Rickmansworth in Hertfordshire; the Colne divides it from Buckinghamshire on the W. The district shows variety of field, wood, and river, with some modern housing development, but it remains one of the most rural parts of the county.

The place appears in Domesday Book as Herefelle ('army open space'— significance obscure). Robert, son of Gilbert, held the manor at Domesday, and it descended from him as part of the honour of Clare, vested in the Duchy of Lancaster, to which a quit rent was paid until 1790. In the late 13th century the de Bacheworth family were lords of the manor; it passed by marriage to Swanland and in the 14th century to Newdegate (later spelt Newdigate). Harefield was exchanged by the Newdegates in 1585 for Arbury in Warwickshire, which became the principal seat of the family; but after Harefield had been in the hands of Lord Keeper Egerton and his wife Alice, Countess of Derby, and others, it was conveyed back in 1675 to Sir Richard Newdigate, grandson of the John Newdegate who had moved to Arbury. The Newdigates remained in possession until the 20th century, the longest time that a principal manor in this county has been held by descent and marriage in the same family.

There was also a manor of Moor Hall, given towards the end of the 12th century[1] to the Knights Hospitallers for a cell to the priory of St John at Clerkenwell. The small manor of Brackenbury has been held continuously by the Newdigate family and was not exchanged with the other lands in 1585; the S. aisle of the church, where the Newdigates are buried, is named the Brackenbury chapel. Breakspear is an ancient estate said to take its name from the family of which the only English pope, Adrian IV, was a member; it was owned by the Ashby family from c. 1474 to 1800.

At the old manor house, Harefield Place, Sir Thomas Egerton entertained Elizabeth with great junketings in 1602. John Milton, living at Horton, near Colnbrook in Buckinghamshire, wrote his *Arcades* in 1632-3 for performance at Harefield. The old house was burnt down in 1660, it is said through Sir Charles Sedley's carelessness with a lighted candle while reading in bed. Its successor, on the same site just SE. of the church, was pulled down in 1814

---

[1] T. Hugo, 'Moor Hall, in Harefield', *Trans. L. Mx. A. S.* OS 3 (1870), p. 1, rejects the date (1221) and donor (Alice de Clare) given by Lysons.

for a new Harefield Place, 3 m. S. towards Ickenham.

The church (St Mary), S. of the village, while not itself of great architectural interest, contains the finest collection of sepulchral monuments in Middlesex: a collection worthy to be ranked with the richest English parish churches.[1] Some of the fittings are also noteworthy. The earliest portion of the existing church (in which some 12th-century work may survive) is the 13th-century chancel. The S. aisle dates from the early 14th century, and the N. aisle and NW. tower from the 16th. The chancel was altered in the 18th century. The plain exterior is mostly faced with cement.

The principal monument is to Alice, Countess of Derby, 1636, who lies in painted effigy possibly by Maximilian Colt of Arras, on an altar-tomb in the SE. angle of the chancel. The lady is represented with long hair, coroneted, in a bodice, gown, and cloak; her three daughters kneel in recesses below. The elaborate curtain canopy is supported by Corinthian columns, and the whole work is enriched with heraldic achievements (*Plate 35 and 36*). On the opposite side of the altar is the large but not so splendid monument of Mary, wife of Sir Richard Newdigate, 1692, with marble effigy in classical draperies, by Grinling Gibbons. So are the two cherubs supporting a sarcophagus on the monument of Sarah, wife of Richard Newdigate, 1695. On the S. wall is a partly recessed table-tomb with canopy of the early 16th century. Other notable 17th-century monuments are to Sir Robert Ashby, 1617, and Sir Francis Ashby, 1623, in the N. chapel, and to Sir John Newdigate (signed by William White and dated 1614), and there are many others to the Newdigate and Ashby families: three Attic urns to Sir

Roger Newdigate's mother and 2 wives by Richard Hayward, 1765 and 1774, and John Bacon, jr., 1800; Bacon also carved the 'tree of life' memorial to C. Parker. The punning ash tree with 'by,' to William Ashby, d. 1760, is probably by Sir Robert Taylor. The whole collection, with the brasses to the Newdigates (from Edetha Newdegate, 1444) and Ashbys (from 1474), presents an historical conspectus of English sepulchral taste from the 15th century to 1800.

The pulpit, an 18th-century three-decker, and the splendidly carved communion rail and reredos, perhaps Flemish work of the late 17th century, are good examples of their kind; the carved font-cover is also 17th-century, and there is some 16th-century glass in the N. chapel and a fine brass chandelier of 1743. Some 15th- and 16th-century funeral helms and gauntlets are suspended in the chancel. Outside the church on the N. side is a monument put up by Mr. Ashby in 1744 in memory of his faithful gamekeeper, Robert Mossendew, with a relief of the man and his dog, and lines complimentary to both. In the churchyard a separate section contains graves of Australian soldiers of the 1914-18 war from Harefield hospital, with a memorial gateway.

Between the church and the village are the Countess of Derby's alms-houses, early 17th-century brick on an H-plan. The village itself is unworthy in appearance, though good buildings occur here and there: the White Horse inn, late 16th-century with additions; the Cricketers, 17th-century; the King's Arms, on the green, with part of the original 15th-century house built into the N. wing; and some others. To the E. is Breakspear House, rebuilt in the 17th century with fragments of earlier

---

[1] See page 170, note 3.

date, and modern wings; there is a 16th-century dovecote in brick with a pyramidal roof. Farther E. is Bourne Farm, 17th-century red brick with blue-brick patterning, much restored. There are a good many other outlying farms of the 16th and 17th centuries N. and S. of the village, mostly in brick, some with weather-boarded barns.

SE. of the village, at Moor Hall, is what remains of the preceptory of the order of St John, now set about with modern cottages and looking rather forlorn. It is a small 13th-century building on two storeys, with lancet windows above, much repaired through the centuries when it was used as a barn. In this portion, called Harefield Moor, were a copper and brass mill until about 1850, a paper mill in 1875, and coal and timber wharves by the Grand Junction canal.

HARLESDEN (D4). *See* WILLESDEN.

HARLINGTON (B5) is a straggling village just N. of the Great West road between Cranford and Harmondsworth, with a parish roughly diamond-shaped, having its N. tip almost on the Uxbridge road W. of Hayes and its S. extremity on Hounslow Heath near Hatton. The village itself stands on the road from Hayes to Hatton and Feltham; Dawley is an outlying settlement to the N. in a desolate area traversed by the main Great Western Railway and the Grand Junction canal, and there is ribbon development along the Bath road in the S. Until about 1910 Harlington was a purely agricultural village, and the market gardens with their cherry trees were a prominent feature of the unexciting scene; but it now presents the usual untidy appearance of W. Middlesex. It forms the S. part of the urban district of Hayes and Harlington.

The place is first mentioned, as 'Hygereding Tun' (Hygered's farm), in 831. The manor, with the small manor of Dawley, was held at Domesday under Roger de Montgomery. When Sir Henry Bennet was raised to the peerage in 1665 he took his title from this place, spelling it 'Arlington,' which no one else has done before or since.[1]

The church (SS. Peter and Paul), W. of the main road carrying heavy traffic through the village, was built in the 12th century; the chancel was added in the 14th century and the W. tower in the late 15th century. The N. aisle was built at the restoration of 1880. The tower has three storeys and a turret with wooden cupola. The timber S. porch dates from the early 16th century, since reconstructed; it protects a fine Norman S. door-way, with round head bearing chevron ornament. The Purbeck marble font, late 12th-century, has a series of round-headed panels on each face.

There are two brasses, to John Monemouthe, rector *c.* 1419 (with the inscription *cujus a[n]i[ma]e propitietur Deus* carefully defaced), and Gregory Lovell and wife, 1545. Against the N. wall of the chancel is a combined monument and Easter sepulchre which formerly contained the Lovell brass. On the S. wall of the nave is a monument to Sir John Bennet, Lord Ossulston, 1686 (the date of his death should be 1695), with busts of him and his two wives. In the chancel and N. aisle are 19th-century tombs of the de Salis family, with recumbent effigies of Count J. F. de Salis (R. C. Lucas, 1836) and Countess de Salis (W. Theed, 1856).

The earliest resident of note at Harlington was William Byrd, composer of Church music, known to have lived there between 1577 and 1592, when he was a gentleman of the Chapel

[1] The spelling was regarded as an error at the time: 'the proper and true name of the place being Harlington', *Continuation of the Life of Clarendon* (ed. 1843), p. 1133. Evelyn (*Diary* to September 1677) says that Henry Bennet was once intended to be parson of Harlington.

Royal and at the height of his composing powers. His house was probably situated near the open space by the village pond.[1] There is a long series of entries in the Middlesex Sessions Rolls mentioning him and members of his household as Roman Catholic recusants.

A rector of some note in his own day was Joseph Trapp, a bad poet who held the living from 1733 to 1747.

Dawley House was bought by Henry St John, Viscount Bolingbroke, from the Bennet family and was his rural retreat from 1726 to 1735; it stood near the present railway and canal. He rebuilt the house with some affectation as a very superior farm, with the motto over the door *Satis beatus ruris honoribus*. He was visited there by Pope, who often went over from Twickenham to try the regimen of asses' milk. Bolingbroke's house was demolished in 1744, apart from some outbuildings.

Dawley manor farm, E. of the road near the church, is still a farm, with good black barns of the 16th century; Church Farm has a similar barn. To the S., at the pond, is Dower House, 16th to 18th centuries; opposite is a notable Baptist church in the classical style of 1879. To the S. is a fine little 18th-century house. The London airport is still confined S. of the Bath road; when, as intended, it overflows to the N. it will take in Harlington village almost up to the church.

HARMONDSWORTH (A5) is a village still recognisable as such on the W. border of Middlesex just N. of the Bath road; the parish included outlying settlements at Longford (on the Bath road), Heath Row (now obliterated by the London airport, to the S.), Perry Oaks (also submerged by the airport), and Sipson (on the lane leading E. to

Harlington). Factories have been established on the Great West road and some rows of suburban dwelling-houses close to it, and the airport is sterilising a huge area in the S.; but agriculture remains predominant in the level landscape. The river Colne separates Harmondsworth from Buckinghamshire on the W. and the Duke of Northumberland's river divides it from Stanwell on the S. It lies within the urban district of Yiewsley and West Drayton.

The name first appears in Domesday Book as 'Hermodesworde' (Heremode's farm); it was 'Harmsworth' in the 15th century and was so pronounced until recent times. The manor belonged to Earl Harold under Edward the Confessor and was given by William the Conqueror to the abbey of Holy Trinity at Rouen. In 1340 Edward III seized the manor, and in 1391 it was conveyed to William of Wykeham, bishop of Winchester, who settled it on Winchester College; in 1544 it was surrendered to Henry VIII and was granted by him in 1547 to Sir William Paget, from whom it descended, together with the neighbouring manor of West Drayton, to the earls of Uxbridge. Hounslow Heath extended over a large part of the parish until enclosure in 1805 and 1815. William Heather, who founded the Oxford chair of music, was born at Harmondsworth *c.* 1584; but its name was known to few until Penguin Books carried it far and wide from their publishing office in the parish (since 1938).

The church (St Mary) stands at the W. end of the village street. The SW. tower, flint below and brick above with battlemented top (*c.* 1500), pinnacles at the angles, and a jolly wooden cupola of about 1700, is a good feature (*Plate 33*), and the interior, light and

---

[1] Fellowes (page 152, note 1), pp. 11, 39.

well kept, has several points of interest. The present S. aisle and S. nave arcade date from the late 12th century; the round-headed doorway is a well-preserved piece of characteristic Norman, with ornament carried down to the ground on both sides. The N. nave arcade, early 13th-century, makes a strange junction at the top of one of the arches with the 16th-century flattened arches of the chancel. The chapel N. of the chancel has an early 16th-century roof of single hammer-beam type. The seating is good; many of the early 16th-century pews have survived. The late 12th-century font is octagonal. There are some heraldic floor-slabs, but no monuments of note, and the brasses disappeared (stolen, it is said, by workmen at the restoration of 1864).

The most noteworthy antiquity in the parish, however, is the remarkable tithe barn immediately W. of the church, built in the 14th or 15th century to store the tithes for the benefit of the absent lords of the manor. The barn is a timber-framed building of 12 bays, 190 ft. long, with boarded walls and a tiled roof; internally the timber structure is arranged in the form of a nave with two aisles, the arcades being represented by two rows of posts on stone bases; the main roof is continued over the aisles without a break. It remained in use for storage of grain for many centuries; the harvest of 1847 filled it so high that the visiting antiquary could not see it properly.[1]

There are some pleasant old buildings on the wide village street; the Five Bells inn, Sun House (formerly an inn), and some cottages date from the 16th and 17th centuries. The Grange is dated 1675. Harmondsworth Hall, S. of the church, was rebuilt during the 18th century.

Longford, on the Bath road, was a settlement more populous than the village centre. A Quaker meeting-house was built in 1676; subscriptions for this meeting were collected in London, Ireland, and Jamaica in 1671 and 1672.[2] It has some good old cottages and fine black barns; the White Horse inn, in brick and tile, has 17th-century portions. All these buildings have been much renovated.

The huge airport, still contained S. of the main road, was opened for civil use in 1946 and has already obliterated the farms of Heath Row and Perry Oaks. Almost on the airport are two pleasing Bath road inns, the Three Magpies, 17th-century with tiled roof, and the Old Magpies, thatched. 'Nimrod' wrote in 1832: 'No house on the road makes such capital rum-and-milk as the "Magpies" does; the coachmen call it "milking the bull".'[3] During levelling of the airfield in the 1939-45 war an ancient earthwork, noticed by John Aubrey in the 17th century[4] and marked on the Ordnance Survey as 'camp,' was found to contain the foundations of a colonnaded building, believed to have been a temple of about 300 B.C.; it is the only one of its kind recorded in Britain.[5]

HARRINGAY (E3). *See* HORNSEY.

HARROW (C3) is the largest and most populous district in Middlesex, extending over 12,500 acres from the N. edge of Wembley to the Hertford-shire border and containing almost a quarter of a million inhabitants. The ancient parish ran S. as far as the river Brent; WEMBLEY and Sudbury have been detached to form, with KINGSBURY, a separate borough on this side. PINNER, in the N., has had a distinct, though not separate, existence

---

[1] C. Innes, *Builder* 5 (1847), p. 579. [2] Beck and Ball (page 112, note 2), pp. 282, 291. [3] 'Nimrod' (page 224, note 2), p. 118. [4] J. Aubrey, *Monumenta Britannica* (MS. in Bodleian Library, Oxford), iii., p. 161. [5] *War and Archaeology in Britain* (Ministry of Works, 1949), p. 16.

through. out history. The modern urban district of Harrow also includes GREAT and LITTLE STANMORE.

Harrow-on-the-Hill is prominently sited on the most conspicuous eminence of central Middlesex, crowned by the spire that Charles II declared to be 'the church visible' when he heard his divines disputing over the meaning of the phrase. From the most remote days this hill has been recognised as an important place, and Harrow's historic celebrity is surpassed in Middlesex only by that of Hampton Court. The name has descended with many variations from its first appearance as 'Gumeninga Hergae' in 767; this is[1] the old English 'hearg,' a heathen temple or shrine (normally in the open air, on a hilltop), but 'gumeninga' is uncertain. Thus the parish name connects the site of the present church with old heathen worships; and antiquity is still acknowledged in commercial Harrow by a cinema of boldly 20th-century aspect which proclaims the ancient name of Herga to the unastonished inhabitants of Wealdstone.

The land recorded in 767,[2] together with more in Harrow, which was acquired by Wulfred, archbishop of Canterbury, was seized by Cenulf, king of Mercia 796-822, and returned by his daughter Cwoenthryth in 825;[3] it was again restored to Canterbury by a priest named Werhard in 832. From that time until 1545 the manor remained in the possession of the archbishops of Canterbury, with some interruption apparently in the 11th century, when Earl Lewin was in occupation in 1066. Like Hayes, the parish was a 'peculiar' of Canterbury, outside the jurisdiction of the bishop of London, and so remained until 1836. Naturally there was friction where such a valuable property was involved: Anselm, about

to consecrate the church in 1094, found that the holy oil had been stolen by an agent of the bishop; fortunately, it was restored in miraculous fashion. Archbishops until Chichele, about 1440, occupied the manor house at Harrow, and later at Headstone, from time to time, and in 1545 Cranmer surrendered the manor to Henry VIII, who granted it to Sir Edward North in 1547. It later descended to the families of Pitts and Rushout, Lord Northwick. The rectory manor was obtained by Christ Church, Oxford, and later shared with North and his successors. Subsidiary manors were Sudbury (Southbury), Woodhall (Pinner), Headstone, Flambards, and Roxeth.

At Domesday Harrow, consisting of 100 hides worth £56 a year, was the largest manor in Middlesex, though Isleworth (£72) was more valuable; pannage for 2,000 swine (equalled only at Edmonton and Enfield) points to a very large proportion remaining wooded. A weekly market was established in 1262, with an annual fair; the market appears to have lapsed about the middle of the 16th century, when the relative importance of Harrow declined, though the fair struggled on until 1866. It was held at the foot of the hill by West Street.[4]

The opening of John Lyon's free school in 1611 and its successful career in the 18th century gave the village new life; but, lying off the main roads from London to the N. and W., it was much less populous than Tottenham, Edmonton, or Enfield on the N., Ealing and Uxbridge in the W., or Chiswick, Isleworth, or Twickenham in the Thames valley. After the London and Birmingham Railway opened a station (at Wealdstone, well over a mile from the church) in 1837, there was settlement around it and along the road through

---

[1] This is the received version; but W. W. Druett, *Harrow through the Ages* (1935), seeks to show that the hill was not occupied as early as other parts and derives the name from 'ard' (Celtic, a hill). [2] There is dispute where the land referred to in the charter of 767 lay: W. D. Bushell, 'The Harrow of the Gumenings', Tract I in *Church Life on Harrow Hill* (Harrow Octocentenary Tracts, 1909); Druett (preceding note), p. 29. [3] Bushell (see preceding note), 'Wulfred and Cwoenthryth', Tract III, holds that 825 was the first time that the Harrow manor came into the hands of Canterbury. [4] E. D. Laborde, *Harrow School Yesterday and To-day* (1948), p. 18.

Greenhill. The Metropolitan Railway station of Harrow-on-the-Hill was opened in 1880, and in the next 20 years the population was more than doubled; most of the new settlement lay between the two stations.

Since then the fields of Harrow have been covered with houses at an astonishing rate. There is some industry in Wealdstone, but in the main the area is a gigantic dormitory, generally of mediocre appearance, relieved by distant views of the hill with the school playing-fields surrounding it and by a few old buildings (*Frontispiece*).

The obvious and visible topographical centre of the district is the church (St Mary), standing at the summit (400 ft.) of the ridge that falls away steeply E. and W., more gently N. and S. This building is equal to its situation in merit and interest, though the details now command more attention than the whole after Gilbert Scott's drastic restoration in 1846-9. (Scott recorded that he was led by the transepts of Harrow and Pinner to adopt a cruciform plan for his earliest churches; there are Middlesex examples at Hanwell and Turnham Green.[1]) Nothing remains of the church consecrated, with difficulty, in 1094; the earliest surviving portions, in the lower part of the tower, are of about 1130-40. The nave, with pillars of Totternhoe stone from Bedfordshire, and aisles date from the first half of the 13th century; the N. and S. transepts are of about 1300. The clerestory and nave roof were added towards 1450, as well as the S. porch and the upper part of the tower. The top of the spire was rebuilt after being struck by lightning in 1765. In 1786 a correspondent of the *Gentleman's Magazine* reported serious dilapidation: the chancel was 'in such a ruinous state that it is dangerous to

enter! There is not a whole pane of glass left in the windows, very large cracks in the walls, and the east window obliged to be propped up to prevent its falling.'[2] The church was patched up, but in 1800 the 12th-century font was thrown out into a garden and a 'marble wash-hand-basin-stand-looking-thing'[3] put in its place; the original font was retrieved in 1846. Charles Lamb visited the church in 1814 and wrote to Wordsworth: 'Do you know it? with its fine long spire, white as washed marble, to be seen, by vantage of its high site, as far as Salisbury spire itself almost'; it had, he said, the 'instantaneous coolness and calming, almost transforming properties of a country church just entered.'[4]

Scott's restoration was thorough. The exterior was faced with flints, for which there was no warrant, and the chancel was worked over in the style of the 14th century, not until then represented in the building.[5] The tower has 12th-century round-headed windows in the N. and S. walls, and a round-headed W. doorway with chevron ornament. The tall octagonal spire is of timber, lead-covered, a fine specimen of ancient carpentry.

The nave roof, flat-pitched with moulded main timbers, is the most striking feature of the interior, with 12 figures, probably apostles, on the wall-posts and 10 figures with musical instruments at the centre of the roof panels; angels with spread wings, divided by rosettes, are carved on the main beams. The font is a late 12th-century round bowl of Purbeck marble carved with primitive ornament. The 17th-century pulpit, given to the church in 1708, is of richly carved oak with a sounding board, and the modern organ-case incorporates pieces of 17th-century panelling.

[1] Scott (page 74, note 1), p. 86. [2] *Gentleman's Magazine*, 1786, part ii., p. 772. [3] W. Hone, *Table Book* [1827], p. 79. [4] *Letters of Charles Lamb* (page 127, note i), i., p. 271. [5] *Builder* 68 (1895), p. 57.

The church contains a fine series of 13 brasses, many mutilated but still of high interest. The earliest is to Sir Edward Flambard, about 1370, in full armour with dog at his feet, and there is one to John Flambard, *c.* 1390. There are two early brasses of rectors, both now without heads: John Byrkhed, 1468, in full vestments, the orphreys of the cope filled with figures of saints; and Simon Marchford, about 1442. The most celebrated brass is the one to John Lyon, founder of Harrow school, d. 1592, and his wife on the first pier of the N. nave arcade. The monuments are of less interest: the biggest are two to William Gerard (father and son), 1584 and 1609 (reassembled); there is a series to headmasters of Harrow school, including Robert Sumner (with epitaph by Samuel Parr), Joseph Drury, and George Butler.

The churchyard, with some good trees, commands fine views SW. and W.; Byron when a Harrow schoolboy used to spend hours on a certain tomb (the Peachey tomb, SW. of the tower), which is consequently now enclosed in an iron railing. Immediately N. of the churchyard is the Grove, on the site of the old rectory, occupied for some years after 1778 by R. B. Sheridan, and a school boarding-house since 1820.

An assortment of 19th-century buildings, of various inspiration, houses Harrow school, lying S. and E. of the church along the ridge (*Plate 12*). The core of the school, and its only building from 1611 to 1819, is the fourth-form room in the W. wing of the Old School, a red-brick building approached by a straight flight of steps; the E. wing and rear were added in 1819. The interior of the fourth-form room, no longer used as a classroom, has interesting old fittings and names carved on the wall from 1660 onwards. New schools were built in 1855 (by F. Barnes), the Vaughan library in 1861 (G. G. Scott), the speech room in 1874 (W. Burges), science school in 1874 (C. F. Hayward), music school in 1890 (E. S. Prior), art school in 1895 (W. C. Marshall), and many since, including the war memorial building (Herbert Baker, 1921). The chapel, flint and stone in Gilbert Scott's most uncompromising style, was erected in 1857 on the site of an outmoded building of 1839, by C. R. Cockerell; previously the boys had attended services in the parish church. The harsh brilliance of the windows at the E. end (Wailes, 1858) was rendered more tolerable by the application of pigment in 1904.

Tablets in the walls of the school buildings commemorate two events, both in their way historic: one marks the site of a well by which Charles I paused on 27 April 1646 on his way with a few companions from Oxford to St Albans and on to the Scots at Newark, never again to come so far south a free man;[1] the other records Lord Shaftesbury's earliest philanthropic resolution, formed out of disgust at the drunken indecency of a pauper's funeral on its way to the churchyard. The list of Harrow boys who have achieved fame is long; perhaps the most representative names are in politics and literature: Spencer Perceval, Goderich, Peel, Aberdeen, Palmerston, Baldwin, and Churchill, prime ministers; Sheridan, Byron, Lytton, C. S. Calverley, Theodore Hook, Anthony Trollope, J. A. Symonds, John Galsworthy, writers; G. O. Trevelyan and G. M. Trevelyan, historians; Cardinal Manning; Lord Shaftesbury; James Bruce, African traveller; William Jones, orientalist; Lord Dalhousie, governor-general of India, and Pandit Nehru, prime minister of India; Lord Rodney; Viscount

[1] P. M. Thornton, *Harrow School and its Surroundings* (1885), p. 84; Peck (page 95, note 3), ii., pp. 350, 360.

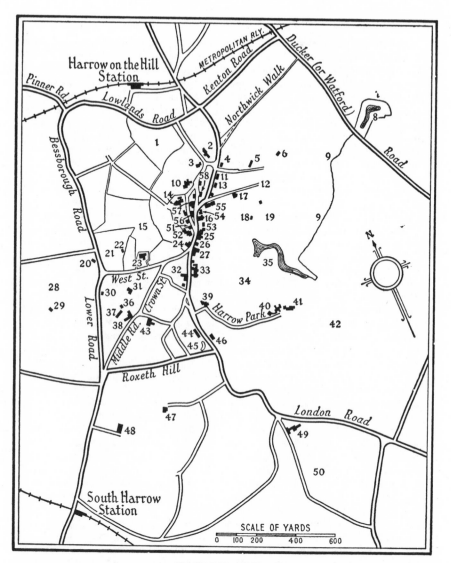

HARROW HILL

1. *Grove Fields.* 2. *Elmfield.* 3. *The Copse.* 4. *Garlands.* 5. *Miniature Rifle Range.* 6. *Wyckoff Stand.* 7. *Ducker.* 8. *30-yard Rifle Range.* 9. *Sheepcote Brook.* 10. *The Grove.* 11. *The Knoll.* 12. *Butler Gate.* 13. *Hillside.* 14. *Parish Church.* 15. *Church Fields.* 16. *School Chapel.* 17. *Music School.* 18. *Boyer Webb Pavilion.* 19. *Parade Ground.* 20. *Fifth Form Pavilion.* 21. *Bessborough Ground.* 22. *Lawn Pavilion.* 23. *Pie Powder House.* 24. *School Stores.* 25. *Headmaster's House.* 26. *Bookshop.* 27. *Moreton's.* 28. *Philathletic Ground.* 29. *Buxton Pavilion.* 30. *Sixth Form Cricket Pavilion.* 31. *Field House.* 32. *Bradleys.* 33. *The Park.* 34. *Park Fields.* 35. *Park Lake.* 36. *Sixth Form Cricket Pavilion.* 37. *Bowling Shed.* 38. *Lower School of John Lyon.* 39. *Newlands.* 40. *Deynecourt.* 41. *Kennet House.* 42. *School Farm.* 43. *Byron House.* 44. *West Acre.* 45. *Moat Pound.* 46. *Manor Lodge.* 47. *Old Sanatorium.* 48. *School Laundry.* 49. *Sanatorium.* 50. *Field let to Lower School of John Lyon.* 51. *Old Schools.* 52. *Druries.* 53. *Vaughan Library.* 54. *New Schools.* 55. *Science School and Museum Schools.* 56 *War Memorial.* 57. *Speech Room.* 58. *Rendalls.*

(All, except 14 and 23, are buildings or properties associated with Harrow School.)

Alexander; William Perkin and Lord Rayleigh, scientists.

Farther along the ridge, in the High Street, the architectural features are less dazzling. There are some good old cottages and shops; parts of the King's Head inn are said to date from 1533. In West Street, behind the Mission House, is the old 'Pie-Powder House,' where the magistrates held their court to control the annual fair. The 18th- and early 19th-century houses in this part of Harrow give it some distinction, which has not been entirely destroyed by the disastrous erections of later times. Matthew Arnold lived from 1868 to 1873 at Byron House, by the junction of Middle Road and Crown Street; 'I cannot tell you,' he wrote to his mother, 'how the old countrified look of the house pleases me.'[1] On the E. slopes, which now look over playing fields and a golf course to the suburban amenities of Wembley, were Julians and Julians Hill, two homes of the Trollope family, who later moved to a farmhouse at Harrow Weald, from which Anthony trudged miserably along the muddy lanes to school; Julians Hill was the model for *Orley Farm*, in which Harrow appears as Hamworth (*Plate 10*). Down the S. slope towards Sudbury are agreeable houses, mostly built since 1890, by A. Mitchell, A. P. Starkey, and others; to the SW. is Roxeth, an ancient hamlet on the Northolt road, now overshadowed by a gas works and in danger of becoming lost in the melancholy aggregation of South Harrow. There is practically nothing left of old Roxeth except the name of an inn, the Timber Carriage; Christ Church (G. G. Scott, 1863), of no special interest in itself, is pleasantly situated in a Victorian picturesque coniferous churchyard on Roxeth Hill.

W. of the railway viaduct is a district that was entirely under grass until the 1930s, when it was built over with such speed that overwrought mapmakers showed rifle ranges and streets of dwellings superimposed on each other.[2] The church of St Paul, Corbins Lane (N. F. Cachemaille-Day, 1938), is a good example of the modern austere school, the lancet windows filled with coloured glass only in the chancel. Otherwise the area is typical of the most recent age of suburbs; the main roads are broad, featureless bus routes, disdaining to follow the wanderings of the country tracks like old Rayners Lane. Part of this district is filled with temporary houses of the 1945 pattern. West Harrow belongs to the preceding period, 1919-39. North Harrow, mostly in the old parish of Pinner, is distinguished by the church of St Paul, on the Ridgeway (A. W. Kenyon, 1937), in yellow brick; there is a bold square tower with windows at the top (*Plate 61*). Inside the roof is a semi-circular vault narrowed at the choir and sanctuary; the aisles are passages only; the finish is off-white plaster, all serious, plain, and harmonious.

The main street of modern Harrow is Station Road, running N. from Harrow-on-the-Hill station through Greenhill to Wealdstone. Only one secular building in it demands notice— the Westminster bank in tortured red brick (B. Fletcher, 1915). St John, Greenhill, at the corner of Sheepcote Lane, is a tolerable building of 1904 with pleasing interior furniture of a more recent date and good clear glass; it replaced a structure of 1866—'of parti-coloured brick, with a prodigious roof,' said Thorne—by Bassett Keeling, perhaps the most regrettable Gothic revivalist. Wealdstone is a dingy district round the railway station of 1837, well rebuilt by the London and North

---

[1] *Letters of Matthew Arnold* (page 159, note 2), i., p. 386. [2] *Authentic Map Directory of London and Suburbs* (ed. 3, c. 1932), p. 37.

Western Railway (G. C. Horsley, 1911). To the W., in Harrow View and Headstone Drive, is the settlement that sprang up when the L.N.W.R. in 1858 offered a free first-class season ticket to Euston for 11 years for every new house over £50 annual value.[1] Farther up the railway are the Kodak works and the printing works of Her Majesty's Stationery Office, the only considerable manufactories in Harrow.

High Road, Wealdstone, continues N. up to Harrow Weald, where the municipal offices are situated in Harrow Weald Lodge, an 18th-century red-brick house horribly gashed with Victorian bow windows. E. is All Saints, Harrow Weald, with nave by W. Butterfield (1845) and a queer tiled and gabled tower (1890). Harrow Weald Park is a cockney-Gothic mansion of 1810 with additional castellation of 1870. Harrow Weald House farm, in Elms Road, is well preserved; there is a tile kiln, relic of an industry once important in this district, near Clamp Hill close by ('clamp' meaning a stack of bricks). The farmhouse where Anthony Trollope lived when his family's fortunes were at their lowest is identified with Durrant's Farm, opposite Wealdstone House. The Weald Stone itself may perhaps be the large stone embedded in the pavement close to the Red Lion inn.[2]

Uxbridge Road has a number of comfortable 19th-century mansions in good grounds; there are a few older buildings, notably the Seven Bells inn, Kenton Lane (17th-century), the Hare, at Harrow Weald common (17th-century), Ashcombe House, Boxtree Lane (18th-century), and Farm Cottage (17th-century). N. of Uxbridge Road the ground is more open.

There is something left of Harrow Weald common, running up to the Watford road and the Hertfordshire border at Bushey Heath. Grim's Dyke is a house on the edge of the common designed in 1872 by R. Norman Shaw, picturesquely timbered in his personal style, for F. Goodall, R.A.; it was occupied by W. S. Gilbert, who died while swimming in the lake, 1911. The earthwork of GRIM'S DYKE itself is separately noticed.

The remaining portion of Harrow, which lies E. of Wealdstone across the railway, is that part of Kenton N. of Kenton Road (the rest is in Wembley). Only one building in its neat, uninteresting roads calls for mention—the church of St Mary (J. H. Gibbons, 1936) in Kenton Road, E. of the station, something more traditional than the other new Harrow churches, with stone dressings to the yellow brick pointed arches and some moulding within. The design has distinction—and this is doubly important to Kenton, for nowhere in Greater London is it easier to get lost for lack of landmarks.

HATCH END (A1). *See* PINNER.

HATTON (B5). *See* BEDFONT.

HAYES (B4) is a large parish, lying across the Uxbridge road between Southall and Hillingdon, which now forms the greater part of the urban district of Hayes and Harlington. The Crane river, or Yeading brook, enters at the N. tip of the parish and forms part of the E. boundary with Southall; Hayes village lies just S. of the Uxbridge road, which runs from Hayes Bridge in the E. to Hayes End on the edge of Hillingdon Heath; Yeading, in the NE. on the road to Northolt, and Botwell in the S. were outlying settlements. The place lies in featureless country, mostly just above the hundred-foot contour; it has a comparatively unspoilt village

[1] *Builder* 16 (1858), p. 296. [2] P. Davenport, 'The Weald Stone', *Trans. L. Mx. A. S.* NS 10 (1951), p. 165.

centre with an ancient church and manor house. Modern housing development has on the whole adopted a better pattern in Hayes than in the neighbouring parishes.

Hayes was mentioned as 'Linga Haese' (*hese*, brushwood) in 793; Yeading is found in 757. The manor was bequeathed to the church of Canterbury in 832. It followed the same alienations as Harrow until 1613, when it was sold by Dudley, Lord North; it was finally bought by Villiers, Earl of Jersey, of Osterley Park.

Hayes contained much heath and uncultivated soil until it was enclosed in 1809. In the middle of the 19th century it was regarded as being the most backward part of Middlesex. As late as 1754 cock-throwing was practised in the churchyard on Shrove Tuesday. In the 19th century a vicar used to come every week from the King's Bench prison and preach with the sheriff's officer behind him in the pulpit; in 1875, according to Thorne, mummers and handbell-ringers still made their rounds at Christmas. Elizabeth Hunt, historian of the parish, wrote in 1861: 'Sure I am that at Yeading dirt, ignorance and darkness reign supreme'; as for Botwell, it was 'a place but little more civilised than Yeading.' Happily things have improved since then. The Grand Junction canal was cut across the S. of the parish in 1798, and the Great Western Railway, running parallel with it, opened its Hayes station at Botwell in 1864. Electric trams were extended from Southall along the Uxbridge road in 1904.

The church (St Mary) lies in a large and well-kept churchyard, diversified with rose-trees, just W. of the road to Harlington and within sight of the Uxbridge road; its situation was delightful until nasty-looking huts for firemen were built just in front of it. It is a building of some interest, heavily restored under Gilbert Scott in 1873. The exterior is finished in flint with red-tiled roofs. The chancel dates from the 13th century, deflecting slightly N. from the line of the nave; there is no chancel arch, and the chancel roof continues some distance into the nave, resting on some grotesque figured corbels on the N. side. The N. aisle is 15th-century work, the S. aisle 16th-century, and the S. porch is an early 16th-century timber structure. The nave roof, also 16th-century, is notable, with moulded ribs and carved bosses showing the emblems of the Passion and the arms of England and Aragon; two modern dormer windows have been inserted in the S. side. On the N. wall is a large 15th-century painting of St Christopher with the child Christ, showing also a hermit, a mermaid, a fish, and an eel. The principal monument is an effigy in judge's robes of Sir Edward Fenner, judge of the King's Bench, 1611, on the N. side of the chancel. In the N. aisle is a stone altar-tomb of Walter Grene, 1456, with brass. There is another brass in the S. aisle on the tomb of Thomas Higate, 1576. In the chancel is a brass to Robert Levee or Lenee, rector *c.*1370; this is the oldest brass remaining in Middlesex. The lych-gate in the churchyard, with its centre-swinging gate under a ridged and gabled roof, is similar to those at Heston, just SE., and at Chalfont St Giles, Buckinghamshire.

E. of the church across the road is the manor house, 16th to 18th centuries, of brick with some timber framing. Hayes (described as Hayes Town on the Congregational church, founded 1788) keeps a faint village air; there is a characteristic old Middlesex cottage on Botwell Road opposite the Royal Oak. Good garden-suburb development of the early 1920s lies S. towards Botwell, which is a newish, undistinguished place centred on the railway station and the extensive works of the 'His Master's Voice' gramophone company. Yeading, N. of the Uxbridge road, contains many houses built since 1930 and a horrible refuse dump by the canal.

The most notable inhabitants of Hayes were Henry Gold, vicar in 1529, who was executed at Tyburn in 1534 as a supporter of the cause of the Maid of Kent, and Robert Wright, rector 1601-23, first warden of Wadham College, Oxford, who resigned because Dorothy Wadham refused to allow him to marry.

As befits its former character, Hayes is haunted; ghosts used to frequent the manor house and grounds in some numbers.

HEADSTONE (c3). *See* PINNER.

HEATH ROW (b5). *See* HARMONDS-WORTH.

HENDON (d3), a borough since 1932, is the third largest Middlesex district, consisting of the ancient parishes of Hendon and Edgware and extending from the heights of Hampstead on the London border to the ridge on the Hertfordshire boundary between Barnet and Elstree in the N. The river Brent cuts off some third of the district S. and E. of the depression formed by its course; in this portion is GOLDERS GREEN, with Child's Hill and part of Cricklewood. To the N. are Colindale, Burnt Oak, and MILL HILL. The Edgware road forms the whole W. boundary, except for a small salient beyond the road near the river Brent. The Welsh Harp, or Brent reservoir, artificially formed in 1838 to supply the Grand Junction canal, lies at the junction of the Silk stream, flowing S. from Edgware, and the Brent, which is formed by the confluence of the Dollis and Mutton brooks on the E., or Finchley, boundary. The district is moderately hilly; Hendon village stands on high ground N. of the Brent on the crossroad from Finchley to the Hyde (West Hendon). It commands an extensive view NW., only inferior in Middlesex to that from Harrow Hill.

Hendon is now a gigantic London dormitory, with some industry on its W. side. An airfield and some wooded country in the Mill Hill area vary the prospect of dwelling-houses. It remained obstinately rural in many parts until the 1914-18 war; the succeeding decades have erased almost every one of the pleasing old brown-brick houses and weather-boarded farms and put in their place rows of pink-brick suburban houses. Apart from Mill Hill ridge, where some antiquity lingers, it is a clean, bright, new-looking place, its style set by the by-pass roads that enmesh it; here 20th-century Middlesex is seen at its most characteristic, with its virtues as well as its evident faults.

'Hendun' ('at the high down') occurs in 959; Dunstan (according to Camden 'a man born for promoting the interest of monkery') prevailed on Edgar to sell him Lotheresleage or Loyersley and gave this, together with other lands in Hendon, to Westminster.[1] Westminster owned Hendon at the Conquest and retained it, apart from a short alienation, until the Dissolution. Hampstead, also owned by the abbey of Westminster, was apparently a chapelry in the mother parish of Hendon from 1333 to 1542-5.[2] Hendon formed part of the endowment of the short-lived bishopric of Westminster; in 1550 it was surrendered to Edward VI and granted

[1] See 'Three Hendon Charters', *Place-Names of Middlesex* (English Place-Name Society, 1942), p. 219 (appendix 1).   [2] The point has been disputed: J. Kennedy, *Manor and Parish Church of Hampstead and its Vicars* (1906), p. 44, concluded that in spite of the use of the word 'chapel' Hampstead was a parish church and was only annexed to Hendon for a short time in the 15th century. This view appears to be no longer tenable: F. C. Eeles, *Parish Church of St. Mary, Hendon* (ed. 2, 1931), p. 30, appendix, 'The Connexion with Hampstead'; N. G. Brett-James, 'Some Extents and Surveys of Hendon', *Trans. L. Mx. A. S.* NS 6 (1932), p. 547.

to Sir William Herbert. It continued in the Herbert family (earl of Pembroke, marquess of Powis) until 1757, when it was sold to Mr. Clutterbuck in trust for David Garrick. The business of the manor court continued to be transacted at the White Bear inn until about 1925.[1] There were smaller manors of Hodford, Frith or New Hall, Clitterhouse (Clitherows), and Renters.

The details of Hendon history may be learned from a series of manor and parish records, including five extents or surveys of the manor covering the period from 1321 to 1754, 'possibly unique in their number and scope.'[2] As the forest was cut back, the fields were devoted principally to grass and to some extent to corn; the Load of Hay inn in Brent Street commemorates the staple crop. There was a fair of sorts from time to time in the 17th and 18th centuries at Hendon, probably on the Burroughs.[3]

Hay does not require a large resident labouring force; the population of Hendon remained small, while the persistence of certain family names is remarkable for Middlesex: Nicoll from 1321 to late 19th century, Brent or Braint from 1321 to 1756, Marsh from 1461 to 1796. From 1600 onwards a few of the best houses were taken by wealthy or retired Londoners—John Norden, surveyor and author of *Speculum Britanniae*, the Middlesex topography of 1593, was one—but the place remained a farming village, cut off from London by the Hampstead ridge. The village centre (Church End) and the nine outlying hamlets were all placed where a patch of gravel cap allowed ponds to form; between them the ungrateful clay repelled settlement.

Things began to change when the Midland Railway station was opened in 1868, but it mostly remained a district

of field and footpath down to the 20th century. Then Hendon was changed in the twinkling of an eye, as historical time goes. Electric trams began on the Edgware road in 1904; the tube railway, opened to Golders Green in 1907, was extended to Hendon in 1923 and to Edgware in 1924. Arterial roads were thrust along the Brent valley and from end to end of the parish. By 1939 there was not much land left unappropriated to suburban uses, though a haystack is still to be seen opposite the bus garage at Church End.

Hendon turned its back on the past and put on a 20th-century look with determination. Still, there are a few historical evidences among the generally uninspired erections of the present age. In the Burroughs, the oldest part of the street leading from West Hendon to the village centre, are a few 18th- and early 19th-century houses, looking careworn, near the rebuilt White Bear inn and the Daniel almshouses of 1729. Up a short lane to the N. is the church (St Mary), commanding a good view from the crest of the ridge. It was of modest size until nearly doubled by additions made on the S. side to Temple Moore's designs in 1915. The exterior is not distinguished; the W. tower seems to be too small for the church and for the weather-vane it carries. Within, however, there are some noteworthy features, though the new nave, chancel, and aisle, built where the old S. aisle stood, with the old S. clerestory now between the two naves, create a curious impression of two separate churches standing side by side. During the most recent restorations (1929-31) remains of a 12th-century chancel were found, but the oldest portion of the present building dates from the middle 13th century; all the rest of the old church—

[1] F. Howkins, *Story of Golders Green* [1923], p. 9. [2] Published by N. G. Brett-James in *Trans. L. Mx. A. S.* NS 6 (1932) and 7 (1937). [3] Dowdell, p. 30, quoting Middlesex County Records, Sessions Book May 1697, fol. 35; E. T. Evans, *History of Hendon* (1890), p. 287.

chancel, nave, and N. aisle—may be of this date. The tower, square, small, and unbuttressed at the outer corners, like Finchley, is 15th-century, repaired in 1783 (date on rain-water heads); the N. chapel was added or rebuilt in the early 16th century. The font is remarkable, a large square bowl decorated with intersecting round-headed arcades of Norman type, about 1150-80. There are some good monuments: in the N. chapel is a semi-recumbent effigy of Sir William Rawlinson, 1703, serjeant-at-law and a commissioner of the Great Seal under William III, in wig and robes, implausibly ascribed to Rysbrack (b. 1694); a draped marble tablet to Edward Fowler, bishop of Gloucester, 1714; and, raised on a plinth in the N. chapel, the most magnificent floor-slab in Middlesex (which lay for years underneath the chancel pavement), a piece of black Flemish marble with a deeply-carved armorial design, to Sir Jeremy Whichcote, 1677. There is a graceful tablet to Charles Colmore, by Flaxman (1807), and a feeble bit of brass on a column to Stamford Raffles, founder of Singapore, d. 1826, also commemorated by an inscription on the floor at the E. end of the new nave. There are remnants of several wall-paintings: two 16th-century black-letter texts below the E. window of the old chancel; a fragment of 13th-century red design on the S. chancel wall; and part of a Stuart royal arms at the E. end of the N. aisle wall. Some fragments and indents of brasses have survived. In the churchyard are some good 18th-century headstones. There are a few old cottages about the entrance to the churchyard, and the rebuilt Greyhound inn stands almost inside it.

In the Burroughs is a row of municipal buildings that play for safety in their looks (town hall, T. H. Watson,

1910; public library, I. M. Wilson, 1932); the Methodist church (Welch and Lander, 1937), at the corner of Egerton Gardens, in speckled brick, is more dashing. Standards fall as the road goes down the hill W. towards the Hyde; but the church of St John, West Hendon, in Algernon Road, S.E. of the station, redeems the district. An uncompleted work by Temple Moore (1896), it is a fine, clean building of the age when the Gothic revival had, in some hands, put off its antiquarian jacket. Though the slender arcade is modelled on the 14th-century church of Austin Friars, its spirit is that of a modern church. A variety of relics from the City have come to rest in it, without incongruity: a font-cover and reredos of the Wren period in the Lady chapel; a fine inlaid pulpit of 1760 from St Michael Bassishaw; and panelling from St Bartholomew, Little Moorfields.

The large houses of old Hendon lay NE. and E. of the church, along Brent Street and Parson Street. If Camden is right, this road and not Watling Street was used in the Middle Ages for entry into London from the NW.[1] Hendon House, occupied probably by John Norden (d. c. 1629), certainly by Sir Jeremy Whichcote (from 1660 to 1677) and Sir William Rawlinson (c. 1694 to 1703), stood just S. of Bell Lane. Beyond Finchley Lane, Hendon Hall and its grounds lie W. of the road; it is a handsome red-brick house, built and elaborately decorated for David Garrick soon after he had bought the manor in 1757. The Corinthian portico, which forms the principal feature on the W. front, is said to have come from Wanstead House, Essex, and before that from the Duke of Chandos' mansion of Canons, Little Stanmore; but this has lately been controverted.[2]

---

[1] W. Camden, *Britannia*, ed. R. Gough 1789), ii., p. 11; J. Norden, *Speculum Britanniae* (ed. 1723), p. 15; R. A. Smith, 'Roman Roads and the Distribution of Saxon Churches in London', *Archaeologia* 68 (2nd ser. vol. 18, 1917), p. 229 and map on p. 246.   [2] Baker (page 125, note 2), p. 447.

Garrick had a memorial to Shakespeare put up at Hendon, as he did at Hampton; it was a brick obelisk, cement-faced, with statues of Shakespeare and three muses round the foot. It just survives in poor condition near Manor Hall Avenue, N. of the Barnet by-pass road, cut off from the grounds of the hall. An octagonal temple on the line of the new road was demolished. Near the house were two more obelisks, with inscriptions to Garrick and to Shakespeare.[1]

On the opposite side of Parson Street was Hendon Place, on the site of one of the oldest Hendon houses. The de Roos family occupied it in the time of Henry III, and it later belonged to the abbots of Westminster; it passed to the Herberts when the manor was made over to them in 1550 and was occupied by Sir John Fortescue (c. 1600), Compton, Earl of Northampton (17th century), John Aislabie (treasurer of the navy 1714-8; chancellor of the exchequer 1718-21; director of the South Sea Company 1718-21; expelled from Parliament 1721), and Charles Abbott, Lord Tenterden (Lord Chief Justice 1818-32). The present house, now occupied by a school, was built about 1756; it has taken the name of Tenterden Hall.

On each side of Parson Street solid mid-Victorian houses in fair-sized gardens were built for London folk who could keep a carriage. Most of them have been pulled down to make way for flats or houses, huddled more closely together. The district is called Holders Hill.

To the W., over the Watford by-pass road and the Midland main line, is Hendon aerodrome, where some of the earliest flying near London was done from 1908 onwards. The Metropolitan Police College is close beside it; the British Museum newspaper library, seriously damaged in the 1939-45 war, is opposite Colindale station, in an area covered with small houses of no particular distinction.

Beyond Colindale, stretching N. and NW. to the borders of Edgware and Mill Hill, in the district generally known as Burnt Oak, is the London County Council's Watling estate, built between 1926 and 1931. The houses, mostly two-storeyed in groups of four, are interesting as examples of the official suburban planning of that era; they are varied, somewhat too varied, in external finish and disposed in different patterns on a careful plan by G. T. Forrest; but the community's buildings—churches, shops, inns—are comparatively obscure or fitted later into the arrangements. The Saturday afternoon street-market between the Edgware road and Burnt Oak station is a recognisable descendant of the same institution in Camden Town.

Besides the people already mentioned, Hendon has had some residents of distinction: Henry Joynes, architect, conductor and comptroller of the building of Blenheim house 1705-15, d. 1754, buried in the churchyard; Charles Johnson, d. 1748, dramatist; Sir Joseph Ayloffe, antiquary, d. 1781, whose researches were used by Richard Gough for his *Sepulchral Monuments*; Nathaniel Hone, portrait painter who caricatured Sir Joshua Reynolds in a picture called 'The Conjuror,' d. 1784; George Carter, d. 1794, who 'though a very indifferent artist, contrived to raise a fortune'; Thomas Crosfield, acquitted in 1796 of attempting to murder George III by a poisoned dart from an air-gun; Abraham Raimbach, engraver, d. 1843; Emily, first wife of Coventry Patmore, original of his 'Angel in the House'; Thomas Woolner, sculptor, d. 1892;

---

[1] N. G. Brett-James, 'The Garrick-Shakespeare Memorial', *Trans. L. Mx. A. S.* NS 10 (1950), p. 55; E. T. Evans, *History of Hendon* (1890), p. 240.

and Thomas Tilling, founder of the carrying and omnibus undertaking, born at Hendon 1825. Among Hendon clergy were: James Townley, vicar 1772-6, author of the farce *High Life below Stairs* (1756); Henry Bate (later Sir Henry Bate Dudley), curate *c.* 1774, co-founder (1772) and editor of *The Morning Post*; Theodore Williams, vicar for 63 years, 1812-75; F. H. A. Scrivener, New Testament scholar, vicar 1876-91.

HESTON (A1) lies between Southall and Hounslow at the N. edge of Hounslow Heath. The name is today used only of the original village centre and the district immediately about it; HOUNSLOW, HOUNSLOW HEATH, and OSTERLEY are separately noticed. The ancient parish stretched from North Hyde, close to Southall, to the Staines road at Hounslow and from the Brent river in the E. to the edge of Cranford in the W. It thus included the N. part of Hounslow, the settlements of Sutton, Lampton, and Scrattage, and most of Osterley Park.

Heston ('farm in the brushwood district') appears first in the early 12th century; it was commonly called 'Heason' and 'Hesson' until recently. Lampton (1376) is 'lamb farm'; Scrattage (1274), or Crached-hedge, 'hurdle enclosure.' In 1300 Heston was a hamlet within the manor of Isleworth; in 1316 it was a manor belonging to the Crown. It was afterwards granted to St Giles' hospital and was surrendered to Henry VIII in 1537. Elizabeth granted it in 1570 to Sir Thomas Gresham, and its later history is noted under OSTERLEY.

The rich brick-earth of the soil has moulded Heston's aspect and economy. From John Norden in 1593 onwards its wheat was celebrated for fineness, and few topographers since have been able to forbear mentioning that Elizabeth's bread was baked from it. The tradition lingered among the inhabitants as late as 1870.[1] By the beginning of the 19th century the earth itself was being dug up and burnt into bricks, to be transported by canal to London, and some to the Midlands. These were the common brown stocks that most London houses are built with. By the 1860s there were complaints that the level of the ground at Heston was constantly changing because of the removal of brick-earth; osiers were sometimes planted in the pits.[2] Houses now cover most of the S. part of Heston, where the Great West road was built in the 1920s.

The church (St Leonard) stands E. of the green. The 15th-century tower and porch were the only portions of the old church to survive when it was 'most disastrously and inexcusably destroyed' in 1865, in spite of strong protests; it is certainly true that its condition was poor—in 1846 there was complaint of its being 'much injured by Messrs. Economy and Compo.'[3] All the same, it was one of the finest and most interesting churches in Middlesex, with work of the 13th, 14th, and 15th centuries, and its disappearance is lamentable. The tower remains one of the best in the county, with four storeys, square-headed windows, and a bold stair-turret at the SW. angle. By the W. doorway is a remarkably well preserved late 15th-century stoup; the W. porch was reconstructed in 1865, largely from the original timbers. The present nave and chancel (J. Bellamy, 1865) seem cold and dark. There is a brass in the chancel to Mordecai Bownell, vicar 1581 (figure lost), and his wife shown in bed with a child, and there are two 17th-century brasses in the S. chapel.

---

[1] Clutterbuck (see page 40, note 3). [2] R. S. R. Fitter, *London's Natural History* (1946), p. 148; Clutterbuck (see preceding note). [3] J. C. Cox, in *Memorials of Old Middlesex*, ed. J. Tavenor-Perry (1909), p. 48; note in *Trans. L. Mx. A. S.* OS 2 (1864), p. 223; *Builder* 4 (1846), p. 210.

There are 17th- and 18th-century monuments, including a charming stele to John Hudleston Watson with lines from *Lycidas*, a monument to Robert Child, of Osterley Park, 1782, by Robert Adam and P. M. van Gelder, and a plain tablet to Sir Joseph Banks, of Spring Grove, traveller and naturalist, d.1820. The carved oak font-cover is of the early 16th century, made up with modern work. The lych-gate, pivoting on a central beam with a weight to return it to the closed position, was perhaps made by the same craftsman as the one at Hayes; it was originally built in the 15th or 16th century. There are good stones in the churchyard.

There is not much else of note at Heston. Just N. of the church is Ye Old Cote, perhaps of the early 16th century, and St Laurence Cottages, to the W., are 17th-century brick. There is a striking village hall in Victorian Tudor (1867). By the canal is the district of North Hyde, where a cavalry barracks was built in 1793; it is now virtually a part of Southall. The airfield, on the W. side of the parish bordering on Cranford, was used by international airlines during the 1930s but has been supplanted for that purpose by the longer runways of Heathrow and Northolt airports.

HIGHGATE (E3) is the W. portion of HORNSEY. The village centre is situated on a cap of sand and gravel overlying the clay ridge running from Hampstead Heath E. to Crouch End; remnants of the woodland that formerly covered all the area divide it from Hampstead and Finchley, SW. and NW., and from Muswell Hill to the N. The settlement and its name had their origin in the bishop of London's tollgate set up in the 14th century at the top of his new road over the ridge, where it rises to 426 ft. The boundary of Hornsey and Middlesex with St Pancras and London runs from the junction of Hornsey Lane up the middle of Highgate Hill to the gatehouse at the top, thence a little S. of Hampstead Lane, thus leaving a considerable part of Highgate in London. The Middlesex portion of Highgate therefore does not include the lower part of Highgate Hill, Highgate cemetery (where Karl Marx and other notables are buried), or the parish church of 1832 and the adjacent parts, which contain some of the most attractive buildings and interesting associations of the place. In this account the London portions, which are historically associated with St Pancras and the manor of Cantelows (Kentish Town), are only briefly indicated.

Apart from the bishop of London's manor house, which probably stood at Lodge Hill, now part of the Highgate golf course close to the Finchley boundary, and was demolished towards the end of the 15th century (if the tradition that stones from it were used to build Hornsey parish church is correct), the earliest known inhabitants of Highgate were a succession of hermits who dwelt on the site of the present school chapel opposite the gatehouse. By 1600 there were a number of good houses on the S. slope, and at the top of the hill Sir Roger Cholmeley had founded the grammar school (1565); the chapel on the site of the hermitage was given to the school (*c.* 1576) and used by the inhabitants as a chapel of ease to Hornsey.

The village grew in favour with wealthy citizens of London during the 17th century. John Norden in 1593 gave it the character of a health-resort: 'Upon this hill is most pleasant dwelling, yet not so pleasant as healthful; for the

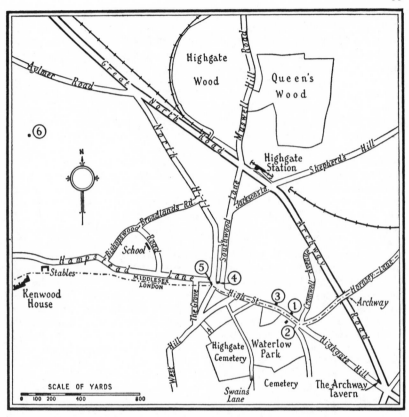

HIGHGATE

*1. Cromwell House. 2. Lauderdale House. 3. Arundel
House. 4. Highgate Chapel. 5. Gatehouse. 6. Site of
Bishop of London's Lodge.*

expert inhabitants here report that
divers who have been long visited with
sickness, not curable by physic, have in
a short time repaired their health by
that sweet salutary air.' Francis Bacon,
however, caught his death in 1626 from
the effects of experimenting on the
preservation of a chicken by stuffing it
with snow, at the foot of the hill; he was
carried to Arundel House, on the W.

side of the hill, and died there. Leaders
of the winning side resided at Highgate
during the Commonwealth, and there
was a strong Nonconformist settlement,
just outside the five-mile radius from
London, dating from 1662. By 1800 it
was a considerable place, rivalling,
though not equalling, Hampstead as a
resort of writers and artists. There was
even a theatre of sorts (in a barn in

Castle Yard) from about 1780 to 1820. The houses then lay along the main North road and in Southwood Lane, which leads from the gatehouse towards Muswell Hill. Archway Road, an easier and more direct route than the old road, was opened, with a tunnel and viaduct (designed by J. Rennie and J. Nash) in 1813 (*Plate 4*); the present bridge (by A. Binnie) dates from 1897. The intervening area was filled up after the Great Northern station, just below the Woodman inn at the top of the Archway hill, was opened in 1867, and horse trams arrived at the foot of the hill in 1871. A cable tramway, the first in Britain, was opened up Highgate Hill in 1884.

The most attractive and interesting building in Highgate is Cromwell House, on the NE. side of the broad sweep of Highgate Hill, half-way between Hornsey Lane and the top. The name, first found in 1833, is misleading: the house was probably built by Richard Sprignell about 1630, and it has no known connexion with Cromwell; Ireton House next door took its name not from General Ireton but from his brother, Sir John Ireton, city merchant and lord mayor in 1658.[1] The house, now the Mothercraft training centre, is a deep-red-brick building of two storeys and attic, with a handsome front on which the brickwork is exceptionally good and varied.[2] There are good plaster ceilings on the first floor, renewed on the lines of the original after a fire in 1865, and there is a remarkable carved oak staircase (1638) with military figures of the period. Additions were made in the 18th century, including the entrance door and the gates and rusticated piers in front, and later. Just N. is a pleasant group with Ireton House and Lyndale House (largely rebuilt about 1730), and Northgate House. As the road narrows

towards the top of the hill there are several smaller 18th-century brick and plaster houses and shops. Opposite are the heavily renovated Lauderdale House (17th-century, now a tea-room for the London County Council's Waterlow Park) to which a story about Nell Gwyn is attached, the site of Andrew Marvell's cottage, and a large Roman Catholic establishment of the Passionist fathers (F. W. Tasker, 1874; additions, 1888).

S. and W. of the gatehouse—a tavern exhibiting no signs of antiquity, except in the narrowing of the road it causes—lies the most agreeable portion of Highgate, at the top of West Hill, with the Grove, large, solid, and handsome 18th-century houses (Coleridge lived at No. 3, 1816-34), and St Michael's church, on the very edge of the hill, built by Lewis Vulliamy in 1832 in the 'impure Perpendicular' style; however impure, its light body and tall spire do not disgrace its situation. It replaced, for the parishioners of Highgate, the ancient chapel at the corner of Southwood Lane opposite the gatehouse; the present building on that site, in a Gothic style, was erected as part of the reconstruction of Highgate school (F. P. Cockerell, 1868). S. T. Coleridge and some of his family were buried in the vault below the chapel. The school, now mostly on the W. side of North Hill, consists of an incongruous assortment of buildings of no great merit. The best-known Old Cholmeleians are G. M. Hopkins, poet, W. W. Skeat, philologist, James Cotter Morison, historian and positivist, and C. Grant Robertson, historian. Nicholas Rowe, poet laureate 1715-8, was at a private school in Highgate before going to Westminster.

North Hill is a broad road with some good houses on the W. side. A. E.

---

[1] The alleged connexion with Cromwell, asserted by the 19th-century historians of Highgate (though not by Lysons) and perhaps an oral tradition somewhat older than 1833, was critically examined by P. Norman (See Bibliography, page 384). It had already been pointed out in 1845 (*Builder* 3 (1845), p. 586, letter from C. J. R[ichardson]), that no connexion with Cromwell or with Ireton had been established. [2] N. Lloyd, *History of English Brickwork* (1925), dates it *c.* 1650; internal decorations prove it to be some 20 years older.

Housman lived at Byron Cottage while writing most of the *Shropshire Lad* poems; George Morland stayed at the Bull tavern to get material for his rural scenes. Where the road begins to fall towards Finchley is Highpoint, a block of flats in cosmopolitan style (Tecton, 1936) and a conspicuous object in any view of the district. The church of All Saints (A. W. Blomfield, 1865) calls for no remark.

Southwood Lane, leading from the gatehouse N. towards Muswell Hill, has some good houses on the E. side, especially at the Highgate end (*Plate 22*), with magnificent views to the SE. The early Highgate Nonconformists established a conventicle in Southwood Lane in 1662, on the site of the existing tabernacle; the first minister (1662-95) was William Rathband, ejected from South Weald, Essex. Highgate dissent was subject to schisms and secessions towards the end of the 18th century: David Williams, founder of the Royal Literary Fund (minister 1769-73), showed sceptical tendencies and was later dignified with the title 'High Priest of Nature'; Rochemont Barbauld (minister 1774-5, husband of Anna Letitia Barbauld, miscellaneous writer) preached a 'liberal' Christianity; and J. B. Pike, minister shortly after, 'adopted various singular opinions not exactly in unison with those of any religious sect' and introduced a liturgy of his own.[1]

W. of Southwood Lane are the Pauncefort almshouses of 1723. Bank Point Cottage, at the corner of Jackson's Lane, is a charming example of a suburban Middlesex dwelling of the early 18th century. Field-Marshal Wade, who has the credit for most of the roads in the Scottish Highlands, lived in a house called Southwood, at the far end of the Lane, after the '45. Across Archway Road are Highgate

Wood and Queen's Wood, as Churchyard Bottom Wood, a plague pit of 1665, was more decorously renamed in 1898. In Archway Road, lower down, is the church of St Augustine (J. D. Sedding, 1885, with additions by H. Wilson).

HIGHWOOD HILL (D2). *See* MILL HILL.

HILLINGDON (B4) lies on the London-Oxford road at the top of the rise from the bridge at Uxbridge—a notable inclination in the uneventful countryside and consequently occupied much earlier than the less defensible site of Uxbridge in the valley. The parish stretches from the Colne above Uxbridge almost to the Grand Junction canal between Hayes and West Drayton. Well wooded and undulating in the N., it presents the familiar dead-level alluvial country in the S. Hillingdon was the ancestor of UXBRIDGE, whose church was a chapel of ease to it until 1842; the modern parish of West Hillingdon is entirely composed of urban Uxbridge.

The earliest form of the name appears to be 'Hildendun' (11th century: 'Hilde's hill'). The manor, with Colham, was held at Domesday by Roger de Montgomery. Colham (or Coleham-cum-Woxebrigge, a fee of the honour of Wallingford) was the more important; the two together covered almost the whole of Hillingdon, Cowley, and Ickenham parishes. After various changes in ownership, Colham passed to the L'Estrange family in 1322 and about 1513 to Stanley, Earl of Derby. It was bought by Sir Robert Vyner in 1669 and in 1782 by Coppinger (later de Burgh).

Hillingdon was a place of some consequence in the Middle Ages. There

---

[1] Lysons, art. Hornsey; J. H. Lloyd, *History of Highgate* (1888), pp. 186, 187 (quoting *Gentleman's Magazine*, 1798); *Transactions of the Congregational History Society* 5 (1912), p. 4.

was a chantry in the church dedicated to St.Thomas of Lancaster (Thomas, Earl of Lancaster, executed 1321), and from 1281 the manor house was occasionally occupied by the bishops of Worcester when travelling to and from London. There was an annual fair. Electric trams arrived in 1904, and a station on the Metropolitan Railway, to the N., was opened in 1923. Cedar House, however, still remains opposite the church, a good brick building of the 17th century named from the cedar planted by Samuel Reynardson in 1683, one of the earliest in England.

The church (St John the Baptist) stands where the main road crosses the ridge 'a long mile' on the London side of Uxbridge; the W. tower, brick faced with flint, boldly placed at the top of the rise, was entirely rebuilt in 1629;[1] it carries a timber cupola above the battlemented parapet. The oldest portion is the chancel arch, about 1260; the nave arcades and the N. and S. aisles date from the middle of the 14th century. At a drastic restoration by Gilbert Scott in 1848 a new chancel, transept, and chapels were built, and there was more restoration in 1902. The roof is modern, with dormer windows in a not unsuitable style. The brasses include one to John L'Estrange, Lord Strange, and his wife, Jacquette Woodville, 1509. The principal monument, on the S. chancel wall, is to Sir Edward Carr, gentleman pensioner to James I, 1637, with kneeling figures of Sir Edward in armour and his wife; opposite is Henry Paget, 1st Earl of Uxbridge, in classical drapery, 1743. The font is Perpendicular, with carved octagonal bowl, supported by lions and savage men. A parochial library in the church, presented by Samuel Reynardson, contains interesting 17th-century books.

Opposite the church is the Red Lion inn, where Charles I stopped for a few hours on 27 April 1646 while escaping from Oxford to the Scottish army at Newark.[2] Hillingdon House was built by Meinhardt, last Duke of Schomberg, in 1717 and was afterwards held by Chetwynd, Talbot, and Rockingham. It is often referred to in Greville's diary and in other memoirs of the 18th and 19th centuries. To the N., up to the Western Avenue, is suburban development of the 1920s and 1930s (*Plate 69*); S. the country is flat and development more scrappy, with market gardens and some old dwellings.

John Rich, 18th-century actor and manager, lived at Cowley Grove in this parish and was buried in the churchyard; he was 'the inventor of the English harlequin' and was noted for the splendid pantomimes he produced at Covent Garden. Major-General Richard Russell, grandson of Oliver Cromwell, was buried at Hillingdon in 1735.

HORNSEY (E3), created a borough in 1903, lies on the London border N. of Islington, bounded E. by Tottenham, N. by Wood Green and Friern Barnet, and W. by Finchley. MUSWELL HILL is on the ridge in the N., HIGHGATE to the W. The S. boundary runs from Manor House, at the E. angle of Finsbury Park, SW. along Seven Sisters Road to Finsbury Park station; the district of Brownswood Park on the London side of the road was transferred to Stoke Newington in 1899. The E. and S. parts of the area are broken and hilly, with two ridges running from the W. to Ferme Park, near Harringay station, and Muswell Hill.

The administrative and shopping centre of the borough is at Crouch End; Stroud Green lies SE. of it, the old

---

[1] J. C. Cox, in *Memorials of Old Middlesex* (1909), p. 51, held that the date 1629 referred only to the doorway and not to the tower itself; but a petition for letters patent authorising the collection of money (1 October 1629) stated that £400 had already been spent on the 'church and steeple' and £400 more was wanted (*M.C.R.*, iii., p. 28). [2] Peck (see page 95, note 3).

church and Hornsey station in the NE., where the New River flows from Wood Green towards Finsbury Park. The district called Hornsey Rise is in London. Hornsey proper, the E. portion of the ancient parish, is mostly a creation of the late Victorian era, with some poor and a good deal of middling layout and building. It contains one first-rate modern work, the town hall at Crouch End.

Hornsey is not mentioned in Domesday Book.[1] It first appears early in the 13th century as 'Haringeie,' developing through many variants to Hornsey; it perhaps means 'hilly region' or possibly 'enclosure of Haer's people.' 'Harringay' was revived in the 19th century and is now used for the NE. part of Hornsey. The name is not free from difficulty, and a considerable pamphlet by Dr. S. J. Madge has been devoted to it. Crouch End (15th-century) signifies the quarter of Hornsey where a cross stood (or at the cross-roads); Stroud Green, also 15th-century, refers to marshy land overgrown with brushwood.

From the earliest mentions of Hornsey the manor belonged to the bishops of London, perhaps forming part of their Stepney properties. They had a residence in the parish, probably at Lodge Hill on the Finchley border in the W.; episcopal documents are dated from 'Haringey' between 1296 and 1335. At Hornsey Great Park in 1387 the Duke of Gloucester and the Earls of Arundel and Nottingham assembled forces to impose their advice on Richard II—a movement that led to Richard's deposition and death. The Duchess of Gloucester was accused in 1441 of having practised some necromancy there to compass the death of Henry VI. From 1647 to 1660 the Church lost the manor, which was sold to Sir John M. Wollaston. There were other manors at Brownswood, in the SE., one of the prebendal manors of St Paul's (often confused with Brondesbury in Willesden),[2] Topsfield, or Broadgates, at Crouch End, Farfields or Farnsfield in the E. portion, and Ducketts, partly in Tottenham. In the manors of Hornsey and the adjoining Cantelows (Kentish Town) lands descended according to the custom of gavelkind—i.e. to all male children in equal shares—as was common in Kent but not elsewhere N. of the Thames.

In the 18th century Hornsey was thoroughly rural, with the influence of London felt only in the establishment of tea gardens and a shooting ground at Hornsey Wood (renamed Finsbury Park after the London borough in 1857). Until about 1870, when the railway began to make significant changes, the district was comparatively open, with some good villas about the hamlets; in April 1866 passengers waiting for the 8.45 at Hornsey station watched a hare being chased and getting away to Haringhey Park.[3] But the end of all this was at hand: Crouch End station was opened in 1867, and Hornsey was already turning into a suburb with a special character of its own; in 1931, 248 in every 1,000 of the occupied population were clerks.[4]

The centre of Hornsey is Crouch End, where, standing back from the High Street, the town hall and its associated buildings (R. H. Uren, 1935) shame their undistinguished neighbours. The unsymmetrical plan, bold tower, and flat brick surfaces owe nothing to traditional ornamental designs. The site and materials are used with an imagination rare, if not unique, in Hornsey, and in a way that would be distinguished anywhere (*Plate 62*).

---

[1] Sharpe (page 12, note 4), p. 209, suggests that Hornsey was a possession of the abbey of St Albans 'lying forfeit in the king's hands when the survey was taken'. It is curious, if this was so, that it was not included with the king's lands enumerated on the first page of the Middlesex survey. S. J. Madge, *Early Records of Harringay alias Hornsey* (1938), p. 31, makes a case for Hornsey being a member of the bishop's principal manor of Stepney. [2] S. J. Madge (see preceding note), p. 49. [3] R. O. Sherington, *Story of Hornsey* (1904), p. 17. [4] *New Survey of London Life and Labour*, dir. H. L. Smith, viii. (London Industries, III) (1934), p. 282.

Tottenham Lane runs NE. past some decrepit ancient cottages to the old and new churches of St Mary. All that remains of the old one is the brick and stone tower, which was built about 1502, to judge from two defaced shields remaining on the W. wall (Thomas Savage, Bishop of London 1496-1501, and William Warham, Bishop of London 1502-3); the upper stages are later. The first church attached to this tower was traditionally said to be built of stone brought from the ruins of the bishops' old mansion on Lodge Hill; it was replaced in 1832 by a new one of white brick, for which 'the Pointed style has been properly adopted,' by G. Smith;[1] this was in turn demolished in 1927, after the nave and chancel of James Brooks' new stone church in the Perpendicular style, designed in 1888, had been built a little way E. If completed with the tower and crocketed spire of 15th-century English type intended for it, this would be the most handsome 19th-century church in Middlesex and a great adornment to Hornsey.[2] As it is, the interior is fine and lofty. Monuments and portions of brasses have been transferred to the new church from the old. The most notable is an incised floor-slab of the late 16th century, showing the figures of George Rey and his two wives; it now stands upright inside the porch. On the E. chancel wall are some fragmentary brasses. There is a marble effigy of Francis Musters, 1680, aged 16, with periwig and cherubs, in the NE. porch, and a miniature monument put up by Margaret, Countess of Cumberland, to Richard Candish, 1601.

N. of the churchyard is Eagle Cottage, a decent 18th-century building with some older panelling inside. A little way W. is the rectory, a pleasant old house with Gothic windows of the early 19th century. Farther along is St George, Priory Road (blitzed), to which the 16th-century octagonal font from the old church was transferred.

The railway effectively detached from Hornsey a small portion lying N. of Finsbury Park and approaching Duckett's Green, close to Turnpike Lane station on the Green Lanes. This portion contains the church of St Peter, Wightman Road (1896), in James Brooks' Early English, in red brick, with two turrets at the W. end.

Hornsey has had some notable rectors: Thomas Westfield, later bishop of Bristol, d. 1644, who never preached, 'except upon extraordinary occasions, more than a quarter of an hour'; Lewis Atterbury, d. 1731, previously at Shepperton; William Cole, d. 1782, antiquary and correspondent of Horace Walpole. John Lightfoot, Hebrew scholar, d.1675, lived at Hornsey; Joshua Toulmin Smith, local government reformer, d. 1869, who lived at Highgate, and Samuel Rogers, the banker poet who refused the laureateship after Wordsworth's death, d. 1855, were buried in the churchyard.

HOUNSLOW (c5) is a suburban town, the modern centre of Heston and Isleworth borough (1932), which lies W. of Brentford where the Staines and Bath roads diverge. It has been a commercial centre with a market since the end of the 13th century. HOUNSLOW HEATH, lying W. of the town, is separately noticed. The place is little but a bustling and unattractive shopping street, with some interest attaching to its historical associations.

The name is found in Domesday as 'Honeslauu,' at that time applied to the hundred later called Isleworth; it means 'the hill of Hund' (probably indicating a personal name, not a dog). A house

[1] *Gentleman's Magazine*, 1832, part ii., p. 12. [2] *Builder* 54 (1888), p.340.

of the Trinitarian or Maturine friars was established about 1211, and a weekly market and annual fair were granted to it in 1296. The friary held land in some of the W. Middlesex parishes, but it was not well endowed. Robert de Hounslow, d. 1430, is recorded as Provincial of the order, which had 12 houses in England and Wales. The priory church survived the Dissolution of the Monasteries and was used as a chapel until demolished in 1828; the place lay, however, within the parishes of Heston and Isleworth, the boundary running down the middle of the Staines road until 1836. The manor was annexed by Henry VIII to the honour of Hampton Court, and was later held by Lord Windsor, Justinian Povey, and Whitelocke Bulstrode, essayist and controversial writer, who bought it in 1705.

At a Parliamentary survey of 1650 Hounslow contained 120 houses, most of them inns and alehouses dependent on travellers; it kept this character until the end of the coaching age. Brewer described it in 1816: 'The chief dependance of the place is on the immense tide of road traffic, which rolls to and from the metropolis with surprising vehemence and bustle ... The principal business of the inns consists in providing relays of post-horses ... All here wears the face of impatience and expedition. The whole population seems on the wing for removal; and assuredly the main street of Hounslow is a place from which the examiner would wish to remove with all the celerity familiar to the spot.'[1] Nimrod, writing in 1832 of a properly turned-out equipage, said: 'Mr. Raby's postillions—for in those days' [about 1800] 'gentlemen's carriages in the country were not driven from the box—were always

Hounslow-bred ones; that is to say, of Hounslow post-boys, having had their education on the road.'[2]

Hounslow is said to have opposed the Great Western Railway of 1835, and a scheme for an atmospheric railway from London in 1845 fell through. Its first station was provided S. of the town on the London and South Western loop line in 1850. But its living had gone with the road traffic, and the place declined. Changes began with the District Railway branch of 1883, and an electric tramway from Hammersmith through Brentford was laid in 1901. The whole area from Whitton (in Twickenham) on the S. towards Heston on the N. became a suburb of common-place type.

The High Street presents few features of interest. The church (Holy Trinity) lies on the N. side, on the site of part of the priory, built of white brick in the semi-Gothic style of 1828; it was destroyed by arson in 1943 (two local schoolboys) but still contains a repaired marble monument of the middle 16th century showing a man in armour and his wife. The town hall, in Treaty Road a little way SW., is a fearsome building of 1904 in brick and terracotta, with an audacious entrance porch in puce glazed tiles. The old council offices, decent Victorian classic of a rural type, now house the Empire cinema on the S. side of the High Street. Opposite is a good late 18th-century shop front, a lonely survival. On the Bath road towards Hounslow West station is a large spired church (St Paul; Habershon and Pike, 1874), and there is a Congregational chapel in Hanworth Road rebuilt in 1835 with a classical front. Otherwise there is nothing that is not mediocre. The place is mostly a collection of streets of the 1880-1914 period, with the better houses in the N.

---

[1] Brayley and Britton, *Beauties of England and Wales* (1816), vol. x., part iv., p. 441. [2] 'Nimrod' (page 224, note 2), p. 18.

and NW. towards the old settlements of Lampton and Sutton.

HOUNSLOW HEATH (B5) is a small piece of open ground between the Bath and Staines roads W. of Hounslow town, the only remaining portion of a large barren tract that extended as far as Stanwell and Harmondsworth until the early 19th century. An act was passed for enclosure in 1545, when the king owned 4,293 acres of waste on the heath, but it escaped all but minor encroachments. Agricultural improvers of the late 18th century denounced the shameful waste of land that it represented, and it was finally parcelled out under a series of enclosure acts between 1789 and 1819; the most important, affecting 7,870 acres in Isleworth, Heston, and Twickenham, was passed in 1813. William James, later a railway engineer, superintended this enclosure,[1] and the heath lost its characteristic appearance of sand and scrub, so that now, except in a few places by the river Crane, there is nothing to remind the traveller of the desolate waste, occupied only by a few small hamlets and beerhouses and by flocks of 'greyhound-like sheep, pitiful half- starved looking animals, subject to rot.' The same agricultural reporter had this district in mind when writing that there were many thousand acres still in a state of nature, and, 'though within a few miles of the capital, as little improved by the labour of man as if they belonged to the Cherokees or any other tribe of American savages.'[2] One writer was scornful of the result: William Cobbett, on his way home to Kensington, found the land between Egham and Hammersmith flat as a pancake and the soil a nasty stony dirt upon a bed of gravel. 'Hounslow Heath, which is only a little worse than the general run, is a sample of all that is bad in soil and villainous in look. Yet this is now enclosed, and what they call cultivated.'[3]

This vacant and useless tract, being crossed by the two western main roads, naturally commended itself to the soldier, the highwayman, and the manufacturer of dangerous substances. Before the sandy wastes of Aldershot were appropriated to the purpose, Hounslow was often a military encampment: in 1267 the people of London under the Earl of Gloucester assembled there in opposition to Henry III; in 1642 the royalist troops, before and after the battle of Brentford; in 1647 the Parliamentary army, mustered under Fairfax; in 1678 Charles II and his army, among whom Evelyn noted 'a new sort of soldiers called *Granadiers*';[4] in 1686-8, James II's army, suspected of dangerous designs on the constitution but ready, as it proved, to welcome the acquittal of the Seven Bishops in 1687.[5] Accommodation of various kinds was provided: James had a wooden Roman Catholic chapel, apparently portable (it was later stabilised at Conduit Street in Mayfair); there was apparently also a camp hospital. Hospital Bridge Road, towards Twickenham on the S. edge of the heath, may refer to this institution.[6]

The heath continued in use as review ground until the 1740s; cavalry barracks were built between the Bath and Staines roads in 1793, and in 1818 some 300 acres were retained as an exercise ground. In 1875 infantry barracks were built farther S., which served for a time as the depot for the Middlesex Regiment and the Royal Fusiliers. These associations are commemorated by the names of inns at the heath end of modern Hounslow—the Hussar, the Light Horse, the Duke

[1] E. M. S. P[laine], *Two James's and Two Stephensons* (1861), p. 15.　[2] T. Baird, *General View of the Agriculture of the County of Middlesex* (1793), p. 7.　[3] Cobbett (page 39, note 2), i., p. 124.　[4] J. Evelyn, *Diary* 29 June 1678.　[5] J. Evelyn, *Diary* 18 July 1691; P. Cunningham, *Handbook for London* (1849), art. Conduit Street.　[6] *Historical Manuscripts Commission, Dartmouth MSS.*, iii. (1896), p. 143; Maxwell (page 38, note 3), p. 49, holds that the name implies medieval ownership by the Hospitallers, otherwise unrecorded.

of Wellington. Hounslow Heath was chosen by General Roy in 1784 for the base line for the triangulation on which the Ordnance Survey was built up; it ran about 5¼ m. from Heathrow to Hampton Hill and is still marked on the one-inch Ordnance map.

The heath was big enough in the 17th and 18th centuries to allow both soldiers and highwaymen to practise on it without much interference from one another. Its reputation as a dangerous stretch for the traveller was approached by only Finchley common; it was infested, especially after the end of William III's and Anne's wars, by marauders who easily defied the rudimentary forces of law and order until in the early 19th century three things combined to suppress them: enclosure of the commons; refusal of licences to the public houses that sheltered them; and mounted police patrols. (It was an ostler from Hounslow who told George Borrow that.[1]) They were an unattractive set of characters, though sentimental writers have tried to persuade their readers otherwise. When they were at last caught, as most of them were, their bodies were strung up on gibbets beside the roads. Some gibbet stumps were dug up when the Hounslow tramway was being laid in 1901.

Two industries, now extinct in Middlesex, have flourished on the SE. corner of the heath: swords and powder. Iron was forged in Isleworth and Hounslow in 1514, and a sword-blade factory was established by Benjamin Stone in 1630. 'Sword-mills' were still in existence near Baber Bridge, where the Staines road crosses the Crane, in 1783.[2] The sword mills closed c.1670 and were converted to gunpowder mills. Powder mills were established near the same spot by the middle of the 16th century, and James

I granted a charter to the Hounslow manufacturers. They were most notable for their explosions, which are recorded at various dates between 1758 and 1915; Horace Walpole complained bitterly of one in January 1772 which damaged Strawberry Hill: 'The north side of the castle looks as if it had stood a siege. The two saints in the hall have suffered martyrdom. They have their bodies cut off, and nothing remains but their heads.'[3] On 11 March 1850 there was an explosion that was felt 50 m. away near Chichester in Sussex and made all the pheasants in the Lavington woods crow at once.[4]

ICKENHAM (B3) is a parish in Uxbridge urban district, lying W. of Ruislip and NE. of Hillingdon, mostly on a flat plain, with its N. extremity verging on the wooded area of Harefield. The Yeading brook meanders about the S. part of the parish. Ickenham has not escaped being built over, but it has escaped the dismal anarchy that prevails S. of the main Uxbridge road. The village green has an air of being a village green, and there are quite rustic farms on the London side of the Metropolitan Railway.

Ickenham means 'Ticca's farm'; it had its 'T' as 'Ticheham' in Domesday. The manor was then held by three knights and one Englishman under Roger de Montgomery. Ickenham manor remained after 1348 in the family of Shordich; Swakeley manor—the name derived from Robert de Swalclyve (Swalecliffe, Kent)—was in the Charlton family from 1350 to 1486 and was bought in 1629 by Sir Edmund Wright; his daughter Catherine married Sir James Harrington, one of the judges of Charles I, who sold it in 1665 to Sir Robert Vyner. In 1750 it was sold to the Clarke family.

[1] G. Borrow, *Romany Rye* (Everyman ed.), p. 145.   [2] Bate (see page 53, note 5), p. 279, quoting Exchequer Accounts, 1514.   [3] H. Walpole to H. S. Conway, 7 January 1772.   [4] Murray's *Handbook for Sussex* (ed. 4, 1877), p. 142.

The village was purely agricultural. In 1904 the Metropolitan Railway's Uxbridge branch cut across the parish. Northolt airfield occupies much of the SE. part of the area, outer-suburban houses and gardens the centre.

The house and park of Swakeleys, occupied since 1929 by the Foreign Office Sports Association, lie NW. of the Uxbridge-Ruislip road. Built by Sir Edmund Wright between 1629 and 1638 in red brick with stone or plaster dressings, it is a good and comparatively unaltered example of the country houses with curved Dutch gables that were being built under Charles I. Sir James Harrington made some alterations a few years later, and Sir Robert Vyner (visited there by Pepys on 7 September 1665) completed the interior decorations; the staircase paintings are attributed to Robert Streater, about 1670-80. An interesting 17th-century wooden screen, painted as stone and marble, is on the ground floor, with busts of Charles I and Fairfax (a third, of Essex, has found its way into the church). The stables and a dovecote are contemporary with the house (*Plate 41*).

The church (St Giles) stands N. of the village green. It is a pleasing little building of flint rubble and brick, with tiled roofs and a wooden bell-turret of the same characteristic NW. Middlesex family as Greenford, Northolt, and Cowley. The nave and chancel were built in the late 14th century; the N. aisle and S. porch were added by William Say about 1575-80—the only surviving example of this period in a Middlesex church. The present vestry on the N. was built as a mortuary chapel about 1640-50, probably by the Harringtons of Swakeleys. The chancel arch and the harsh N. nave arcade were rebuilt during the 19th century. Modern dormer windows have been inserted to light the interior. A brass of 1584 and monuments clown to 1940 commemorate the Shordich family, and there are two brasses to the Says. A charming marble effigy of the infant son of Sir Robert Clayton, 1665, lies on the S. window-sill of the chancel with the words 'Of such is yᵉ Kingdom of Heaven'; the same child is also commemorated on the monument of his father, founder of St Thomas's and Christ's hospitals, at Bletchingley, Surrey. There are slabs to the Harringtons and Vyners, a 17th-century bust of the Earl of Essex in armour from the screen at Swakeleys, and a tablet by Thomas Banks to J. G. Clarke, 1800. Bits of 16th-century wall painting remain in different places. An unsuitable carved representation of Leonardo's 'Last Supper' adorns the S. chancel wall.

SE. of the church are Ickenham Hall, an 18th-century house, and Manor Farm, with a moat, dating from the early 16th century. The fields beyond are quaintly rural for Middlesex, with aircraft roaring overhead most of the time. There are other old farms and barns in the parish; the barns include one of 5 bays at Milton farm, SW. of the church.

The only inhabitant of Ickenham to achieve more than local note was Roger Crab, a Commonwealth soldier who developed eccentricities of belief and diet, was given to quackery and prophecy, and died at Bethnal Green in 1680.

ISLEWORTH   (c5)   (pronounced *eyezelw'th*) is a large area extending from the Thames between Twickenham and SYON HOUSE (noticed separately) SW. to the boundary of Feltham on Hounslow Heath and N. to Osterley Park and the edge of Hanwell. The ancient parish included the parts of HOUNSLOW (noticed separately) S. of the London-Staines road. The Brent forms part of its boundary on the NE., and the Crane flows out into the Thames at the S. It has formed part of Heston and Isleworth borough since 1932.

Isleworth has various aspects: most of its river front has happily been preserved as the park of Syon House; the riverside village has been subject to the process of change and decay, though traces of occupation by aristocrats and substantial citizens remain; the SW. corner is comparatively open, retaining some of the market gardens for which the place was once famous; the NW. is mostly plain suburban, though remains of a Victorian building speculation give a different character to Spring Grove.

The name is found in the earliest recorded Middlesex charter, a copy of a list dated 695 recording gifts to the nuns of Barking; it appears there as 'Gislheresuuyrth,' from a personal name, Gislhere.

The manor, which then included Heston and Twickenham, was granted by William the Conqueror to Walter de St Valéry. It was vested in the Crown in 1227, and in 1229 Henry III gave it to his brother Richard, Earl of Cornwall and King of the Romans. In 1264 Hugh le Despenser went out to Isleworth, according to Holinshed's chronicle, 'with a great multitude of the citizens of London, and they spoiled the manor-place of the king of Romans and destroyed his water-mills and other commodities that he there had.' When Henry had suppressed the barons' revolt, London had to pay 1,000 marks as reparation. The manor remained vested in the Crown and was annexed to the duchy of Cornwall. In 1421 Henry V by act of Parliament transferred the manor to his new convent of Brigittine nuns at Syon. The Crown

retained it after the Dissolution until James I granted it in 1604 to Percy, Earl of Northumberland, from whom it descended to the dukes of Northumberland, who still hold it. There were sub-manors at Worton, or Eyston's, and Wyke. Records of several commotions attending the beating of Isleworth bounds have survived: in 1439 judgment was given that, for preservation of the peace, the Isleworth procession should perambulate the parish bounds on Monday or Tuesday in procession-week, the Twickenham procession on Wednesday[1]; some 100 years later there is evidence of an affray between Isleworth and Heston parties on the same errand[2]; and in 1582 Isleworth and Hanwell processions collided at Brentford bridge.[3]

A copper and brass mill was established at Isleworth about 1582. The ore was brought from Worley Hill, in the Mendips, and Norden (1593) reported 'many artificial devices' employed on the work.[4] The mill was probably on the site of the present brewery, and Brazil Mill Lane (now St John's Road) is thought to have been named from it; the mill was marked as 'decayed' on a map of 1623.

In the 17th and 18th centuries Isleworth provided residences for the court and the City. It was a scattered parish, with separate settlements noted by Lysons in 1794 at Isleworth, Hounslow, Worton, Rails-head, Brentford End, Whitton Dean, Smallbury Green, Sion Hill, Wyke Green, and Brazil Mill Lane. Between the hamlets the ground was largely devoted to fruit-gardens; raspberries were cultivated, especially for distilling, and table fruit was carried to Covent Garden market by women who came up to work during the season 'principally from Shropshire and the neighbourhood of Kingsdown in Wilt-

[1] *H.C.M.* 6 (1904), p. 160.   [2] Lysons, art. Isleworth.   [3] M. Sharpe, *Account of Bygone Hanwell* (1924), p. 76.   [4] See Part I, page 53.

shire'; they carried their loads on the head and were said to make 5 m. an hour.[1] Water for the gardens was lifted from wells by a bucket suspended from a counter-balanced pole, like the *shaduf* of the Nile valley. There was also a pottery, from 1750 to about 1830 near Railshead Creek and then removed to the Hanworth road at Hounslow until it ceased work about 1855; it produced first common Welsh ware and earthenware, and later earthenware in bright colours, looking like bronze and red sealing-wax. Apparently it did not produce porcelain.[2]

An early experiment in co-operative ownership began at Isleworth in 1801, when about 120 members of the Good Intent Society jointly acquired a corn mill. The transaction got some notoriety when hundreds of men joined the society and thus, as they claimed, became entitled to freeholders' votes, which they used for Sir Francis Burdett at the election of 1802. After much controversy, Burdett was unseated in 1806.[3]

Dissent does not seem to have been strong at Isleworth, but there was a Roman Catholic chapel in the middle of the 18th century, the only one at that date in rural Middlesex. It was established in Shrewsbury House (by Lion wharf, in the middle of the village) where Lady Shrewsbury, d. 1752, lived as an avowed Roman Catholic after the Duke of Shrewsbury's death in 1718. The registers date from 1746, with entries referring to Brentford, Hayes, Hounslow, Teddington, Twickenham, Sunbury, and some places on the Surrey side.[4]

In 1801 Isleworth was the most populous of the Middlesex Thames-side places, but while it grew steadily it did not increase so fast as Chiswick or Twickenham. The London and South Western Railway opened its Hounslow loop with a station at Spring Grove in

1849; trams arrived in 1901-2. The 20th century has so far left Syon park untouched; the parish church has been burnt out and so followed most of the surrounding buildings into dilapidation; public institutions fill much of the ground N. of the village, and a gigantic sewage purification works at Mogden occupies the SW. Isleworth is, in the elegant modern phrase, 'ripe for redevelopment.'

The centre of old Isleworth is a riverside group by the S. lodge of Syon park, where a ferry plies to the opposite bank; there is a picturesque look about the place from certain angles. Ferry House (gutted), with the Syon House garden pavilion or boathouse overlooking the river (J. Wyatt, c. 1800), used to form a charming scene. Ferry House was rebuilt to the original design 1951-2 and with the boathouse (now established as having been designed by Robert Mylne) continues to form a charming scene. The church (All Saints) was a curious jumble; the small tower, late 15th-century, has square-headed windows and a battlemented top with corner pinnacles; the nave was a rectangular classical building of 1706, said to derive in part from a design by Wren,[5] with round-headed windows and N., W., and S. galleries; the chancel was an incongruous Gothic addition of 1866. The body of the church was burnt out, not by enemy action, in 1943. There were several brasses, including one to Margaret Dely, 'a sister professed in Syon,' 1561, and a man in armour, c. 1450. The monuments included a draped tablet to Sir Theodore de Vaux, physician to Charles II, 1694; George Keate, by Nollekens, 1794; Sir Orlando Gee, by Francis Bird, 1705; and Mrs. Dash, by William Halfpenny, about 1758; the two last, under the tower, are least seriously damaged. There have been some notable vicars: John Hall, hanged at

---

[1] Lysons, art. Isleworth. [2] See page 54, note 2. [3] Bate (see page 53, note 5), pp. 124, 224. [4] See page 114, note 3. [5] This tradition goes back well into the 18th century (Lysons, art. Isleworth), The Wren Society (vol. xix. (1942), p. xii.) do not dismiss the possibility.

Tyburn 1535 for denying Henry VIII's supremacy in the Church; Nicholas Byfield, Calvinistic writer (father of Adoniram Byfield, clerk of the Westminster assembly under the Commonwealth), d. 1622; William Grant, who published a pamphlet in 1641 entitled *The Vindication of the Vicar of Isleworlh, in the County of Middlesex, from a Scandalous Pamphlet*; and William Drake, antiquary and philologist, d. 1801.

Close to the church, by the waterside, is the ancient London Apprentice inn, with an 18th-century bay window added to the first floor in 1905; at some periods it used to stay open all night for river travellers.[1] Beyond is the old village, with a few features of good antiquity relieving a general down-at-heel appearance. The Tolson almshouses in Church Street are as ugly as 1860 could make them; the Ingram group, dated 1664, is a pleasant brick building on Mill Plat.

The principal houses of the riverside were Lacy House, built for James Lacy, patentee of Drury Lane theatre, later occupied by R. B. Sheridan; Kendal House, occupied by Mme von der Schulenburg, Duchess of Kendal, d. 1743, converted into a place of entertainment, 1750; Gumley House, Twickenham Road, about 1700, with modern additions as a Roman Catholic convent; Isleworth House (E. Blore, 1832); Gordon House; St Margaret's House (L. Vulliamy, 1852), at the head of the reach above the ferry. Nearly all have been demolished; the few survivors house institutions. Almost opposite Gumley House is a tablet on 158 Twickenham Road recording that Vincent van Gogh lived there in 1876, when he taught Bible history at Mr. Jones's chool and preached on Sundays in Bible Christian chapels at Turnham Green and Richmond.[2]

St John's Road, the modern name for Brazil Mill Lane where the brass mill stood, leads to the 19th-century settlement called Spring Grove (formerly Smallbury Green) round the railway station. The church of St John (1857) is a stone building in the Early English style of that date, with a good tower.

N. of the London road, on the site of the Spring Grove estate, are large houses of the 1850s built by an unfortunate speculator who tried to establish a fashionable suburb of villa residences. The house of Spring Grove was altered and extended 1892-4 for Andrew Pears, of Pears soap works, having previously been occupied by Sir Joseph Banks, explorer, naturalist, and president of the Royal Society, d. 1820 and buried at Heston; it is now used for a secondary school and polytechnic. The church of St Mary, Osterley Road, is an unpleasant object (J. Taylor, jun., 1856) covered with hairy creeper. Just W., in Witham Road, R. L. Stevenson attended Burlington Lodge school (now St. Vincent's) in 1863. To the E. is the Borough Road teachers' training college; the main block, in the style of Gothic then considered appropriate for educational buildings, was erected for the International College by J. Norton and P. E. Masey in 1867. Frederick Delius and Maurice Hewlett attended the International College.

There remain some former inhabitants of Isleworth who cannot be associated with any particular building: George Calvert, Lord Baltimore, secretary of state to James I and original grantee of Maryland, d. 1632; Dorothy Sidney, whom Edmund Waller courted in verse as 'Sacharissa,' b. 1617; Peter Scheemakers, sculptor, an inhabitant in 1771; and George Keate, d. 1797, author of *The Distressed Poet* (an account of a quarrel with Robert Adam, the

[1] *H.C.M.* 7 (1905), p. 245. [2] See page 162, note 1.

architect), *Sketches from Nature in a Journey to Margate* (in imitation of Sterne), and *An Account of the Pelew Islands.* Margaret Howard, whose wedding to Roger Boyle at St Martin in the Fields in 1641 was the occasion of Sir John Suckling's *Ballad on a Wedding*, was born at Syon House.

KEMPTON (B6). *See* SUNBURY.

KENSAL RISE (D4). *See* WILLESDEN.

KENTON (C3). *See* HARROW and WEMBLEY.

KILBURN (D4). *See* WILLESDEN.

KINGSBURY (D3) (now in Wembley borough) lies W. of Hendon between the outskirts of Edgware in the N. and Wembley Park station in the SW. It is separated by the Brent, here dammed to form the Welsh Harp reservoir, from Willesden on the S. and by the Edgware road from Hendon to the E. The land is the heavy clay of NW. Middlesex, with a few undulations but no prominent features; in earlier centuries mostly wooded, it was turned over to grass-farms supporting a small population and then to the suburban houses that have submerged the little hills and the plain between Hendon and Harrow. The ancient church lies at the extreme S., overlooking the Brent valley and its reservoir; in the 19th century a settlement grew up at Kingsbury Green farther N., on the road from Hendon to Harrow, and between 1920 and 1940 almost the whole district was filled up.

The name Kingsbury—the king's manor or stronghold—is first found about 1044-6. The original name of the manor appears to have been 'Tunworth.' There were two manors at the time of Domesday: one belonged to Westminster Abbey.[1] It was held under

the Earl of Lancaster in 1317 and in 1439 was bought, like Edgware, for All Souls College, Oxford. The other, later called Freren *alias* Kingsbury, belonged to the priory of St John of Jerusalem; after the Dissolution it was granted to St Paul's.

Kingsbury has no recorded history. Its only noteworthy association is with Oliver Goldsmith, who lodged in a cottage in Hyde Lane in 1768 and wrote *She Stoops to Conquer* (1771) and *Animated Nature* (1772-4) at Mr. Selby's, a farmhouse on the Kingsbury side of the Edgware road near the 6th milestone.[2] Joshua Reynolds, Johnson, and Boswell visited him there.[3] Trams along the Edgware road began to operate in 1904; settlement spread northward from Wembley Park station, very slowly after its opening in 1894, faster after 1920; and stations on the new Metropolitan Railway line to Stanmore were opened in 1932 and 1934 called Kingsbury and Queensbury (a coined name) in the NW. part of the district.

The old parish church (St Andrew) stands on a knoll overlooking the Brent. It is an antiquarian's puzzle. The walls contain some Roman material, and the W. angles of the nave have quoins of modified 'long-and-short' type, which generally indicate late pre-Conquest work; on the other hand there are indications that the whole building was reconstructed in the 13th century, when the chancel was certainly built. The church is a plain rectangle, with a simple wooden bell-turret (rebuilt in 1870) of a type familiar farther W. in Middlesex, as at Northolt and Ickenham. It was carefully restored in 1888, when the S. door-arch of the 12th century was brought to light and the timber porch added, to a design taken from an old engraving preserved in the

---

[1] Edgware was perhaps included within this manor at Domesday (*Trans. L. Mx. A. S.* NS 7 (1937), p. 159). [2] There are suggested identifications in *Mx. & H. N. & Q.* 1 (1895), pp. 31, 82. [3] J. Boswell, *Life of Samuel Johnson* (Oxford ed., 1933), i., p. 460 (April 1772).

Guildhall library. The W. gallery and ceiling disappeared at this time.[1] The font is 13th-century, and the lectern is formed from a late 17th-century carved oak figure of an angel, probably from a demolished City church. By the 1930s, however, this church had become far too small, and St Andrew, Wells Street (Dawkes and Hamilton, 1847), was brought from Marylebone and re-erected just NW.

Kingsbury Green, with a church (Holy Innocents, 1884) on the road to Hendon, has nothing to commend it. Slough Lane and Honeypot Lane no longer wear the clay surfaces commemorated in their names; 'honey,' in old Middlesex field names, has the significance of something gluey. At Roe Green, N. of Kingsbury Road, is a housing estate (Sir Frank Baines) for munition workers of the 1914-18 war, with a village green consciously worked into the scheme and all the existing trees retained. It is a pity that more of modern Kingsbury does not look like this.

Stag Lane, farther N., gave its name to an aerodrome prominent in the earliest days of aviation, later cut up for building. There are one or two weather-boarded cottages at the S. end of Stag Lane, a weird outburst of towers and battlements in Buck Lane, and some artificial old-world creations heavy with thatch and make-up. For the rest, Kingsbury merges with Kenton and Stanmore in an unremarkable region of pink-brick houses, recreation grounds, small factories, road roundabouts, and bus stops.

LALEHAM (A6) is a pleasant Thames-side village 2 m. SE. of Staines, where Dr. Thomas Arnold and his son Matthew lived for some years. A few acres on the Surrey side of the river opposite the village are in Middlesex; Surrey correspondingly takes some of the left bank 1½ m. lower down opposite Chertsey lock. The parish is completely flat, and the fields share the featureless nature of the W. part of Middlesex.

Laleham (*lael*, withy; *hamm*, bend in the river) belonged to Westminster Abbey in 1254. It was annexed to the honour of Hampton Court under Henry VIII and in 1606 was granted by the Crown to Spiller; it was later owned by Lowther, Earl of Lonsdale, and Bingham, Earl of Lucan. The roads and riverside through the village have been fully built up except where the park of Laleham House runs down to the Thames. Among much indifferent modern building the Three Pigeons, a 17th-century inn, and Dial House with a sundial dated 1730 are noteworthy; both are on the Shepperton road.

The church (All Saints) has a patchwork brick exterior with a short brick W. tower built in 1732, of curious design with four stone pilasters surmounted by a brick battlement. The nave arcades date from the late 12th century; a N. chapel was added in 16th-century red brick; the N. aisle and chancel are 19th-century, though the 16th-century brick chancel arch survives. A large painting by G. Harlow, 1811, hangs at the W. end. The best monument is in the chancel to Sir George Perrott, Baron of the Exchequer, 1780, by W. Tyler, and there is one by Chantrey to Henrietta Hartwell, 1818.

Laleham House, S. of the village, is a plain mansion with a Tuscan portico, designed by J.B. Papworth in 1803 for the Earl of Lucan. The 3rd Earl, d. 1888, commanded the Heavy Brigade of cavalry at Balaclava.

Dr. Thomas Arnold taught private pupils at Laleham from 1819 until his appointment as headmaster of Rugby

[1] *Builder* 59 (1889), p. 225.

in 1828. A brass tablet on the N. wall of the church commemorates him. Matthew Arnold, born at Laleham on 24 December 1822, is buried in the churchyard with three sons who died in childhood. He lived in the village as a pupil of his uncle John Buckland from 1830 to 1836 and, like his father, often revisited it. After one visit he wrote to his mother (2 January 1848): 'Today after morning church I went up to Pentonhook. I was yesterday at the old house and under the cedars and by the old pink acacia.' The cedars still stand by the Ashford road, but there is not much else about Laleham except its church that Matthew Arnold would recognise.

LAMPTON (c5). *See* HESTON.

LITTLE STANMORE (c2). *See* STANMORE, LITTLE.

LITTLETON (b6) is a parish 3 m. SE. of Staines, shaped like a wedge with the point running down to the Thames at Chertsey bridge. The area is quite flat and devoted to agriculture, pleasantly diversified with trees. The small village lies 1m. from the river, just N. of the Staines-Shepperton road.

The name is first found in 1042; it signifies a small enclosure or farm. The manor was apparently detached from Laleham during the 12th century; it was held by Blunt, Windsor of Stanwell, Seymour, Earl of Hertford, and others, and was bought in the 18th century by the Wood family, who had held the manor of Astlam within the parish since 1660.[1] The Woods, of whom General Sir David Edward Wood, d. 1894, was the most distinguished figure, lived at Littleton Park until it was burned down in 1874. Their house was contemporary with the William-and-Mary portion of Hampton Court and may have been built by the same workmen. After rebuilding it was occupied by the Burbidge family; now, with appropriate additions, it houses film studios.

The church (St Mary Magdalene) is a small and attractive building with 12th-century work in the main fabric and a 15th-century brick clerestory above; the tower, dating from the early 16th century, had an unroofed upper stage added in the 18th century. The chancel, longer than the nave, has a brick mausoleum on the N., built for the Woods in 1705 and later extended. The interior has some good fittings: 17th-century Flemish carved communion rails; simple 15th-century pews; a good 18th-century pulpit; an octagonal font of the 13th century; a heavy iron-bound chest; and 15th- or early 16th-century screen and stalls. There is a brass to Blanche Vaughan, 1553. The nave is decked with a series of 24 colours of the Grenadier Guards presented by Colonel, later General, Thomas Wood in 1855. The most noticeable monument in the churchyard is the extremely large tomb of Sir Richard Burbidge (1917) and Sir R. Woodman Burbidge (1945).

The rectory, E. of the church, and parts of the old manor house contain old work. Almost the whole area N. of the village, including the settlement of Astlam and the only considerable wooded area in SW. Middlesex, was submerged by the huge Queen Mary reservoir, opened in 1925, whose embankment frowns down on the church. It has a central breakwater to reduce the force of the waves on its banks.

Chertsey, sometimes called Littleton, bridge is the successor to a ferry mentioned in 1299. About 1535 Leland noted 'a goodly bridge of timber, newly repaired' there; the present one, of

[1] Table of lords and tenants of Littleton manor, T. C. Wignall, *Life of Commander Sir Edward Nicholl* (1921), p. 228.

7 stone arches, was designed by James Payne and opened in 1785.

LONGFORD (A5). *See* HARMONDS-WORTH.

MIDDLESEX GUILDHALL (E4), though not situated within the administrative county, demands notice in an account of Middlesex because of the historical associations of its site and because it is the county council's headquarters.[1] Moreover, the building has architectural merit of its own.

The site in Parliament Square, occupied by the old belfry of the abbey of Westminster and later by the Three Tuns tavern, was used as a market from 1750 to about 1800; the justices for the Liberties of Westminster then took it over, and a new guildhall was built in 1805 (octagonal, with Doric portico, by S. P. Cockerell). It became the headquarters of the new Middlesex County Council, in exchange for the sessions house at Clerkenwell, by agreement with the County of London after the Local Government Act of 1888, and a new guildhall of indeterminate neo-Tudor appearance was put up (F. H. Pownall, 1893). The foundations of the old belfry, with great cellars once used as a sanctuary, remained until this building gave way to the present one in 1913.

Challenged by the fearful difficulty of designing a new building in a square containing Westminster Abbey and St Margaret's church on the S. and Westminster Hall and Charles Barry's Houses of Parliament on the E., not to mention J. M. Brydon's Edwardian-classic Ministry of Health on the N., the architect (J. S. Gibson) adopted a mature Gothic style, simple and generally unostentatious, in Portland stone. Only the central porch and the tower above are full of decorative feature; otherwise the exterior is comparatively plain except in the window details. It is thus harmonious with its surroundings, yet distinctive: one of the best 20th-century buildings in inner London.

The porch bears decorative stone carvings (H.C. Fehr) of historic Westminster and Middlesex scenes (Magna Carta island at Runnymede being annexed to Middlesex for the purpose); the effect is rich without being heavy. Inside are a handsome staircase and council chamber, the county memorial of the 1914-18 war, and some good and more interesting portraits. These include Sir Baptist Hicks, Viscount Campden (d. 1629), by Van Somer; Sir John Fielding, d. 1780, by N. Hone; William Mainwaring, chairman of Quarter Sessions 1781-1816, by Gainsborough; Hugh Smithson, Duke of Northumberland, d. 1786, by Reynolds. The Middlesex county records, running in a continuous series since 1549, are at present housed on the lowest floor, and they are constantly being added to as manorial and other private documents are deposited there for safe keeping.[2]

MILL HILL (D2) lies at the N. of Hendon borough, between Edgware on the W., Elstree on the N., and Totteridge, in Hertfordshire, on the E. The main feature is a well-defined ridge; the old village is disposed along it, clearly distinguished from the modern settlement, mostly built up between 1920 and 1940, to the S. and W. about the Watford by-pass road and the railway stations. The ridge retains an open aspect and enjoys good views, with extensive tracts reserved from building by the grounds of Mill Hill school on the W. and the London

[1] C. W. Radcliffe. *Middlesex* (1939).   [2] See Bibliography, section A, page 371.

'Green Belt' on the E. and N. There are some attractive, if not specially notable, old domestic buildings; a selection of notable, if not always attractive, new ones for institutions of various kinds; and a striking church in the new quarter.

Mill Hill cannot be certainly traced farther back than 1547. It first comes into notice as anything more than a farming hamlet at the Restoration period, when it provided a convenient retreat for Richard Swift, the ejected puritan incumbent of Edgware, to set up a school about 1665 and for Quakers to assemble at meetings which George Fox sometimes visited. Lord Russell, executed for complicity in the Rye House plot, 1683, had a house at Highwood; Peter Collinson, botanist, established a celebrated garden on the W. side of the Ridgeway about 1750; and Belmont was built for Sir Charles Flower, lord mayor of London, about 1765. Apart from sporadic development at the Hale, the district remained rural, with a number of good houses and the institutions on the higher ground, until about 1925. Since then the lower parts have been almost completely filled up.

The road from Hendon climbs up Bittacy Hill to the Ridgeway. On the E. side are the melancholy buildings of the barracks named after Colonel Inglis, the heroic commander of the 57th Foot at the battle of Albuera. Farther E., on the Finchley border, are Frith Manor House, late 18th-century successor to a Westminster Abbey property, and Nether Court (Elizabethan of 1882). At the top of the hill is the Medical Research Laboratory (M. Ayrton, 1950), a tall building, not ill-looking though it usurps too much of the skyline. On the NE. beyond Burton Hole Lane is Littleberries, a charming

17th-century house, popularly associated with Nell Gwyn; incongruous additions were made during conversion into St Vincent's convent, including a chapel by F. W. Tasker (1887).

On the SW. of the Ridgeway are the main buildings of Mill Hill school, which, like most English public schools, is an architectural mess. They stand on the site of Peter Collinson's Ridgeway House and botanical garden; the main block presents to the road a seemly and dignified brown brick front, with a classical portico and flat pilasters, weak but not without charm, by William Tite (1825). The war memorial gateway in front (S. Hamp, 1921) is classical in another convention. The opposite side of the school building is a fine elevation with bold portico, commanding good wooded views SW. The chapel, at the NW. end of the range, is a red-brick basilica (B. Champneys, 1896). Included in the buildings is J. A. H. Murray's 'scriptorium,' where three tons of paper slips bearing quotations were sorted and stored before publication of the *New* (or *Oxford*) *English Dictionary* began in 1884. Murray was a master from 1870 to 1885. School boarding houses are in Wills Grove, S. of the main buildings; Burton Bank (S. Hamp, 1935) is a modern work of some note.

Farther along the Ridgeway is the church of St Paul, built in 1829 in cockney-Gothic, with pinnacles at the corners but no tower or spire; a dispute between William Wilberforce, of Highwood Hill, largely responsible for its erection, and Theodore Williams, vicar of Hendon, who was much opposed to Evangelicals in general,[1] delayed its consecration until 1836. Beyond, on Hammers Lane, is a group of weatherboard cottages (*Plate 20*); opposite is Belmont (1765, attributed to the brothers Adam), now occupied

[1] Demetrius Boulger, *Life of Sir Stamford Raffles* (1897), p. 387.

by Mill Hill junior school. W. of the road as it descends is St Mary's abbey, a Franciscan convent; SW. of it, approached from Lawrence Street, is St Joseph's college for foreign missionaries (Goldie and Child, 1871), surmounted by a large and conspicuous gilded statue of the saint, known to irreverent locals as 'Holy Joe.' Cardinal H. A. Vaughan, d. 1903, founder, was buried in the grounds.

Beyond a dip in the road is the picturesque settlement of Highwood Hill. Highwood Ash, E. of the road, is an early 18th-century house; the Rising Sun inn, looking down the hill, is older. Highwood House, a pleasant, undistinguished building (J. Johnson, c. 1780), the first house on the road to Totteridge, was Stamford Raffles' home during his short retirement (1825-6) after his proconsulship in Java and Singapore. The 17th-century Lord Russell had a house here, where his widow continued to live after his execution in 1684. A well in the garden of Highwood Park is inscribed: 'Mrs. Rachell Russells gift, June y.10. 1681'; at one period its water was considered to have medicinal virtues.[1] Almost opposite is Highwood Hill, where William Wilberforce, Evangelical and emancipator of the slaves, lived from 1826 until 1831.[2] Raffles and Wilberforce owned the hamlet between them.

To the N. is Moat Mount, home of Serjeant E. W. Cox, d. 1879, Proprictor of *The Law Times* and founder of *The Field* and *The Queen*. Mary Porter, actress, d. 1765, lived close by. From here the country is more or less open to the Hertfordshire border at Barnet Gate.

Below the ridge at Mill Hill there is not much of note, except Copt Hall, E. of Page Street at the corner of Bunns Lane, S. of the school. This is a three-storey red-brick house, rebuilt in 1624 for Randall Nicoll, and much altered since. The district near the by-pass road junctions and the stations at the Hale has some churches in assorted styles of the early 20th century; farther W., in Dean's Lane, almost in Edgware, is the striking John Keble church (D. F. Martin Smith, 1935). The exterior is finished in yellow-brown brick, with a W. belfry; inside it is light, austere, and strong, though the flat roof, with a jazzy criss-cross effect, is not happy. The plan is the least conventional of any Middlesex church, square, without chancel, the choir being disposed in the centre of the space. The whole building is bold and lively.

MIMMS, SOUTH (D1) bounded N., W., and S. by Hertfordshire and E. by Enfield, is the most northerly part of Middlesex. POTTERS BAR, the ribbon development along the Great North road and the railway to the E., has given its name to the modern urban district. South Mimms itself, lying on the St Albans and Holyhead road, is one of the two or three remaining villages in Middlesex. Much of the land is agricultural; there are two large private estates, Wrotham Park and Dyrham Park, a good-looking church of much interest, Knightsland Farm with remarkable 16th-century wall-paintings, and some other antiquities of note, including the remnants of a motte-and-bailey castle.

'Mimes' (of uncertain derivation) appears in Domesday as a 'berewick' within Geoffrey de Mandeville's manor of Edmonton;[3] 'South' was added, in distinction from North Mimms in Hertfordshire, from the 13th century. In 1268 Roger de Leuknore was lord of the manor, by that time independent of Edmonton. Leuknore held it till

[1] *Country Life* 104 (1948), p. 1114. [2] Boulger (see page 310, note 1), p. 349; *Stamford Raffles* (page 127, note 5), p. 590. [3] The Domesday entry under Edmonton (p. 129b, col. 2) – *Ad hoc manerium jacuit et jacet una Berewica quae vocatur Mimes* – is not mentioned by Lysons (1800), Cass (1877), or Brittain (1931), who take South Mimms to have been part of Enfield.

1479; by 1567 Edward, Lord Windsor, was in possession under the Crown, and in 1661 it was in the Salisbury family. Smaller manors were Oldfolds, property of the Frowycks from the 13th century to 1527; Wyllyotts, at Potters Bar, retained by the Leuknores until 1562; and Derhams or Durhams.

A windmill existed at South Mimms in 1289—the earliest certain English example. The battle of Barnet took place in 1471 at the S. end of the parish, probably near Kitts End. Telford's Holyhead road reconstruction of 1826 replaced the winding road by a new direct highway driven at an angle through the village street. Potters Bar, to the NE., and Barnet Side, in the S., indistinguishable from Chipping Barnet itself, supported Methodist chapels by 1800 and grew rapidly in the middle of the 19th century. South Mimms urban district, which consisted of West Barnet or Barnet Side, was detached from Middlesex and added to Barnet, and Hertfordshire, in 1896. The Great Northern Railway cut across the Potters Bar side in 1850, and in 1927 the Barnet by-pass road was driven through the parish E. of the village. Since then houses have spread W. from Potters Bar, but they have not yet effaced the rural character of the district.

The church (St Giles), E. of the old village street, just W. of the newer St Albans road, is a building of much detailed interest with a bold and handsome W. tower, having a SE. stair-turret and the square-headed belfry windows typical of 15th-century Middlesex towers. The exterior is faced with flints, perhaps obtained from the chalkpits to the N. The chancel was built in the 13th century, the nave about 1400. The N. aisle and arcade with four-centred arches were added early in the 16th century, and the red-brick chapel

N. of the chancel was built under the will of Henry Frowyck, d. 1527. G. E. Street restored the church in 1877. Not all the fittings recently introduced produce a happy effect.

The Frowyck family figures prominently inside the church. There is a brass in the chancel to Henry Frowyck, 1386, and one in the W. tower to Thomas Frowyck, 1448. The altar-tomb with canopy against the N. chancel wall is probably to Henry Frowyck, d. 1527, in spite of the letters R and (?) H on bosses. The baluster-shaped supporters of the canopy show Renaissance influences at work on the Gothic—influences not present in the canopied tomb in the N. chapel of another Frowyck (perhaps Thomas, d. about 1500) with an effigy in plate armour.[1] There is an interesting series of early 16th-century painted glass windows in the N. chapel and N. aisle, showing figures kneeling at prayer-desks; fragments of the inscriptions remain. There is a notable wooden parclose screen (early 16th-century) dividing the chapel from the church, with 15 bays on the S. and 10 on the W. On the S. wall of the nave is a curious wall monument with a death's head; it used to bear this inscription:

[Be b]oulde, looke on, why turn awaye thyne eyne,
This is no stranger's face, the phesnamey is thyne.[2]

The principal object in the churchyard is a large monument to Sir John Austen, three times M.P. for Middlesex, d. 1742.

The village street contains some attractive buildings: the surviving inns (two out of some dozen at the height of the coaching age) are both old houses, the Black Horse of red brick, early 18th-century at latest, and the White Hart, with plaster pargeting on its 18th-

---

[1] For the ascription to this Thomas Frowyck, see F. C. Cass, *South Mimms* (1877), p. 66, and F. Brittain, *South Mymms* (1931), p. 21. If it is right, the date 'c. 1530-40' given by the Royal Commission on Historical Monuments, *Middlesex* (1937), p. 94, is some 30 years too late, which the style of the monument appears to confirm. [2] Lysons, art. South Mimms; F. C. Cass, *South Mimms* (1877), p. 57; not in Brittain. The bracketed letters are my conjecture. Other suggestions have been made – '[You sh]oulde' (*Gentleman's Magazine*, 1830, part i., p.110), and '[Both young and] oulde' (W. Jerrold, *Highways and Byways in Middlesex* (1909), p. 339), but these fail to agree with the singular 'thyne'.

century front to the old road. Sparrow farm, about 30 yds. SW. of the Black Horse, was built c.1500. At the S. end are some agreeable houses of the 18th and 19th centuries.

Most of the farm buildings scattered about the parish have some old and pleasing features. Knightsland farm, W. of the Barnet road about 1 3/4 m. SE. of the church, is a 16th-century building cased with 18th-century brick. It has some early 16th-century linen-fold panelling inside and a remarkable series of late 16th-century wall-paintings in a first-floor room representing the parable of the Prodigal Son.

Dyrham Park, W. of Knightsland, takes its name from the Durham family, first heard of at South Mimms in 1340. It was owned by Frowyck from 1368 until the 16th century, and later by Austen, Keppel, Earl of Albemarle, Bethell, and Trotter. The mansion dates from the early 19th century; the imposing entrance gateway appears to be an 18th-century design—perhaps of 1736—and not, as suggested in most accounts, a triumphal arch erected by General Monk to celebrate the Restoration of 1660 (*Plate 27*).[1]

Wrotham Park, lying just W. of the Great North road immediately beyond Hadley Common, was an estate bought by Admiral John Byng about 1749, on which he built a house designed by Isaac Ware, in red brick (later stuccoed) with a handsome Ionic portico on the main front (*Plate 42*). The name was taken from the family's Kentish home. After Byng's trial and execution in 1756-7 for alleged cowardice in the Minorca campaign, the house went to George Byng, M.P. for Middlesex with Wilkes, and to his son George, M.P. from 1790 until 1847. It descended to a younger brother, created Earl of Strafford in 1847.

S. of Dyrham, on the county border, is Fold farm, the house and two barns of 17th-century date. The farm occupies the site of the Frowycks' manor-house; a moat in good preservation was probably part of it. Blanch farm, about 3/4 m. S. of the church, Mimms Hall, about 3/4 m. NE. of the church, and barns at Bridgefoot farm and Bentley Heath farm, E. and SE. of the church, are 16th- and 17th-century buildings.

There are remains of a motte-and-bailey castle, unknown until 1918, near the chalk-pit W. of the Barnet by-pass road in the N. of the parish. It is conjectured that this may have been constructed by Geoffrey de Mandeville the younger about 1140.[2]

MOOR HALL (a1). *See* HAREFIELD.

MUSWELL HILL (E3) (no longer pronounced Muzzle Hill) is the NW. portion of Hornsey borough, divided from the rest by a belt of park and wood from Alexandra Park in the SE. to Highgate Wood on the main North road. It lies on the ridge running E. from Hampstead to Wood Green; to the N. it touches Friern Barnet near the North Circular road, and in the W. it merges with East Finchley in the district of Fortis Green. It was celebrated in medieval times for its holy well, lying close to the hill leading from Hornsey, which was the main road from London to the north until the 14th century. Suburban settlement began in earnest at the end of the 19th century, and it is mostly a pleasant place built within the last 60 years, without any special distinction except some good views to the S.

The name, first found in 1152, derives from 'mossy spring'; the hill itself was called 'Pinn's Knoll' until the 17th century. The well was situated near

[1] Brittain (page 312, note 1), p. 51.   [2] *Trans. L. Mx. A. S.* NS 7 (1937), pp. 175, 464.

the house Monkswell in Muswell Road, almost opposite Coniston Road; there was a tradition that a king of Scotland— perhaps Malcolm IV (1153-65)—was cured by its water. An area of 69 acres adjoining the well was granted about this time by the bishop of London to the priory of St Mary, Clerkenwell, and it remained 'Clerkenwell Detached' until 1900. In 1540, after the dissolution of Clerkenwell nunnery, there was a chapel at Muswell with a 'Priest's Chamber' over the gate.

The ridge, being clay with some glacial drifts and therefore almost waterless, unlike the sand and gravel at neighbouring Highgate, was not settled until the 19th century. Topham Beauclerk, friend of Johnson and Horace Walpole, had an estate, the Grove, on the slope of the hill, now part of Alexandra Park. Tom Moore lived in 1817 in a cottage at the foot of the hill. Mazzini, the Italian republican, often visited the Ashurst family at the Grove in the 1840s. Frederic Harrison, author and positivist, d. 1923, lived at Muswell Hill 1831-40, and W. E. Henley, poet and critic, 1896-9.

The Great Northern Railway opened its station at Muswell Hill in 1873, and the place became a middle-class suburb. The Broadway is a tolerable specimen of the suburban building of its age, with a variety of churches from St James (J. S. Alder, 1901; blitzed) to non-conformist chapels of Edwardian date. Farther N. are newer districts, especially along Colney Hatch Lane, where a Roman Catholic church revives the dedication to Our Lady of Muswell (1938) and a new church of St Peter le Poer (1910) continues the parish name transplanted from the City.

NEASDEN (D3). See WILLESDEN.

NEW   BRENTFORD   (C5).   See BRENTFORD.

NEW   SOUTHGATE   (E2).   See SOUTHGATE.

NORTHFIELDS (C4). See EALING.

NORTHOLT (B4) lies in the clay country between the Uxbridge road and Harrow; it is mostly flat, but the N. tip runs up to the slope of Harrow hill. The Grand Union canal's Paddington branch runs across the SE. corner between Greenford Green and Yeading. West End is a hamlet to the SW.; Wood End, now built over, was another towards Harrow. It has been included in Ealing borough since 1930.

The name first appears in 960; until the 19th century 'Northall' and 'Northhold' were as common as the received spelling.[1] It means 'north angle or nook of land,' in distinction from Southall. The manor was given by the Conqueror to Geoffrey de Mandeville and was granted in 1398 to the abbey of Westminster. After the Dissolution it was held by the bishop of Westminster until 1550 and then by Wroth. Lord Carnarvon, later Duke of Chandos, bought it in 1716, and it was afterwards owned by Villiers, Earl of Jersey. There was a subsidiary manor at Down Barns.

Northolt has always been an obscure, sleepy place; it has not entirely lost that aspect in spite of suburban develop- ments and a monstrous airport. Its growth was restricted by scarcity of water—the vicar sank new wells in 1791 to remedy it—and because it was very inaccessible, with as much as a square mile unserved by any road or lane, until the Paddington canal was cut in 1801. It was the last Middlesex parish to get its enclosure act, in 1825. Even then,

---

[1] Lysons wrote 'Northall', Tremenheere in 1843 (see page 40, note 2) 'Northold'.

only 3 houses were built at the hamlet of West End between 1837 and 1935.[1] After the railway arrived in 1905, development began very slowly. In the 1930s the Western Avenue was driven through the parish just S. of the church, and Northolt airport spread over the NW. part. S. of the Western Avenue, about West End and Down Barns, there are still fields and old houses waiting for something to happen to them.

The church (St Mary), E. of a village green on an eminence falling away to the SE., is a simple aisleless building with whitewashed exterior, red-tiled roof, and bell-turret with low spire at the W. end like Ickenham and Cowley. The nave was rebuilt and perhaps widened to the S. about 1300; the chancel and the square bell-turret were rebuilt probably in the 16th century. The S. porch is a mean early 19th-century object which is to be removed. The interior is plain and light, with a certain rustic charm; a wooden gallery of 1703 fills the W. end. The E. window of the chancel, whose tracery and glass came from the Gothic court of the 1851 exhibition in Hyde Park, was unhappily destroyed by enemy action in the 1939-45 war. There are 3 brasses. The font is a late 14th-century octagonal bowl with carved panels including the arms of Sir Nicholas Brember, lord mayor, d. 1388; the carved oak cover is dated 1624. On the E. wall of the nave is a carved and painted Stuart coat-of-arms.

There is not much else of note in the place: ruins of a pigeon house in the grounds of Islip manor, NW. of the church; Moat farm and Court farm, 17th-century, with barns to the NE.; and Down Barns, a brick house, c. 1700, with a great old chimney stack on the W. side, standing remotely on a ridge S. of the airfield where the last of the once numerous shooting towers of Middlesex are still to be seen.

Some of the Northolt clergy have been celebrated. Richard Northall, archbishop of Dublin, d. 1397 (perhaps an early inhabitant); John Maplet, d. 1592, author of *A Greene Forest* (natural history alphabetically arranged) and *A Diall of Destiny* (astrology); Robert Malthus, a Commonwealth intruder who proved obnoxious to the parish,[2] great-grandfather of Thomas Malthus the demographer; Goronwy Owen, curate 1755, poet and first secretary of the Honourable Society of Cymmrodorion, later master of William and Mary College, Williamsburg, Virginia (tablet with Welsh inscription). S. C. Demainbray, d. 1782, experimental scientist, lived in the parish.

NORTHWICK PARK (c3). *See* WEMBLEY.

NORTHWOOD (B3) is the part of Ruislip ancient parish bordering on Hertfordshire, lying between Pinner and Harefield; it was a mere hamlet until 1850, with much of the land in pasture and many of the inhabitants engaged in hewing and preparing firewood from the remainder for sale in the London market. Lying on the road, and from 1887 on the Metropolitan Railway, linking Harrow and Pinner with Rickmansworth, it developed rather more in line with them than with Ruislip, from which a belt of woodland made, and makes, a separation. Its name was admitted, as a junior partner, to the Ruislip-Northwood urban district of 1904. It is an outer suburb of mixed character: commonplace development round the station, middling on the Pinner side near Northwood Hills station (1933), superior houses, many of the 1890-

[1] Willatts, p. 209. [2] Reasons for the dispute are discussed in Part I, page 111, and note 3.

1914 period, in more spacious layout to the NW. and W.[1]

The church (Holy Trinity; S. S. Teulon, 1854) on the Rickmansworth road deserves a cautionary glance; it is characteristic flinty mid-Victorian Gothic. There are striking monuments in the churchyard, including one to Sir Robert Morier, d. 1893, ambassador to St Petersburg, with a gigantic cross of Siberian jasper. Several of the Grosvenor family, of Moor Park, Hertfordshire, were buried there. Beyond is the large Mount Vernon hospital; S., at Haste Hill, towards Eastcote, is St Vincent's hospital. In Hallowell Road, E. of the station, are good Presbyterian and Roman Catholic churches (1914 and 1923); in Gatehill Road, at the top of High Street, NE. of these, is a 17th-century brick farmhouse.

NORWOOD[2] (c4) is a small portion of SOUTHALL borough, lying between the Grand Junction canal and OSTERLEY Park. It was an ancient ecclesiastical precinct and the original parochial centre of Southall.

At Domesday Norwood was included within the archbishop of Canterbury's manor of Hayes, but it was a separate manor in 1481. It passed to Fiennes, Lord Dacre, c. 1580 and to Francis Awsiter c. 1600. It was sold by the Awsiter family in 1756 in trust for Mrs. Child and descended to Villiers, Earl of Jersey, of Osterley Park. The church formed a separate precinct or chapelry of Hayes until 1871. Most of the bricks used for the building of Buckingham Palace came from John Nash's kilns at Norwood.[3]

Apart from the green, which remains pleasant and tree-shaded with substantial houses round it, the only object of interest in Norwood is the church (St Mary) at the E. end. There are 12th-

century fragments in the nave; the chancel was probably added or rebuilt in the 13th century. It is said to have been rebuilt under Archbishop Chichele in 1439, but this seems to apply only to the roofs and some windows. The timber-framed S. porch was added in the late 15th century and extensively rebuilt in the 19th, when the whole N. side of the church and the red-brick SW. tower were added; the tower (1898) replaced a timber W. spire. There is some late 16th- or 17th-century foreign glass in the nave. In the chancel is a fine tomb ascribed (by a modern hand) to Edward Cheeseman, cofferer to Henry VII, and his son Robert, 1556, with a helm and sword above. There are brasses in the chancel; a life-size semi-recumbent effigy of John Merrick of Norcut, 1749; and a black floor-slab to John Merrick, 1663.

OLD   BRENTFORD   (c5).   See BRENTFORD.

OSTERLEY (c5) is the house and park formerly belonging to the Earls of Jersey, lying W. of the lower Brent; it now also denotes a modern district of Isleworth and Hounslow lying about the Great West road, S. of the park. The house is a fine example of 18th-century remodelling of an earlier building; it has an admirable portico and handsome interior decorations by Robert Adam. The park, though level, is agreeable, and doubly so by reason of the relief it gives to the surrounding miles of suburban building. The name means 'sheepfold clearing,' not, as might be supposed, 'east meadow.'

In 1530 the manor was owned by the convent of Syon at Isleworth; it was granted to Henry Courtenay, Marquess of Exeter (attainted 1538), Edward Seymour, Duke of Somerset, Lord

---

[1] Towerwood (R. A. Briggs, 1893) illustrated in A. H. Gardner, *Outline of English Architecture* (1945), opp. p. 104. [2] 'Norwood, Middlesex', has proved a stumbling-block even to the learned: Clapham, *Modern Britain*, i., pp. 461, 463, amended the spelling of his authority, Tremenheere (see page 40, note 2), to 'Northwood'; but Northwood was, and is, quite a different place. [3] Summerson (page 49, note 6), p. 264.

Protector (attainted 1552), and in 1562 to Sir Thomas Gresham, merchant and founder of the Royal Exchange, whose family fortunes had been established by his father Sir Richard Gresham, d. 1549, out of monastery lands.[1] Thomas Gresham built a paper mill at Osterley in 1565 and completed a new mansion, whose design with corner turrets still peeps through its 18th-century veil. The place was very splendid in his day, and Gresham entertained Elizabeth with acceptable diversions in 1576. Some of the local people seized the occasion to call attention to their grievances by tearing up the enclosing fence of the park.[2] After the death of Gresham's widow in 1596, Sir Edward Coke, Attorney-General, later Lord Chief Justice, lived in the house. George Fielding, Earl of Desmond (who abducted his own wife on returning from foreign travel in 1635), lived there from 1639; Sir William Waller, Parliamentary general, from 1655 to 1668; and later Nicholas Barbon, son of 'Praise-God Barebones,' economist, promoter of fire insurance, and London building speculator, d. 1698.

Some building was done during Barbon's occupation, and a staircase and panelling survive. In 1710 the estate was sold to Sir Francis Child, banker, d. 1713, and it remained the property of the Child family, passing by marriage in 1804 to Villiers, Earl of Jersey. Remodelling and interior redecoration of the house were begun in 1761 by Robert Adam, at the same time as he was dealing with Syon; it was completed by 1780. During the 19th century it was celebrated as a Conservative country house. In the 1939-45 war it housed the Home Guard training school, and in 1949 the house and park became the property of the Ministry of Works.

Horace Walpole visited Osterley when it was new in 1773 and wrote a characteristic letter to the Countess of Upper Ossory: 'On Friday we went to see—oh, the palace of palaces!—and yet a palace *sans crown, sans coronet,* but such expense! such taste! such profusion! and yet half an acre produces all the rents that furnish such magnificence. It is a Jaghire got without a crime. In short, a shop is the estate, and Osterley Park is the spot. The old house I have often seen, which was built by Sir Thomas Gresham; but it is so improved and enriched, that all the Percies and Seymours of Syon must die of envy. There is a double portico that fills the space between the towers of the front, and is as noble as the Propylaeum of Athens. There is a hall, library, breakfast-room, eating-room, all *chefs d'oeuvre* of Adam, a gallery one hundred and thirty feet long, and a drawing-room worthy of Eve before the Fall. Mrs. Child's dressing-room is full of pictures, gold filigree, china and japan. So is all the house; the chairs are taken from antique lyres, and make charming harmony; there are Salvators, Gaspar Poussins, and, to a beautiful staircase, a ceiling by Rubens. Not to mention a kitchen garden that costs £1,400 a year, a menagerie full of birds that come from a thousand islands which Mr. Banks has not yet discovered, and then, in the drawing-room I mentioned, there are door-cases and a crimson and gold frieze, that I believe were borrowed from the Palace of the Sun; and then the Park is—the ugliest spot of ground in the universe—and so I returned comforted to Strawberry.' Five years later, on another visit, he did not care for it so much.[3]

The material of the house is striking red brick, with turrets at the angles of the almost square plan. A flight of steps

[1] R. H. Tawney, *Religion and the Rise of Capitalism* (Penguin ed., 1938), p. 133. [2] *M.C.R.* i., p. 97 (6 May 1576). [3] Horace Walpole to the Countess of Upper Ossory, 21 June 1773; to Rev. William Mason, 16 July 1778.

leads to a handsome Ionic portico, one of Adam's finest external works, whose colonnade closes a court. The main staircase has Rubens' picture of the Apotheosis of William of Orange let into the ceiling. The ceiling and mantelpiece of the breakfast-room perhaps date from 1755-60, before Adam's work was begun, and may have been carried out by Sir William Chambers. The library (from which the principal treasures, including fifteen Shakespeare folios, were sold in 1894) and dining-room are decorated with pictures by Antonio Zucchi and Angelica Kauffmann. The gallery, 130 ft. long, on the garden front contains mantelpieces and other work in William Kent's style, about 1740. The drawing-room and tapestry-room show Robert Adam in his most skilful, ornate, and richly-coloured vein, and there is an Etruscan room, with paintings done to Adam's direction, beyond. Throughout there are notable pictures and furniture, mostly elegant and occasionally sumptuous; the state bed is indeed amazing. Osterley is a magnificent example of Adam's talents during the 20 most productive years of his life, with something of genius in the best work.

Outside are Gresham's stables, with 17th-century alterations. There is an ornamental water in the park, and good elms line the public lane from Norwood to Wyke Green. On Windmill Lane, a sequestered road E. of the park, are Wyke farm and the Hare and Hounds inn, pleasant brown houses of the late 18th century.

PALMER'S GREEN (E2). *See* SOUTHGATE.

PARK ROYAL (c4). *See* TWYFORD and WILLESDEN.

PERIVALE (c4) is a small parish in the Brent valley between Sudbury and Ealing. The tiny village—no more than church, manor house, and some farms— lay in the SW. corner; in the N. it extended as far as the S. slope of Horsendon Hill, where the Paddington canal was cut in 1801. The Great Western's Greenford railway was pushed through in 1904, but no main road crossed the district until the Western Avenue of the 1920s.

The place was called Greenford Parva, or Little Greenford, from 1254 until 'Pyryvale' appeared in 1508 ('pirie'—a pear tree—and 'vale'). The manor was granted by Edward II to Henry de Beaumont, from whom it passed through many different hands.

Until recently Perivale was a place pleasurably discovered by Londoners and topographers for its small size and remoteness so near to London, only 8 m. from Hyde Park Corner. It lay behind the natural impediments of the Brent and the ridge N. of Ealing, and there was nothing but hay-farming in the parish. Ghosts (of Simon Coston, d. about 1666, and Thomas Bowler, executed for an attempted murder at Alperton, 1812) used to haunt what dwellings there were, and there was a miser at Perivale mill. There was not even a village inn. In 1836 a motion to provide a new font and cover for the church was negatived 'because there are no christenings for parishioners of Perivale, nor likely to be any.' Since 1925, however, factories and houses have sprung up in the middle part; but S. towards the river there are meadows, and the district is not completely filled with building.

The church and rectory survive from Perivale's secluded past. The dedication of the church is unknown (St James, given on early Ordnance Survey maps, has no authority). It is a simple aisleless structure of rubble and flint, of a decidedly rustic type. The chancel, with a low-side window, may be late 13th-century; the nave is not certainly earlier than the 15th century. The timber W. tower, weather-boarded and surmounted by a pyramidal tiled roof, was probably added in the 16th century. A S. porch was built in the 17th century. Much restoration went on in the 19th century, and a new chancel arch was built; refined taste, as expressed in *The Builder* of 1868, would have swept away 'all the rest of the Puritanical and Georgian anomalies, especially the Punch and Judy construction called the tower,'[1] but happily Punch survived the restorers. There is a brass to Henry Myllet, 1505. The font is a 15th-century octagon; the cover (1665) is of carved oak. There are also some fragments of 15th-century painted glass in the chancel windows and several 17th-century monumental tablets. The churchyard contains some wooden headboards.

The rectory, N. of the church, presents to the view little older than the 19th century, but it has a middle portion of the 15th and work of most centuries since. The manor house, opposite the rectory to the W., and the five farm houses have disappeared. Their place has been taken by semi-detached dwellings and some factories.

PINNER (B3), the NW. portion of Harrow urban district, lies against the Hertfordshire border, with Harrow Weald on the E. and Ruislip and Northwood on the W. The old parish also included the settlements of Headstone (SE., towards Harrow), Pinner Green (NW.), Hatch End (NE.), and the district now called Rayners Lane (S.). The country varies from undulating high ground in the N. to flat plain in the S.; most of it is pleasantly broken and was wooded until recently. The Pin brook passes through the old village on its way from its source N. of Harrow Weald to join the Colne at Uxbridge. Pinner is an agreeable place with a good many evidences of a respectable antiquity, among suburban developments which are mostly of a superior type.

Pinner first appears, as 'Pinnora,' in 1232. *Ora* means 'bank or edge,' the *Pin* part is obscure. The oldest thing about the place is the earthwork of GRIM'S DYKE; Pinner Park, NW. of the church, may be the remnant of a hunting enclosure at the original W. end of the dyke.[2] The church, dedicated in 1321, was a chapel of ease to Harrow. Harrow manor and parish extended over Pinner, though the hamlet had defined rights of self-government throughout, including an 'immemorial immunity,' reasserted in 1699, from the Harrow church rate. A weekly market and two annual fairs were granted in 1336; there was another market at Harrow, a commentary on the difficult communications over the clay roads— the 'illness of the way' between the two places was adduced in 1649 as a reason for establishing a separate parish of Pinner,[3] which was done in 1766. A small nonconformist academy was established at Pinner in 1696 by T. Goodwin, jr., but it can only have lasted for a few years.[4]

In the 19th century there were at Pinner numerous houses with fair-sized grounds kept by Londoners while it still preserved a good deal of its ancient manners and aspect. Good houses were already being built when there was no better communication from London than barge to Northolt and thence on foot, or a daily four-horse coach. More

[1] *Builder* 26 (1868), p. 736. [2] Braun (page 69, note 1), p. 374. [3] *H.C.M.* 1 (1899), p. 320.
[4] *Transactions of the Congregational History Society* 6 (1951), p. 137.

building took place after a station was opened in 1844 at Hatch End. In 1886 the Metropolitan Railway opened a station in the village, and from that time the W. side of the parish was more rapidly built up, with some good houses of the period 1890-1914. After 1920 suburban development of a more commonplace sort filled up the SW. corner towards Rayners Lane and Eastcote, the SE. round Headstone, and the N. at Pinner Green; and since 1945 a large London County Council estate has covered the fields E. of the railway at Headstone Lane, running into Harrow Weald. Nevertheless, considerable tracts of open land have been judiciously reserved, including the greater part of Pinner Park.

The village street, with some good old houses somewhat self-consciously dated and kept in order, is overlooked by the church (St John the Baptist) from the E. It was built early in the 14th century (consecrated 1321); the tower and S. porch were added in the 15th century. There have been frequent restorations since 1811; the S. chapel was added in 1859, and the whole building was drastically renovated by J. L. Pearson in 1880 leaving the interior bare and dull. The W. tower is the best feature, with square-headed windows, a staircase turret at the NE. angle, and a large wooden cross of 1637, cased in lead, rising from the low pyramidal top. The best internal fittings are a finely-carved 18th-century communion rail and a table (now in the vestry) of about 1700. Also in the vestry is a chrisom brass to Anne Bedingfeld, 1581. There are 17th-century monuments, including one to Sir Bartholomew Shower, 1701, whom Macaulay called 'a servile and cruel sycophant, an unprincipled Tory, a base and hard-hearted pettifogger';[1] he prosecuted the Seven Bishops for

the Crown. In the chancel are three good black marble floor-slabs of 1681-3 with achievements of arms. In the churchyard is a monstrous monument to the parents of J. C. Loudon, agricultural writer, c. 1810, which has given rise to a silly legend.

High Street, where the modern descendant of the ancient fair still takes place on the Wednesday after Whit Sunday, contains as good a selection of old buildings of modest size as can be found together in Middlesex. At the top, just N. of the church, is an 18th-century red-brick house, now the Conservative Club, which was a temperance tavern called the Cocoa Tree c. 1880. Opposite is Church Farm, of the 17th and 18th centuries. The Queen's Head inn and the houses and shops down the High Street have interesting, and some good, features dating from the early 16th to late 18th centuries. There are more old cottages in Love Lane and Waxwell Lane to the N.; Waxwell Farm House, red brick with timber framing, rebuilt and extended in 1898, remains pleasing. S. of the church is Pinner House, with a pediment carried on two pilasters, an agreeable piece of 18th-century vernacular building. East End Farm (still a farm), NE. of the church in Moss Lane, and Tudor Cottage, just S., are late 16th-century buildings; the farm outbuildings are weather-boarded. W. of the village not so many old houses have survived: Sweetmans Hall, West End Lane, is one.

About 1 m. E. of the church, in a public park, is Headstone Manor, a 2-storey house containing portions of the building in which medieval archbishops of Canterbury probably resided while at Harrow. It is partly timber-framed, partly brick; the middle part of the present house is the oldest

---

[1] Lord Macaulay, *History of England* (World's Classics ed.), ii., p. 324.

portion, probably dating from the 14th or 15th century. The main block was rebuilt in the late 16th century, and, though there have been a good many alterations and additions, the place contrives to retain an air of comfortable retirement. Two handsome barns flank the house; one, of about 1600, is a grand building, timber-framed and weather-boarded, 10 bays long. There are considerable remains of a moat (*Plate 31*). Just NW. of Headstone Lane station is Park Gate, a fine 2-gabled brick farmhouse. Races of a rough kind were held at Headstone until 1903; latterly they usually ended out of the control of the local police force.

Hatch End was the outlying settlement of Pinner towards Harrow Weald. The station was well rebuilt in 1911 (G. C. Horsley). The church of St Anselm, W. of the station, of 1895-1905, gave rise to a celebrated ecclesiastical suit about ritual when a rood-screen was first erected there. SE. of the station are the Royal Commercial Travellers' schools; the principal block is in the Elizabethan Gothic of 1856 (Lane and Ordish); numerous additions include work by Batterbury and Stonhold in 1914, with highly picturesque half-timbering. The course of GRIM'S DYKE in this district is separately noticed.

In the N. of the parish were Woodhall, near Hatch End, one of the old sub-manors, and Pinner Hill, which retains good open views to the S. A curious building, Woodhall Towers, now the estate office in Woodhall Drive, and an isolated tower at Gregory's Farm, in Pinner Hill Road, were built in 1862-4 by A. W. Tooke out of admiration, it is charitably alleged, for styles of exterior decoration seen in Belgium.

In the SW. part of Pinner, towards Eastcote, are the Grove, where the Milman family, including Henry Milman, dean of St Paul's, author of *The History of the Jews*, lived about 1820, and Pinner Place (the Marsh), which belonged to John Zephaniah Holwell, survivor of the Black Hole of Calcutta, later governor of Bengal, d. 1798. Bulwer Lytton wrote parts of *Eugene Aram* in 1831-3 at Pinner Wood House; Mr. Tilbury, inventor of the carriage named after him, lived at Old Dove House, Pinner Park. Henry Pye, poet-laureate, d. 1813 (tablet in church), James Gairdner, historian, d. 1912, George Gissing, novelist, d. 1903, Barry Pain, novelist, d. 1928, Liza Lehmann, singer and composer of *In a Persian Garden*, d. 1918, and Nelson's daughter Horatia (Mrs. Ward, d. 1881) also lived at Pinner.

PONDERS END (F2). *See* ENFIELD.

POTTERS BAR (E1), the E. portion of South Mimms ancient parish, bordering on Enfield Chase, grew during the 19th and still more during the 20th centuries to be the predominant partner and gives its name to the urban district. The ancient moot of Edmonton hundred may have met near Potters Bar.[1]

The name is first found in 1509; the bar was probably one of the gates of the chase. The hamlet supported a Baptist chapel by 1789, and in 1801 a pair of stocks was required there 'for the punishment of bad, disorderly people.' The houses were strung out along the Great North road on the ridge from Hadley Green past Ganwick corner to Potters Bar itself, where there were some of good size; the Great Northern Railway station (1852) about 1 m. W. of the road caused a new settlement near Wyllyotts manor house. There has been some recent

[1] F. W. M. Draper, 'The Edmonton Hundred 'Moot Plain'', *Trans. L. Mx. A. S.* NS 10 (1951), p. 149.

development stretching farther W. from the station towards South Mimms village, but so far not much E. of the main road.

Wyllyotts manor, now council offices, immediately W. of the station, is the only feature of interest in the place. The present building, well restored *c.* 1923, may have been the barn to the original manor house of the Leuknores; it is, perhaps rather conservatively, attributed to the 16th century, the house to the E. *c.*1600. The two form a pleasing picture of timber-frame construction, skilfully prevented from going to decay like most of the surviving Middlesex examples (*Plate 32*).

The churches of Potters Bar, though not beautiful, are curious: E. of the Great North road is St John (1835, abandoned and dilapidated), churchwarden's Norman of an uncommon type; almost opposite is its unfinished successor, St Mary and All Saints (1914); at Bentley Heath, to the S., is Trinity chapel (S. S. Teulon, 1866), quaintly described by Thorne as 'semi-Norman.'

Among the modern secular buildings, to which Banister Fletcher contributed some characteristic houses, there is nothing noteworthy. The Duke of York inn at Ganwick corner is a good plain house of the late 18th century.

POYLE (A5). *See* STANWELL.

PRESTON (C3). *See* WEMBLEY.

QUEENSBURY (C3). *See* KINGSBURY.

ROXETH (C3). *See* HARROW.

RUISLIP (B3) (pronounced *Rizelip* or *Ry-slip*) lies in the NW. of Middlesex between Northolt and the Hertfordshire boundary near Rickmansworth, with Harrow and Pinner on the E., Ickenham

and Harefield on the W. It includes Ruislip old village and the settlement of Eastcote, in undulating and wooded country at the centre of the district; NORTHWOOD, on the Hertfordshire border (separately noticed); and a flat plain S. of the old village in an area which was until about 1910 one of the most deserted parts of the county. N. of the village the Pin brook flows on its way to join the Colne at Uxbridge; one of its tributary streams, dammed to form a canal reservoir *c.* 1839, has created a lake that lends picturesqueness to the surrounding woods. Ruislip and Eastcote are the best examples in Middlesex of suburban development decently carried out, with reasonable conformity of new building with old and a sensible conservation of natural and historical features.

The place first appears as 'Rislepe' ('rush' and 'leap') at Domesday when Ernulf de Hesdin was in possession; a hunting park was specially noted—*parcus est ibi ferarum silvaticarum*; this is connected by some writers with the Middlesex Grim's Dyke.[1] De Hesdin was apparently implicated in conspiracy against William Rufus in 1096; he died at Antioch during the first Crusade in 1098, and the manor passed to the abbey of Bec Hellouin in Normandy, the abbey of Lanfranc and Anselm. It was under the management of Ogbourne priory, Wiltshire, until its dissolution in 1414,[2] and it was then granted by Henry IV to his third son, John, Duke of Bedford (d. 1436). In 1461 Ruislip and Northwood were granted by Henry VI to King's College, Cambridge, which retained them from that time. There was a sub-manor of Southcote; Eastcote was held by the Hawtreys from the 16th century to about 1800.

Ruislip itself lay off the main roads

---

[1] Braun (see page 69, note 1).   [2] M. Morgan, *English Lands of the Abbey of Bec* (1946).

and stayed rather remote; in 1896 it was remarked that one might be 100 m. from London there.[1] Its occupations were entirely agricultural, with most of the land in pasture; there was some trade in timber and firewood for London, and there is still a sawmill in Bury Street. In 1904 the Metropolitan Railway branch from Harrow to Uxbridge was opened with a station at Ruislip. This began a development which, under town-planning control, was reasonably contained and satisfactory. The urban district council was one of the earliest to use the powers given by the Housing and Town Planning Act of 1909 and in 1934 it took a case to arbitration to compel alterations to an architect's design for a house which it considered eccentric and out of character with the district.[2] Some of the later building, however, in the flat plain S. of the Metropolitan Railway, running down to Northolt airport, is a long way inferior to the earlier development.

The High Street, though good of its kind, is undistinguished except at the N. end, where a row of ancient cottages backs on the churchyard (*Plate 30*) and partly obscures the church (St Martin), E. of the road junction. A board describes it misleadingly as a 'priory church'—the priory was in Wiltshire. The nave was built in the middle 13th century, the tower, chancel, and S. aisle in the 15th and the N. aisle about 1500. At a fierce renovation under Gilbert Scott in 1870 the 3 dormer windows originally in the roof were removed, but one has since been put in. The 13th-century nave arcades are good, with alternate round and octagonal columns; the S. arcade is somewhat earlier than the N.[3] The aisle windows are 4-centred with depressed heads. The tower has a battlemented parapet but not an angle staircase. The 15th-century roofs

throughout the church, especially in the chancel, are good examples of their kind. The brasses and monuments are of interest, with the Hawtrey family of Eastcote predominating; the monument to Raphe and Mary Hawtrey, 1638 and 1647, is by John and Matthias Christmas. Mary (Hawtrey), wife of Sir John Bankes, Chief Justice of the Common Pleas, the lady who commanded the garrison of Corfe Castle, Dorset, against the Parliamentary forces, 1643 and 1645-6, is also commemorated. A fair amount of old furniture survived restoration: some ancient seating; an early 17th-century carved oak pulpit, now lacking its sounding-board; two massive early 16th-century oak chests; a bread cupboard to contain the gift of Jeremiah Bright, d. 1697 (with bread); and a copy of Bishop Jewel's *Apology*, 1611, in leather binding tooled with royal badges. Some fragmentary remains of wall paintings, including traces of scenes from the life of a saint (perhaps St Martin), appear above the N. and S. arcades in red and yellow; and on the face of the rood-loft staircase in the N. aisle is a figure of St Michael weighing a soul, with the Virgin on his left and St Lawrence with a gridiron below.

Many buildings of the 16th and 17th centuries and earlier remain, most in good condition and adapted for modern occupation; some houses and farms that would be notable survivors in other Middlesex areas do not call for special notice at Ruislip. Manor Farm, just N. of the church, marks the site of the Ruislip cell of the Benedictine priory of Ogbourne. The present house is probably of the early 16th century, with additions; there is early 18th-century panelling inside. The barn, timber-framed and weather-boarded, with an admirable roof, is of about

[1] *Mx. & H. N. & Q.* 2 (1896), p. 108. [2] J. T. Cattle and others, *Short History of Ruislip* (1930), p. 25; *Builder* 146 (1934), pp. 747, 1059. [3] F. H. Mansford, *Builder* 129 (1925), p. 420, considers that the S. aisle and vestry represent the original Norman structure.

1600; it has been well restored. The farm stands within the bailey of a motte-and-bailey castle, presumably de Hesdin's. The earthwork, partly obliterated by a later moat, can be detected, and to N. and NE. the bounds of a much larger enclosure, the hunting park of Domesday; there are also traces of an enclosure round the village.[1]

At the top of the village street, in the angle of the Eastcote and Rickmansworth roads, is the old post office, with a chimney stack built of thin 16th-century brick; on the S. side of Eastcote Road, just N. of the church, is a good row of 17th-century red-brick and timber almshouses. 1-15 High Street, near the church, are pleasing restored houses of about 1600; the Old Swan inn, opposite, dates from 1500 and 1600, with too much added. There are many good old houses in Bury Street, leading N., from The Old House and Mill House near the church as far as the dingy settlement of Ruislip Common with its Lido on the reservoir. S. of the station are Field End Farm and Shirley Farm, of timber-frame construction with weather-boarded barns of characteristic Middlesex type.

Eastcote (*Plates 70 and 71*) has still 25 buildings recorded by the Royal Commission on Historical Monuments as earlier than 1714, a remarkable number for a Middlesex hamlet. Eastcote House, NW. of the station, is a mansion of about 1600, with 17th-century stables, refaced in the 18th century, with additions; Park Farm and Sigers House, to the SE., are both 17th-century houses; Haydon Hall farm, in Joel Street, was built *c.*1700. Field End farm, with its dovecote and 16th-century barn of unusual height, is a fine example of the old comfortable Middlesex house. This corner of Eastcote, with Field End House and

Field End Lodge close by, shows how modern suburbs might have wrought the old into the new as town overran country if they had tried to.

The modern church of Eastcote (St Lawrence; C. Nicholson, 1933) is in Bridle Road, Field End Road. At Ruislip Manor, the name given to a newer settlement S. of Eastcote Road, is the church of St Paul (N. F. Cachemaille-Day, 1936).

ST MARGARET'S (c5). *See* TWICKENHAM.

SCRATTAGE (c5). *See* HESTON.

SHEPPERTON (B6), the most southerly parish of Middlesex, lies on the Thames where it makes a deep curve between Staines and Hampton Court. Shepperton (and Middlesex) takes in a few acres on the S. bank near Chertsey, where the county boundary indicates the ancient main channel of the river. The village lies near the river, with outlying settlements at Lower Halliford, 1 m. E., and Shepperton Green, round the station 1 m. N. The parish is entirely flat. There are pleasant stretches near the river; the buildings and associations of the old village are the only features of interest.

The name is first found as 'Scepertune' (shepherd's farm) in 959. An early Saxon cemetery, ascribed to the 5th or 6th century, has been unearthed, but most of the remains have disappeared. The manor belonged to Westminster Abbey at Domesday; it was alienated by abbot Gervase in the 12th century, and it was thereafter in private hands.

Early in the 19th century Shepperton must have been a lively place: there was a good deal of prize-fighting (Tom Belcher fought Dutch Sam on

---

[1] H. Braun, 'Earliest Ruislip', *Trans. L. Mx. A. S.* NS 7 (1937), p. 99, refers the park to the pre-Saxon, and possibly to the prehistoric, age.

Shepperton Range), and a sporting parson, John Hubbard, read a burial service in top-boots and hunting dress. The village's only historian, an anonymous inhabitant of 1867, declared that in the early part of the century the bulk of the inhabitants were 'in a state of great ignorance and depravity'; in 1856 there were still one-roomed cottages.[1] A branch railway arrived in 1864. The village itself is still quiet, but modern development has not spared the rest of the parish; gravel pits disfigure the inland parts, and there has been a good deal of disagreeable building.

The church (St Nicholas), the rectory, and the King's Head inn form a charming group at the centre of the old village. There is a story that the church was not originally on this site, but stood on piles in the river, from which it was removed after serious flooding. This tradition is unknown to writers before about 1820;[2] the evidence for it (a picture of Oatlands by Anthony van der Wyngaerde painted in 1548, now in the Bodleian Library, Oxford) is not conclusive. The whole building was reconstructed in 1614, with much old material used again, including some 12th- and 13th-century work. The tower was rebuilt in 1710.

As it is now, the church is a picturesque jumble. The plan is cruciform; there are bricks, tiles, freestone, and flints in the walls, and the tower is rectangular, like Littleton, with a brick battlemented top. Inside it is dark, but not over-restored; galleries remain at the W. end, with painted Hanoverian arms, and in the N. transept. Tile best monument is a modern tablet in the chancel to Lord Blythswood, lord of the manor of Halliford (1908). There are some handsome stones in the churchyard; two of them bear singular

Latin inscriptions to negro servants, Benjamin Blake, *Davo aptior, Argo fidelior, ipso Sanchone facetior*, and Cotto Blake, who both died in 1781. There is also a charming epitaph by Thomas Love Peacock on his daughter Margaret, d. 1826, aged 3.

The rectory, NW. of the church, is a noteworthy building, its main internal structure being timber framing of 15th- or early 16th-century work. The front is a symmetrical and well proportioned 18th-century design in warm red brick, with dormer windows and projecting wings (*Plate 38*). There is a good 18th-century staircase inside, and the hall has the original moulded ceiling-beams.

There are other old buildings in the parish: Ivy Cottage, 80 yds. N. of the church, and White Cottage at Shepperton Green date from the 16th century. There is a 17th-century barn at Manor Farm with timber frames and weather-boarding.

The principal figures in the history of Shepperton are three clerics: William Grocyn, scholar, one of the earliest teachers of Greek at Oxford, friend and correspondent of Erasmus (who may have visited him there and whose ghost is alleged to have been seen), rector 1504-13; Lewis Atterbury, rector 1707-31, who had the church tower rebuilt; and J. M. Neale, leader of the High Church movement and author or translator of one-eighth of *Hymns Ancient and Modern*. Neale lived at Shepperton 1823-9 and wrote in 1844 an historical romance, *Shepperton Manor*, with the manor house, church, and ferry for the site of its principal scenes. (George Eliot's 'Shepperton' in *Scenes from Clerical Life* is not this place, but Chilvers Coton in Warwickshire.)

Cowey Stakes a few yards W. of Walton bridge, was supposed by the earlier antiquaries from Camden to

---

[1] Anon, *History of Our Village* (1867), pp. 50, 56, 59. [2] The story is mentioned by W. E. Trotter, *Select Illustrated Topography of Thirty Miles around London* (1839), p. 139, and Anon, *History of Our Village* (1867), p. 40, as a doubtful tale; its first appearance was not in C. Dickens, *Dickens's Dictionary of the Thames* (1880), p. 191, as implied by J. C. Cox in *Memorials of Old Middlesex* (1909), p. 65. Lysons in 1800 and J. M. Neale, writing his romance *Shepperton Rectory* about James I's reign in 1844, were unaware of it.

Guest to be the ford at which Caesar crossed the Thames in his second invasion of Britain, 54 B.C. The theory never found complete acceptance, because the stakes ran in parallel rows across the river; if they were intended for defence they should have run along it.

Lower Halliford is a settlement close to a sharp bend of the Thames E. of Shepperton village; the name is taken from the ford not over the Thames, but over its small tributary the Ash. Thomas Love Peacock lived there during the latter part of his life until his death in 1866, and George Meredith, his son-in-law, for a few years after 1851. Just beyond is Walton bridge, an ungracious structure of iron lattice girders (E. T. Murray, 1863).

SIPSON (B5). *See* HARMONDSWORTH.

SOUTH MIMMS (D1). *See* MIMMS, SOUTH.

SOUTHALL (B4) is a borough (1936) on the Uxbridge road W. of Hanwell. The boundaries are those of the ancient parish of NORWOOD, extending to the Brent on the E. and the Crane, or Yeading brook, which divides it from Hayes, on the W. It is a typical modern town of the W. Middlesex gravel plain, with a few traces of the past to relieve its generally unattractive appearance. The part N. of the Uxbridge road, on clay, was developed latest. It was first mentioned as 'Suhall' in 1198—'the south nook or corner,' in distinction from Northolt. The portion on the main road was formerly called Northcote; Southall lay about the manor house to the S.; and Norwood was a settlement round a green farther S. towards Heston.

The manor was held under the archbishop of Canterbury by a succession of families including Shoredych, Cheeseman, Fiennes, Lord Dacre, and Villiers. There was a manor farm of Waxlow in the N.; the name, probably associated with Uxbridge and Uxendon, is continued by the local telephone exchange. A field N. of Hayes bridge, on the W. side, was called Hellthorn, possibly indicating the assembly-place of the old hundred of Elthorne.[1]

The Uxbridge road does not appear to have had any important effect on Southall until 1698 when Francis Merrick was granted a charter for a weekly cattle market and two annual fairs at Northcote. There is still trade in cattle near Southall Park, which consists of the grounds of Merrick's house (later a private lunatic asylum kept by Sir William Ellis[2]). The Grand Junction canal was built in 1798 from the Brent by Hanwell to the SW. corner against Hayes, where the Paddington branch was brought in from Greenford to form Bull's Bridge Junction in 1801; brickworks, timber wharves, and factories were established along the canal banks. A station on the Great Western line was opened in 1839. Electric trams arrived from Ealing in 1901. Some suburban settlement began round the station in the 1840s.[3] Industries have multiplied in the S., and a gigantic gasholder dominates most of the views.

The most interesting feature of Southall is the 16th-century timber-framed manor house, on the main street S. of the station. It is a black-and-white gabled Elizabethan manor, now unique of its kind in Middlesex, built in 1587 by Richard Awsiter, consisting of a central hall with cross wings N. and S. It was prettified in 1840, and the interior panelling and fittings, though of interest, include a good deal of modern work.[4] The house is now used

---

[1] Sharpe (see page 12, note 4), p. 179; the suggestion is not taken up in the English Place-Name Society's Middlesex volume (1942). [2] Mogg (page 138, note 2), p. 231. [3] MS. Diary of B. J. Armstrong (see Part 1, pp. 78-9). [4] There are Awsiter arms in the carving, though none were recorded at the Middlesex visitation of 1663.

for local government offices. The old church of St John, to the SW., is a white-brick affair of 1835 with a pinnacle; the new church lies E. of the road. N. of the railway, at the junction of South Road (with a noteworthy cinema of about 1930 in the Chinese style) and Uxbridge Road, is the centre of modern Southall on the site of the former hamlet of Northcote. To the W. towards Hayes Bridge, in Lancaster Road, is St George (1906), built partly with funds raised by the sale of St George, Billingsgate, with its organ-case (Richard Bridge, 1753), similar to the case at Enfield.

In Dormer's Wells Lane, in the NE., perhaps at the right-angle turn at Telford Road, is the site of an old moated house occupied by Cheeseman from 1328 and inherited by Fiennes, Lord Dacre.[1] The rest of Southall in this direction up to the Greenford border consists of houses built since 1930, with schools and recreation grounds to suit (*Plate 59*).

The E. end of the borough is occupied by St Bernard's Hospital (noticed under HANWELL), and the parts S. of the canal by NORWOOD and OSTERLEY Park, which are noticed separately.

SOUTHGATE (E2) is a borough (1933), until 1881 the W. part of Edmonton parish and manor, bounded on the N. by Enfield Chase, W. by the tongue of Hertfordshire containing East Barnet, and S. by Wood Green. The old village is situated on the highest ground, on the W. side; WINCHMORE HILL, Palmer's Green, and Bowes Park are, from N. to S., places on the Green Lanes (Enfield road), which runs through the E. part. New Southgate is a district in the SW. formerly known as Colney Hatch; a portion in the N. is called Oakwood. The Pymmes brook

flows S. of Southgate and Palmer's Green towards the Lea; the New River enters at the NE. corner and runs down to Wood Green. Though Southgate's development, which took place largely in the 20th century, has not been quite exemplary, the place is mostly open and variegated, with some old houses and good trees remaining, and it is the most agreeable of the northern suburbs.

The name, first found in 1370, refers to the S. gate of Enfield Chase. The hamlet was considerable enough for Sir John Weld to secure permission for a chapel to be built there in 1615, stated to be the first example after the Reformation of a second building being consecrated within a parish.[2] It was a little brick building in the grounds of Arnolds, the Welds' house. In the 18th century a number of mansions were built: Minchenden House, about 1747 (demolished 1853), which passed by marriage to James, 3rd Duke of Chandos; Grovelands, by John Nash; Cannons or Cullands Grove; and some smaller houses, of which Eagle Hall was kept as a school by Leigh Hunt's father, Isaac Hunt. Early in the 19th century it was a charming place: Leigh Hunt felt it 'a pleasure to me to know that I was even born in so sweet a village as Southgate ... Southgate is a prime specimen of Middlesex. It is a place lying out of the way of innovation, therefore it has the pure, sweet air of antiquity about it.' Henry Crabb Robinson, the diarist, found 'no distant prospect from the Green, but there are fine trees admirably grouped, and neat, happy houses scattered in picturesque corners and lanes.'[3]

The principal estate was Arnolds, or Arnos Grove, lying S. of the green. The Weld family removed to Lulworth, Dorset, about 1622; the old house was bought by James Colebrooke in 1719

[1] T. Barrett-Lennard, *Account of the Families of Leonard and Barrett* (1908), p. 222. [2] J. W. Round [pseud. J. F. Bunting], *Story of Southgate and Winchmore Hill* [1906], p. 15. [3] Leigh Hunt, *Autobiography* (World's Classics ed.), p. 46; H. C. Robinson, letter to Mrs. Clarkson, 13 August 1812.

and a new one built slightly E. shortly afterwards. Lord Newhaven made additions about 1776. In the 19th century it was owned by the Walker family, the founders of Middlesex county cricket; a tablet on the E. front commemorates them. V. E. Walker was, according to Lillywhite's *Guide to Cricket* (1859), 'undoubtedly the best all-round cricketer in the world.' From 1858 to 1863 Sixteen of Southgate could challenge a United All England team; the sixteen won in 1858 by 59 runs, and in 1859 by 12 wickets. Since 1928 Arnos Grove has housed electricity offices, with additions N. and S.; the central block remains a handsome piece of 18th-century building, with staircase frescoes by Lanscroon, a pupil of Verrio, about 1723, and some good late 18th-century interior decoration. Arnos Grove station (C. Holden, 1932), some distance SW. on the North Circular road, is the most successful of the Underground's stations on the Piccadilly line extension; it combines brick, glass, and concrete in a useful and satisfying way (*Plate 64*).

Gilbert Scott's church (Christ Church, 1863), W. of the green, is coldly Decorated, with some stained glass by Burne-Jones and Rossetti. The octagonal broach spire is a landmark (*Plate 60*). To the NE. are pleasant houses— Essex House and Arnoside, a good 18th-century pair, with a seemly group of the early 19th century round the corner in the High Street, and some old cottages farther along. The Underground station (1933) is more adventurous in appearance than most of Southgate. N. to Oakwood and NE. to Winchmore Hill the 20th-century houses are undistinguished. Southgate Grove, or Grovelands, now a convalescent home in a public park, is one of Nash's most

successful country houses in his early unacademic classical manner (1797) (*Plate 9*). To the S., down Alderman's Hill, is Broomfield Park, where the house, containing 16th-century portions and a staircase painted by James Thornhill, has recently been 'half-timbered' with unhappy effect. It still shows a presentable aspect to the E.

Palmer's Green, still in 1875 'a little gathering of houses on the road to Enfield,' grew only slowly after the railway arrived in 1871 and owes its present form to the tramway extension from Wood Green to Enfield in 1907-9; the parades of shops and roads of houses are middle-class Edwardian. The church (St John; J. O. Scott, 1905) does not merit more than a glance; the Congregational church (1907) a little way N. is superior. The best building in Palmer's Green is the admirable group of Skinners' almshouses in the cottage style at the N. end of the shops (W. Campbell Jones, 1895); the 17th-century figures of a man and a woman on the gate piers were brought from the old building at Great St Helen's in the City.

The late-Victorian district of Bowes Park, S. of Palmer's Green, lies mostly in Southgate borough. It has a church, St Michael at Bowes, Palmerston Road, by Gilbert Scott (1874) in his characteristic style of heavily rusticated stone, with a candle-snuffer spirelet.

A settlement on the W. side of the district grew up suddenly in the 1850s and 1860s. The huge asylum at Colney Hatch (or Bet's Stile, as it was first called) rendered that name opprobrious to most of the inhabitants, and New Southgate was adopted in preference. The asylum building is noticed under BARNET, FRIERN. New Southgate itself contains a Gilbert Scott church (St Paul, 1873; blitzed) and nothing else of note.

SPRING GROVE (c5). *See* ISLEWORTH.

STAINES (a5) is a town, probably on the site of the Roman-British settlement Ad Pontes, at the SW. extremity of the county where the road from London through Brentford and Hounslow crosses the Thames on its way to Salisbury and Exeter. The town has little to show for its history, though there is a pleasant quarter in Church Street; suburban development has spread along the roads to the E. and S. It is separated by the Colne from Buckinghamshire and by the Thames from Surrey. The N. part, meadow-land intersected by streams, is known as Staines Moor. The name (first found in 969) means 'stones,' but its significance is uncertain.

The manor belonged to the abbey of Westminster at Domesday; after the Dissolution it was transferred to the Crown, and in 1613 it was granted to Lord Knyvett, of Stanwell. There were also manors at Grove Barns and Yeoveney.

The most important thing about Staines has always been its bridge, after London Bridge one of the earliest across the Thames. The town clustered around the E. or Middlesex end of the bridge, with a weekly market granted in 1228 and still in existence. A new bridge, by Thomas Sandby, was built under an act of 1791 and opened in 1797. Soon afterwards it was found to be in danger of collapse; an iron bridge in substitution, completed in 1803, also proved a failure. Another iron bridge was built, which also gave way. Finally the present bridge was built in granite by George Rennie and opened in 1832.

The place, in spite of its position, remained singularly unaffected by historic events—Magna Carta, at Runnymede 2 m. away, excepted. In 1549 the inhabitants petitioned the Privy Council against an order to demolish the bridge on account of the rebellion in the west. It was apparently broken down in the Civil War.[1]

Until late in the 19th century Staines remained a fairly quiet country town: about 1840 there was a Literary and Scientific Institution, the malting trade was falling off, and there was an annual onion fair.[2] The London and Windsor Railway was opened through Staines in 1848, and some manufactures were established: besides a brewery, which supported the local bank of Messrs. Ashby (1796),[3] there were mustard mills, papier-mâché mills, and linoleum works. The town has now developed into a characteristic agglomeration of the outer suburban area with some local industries and streets of dormitory houses.

The main street is bustling and mostly new and ugly; the post office and bus garage are good. The Blue Anchor and White Lion are the only old inns to survive, both with modern additions; the Commercial Hotel, at the river end of the street on the S. side, is a decent 18th-century house.

Church Street runs N. from this point, with several good old houses and cottages. The old church (St Mary) was according to Lysons a Gothic structure with a Saxon (i.e. Norman) chancel door, the nave partly rebuilt in brick, and a square embattled W. tower of 1631. That structure fell down one Sunday morning, and the present nave and chancel were built to replace it in the Gothic style of 1828 (J.B. Watson); the old tower, with an inscription asserting that it was built by Inigo Jones in 1631, still stands at the W. end. The interior still answers to Thorne's description—'large, bald, and uninteresting.'

[1] Thacker, *Locks and Weirs* (page 52, note 4), pp. 388, 390. [2] Trotter (see page 325, note 2), p. 144. [3] P. W. Matthews and A. W. Tuke, *History of Barclay's Bank, Ltd.* (1926), p. 292.

Outside the churchyard are Duncroft House, perhaps of 1631, altered but attractive, and St Mary's Cottage, early 18th-century brick. On the river bank is 'London Stone,' marking the W. limit of the old jurisdiction of the City of London over the Thames waterway. The stone now in position, no doubt the successor to a much older one (the date 1285 used to appear on it), seems to have been put up in the 16th century; the pedestal and plinth were reset in 1781. The inscription reads: '[G]od preserve y⁰ Citty [of London].'

S. from the High Street, in Laleham Road, is a pleasing Congregational church (W. Higgins, 1836), a severe little classical building with four Ionic columns in the portico, sadly marred by a nasty sign across it (*Plate 47*). Nonconformity was strong in SW. Middlesex, and there has been a Quaker meeting since 1676; the present house was built in 1844 (S. Dawkes).[1] Farther S. between the Laleham Road and the river is the church of St Peter (G. H. F. Prynne, 1893), largely built at the cost of Sir Edward Clarke, d. 1932, who is buried there. It is a successful example of late-Victorian red-brick Gothic; the exterior is nothing memorable, but inside, with its brass fretwork pulpit and pink, blue, and mauve glass, it is interesting and individual.

STANMORE (B2) lies between Watling Street, separating it from Edgware to the E., and Harrow Weald on the SW. It is divided roughly N. and S. into Great Stanmore on the W. and LITTLE STANMORE, or Whitchurch, on the E. Both now form part of Harrow urban district.

Great Stanmore village lies at an angle of the road from London to Watford. To the N. the district retains much of its original wooded character with large houses in their own grounds, rising to Stanmore Common on the Hertfordshire border near Bushey Heath. The ground here is 510 ft. above sea level, the highest point in Middlesex.

The name is first found as 'Stanmere' (stony pool or mere) in a 12th-century copy of a charter of 793. The manor belonged to St Albans abbey before the Conquest, but was held by Edmer Atule, the king's thane, in 1066; it was then granted by the Conqueror to his half-brother Robert, Earl of Mortain,[2] but was restored to St Albans between 1097 and 1104. By 1300, after further interruptions of tenure, it was leased to the priory of St Bartholomew, Smithfield.[3] After the Dissolution it was first granted to Sir Peter Gambo, a Spaniard murdered by a Fleming near St Sepulchre's church, Newgate, in 1550. In 1604 it was granted to the Lake family, under whom the Burnells were in possession. In 1714 it was bought in trust for the Earl of Carnarvon (Duke of Chandos, 1719), and it later passed to Earl Temple.

Stanmore lived entirely from agriculture until well into the 19th century, when Clutterbuck's brewery was built. There were several large country houses with extensive grounds, and the influence of London was not much felt until a branch railway from Harrow, running to a discreet little station looking like a chapel, was opened in 1890; it was stipulated that there were to be no Sunday trains, and there were none till 1935. The Metropolitan's electric line from Wembley arrived in 1932. Between 1930 and 1939 almost all the open country S. of the village down to Kenton was built over with semi-

---

[1] Beck and Ball (page 112, note 2), p. 282. [2] Sir Montagu Sharpe, *Middlesex in British, Roman, and Saxon Times* (ed. 2, (1932), pp. 207, 221, and *Middlesex in the Eleventh Century* (1941), map, identifies this manor with Little Stanmore and Roger de Rames' manor with Great Stanmore; but this view has not been generally accepted: P. Davenport, *Old Stanmore* (1933), text opposite plate II. [3] W. W. Druett, *Stanmores and Harrow Weald through the Ages* (1938), p. 34.

detached houses of standard Middlesex patterns.

The village could have been one of the most charming in suburban Middlesex, but its appearance has been spoiled. A few good old buildings remain: tenements on the S. side of Church Road, at the E. end, are late 16th-century, and the house almost opposite was built perhaps 100 years later; here and there are some other old buildings, especially S. of the church, where a tithe barn has been converted into cottages and old timber from elsewhere in the parish has been worked into a church hall. But the new buildings are not good, and the centre of Stanmore is a mess.

The small medieval church, probably dedicated to St Mary,[1] stood some 700 yds. SSW. of the present one, near a spot marked by a tombstone to Baptist Willoughby, incumbent 1610-11, now lying in the garden of a house called Haslemere, Old Church Lane. A new church (St John) was built at the cost of Sir John Wolstenholme and consecrated by Archbishop Laud in 1632—an action that, described as the approval of a private chapel, was afterwards used against him by the Puritan party as evidence of Romish practices. It is a remarkable example of brickwork, with a bold W. tower and a rectangular body without structural distinction between nave and chancel. The windows and S. door are round-headed; the S. porch is attributed to Nicholas Stone.[2] The N. annexe was added in the 18th century. About 1845 the condition of the church caused anxiety; although it could probably have been repaired, it was abandoned and a new church built farther E. The roof was removed, and the whole building was allowed to fall into decay. In spite of its alleged poor condition, the tower still stands and most of the walls are complete, except that the middle of the S. side has fallen (*Plate 34*).

The 1849 church (St John, by H. Clutton) is a cold and featureless thing, though the monuments are interesting. These were gradually transferred from the old building, but many of them are ungraciously skied or huddled in the base of the tower. In the N. aisle are a pleasing wall-monument showing the kneeling figures of John Burnell and his wife, 1605 (kept clean and in good repair by the Clothworkers' company), and a white marble effigy of Sir John Wolstenholme, 1639, partly by Nicholas Stone (not by Thomas Stone, as stated in the church). Under the tower is a massive representation of John Wolstenholme, 1669, with reclining figures in a four-poster bed. At the W. end of the nave are some charming monuments to the Dalton family, including one by John Bacon, jr., 1791. At the E. end of the S. aisle is a recumbent effigy of Lord Aberdeen, prime minister, d. 1860 by J. E. Boehm. There are two fonts: the one in use is a stone object given by Queen Adelaide, whose patronage is commemorated by Willement's E. window; the other, of white marble bearing the Wolstenholme arms, with a carved oak cover, was the work of Nicholas Stone, 1632. Some of the bells are said to have come from Little Stanmore church in 1720. In the churchyard W. of the S. door a winged female figure marks the grave of W. S. Gilbert, dramatist, who died at Grim's Dyke, Harrow Weald, 1911.

The great houses were Bentley Priory and Belmont (later called Stanmore Park and Stanmore House). The small priory of Bentley was suppressed early in Henry VIII's reign before the general Dissolution. In 1766 the estate was bought by James Duberly, army contractor, who built a new house; in

---

[1] Davenport (see page 330, note 2), p. 31. [2] On Nicholas Stone and the porch, font and Wolstenholme monument, see Walpole Society, vol. vii. (1919), pp. 11, 19, 79.

1790 the Marquess of Abercorn had additions made by Soane. It was visited by many distinguished people: Scott revised *Marmion* and added the lines on Fox during a visit to the Priory[1]; Lord Aberdeen lived in it, and his son took his title from Stanmore; Queen Adelaide rented the Priory for a time and died there, 1849. Additions were made during the ownership of Sir John Kelk, contractor for the Albert Memorial and other large works, 1854-82. It is now the headquarters of R.A.F. Balloon and Fighter Commands. Belmont, so named from an artificial hill in the grounds with a summer-house on top, was bought in 1729 by Andrew Drummond, banker, and was later occupied by Lord Castlereagh and G. C. Glyn, Lord Wolverton, banker and first chairman of the London and North Western Railway; the house is attributed to Henry Holland.[2] There are other houses of the later 18th and 19th centuries N. of the church, including some in the Gothic taste—Aylwards, 18th-century Gothic on an older core, and Stanmore Hall. The Manor House, formerly the Croft (1901), is a pastiche of Tudor materials.

Other inhabitants recorded in the histories are John Warner, warden of All Souls, Oxford, and first regius professor of medicine (1546), d. 1565; Lord Henry Beauclerk, d. 1761; Charles Hart, actor, 'the Roscius of his age,' d. 1683; and Aaron Capadoce, a Jew, d. 1782, 'supposed to be one hundred and five years of age' and sent to Holland to be buried. Samuel Parr, whig writer, unsuccessful candidate for the headmastership of Harrow in 1771, kept a rival school at Stanmore for a few years.

STANMORE, LITTLE, or WHIT-CHURCH (C2), lies between Watling Street and Great Stanmore, N. of Kingsbury. It has never had a village centre, but it contained that part of Edgware lying W. of the main road. The central part of the parish was filled by Canons Park, first a religious house, later the palatial seat of the Duke of Chandos; the church lies just S. Most of Little Stanmore is now indistinguishable from the neighbouring parts of Harrow urban district, of which it has formed part since 1930, but the church and the historic associations of Canons give it a special character.

The place was known as Little Stanmore throughout the Middle Ages; 'Whyt Churche' occurs in the 16th century, presumably from the colouring of the church walls. The manor 'in Stanmore' was given by William the Conqueror to Roger de Rames[3] and was later held by the priory of St Bartholomew, Smithfield. After the Dissolution it was granted in 1544 to Hugh Losse, whose descendants sold it in 1604 to Sir Thomas Lake, secretary of state to James I. It was sold about 1710 to James Brydges (Earl of Carnarvon 1714, Duke of Chandos 1719), who had married Mary Lake in 1696.

Little Stanmore remained a modest place throughout the 19th century. The electric tram line from Cricklewood to Edgware in 1904 marked the beginning of the change. Only in the N., towards the Hertfordshire border near Brockley Hill, is there still open and wooded country.

The estate of Canons,[4] or Canons Park, was so named from being the property of the Augustinian canons of St Bartholomew, Smithfield; no trace of any monastic building remains. The manor house of the 16th-century owner, Hugh Losse, was probably the building in the main street of Edgware later converted into the Chandos Arms.

---

[1] 'The press copy of Cantos I and II of *Marmion* attests that most of it reached Ballantyne in sheets franked by the Marquis [of Abercorn] or his son-in-law Lord Aberdeen': J. G. Lockhart, *Life of Sir Walter Scott* (Everyman ed.), p. 162.   [2] Keane (page 134, note 2), p. 138; note in D. Stroud, *Henry Holland, 1745-1806* (1950).   [3] See page 330, note 2; on the possible inclusion of Edgware, Druett (page 330, note 3), p. 49.   [4] Spelt 'Canons' and 'Cannons' indifferently; the first Duke of Chandos could not make up his mind.

It is a 16th-century house, now condemned. Another house, traditionally ascribed to John Thorpe, was built for Sir Thomas Lake,[1] but it was pulled down for a new mansion begun in 1715. James Brydges had amassed a sizeable fortune—perhaps £600,000—from his tenure of the paymaster-generalship during Marlborough's wars and spent between £200,000 and £300,000 of it on the new house and grounds. Like many other people who have had houses built for themselves, he had not meant to spend half as much as he did.[2] The architectural history of the house is not by any means clear: John James of Greenwich is reported to have designed the main front; William Talman, James Gibbs, architect of St Martin-in-the-Fields, John Price, and Edward Shepherd, who built Goodman's Fields and Covent Garden theatres, were also associated with it as architects; and Vanbrugh was consulted (*Plate 13*).[3] The place, though not particularly large, was designed to seem so; it stood at an angle to the main avenue so that two sides should be seen by the approaching visitor. The interior was decorated with frescoes by Bellucci, Laguerre, and William Kent. Defoe was immensely struck by it: 'This palace is so beautiful in its situation, so lofty, so majestic the appearance of it, that a pen can but ill describe it, the pencil not much better.'[4]

Chandos was generally supposed the object of Pope's scorn, in the lines on Timon's villa in the *Epistle on False Taste* addressed to the Earl of Burlington in 1731. In spite of Pope's denials, which Chandos accepted, controversy continues whether he can have had anything but Canons in mind.[5] His biting couplets have long outlived the house; the lines on the chapel are remembered:

> *On painted ceilings you devoutly stare,*
> *Where sprawl the saints of Verrio or Laguerre ...*
> *To rest the cushion and soft dean invite,*
> *Who never mentions Hell to ears polite.*

From 1720 onwards the duke's fortunes declined; but it was his son, heavily in debt when he succeeded in 1744, who found it impossible either to carry on Canons or to dispose of it. He had it sold by auction in separate lots beginning in 1747; he realised £11,000 for what had cost a quarter of a million. The distribution and survival of some of the materials and fittings is curious. A few portions were worked into the later house. The main portico is said to have gone to Wanstead House, Essex, which witnessed a similar though less rapid rise and reversal of fortune in the Child and Tylney families; the Wanstead portico was sold to Hendon Hall, only a few miles from Canons, where the pediment and capitals still exist, carried on brick columns, but it is difficult to identify these with anything known of Canons. The great staircase was built into William Kent's Chesterfield House in Mayfair, with no alteration except the substitution of an earl's for a duke's coronet over the initial 'C'; when Chesterfield House was demolished in 1934 it went to Harewood House, Yorkshire. Grinling Gibbons' famous carving of the Stoning of St Stephen went to Bush Hill Park, Edmonton, later to Wivenhoe, Essex, and then to the Victoria and Albert Museum; a Grecian temple from the grounds to Old Park, Enfield; gateways and other ironwork to Hampstead parish church, the Durdans, Epsom, and Wotton, Buckinghamshire; the

---

[1] Plan in 17th-century hand in the Soane Museum. [2] 'I very well remember that the late truly noble-spirited Duke of Chandos, to whom I had the honour of being known, assured me that the greatest part of his buildings at his Grace's seat at Cannons, near Edgware in Middlesex, cost his Grace considerably more than double the sum proposed by his surveyors and workmen': B. Langley, *London Prices of Bricklayers' Material and Works* (1748), p. xii. [3] *Country Life* 40 (1916), p. 518: C. H. C. and M. I. Baker, *The Life and Circumstances of James Brydges, First Duke of Chandos* (1949), which includes much new material requiring substantial modification of all earlier accounts; I. Dunlop, 'Cannons, Middlesex: a conjectural Restoration', *Country Life* 106 (1949), p. 1950. [4] Daniel Defoe, *Tour through England and Wales* (1724-6) (Everyman ed.), ii., p. 6. [5] G. Sherburn, '"Timon's Villa" and Cannons', *Huntington Library Bulletin* no. 8 (1935), p. 131, holds that Pope's denial may be accepted.

pulpit, altar, font, and some pews from the private chapel, carved by the school of Gibbons, to Fawley church, Buckinghamshire; the stained glass and ceiling paintings by Bellucci to Great Witley, Worcestershire; and the organ to Holy Trinity, Gosport, Hampshire. A statue of George I in lead, from an island in the lake, 'helped to make Leicester Square hideous'; another, representing George II, was put up in Golden Square in 1753. It is not now believed that the iron railings at New College, Oxford, came from Canons garden.[1]

The second duke moved to Minchenden House, Southgate, and the estate was bought by Hallett, a cabinet-maker of Long Acre, who built a modest house about 1754 with some of the materials of the old one. Later it was owned by Captain Dennis O' Kelly (d.1788), owner of a celebrated talking parrot and of Eclipse, the most famous racehorse on the English turf, proverbially remembered in the phrase 'Eclipse first, the rest nowhere.'[2] An extra storey was added to Hallett's house c. 1910. In 1930, after successive portions of the park had been sold for building and a golf course, the house was taken over by the North London Collegiate School for girls, founded in Camden Town by Miss Frances Buss in 1850, and most of the remaining grounds were acquired by the Harrow urban district council.

The parish church (St Lawrence) stands on the N. side of Whitchurch Lane, about ½ m. W. of Edgware. There was a religious brotherhood on the site in 1272, but the earliest part of the present building is the small 16th-century W. tower, of red brick and rubble rendered with cement. All the rest was rebuilt in 1715 (date on rainwater heads) at the expense of the Duke of Chandos, to the design of John

James (or less probably John Price).[3] It is said that a new tower would have been provided also if the church-wardens had not displayed indecent haste in anticipating the gift by selling the old bells to Great Stanmore. This was a different building from the private chapel of Canons, which was demolished with the house in 1747 and the fittings distributed.

Apart from a 19th-century altar screen of knobbly pattern and the window glass on the S. side, the interior is much as the duke left it. It is unique of its kind in England; the walls and ceilings are panelled and covered with fresco in colour and *grisaille*, with the bold modelling, light and shade, and eye-deceiving perspectives of the baroque school. This is probably the work of Louis Laguerre.[4] At the W. is the ducal pew, like a theatre box, with an imitation of Raphael's Transfiguration in the half-dome above. The pews are of original oak, with iron rings where the service books were chained. Behind the altar is the organ, which many authorities, including the Royal Commission on Historical Monuments, call Handel's organ. It is certainly the instrument which, renovated and altered at different times, stood in the church during those years, with black keys for the naturals and white for the accidentals; it was built by Jordan, and the case by Gibbons or his school. But the association with Handel is only presumptive; he may have lived for a short time at Canons, and he may have attended the services at the parish church as well as the private chapel. If he did, he probably played the organ, but he would not need to compose on it, as stated on the plate now affixed.

On the N. side is the Chandos chapel, completed by Gibbs in 1735; it is in fact a mausoleum housing the

[1] *Country Life* 35 (1914), p. 708; J. Starkie Gardner, *Ironwork, Part III* (Victoria and Albert Museum guide 1922), pp. 129, 147; G. Nares 'Wotton House, Aylesbury', *Country Life* 106 (1949), p. 39; C. Hussey, 'Witley Court, Worcestershire', *Country Life* 97 (1945), p. 992; criticism of the George I statue, L. Stephen, in *Dictionary of National Biography*, art. James Brydges. [2] Eclipse was not buried in the park; his skeleton was preserved and finally given to the Natural History Museum; his skin was stretched on a wooden frame and kept by a Stanmore vet.: L. Weaver, 'Canons Park', *Country Life* 40 (1916), p. 518. [3] Baker (see page 333, note 3), p. 117; M. Whiffen, *Stuart and Georgian Churches* (1947), pp. 26, 40, 98-9. [4] It is often attributed to Verrio, apparently on the sole authority of Pope's lines; but Verrio died in 1707.

huge tomb of the first duke and his first two wives, possibly by Grinling Gibbons. The monument to Lady Carnarvon is by Sir Henry Cheere (1738).[1] When Victor Schoelcher, Handel's biographer of 1857, visited the place he found the marble statue of the duke 'in the last state of dilapidation. The wind whistles through the broken windows of its funereal abode, and the plaster of the roof, detached from its skeleton of laths, powders his enormous wig and soils the imperial robe that drapes his shoulders.'[2] The frescoes here and throughout the church were skilfully restored by W. P. Starmer in 1937, and the whole building is now in better order. Some old service books and a copy of the 'vinegar Bible' (by Baskett, Oxford, 1716) are preserved by the organ. In the churchyard opposite the S. wall of the church is an early tombstone, to John Francklin, 1597 (the recut inscription gives the old-style date, 1596). There is also a stone to William Powell with an inscription affirming him to be the harmonious blacksmith of the Handel legend.[3]

Behind the rectory (A. Salvin, 1852) is a group of brick almshouses in a half-H-shaped block, now dilapidated and condemned. They were founded before 1642, by Mary Lake. The most notable incumbent of Little Stanmore was J. T. Desaguliers, d. 1744, of Huguenot extraction, an experimental scientist credited with invention of the planetarium, who built seven steam pumping engines; the first (1717-8) was for Peter the Great's palace garden at St Petersburg.[4]

The remaining old houses in the parish are nearly all on the W. side of Edgware High Street, from the White Hart inn up to no. 95. These date from the late 16th and 17th centuries, some with rebuilt fronts; many of them are in poor condition. At the extreme N. of the parish are Brockley Hill Farm and Lymes Farm, both weatherboarded with large barns. BROCKLEY HILL is separately noticed.

STANWELL (B5) is a large parish in the SW. of the county with Harmondsworth on the N., Bedfont on the E., and Staines and Ashford on the S.; the numerous streams of the Colne run through the W. portion, one of them providing the county boundary with Buckinghamshire. Lying between the two great roads passing through outlying parts of the parish—the Great West road to the N. and the Staines road to the S.—and protected from development by Metropolitan Water Board reservoirs, Stanwell village remains one of the least spoiled in the county.

The parish contains, as well as the village of Stanwell itself, the settlements of West Bedfont, Stanwellmoor, and Poyle, and the Middlesex portion of Colnbrook. It appears in Domesday as 'Stanwelle,' meaning 'stony stream or spring'; the manor was then held by Walter FitzOther; his eldest son William assumed the surname of Windsor, being warden of Windsor castle. It continued in the Windsor family until 1543, when Henry VIII, who had an eye for land in SW. Middlesex, told Andrew, Lord Windsor, that he must exchange it for Bordesley abbey, Warwickshire. At this time the manor was very large; portions lay in Berkshire, Buckinghamshire, Hampshire, and Surrey. James I granted Stanwell to Sir Thomas Knyvett in 1603. There were also manors at West Bedfont, Shipcote or Hammonds, and Poyle. Poyle—a 13th-century family name from de l'Apulie (Apulia in

[1] Baker (see page 333, note 3), pp. 413, 449; the duke's monument has formerly been attributed to André Charpentier. [2] V. Schoelcher, *Life of Handel* (1857), p. 61. [3] For the Handel legends, see Part I, pages 152-3. [4] R. H. Thurston, *History of the Growth of the Steam-Engine* (ed. 5, 1895), p. 44; R. L. Galloway, *Steam-Engine and its Inventors* (1881), p. 81 (who gives Desaguliers the credit that he 'invented or contrived a few trifles for himself').

Italy)—was granted by Elizabeth to Nicholas Hilliard, miniaturist, for 21 years in 1587.[1] At Poyle and Colnbrook several factories were established; paper mills from the early 16th century, and leather dressing and glue-boiling in the 18th.[2] The Great Western Railway slightly disturbed the rural peace by opening its Staines branch with a station at Colnbrook in 1884.

The church (St Mary) stands at the W. end of the village street; its tall spire forms a conspicuous landmark in the flat Middlesex plain. The nave arcades, with alternate round and octagonal pillars, date from about 1250, the chancel, S. aisle, and tower (above the bottom stage) and spire from the 14th century; the clerestory was added in the 15th century. The E. wall of the chancel was rebuilt in 1774, and the N. aisle was completely reconstructed in 1862. There is some chequer-work in flint, uncommon in Middlesex, on the upper stage of the tower. The chancel, which is lower than the nave, has 14th-century wall arcading on the N. and S. walls, somewhat damaged. It has been suggested that this may represent seating provided for the monks of Chertsey abbey; since the direct connexion with Chertsey began in 1415, the story may be dismissed.[3] The Knyvett monument on the N. chancel wall, showing Thomas, Lord Knyvett, and his wife kneeling, is elaborate and striking; it was cut by Nicholas Stone in 1622 and cost £215. There is a brass in the chancel to Richard de Thorp, rector, 1408. Two piscinae, with credence and aumbry, were discovered in 1950 when pews and panelling were removed.[4]

An attractive feature of the village is the 17th-century school house built of brick with a tile roof, founded by the will of Lord Knyvett in 1624 and very little altered since (*Plate 58*). There is

an ancient manor house at Poyle with fragmentary remains of early work, substantially rebuilt in the 18th century; Hammond's farm is a brick building of about 1700; and there are some timber-frame cottages here and there in the parish. Stanwell Place, W. of the village, stands on the site of the ancient manor house.

The families of Windsor and Knyvett were conspicuous in the history of Stanwell; Sir Thomas Knyvett, gentleman of the privy chamber under James I, in 1605, on information given in a letter to Lord Monteagle, was sent to search the vaults of the House of Commons and so discovered the Gunpowder Plot. Among Stanwell worthies of the following century were Dr. Bruno Ryves, a high royalist described as 'a noted and florid preacher,' who was deprived of the living during the Civil War and reinstated at the Restoration, later rector of Acton, and Sir John Bankes, Lord Chief Justice, whose widow conducted the famous defence of Corfe Castle against the Parliamentary troops and is commemorated in Ruislip church.

The portion of Colnbrook within Middlesex is in Stanwell parish. The principal interest of the place lies in its inns, especially the George and the Ostrich, both on the Buckinghamshire side. In Middlesex, however, is the house called King John's Palace, late 16th- or early 17th-century, on an L-shaped plan, with later additions. The whole now forms a hollow square round a court; there is some simple decorative work on the plaster. The Star and Garter and White Hart inns and other houses are old and pleasing.

The most famous of all apples, Cox's Orange Pippin, was first grown at the back of a modest house, Lawn Cottage, just W. of Colnbrook station on the N.

[1] *Dictionary of National Biography*, art. N Hilliard, wrongly places this manor of Poyle in Stanmore, Middlesex. [2] *V.C.H.* ii., p. 196; Summers (page 112, note 9), p. 58. [3] J. B. Firth, *Middlesex* (1906); J. C. Cox in *Memorials of Old Middlesex*, ed. J. Tavenor-Perry (1909), p. 70. [4] *Times*, 2 June 1950.

side of the Bath road, by Richard Cox, d. 1845, buried at Harmondsworth. The apple's popularity grew slowly after it was first shown in 1857; the original tree was blown down in 1911.[1]

STONEBRIDGE PARK (D4). *See* WILLESDEN.

STRAND ON THE GREEN (C5) is a single row of houses facing the Thames at the Kew bridge end of Chiswick. It is a picturesque relic of 18th-century Middlesex, in places over-preserved, and much knocked about by a railway bridge and dreary buildings of the late 19th century. The place consisted only of fishermen's cottages until about 1770, when some more pretentious houses were built and some of the existing ones refronted. Fishing, boat-repairing, and beer-selling have been the principal occupations. The Bull's Head and the City Barge are the only survivors of the old inns. The barge referred to was the *Maria Wood*, the state craft in which the Lord Mayor made his journeys by river until well into the 19th century; it was laid up opposite when not in use. No. 55, Old Ship House, is good; Zoffany House farther on is the best in the row, in red brick (the others are all brown). It is named from John Zoffany, who took the house about 1780 and had it until his death in 1810; his painting of the Last Supper, with Strand on the Green fishermen as models for the disciples, is still in St George's church, New Brentford.

The Strand runs on past good late 18th-century building, each house or pair of houses in the terrace slightly different, to Strand on the Green House at the end; there are a few 20th-century insertions, doing their best in the face of the elegant plainness of the 1780s.

Apart from Zoffany, the most noteworthy inhabitant was Joe Miller, d. 1738, comic actor and putative father of *Joe Miller's Jest Book*, a collection of jokes that grew marvellously as time went on.

STRAWBERRY HILL (C5) was Horace Walpole's Twickenham house, reconstructed between 1750 and 1776 in a 'Gothic' style which, if not particularly admirable in itself, had a profound influence on the development of architectural taste. The name is now applied to the SE. district of Twickenham.

The earliest building on the site was a modest tenement built for a coachman in 1698. Walpole took it in 1747 from Mrs. Chenevix,[2] a toy-seller, changed its name from Chopped Straw Hall to Strawberry Hill, and proceeded to enlarge the grounds to 14 acres and turn the cottage first into a villa and then into something combining a mansion, an abbey, and a castle. Walpole, Richard Bentley (son of the critic), and John Chute made the designs in conjunction, by working up drawings of surviving Gothic buildings, sacred and profane. Walpole affected to regard it as a personal fantasy, a 'romance in lath and plaster'; 'it was built to please my own taste, and in some degree to realise my own visions'; but it was not 'so Gothic as to exclude convenience and modern refinements in luxury.'[3] Writing to Miss Berry in October 1794, at the end of his life, Walpole judged it more harshly than he would have borne from others: 'Every true Goth must perceive that [my rooms] are more the works of fancy than of imitation.'

In 1750 the sense of period in decoration was not so strongly developed as it has since become, and

[1] See page 42, note 1. [2] This name was spelt 'Chevenix' by Lysons and appears so in most of the guide books. [3] H. Walpole, *Description of ... Strawberry Hill* (1784), preface.

in the result Strawberry achieved a highly individual style, much deplored by 19th-century Goths but appealing in its own way. It was, however, not an exceptional product of one man's taste, but the most notable example of the fashion begun by Sanderson Miller's Edgehill tower, Oxfordshire, 1746, and Hagley, 1747.[1] Most judgments have been unfavourable: Lady Townshend objected to the lack of bedrooms: 'Lord God! Jesus! What a house! It is just such a house as a parson's, where the children lie at the foot of the bed.'[2] (She had not seen the 19th-century parsonage.) William Beckford called it 'a species of Gothic mousetrap'[3]—a criticism from which his Fonthill Abbey was presumably exempt; and critics since have not left much about it uncriticised. Its importance in the history of architecture, however, lies not so much in what it was as what it did. It established a serious competitor to the classical vernacular that ordinary builder-craftsmen of its day were using so happily. Its sham battlements and stained-glass windows led straight to the builder's house of the next century, when gimcrack fashions left little room for craftsmanship.

As Walpole left it, the house was an irregular structure on three floors, with a large round tower at the W. end and a small spired turret; the building was battlemented overall, with crocketed pinnacles at the angles (*Plate 16*). There were a small cloister (where Walpole's cat was drowned in a blue-and-white vase), a chapel in the grounds, built by Gayfere, master mason of Westminster Abbey, in 1771, and a cottage in the flower-garden. Inside the house was an immense collection of high-class bric-à-brac, including miniatures, china, sculpture, stained glass, Charles II's warming-pan, and Wolsey's red hat; it

took the auctioneer George Robins 24 days to sell the lots in 1842.

Almost every personage of note from the royal family downwards visited Strawberry during Walpole's lifetime; it was so popular that for all but the most distinguished visitors excursions had to be organised and tickets obtained in advance. On his death in 1797 Mrs. Damer, sculptress, took it over; she relinquished it to Lady Waldegrave in 1811. It then became somewhat decrepit until it was lavishly refurbished and extended in the 1860s when the parties given by another Lady Waldegrave rivalled those of a century before. In 1925 the buildings were remodelled by Pugin and Pugin to serve as St Mary's training college for Roman Catholic teachers, removed from Brook Green, Hammersmith. It was slightly damaged by a fire bomb in the 1939-45 war; still, much of the fabric of Walpole's vision remains intact.

Little Strawberry, demolished in 1883, the last house in Twickenham on the lower Teddington road, was also Walpole's property. Kitty Clive, actress, lived in it from 1769 to 1785, and Walpole naturally called it 'Cliveden'; in 1791 he let it to his beloved Miss Berrys and their father.

STROUD GREEN (E3). *See* HORNSEY.

SUDBURY (C3). *See* WEMBLEY.

SUNBURY (B6) lies on the Thames between Shepperton and Hampton. The parish includes Sunbury Common, a modern settlement round the railway station 1 m. N. of the river, Charlton, 2 m. W. of the village near Littleton reservoir, Upper Halliford, bordering on Shepperton, and Kempton, to the NE. The riverside is delightful in places, and the village contains some pleasant

---

[1] K. Clark, *Gothic Revival* (1928), p. 50. [2] H. Walpole to R. Bentley, 3 November 1754.
[3] Quoted in S. Sitwell, *British Architects and Craftsmen* (1945), p. 165.

old houses and a church which is remarkable in its own style. Away from the river waterworks and modern housing development have spoiled whatever quiet charm the flat countryside may have had.

The name appears first as 'Sunnabiri' in 969, meaning 'Sunna's stronghold.' The manor was confirmed by Edward the Confessor to the abbot of Westminster in 1066. In 1222 it was ceded to the bishop of London, and during the 16th century it was vested in the Crown. In 1603 James I granted it to Robert Stratford. The manor of Kenington or Kempton was held at Domesday by Robert, Earl of Mortain, whose son William forfeited it to Henry I in 1104. It was used as a royal residence during the reigns of the first Henrys and Edwards; an inventory of the palace, with its dilapidations, taken in 1331 has survived. It was sometimes called 'Col (or Cold) Kennington.' This manor, with Hanworth, was granted in 1558 to Anne, Duchess of Somerset, widow of the protector; in 1594 it passed to the Killigrew family. Halliford manor was taken by the Crown at the Dissolution, and in 1637 it was granted to Queen Henrietta Maria. It was afterwards part of the property of Catherine of Braganza, queen of Charles II.

Nothing of consequence has ever happened at Sunbury. Admiral Hawke lived there from 1771 to his death in 1781, and Anthony Trollope was at a private school for a short time after leaving Harrow in misery. The railway arrived in 1864, and since then the village has grown without grace, like the others of the upper Middlesex Thames-side.

Sunbury church supplies an instructive commentary on the changes of taste and fashion in ecclesiastical architecture since 1750. In 1751 the church was demolished (Lysons says 'on Easter Monday'), and a new one was built by Mr. Wright, clerk of the works at Hampton Court, and consecrated in 1752. It was of brown brick, with a plain body and a W. tower surmounted by a cupola. J. H. Sperling wrote in 1849 that it held out 'no inducement to the ecclesiologist to prolong his walk thither,' and in 1856 S. S. Teulon was commissioned to turn it into something more seemly. He reconstructed the interior in what was quite seriously called the Byzantine style, similar to his later efforts at Ealing; this did not involve altering the round-headed windows. In the judgment of the time 'instead of a plain brick barn, it is now a glittering Byzantine temple.' The interior, which is happily too dark to be easily seen, contains galleries supported on cast-iron columns; the walls and roof are heavily ornamented, and the stone pulpit is picked out with startling inlay. The exterior, apart from the tower, which was allowed to retain its original appearance, was overlaid with polychromatic brick, and a W. porch and narthex were added. There is a tablet to Richard Billingsley, 1689, and one in the organ chamber to Francis and John Phelips, 1679 and 1681, and there are some good old tombstones in the churchyard.

A few good houses are left in the village; Ivy House, Rossell House, Hawke House, and the Three Fishes inn are the oldest. The Magpie hotel commemorates on a tablet the first meeting of the Grand Order of Water Rats, 1889. Towards Hampton, overlooking the river, is Sunbury Court (formerly Sunbury Place), an early 18th-century red-brick house with portico, now a Salvation Army youth centre.

Beyond is one of the few striking 19th-century Gothic houses in the county. To the N. is Kempton Park, a racecourse since 1889, with a Gothical mansion and outhouses put up about 1815.

The road from the river to Sunbury Common, by the station, runs past solid 19th-century mansions in large grounds; many are being broken up. The settlement of Sunbury Common has a regrettable appearance, redeemed only by the Middlesex County Council's Kenyngton Manor school.

NW., on the edge of the huge Queen Mary reservoir, is the isolated hamlet of Charlton: a strange survival in Middlesex today, with some 200 inhabitants, but no public transport, shop, school, electricity, post office, or church. The Harrow inn is one of the oldest domestic buildings in the county, with parts about 1500 (*Plate 29*).

SWAKELEYS (B3). *See* ICKENHAM.

SYON HOUSE (C5), in a park lying on the Thames at the NE. corner of Isleworth parish, is the last of the great riverside mansions near London remaining in private ownership. Commemorating by its name the greatest medieval monastic foundation of Middlesex and incorporating in its fabric the work of many different centuries, Syon is a monument of historic importance only excelled in Middlesex by Hampton Court, and the decorative beauties of its 18th-century interior are set off by the great charm of its site.

Syon was originally a Brigittine nunnery, one of a pair (with Sheen, on the Surrey bank) founded by Henry V in 1415. The monastery was removed from Twickenham to the Isleworth site *c.* 1431.[1] It was disaffected to Henry VIII, but not (as sometimes stated) dissolved specially on that account.

In the succeeding centuries it housed a succession of distinguished persons: Catherine Howard, Henry VIII's fifth queen, 1541-2; Edward Seymour, Duke of Somerset, protector, executed 1552; John Dudley, Duke of Northumberland, and Lady Jane Grey, both executed 1553; the nuns, recalled from the Netherlands, 1557-8; Henry Percy, Earl of Northumberland, involved in the Gunpowder Plot; Charles I's children; Charles II during the plague, 1665; and the dukes of Northumberland of the 1766 creation, who still hold it.

The house, three storeys with battlemented top and angle turrets, is built on a hollow square which probably reproduces the ground-plan of the nuns' cloister of the abbey; part of the 15th-century undercroft remains. Protector Somerset reconstructed the house in handsome style, 1547-52, substantially in its present shape. Henry, Earl of Northumberland, improved the property in the early 17th century; his successor Algernon restored the building about 1659. The arcade on the river front may have been the work of Inigo Jones; it has certainly been altered a good deal. The principal rooms on the first floor were reconstructed by Robert Adam from 1761 onwards, and he also built the gateway and screen on the main Brentford-Hounslow road. The house was almost entirely recased in 1819-25. The final touch to the exterior was given in 1874 by the erection on the river front of the Percy lion, transferred from old Northumberland House at Charing Cross. The exterior is familiar to the visitor to Kew Gardens or the passer on Thames steamer or towpath as an agreeable, if not specially attractive, feature of the river's most charming reach near London.

[1] On Henry V's foundation, see Shakespeare, *Henry V*, Act iv, scene 1:
    'I have built
Two chantries, where the sad and solemn priests
Sing still for Richard's soul.'
For the monastery, see Part I, p. 107.

Within, however, there is a striking contrast to the cool levels of the water-meadows and the plain rectangularity of the fronts. Robert Adam's planning and decoration were bold and vigorous, with a dashing use of colour that must have been startling in 1765, as indeed it seems opulent today. The entrance-hall, as a foil to the living-rooms, is a high, airy apartment, in black and white, with strongly patterned marble floor; at one end columns stand free as a screen across a staircase, concealing the rise to the next room. This is the anteroom, brilliantly coloured with scagliola floor, *verde antico* columns surmounted with gilded classical figures, and painted ceiling, in yellow, brown, and red. Adam again employed his favourite trick of running a screen of disengaged columns across the end of the room, making it almost square in effect. A massive Sèvres vase, mostly gold, pink, and blue, dominates the piece; this was presented by Charles X of France to the duke of Northumberland who attended his coronation (1825).

The dining-room again has a screen at each end across an apse; statues supply most of the decoration. The walls have frieze panels in chiaroscuro, like the entrance hall.[1] The red drawing-room, with patterned hangings of plum-red Spitalfields silk, is warm and rich, with a carpet woven to order by T. Moore of Moorfields in 1769. The ceiling, of little panels filled with painted scenes, displays Adam's manner carried to extreme. Throughout these rooms are handsome statues after the antique, and the plaster work by Joseph Rose is very fine.

The gallery is a 16th-century room running the whole length of the E. side, 136 ft. long; all Adam's skill at breaking up the distance cannot quite overome

the difficulty presented by its width of only 14 ft. The pilasters were painted by Pergolesi, and the representations of the earls of Northumberland in medallions are interesting, if hardly all authentic. The 19th-century print room has portraits of the Percys. In the passage beyond are more paintings and a fine map of Isleworth hundred (Moses Glover, 1635), with the S. at the top. If Adam's reconstruction had been completed, the central courtyard would have become a domed saloon; it was in fact covered over temporarily for a party in 1768.

In front of the W. side of the house are two garden lodges, facing the lane across the park, which date from the early 17th century, with 18th-century Venetian windows. On the main road is a splendidly conceived gateway, with open ironwork, surmounted by another lion and flanked by lead sphinxes. Walpole had a grumble about 'the magnificent gateway and screen for the Duke of Northumberland, which I see erecting every time I pass. It is all lace and embroidery, and as *croquant* as his frames for tables; consequently most improper to be exposed in the high road to Brentford. From Kent's mahogany we are dwindled to Adam's filigree. Grandeur and simplicity are not yet in fashion.'[2] Our own age may be grateful to the noble patron who was content to pay for such filigree on the Brentford road; it is elegance unsurpassed (*Plate 28*).

The gardens, already notable for the improvements made by William Turner, father of scientific botany in England, d. 1568, were replanned by Lancelot ('Capability') Brown in the middle 18th century. They contain magnificent trees and shrubs and a conservatory of 1827 by Charles Fowler, architect of glass-and-iron

[1] These were possibly meant to be sketches for plaster work: J. Lees-Milne, *Age of Adam* (1947), p. 110. [2] Horace Walpole to Rev. W. Mason, 29 July 1773.

buildings at Covent Garden and Hungerford markets that show Paxton's Crystal Palace of 1851 to have been descended from a line of ancestors. The Syon glasshouse is attractive without being good-looking—the dome is too large. The stables NE. of the house are on the site of early buildings, perhaps belonging to the abbey.

Some attractive smaller houses stand to the N., including Syon Gardens (*Plate 11*), and on the main road—Syon Lodge and Syon Park House (*see* BRENTFORD). Still farther N., where the Great West road now runs, was Syon Hill, where the Duke of Marlborough had a house about 1795.

TEDDINGTON (c6), since 1937 part of Twickenham borough, lies on the Thames below Hampton Wick, with a strip running W. through Fulwell towards Hanworth. It is now a residential suburb, with some relics to indicate where the old village stood.

The name originally appears as 'Tudington,' meaning 'Tuda's farm.' The silly old story that it means Tide-End-Town has been too often repeated.[1] The manor belonged to Westminster Abbey until it was surrendered to Henry VIII; it afterwards remained Crown property. Elizabeth leased it in 1572 to Sir Amyas Paulet, keeper of Mary, queen of Scots. The London & South Western station was opened in 1863; electric trams began running in 1903, and much building was done at this period. Teddington became the effective up-river limit of tidal waters when the lock was built in 1811; it is now the frontier of the jurisdictions of the Port of London Authority and the Thames Conservancy Board. There was a large candle factory in the 19th century, with wax-bleaching grounds covering 4 acres.

Though overshadowed in fame by Twickenham, Teddington has had some notable inhabitants. Elizabeth's Earl of Leicester was living there in 1570; Matthew Rendall or Randall, appointed curate 1638, was suspended for preaching a sermon over an hour long; William Penn, founder of Pennsylvania, dated his letter rebutting a charge of popery from Teddington, 1688. Sir Orlando Bridgeman, royalist, Lord Keeper of the Great Seal 1665, Henry Flitcroft (son of a Hampton Court gardener), architect of Wentworth Woodhouse and Woburn Abbey, d. 1769, Paul Whitehead, poet, d. 1774, and John Walter, printer, founder of *The Times*, d. 1812, are buried in the church. Thomas Traherne, metaphysical poet, chaplain to Sir Orlando Bridgeman and minister of Teddington, was buried in the church, 1674; his admirers have not yet erected a permanent memorial to him. Stephen Hales, minister 1709-61, was a natural philosopher of various interests; Peg Woffington, comic actress, d. 1760, lived in the parish (tablet in the church); she acted Polly Peachum in *The Beggar's Opera* in Madame Violante's Lilliputian company at the age of 8 and became one of the favourites of the 18th-century stage. She was said to be one of the few actresses of her day who would allow her face to be made up.[2] Alexander Herzen, leader of the 19th-century liberal exiles from Russia, occupied Elmfield House, 1863-4;[3] R. D. Blackmore, d. 1900, author of *Lorna Doone*, lived at Gomer House and owned market gardens.

Little is left of the Teddington that these characters knew. Two churches now confront each other at the W. end of the High Street, the modest old parish church (St Mary) to the N. and an unfinished edifice of the late 19th century (St Alban) opposite. St Mary is

[1] By Napoleon III in his *Vie de Jules César*, so recently as 1940, in *Middlesex* (ed. A. Mee), p. 182. In historic times the tide flowed much higher up the river.   [2] Aaron Hill, quoted in *Johnson's England* (page 153, note 4), ii., p. 181.   [3] E. H. Carr, *Romantic Exiles* (Penguin ed.), p. 429 (appendix C).

a plain little building, largely reconstructed in the 18th and 19th centuries; the S. aisle is early 16th-century brickwork with some black brick patterning. The N. aisle and W. tower were built 1753-4. There is a brass of 1506 and a monument to Sir Orlando Bridgeman, 1674. St Alban, across the road, is a vast fragment with copper-sheathed roof, by W. Niven (1886); the original design ran to a N. tower and W. front with two spires. The apsidal chancel and part only of the nave have been completed. The interior is enriched with costly fittings in the different ecclesiastical tastes of the last 65 years. The other Teddington churches are SS. Peter and Paul, Broad Street (G. E. Street, 1866), in yellow and red brick, and St Mark, South Teddington (C. A. Farey, 1939), a plain and seemly yellow-brick building with a low pyramidal spire. Elmfield House, now municipal offices, is a late 18th-century brick building, a rare survival of old Teddington.

A large part of Bushy Park (*see* HAMPTON COURT) lies within Teddington; the ranger's house became the nucleus of the National Physical Laboratory when it was established in 1900. New buildings have been added to the W. of Bushy House. Farther W. is the district of Fulwell; King Manoel of Portugal lived at Fulwell Park after his exile from Lisbon in 1910.

TOTTENHAM (F3) is a borough (1934) on the borders of London and Essex, lying astride the road from London to Waltham Cross; Wood Green, to the W., was separated from it in 1888. The area is flat, and the river Lea, the E. boundary, is the only evident natural feature. The High Road, on the line of the Roman road from London to Lincoln, runs N. through

the old village centre. Most of Tottenham owes its present aspect to the years from 1871 to 1900, when working-class London flowed out over the Stoke Newington border and submerged the large, comfortable houses with their gardens that used to line the High Road. Only in the NE. corner was much room left by 1918, and that was already earmarked by the London County Council for its White Hart Lane housing estate. There are two old buildings of unusual interest, Bruce Castle and the Priory, by the church; but on the whole it is an unprepossessing place.

It was 'Toteham' in Domesday Book, 'Totta's farm' or 'lookout place'; later it was often 'Tottenham High Cross.' The history of the manor, according to the judicious Lysons, 'affords a very striking instance of the instability of honours and property in the early periods of our annals.' Under Edward the Confessor it was the property of Earl Waltheof of Northumberland; he plotted against William soon after the Conquest and was beheaded in 1075, but his widow Judith, niece of the Conqueror, still held it at the Domesday Survey of 1086. It passed early in the 12th century to David, son of Malcolm III of Scotland, who secured all the lands previously held by Waltheof; it then descended to David, Earl of Angus, Galloway, and Huntingdon, d. 1219, and in 1254 was divided between three co-heirs, Robert de Brus, John de Baliol, and Henry de Hastings. One portion remained in the Bruce family until Edward II seized it in 1306 on Robert Bruce's assertion of his right to the crown of Scotland. The reunited manor was held by Hare, Lord Coleraine, from 1626 to 1749. There were smaller manors called Mockings, Ducketts (partly in Hornsey), Willoughby (partly in Edmonton), Twyford, and Stoneleys.

An alliterative poem, 'The Tournament of Tottenham,' has survived in a manuscript at the British Museum, reprinted in Percy's *Reliques of English Poetry*,[1] telling how Randall the reeve appointed a tournament for his daughter Tybbe as the prize, with flails as weapons, and how there came to it

> ... *alle the men of that contray*
> *Of Hisselton, of Hy-gate, and of Hakenay.*

It is a strange piece, perhaps a mid-15th-century parody.

Tottenham's earliest economic importance was as the river head on the Lea; barges were plying to it in 1448.[2] It was never a market town. Wells in the parish enjoyed some celebrity, especially St Loy's Well with a hermit's cell not far away, near Philip Lane, and Bishop's Well, near the Moselle (or Muswell) brook. As trade and navigation moved higher up the valley in the 16th and 17th centuries, Tottenham became a pleasant country retreat for substantial citizens; this character lasted until well into the 19th century. In 1724 it was thought of as a healthy place: 'the Air is wholesome and temperate, and has no Bogs, Moors, or Fens to infect and distemper it' (in spite of the Lea marshes).[3] Its position marked it out as suitable for private schools, and there was an influential Quaker body. In 1795 the only manufactures were corn and oil mills by the Lea crossing at the Hale; in 1815 a silk mill was built, soon afterwards converted to lace-making; in 1837 it went over to rubber manufacture, but the stench of naphtha was too much for the district.[4] Tottenham was a receiving station for cattle and sheep from the eastern counties, which were driven on to London markets after a rest in 'lairs' or pens beside the railway station at the Hale.[5] Between 1868 and 1878 the original railway of 1840 up the Lea valley was supplemented with a network covering the parish. Tramways began to work up the High Road in 1881 (electrified 1904).

The new railways of the 1870s, with their workmen's trains, and the trams brought thousands of London wage-earners out to live in Tottenham, almost all in the E. half of the district, and factories soon followed.

Almost everything of note lies on or close to the High Road, a broad street with some trees at the S. end. The church of St Anne (1861, T. Bury) gives its name to the street, formerly Hanger Lane, running NW. Seven Sisters Road (completed 1833) is supposed to be named from a group of seven elm trees at Page Green, where it joins the High Road; legend has not neglected them. To the E. is the district of the Hale, a Middlesex name found also at Mill Hill, meaning 'angle or corner;' the Ferry Boat inn is its only attractive feature (*Plate 39*).

A slight rise, dignified by Izaak Walton's Piscator with the name of Tottenham Hill, leads from Seven Sisters past Tottenham Green to the High Cross. W. of the Green are the dull and dignified municipal buildings (A. S. Tayler and A. R. Jemmett, 1905); opposite is the Prince of Wales Hospital, which grew out of an institution founded by Dr. Michael Laseron in 1868 for training Protestant deaconesses as nurses, on the model of the German institution at Kaiserswerth; to the N. is the church of Holy Trinity, High Cross (J. Savage, 1830; blitzed)—'Early English of impure character,' according to Thorne. At the top of the rise, on the right, is the High Cross—a brick object

---

[1] *Oxford Book of Light Verse*, ed. W. H. Auden (1938), p. 41. [2] *H.C.M.* 13 (1911), p. 231. [3] Cox (page 44, note 1), iii., p. 34. [4] Dean (page 54, note 5). [5] Murray's *Handbook for Essex, Suffolk, Norfolk, and Cambridgeshire* (1870), p. 83; the same statement appears in ed. 3 (1892), p. 89, but it was almost certainly out of date by then; description of cattle arriving by rail at Tottenham for Londoners' Christmas dinners, *Illustrated London News* 27 (1855), p. 751.

of about 1600, stuccoed over in 1809 with embellishments in the Gothic taste. An older wooden wayside cross stood on the site, but there was not one of the Eleanor crosses here.

Farther N., at the junction of Bruce Grove, the shopping centre now congests the High Road. Bruce Grove, where most of the old Quaker families had their houses, leads NW. to Bruce Castle and the parish church. Bruce Castle, which has retained its name from the comparatively brief association of the Scottish family with the manor from 1254 to 1306, appears to date from the late 16th century. It is built of red brick with stone dressings, with a projecting central porch on the S. surmounted by a clock tower and cupola, and semi-octagonal wings. Only the central feature retains the elaborate ornament of the original building; 18th-century and later alterations have left the rest very plain. On the N. front is a handsome cornice and pediment containing the Coleraine arms (about 1720); inside there are some agreeable 18th-century fittings, perhaps more than might be expected from its history. It was bought by the brothers Rowland, Edwin, and Frederick Hill in 1827 as a branch for their successful Hazelwood school, Birmingham; Rowland left the partnership in 1833 and devoted himself to postal reform. It remained a school until 1891 (Birkbeck Hill, Johnsonian scholar, was headmaster 1859-76) and was then bought by the local council. A museum of postal history is now housed in the main part of the house. A little way SW. is a circular brick tower, apparently of the 16th century, of uncertain origin.

To the N., left of the road to the church, is the Priory, now the vicarage, a charming house of about 1620 refaced early in the 18th century, with fine plaster ceilings, overmantels, and fireplaces inside. In the garden is a good early 18th-century wrought-iron gate, with overthrows, from the old vicarage.

The parish church (All Hallows) stands at the NW. corner of Bruce Castle Park, about ¼ m. W. of the High Road. It is an architectural jumble with some good features; the thin W. tower spoils its appearance (*Plate 1*). The oldest portion is the lower part of the tower (early 14th-century); later in that century the nave and 'old chancel' (now part of the nave) were rebuilt. About 1500 the S. aisle was rebuilt and the whole church extended to the E.; the upper part of the tower was added late in the 18th century. The present N. aisle dates from 1816, and in 1875 W. Butterfield added a harsh new chancel, transepts, and vestries. The best feature of the church is the S. porch, in brick with black brick patterns and stone dressings, of about 1500; it has a chamber above the porch itself and a battlemented parapet and moulded chimney stack. The principal monuments are one of black and white marble (N. aisle) to Mary, wife of Sir Robert Barkham, 1644, with busts by Edward Marshall of both of them and a row of 12 pretty children; (in the S. aisle) to Richard and Elizabeth Kandeler and also to Sir Ferdinando and Anne Heyborne, with two pairs of kneeling figures, *c.* 1620, and to Sir John Melton, 1640. There is some notable French glass of about 1600 in the W. window of the N. aisle. There is a plain early 17th-century communion table in the N. transept. The sanctus bell (French, 1663) is said to have been the garrison bell at Quebec, taken in 1759. There are some good 18th-century headstones in the churchyard.

Most of the remaining old buildings in Tottenham lie on the High Road north of Bruce Grove; they might enhance the appearance of this slovenly thoroughfare, but they are generally in poor condition. At the extreme N. of the parish is Brook House, left of the road, with a pleasant front.

The N. district is unattractive; the Northumberland Park area, genteel houses built after the station was opened in 1840, is shabby. St Mary, Lansdowne Road (J. E. K. Cutts, 1887), was a Marlborough College mission church. The Hotspurs' football ground, not far away, supplies Tottenham with most of the attention it gets from the outside world. Asplin's farm, 17th and 18th centuries, now lies among factories immediately E. of the Northumberland Park level-crossing. N. of White Hart Lane, near the station, are two good 18th-century houses, one with a pillared porch.

Farther W. along White Hart Lane where it makes some remarkable right-angle turns are Tottenham College, in academic Tudor of the 1930s, and St Katherine's training college, on the N. side, a remarkable building (A. Blomfield, 1879) for its date, using Wren idioms, large rectangular windows, and high dormers. Beyond, farther W., is the London County Council's housing estate, seen to best advantage in Roundway, begun in 1902 and built over the next 30 years. The houses are not bad, but the planning of shops and services, with the arterial road running through the middle, is faulty. The church of St John the Baptist (J. Seely and P. Paget, 1939) is an example of the modern style. S. of this, West Green Road contains some decent houses that have passed their best days.

Some of the houses and institutions that have disappeared deserve mention: the almshouses founded by Balthasar Sanchez (d. 1600), a court confectioner

of Spanish origin, which stood where the ugly shops 578-592 High Road still bear his name; Reynardson's house, on the N. side of the Green, built 1590, a famous Quaker boarding-school, demolished 1810; Grove House, its successor as a school from 1828 to 1879, where Lord Lister, J. H. Shorthouse, author of *John Inglesant*, W. E. Forster, and A. Waterhouse, architect, were educated; the Black House, E. of the High Road opposite White Hart Lane, residence of George Hynningham, of Henry VIII's household, and later of Sir Hugh Smithson, ancestor of the present duke of Northumberland of Syon House, Isleworth. Other inhabitants were Sir Julius Caesar, Master of the Rolls, 1557 (son of Cesare Dalmare, physician to Queen Elizabeth), and his son Sir Charles Caesar; Sir Abraham Reynardson, royalist lord mayor of London 1648-9, who refused to proclaim the abolition of royal power and was deposed and imprisoned; William Baxter, schoolmaster and antiquary, nephew of Richard Baxter the nonconformist, d. 1723; Priscilla Wakefield, a Friend, who began a children's savings bank in 1798 and enlarged it into the first genuine savings bank of the modern kind in 1804; William Hobson, building contractor for Newgate prison, some of the Thames docks, and (though a Quaker) the Martello towers;[1] Thomas Shillitoe, d. 1836, a zealous Friend of the early 19th century; John Williams, missionary to Polynesia, b. at Tottenham 1796; Luke Howard, d. 1864, chemist and author of *The Climate of London* (1818), a pioneer in the classification of clouds; Charles Bradlaugh, radical M.P., who lived in Northumberland Park, 1866.

Tottenham has been assiduously, though not yet adequately, dealt with by some notable chroniclers: after

---

[1] *Builder* 103 (1912), p. 419.

William Bedwell, vicar and orientalist, 'the first noteworthy Arabist of the new age,'[1] who wrote a history in 1631 (one of the earliest English histories of towns or villages), Lord Coleraine collected a manuscript history first printed in 1790; there has been a history sold for a farthing (1890); and F. Fisk's work (1913 and 1923) was written, set up, printed, bound, and sold by the same man. A place inspiring such devotion deserved to be better looked after.

TWICKENHAM (c5) is an extensive district on the Thames between Teddington and Isleworth. The E. part of the ancient parish contained most of the settlements until the 20th century: the old village just inland from the river at Eel Pie island; 17th- and 18th-century ribbon development along the river (STRAWBERRY HILL is separately noticed); and the W. approach to Richmond bridge, in the district called St Margaret's, bordering on Isleworth. The W. part, with the hamlet of Whitton, extended as far as Hounslow Heath. Twickenham now presents several distinct aspects: old-established houses and parks by the river, somewhat cut up but on the whole well preserved; 19th-century houses, mostly large and once comfortable, round the railway stations; and modern dwellings filling up all the remaining spaces except where light industries have established a few factories. The banks of the Crane have been preserved from the border of Hanworth on the extreme W. to St Margaret's in the NE. Twickenham became a borough in 1926.

The name appears in the second oldest Middlesex charter—one of 704 in which Suebraed, king of Essex, granted land at *Tuicanhom in provincia quae nuncupatur Middelseaxan*; it prob-ably means 'Twica's *hamm*' (bend in the river). It was not mentioned in Domesday Book, being included in Isleworth. Most of the parish lay within the manor of Syon.

By 1600 houses for the nobility were being built at Twickenham, pleasantly situated on the road to Hampton Court. Francis Bacon lived at Twickenham Park in the NE. corner from about 1592 to 1606, and during the 17th century it became popular with the wealthy. There were some political commotions under the Commonwealth: the puritan Parliament found time in the spring of 1645 to pass an ordinance abolishing the custom of dividing two great cakes on Easter day in the church (later bread was thrown from the top of the tower to be scrambled for in the churchyard, something like the 'pancake greaze' at Westminster[2]); in 1649 Sir Thomas Nott, of Twickenham Park, apparently had the accession of Charles II publicly proclaimed, giving rise to a riot;[3] and in 1659 Thomas Willis, the intruding minister, preached against Sir Thomas Middleton, Sir George Booth, and others arming to secure Charles's return; early in 1660 he gave thanksgiving for delivery from 'that bloody family' of Stuarts. He was ejected at the Restoration and arraigned at the sessions for these offences; but he later conformed, became vicar of Kingston-on-Thames, and was actually appointed one of Charles's chaplains.[4]

After the Restoration Twickenham became increasingly popular, and in the 18th century the river was lined with houses of the great, the rich, and the literary: Pope and Horace Walpole were the successive geniuses of the place. Fruit-gardens, lamprey-fishing, and a linseed mill were the only commercial enterprises of any consequence existing in 1800; Batty

[1] A. J. Arberry, *British Orientalists* (1943), p. 16. [2] R. S. Cobbett, *Memorials of Twickenham* (1872), p. 173. [3] *Mx. & H. N. & Q.* 1 (1895), p. 114, quoting Parliamentary Council of State, 25 August 1649. [4] *M.C.R.*, iii., p. 308; A. G. Matthews, *Calamy Revised* (1934), art. T. Willis.

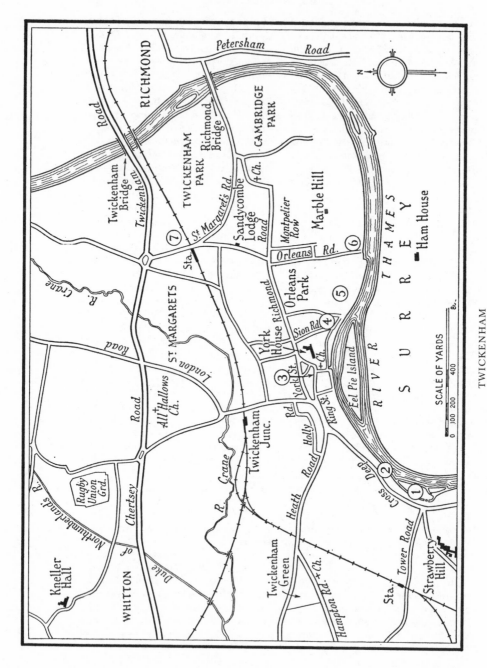

TWICKENHAM

1. *Radnor House.* 2. *Pope's Villa.* 3. *Aragon House.* 4. *Mount Lebanon.* 5. *Orleans House.*
6. *Ragman's Castle.* 7. *Ailsa Park Villas.*

Langley the architect, born at Twickenham 1696, published in his *Pomona, or the Fruit-Garden Illustrated* (1728) the days the different fruits ripened there in 1727. Even after the opening of the railway in 1849 little industrial development took place. A tramway was laid from Isleworth through to Teddington in 1902-3. Twickenham has managed to preserve much of the characteristic charm of its riverside and to build some good suburbs in the newer districts; but some deplorable things were done, and the shopping centre of modern Twickenham is a sad commentary on the taste of Pope's and Walpole's 20th-century successors.

Radnor House, built for John Robartes, Earl of Radnor, d. 1757, stood first downstream from Strawberry Hill. The house, by then an ugly object, was blitzed in 1940; the gardens are a public park.

Pope's villa, where he lived from 1719 to 1744, was a few yards nearer to Twickenham; a convent building stands on part of the site. The garden with its weeping willow and grotto, reached by a tunnel under the Teddington road, was Pope's special pride, and his own taste, combined with the professional aid of Kent and Bridgman, began a movement towards informal design in gardening. The house was pulled down in 1807 and a new one built 100 yds. N. In 1840 this in turn was demolished, and the main part of the present gingerbread affair called Pope's Villa was put up. H.Labouchère, politician and founder of *Truth*, d. 1912, later lived in it. Thomas Hudson, painter, d. 1779, lived in a house on part of the site.

Cross Deep, close by, is an 18th-century house with good iron gateway, but the 19th and 20th centuries have obliterated the rest of the mansions that stood on this side of the church and erected instead their own idea of a suburb. King Street, the centre of modern Twickenham, lacks character; what character there is in an Egyptian-style cinema could well be spared. Modern times have passed by Church Street, a narrow lane, and Bell Lane, where some undistinguished 17th-century building remains; and there are one or two old houses on the embankment opposite Eel Pie island. The island—properly Twickenham Ait—has refreshed excursionists since Henry VIII's reign. In Dickens' day it was a favourite spot for cockney outings— Miss Morleena Kenwigs, in *Nicholas Nickleby*, went there for a picnic.

W. of the lane leading to the church is Arragon House, probably the remains of the old manor house; it is doubtfully associated with Katharine of Aragon, and Catherine of Braganza is said to have lived in it for a time. Samuel Scott, marine painter, d. 1772, and W. Marlow, landscape painter, d. 1813, occupied it (*Plate 15*).

E. of Arragon House, well situated when seen from the river, is the parish church (St Mary), with a classical brick body built on to a 15th-century stone W. tower. The old church fell down in 1713, and the present one, quaintly described by the Royal Commission on Historical Monuments as 'a Renaissance building of some interest,' was built in 1714-15 to the designs of John James, architect of St George, Hanover Square. The interior is galleried, with a plaster ceiling, coved at the sides; the reredos, staircases, font, and doors are contemporary with the church, and the 18th-century pulpit remains; but the rest of the interior was heavily reconstructed in 1859 and 1871. In all, the interior is interesting rather than attractive. Some monuments survive from the old church, including a brass of 1443. Some 18th-century monuments have notable associations: one to Pope, d. 1744, put up in 1761 by Warburton, the sculpture by Prince Hoare;[1] one (by F. Bird) erected by Pope to his parents, 1717 and 1733, with the words *et Sibi* at the foot; a tablet to Nathaniel Pigott, barrister, d. 1737, with inscription by Pope; and a stone on the outside wall of the chancel to Mary Beach, Pope's nurse, d.1725. Close to it is an inscription to Kitty Clive, actress, d. 1785. Many of the monuments inside the church are difficult to see.

Just NE. of the church is Twickenham's most handsome building, York House, now used as council offices. It is a symmetrically-designed red-brick building of the late 17th century, three storeys on H-plan with slightly projecting wings (*Plate 44*). There is 17th-century panelling and wooden staircase, spoilt by insertion of a lift, inside. The name is probably owing to a 15th-century owner and not to James, Duke of York (later James 11);[2] when his daughter, later Queen Anne, lived in the house as a child *c.* 1665, Edward Hyde, Earl of Clarendon, his father-in-law, was the owner. It was occupied by Mrs. Anne Damer, sculptor, d. 1820, and by the Orleanist Comte de Paris from 1864 to 1871. There are agreeable gardens to the S.; amateurs of the curious should cross the bridge into the riverside garden where some remarkable statuary is displayed.

Immediately E. of York House is Sion Row, dated 1721 on the street tablet, a delightful terrace of small houses, damaged by one ugly Victorian bow window. Laetitia Hawkins, tattling writer, lived in Sion Row and left *Anecdotes*, of which many refer to Twickenham. Ferry House, at the river end, is attractive. The next piece of ground was occupied by Mount Lebanon, where the Prince de Joinville, 3rd son of Louis Philippe, lived from 1866 to 1871. The next estate was called Orleans House from its connexion with the exile from France of Louis Philippe and his family in 1800 and again after 1852. The house has been demolished, except the 'octagon room,' built by James Gibbs[3] for James Johnstone about 1720, but the grounds remain as a public park.

Downstream is Marble Hill (the name is probably a 17th-century corruption of 'Mardle's Hill'). The house was built by Robert Morris[4] about 1725 for Mrs. Howard, Countess of Suffolk, mistress of George II; Swift and Pope had a good deal to say about it. The house was rented by Mrs. Fitzherbert, and she was living there at the time of the marriage ceremony between her and the Prince of Wales in 1785. The estate was bought in 1902[5] to preserve the historic view up the Thames from Richmond hill, the view that Jeanie Deans admired and Constable, Turner, and many others have sought to capture. At the NW. corner of the park is Montpelier Row, a tall and handsome terrace dated 1720; Tennyson lived at the end house, on the corner of Chapel Road, 1851-2. Close to Marble Hill stood Little Marble Hill, occupied by Kitty Clive, actress, before she moved to Little Strawberry Hill, and Ragman's Castle, where Hannah Pritchard, actress, d. 1768, lived for some years.

The land in the loop of the river between Marble Hill and Richmond bridge (J. Payne, 1777), called Cambridge Park, commemorates Richard Owen Cambridge, wit and writer, d. 1802; the church of St Stephen (1875) was built for the suburb that succeeded the big houses. To the N. is the district called St Margaret's; this was the site of Twickenham Park, where the nunnery of Syon was established from 1414 to c.1431, when it removed to Isleworth. Francis Bacon lived there from about 1592 to 1606. Lucy, Countess of Bedford, lived in the house from 1607 to 1618; she was a patron of John Donne, who wrote a poem called *Twicknam* (*sic*) *Garden*. John, Lord Berkeley of Stratton had the park from 1668 to 1678; the house was pulled down about 1820. The estate stretched N. into Isleworth parish, and the house stood on the boundary, so that when the parishes were beating bounds a representative had to pass through the house while the company were singing the Hundredth Psalm in the hall.

Two of the 19th-century houses in St Margaret's, built when the large estates were cut up, have interesting associations: 2 Ailsa Park Villas, opposite the station, where Dickens lived in 1838 and 1839 while writing *Nicholas Nickleby*; and Sandycombe Lodge to the SE. in Sandycombe Road, a charming little house designed for himself by J. M. W. Turner in 1813, where he lived till 1825.

There are some good old houses by London Road in the centre of Twickenham, notably by the Crane river N. of the railway bridge and in Holly Road, just behind. Twickenham Green, to the W., is an early 19th-century district; there is a white brick church (Holy Trinity) by G. Basevi (1841; enlarged F. T. Dollman, 1863). Near the railway bridge over Heath Road was Twickenham House, where Sir John Hawkins, Middlesex magistrate, editor of Walton's *Compleat Angler*, author of *The History of Music* and *Life of Dr. Johnson*, d. 1789, lived for many years. It was afterwards a

private lunatic asylum. Next door was Saville House, where Lady Mary Wortley Montagu lived after 1720, in order to be near to Pope; a quarrel followed. Somewhere near was a timber house where Henry Fielding lived in 1747 and 1748. N. of the Green, Paul Whitehead, poet, d. 1774, lived in a house called Colne Lodge (there has been a good deal of confusion between the river names Crane and Colne). On the E. side of Hampton Road, just short of Fulwell (in Teddington), is Fortescue House, formerly Wellesley House: the name was transferred with the Metropolitan Police orphanage from the middle of the village about 1880. In a small cottage on the Staines road lived Joanna Southcott, prophetess, d. 1814; there were traces of attachment to her in the district 50 years later.[1]

The NW. portion of Twickenham is Whitton, a hamlet until 1862. The Chertsey road, running N. of the Crane to the edge of Hounslow Heath, is an uninteresting by-pass except for the church of All Hallows, on the S. side just W. of London Road. The tower, standing boldly in the flat surroundings, is Wren's tower of All Hallows, Lombard Street, re-erected 1940; the body of the church, linked to it by a cloister, is by R. Atkinson. Woodwork, monuments (including a bust of E. Tyson by Edward Stanton), and floor-slabs from the old church have been worked into the new; the pulpit, panelling, reredos, and organ case, all of 1694, are particularly good, but the roof fails to make a happy effect.

To the NW., in Whitton Road, are the Rugby Union football ground and Kneller Hall, the military school of music. The house has had a chequered history; it was built in 1709-11 (perhaps to a design by Vanbrugh[2]) for Sir Godfrey Kneller, portrait-painter, who

---

[1] Cobbett (see page 347, note 2), p. 345. [2] Whistler (page 7, note 1), p. 297.

during his residence there had some unedifying squabbles with Pope. It was then called Whitton House. About 1820 it was considerably altered by Philip Hardwick; in 1847 it became a teachers' training college under Frederick Temple, later archbishop of Canterbury, with F. T. Palgrave, critic and anthologist of *The Golden Treasury*, as vice-principal 1850-5. At this time it was further enlarged by G. Mair, who arranged the front allegedly after the style of Wollaton Hall, Nottingham, a mansion of 1580-8. It became the military school of music in 1857. It is a more pleasing object than the tale of its refashionings would suggest.

Murray Park, to the W., is all that remains of the grounds of several extensive 18th-century seats. Whitton Place was built about 1725 by James Gibbs for the Earl of Islay, and the grounds planted with conifers and exotics; this was the nobleman of whom 50 years later Johnson pronounced: 'Archibald, Duke of Argyll, was narrow in his quotidian expenses.' Sir William Chambers, designer of Kew Gardens and architect of Somerset House, d. 1796, bought the house and part of the grounds; he turned it into an Italian villa, pulled down *c.* 1847.[1] Sir John Suckling, poet, was born at Whitton, 1609.

After 1850 Whitton grew quickly owing rather to the spread of Hounslow S. past its railway station than to growth of Twickenham to the N. The church (SS. Philip and James; F. H. Pownall, 1862) is a little stone-built affair, in the Victorian version of Early English, with a small pepper-pot turret at the W. end.

TWYFORD (c4)—properly West Twyford, in distinction from East Twyford in Willesden[2]—is a singular little parish of 281 acres at the SW.

extremity of Willesden, S. of the Brent, which consisted until 1900 only of the manor house and its appurtenances. It is divided between Ealing and Willesden boroughs. Cows are still to be seen grazing in fields, and it is the nearest place to London where the motorist is requested to 'Beware Cattle Crossing.' In spite of the factories of Park Royal on the E. and suburban building along the North Circular road on the N., it retains some air of 19th-century rural Middlesex.

'Tueverde' (two fords) appears in Domesday as a separate manor. It was one of the ancient domains of St Paul's. It passed to various owners, including John Lyon, founder of Harrow school, until it was bought in 1806 by Thomas Willan, proprietor of the Bull and Mouth tavern, a celebrated coaching inn off Aldersgate. The manor house, the only dwelling in the parish, was taken down and a new house, called 'Twyford Abbey,' built in 1808 in the cockney-Gothic style of the period, to the designs of W. Atkinson, who later built Abbotsford for Sir Walter Scott. The house was bought by the Alexian brothers, a Roman Catholic order, in 1902 and has since been occupied by them as a nursing-home; additions including a chapel were built in 1904.

The little church (St Mary), standing just W. of the manor house, was also completely reconstructed in 1808, in yellow brick with four corner pinnacles.[3] The preceding church is said to have been rebuilt by Robert Moyle in the 16th century. There are a few old monuments. Services at Twyford church were intermittent; about 1800 there were six a year, but at the end of the 19th century no Sunday service was held for 4 years together (1893-7). After the sale of the manor and advowson to the Roman Catholic community (with

[1] J. Boswell, *Journal of a Tour to the Hebrides with Samuel Johnson, LL.D.* (Oxford ed., 1930), p. 393; drawings of the house as designed by Gibbs and Chambers, A. E. Richardson, *Introduction to Georgian Architecture* (1949), p. 48. [2] There has been a good deal of confusion, particularly in the ecclesiastical writers, between East and West Twyford; I. M. (Mrs. Basil) Holmes, *West Twyford, Middlesex* (1908; ed. 2, 1936), corrects it. [3] Atkinson is credited with the design of Twyford chapel (presumably the church) as well in *Dictionary of Architecture*, i. (1856), p. 119.

consequent lapse to the Crown of the right of presentation), the church was restored and reopened in 1907.

Modern development first laid its hand on this curiously sequestered corner in 1900 when the Park Royal estate, partly in the E. of the parish, was bought by the Royal Agricultural Society for use as a showground. In 1903 Park Royal stations were opened, and some building began. In 1937 a new red-brick mission hall was built NW. of the church for the needs of the immigrants who had arrived to occupy houses built W. and N. of the church since the North Circular road had been driven through the parish along the line of the Brent.

UXBRIDGE (A4) is one of the former market towns of Middlesex, lying on the W. border where the London-Oxford road dips to cross the streams of the Colne and enter Buckinghamshire. The town, though ancient, was not certainly a borough in the Middle Ages,[1] and its church was a chapel of ease to Hillingdon until 1842; much of the E. part of the town is ecclesiastically in West Hillingdon parish (here treated as part of Uxbridge). It is now a suburban town under the influence of London, but its main street shows evidence of a vigorous independent economic life lasting until less than 100 years ago.

The name of the town is first found as 'Oxebruge' c.1145; it apparently refers to the 7th-century tribe of Wixan. The town lay within the manor of Colham (see HILLINGDON) until 1669. The manor was sold in 1695 to seven inhabitants of the town and vested in a trust, which still administers the manorial affairs, in 1729.

The earliest indication of the milling trade, which became a prime occupation in the 18th and 19th centuries, is perhaps to be found in the Domesday mention of 'half a mill' in Colham (half being in Buckinghamshire).[2] A market charter was granted c.1170; by Leland's day, about 1540, it was 'a celebrated market once a week,'and it became important, with a market-house built in 1561 and a successor in 1789 to accommodate the sale of corn. The town was influential enough to be selected as the scene of Protestant burnings in 1555; the victims were not local men. The townsmen contested the right of the manor-owner, Alice Countess of Derby, of Harefield, to take tolls from the market in 1630 and, failing at law, rioted against the tolls. In 1645 it was in effect a frontier town occupied by the Parliament forces, to which the Royalists sent commissioners to negotiate for agreement, without success. Dissent and Quakerism flourished in the late 17th and 18th centuries, especially among the millers and merchants. The Uxbridge Old Bank, founded by Norton and Mercer in 1791, was taken over by Hull and Smith, Quaker millers, in 1820.[3] The Grand Junction canal of 1798 put Uxbridge in direct communication with Brentford and London on one side and with the Midlands on the other; there was a 'passage-boat' to Paddington from 1801. West Drayton, on the Great Western line, was the nearest railway station from 1838 to 1856, when a branch was opened to the town;[4] in 1904 the Metropolitan line from Harrow was opened. The end of the electric tramway from Shepherd's Bush reached Uxbridge in 1904.

Long united to Hillingdon, Uxbridge chafed under its administration. There was an appeal in 1628 to Laud, then bishop of London, about payments to

[1] G. Redford and T. H. Riches, *History . . . of Uxbridge* (1818), make the best case they can for Uxbridge having been a borough; the evidence is not conclusive. [2] Sharpe (page 12, note 4), p. 213, identifies this mill with Mercer's Mill, standing on an island. [3] Matthews and Tuke (page 329, note 3), p. 290. [4] There is a story that the inhabitants objected to the Great Western main line passing through the town and got it diverted (M. S. Briggs, *Middlesex Old and New* (1934), p. 205n.); but it is an unlikely tale (see Part I, page 78 and note 1).

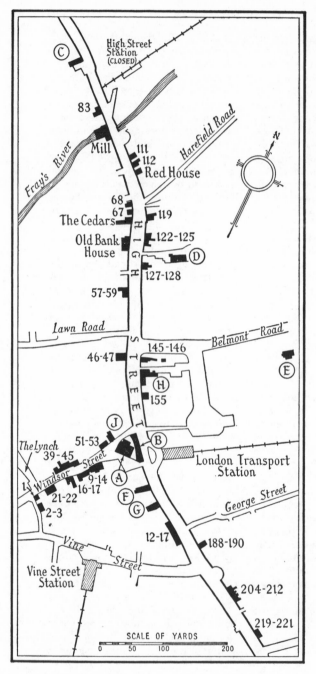

UXBRIDGE

A   St Margaret's Church
B   Market House
C   Treaty House
D   Old Meeting
     Congregational Church
E   Friends' Meeting House
F   The Three Tuns
G   The King's Arms
H   The George
J   The Queen's Head
(The figures shown on the plan
refer to the street numbers of the
remaining houses dating from
before 1700)

Hillingdon church, and at the Commonwealth visitation of 1649 Uxbridge applied to be made a separate parish. By 1800 it had become a flourishing market town, the agricultural centre of a strip of NW. Middlesex and a good deal of E. Buckinghamshire which sent its corn to the mills. The connexion with Buckinghamshire was close: there is a monument by Burgiss, an Uxbridge mason, in Fleet Marston church, near Aylesbury;[1] the Congregational church lay within the Berks., South Oxon and South Bucks. Association;[2] the *Buckinghamshire Advertiser* newspaper, begun as *Broadwater's Journal* at Amersham in 1840, was transferred to Uxbridge in 1860 and claimed to cover the area from Hammersmith to Oxford and Staines to Watford.[3] Uxbridge formed its Yeomanry Cavalry in 1797 (the name was changed to Middlesex Yeomanry Cavalry in 1871); it had a Harmonic Society in 1854[4] and public subscription libraries in 1811 and 1815;[5] and a theatre existed, if it did not flourish, in the 1840s.[6] The town was paved and lighted under powers given by an act of 1806, but the 'liberties of Hillingdon,' extending half-way down this High Street, were not. The 19th century saw these anomalies slowly adjusted. In 1875 there were, in addition to corn mills on the Colne and wharves and timber mills by the canal, breweries and an iron foundry. Steam engines for canal craft were built at Uxbridge from about 1885.[7]

In the 20th century Uxbridge has lost most of its character and become assimilated to suburban Middlesex, but there still remain in and near the High Street old houses of the 16th-18th centuries, often behind new ungracious fronts, and there are some things of merit towards the river.

The centre of the town is where the London Transport station (1938; good concrete interior) faces the market house of 1789, with a large room on the upper storey supported on 51 wooden columns. Behind the market hall, on a cramped site, is the church (St Margaret). It is almost square in plan, with a tower on the N., and there is no churchyard; the burial ground is about 150 yards SW. The tower, apparently late 14th-century (much rebuilt about 1820), is the oldest portion; it is surmounted by a wooden cupola of about 1700. The nave and N. aisle date from the early 15th century; the S. aisle, wider than the nave, was rebuilt in the late 15th century as a gild chapel of St Mary and St Margaret, with a good hammerbeam roof, and the chancel was rebuilt at the same time. The N. chapel was rebuilt in the 16th century; the whole church was restored in 1872. There is a handsome monument in the chancel to Leonora Bennet, 1638. The late 15th-century font, well preserved, has an octagonal bowl with side panels bearing a rose and a leopard's face alternately.

Windsor Street, SW. from the church, contains several 17th-century houses, mostly refronted; the Queen's Head inn has portions of about 1500. This street was formerly called the Lynch; the burnings of 1555 took place in it. To the E. is Vine Street, which may refer to the vineyard in Colham manor at Domesday.[8] The High Street E. of the market hall has some old houses on the S. side as far as Vine Street (including the Three Tuns and King's Arms inns, partly dating from about 1500), and on the N. side beyond (Nos. 188-221); most now have poor fronts. Farther E., S. of the street, is Gilbert Scott's yellow church of St Andrew (1865), with an ugly broach spire; it is an unpleasing object. The cemetery

---

[1] *Murray's Buckinghamshire Architectural Guide*, ed. J. Betjeman and J. Piper (1948), p. 118. [2] Summers (see page 112, note 9), p. 66. [3] *Buckinghamshire Advertiser*, 5 November 1948. [4] Stonham and Freeman (page 101, note 4), p. 43. [5] Redford and Riches (page 353, note 1), pp. 138, 139. [6] Playbills in Public Library. [7] C. N. Hadlow, 'Horse Power', *Lock and Quay* 2 (1950), p. 61. [8] It used to be called Blind Lane or Woolwind Lane; but several gardens on the E. side 'were formerly called the Vineyard': Redford and Riches (see page 353, note 1), p. 77.

contains two spiky chapels by B. Ferrey (1867).

W. of the market hall, as the High Street descends to the river, there are 18th-century country-town houses of a good class, notably the Old Bank House (*Plate 40*) and the Cedars, with charming curved ends. The Chequers inn is a good 19th-century successor to a much older building. On the river are the mills that earned modest fortunes in the 18th century. At the end of the town, S. of the road, is the Old Treaty House, now the Crown inn, which is the NW. wing and part of the main block of Sir John Bennet's house, used in 1645 for the abortive discussions—called 'treaty' only in the sense of 'negotiations'—between King and Parliament. It is an early 16th-century building, with alterations and details of most later periods (*Plate 6*).

Chapels of the two influential dissenting sects lie off the High Street: the Old Meeting, Congregational, deriving descent from ejected ministers of 1662, the building completed in 1716 and heavily reconstructed in 1883 (*Plate 46*); and the Friends' Meeting House, a plain decent building of 1817 beside Belmont Road, successor to one of about 1690. The town is full of yards and alleys; they sometimes afford pleasing views of the gardens and backs of houses, often more attractive than their fronts.

N. of the High Street the town runs up to Uxbridge Common. It was long used for the yeomanry's exercises, and there was a regular cricket ground in 1818. A church was built for the district in 1837. To the S. there are houses, with some factories, in the direction of Cowley.

UXENDON (c3). *See* WEMBLEY.

WEALDSTONE (c3). *See* HARROW.

WEMBLEY (c3) was a hamlet of Harrow until 1894; in 1937 it became a borough, including Sudbury, Alperton, Preston, part of Kenton, and KINGSBURY. It lies between the Brent, which divides it from Willesden, and the SE. slopes of Harrow Hill.

The earliest mention of Wembley is in 825, as 'Wemba lea'—'Wemba's clearing'; it does not appear in Domesday. The pronunciation 'Wembley' used to be common. The manor-farm belonged to Kilburn priory. In 1543 it was granted to Richard Page and remained in that family till 1802. The title to Wembley Park then became obscure, and several persons attempted to disturb later owners without success; these claimants conceived that there were 'Page millions' to be had.[1] The manor of Uxendon, at Preston, passed from Travers to Sir Nicholas Brember about 1376; in the 15th century it passed to the Bellamy family, who were in occupation at the time of the Babington plot (1586). At 'Tokynton,' or Oakington, there was in 1547 a chapel of ease to Harrow.

Wembley was entirely given over to grass-farms until a station was opened on the London and Birmingham Railway in 1845. The Metropolitan Railway, extended through the district in 1880, did not think it worth building a station at Wembley[2] until 1894, in connection with a grandiose scheme of Sir Edward Watkin's for building a sort of Eiffel Tower, but 175 ft. higher, in Wembley Park. The tower never got above the first stage. Electric trams were laid along the Harrow Road to Wembley in 1908 and Sudbury in 1910; and after the 1914-18 war building began in earnest.

The British Empire Exhibition of 1924 and 1925 was held in the grounds of Wembley Park, where thousands of

---

[1] A certain Mrs. Davey publicly laid claim to the estates and excited so much hostility that she had to be escorted out of Harrow by police: W. W. Druett, *Harrow through the Ages* (1935), p. 160. [2] Foley, p. 62.

people daily visited the massive display buildings, the pavilions of Dominion and colonial governments, and an amusement park. It marked the peak of the post-war recovery. The outline plan of the exhibition grounds and buildings was designed by J. W. Simpson and M. Ayrton, who were also the architects of the most important buildings. These were executed in various neo-classic and national styles. They had a look of permanence, before the modern fashion of making exhibitions look as though they are built of bent cardboard. Few of the exhibition pavilions survive.

The Stadium remains the dominating feature of the scene. This vast arena accommodated, with some difficulty, 120,000 people for the football cup final of 1923; the buildings (J. M. Simpson and M. Ayrton, 1923), concrete-finished, with four domed towers, are imposing enough for their purpose. Adjoining the stadium is the Empire swimming pool, a reinforced-concrete building of ingeniously balanced construction (E. O. Williams, 1934).

NE. of Wembley Park station, on Forty Lane in the Kingsbury part of the borough, are the municipal offices (C. Strange, 1935) in somewhat bleak yellow-grey brick; the rectangular masses are not relieved by a central feature, but the building is bold and a child of its age, which is a virtue in modern town halls. NW. is the site of Uxendon manor-house, where the unhappy Bellamy family sheltered Roman Catholic priests and conspirators in Elizabeth's reign.[1] The hamlet of Preston, with the farmhouse of John Lyon, founder of Harrow school, used to lie beyond; now all this district is given over to Gardens, Ways, and Crescents, running up to Kenton Road. Where Honeypot Lane joins the Kingsbury-Kenton road at Kingsbury Circle, the old meeting-place of the moot of Gore hundred was identified, as building was fast advancing upon it, in 1935.[2]

The NW. corner, with good views up to Harrow hill, is named Northwick Park, from the last lords of the manor of Harrow. North Wembley has modern factories beside the railway; Sudbury, to the W., consists of a ribbon of 19th-century building along the Harrow road as it wanders towards Sudbury Hill, with 20th-century houses behind. The church in Harrow Road (St Andrew; C. Waymouth, 1925) is of a barn-like type, not unhandsome. S. of Wembley, about the Ealing road, is Alperton, with factories on the Grand Union canal and North Circular road, and houses of an earlier period, 1890 to 1910, than most of Wembley. Oakington, covering the old manor farm S. of the Stadium, is a pleasant suburb (part designed by O. Hill, 1924), with the church of St Michael, Tokyngton (C. A. Farey, 1933). The original settlement of Wembley lies on the High Road about Wembley Central station; the church (St John, 1845) is an early design of G. G. Scott.

WEST DRAYTON (A4). *See* DRAYTON, WEST.

WEST TWYFORD (C4). *See* TWYFORD.

WHETSTONE (D2). *See* BARNET, FRIERN, and FINCHLEY.

WHITCHURCH (C2). *See* STANMORE, LITTLE.

WHITTON (C5). *See* TWICKENHAM.

WILLESDEN (D4) is a borough (1933), roughly triangular in shape, lying

[1] See page 109, note 1. [2] H. Braun, 'The Hundred of Gore and its Moot-Hedge', *Trans. L. Mx. A. S.* NS 7 (1937), p. 218; P. Davenport, 'The Site of the Gore Hundred Moot', *Trans. L. Mx. A. S.* NS 10 (1951), p. 145.

between Hendon, Wembley, and Acton, with one corner jutting deeply into the county of London. The Edgware road divides it on the NE. from Hampstead and Hendon, the river Brent on the NW. from Wembley, and a line on the S. corresponding to no recognisable features from Paddington and Acton. Within these limits are, as well as Willesden itself (Church End), the districts of Queen's Park, Kensal Rise, Harlesden, Stonebridge Park, Willesden Green, Dollis Hill, Neasden, and half of Cricklewood and Kilburn, with part of the ancient parish of West TWYFORD; but almost all the railway junction for which Willesden is notorious lies outside the borough. The Brent valley, soured with electricity generating stations and railway sidings, is the principal natural feature, the Brent reservoir, or Welsh Harp, a striking artificial one; the ground rises from them to elevations over 200 ft. in the N. and E. parts.

The place first appears as 'Wellesdune' in 939; it perhaps means 'hill of the spring.'

Domesday states that Willesden was one of the ancient properties of St Paul's; the villagers were paying rent for all the land, and none was retained in demesne.[1] In 1150 a new arrangement was made, and eight of the prebendal stalls were named from and directly supported by specific portions of the Willesden estates—Brondesbury,[2] Chamberlainwood, Harlesden, Mapesbury, Neasden, Oxgate, East Twyford, and Willesden. In the late Middle Ages it was a celebrated place of pilgrimage, being denounced in the same breath as Walsingham by 16th-century reformers.[3]

It remained entirely rural well into the 19th century (*Plate 51*). J. J. Park, historian of Hampstead, remarked in 1818: 'The parish of Willesden has somehow or other escaped the general resort of London traders, and the whole property of the parish is contained in some half-dozen farms and two or three extensive seats.'[4] There is therefore little of any antiquity to be seen in Willesden compared with Tottenham, which, lying no nearer to London, was comparatively thickly settled and still has plenty of evidences of the 17th and 18th centuries. In 1822 the *Gentleman's Magazine* could write of the 'delightful prospect of the country' seen from Maida Hill; the railway station of 1844 was put up, it was alleged, only for the benefit of the manager, for there was no prospect of traffic. Willesden junction became one of the most famous railway exchange-points of the 19th century, with such a complicated layout that legends arose about the ghosts of passengers who expired while trying to find the way out.[5] More railways were opened between 1861 and 1880; a horse tramway began to ply down the Harrow road by 1890, electrified and extended to Wembley in 1906-8. Beginning c.1900, and faster after 1920, factories were built in the SW. corner, bordering on North Acton and Park Royal, and along the line of the North Circular road along the Brent valley. Apart from manufacturing industries, there is a concentration of laundries in the borough; the reason for their establishment at Willesden and Acton is said to be that the brickmakers of the district, who had a seasonal occupation, chose to marry laundresses or ironers to ensure some earnings for the family in the winter months.[6]

Willesden begins about 2 m. NW. from the Marble Arch, with Kilburn Park, or Carlton ward, S. of the Euston main line; it is a dreary district that seems properly to belong to

[1] Clapham, *Concise*, p. 53: 'At Willesden business methods obtrude. St. Paul, in the person of his canons, has abandoned demesne altogether... Most Saints were absentees'. [2] Sometimes confused with Brownswood (South Hornsey), a different prebend altogether: S. J. Madge, *Early Records of Harringay alias Hornsey* (1938), p. 49. [3] Nothing is known of this shrine except the reformers' denunciations: references collected by J. G. Waller, 'On the Pilgrimage to Our Lady of Wilsdon', *Trans. L. Mx. A. S.* OS 4 (1875), p. 173. [4] J. J. Park, *History and Topography of Hampstead* (ed. 2, 1818), p. 135. [5] *H.C.M.* 1 (1899), p. 198; G. P. Neele, *Railway Reminiscences* (1904), p. 74; the story is not true, but it serves to indicate the poor prospects for traffic. On Willesden Junction, M. Robbins, *North London Railway* (ed. 3, 1946), p. 14. [6] *New Survey of London Life and Labour*, dir. H. L. Smith, v. (London Industries II, 1933), p. 345.

Paddington. The tall spire of J. L. Pearson's church of St Augustine, 50 yds. within London, stands over this quarter; it is one of his most mature works, looking decidedly French outside, with a vaulted interior, handsome and sombre. The public baths and laundry in Granville Road, in orange brick, are the only architectural alleviation of the general drabness. N. of the railway, Kilburn (*Plate 50*) (where the original Willesden manor house stood), Queen's Park, and Kensal Green are commonplace, or worse, suburbs of 1860-1900; Brondesbury has more pretensions. Christ Church, Willesden Lane (R. B. King, 1866; blitzed), is a spacious cruciform church of the Decorated revival; the church hall, farther W. along Willesden Lane, is a pleasing small building (T. A. Lodge, 1922). To the W. is a portion stretching across the ancient parish from Cricklewood to Kensal Green which was formerly the manor of Malourees; it belonged to All Souls College, Oxford, commemorated by Chichele Road and All Souls Avenue. Most of it S. of the Metropolitan Railway was left untouched until after 1920; then it was filled up with semi-detached houses of orthodox pattern. Willesden Green is a child of the Metropolitan Railway (1879); there is a church by James Brooks (St Andrew, 1886), and St Gabriel, Walm Lane (1898), is a decent edifice in rusticated stone with a saddleback tower.

High Road, not straightened since its origin as a country byway, leads W. to Church End, where the old parish church (St Mary) lies out of the way W. of Neasden Lane. It contains no work earlier than about 1250 though the font is 12th-century Norman and remains of a narrow Norman window were found at the reconstruction of 1872.

The S. nave arcade dates from the middle 13th century; the chancel was rebuilt about 1400 and the tower, at the SW, about the same period. The S. chapel was added in the 16th century. In the first half of the 19th century its appearance of venerable antiquity made it a favourite subject for sketching; but in 1852 it was restored and the nave extended W., and the N. aisle was added in 1872. The tower bears a sundial dated 1732. A carved boss from the old nave roof (15th-century) is preserved in the public library. There are good brasses in the chancel, including Bartholomew Willesden, comptroller of the great roll of the Pipe, 1492, and some 17th-century monuments. The 12th-century font, of Purbeck marble, has simple, almost rude, carving on a tapering square bowl; there is a late 16th-century carved communion table, and a fine late 14th-century door, with carved intersecting tracery. In the churchyard a slab on stilts marks the tomb of Charles Reade, author of *The Cloister and the Hearth*, d. 1884.

The districts N. of the High Road are comparatively open, with the wooded knoll of Dollis Hill (Gladstone Park) looking S. over them. Dollis Hill House (1824), where W. E. Gladstone often stayed between 1882 and 1894, crowns the top of the hill, with the Post Office Research Station (A. R. Myers, 1933) and the hospital of St Andrew (R. L. Curtis, 1912), both seemly buildings, behind. St Francis of Assisi, Gladstone Park (J. H. Gibbons, 1933), and St Paul, Oxgate (N. F. Cachemaille-Day, 1939), are Willesden's Anglican churches in the modern manner. To the N., in Coles Green Road, are what remains of Old Oxgate Farm (about 1600) and Willesden Paddocks (early 18th-century, much altered).

Neasden, SW. across Dudden Hill Road, has a group of buildings of about 1700—the Grove, the Grange, and the Cottage, now decrepit—at the top of Neasden Lane. Sir William Roberts, d. 1662, a prominent adherent of the Parliament side in the Civil War and one of the 1657 house of peers, lived at Neasden; the story that Oliver Cromwell owned a house there is unfounded. The Methodist church on the slope towards Kingsbury bridge (E. B. Glanfield) is a good specimen of modern church building, superior to the surrounding dwellings but recognisably of the same age.[1]

SW. of Neasden, where the Harrow road crosses the Brent, was a stone bridge, first recorded in 1745, that gave its name to the district. George Morland, painter, lived for a time at the Coach and Horses inn by the bridge. 'Stonebridge Park,' wrote Thorne in 1875, 'is a cluster of 60 or 80 smart new villas for City men.' It is not so now, but a continuation of the crowded and unsightly district of Harlesden, lying immediately N. of Willesden Junction. Harlesden is an ancient place, described in Domesday as a manor of St Paul's separate from Willesden; today it has no attractions to offer the visitor and few, perhaps, for the inhabitant. Farther SW. Willesden expires on the edges of Twyford, Park Royal, and the unlovely scenery of North Acton Road, where only the handsome blocks of Giles Scott's Guinness brewery (1936) are grateful to the eye. These are in the best manner of unadorned modern industrial building (*Plate 65*).

Two 19th-century novelists lived in Willesden: Harrison Ainsworth, who was pleased to make a romance about Jack Sheppard the highwayman operating at Willesden and being buried in the churchyard; and Mrs. Craik (née Mulock), d. 1887, author of *John Halifax, Gentleman.* A slighter association may be claimed by Walter Map, or Mapes, canon of St Paul's, *fl. c.* 1180-1200, characterised as 'medieval author and wit,' from whom the Mapesbury prebendal stall and manor were named.

WINCHMORE HILL (E2) is the NE. part of Southgate, lying between Palmer's Green and Enfield. A rural hamlet known by a few Londoners at the end of the 18th century, it grew slowly until the railway (1872) and the electric tram (1909) made it accessible, and most of the district has been covered with houses of the better sort since 1900. The greater part of Bush Hill Park lies within the Southgate boundary, though the station and suburb of that name are in Edmonton.

The name 'Wynsemerhull' first appears in 1319; its derivation is doubtful. It was close enough to London, and obscure enough, to be a useful retreat for the Society of Friends in the 17th century, and a meeting was begun there in 1662; George Fox was often there between 1681 and 1690 A meeting house was completed in 1688 and rebuilt in 1790. There was also a curious 19th-century sect, the Udallites, with a chapel in Vicarsmoor Lane.[2]

The Green, W. of the main road and the railway, has some good old houses round it. Farther W. is the church (St Paul, 1828), an early revived-Gothic building of the Perpendicular persuasion, in white brick, with no aisles, a W. gallery, flat ceiling, and an apsidal chancel added later. Almost opposite is the unassuming meeting house, with the Friends' graveyard at the side (*Plate 45*). John Fothergill, surgeon, d. 1780, is the most celebrated of those buried there—'the Westminster

---

[1] Illustrated in M. S. Briggs, *Puritan Architecture* (1946), plate xxii. [2] J. W. Round [pseud. J. F. Bunting], *Story of Southgate and Winchmore Hill* [1906], p. 58; the sect is unknown to J. H. Blunt, *Dictionary of Sects, Heresies, Ecclesiastical Parties, and Schools of Religious Thought* (1874).

Abbey of the Friends of Middlesex where our kings, statesmen and poets repose.'¹ N. of this is Vicarsmoor Lane, where Thomas Hood lived in Rose Cottage from 1829 to 1832. Sharon Turner, historian, d. 1847, also lived at Winchmore Hill.

In the N. of the district the Beggars Bush fair used to be held on the edge of Enfield Chase; it was removed there from Theobalds Park in 1615 and continued to be held immediately before Barnet Fair into the 20th century. Bush Hill Park, a large 18th-century brick mansion now surrounded by a golf course, was occupied by the Sambrooke and Mellish families; Grinling Gibbons' famous wood carving of the stoning of St Stephen, now in the Victoria and Albert Museum, was long in the hall. Sir Hugh Myddleton had a house on the E. side of Bush Hill, where his New River now winds agreeably among the suburban roads (*Plate 53*); the sluice house and Bush Hill Cottage impart a Regency touch to the scene. The most noticeable building on this side, The Wells with its curious tower, was a late 19th-century waterworks.

The district of Grange Park lies N. of Winchmore Hill, where Enfield, Edmonton, and Southgate meet. It has been built up almost entirely since 1920, with two good churches: St Peter, Vera Avenue (C. A. Farey, 1941), and the Methodist Church in the Orchard, E. of the station (C. H. Brightiff, 1938), which is the best of its kind in the county.

WOOD GREEN (E3), lying between Southgate and Hornsey, was formerly the NW. portion of Tottenham parish, detached in 1888; it became a borough in 1933. It has no distinguishing feature except the deplorable Alexandra Palace scowling over it from a ridge running in from the W. side.

The name is first found in 1502; most of the land appears to have been within the Ducketts manor of Tottenham. A pottery on White Hart Lane, in the NE. corner, has existed since the 17th century; latterly it has specialised in flower-pots. Otherwise agriculture was the only occupation. The Great Northern railway station was opened in 1859; trams were laid from Finsbury Park in 1887; and the Piccadilly tube station was opened in 1932.

Most topographers of Middlesex, in a tradition not lightly to be disregarded, confine their accounts of Wood Green to the almshouses. There were no considerable estates until the 19th century; then the fields were cut up for terrace houses without the intervening stage, found in most of the adjoining districts, when the area was covered by large houses and gardens. Exceptional for Wood Green, Earlham Grove House, E. of the main road towards the N., is a decent 19th-century brick mansion, now council offices. The church (St Michael), at the junction of the road to Colney Hatch, was built in 1865-74 (H. Curzon) and looks it. Opposite are the Printers' almshouses, in Victorian-Tudor style (W. Webb, 1850, enlarged 1870); the Fishmongers' almshouses are close by. The town centre is at the crossing of Green Lanes and Lordship Lane, leading E. to Tottenham. In the SE. corner is the Noel Park estate, laid out in 1883, the best that good ordinary developers could do at the time; the effect is mild and depressing. The E. side touches the London County Council White Hart Lane estate. NE. are Devonshire Hill and Chitts Hill, the last portions of the borough to be built over; N. is Bowes Park station, but most of that district is in Southgate borough.

To the W. the gigantic slothful bulk

---

¹ Diary of James Jenkins, quoted by I. L. Edwards, *Journal of Friends' Historical Society* 35 (1938), p. 23.

of the Alexandra Palace spoils the outlook. Alexandra Park, a pleasure ground with a racecourse, was laid out in 1863 on the site of Tottenham Wood farm as a North London counterpart to the Crystal Palace at Sydenham; the palace building, with a gigantic organ by Willis, was opened in 1873 and burnt down within a month; unhappily it was rebuilt in 1875 to J. Johnson's design, strikingly ugly even for the 1870s, of uncertain parentage, perhaps inspired by Paris and Vienna exhibition buildings. It has been turned to various uses, barrack, transit camp for Belgians, prison camp, and government offices during the 1914-18 war; latterly the E. end has been converted to house the B.B.C. television studios, and such looks as it had have been knocked about in the process.

WOODSIDE PARK (D2). *See* FINCHLEY.

YEADING (B4). *See* HAYES.

YEOVENEY (A5). *See* STAINES.

YIEWSLEY (A4) is the settlement N. of the Great Western railway at West Drayton which has given its name to the urban district; it was the S. part of Hillingdon parish. The name derives from 'Wiveslege' (1235), 'Wife's wood or clearing.' It is a 19th-century township, with factories, mills, and a London rubbish-tip on the Grand Junction canal and the Colne river.

The De Burgh Arms inn, by the station, is a 17th-century house, much altered; the Red Cow inn, a little way N., is timber-framed. The church (St Matthew, G. G. Scott, 1869; altered C. A. Nicholson, 1897) lies farther N. On the Cowley boundary is the Grange, a house of about 1700, timber-framed with brick casing. The rest is mostly unattractive, apart from a good modern school (Evelyn's) in Appletree Avenue (W. T. Curtis and H. W. Burchett, 1936).

APPENDICES

TABLES OF POPULATION

1. RECORDED BAPTISMS

	1580-1589	1630-1639	1680-1689	1730-1739	1780-1789	
ACTON	-	-	-	327	382	
BARNET, FRIERN	-	-	84	118	111	
BRENTFORD & CHISWICK						
New Brentford	-	-	273	273	434	
Old Brentford	-	-	-	-	-	In Ealing
Chiswick	-	-	534	768	1,004	
EALING						
Ealing	298	-	-	983	1,476	
Greenford	47	81	58	94	137	
Hanwell	47	52	74	83	114	
Northolt	69	100	114	101	102	
Perivale	-	-	-	14	-	
West Twyford	-	-	-	-	-	13 between 1722 and 1794
EDMONTON	434	421	696	815	1,263	
ENFIELD	753a	729	815	1,081	1,257	
FELTHAM						
East Bedfont	-	-	-	65	148	
Feltham	-	-	71	80	119	
Hanworth	-	58	67	71	119	
FINCHLEY	266	383	223	267	439	
HARROW						
Harrow on the Hill	-	-	} 478	526	576	
Pinner	-	-				
Great Stanmore	-	88	149a	-	269	
Little Stanmore	91	136	169	129	184	
HAYES & HARLINGTON						
Harlington	82	78	64	98	110	
Hayes	154	208	150	193	221	
HENDON						
Edgware	-	-	-	140	130	
Hendon	-	-	466	413	489	

For notes, see page 367

	1580-1589	1630-1639	1680-1689	1730-1739	1780-1789	
HESTON & ISLEWORTH						
Cranford	32	38	40	51	69	
Heston	284	265B	249	200C	607	
Isleworth	263	539	618	616	1,247	
HORNSEY	-	-	-	187	342	Note K
Highgate	-	143D	334	337	389	
POTTERS BAR						
(South Mimms)	212	279	-	436	330E	
RUISLIP-NORTHWOOD	-	-	279F	246	366	
SOUTHALL (Norwood)	-	-	116	134	157	
SOUTHGATE	-	-	-	[202]	[264]	Included in Edmonton
STAINES						
Ashford	-	-	40F	-	55	
Laleham	-	-	-	-	90	
Staines	80G	96G	88G	340	425	
Stanwell	-	198H	-	242	263	
SUNBURY-ON-THAMES						
Littleton	37	22	33	53	56	
Shepperton	-	116	102	157	227	
Sunbury	99	128	139	330	395	
TOTTENHAM	240	339	381	373	706	
TWICKENHAM						
Hampton }	105	227	274	321	398	
Hampton Wick						
Teddington	40 a	54 a	130 a	129 a	194 a	
Twickenham	162	-	536 a	728	876	
UXBRIDGE						
Cowley	33	49	-	45	43	
Harefield	153	198	139	200	236	
Hillingdon	211	305	255	326	389	
Ickenham	60	61	58	67	88	
Uxbridge	352	418	356	532	696	
WEMBLEY						
Kingsbury	-	-	-	88J	65	
Wembley	-	-	-	-	-	In Harrow
WILLESDEN	-	175	156	141	249	

	1580-1589	1630-1639	1680-1689	1730-1739	1780-1789	
WOOD GREEN	-	-	-	-	-	In Tottenham
YIEWSLEY & WEST DRAYTON						
Harmondsworth	-	-	168	194	211	
West Drayton	98	96	97	123	115	
Yiewsley	-	-	-	-	-	In Hillingdon

A 1589-1598. B 1629-1638. C *Known to be inaccurate owing to vicar's absence.* D 1635-1644. E *Many baptised at Hadley and Barnet.* F 1700-1709. G *Registers imperfect before* 1700. H 1632-1641. J 1733-1742. K *About four-fifths in Hornsey parish, but not included in Hornsey figures.* a: *Shorter period extended arithmetically to decennium.*

2. CENSUS TABLES

				Census Year				
	1801	1851	1881	1911	1931	1951	1961	1991
ACTON (*Note* A)	1,425	2,582	17,126	57,497	70,008	67,424	65,586	-
BARNET, FRIERN (*Note* A)	432	974	6,424	14,924	22,715	29,164	28,813	-
BRENTFORD & CHISWICK	-	-	-	-	63,217	59,354	54,833	118,142 (inc. Isleworth)
New Brentford (*Note* B)	1,443	2,063	2,138	2,093	-	-	-	-
Old Brentford	B	B	B	14,478	-	-	-	-
Chiswick	3,235	6,303	15,663	38,697	-	-	-	-
EALING	-	-	-	-	116,771	187,306	183,077	264,867 (Borough)
Ealing (*Note* B)	5,035	9,828	25,748	x61,222	-	-	-	-
Greenford	359	507	538	843	-	-	-	-
Hanwell	817	1,547	5,178	19,129	-	-	-	-
Northolt	336	614	496	685	-	-	-	-
Perivale	28	32	34	95	-	-	-	-
West Twyford (*Note* C)	8	21	75	126	-	-	-	-
EDMONTON (*Note* D)	5,093	9,708	23,463	x64,797	77,658	104,244	91,956	-
ENFIELD (*Note* A)	5,881	9,453	19,104	56,338	67,752	110,458	109,542	250,750 (Borough)
FELTHAM (*Note* A)	-	-	-	-	16,066	44,830	51,047	120,596 (inc. Heston)
East Bedfont (*Note* A)	456	1,035	1,452	2,426	-	-	-	-
Feltham (*Note* A)	620	1,109	2,909	5,135	-	-	-	-
Hanworth (*Note* A)	334	790	1,040	2,188	-	-	-	-
FINCHLEY (*Note* A)	1,503	4,120	11,191	39,419	59,113	69,990	69,370	-
HARROW	-	-	-	-	96,656	219,463	209,080	194,893 (Borough)
Harrow on the Hill (*Note* E)	2,485	4,951	10,277	x31,217	-	-	-	-
Pinner	761	1,310	2,519	7,103	-	-	-	-
Great Stanmore	722	1,180	1,312	1,843	-	-	-	-
Little Stanmore	424	811	862	1,761	-	-	-	-
HAYES & HARLINGTON (*Note* F)	-	-	-	-	22,969	65,609	67,915	-
Harlington	363	872	1,538	2,374	-	-	-	-
Hayes	1,026	2,076	2,891	2,594	-	-	-	-
HENDON (*Note* A)	-	-	-	-	115,640	155,835	151,843	-
Edgware	412	765	816	1,233	-	-	-	-
Hendon	1,955	3,333	10,484	38,806	-	-	-	-

	1801	1851	1881	1911	CENSUS YEAR 1931	1951	1961	1991
HESTON & ISLEWORTH	-	-	-	-	76,254	106,636	103,013	-
Cranford (*Note* F)	212	437	503	615	-			-
Heston	1,782	5,202	9,754	15,368	-		-	-
Isleworth	4,346	7,007	12,973	27,495	-		-	-
HORNSEY (*Note* G)	2,716	7,135	37,078	x84,592	95,416	98,134	97,962	-
HOUNSLOW (Borough)	-	-	-	-	-	-	-	204,397
POTTERS BAR (*Note* H) (South Mimms)	1,698	2,825	4,002	x2,805	5,720	17,163	23,376	-
RUISLIP-NORTHWOOD (*Note* A)	1,012	1,392	1,455	6,217	16,035	68,274	72,791	-
SOUTHALL (Norwood) (*Note* I)	697	2,693	6,681	26,323	38,839	55,940	52,983	-
SOUTHGATE (*Note* D)	D	D	D	33,612	56,063	73,376	72,359	-
STAINES (*Note* A)	-	-	-	-	21,336	39,983	49,838	-
Ashford	264	497	1,484	6,763	-			-
Laleham	372	637	544	478	-			-
Staines	1,750	2,577	4,629	6,755	-			-
Stanwell	893	1,723	2,156	2,265	-			-
SUNBURY-ON-THAMES (*Note* A)	-	-	-	-	13,449	23,396	33,437	-
Littleton	147	106	126	399	-			-
Shepperton	731	807	1,285	2,337	-			-
Sunbury	1,447	2,076	4,297	4,607	-			-
TOTTENHAM (*Note* J)	3,629	9,120	46,456	137,418	157,667	126,921	113,249	-
TWICKENHAM (*Note* A)	-	-	-	-	79,299	105,645	100,971	-
Hampton	1,722	3,134	4,776	9,220	-			-
Hampton Wick	793	1,668	2,164	2,417	-			-
Teddington	699	1,146	6,599	17,847	-			-
Twickenham	3,138	6,254	12,479	29,367	-			-
UXBRIDGE (*Note* K)	-	-	-	-	31,887	55,944	63,941	-
Cowley	214	344	498	x1,021	-			-
Harefield	951	1,498	1,503	2,402	-			-
Hillingdon	1,783	6,352	9,295	x3,068	-			-
Ickenham	213	364	376	396	-			-
Uxbridge	2,111	3,236	3,346	x10,374	-			-
WEMBLEY (*Note* E)	-	-	-	-	65,799	131,369	124,892	-
Kingsbury	209	606	759	821	-			-
Wembley	E	E	E	10,696	-			-
WILLESDEN (*Note* C)	751	2,939	27,453	154,214	185,025	179,647	171,001	-

	1801	1851	1881	CENSUS YEAR		1951	1961	1991
				1911	1931			
WOOD GREEN (Note J)	J	J	J	49,369	54,308	52,224	47,945	-
YIEWSLEY & WEST DRAYTON (Note K)	-	-	-	-	13,066	20,488	23,723	-
Harmondsworth	879	1,307	1,812	2,081	-	-	-	-
West Drayton	515	906	1,009	1,668	-	-	-	-
Yiewsley	K	K	K	4,315	-	-	-	-

A   *Boundaries substantially unchanged throughout.*
B   *Old Brentford included in Ealing in 1801, 1851, and 1881.*
C   *Part of West Twyford now included in Willesden.*
D   *Southgate included in Edmonton in 1801, 1851, and 1881.*
E   *Wembley included in Harrow on the Hill in 1801, 1851, and 1881.*
F   *Part of Cranford now included in Hayes and Harlington.*
G   *Hornsey included in South Hornsey later tranferred to Stoke Newington, London in 1801, 1851, and 1881.*
H   *Potters Bar (South Mimms) included part of Barnet, later transferred to Barnet, Hertfordshire in 1801, 1851, and 1881.*
I   *Boundary revision between 1881 and 1911 added 700.*
J   *Tottenham included Wood Green in 1801, 1851, and 1881.*
K   *Hillingdon included Yiewsley in 1801, 1851, and 1881; Cowley, Hillingdon, and Uxbridge boundaries revised between 1881 and 1911.*
x   *Considerable change in area between this census and the preceding one.*

General Note: The 1951 census figures are provisional.

1991 Census information is available for separate parishes. Here is a table of population for Spelthorne Division.

Ashford Common	6101
Ashford East	5784
Ashford North	4297
Ashford Town	7190
Ashford West	2367
Halliford and Sunbury West	6506
Sunbury Common	6981
Sunbury East	6157
Laleham	7330
Shepperton Green	5274
Shepperton Town	6315
Staines East	6983
Staines Town	6291
Stanwell North	4992
Stanwell South	4325
The Moors (Stanwell)	3094

BIBLIOGRAPHY

WRITTEN materials for the study of Middlesex history and topography are treated here in three sections:

A. Manuscript sources;

B. Printed books dealing with the whole county;

C. Books, pamphlets, and articles on particular places.

The lists are selective and do not profess to be complete; they are meant to be a guide. Some comment is made in section B on the usefulness of the works mentioned; in section C a few general histories of parishes have been indicated with a star, Baedeker-like, to show that they are particularly valuable for further study.

These lists do not attempt to deal with the following classes of printed materials: official publications of the county and county district councils; newspapers; 'official guides,' which, though naturally inclined to gratify civic pride, occasionally contain useful information; directories; local news-sheets, parish magazines, and pamphlets. Books on particular subjects—the Thames, ecclesiastical affairs, railways, for example—are referred to in the notes on the section of the text concerned.

A. MANUSCRIPT SOURCES

One of the most valuable historical treasures of Middlesex is the collection of the sessions records, which run tolerably complete from Epiphany Term 1549 down to the present time—a series rivalled by Norfolk but hardly by any other English county. The Middlesex records underwent several vicissitudes of neglect and spoliation—at one time in William III's reign many of them were transported by the Clerk of the Peace to his 'country house in Holborn.' In 1882, under direction of the justices, all sessions records relating to the county were collected and properly housed in the Sessions House at Clerkenwell. After litigation arising out of the Local Government Act of 1888, which established London as a separate county, it was decided that the Lord Lieutenant and Custos Rotulorum of Middlesex was responsible for the safe custody of all these records, and in 1898 the Middlesex County Council was empowered to incur expenditure from the county rate on preserving, arranging, indexing and classifying, and publishing the records. This work has since gone forward, and the documents are now well cared for and accessible to the student.

Selections from the records have been published as follows: *Middlesex County Records*, ed. J. C. Jeaffreson, i, 1550-1603 [1886]; ii, 1603-25 [1887]; iii, 1625-67

(1888); iv, 1667-88 (1892); ed. W. J. Hardy, v, 1689-1709 (1905). *Middlesex Sessions Records*, which comprise complete calendars of the years covered, have been published as follows, ed. W. le Hardy: i, 1612- 14 (1935); ii, 1614-15 (1936); iii, 1615-16 (1937); iv, 1616-18 (1941). *Middlesex County Records Reports, 1902-1928* (1928), by W. J. Hardy and W. le Hardy, is a series of reports made to the magistrates by the keepers of the records, which contain a good many references to the documents and quotations from them. There are duplicated calendars of the Sessions Orders down to 1751.

The County Record Office at the Middlesex Guildhall also houses the memorials from the Middlesex Registry of Deeds, comprising a record of all land transactions within the county from 1709 to 1837. The later records of the Middlesex Registry, down to 1938, are in the custody of the London County Council owing to lack of storage room at the Middlesex Guildhall. All manner of other documentary records, manorial, ecclesiastical, and private, have been added to the official records in the keeping of the County Archivist; there is a table of manorial documents in *Trans. L. Mx. A. S.* NS 10 (1951), p. 252; 11 (1952), p. 93 (in progress).

The other principal manuscript sources for Middlesex are manor court rolls and parish registers. Manorial records have been much scattered, when they have survived; they are to be found, for instance, at the Middlesex Guildhall, at All Souls College, Oxford (for Edgware), at King's College, Cambridge (for Ruislip), in the Westminster Abbey archives, among the records of the Church Commissioners now deposited at the Public Record Office, and among documents still in private possession, like the Isleworth records, belonging to the Duke of Northumberland, at Syon House.

A good many of the parish registers have been printed; there is a convenient list of transcripts in *Trans. L. Mx. A. S. NS* 8 (1940), p. 81. Two volumes of a *Calendar to the Feet of Fines for London and Middlesex*, edited by W. J. Hardy and W. Page, were published: i, Richard I to Richard III (1892); ii, Henry VII to Michaelmas 1569 (1893). There are references to places and persons in Middlesex scattered up and down the *Reports* of the Historical Manuscripts Commission.

B. GENERAL TOPOGRAPHICAL WORKS

No bibliography solely devoted to Middlesex topographical books has been published, and there is no general list of British topography more recent than J. P. Anderson, *The Book of British Topography* (1881), and A. L. Humphreys, *A Handbook of County Bibliography* (1897).

The first topography of Middlesex, and one of the earliest published about a single English county, is J. Norden, *Speculum Britanniae: The First Parte: An historicall and chorographicall Discription of Middlesex* (1593; reprinted, with Hertfordshire, 1637 and 1723). Additional passages on Middlesex, from the British Museum Harleian MS 570, are printed in the introduction to *Speculi Britanniae Pars* (Essex), ed. H. Ellis (Camden Society, 1840). Though his book is not of much value for topographical detail, the general descriptions are charming; some passages are quoted on pages 32-34.

Of topographies covering the whole kingdom, *The Itinerary of John Leland* (*c.* 1534-43) contains many useful particulars; the edition by L. Toulmin Smith (1905-10) is the best. W. Camden, *Britannia* (1586 in Latin; translated by P. Holland, 1610), contains a detailed account of Middlesex, and the edition by R. Gough, of Enfield (1789; ed. 2. 1806), enlarged and continued down to his own day, is full and useful. M. Drayton, *Poly-Olbion* [1612-22], celebrates the county's qualities in verse. J. Speed, *The Theatre of the Empire of Great Britain* (1627), and T. Cox, *Magna Britannia et Hibernia Antiqua et Nova*, vol. iii (1724), are the most informative of the older topographers.

J. Bowack, *The Antiquities of Middlesex* (1705-6), contains Chelsea and Kensington in vol. i, Fulham, Hammersmith, Chiswick, and Acton in vol. ii; 'a third was promised, containing the parishes of Ealing, New Brentford, Thistleworth, and Hanwell, but the author proceeded no further, not finding or deserving encouragement.' *A Description of the County of Middlesex*, printed by R. Snagg (1775), and L. Pope, *The History of the County of Middlesex* (1795), both unfinished, add little to knowledge.

The classic account of Middlesex topography is D. Lysons, *The Environs of London*, vols. ii and iii (1795; reissued with supplement, 1811) and *An Historical Account of those Parishes in the County of Middlesex which are not described in the Environs of London* (1800). These handsome quartos, with adequate plates, are the foundation on which all later antiquarian writings have been firmly based. The century and a half that has passed since their publication has brought to light remarkably few errors in Lysons' careful investigations into manorial and ecclesiastical affairs. Economic history is touched on only incidentally, but some useful references are to be found. The extra illustrated copy in the Guildhall library of the Corporation of London is particularly valuable for prints of the parish churches before 19th-century restorations.

In the years 1800-20 a crop of descriptions of the country round London was put forth. None of these books is of much value; most were content to copy out earlier authors. The best are H. Hunter, *London and its Environs* (1811; some copies have the name of John Aikin on the title-page); D. Hughson [i.e. D. Pugh], *London: being an accurate History and Description of the British Metropolis and its Neighbourhood* (1805-9); and B. Lambert, *History and Survey of London and its Environs* (4 vols., 1806). Of the same sort were W. Ellis, *The Campagna of London* [1791-3]; Anon., *Ecclesiastical Topography: a Collection of one Hundred Views of Churches in the Environs of London* (2 vols., 1807); and J. Hassell, *Picturesque Rides and Walks, with Excursions by Water, Thirty Miles round the British Metropolis* (2 vols., 1817); in general their plates are more useful than their text. Meanwhile, successive editions of *The Ambulator, or the Stranger's* [later, *a Pocket*] *Companion in a Tour round London* (ed. 1, 1774; ed. 12, 1820) were appearing—a small volume arranged alphabetically, pleasant enough to read but of no great value.

The reports to the Board of Agriculture give more information on the state of the county at the time: T. Baird, *General View of the Agriculture of the County of Middlesex* (1793); P. Foot, with the same title (1794); and, best of the three, J. Middleton, *View of the Agriculture of Middlesex* (1798; ed. 2, 1807). Mr Middleton, a land surveyor of Merton and Lambeth, Surrey, did not confine his attention to agriculture but described many aspects of social and economic life, based on personal inquiry. It is curious that, when approached for information by Brayley and Britton for their *Beauties of England and Wales* (1816), he declined to communicate any intelligence to them, owing to 'a distaste for the county of Middlesex.'

E. W. Brayley and J. Britton's *Beauties of England and Wales* dealt with London and Middlesex in vol. x, which comprised 5 separate parts; Middlesex was described, with good engravings, in part 4, written by J. N. Brewer (1816). G. A. Cooke, *Topographical and Statistical Description of the County of Middlesex* (c. 1800-10; ed. 2, c. 1825); W. E. Trotter, *Select Illustrated Topography of Thirty Miles Round London* (1839); J. F. Murray, *Environs of London: Western Division* (1842); and W. Keane, *The Beauties of Middlesex* (1850)–the last dealing mainly with landscape gardening–all have something to add. J. H. Sperling, *Church Walks in Middlesex* (1849; ed. 2, 1853), gives a sharp picture of the church buildings before most of them were restored away. Historical works of the same period are W. Pinnock, *The History and Topography of Middlesex* (1835), and S. Tymms, *A Compendium of the History of Middlesex* (c. 1841), the latter including some useful economic information. 19th-century county geographies include *The Counties of England and Wales (No. 1) Middlesex* (1855); W. Lawson, *Geography of the County of Middlesex* (1872); W. Hughes, *The Geography of Middlesex* (1872); and T. Murby, *Middlesex* (1874).

Middlesex did not find a place of its own in the well-known series of Murray's Hand Books to the Counties of England, the unacknowledged source of most later guide-book writing, but it was included in James Thorne's *Handbook to the Environs of London*, published by Murray (1876). This is a first-class descriptive account, and many of the historical notices have not been improved on in more recent writings–indeed, too many of Thorne's successors have been content to copy him out. While still firmly grounded on the foundations laid by Lysons, Thorne drew into his descriptions copious quotations from literary sources, especially of the 18th century, and he had a quick perception of the picturesque in contemporary scenes.

In the next 30 years Middlesex topography made little progress. F. T. Cansick, *A Collection of Curious and Interesting Epitaphs of Middlesex* (vol. iii, 1875), transcribed inscriptions from Hornsey, Tottenham, Edmonton, Enfield, and Friern Barnet; J. A. Brown, *Palaeolithic Man in North-West Middlesex* (1887), ranged from Ealing to Tierra del Fuego; E. Walford, *Greater London* (1882-4; reissued 1885, 1893), though produced and illustrated in a popular style, is nevertheless a careful work, covering the whole of Middlesex, apart from Chiswick, Hornsey, Tottenham, and Edmonton, on the London border, which were included in W. Thornbury and E. Walford, *Old and New London* (1873-8; 1893; 1898). Some footpath guides were produced in these years: H. J. Foley, *Our Lanes and Meadowpaths* (c. 1890), is still useful; H. S. Vaughan, *The Way about Middlesex* (1896), and A. Holliday (pseud.), *Rambles Round London: Over the Northern Heights* (2 parts, 1896-7), less so.

Between 1900 and 1910 several books on Middlesex appeared in series intended to cover all the English counties; R. H. E. Hill, *Picturesque Middlesex* (illustrations by D. Moul, 1904), and A. R. H. Moncrieff, *Middlesex* (illustrations by J. Fulleylove, 1907), would probably not have been written for any other reason. J. B. Firth,

Middlesex (1906; revised, perhaps not thoroughly enough, 1930), is a good volume in the Little Guides series; W. Jerrold, *Highways and Byways in Middlesex* (illustrations by H.Thomson, 1909), is a delightful book, a gossiping, literary saunter through the old rural county that the electric trams were quickly transforming. *Bygone Middlesex*, ed. W. Andrews (1899), and *Memorials of Old Middlesex*, ed. J. Tavenor-Perry (1909), are collections of essays by different hands; the latter is valuable, especially for an article on the ancient churches by J. C. Cox. *Middlesex Biographical and Pictorial* (1907) is a curious work, composed of biographical sketches of prominent inhabitants, presumably supplied by themselves, with some odd information not otherwise preserved; T. Press, *The Book of Middlesex* (1930), is of a similar character. School books of the period are V. G. Plarr and F. W. Walton, *A School History of Middlesex* (1905), mostly about London, and G. F. Bosworth, *Middlesex* (Cambridge County Geographies, 1913).

One volume, the second, of the Middlesex *Victoria County History*, ed. W. Page, was published in 1911; no other has yet appeared.[1] It contains sections on earthworks; political history; social and economic history; industries; agriculture; forestry; sport; and the first part of the topography of Spelthorne hundred– Ashford, Bedfont, Feltham, Hampton, Hanworth, Laleham, and Littleton. Some of these are admirable, especially the account of Hampton Court; but the economic sections are generally incomplete and out of date.

Middlesex has, naturally enough, incurred something less than its share of writing in the personal, romantic vein that counties like Sussex and Devon suffer from. Good examples are C. G. Harper, *Rural Nooks round London* (1907), and W. G. Bell, *Where London Sleeps* (1926); others are Mrs. A. Bell, *The Skirts of the Great City* (1907), G. Maxwell, *Just Beyond London* (1927) and *The Fringe of London* (1931), not to mention a string of such publications about the Thames. A. Mee, *Middlesex: Little Home County* (1940), is the latest in this tradition; it contains some information not easily found elsewhere, but its manner is not likely to appeal to anyone who has read so far in this book. Its Middlesex geese are all swans. M. S. Briggs, *Middlesex Old and New* (1934), is an astringent book that gives the best general survey of the modern county. There are several 'planning' publications: Adams, Thompson, and Fry, *West Middlesex* (1924), *North Middlesex* (1928), and *The Thames from Putney to Staines* (1930); Greater London Regional Planning Committee, *Reports*, vols. i (1929) and ii (1933); and P. Abercrombie, *Greater London Plan 1944* (1945).

The 1930s were fruitful for the scientific study of Middlesex history. C. E. Vulliamy, *The Archaeology of Middlesex and London* (1930), is an excellent handbook; Sir Montagu Sharpe, *Middlesex in British, Roman, and Saxon Times* (ed. 1, 1919; ed. 2, 1932, incorporating and enlarging earlier pamphlets entitled *Antiquities of Middlesex*, 1905-16), though its main conclusions are difficult to accept for reasons indicated on pages 16-17, is indispensable for study of the earlier periods; the Royal Commission on Historical Monuments, *Middlesex* (1937), a handsome and copiously illustrated volume, deals authoritatively if conservatively with antiquities down to 1714; and the English Place-Name Society's volume XVIII, *The Place-Names of Middlesex* (1942), in succession to J. E. B. Gover, *The Place Names of Middlesex* (1922), deals faithfully, if not finally, with its subject. Two books produced primarily for schools are useful in their own way; T. M. Pope, *Middlesex in Prose*

---

[1] See p.392 for a full list of V.C.H. *Middlesex* volumes.

and Verse (1930), is an anthology which may be supplemented by J. D. Mortimer, *An Anthology of the Home Counties* (1947); *The Middlesex Book of Verse* (*c.* 1930), on the other hand, is a selection of work by students at the Middlesex Education Committee's secondary schools; C. W. Radcliffe, *Middlesex: The Jubilee of the County Council 1889-1939* (1939), is largely devoted to the county administration but also includes a sketch of historical development. Two important books on economic aspects are D. H. Smith, *The Industries of Greater London* (1933), principally about Middlesex, and E. C. Willatts, *Middlesex and the London Region* (vol. 79 of *The Land Utilisation Survey of Britain,* 1937). A. H. Hyatt, *Thoughts from a Middlesex Garden* (1901), is not of topographical interest. T. C. F. Prittie, *Mainly Middlesex* (1947), and *Middlesex* (1952), are about cricket.

Periodicals dealing particularly with Middlesex have been *The London and Middlesex Notebook,* ed. W. P. W. Phillimore (1 vol. only, 1891-2); *Middlesex and Hertfordshire Notes and Queries,* ed. W. J. Hardy (vols. 1-4, 1895-8), succeeded by *The Home Counties Magazine,* ed. W. J. Hardy (vols. 1-14, 1899-1912), together forming a valuable series; and *Transactions of the London and Middlesex Archaeological Society* (old series, vols. 1-6, 1860-1890; additional proceedings at evening meetings, 1860-1874; new series, vol. 1, 1905, in progress, ed. C. Welch, A. Bonner, S. J. Madge, W. Martin, N. G. Brett-James, F. W. M. Draper), in which, though the balance has shifted from time to time, the preponderance of interest is naturally in London. Articles and paragraphs on Middlesex from *The Gentleman's Magazine,* 1731-1868, are usefully extracted in *Topographical History of Leicestershire, Lincolnshire, Middlesex, and Monmouthshire,* ed. G. L. Gomme (Gentleman's Magazine Library, 1896).

Three works on the county have appeared since this book was written: N. Pevsner, *Middlesex* (1951), in 'The Buildings of England' series, a useful and detailed handbook on architectural features and church furnishings, N. G. Brett-James, *Middlesex* (1951), and the *Report* of the survey for the county development plan (1952), which contains some statistical material that would usefully have supplemented Chapters III-VII of this book.

C. LOCAL BIBLIOGRAPHY

Topographical and historical writings on Middlesex places are set out in the following list, arranged alphabetically by ancient parishes and the few other districts separately noticed in Part II. Under each parish the works are divided into (i) books containing general topographical and historical accounts (among which not more than one is starred if it is particularly useful for further study) and (ii) books, pamphlets, and a few articles on particular districts and buildings. The date of publication of books and pamphlets is given, where known; the place of publication is stated where it is outside London. In the case of articles, reference is made to the first page.

The word 'Nil' appearing under a parish, or no entry under the heading (i), must not be taken to mean that nothing has been written about it, but only that nothing has been separately published. Valuable particulars of every parish will be found in the general works named in section B, especially in Lysons (1795-1800) and Thorne (1876).

Comparatively few of the locally-published works are to be found in the British Museum or any other central library, and details of some have had to be included at second hand.

ACTON
(i) P. Jolliffe, *Acton and its History* (Ealing, 1910).
    W. K. Baker, **Acton, Middlesex* (Acton, ed. 2, 1912).
    H. Mitchell, *Records and Recollections of Acton* (Ealing, 1913).
(ii) *East Acton Manor House* (Committee for Survey of Monuments of Greater London, 1921).
    J. E. Lush, *Berrymead–or Berrymede–Priory, Acton* (Acton [1923]).
    Builder: Our Lady of Lourdes, 77 (1899), p. 110; St Peter, Southfield Road, 106 (1914), p. 702; 130 (1926), p. 120; Old Oak and Acton Wells estates, 118 (1920), p. 728; Bromyard Avenue government offices, 123 (1922), p. 312; West Acton housing scheme, 125 (1923), p. 614b; 145 (1933), p. 778; St Saviour, Old Oak Road, 139 (1930), p. 1.

ASHFORD
(ii) *Builder:* Welsh schools, 15 (1857), p. 291.

BARNET, FRIERN
(ii) *Builder:* Colney Hatch asylum, 5 (1847), p. 585; 9 (1851), p. 415; Methodist church, 141 (1931), p. 20.

BEDFONT
(ii) E. A. Ebblewhite, 'The Village and Church of Bedfont, Co. Middlesex', *Journal of the British Archaeological Association* 49 (1893), p. 120.

BRENTFORD
(i) T. Faulkner, *The History and Antiquities of Brentford, Ealing, and Chiswick* (1845).
    F. Turner, *Brentford: Literary and Historical Sketches* (1898); **History and Antiquities of Brentford* (Brentford, 1922).
    M. Sharpe, *Bregantforda and the Hanweal* (Brentford, 1904); *Some Account of Bygone Hanwell and its Chapelry of New Brentford* (Brentford, 1924).
(ii) Boston House, *Country Life* 15 (1904), p. 272.
    M.N.E., 'The Poetry of Brentford', *Athenaeum* (1847), p. 1196.
    Published at Brentford: M. Hawke and R. Vincent, *The Ranger: a Collection of Periodical Essays* (2 vols., 1794-5); *The Brentford Miscellany*, by members of the Mechanics' Institution (1843).

BROCKLEY HILL
    References to earlier writings in C. E. Vulliamy, *The Archaeology of Middlesex and London* (1930), pp. 202, 297, and Royal Commission on Historical Monuments, *Middlesex* (1937), p. 16.
    H. Braun, 'Some Earthworks of North-West Middlesex', *Trans. L. Mx. A. S.* NS 7 (1937), p. 365.
    F. Cottrill, 'A Note on the Trial Excavation at Brockley Hill', *Trans. L. Mx. A. S.* NS 7 (1937), p. 686.
    K. M. Richardson, 'Report on the Excavations at Brockley Hill, Middlesex, August and September 1947', *Trans. L. Mx. A. S.* NS 10 (1951), p. 1.
    S. H. Applebaum, 'Sulloniacae–1950', *Trans. L. Mx. A. S.* NS 10 (1951), p. 201.

CHISWICK

(i) T. Faulkner, *The History and Antiquities of Brentford, Ealing, and Chiswick* (1845).
W. P. W. Phillimore and W. H. Whitear, *Historical Collections relating to Chiswick* (1897).
L. C. Sanders, *Old Kew, Chiswick and Kensington* (1910).
W. Draper, *Chiswick* (1923).
M. Gilbert, *Chiswick: Old and New* (1932).

(ii) R. Jenkins, *A Sketch of the History of Turnham Green* (Turnham Green, 1849).
L. W. T. Dale, *Notes on Chiswick Church* (1884).
F. W. Isaacs, *Brief Notes on Chiswick Church* (1919).
Chiswick House, *Trans. L. Mx. A. S.* NS 9 (1948), p. 107; *Journal of the London Society* No 294 (1947), p. 43; *Country Life* 4 (1898), p. 464; 9 (1901), p. 512; 14 (1903), p. 336; 43 (1918), pp. 130, 160; 60 (1926), p. 308; 66 (1929), p. 181.
Builder: Congregational church, Turnham Green, 45 (1883), p. 150; houses on Chiswick Mall, 53 (1887), p. 491; 92 (1907), p. 775; Hogarth's house, 58 (1890), p. 98; 80 (1901), p. 606; ironwork gates, 93 (1907), p. 172.

COWLEY

Nil; references in Hillingdon and Uxbridge histories.

CRANFORD

(ii) Cranford Park, *Country Life* 77 (1935), p. 240.

DRAYTON, WEST

(i) A. H. Cox, *West Drayton: Village of a Thousand Years* (West Drayton, 1948).
S. J. McVaigh, *West Drayton: Past and Present* (West Drayton, 1950).
(ii) A. H. Cox, *Saint Martin, West Drayton: A Church with a History* (West Drayton [1948]).

EALING

(i) T. Faulkner, *The History and Antiquities of Brentford, Ealing, and Chiswick* (1845).
D. F. E. Sykes, *Ealing and its Vicinity* (Ealing, c. 1895).
E. Jackson, *The Annals of Ealing* (1898).
C. Jones, *Ealing from Village to Corporate Town, or Forty Years of Municipal Life* (Ealing, 1902); *A Decade of Municipal Progress (1901-1911) ... in Ealing* (c. 1912).
C. M. Neaves, *History of Greater Ealing* (Brentford, 1930; ed. 2, 1931).
(ii) I. M. (Mrs. Basil) Holmes, *The Home of the Ealing Free Library* (Ealing, 1902).
A. T. Bolton, *Pitzhanger Manor* (Soane Museum, 1918).
Gunnersbury Park, *Country Life* 8 (1900), p. 56.
Builder: Christ Church, 10 (1852), p. 441; St Peter, 57 (1889), p. 350; 61 (1891), p. 78; Westminster bank, West Ealing, 102 (1912), p. 259; town hall extension, 140 (1931), p. 760.

EDGWARE

(i) T. J. Relf, *Ye Booke of Olde Edgware* (Edgware, ed. 2, c. 1924).
(ii) C. R. L. Fletcher, 'All Souls College v. Lady Jane Stafford, 1587', *Collectanea*, 1st series (Oxford Historical Society, 1885), p. 179.
D. G. Denoon and T. Roberts, 'The Extent of Edgware, A.D. 1277', *Trans. L. Mx. A. S.* NS 7 (1937), p. 158.
C. F. Baylis, 'The Omission of Edgware from Domesday', *Trans. L. Mx. A. S.* NS 11 (1952), p. 62.
References in Anon., *The Twelve Churches; or, Tracings along the Watling Street*

(1860).
Builder: chapel of St Mary of Nazareth, 58 (1890), p. 359; 99 (1910), p. 49.

EDMONTON
 (i) W. Robinson, *The History of Antiquities of the Parish of Edmonton* (1819).
    F. Fisk, *The History of the Parish of Edmonton* (Tottenham, 1914).
    [H. J. Griffin], *Historical Articles on Old Tottenham and Edmonton* (Tottenham, 1926).
    G. W. Sturges, **Edmonton Past and Present* (2 vols., Edmonton, 1938 and 1941);
    The Teaching of Local Geography, with particular reference to Edmonton, Middlesex (Edmonton, 1946); *The Edmonton Heritage* (Edmonton, 1947).
 (ii) J. W. Ford, *Sketch towards a History of Bush Hill Park* (Enfield, 1904).
    G. W. Sturges, *Schools of the Edmonton Hundred* (Edmonton, 1949).
    Builder: St John, Dysons Lane, 132 (1927), p. 484; housing scheme, 123 (1922),
    p.829.

ENFIELD AND ENFIELD CHASE
 (i) W. Robinson, *The History and Antiquities of Enfield* (1823).
    J. Tuff, *Historical, Topographical, and Statistical Notices of Enfield* (Enfield, 1858).
    E. Ford and G. H. Hodson, *A History of Enfield* (Enfield, 1873).
    E. W. Kempe, *Enfield and its Environments* (Enfield, *c.* 1888).
    W. Round [pseud. J. F. Bunting], *Rambles round Enfield* (Enfield, 1905, 1911).
    A. H. Hyatt, *A Guide to Enfield and its Neighbourhood* (Enfield, 1908).
    Various authors, *Recollections of Old Enfield* (Enfield, 1911).
    C. W. Whitaker, **An Illustrated Historical, Statistical and Topographical Account ... of Enfield* (1911).
    V. H. Allemandy, *Enfield: Past and Present* (Enfield, 1914).
    M. Phillips, *Jaunts from Enfield with Bicycle and Camera* (Enfield [1915]; *Enfield: Past and Present* (Enfield, 1917).
    Anon., *The History of Enfield* (Enfield, 1930).
 (ii) P. Hardy, *Hints for the Benefit of the Inhabitants of Enfield in particular, but applicable to every Parish in England* (poor-law administration), (Tottenham, ed. 4, 1813);
    The Charities of Enfield (Tottenham, 1834).
    H. C. Weld, *An Account of the Origin ... of the Charities of Enfield* (Enfield, 1895).
    W. H. F., *Churches of the Deanery of Enfield* (Enfield, 1898, 1901).
    H. D. Sykes, *The Old Palace, Enfield* (Enfield, 1907).
    S. Smith, *A Short History of the Enfield Grammar School* (Enfield, 1931).
    F. Wilson, *Memories of Forty Hill, Enfield* (Enfield, 1947).
    C. Boutell, paper on Tiptoft brass, Enfield parish church, *Trans. L. Mx. A. S.* OS 1 (1860), p. 67.
    C. E. Thomas, 'Enfield', *H.C.M.* 12 (1910), pp. 213, 256.
    Trent Park, *Country Life* 13 (1903), p. 240; furniture, 68 (1930), p. 497; 69 (1931), pp. 40, 66; gardens, 69 (1931), pp. 237, 807.
    Builder: Chase Side Congregational church, 33 (1875), p. 1131; London and Provincial bank, 72 (1897), p. 39.

FELTHAM
 (ii) *Builder:* Middlesex industrial school, 15 (1857), p. 26; St Catherine, 139 (1930), p. 55; Longford school, 150 (1936), p. 784.

FINCHLEY
 (i) J. R. Biggers, *Finchley and the Neighbourhood* (1903).

W. B. Passmore, *Bygone Finchley* (Finchley, 1904-5: reprinted *Mx. & H. N. & Q.* and *H.C.M.*).
C. Wilkinson, *Finchley* (Finchley, 1909).
A. Latimer, *The Illustrated Story of Finchley* (Birmingham, n.d.).
C. O. Banks, *The Romances of the Finchley Manor* (vol. 1, Finchley [1929]).
(ii) T. F. Peacock, 'Finchley', *Trans. L. Mx. A. S.* evening meetings 1872, p. 79.
Parish Church (judgments of the Consistory Court), *Trans. L. Mx. A. S.* NS 6 (1932), pp. 208, 662.
Builder: Christ Church, 28 (1870), p. 147; parish church restoration, 104 (1913), p. 53; Christ College new building, 133 (1927), p. 771.

GOLDERS GREEN AND HAMPSTEAD GARDEN SUBURB
(i) General histories of HENDON; also:
M. E. Wilson, *Wyldes and its Story* (Hampstead, 1904).
J. E. Whiting, *Golder's Hill, Hampstead* (Hampstead, 1898; ed. 3, 1909).
B. W. Dexter, *Cricklewood* (*c.* 1908).
E. J. Davey, *Golder's Hill and Wylde's Farm* (Hampstead, 1907).
F. Howkins, *The Story of Golders Green and its remarkable Development* (Golders Green [1923]).
H. Barnett, *The Story of the Growth of the Hampstead Garden Suburb* (1928).
The Hampstead Garden Suburb: its Achievements and Significance (Hampstead Garden Suburb [1937]).
(ii) F. Hitchin-Kemp, 'Clitterhouse Manor, Cricklewood', *Trans. L. Mx. A. S.* NS 5 (1926), p. 269.
F. Marcham, 'Eton College Property in Hampstead and adjacent Parishes', *Trans. L. Mx. A. S.* NS 6 (1930), p. 310.
Builder: St Peter, Cricklewood, 82 (1902), p. 321; Hampstead Garden Suburb, 97 (1909), pp. 48, 89; 98 (1910), pp. 101, 297; 103 (1912), p. 250; crematorium, 100 (1911), p. 782; 131 (1926), p. 446; 137 (1929), p. 472; 141 (1931), p. 308; St Edward the Confessor, 109 (1915), p. 458; All Souls, Hoop Lane, 132 (1927), p. 270; Orpheum cinema, Temple Fortune, 139 (1930), p. 644; St Alban, 142 (1932), p. 346; 145 (1933), p. 48.

GREENFORD
(ii) A. Heales, 'Greenford Church', *Trans. L. Mx. A. S.* OS 4 (1871), p. 151.

GRIM'S DYKE
References to earlier writings in C. E. Vulliamy, *The Archaeology of Middlesex and London* (1930), pp. 270, 299, and Royal Commission on Historical Monuments, *Middlesex* (1937), xxvii.
H. J. W. Stone, 'The Pinner Grims Dyke', *Trans. L. Mx. A. S.* NS 7 (1937), p. 284.
H. Braun, 'Some Earthworks of North-West Middlesex', *Trans. L. Mx. A. S.* NS 7 (1937), p. 379.
R. E. M. Wheeler, *London and the Saxons* (1935), p. 59.
J. N. L. Myres, *Journal of Roman Studies* 26 (1936), p. 87.

GUNNERSBURY
See EALING.

HAMPSTEAD GARDEN SUBURB
See GOLDERS GREEN.

HAMPTON AND HAMPTON WICK

(i) H. Ripley, *The History and Topography of Hampton-on-Thames (1885).
   B. Garside, Incidents in the History of Hampton-on-Thames during the 16th and 17th Centuries (Hampton, 1937).
(ii) W. Jackson, Abstract of Hampton Parish Documents in 1816 (Hampton, 1816).
   B. Garside, The History of Hampton School from 1556 to 1700 (1931; ed. 2, 1950); The Parish Church, Rectory, and Vicarage of Hampton-on-Thames during the 16th and 17th Centuries (Hampton, 1937); Their Exits and their Entrances (Hampton parish registers, 16th and 17th centuries) (Hampton 1947); The Ancient Manor Courts of Hampton-on-Thames during the 17th Century (2 parts, Hampton 1948 and 1949); The Manor, Lordship, and West Parks of Hampton Court during the 16th and 17th Centuries (Hampton, 1951).
Garrick's villa, Country Life 40 (1916), p. 756.
Builder: Garrick's villa, 34 (1876), p. 1240; 98 (1910), p. 686.

HAMPTON COURT

A. General Histories and Descriptive Works
   G. Bickham, Deliciae Britannicae, or the Curiosities of Hampton Court and Windsor Castle (1742; ed. 2 [175-]).
   E. Law, *The History of Hampton Court Palace (3 vols., 1885-91); A Short History of Hampton Court (1897; ed. 2, 1906; new ed. (to 1688 only), 1924).
   W. H. Hutton, Hampton Court (1897).
   J. Cartwright, Hampton Court (1910).
   W. Jerrold, Hampton Court (1912).
   E. Yates, * Hampton Court (1935).
   P. Lindsay, Hampton Court: a History (1948).
B. Guide Books
   The Hampton Court Guide (Kingston, 4 editions, 1817-19).
   The Stranger's Guide to Hampton Court Palace and Gardens [1825 and editions to 1842; later editions by John Grundy].
   E. Jesse, A Summer's Day at Hampton Court (1839 and later editions).
   F. Summerly [pseud. Sir H. Cole], A Handbook for the Architecture ... of Hampton Court (1841, editions to 1859).
   E. Law, The New Guide to ... Hampton Court (1882 and later editions).
   E. M. Keate, Hampton Court Palace: a short popular Guide (1932).
   E. E. Kilburne, Hampton Court Palace: a History and Guide for Catholics [c. 1932] (16th-century work only).
   G. H. Chettle, Hampton Court Palace (1947).
   In other languages: A. Hirschig, Het Kasteel Hampton Court nabij London (Alkmaar, 1859); Le Palais de Hampton Court [London, 1862].
C. Parks and Gardens
   E. Law, The Chesnut Avenue in Bushey Park, Hampton Court (1919); Hampton Court Gardens: Old and New (1926).
   M. Sands, The Gardens of Hampton Court (1950).
D. Pictures
   H. G. Clarke, The Royal Gallery of Hampton Court Palace (1843; French translation, 1851).
   E. Law, An Historical Catalogue of the Pictures in the Royal Collection at Hampton Court (1881); The Royal Gallery of Hampton Court Illustrated (1898); Mantegna's 'Triumph of Julius Caesar' (1921).
   E. C. Jerrold, The Fair Ladies of Hampton Court (1911).

E. *Other Subjects*

C. H. Collins Baker, *Catalogue of the Pictures at Hampton Court* (Glasgow, 1929).
W. Ormsby Gore (Lord Harlech), *The Triumph of Caesar* ([1935]; ed. 2, 1949).
J. Laver, *The Ladies of Hampton Court* (1942).
E. Law, *The Haunted Gallery of Hampton Court and its Associations with Shakespeare* (1918); *Cardinal Wolsey at Hampton Court* (1923); '*My Lorde Cardinall's Lodgynges*' (*c.* 1924); *King Henry VIII's Great Kitchen at Hampton Court* (n.d.); *King Henry VIII's New Wyne Seller at Hampton Court* (1927).
H. C. Marillier, *The Tapestries at Hampton Court Palace* (1931; ed. 2, 1951).
[P. A. Negretti and M. G. L. Bruce], *Royal Tennis Court, Hampton Court Palace* [1950].

F. *Miscellaneous*

F. Streeter, *Hampton Court: a descriptive Poem* (1778).
Hampton Court; or the Prophecy Fulfilled (poem) (1844, 3 vols.).
Hampton Court, Hampton Wick, and Hampton-on-Thames Wills and Administrations, ed. H. T. McEleney (1922).
E. M. Keate, *The Jackanapes Jacket: a thrilling story of a murder at Hampton Court* [1931].

G. *Articles and Extracts*

E. M. Keate and C. R. Peers, 'Hampton', *V.C.H.* ii., (1911), p. 319 (full references to original sources).
Royal Commission on Historical Monuments, *Middlesex* (1937), art. Hampton.
Wren Society, vol. 4 (1927), 'Hampton Court Palace'; supplementary notes, vol. 7 (1930), p. 197.
Country Life: 13 (1903), p. 400; state apartments, 83 (1938); p. 673; furniture, 98 (1945), pp. 560, 692, 817, 918; beds, 35 (1914), p. 562.
Old Court House, *Country Life* 84 (1938), p. 330.
R. G. Rice, 'Notes on Huntington Shaw, Blacksmith', *The Archaeological Journal* 52 (2nd ser., vol. 2, 1895), p. 158.
Builder: 49 (1885), p. 116; 54 (1888), p. 212 (Fountain Court); 61 (1891), p. 294 (Great Hall); 78 (1900), p. 422 (colonnade to King's staircase); 90 (1906), p. 264 (Wren work); 91 (1906), p. 144 (Lion gates); 96 (1909), p. 96 (bridge); 99 (1910), p. 759 (Tijou); 125 (1923), p. 760: 132 (1927), p. 275; 133 (1927); p. 968; 138 (1930), p. 595 (old crown glass); Hampton Court bridge, 144 (1933), p. 769.

HANWELL

(i) M. Sharpe, *Bregantforda and the Hanweal* (Brentford, 1904); *Some Account of Bygone Hanwell and its Chapelry of New Brentford* (Brentford, 1924).
(ii) M. Sharpe, 'The Mending of the Brynt Bridge' (in 1530), *Trans. L. Mx. A. S.* NS 5 (1928) p. 449.
Builder: St Thomas, Boston Road, 146 (1934), p. 634.

HANWORTH

(ii) J. G. N[ichols], 'Answer filed in Equity respecting the Park and Common at Hanworth' (enclosure litigation *c.* 1675), *Trans. L. Mx. A. S.* OS 1 (1860), p. 183.

HAREFIELD

(i) W. F. Vernon, *Notes on the Parish of Harefield* (1872).
W. Goatman, *Harefield and her Church* (Harefield, [1947]).

(ii) H. S. Cochran, *St Mary's, Harefield* (Rickmansworth, 1926; ed. 3, 1936); *More about Harefield Church and Parish: Extracts from the Rate Books* (2 vols., Richmansworth, 1927); *The History of Moor Hall* (Rickmansworth, 1937).
T. Hugo, 'Moor Hall, in Harefield', *Trans. L. Mx. A. S.* OS 3 (1870), p. 1.

HARLINGTON
(ii) H. Wilson, *Eight Hundred Years of Harlington Parish Church* (ed. 1, Uxbridge, 1909; *ed. 2, enlarged, with notes on the village, Rochester, 1926).
Builder: church, 125 (1923), p. 849.

HARMONDSWORTH
(ii) A. Hartshorne, 'The Great Barn, Harmondsworth', *Trans. L. Mx. A. S.* OS 4 (1875), p. 417.
J. C. Taylor, 'The Old Parish Church at Harmondsworth, Middlesex', *Trans. L. Mx. A. S.* NS 1 (1905), p. 347.
Builder: church and tithe barn, 5 (1847), p. 579.

HARROW
(i) *The Visitor's Companion to Harrow on the Hill* (c. 1837).
Handbook for the Use of Visitors to Harrow on the Hill, ed. T. Smith (1850).
A. Rimmer, *Rambles round Eton and Harrow* (1882; ed. 2, 1898).
G. H. Hallam, *Official Guide to Harrow and Harrow School* (1931).
W. M. Keesey, *Harrow: a Sketch Book* (1914; ed. 2, 1933, ed. C. du Pontet).
W. W. Druett, *Harrow through the Ages* (Uxbridge, 1935; ed. 2, 1936); *The Stanmores and Harrow Weald through the Ages* (Uxbridge, 1938).
E. D. W. Chaplin, *The Book of Harrow* (1948).
(ii) Harrow School: R. Pitcairn, *Harrow School* (1870).
P. M. Thornton, *Harrow School and its Surroundings* (1885).
E. J. L. Scott, *Records of the Grammar School founded by John Lyon* (Harrow, 1886).
E. W. Howson and G. T. Warner, *Harrow School* (1898).
J. F. Williams, *Harrow* (1901).
A. D. Fox, *Harrow* (1910).
Harrow in Prose and Verse, ed. G. T. Warner [1913].
P. H. M. Bryant, *Harrow* (1936).
E. D. W. Chaplin, *Winston Churchill and Harrow* (1940).
E. D. Laborde, *Notes on the School Buildings* (Harrow, 1937); *Harrow School Yesterday and To-day* (1948).
Country Life 76 (1934), pp. 36, 64.
S. Gardner, *Architecture and History of Harrow Church* (Harrow, 1895).
W. D. Bushell, *Church Life on Harrow Hill* (Harrow Octocentenary Tracts I-XIII) (Cambridge, 1909); *Architecture and History of ... St Mary, Harrow* (Cambridge, 1901; ed. 2, 1912).
A. Heales and J. G. Nichols, article on brasses in church, *Trans. L. Mx. A. S.* OS 1 (1860), pp. 269, 276.
W. D. Cooper, article on parish registers with special reference to Page and Bellamy families, *Trans. L. Mx. A. S.* OS 1 (1860), p. 285.
'Harrow Pie House', *Trans. L. Mx. A. S.* NS 6 (1932), p. 399.
P. Davenport, 'The Weald Stone', *Trans. L. Mx. A. S.* NS 10 (1951), p. 165.
T. L. Bartlett, *The Story of Roxeth* (East Molesey, 1948).
Builder: church, 15 (1857), p. 677; 68 (1895), p. 57; houses by Arnold Mitchell, 64 (1893), pp. 408, 469; 69 (1895), p. 84; 102 (1912), p. 365; Orley Farm school, 83 (1902), p. 606; Lloyd's bank, 96 (1909), p. 468; Westminster bank,

113 (1917), p. 24; school war memorial buildings, 119 (1920), p. 119; houses by A. P. Starkey, 126 (1924), p. 17; 134 (1928), p. 624; 136 (1929), p. 199; National Provincial bank, 131 (1926), p. 1024.

HAYES
(i) E. Hunt, *Hayes Past and Present* (1861).
   T. Mills, *History of the Parish of Hayes* (1874).
(ii) *Builder:* St Anselm, 132 (1927), p. 974; 135 (1928), p. 216; 141 (1931), p. 465; housing estate, 145 (1933), p. 778.

HENDON
(i) E. T. Evans, *The History and Topography of the Parish of Hendon, Middlesex* (1890).
   N. G. Brett-James, **The Story of Hendon* (Hendon, 1931); *Some Extents and Surveys of Hendon* (1936).
(ii) F. C. Eeles, *The Parish Church of St Mary, Hendon* (ed. 2, 1931).
   A. G. Clarke, *The Story of Goldbeaters and Watling* (Mill Hill, 1931).
   R. Durrant, *Watling* (1939).
   N. G. Brett-James, 'Some Extents and Surveys of Hendon', *Trans. L. Mx. A. S.* NS 6 (1932), p. 547; 7 (1937), p. 1; p. 234; p. 528 (the first three articles reissued as *Some Extents and Surveys of Hendon* (1936), above).
   N. G. Brett-James, 'The Garrick-Shakespeare Memorial', *Trans. L. Mx. A. S.* NS 10 (1951), p. 55.
   Builder: St John, West Hendon, 67 (1894), p. 377; council offices, 87 (1904), p. 492; Ambassador cinema, 142 (1932), p. 462; Midland bank record office and store, Colindale, 144 (1933), p. 625.

HESTON
(i) G. E. Bate, *A History of the Urban District of Heston and Isleworth* (Hounslow, 1928); *And So Make a City Here* (Hounslow, 1948).
(ii) A. Heales, 'Heston Church', *Trans. L. Mx. A. S.* OS 2 (1864), p. 204.
   Builder: church, 4 (1846), p. 210; 23 (1865), p. 67.

HIGHGATE
(i) General histories of HORNSEY; also:
   W. S. Gibson, *The Prize Essay of the History and Antiquities of Highgate* (1842).
   F. Prickett, *History and Antiquities of Highgate, Middlesex* (Highgate, 1842).
   W. Howitt, *The Northern Heights of London* (1869).
   J. H. Lloyd, **The History, Topography, and Antiquities of Highgate* (Highgate, 1888).
   J. Sime, *Historical and Literary Associations of Old Highgate* (1905).
   W. K. Jealous, *Highgate Village* (Hampstead, 1919).
   P. W. Lovell, *An Afternoon in Old Highgate* (1926).
   P. W. Lovell and W. McB. Marcham, *The Village of Highgate* (The Parish of St Pancras, vol. i) (London County Council and London Survey Committee, 1936; does not include any Middlesex buildings).
   S. W. Kitchener, *Old Highgate* (Highgate, 1949).
(ii) P. Norman, *Cromwell House Highgate* (1917); *Cromwell House, Highgate* (London Survey Committee, 1926).
   C. A. Evors, *The Story of Highgate School* (1938; ed. 2, 1949).
   Builder: Cromwell House, 3 (1845), p. 586; St Augustine, Archway Road, 71 (1896), p. 212; Archway, 103 (1912), p. 754; Highpoint flats, 150 (1936), p. 345.

HILLINGDON
(See also UXBRIDGE)
 (i) R. de Salis, *Hillingdon through Eleven Centuries* (Uxbridge [1926]).
(ii) *Builder:* cemetery chapels, 25 (1867), p. 275.

HORNSEY
 (i) C. Nicholson, *Scraps of History of the Northern Suburb of London* (1879).
     R. O. Sherington, *The Story of Hornsey* (1904).
     S. W. Kitchener, *Old Hornsey: Some Gleanings from the Past* (Hornsey, 1942).
     References in W. Howitt, *The Northern Heights of London* (1869), and J. H. Lloyd,
       The History, Topography, and Antiquities of Highgate (Highgate, 1888).
(ii) *Court Rolls of the Manor of Hornsey, 1603-1701*, ed. W. McB. and F. Marcham
       (1929).
     S. J. Madge, *The Origin of the Name of Hornsey* (1936); *The Early Records of Harringay
       alias Hornsey* (Hornsey, 1938); *The Medieval Records of Harringay alias Hornsey*
       (Hornsey, 1939).
     C. J. M. Sidey, *Short History of Hornsey Old Church* (1911).
     W. McB. Marcham, 'The Court Rolls of Hornsey', *Trans. L. Mx. A. S.* NS 6
       (1932), p. 314; 'The Village of Crouch End, Hornsey', *Trans. L. Mx. A. S.* NS
       7 (1937), p. 393.
     F. W. M. Draper, *Literary Associations of Hornsey* (Hornsey, 1948); 'Two Studies in
       the Hornsey Church Books', *Trans. L. Mx. A. S.* NS 10 (1951), p. 41.
     Builder: St Mary, 54 (1888), p. 340; St Peter, Wightman Road, 71 (1896), p. 140;
       town hall, 145 (1933), p. 573; 149 (1935), p. 834.

HOUNSLOW AND HOUNSLOW HEATH
 (i) General histories of HESTON and ISLEWORTH; also:
     E. R. Milton, *Hounslow through the Ages* (Hounslow, 1931).
     G. S. Maxwell, *Highwayman's Heath* (Hounslow, 1935; ed. 2, 1949).
(ii) W. Wilkes, *Hounslow-Heath: a Poem* (ed. 1, anonymous, 1747; ed. 2, 1748; ed. 3,
       notes by W. Pinkerton, 1870).
     D. Loinaz, 'Hounslow and Hounslow Heath', *H.C.M.* 14 (1912), p. 241.
     G. E. Bate, *A History of the Priory and Parish Church of the Holy Trinity, Hounslow*
       (Hounslow, 1924).

ICKENHAM
(ii) W. H. Godfrey, *Swakeleys* (London Survey Committee [1934]).
     Swakeleys, *Country Life* 26 (1909), p. 526; 61 (1927), p. 61.
     F. D. Bawtree, 'Ickenham and its Hermit', *Mx. & H. N. & Q.* 1 (1895), p. 160.

ISLEWORTH
 (i) G. J. Aungier, *The History and Antiquities of Syon Monastery, the Parish of Isleworth,
       and the Chapelry of Hounslow* (1840).
     G. E. Bate, *A History of the Urban District of Heston and Isleworth* (Hounslow, 1928);
       And So Make a City Here (Hounslow, 1948).
(ii) G. E. Bate, *The History of Isleworth Charity School* (n.d.).
     'Parish Registers of Isleworth, Middlesex', Catholic Record Society *Miscellanea
       VIII*, 13 (1913), p. 299.
     Builder: St Margaret's house, 10 (1852), p. 424; St Mary, Spring Grove, 14
       (1856), p. 691; International College, 25 (1867), p. 129.

KINGSBURY
(ii) S. Potter, *Old Kingsbury Church* (ed. 2, 1928).
      Builder: church, 51 (1886), p. 51; 56 (1889), p. 225; Roe Green housing scheme,
      114 (1918), p. 5; 116 (1919), p. 40 (supplement ix).

LALEHAM
(ii) E. M. R[ogers], *All Saints, Laleham* (Laleham, 1951).

LITTLETON
 (i) W. M. Wood, *Littleton, Middlesex* (n.d.).

MIDDLESEX GUILDHALL
      Builder: 100 (1911), p. 271; 105 (1913), p. 519; 108 (1915), p. 272.

MILL HILL
 (i) General histories of Hendon; also:
      N. G. Brett-James, **The Story of Mill Hill Village* (Reigate, c. 1925).
(ii) D. G. Denoon, *How Mill Hill got its Name* (Mill Hill, 1932).
      N. G. Brett-James, *The History of Mill Hill School 1807-1907* [1909]; *The History
      of Mill Hill School 1807-1923* (Reigate [1925]); *Mill Hill* (i.e. school), 1938.
      Builder: foreign mission college, 29 (1871), p. 966; St Vincent de Paul chapel, 52
      (1887), p. 1914; St Mary's chapel, 56 (1889), p. 318; Congregational church,
      119 (1920), p. 516; John Keble church, 147 (1934), p. 589; 150 (1936), pp. 913,
      1042.

MIMMS, SOUTH, AND POTTERS BAR
 (i) F. C. Cass, *South Mimms* (1877).
      F. Brittain, **South Mymms* (Cambridge, 1931); *Tales of South Mymms* (Cambridge,
      1952).
(ii) 'South Mymms Castle', *Trans. L. Mx. A. S.* NS 7 (1937), pp. 175, 464.
      Wrotham Park, *Country Life* 44 (1918), pp. 404, 458; *Trans. L. Mx. A. S.* NS 9
      (1948), pp. 1, 106.
      A. H. Seabrook, 'Wyllyotts Manor', *Trans. L. Mx. A. S.* NS 5 (1926), p. 289.
      F. C. Cass, 'The Battle of Barnet', *Trans. L. Mx. A. S.* OS 6 (1890), p. 1.

MUSWELL HILL
 (i) General histories of HORNSEY; also:
      F. W. M. Draper, *Muswell Hill Past and Present* (Hornsey, 1936).
(ii) F. W. M. Draper, 'Muswell Farm; or Clerkenwell Detached', *Trans. L. Mx. A. S.*
      NS 6 (1932), p. 633.
      W. McB. Marcham, 'More Facts concerning 'Clerkenwell Detached' at Muswell
      Hill', *Trans. L. Mx. A. S.* NS 7 (1937), p. 610.
      J. F. Connolly and J. H. Bloom, *An Island of Clerkenwell: Notes on the Chapel and
      Well of Our Lady of Muswell* (Rochdale, 1933).

NORTHOLT
(ii) K. Cochrane-Holroyd, *The History of the Parish Church of Northolt* (Cricklewood,
      1930).

OSTERLEY
      Earl of Jersey, *A Guide to Osterley Park, Isleworth* (Osterley, 1939).

Osterley Park, *Country Life* 60 (1926), pp. 782, 818, 858, 907, 938, 972, 981; 85 (1939), p. 579; 86 (1939), p. 8.

PERIVALE
(i) J. A. Brown, **The Chronicles of Greenford Parva* [1890].
(ii) *Builder:* church, 26 (1868), p. 736; Hoover factory, 142 (1932), p. 389.

PINNER
(i) W. W. Druett, *Pinner through the Ages* (Uxbridge, 1937).
    E. M. Ware, *Pinner in the Vale* (Pinner, 1937).
    Panorama of Pinner Village, ed. J. W. Ferry (Pinner, 1947).
(ii) *Historical Guide to St John's, Pinner* (Harrow, 1921).
    W. M. Hind, 'Pinner Church', *Trans. L. Mx. A. S.* OS 3 (1870), p. 171.
    A. Hartshorne, 'Headstone House, near Harrow', *Trans. L. Mx. A. S.* OS 3 (1870), p. 185.
    Builder: Commercial Travellers schools, 12 (1854), p. 158; 107 (1914), p. 272; 115 (1918), p. 228; Waxwell Farm, 77 (1899), p. 201; Moss Cottage, 86 (1904), p. 391.

POTTERS BAR
    See Mimms, South.

RUISLIP
(i) J. J. Roumien, *History of the Parish and of the Church* (1875).
    Descriptive Guide to Ruislip (Ruislip, c. 1913).
    J. T. Cattle and others, ed. J. Hooper, **A Short History of Ruislip* (Ruislip, 1930).
(ii) H. Braun, 'Earliest Ruislip', *Trans. L. Mx. A. S.* NS 7 (1937), p. 99.
    Builder: Ruislip Manor estate layout, 100 (1911), p. 18; church, 129 (1925), p. 420.

SHEPPERTON
(i) *The History of our Village; or a few Notes about Shepperton, Ancient and Modern*, by One of its Inhabitants (1867).
(ii) S. J. Madge, 'The Economy of the Manor of Halliford, Middlesex, as described in the Parliamentary Survey of 1650', *Trans. L. Mx. A. S.* NS 4 (1922), p. 404.

SOUTHALL AND NORWOOD
(i) S. G. Short, *Southall and its Environs* (1910).

SOUTHGATE AND WINCHMORE HILL
(i) J. W. Round [pseud. J. F. Bunting], *The Story of Southgate and Winchmore Hill* (Enfield [1906]).
    H. C[resswell], *Winchmore Hill: Memories of a Lost Village* (1907; ed. 2, Dumfries, 1912).
    T. Mason, *The Story of Southgate and other Local Essays* (Enfield, 1947; ed. 2, 1948); *A Southgate Scrap-Book* (Enfield, 1948).
    H. W. Newby, *'Old' Southgate* (Southgate, 1949).
(ii) 'Southgate', *H.C.M.* 11 (1909), p. 167.
    W. A. Bettesworth, *The Walkers of Southgate* (1900).
    Builder: St Michael at Bowes, 30 (1872), p. 864; Skinners' almshouses, Palmer's Green, 68 (1895), p. 395; Broomfield Park, 99 (1910), p. 181; Grovelands Park, 99 (1910), p. 695; Underground Stations, 143 (1932), p. 599.

STAINES
(ii) W. Marratt, 'A Short Account of the Antiquities of Staines', *Trans. L. Mx. A. S.*
      OS 5 (1881), p. 519.
      Builder: St Peter, 64 (1893), p.490.

STANMORE
 (i) P. Davenport, *Old Stanmore* (Stanmore, 1933).
W. W. Druett, *The Stanmores and Harrow Weald through the Ages* (Uxbridge, 1938).
(ii) *H.C.M.* 3 (1901), p. 70.
      References in Anon., *The Twelve Churches; or, Tracings along the Watling Street*
      (1860).
      Builder: Bentley Priory, 97 (1909), p. 91.

STANMORE, LITTLE, AND CANONS
 (i) B. J. Armstrong, *Some Account of the Parish of Little Stanmore, alias Whitchurch*
      (1949; ed. 2, 1861; ed. 3, ed. E. Cutler, Edgware, 1895; ed. 4, Edgware, 1908).
      W. W. Druett, *The Stanmores and Harrow Weald through the Ages* (Uxbridge, 1938).
(ii) C. L. Holness, *A Short Guide to the Parish Church of Little Stanmore* (1937; ed. 2,
      1942; ed. 3, 1949); *Reminiscences of a Verger* (Little Stanmore [1947]).
      Canons:
      C. H. Collins Baker and M. I. Baker, *The Life and Circumstances of James Brydges,
      First Duke of Chandos* (Oxford, 1949).
      Country Life 35 (1914), p. 708; 40 (1916), pp. 518, 615; 106 (1949), p. 1950.
      W. Myers, 'Canons, Edgware', *The North London Collegiate School 1850-1950:
      Essays in Honour of the Frances Mary Buss Foundation* (1950), p. 158.
      C. Gildon, *Cannons, or the Vision* (verse) (1717).
      S. Humphery, *Cannons, a Poem* (1728).
      For the Handel association, see Note 1 to page 153.
      References in Anon., *The Twelve Churches; or, Tracings along the Watling Street*
      (1860).
      Builder: Metropolitan Railway stations, 143 (1932), p. 1055.

STANWELL
(ii) T. Pitt, 'Stanwell and Colnbrook,' *H.C.M.* 9 (1907), p.40.
      A. Heales, 'The Church of Stanwell and its Monuments', *Trans. L. Mx. A. S.* OS
      3 (1870), p. 105.
      C. O. Banks, 'Sir Richard de Wyndesore, of Stanwell, Middlesex', *Trans. L. Mx.
      A. S.* NS 6 (1932), p. 358.

STRAND ON THE GREEN
      See general histories of CHISWICK; also:
      J. Tavenor-Perry, 'Strand on the Green', *H.C.M.* 13 (1911), p. 109.

STRAWBERRY HILL
      (See also TWICKENHAM.)
      H. Walpole, *A Description of the Villa of Mr. Horace Walpole* (1784; ed. 2, 1788).
      Strawberry Hill Accounts, ed. P. Toynbee (1927); *Journal of the Printing Office at
      Strawberry Hill*, ed. P. Toynbee (1931).
      W. S. Lewis, *The Genesis of Strawberry Hill* (New York, 1934).
      Country Life: 56 (1924), pp. 18, 56.

SUNBURY

(i) C. E. Goddard, *An Historical Account of the Parish of Sunbury (Middlesex)* (Sunbury, 1890).

(ii) S. J. Madge, 'The Economy of the Manor of Halliford, Middlesex, as described in the Parliamentary Survey of 1650', *Trans. L. Mx. A. S.* NS 4 (1922), p. 404.

W. H. Tapp, *The Sunbury Charter* (Sunbury [1951]).

W. H. Tapp and F. W. M. Draper, 'The Saxon Charter of Sunbury-on-Thames', *Trans. L. Mx. A. S.* NS 10 (1951), p. 302.

Builder: church and village, 17 (1859), p. 414.

SYON HOUSE

G. J. Aungier, *The History and Antiquities of Syon Monastery, the Parish of Isleworth, and the Chapelry of Hounslow* (1840).

Syon House: its Pictures, Galleries, and Gardens (1851).

Helen, Duchess of Northumberland, *Syon House, Middlesex* (privately printed, 1929).

Syon House: a Brief History and Guide (Syon, 1950).

Syon House: the Story of a Great House (Syon, 1950).

Country Life: 5 (1899), p. 112; 46 (1919), pp. 728, 802, 838, 874.

TEDDINGTON

(i) K. Ingram, *A Short History of the Parish of Teddington* (Teddington, 1909).

(ii) [H. T. Dade], *The Parish church of St Alban the Martyr Teddington-on-Thames and the Old Parish Church of St Mary* [1947].

Builder: St Alban, 55 (1888), p. 233; 57 (1888), p. 460; 121 (1921), p. 805.

TOTTENHAM

(i) W. Bedwell, *A Briefe Description of the Towne of Tottenham Highcrosse in Middlesex* (1631; ed. 2, 1717, bound with R. Butcher, *The Survey and Antiquity of the Town of Stamford*).

Henry Hare, 3rd Lord Coleraine (d. 1749), manuscript history in Bodleian Library, Oxford (printed in Oldfield and Dyson, 1790).

H. G. Oldfield and R. R. Dyson, *History and Antiquities of Tottenham* (1790; ed. 2, 1792, R. Dyson only).

W. Robinson, *The History and Antiquities of the Parish of Tottenham High Cross* (1818; ed. 2, 1840).

G. L. Wilson, *Farthing Illustrated History of Tottenham* (1 part issued, Tottenham, 1890).

[-. Freeman], *A Short History of Tottenham and Bruce Castle* (1891).

F. Fisk, *The History of Tottenham* (1st series, Tottenham, 1913; 2nd series, Tottenham, 1923).

[H. J. Griffin], *Historical Articles on Old Tottenham and Edmonton* (Tottenham, 1926).

W. J. Roe, *Ancient Tottenham* (Tottenham [1949]).

(ii) W. J. Hall, *Notes with Reference to All Hallows' Church* (1861; ed. 2, 1862).

G. Waight [i.e. Weight], *The History and Description of Allhallows Church, Tottenham* (Tottenham, 1876).

W. J. Roe, *All Hallows, the Mother Church of Tottenham: a Short History* (Tottenham, 1930; ed. 2, 1948).

T. Compton, *Recollections of Tottenham Friends and the Forster Family* (1893).

A. Hill, *Reminiscences of 72 Years in Tottenham* (1899).

H. Couchman, *Reminiscences of Tottenham* (1909).

[E. Shorthouse], *Grove House School* (1913).

J. A. Heraud, *Tottenham* (poem) (1820).

[J. Dean], *Tottenham and its Institutions in 1843* (Tottenham, 1843).

C. H. Rock, *A Guide to the Collection illustrating the History of the Post Office* (Tottenham Museum, 1938; contains sections on Bruce Castle and on Tottenham postal history).

G. H. Lake, *The Railways of Tottenham* (1946).

Builder: St Katharine's training college, 41 (1881), p. 185; St Mary, Lansdowne Road, 49 (1885), p. 694; town hall, 90 (1906), p. 409; White Hart Lane estate, 105 (1913), p. 449; 114 (1918), p. 173; 133 (1927), p. 354.

TWICKENHAM

(See also STRAWBERRY HILL.)

(i) A Lady [J. Pye], *A Short Account of the Principal Seats and Gardens in and about Twickenham* (1760; ed. 2, 1767).

A Peep into the Principal Seats and Gardens in and about Twickenham (1775).

E. Ironside, *History of Twickenham* (1797).

R. S. Cobbett, **Memorials of Twickenham* (1872).

(ii) Houses, *Country Life* 46 (1919), pp. 420, 464, 508, 605, 648, 692, 824, 913, 1089.

York House, Twickenham (Twickenham Borough Council [1948]).

Radnor House, *Country Life* 82 (1937), pp. 12, 83, 340.

Sandycombe Lodge, *Country Life* 110 (1951), p. 40.

Marble Hill House (London County Council, 1930; 1951); *Country Life* 39 (1916), p. 394.

F. C. Hodgson, *Thames-Side in the Past* (1913).

C. J. Thrupp, 'Twickenham and its Worthies', *Trans. L. Mx. A. S.* OS 6 (1890), p. 449.

'The Literary Suburb of the 18th Century', *Fraser's Magazine* 61 (1860), pp. 124, 267, 387, 834; 62 (1860), p. 94.

Builder: Sandycombe Lodge, 73 (1897), p. 219; Marble Hill, 89 (1905), p. 316; St Mary's college, Strawberry Hill, 129 (1925), p. 736; Luxor cinema, 137 (1929), p. 867; Twickenham bridge, 144 (1933), p.723.

TWYFORD, WEST

(i) I. M. (Mrs Basil) Holmes, *West Twyford, Middlesex* (1908; *ed. 2, Ealing, 1936).

UXBRIDGE

(i) G. Redford and T. H. Riches, *The History of the Ancient Town and Borough of Uxbridge* (Uxbridge, 1818; reprinted 1885).

J. King, *Guide to Picturesque Uxbridge* (Uxbridge, 1904).

S. Springall, *Country Rambles round Uxbridge* (Uxbridge, 1907).

(ii) A. D. Perrott, *The Story of Uxbridge Parish Church* (ed. 5, c. 1948).

W. S. Cooper, 'Notes on Uxbridge and its Former Inhabitants', *Trans. L. Mx. A. S.* OS 2 (1864), p. 113.

G. Eves, 'Antiquities of Uxbridge', *Trans. L. Mx. A. S.* OS 2 (1864), p. 154; *Gentleman's Magazine* NS 11 (1861), p. 517.

S. W. Kershaw, 'The Treaty House, Uxbridge: its History and Associations', *Trans. L. Mx. A. S.* OS 5 (1881), p. 504.

Builder: St Andrew, West Hillingdon, 22 (1864), p. 632.

WEMBLEY
(See also HARROW.)
(ii) D. Maxwell, *Wembley in Colour* (1924; British Empire Exhibition).
H. Braun, 'The Hundred of Gore and its Moot-Hedge', *Trans. L. Mx. A. S.* NS 7 (1937), p. 218.
P. Davenport, 'The Site of the Gore Hundred-Moot', *Trans. L. Mx. A. S.* NS 10 (1951), p. 145.
W. D. Bushell, 'The Bellamies of Uxendon', *Trans. L. Mx. A. S.* NS 3 (1917), p. 71.
Builder: St James, Alperton, 102 (1912), p. 726; Oakington garden suburb, 123 (1922), p. 696; St Andrew, Sudbury, 127 (1924), p. 209; stadium and exhibition buildings, 123 (1922), p. 577; 125 (1923), p. 615; 126 (1924), p. 216; Empire pool, 145 (1933), p. 704; 147 (1934), pp. 152, 346; municipal buildings, 148 (1935), p. 959.

WILLESDEN
(i) C. Biddiscombe, *The Willesden Local Guide and History* (historical survey by F. Hitchin-Kemp) (Willesden, 1905).
S. Potter, *The Story of Willesden* (1926).
(ii) E. T. Slater, *Dollis Hill and its Memories of Gladstone* (1906).
J. S. Bridges, *Dollis Hill House* (1920).
B. Hutchinson, *Willesden and the New Towns* (Central Office of Information social survey, 1947).
The Willesden Survey, 1949, ed. J. C. Morris (Willesden, 1951).
J. G. Waller, 'On the Pilgrimage to Our Lady of Wilsdon', *Trans. L. Mx. A. S.* OS 4 (1875), p. 173.
F. A. Wood, 'The Parish of Willesdon', *Trans. L. Mx. A. S.* OS 4 (1875), p. 189.
Willesden Junction, *H.C.M.* 1 (1899), p. 198.
Builder: housing estate, Queen's Park, 33 (1875), p. 933; St Andrew, Willesden Green 50 (1886), p. 59; 69 (1895), p. 314; St Michael, Stonebridge, 61 (1891), p. 48; St Andrew's hospital, 103 (1912), p. 717; Post Office research station, 146 (1934), p. 57; Guinness brewery, 150 (1936), p. 916.

WINCHMORE HILL
See SOUTHGATE.

WOOD GREEN
(i) See general histories of TOTTENHAM, especially, F. Fisk, *The History of Tottenham* (2nd series, Tottenham, 1923).
(ii) *Builder:* printer's almshouses, 7 (1849), p. 270; Alexandra Palace, 32 (1874), p. 658; Noel Park estate, 44 (1883), p. 880; almshouses from St Leonard, Shoreditch, 89 (1905), p. 620; Our Lady of Compassion, Linacre Road, 96 (1909), p. 283; St Paul, 85 (1903), p. 316.

YIEWSLEY
(ii) *Builder:* church, 72 (1897), p. 361; 107 (1914), p. 556.

THE VICTORIA HISTORY OF THE COUNTY OF MIDDLESEX

Volume I
Edited by J. S. Coburn, H. P. King and K. G. T. McDonnell, 1969, Oxford University Press.
General volume covering the whole of the county under subject headings.

Volume II
Edited by William Page, F.S.A., 1911, Oxford University Press.
Completes chapters covering the whole of the county under subject headings. Covers the parishes of Ashford, East Bedfont with Hatton, Feltham, Hampton with Hampton Wick, Hanworth, Laleham, Littleton.

Volume III with Index to Volumes II and III
Edited by Susan Reynolds, 1962, Oxford University Press.
Parishes of Shepperton, Staines, Stanwell, Sunbury, Teddington, Isleworth, Heston, Hounslow, Twickenham, Cowley, Cranford, West Drayton, Greenford.

Volume IV
Edited by J. S. Coburn and T. F. T. Baker, 1971, Oxford University Press.
Parishes of Hanwell, Harefield, Harmondsworth, Hayes, Norwood (including Southall), Hillingdon (including Uxbridge, Ickenham, Northolt, Perivale, Ruislip), Edgware, Harrow (including Pinner).

Volume V
Edited by T. F. T. Baker, 1971, Oxford University Press.
Parishes of Hendon, Kingsbury, Great Stanmore, Little Stanmore, Edmonton, Enfield, Monken Hadley, South Mimms, Tottenham.

Volume VI
Edited by T. F. T. Baker, 1980, Oxford University Press.
Parishes of Friern Barnet, Finchley, Hornsey (including Highgate).

Volume VII
Edited by T. F. T. Baker, 1982, Oxford University Press.
Parishes of Acton, Chiswick, Ealing and Brentford, West Twyford, Willesden.

Volume IX
Edited by T. F. T. Baker, 1989, Oxford University Press.
Parishes of Hampstead and Paddington.

THE MIDDLESEX BIBLIOGRAPHY

Four volumes plus Supplement, published by Middlesex Local History Council, c.1960-1965.
Vols.1-4 list books published up to 1956.
Supplement (1968) lists books published 1956-1965.

INDEX